ASPECTS OF

Anglo-Saxon Archaeology

SUTTON HOO AND OTHER DISCOVERIES

ASPECTS OF
Anglo-Saxon Archaeology

SUTTON HOO AND OTHER DISCOVERIES

RUPERT BRUCE-MITFORD

Keeper of Medieval and Later Antiquities in the British Museum

LONDON
VICTOR GOLLANCZ LIMITED
1974

ISBN 0 575 01704 X

Book designed by Richard Hayes

CORRIGENDA

p.230 line 31 after 'elucidation' insert footnote reference '9' and on p.231 for footnote reference 9 read 9[a].

p.251 footnote 9 to read: I am much indebted to Mrs. V. H. Fenwick for her assistance in the latter stages of the work, particularly for her active interest in the technical problems of the helmet and liaison work with the Research Laboratory.

Footnote 9[a] to read:

O. Doppelfeld, *Germania* 42, 1964, 1-45 10 By mercury gilding, which can be seen in several cases. I am indebted to Dr. Hilda Davidson for the reference to Freyr's boar.

PRINTED IN GREAT BRITAIN
BY EBENEZER BAYLIS AND SON LTD
THE TRINITY PRESS, WORCESTER, AND LONDON

Contents

List of Plates

(*Where not otherwise acknowledged plates and figures are reproduced by courtesy of the Trustees of the British Museum*)

List of Figures

2

Acknowledgements

A number of the chapters in this book, here substantially revised and expanded, formerly appeared elsewhere. I am grateful to the editors and publishers of the following journals and books for permission to re-issue in the present volume material which they had previously printed:

Chapter One	*Proceedings of the Suffolk Institute of Archaeology and Natural History* XXV, 1949, pp. 1–78.
Chapter Two	*Proceedings of the Suffolk Institute of Archaeology and Natural History* XXIV, 1948, pp. 228–51.
Chapter Three	*Proceedings of the Suffolk Institute of Archaeology and Natural History* XXVI, 1952, pp. 1–26.
Chapter Five	*Antiquity* XLII, 1968, pp. 36–9.
Chapter Six	*Acta Archaeologica* XXXVIII, Copenhagen, 1967, pp. 199–209; and *Antiquity* XLIV, 1970, pp. 146–8.
Chapter Seven	*Antiquity* XLIV, 1970, pp. 7–13.
Chapter Eight	*British Museum Quarterly*, Vol. XXXVI, Nos. 3–4, Autumn 1972.
Chapter Nine	R. H. Hodgkin, *A History of the Anglo-Saxons* II, 3rd Ed., Oxford University Press, 1952; a note (pp. 752–4) from the appendix on the Sutton Hoo Ship Burial by R. L. S. Bruce-Mitford.
Chapter Ten	*Frühmittelalterliche Studien*, Jahrbuch des Instituts für Frühmittelalterforschung der Universität, Münster, Berlin, 1968, Band 2, pp. 233–6.
Chapter Twelve	Ritchie Girvan, *Beowulf and the Seventh Century*, London, Methuen, 1971, pp. 85–98.
Chapter Fourteen	*The Relics of St Cuthbert*, The Dean and Chapter of Durham, 1956, pp. 308–25 and 542–4.
Chapter Fifteen	*Dark Age Britain*, Studies presented to E. T. Leeds, edited by D. B. Harden, Methuen, 1956, pp. 171–201.

Blocks have been kindly lent as follows:

Plates 14b; 15a; 17; 46a, b; 47a, b; 48; 49; 50; 51; 52; 53; 54; 111; Figs 1; 4; 5; 7; 8; 9; 26; 27; 28; 29; 30; 60 – by The Trustees of the British Museum.

Plates 28; 29; 30; 39; 40; 41; 42; 43a, b; 44 a–d; 45; Figs 22; 23; 24; 25 – by The Editorial Board of *Antiquity*.

Plates 33 a–c; 34a, b; 35a, b; 36a, b; Fig 19 – by The Editorial Board of *Acta Archaeologica*.

Plates 56; 57a, b; 58a, b; 59a, b; 60 – by The Editorial Board, *Mittelalterliche Studien* and Prof. Dr Karl Hauck, Münster.

Plates 94 a–d; 95 a–e; 96 a–e; 97 a–d; 98 a–d; Fig 51 – by The Dean and Chapter of Durham Cathedral.

Preface

This book is primarily a re-publication of twelve selected papers and notes by myself which have appeared in various learned journals, or in books, over the last twenty-five years. All have been brought up to date and some substantially re-written. In addition the book contains four papers not previously published, 'The Benty Grange helmet, and other supposed Anglo-Saxon helmets', 'Six pieces of cloisonné jewellery', 'Basil Brown's Diary of the 1938 and 1939 excavations at Sutton Hoo', and 'A glass vessel from Deal'. The book, originally, was thought of as a device to simplify footnote references in the volumes of the British Museum definitive publication on the Sutton Hoo Ship-burial, Volume 1 of which is in the press. In that major publication this book is cited throughout. I hope that this assembly of material, mostly connected with the ship-burial, will at the same time be of use to all students whose interest may lie within the wide and varied fields on which the ship-burial impinges. Many of the papers here re-published are difficult to come by and yet are still in demand, for the importance of the Sutton Hoo discovery has steadily increased with the years, with a growing literature and with our fuller knowledge of the nature of its contents. Some items such as the Sutton Hoo helmet, the lyre, and the re-excavation of the ship in 1966–7, will be exhaustively treated in the major publication; but that will be an expensive work and these shorter and more readily accessible accounts may prove useful for convenient reference.

I owe a particular debt of gratitude to Miss Marilyn Luscombe who has undertaken the great bulk of the editorial work on the volume, a labour without which the book would certainly not have seen the light of day.

RUPERT BRUCE-MITFORD

British Museum,
London, W.C.1.
October, 1973.

CHAPTER ONE

The Sutton Hoo Ship-burial: Comments on general interpretation

INTRODUCTION

The Sutton Hoo ship-burial was discovered over thirty years ago. During the succeeding years, treatment and study of the finds has proceeded and Migration and Merovingian period archaeology has advanced. The deep significance, in many fields of study, of the Sutton Hoo discovery has becoming increasingly evident. Yet much uncertainty prevails on general issues. Many questions cannot receive their final answers until the remaining mounds of the grave-field have been excavated. Others can be answered, or at any rate clarified, now. My hope in this chapter is to clarify the position of the burial in English history and archaeology.

To illustrate the need for such clarification we may note that it has been said by one writer that 'practically the whole of the Sutton Hoo ship-treasure is an importation from the Uppland province of Sweden. The great bulk of the work was produced in Sweden itself.'[1] Another writer claims that the Sutton Hoo ship-burial is the grave of a Swedish chief or king.[2] Clearly, we must establish whether the ship-burial is part of English archaeology, or of Swedish, before we can begin to draw inferences from it.

The identity of the person buried, or commemorated, and our historical appreciation of the monument, depend not only on whether the grave was English or Swedish but on whether, if English, it was that of an East Anglian king, or of someone else. One must also consider whether it was pagan or Christian and whether or not it originally contained a body, or was constructed as a cenotaph. Many opposing views have been expressed on these subjects and it is desirable that a considered assessment of the issues should be offered to students, even though certainty may never be possible.

Two articles in which these questions have been discussed appeared together in *Fornvännen* (h. 2–3, 1948). They are '*Sutton Hoo och Beowulf*' (Sutton Hoo and Beowulf) by Professor Sune Lindqvist, former Professor of Northern Archaeology in Uppsala University and '*Sutton Hoo: en svensk kunga- eller hövdinggrav?*'

(Sutton Hoo: the grave of the Swedish king or prince?) by Professor Birger Nerman, former Director of the Statens historiska Museum, Stockholm. Professor Lindqvist's paper appeared in English translation in *Antiquity*, 1948, 131–140.

In maintaining that the grave is that of a Swede, Nerman claimed the use of a boat and other general aspects of the funeral arrangements as Swedish.[3] As far as the objects that make up the burial-deposit are concerned, he claimed only three pieces out of the lengthy grave-inventory – the sword, the helmet and the shield – as made in Sweden. The rest he seemed prepared to regard as objects acquired in Suffolk by his Swedish intruder, whether as gifts, as spoils taken in fighting, or as rewards for services rendered. On this basis it may not seem to matter much to English archaeology whether the man buried or commemorated was a Swede or not. The silver dishes and other silver pieces, the Coptic bowl, the Merovingian coins and the hanging-bowls (if made in Ireland or the Celtic North or West) would remain imports into Suffolk and a part of English archaeology, even if they eventually came into the hands of a Swedish intruder. The bulk, at any rate, of the gold jewellery and most of the remaining finds are, in Nerman's view and indeed by common consent, local English work.

Questions of first importance do, nevertheless, depend upon the identity of the buried or commemorated man. The meaning of the direct link between England and Sweden, now revealed for the first time and beyond all question, at Sutton Hoo,[4] depends wholly upon whether the Swedish traits occur in the grave of a stray Swede or in that of an established English king. Before this important question can be satisfactorily discussed it is necessary to clarify related questions: whether the monument is a king's or not, whether it is pagan or Christian, whether it was grave or cenotaph.

The cenotaph question has been the subject of a special study[5] and will not be discussed here in detail but the findings will be summarized. We must, however, consider in some detail the question of the supposed royal character of the burial, the prospects of identifying the person buried or commemorated and the pagan or Christian character of the monument.

IS THIS A KING'S BURIAL?

In an essay of great distinction published in 1940 on the question of the identity of the man for whom the Sutton Hoo treasure-ship was buried the late Professor H. M. Chadwick wrote:

> I find it impossible to believe that in the times with which we are concerned

> a treasure of such amount and value can have belonged to anyone except a king. According to heroic standards then recognised all men of the highest rank were dependent upon the king and expected to present to him, as their lord, everything that they acquired by their exploits—though doubtless they looked for rewards. We may refer to *Beowulf* 2052 ff. where the hero, on his return home, presents to the king and queen all the treasures which have been given to him at the Danish court. There is no evidence that England in the seventh century possessed a wealthy independent class whether mercantile, industrial or professional. It does not necessarily follow that the person buried or commemorated was himself a king. We know of extravagant funeral honours paid by kings to their mothers and wives; and this funeral may have possibly been in honour of the father or other near relative of a king. But on the whole it is not very likely. The great funerals we hear of in early Teutonic history and tradition are those of kings themselves; we may thus cite e.g. *Jordanes Get.* 49 and *Beowulf* 3134 ff. At all events it is difficult to believe, that a cenotaph on this scale can have been intended for anyone except a king.[6]

The royal status of the grave is further discussed in Chapter 2.[7] What is said there should be read in conjunction with Chadwick's treatment of this subject in the article quoted and with the most recent assessment in Chapter X of Volume I of the British Museum's definitive publication, *The Sutton Hoo Ship-Burial* (1974).

It seems impossible to doubt that the Sutton Hoo burial is royal in the sense that it reflects a royal court, the top stratum of Anglo-Saxon society. The treasures, if not actually personal to a king, may legitimately be regarded at least as 'tribal treasures' (*Þeodgestreon*, *Beowulf* 1218–19) such as were distributed by him from the national treasure-store.

The set of ten[8] silver bowls, probably, and certainly the pair of spoons,[9] have a specifically Christian character.[10] We read in Bede of gifts from Popes to Saxon kings and queens, converts or prospective converts. 'Numerous gifts of every kind . . .'[11] '. . . a robe embroidered with gold and a garment from Ancyra';[12] 'a silver mirror and an ivory comb adorned with gold'.[13]

The spoons and perhaps the set of silver bowls seem likely to have come into this category of gifts to royalty. We do not read of any general distribution of such gifts. Important nobles might well, for all we know, as converts or prospective converts, receive from a bishop an individual token of this kind. We would not expect to meet such gifts in the archaeological record, as I do not believe they would normally be placed in the grave of such a recipient, if he were a Christian. There is a body of opinion that can regard lavish burials such as those at Sutton Hoo[14] and Taplow[15] as the graves of Christians. If this is right, we might certainly expect to find such baptismal or conversion gifts amongst grave-goods. Except at Sutton Hoo, however, we do not. The fact remains that classical silverware, whether acquired by ecclesiastical gift or Continental trade, is excessively rare not only in Anglo-Saxon but in continental Germanic archaeology of this period. I can quote only the phalerae from Ittenheim[16] and the odd spoon, such as that from the princely grave at Krefeld-Gellep,[17] as instances of Mediterranean silver in the classical tradition occurring in a Germanic grave of this period (sixth to seventh centuries). I know of no other instance on the Continent and no single piece of Mediterranean silver has come to light in any Anglo-Saxon grave, other than the Sutton Hoo ship-burial. Nothing of the kind, so far as we can tell, occurred in the rich seventh-century burials at Taplow and Broomfield, or rewarded those industrious early gatherers of Saxon grave-goods, Faussett, Douglas and Akerman. This is the more remarkable because oriental and Mediterranean imports in general – Coptic bowls, ewers, copper and bronze pails, amethyst beads, cowrie shells and so on – are common in South Germany, the Rhineland and South-East England in the sixth and first half of the seventh centuries.[18] It seems highly unlikely that the sixteen notable pieces in the Sutton Hoo grave, comprising items of diverse dates and origins, could have been accumulated anywhere at this time except in a royal treasury and by a royal family, especially since we may reasonably suppose that the entire holding of silver was not disposed of in the grave. Other, perhaps finer pieces must have been retained in the family's possession or royal treasure-store, so that the accumulation of silver held can be supposed to have been in fact much greater than revealed in the grave. When we hear in literary sources of the use of a silver dish in Anglo-Saxon England at this time, a piece that seems to be in the category of the Anastasius dish or at the least of the bowl with classical head from Sutton Hoo, the context is royal.[19] Such considerations, together with those brought forward by Chadwick and myself in the other discussions of this subject already referred to,[20] seem to leave no reasonable doubt that the Sutton Hoo grave is of royal standing.

Is there any justification for claiming that it is the burial of the king himself? Can we say with any confidence that it is not the grave of a king's father, uncle or son? Ene, younger brother of Raedwald and father of four East Anglian kings, may have died within the margins now fixed for our burial by the coins and the general historical context (after 620–5, before *c.* A.D. 640). He seems to have been born about 570–80[21] and thus would have reached an age of some fifty to seventy years. One might expect a father of kings, whose life had spanned the great phase and been linked with the great personalities of early East Anglian history, to receive conspicuous honours at the hands of his surviving royal sons or grandchildren. This is speculation, but it illustrates the need for caution. Ene would be a reasonable candidate for such honours. Or again, to add a category to those mentioned by Chadwick, might it not be the grave of a distinguished visitor, perhaps related to the East Anglian royal family, who died on his visit? Nerman has already suggested the foreign visitor explanation of the burial.[22] The burial of any of these persons would be at the royal level. It would contain gifts and no doubt heirlooms from the royal treasury and the siting of the burial near a royal centre (in this case Rendlesham) would be natural.

The distinguished foreign visitor theory arises from the view already referred to that boat-burial is not a Saxon but, on the contrary, at this date a distinctively Swedish custom and that the dead man's most cherished weapons were of Swedish make – helmet, shield and sword, together with an object of special social or symbolic significance, the shield-ring (in the general semblance of a sword-ring), not at the time of Nerman's paper recognized as Swedish. These facts have to be explained. The distinguished foreigner theory would account for them, if the foreigner were a Swede; so this possibility, as well as the possibility that the grave is that of a near relative of an English king, must be given serious consideration.

We may here echo Chadwick's comments on these possibilities – that they do not seem very likely. Whatever may be theoretically possible, in practice all burials of an equivalent scale or richness known in literature and in archaeology are known to be, or are with good reason held to be, those of kings themselves.[23] The very great richness of the Sutton Hoo burial, the unique character of many of the pieces it contained, the outstanding quality of everything present (though some of the imported silver, by classical standards, has a somewhat provincial look), even the great size of the ship, suggest that it was a king's grave.[24] It may be doubted that any relative or visitor, however distinguished, other than a king, would have received such lavish treatment.

We must also note Chadwick's point that at all events it is difficult to believe that a *cenotaph* on this scale can have been intended for anyone except a king. Scientific study of the cenotaph problem, over many years, concluded in 1973, suggests that a body may have been lain in the region of the burial-deposit between the Anastasius dish and the west end of the burial-chamber – a region that included the space in which the sword and jewellery lie.[25] The evidence is a matter of chemical traces which cannot be interpreted with certainty – artefacts of bone or ivory and animal bone will yield phosphatic traces. It cannot be shown that the phosphate source is human and there are certain factors in the lie of the relevant grave-goods as found which are difficult to reconcile with the original presence of a body.

As has been said elsewhere[26] the question whether the grave is that of a king or of some other royal person depends, more perhaps than on anything else, upon the interpretation of two objects in the grave, the long iron stand with a spike at the bottom and the giant 'whetstone' or stone bar. They were formerly identified as a standard and a sceptre.[27] If they are, then they must surely be symbols of not merely rank but of office, such as can only at this date have been proper to the king himself and to no one else. It is necessary to examine these two objects more closely and if possible to establish their true character.

THE WHETSTONE (Plate 1)

The fact is that the character of the 'whetstone' has been radically changed and clarified by the recognition that the bronze pedestal, twisted iron wire ring and stag-figure, previously associated with the iron stand, constitute the missing finial from its squat end. There was not, as has hitherto been supposed, another saucer, similar to that surviving at the opposite end. The stone bar has thus ceased to be a supposedly symmetrical object with two ends of approximately the same design. It has now acquired a top and bottom; and since one cannot suppose the object to have been used with the stag standing on its head, the saucer at the opposite end becomes the bottom feature and is reduced to something functional. It fits naturally and comfortably onto the knee cap and at once evokes a picture of the seated king with the stone bar held in the hand, its lower end resting on the knee. The red-painted lobed ends and the carved human faces, perhaps male and female mixed, add to the portentousness and aura of this staff. It can scarcely be anything but a ceremonial object, associated not so much with an individual as with an office. In its context of a secular warrior-type *fürstengrab* it can hardly be other than an emblem of *kingly* office. If it were not for the grave-inventory, typical of warrior and princely graves, we might consider the object as of purely religious significance, a cult object of power, and the burial conceivably that of a personage such as Coifi, the high priest of the pagan Northumbrians (Bede, *Historia Ecclesiastica*, Bk. II, Chapter 13) but possessed of private wealth (Coifi was a poor man). In what is evidently a secular grave, however, the object can only be seen as a sceptre, indicating a king. A giant whetstone would be a natural enough symbol for the power of a king, the giver and master of the swords of his war-band, the head of a fighting élite in an heroic period. Kendrick said of it, before its full impressiveness was revealed by the restoration to it of the stag and ring:

> nothing like this monstrous stone exists anywhere else. It is a unique, savage thing; and inexplicable except perhaps as a symbol, proper to the king himself, of the divinity and mystery which surrounded the smith and his tools in the northern world.[28]

No comparison can properly be drawn between this astonishing object and the plain, strictly functional, often well-worn whetstones common in rich Swedish burials of the period; for instance the earlier boat-graves at Vendel, or the royal mounds at Old Uppsala.[29] None of these show anything of the elaboration or ornate character of the Sutton Hoo piece. There is also a difference in scale. The longest of those quoted, in Vendel graves 4 and 1, are 31.2 and 28 cms in length.[30] The Sutton Hoo stone without the bronze fittings at either end is 60 cms long. It is not in all cases possible to tell the original length of the whetstones found in the royal mounds at Old Uppsala but the thickness of the largest fragment is approximately 3.3 cms;[31] that from Sutton Hoo reaches 5 cms. In bulk and weight the Sutton Hoo object greatly exceeds any functional whetstone known. In both Germanic and Celtic contexts in Britain, whetstones with faces carved at one end at least (only one end survives in most cases) are known (Plate 7c and d). None matches the Sutton Hoo example in size or in its ceremonial elaborations. In addition to the two from the Celtic west illustrated here, there are larger scale fragments with heads from Hough-on-the-Hill, Lincolnshire – a stray find – and from Lochar Moss in Dumfriesshire (both the latter are illustrated in the British Museum's definitive publication, Vol. II). The date of the Dumfries stone is uncertain – a matter of style – the Welsh and Irish examples are regarded as of 'Dark Age' date.[31a] That sceptres of a more conventional (Roman) kind were not attributes of royalty known to Germanic kings at this period may perhaps be inferred from the signet ring of the Frankish king Childeric I (d. 481), which gives a representation of the king holding not a sceptre but a spear.[32] Although the Sutton Hoo object cannot be paralleled in archaeology or so far as I know from literary sources and although all its features cannot be readily explained, its identification as a royal sceptre seems inevitable.

THE IRON STAND OR 'STANDARD' (Fig 1)

The second object which must be considered as relevant to the identification of the grave as that of a king is the iron stand. In the official report of the excavations in *Antiquaries Journal*, Vol. XX, 1940, it was called a flambeau. Phillips said of it:

> It seems to have been a portable flambeau which could have been stuck in the ground where required. Its head would be wound round with tow soaked in oil; the bull's heads playing their part in helping to retain the combustible material in place.[33]

This suggestion recurs in the *Antiquity* XIV account of the finds and the *British Museum Quarterly*, XIII, 1939 (p. 113), apparently following Mr Phillips' lead, called it a lampstand. The mounting of the stag and its ring on the top of this stand, when this connection was made, altered the concept of its use. I wrote of this at the time in the following terms:

> When these suggestions (i.e. portable flambeau etc.) were being put forward it was not known that the cruciform projections terminating in bull's heads at the upper end of the object were not the top of it but had in fact themselves been surmounted by a vertically set ring of twisted wires, on top of which in turn was set an exquisitely modelled cast bronze stag.[34] These additions transform the character of the object giving it added height and a more ornate and impressive appearance. It seems extremely improbable that so delicate an arrangement as the ring, which is made up of four individually twisted strands of wire, about one eighth of an inch thick, held together by fluted bronze strip-clips, of the kind familiar in Saxon archaeology on the rims of ornamented cups and drinking-horns, would have remained intact in the heat of flames such as would accompany its use as a flambeau or beacon. Nor would the delicate antlers of the stag stand up to the heat, or to repeated alternations of heat to cold, for long. The illumination of the stag by flames beneath and around it might have made a spectacle but it is most unlikely that so rare an object would have been given over to the constant action of flames and intense heat and the fouling of smoke. The fact is that this stag is a great rarity, unique in the Germanic world of this time as sculptural work and in its sensitivity, life-like appearance and delicate stylisation. It does not seem to belong to the Germanic art-world at all, and may have been made in distant parts, possibly even in a distant age.[35] The stag and ring in fact show no signs of exposure to heat. In view of this new knowledge of the nature of the object the portable flambeau or beacon explanation can be ruled out.

The lampstand possibility was not ruled out by the supposed presence of the stag and ring on top. The horizontal openwork grid (Fig 1) might have functioned as an elevated portable platform on which small float-wick lamps, each giving a comparatively small tongue of flames, could be set. The wire ring, stag and bulls' heads could be merely ornamental and would not have been subjected to intense flames and heat. Even with this restricted use for lighting, the stag and upper parts of the object must have become blackened and dirty and there would not seem to be any purpose, other than a spectacular one, for continuing the object above the level of the lamp-carrying platform for twenty inches, as seemed to be the case. There were no fragments in the burial of pottery or other vessels such as might have been employed as lamps in conjunction with the stand.[36] No such objects are known in Germanic archaeology. One might imagine pottery cressets used in this way like those discovered in quantities on the late Saxon town site at Thetford.[37] These are hemispherical cups perched on clay spikes, which could be accommodated in the open portions of the grid. Individual lamps could be picked out and carried away in the hand and replaced in the grid when finished

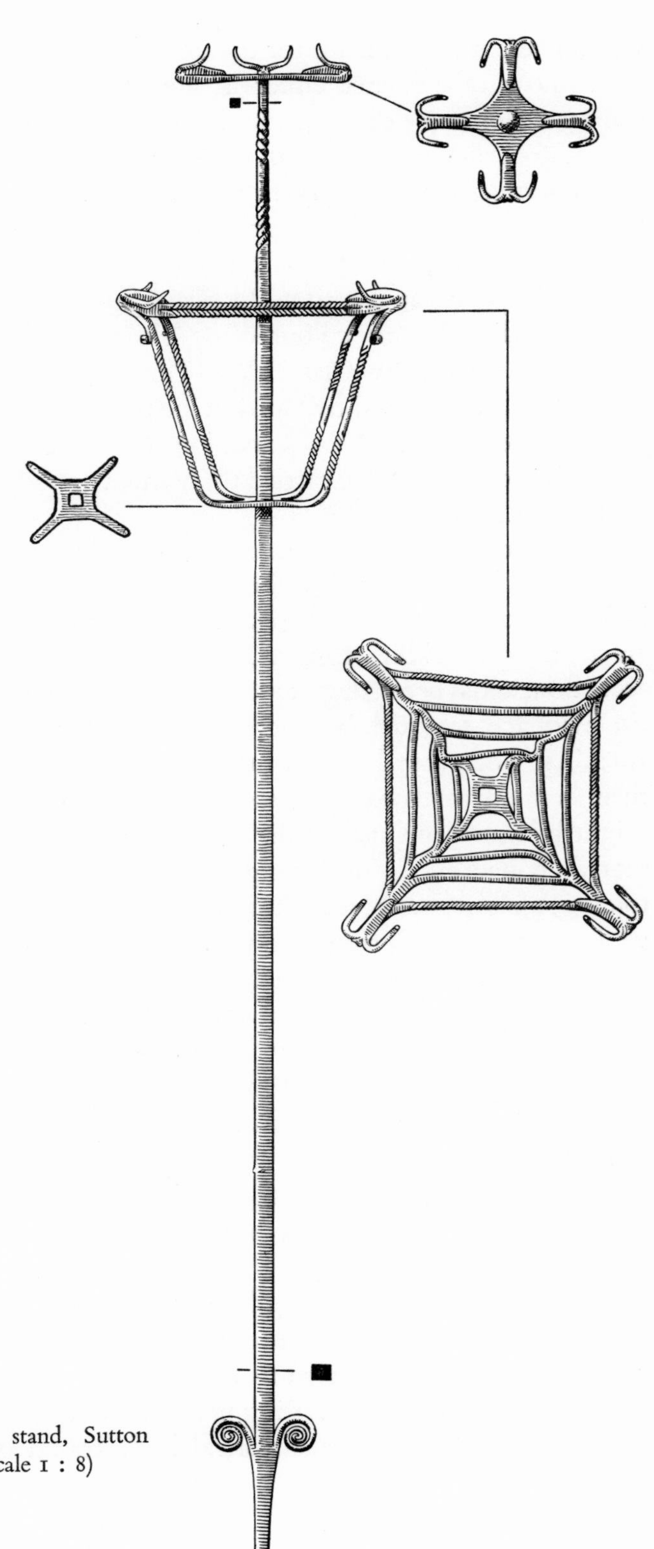

Figure 1 The iron stand, Sutton Hoo, with details (Scale 1 : 8)

with. There is no evidence for the use of such cressets in the seventh century, nor do I know of evidence either in literary sources or in archaeology that such elaborate lighting devices as the iron stand were used. There is no reference to anything of the kind in the hall scenes in *Beowulf* and indeed references to artificial lighting are curiously absent from the poem. A lampstand of the kind visualized would only be a practical proposition indoors and only then if the floor of the building was an earthen one. It is not unlikely that the floors of important royal halls were paved at this time. In *Beowulf* (line 752) the floor of Hrothgar's hall Heorot is described as 'coloured' or 'gleaming' (*fag*: '*on fagne flor feond treddode*', which is rendered by Clark Hall 'The fiend stepped onto the many-coloured paving of the floor' and by Gordon 'he trod the gleaming floor').[38] A stone pavement was encountered in excavations on the earthen platform at Old Uppsala which is thought to have carried the Vendel period (later sixth, seventh and eighth centuries A.D.) royal hall.[39]

It has also been suggested that the Sutton Hoo iron stand is a portable weapon-rack. For this purpose it is quite impracticable. It has a tendency to be top-heavy in itself and the treads and spike at the bottom would be insufficient to keep it erect under a weight of gear. The openings in the grid are too narrow for the reception, as has been suggested, of spear shafts. There is no literary or archaeological evidence for such weapon-racks. In *Beowulf* (1242–7) we read how the warriors, when they lay down to sleep in the hall, set their shields at their heads, their helmets, mailcoats and spear-shafts on the bench above each man. Spears might be leaned up against the edges of the grid of the Sutton Hoo stand, their shafts retained by the projecting bulls' heads at the corners but it seems pointless to carry a cumbrous object about in the field, just to rest spears against, when the wall or ground, or a simple improvisation would do as well. Suggested uses for the iron stand have even included from one authority, though perhaps not seriously meant, the hanging of enemy scalps. Such an idea might suit a barbarian milieu like that represented by the Nagy-Szent-Miklos treasure, on whose golden cups scenes of scalping occur,[40] but it would be wholly out of place, as an historian must know, in the context of Anglo-Saxon kingship on the eve of Christianity or in its early years. None of the foregoing suggestions has anything positive to support it; but the removal of the stag and ring removes the prime objection to the flambeau theory. It also makes the standard identification less convincing, although it does not rule it out.

Before we pass to the standard possibility, it is necessary to consider the historical setting in which the Sutton Hoo burial occurs. It will be seen at once that by contrast with other unsupported theories as to the use of the object, the concept of a standard fits the historical setting in a natural way and receives both archaeological and literary support. The historical background of Sutton Hoo is, as we shall

Plate 1 The Sutton Hoo sceptre
Height 82 cms (2 ft 9½ ins)

3

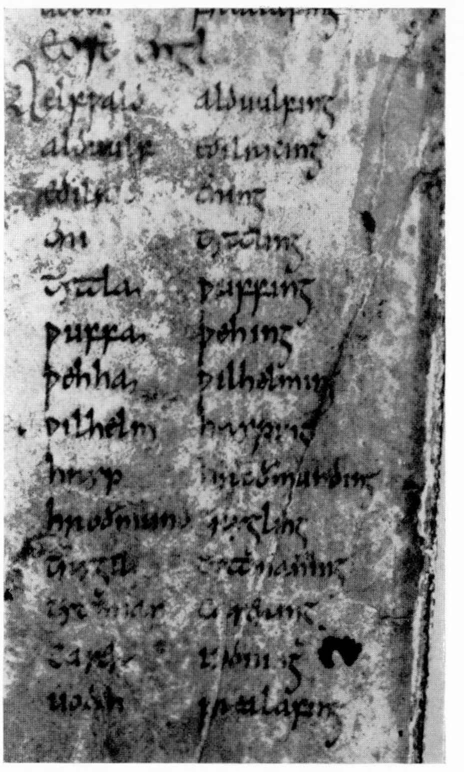

a

	Eost Engla
Aelfwald	Alduulfing
alduulf	eðilricing
eðilric	ening
eni	tyttling
tyttla	wuffing
wuffa	wehing
wehha	wilhelming
wilhelm	hryping
hryp	hroðmunding
hroðmund	trygling
trygil	tyttmaning
tyttman	casering
caser	uodning
uoden	frealafing

b

2

Plate 2 One of the set of ten shallow silver bowls from the Sutton Hoo ship-burial (Scale approx. 3 : 5)

Plate 3 Genealogy of the East Anglian Kings (British Museum MS. Cotton Vespasian B.VI. Folio 109 v). Early ninth century; with transcription

b

a

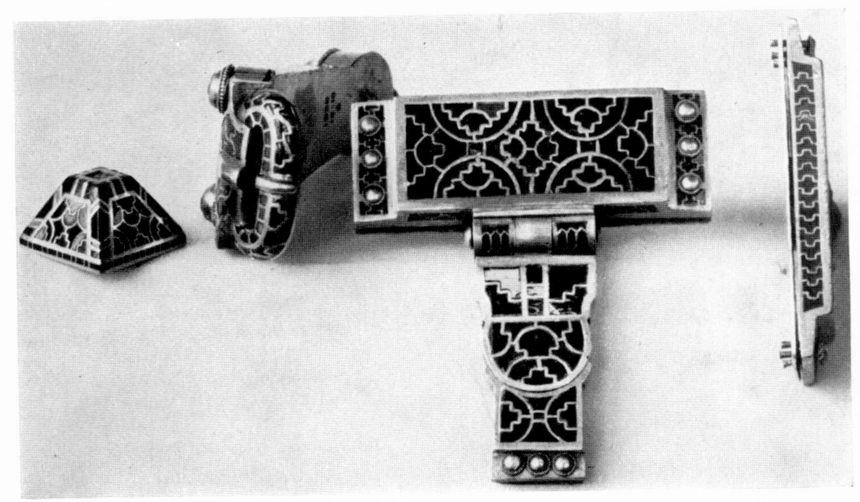

c

Plate 4 Gold jewellery from the Sutton Hoo ship-burial: *a*, Rectangular strap-mount; *b*, Hinged bar set with garnets, from the frame of the purse-lid; *c*, Various pieces photographed to show garnets set in edges and, in the T-shaped mount, in the hinge (Scales *a* 1 : 1 the rest reduced, except for the right-hand mount, which is 1 : 1)

Plate 5 Seventh-century Anglo-Saxon pendant gold crosses: *a*, Ixworth, Suffolk; *b*, Thurnham, Kent; *c*, Cruciform design from a scabbard boss, Sutton Hoo. (Scales all 1 : 1)

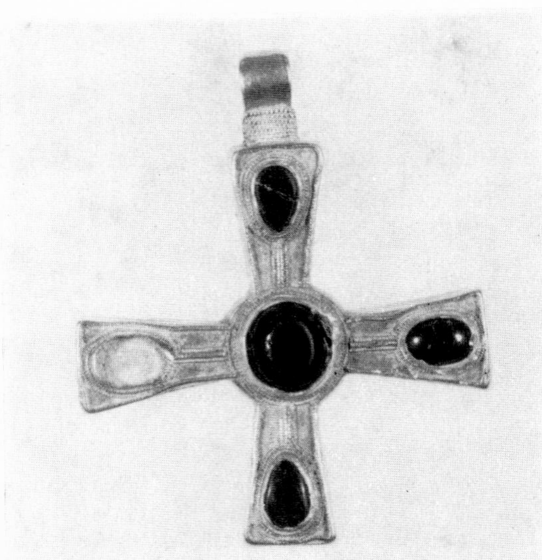

b

c

a

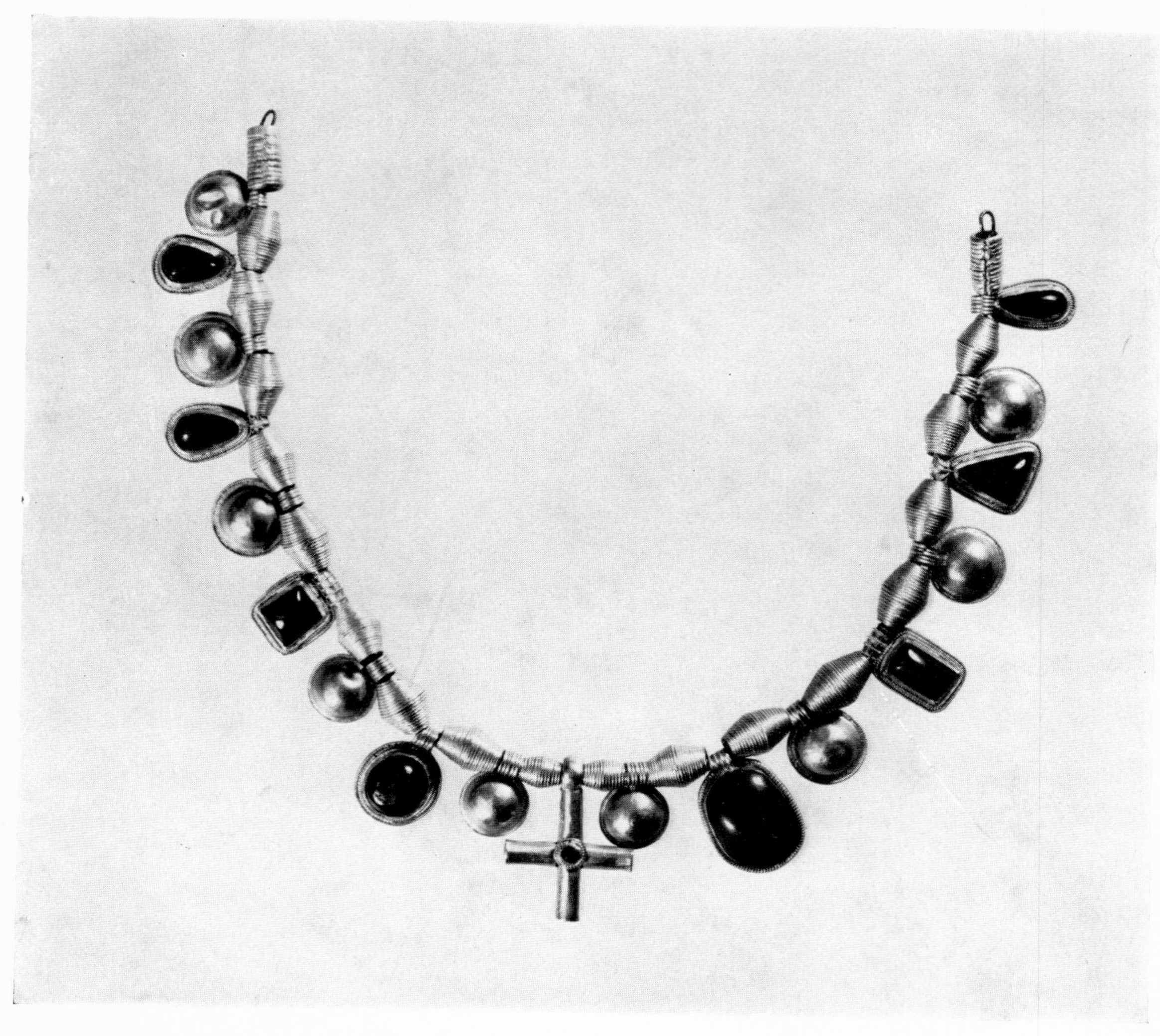

Plate 6 The Desborough necklace (Scale 3 : 4). Gold and cabochon garnets. 7th century A.D.

see, most important. The stone sceptre, to judge by its human faces, which are really all that we can parallel about it, might perhaps be claimed as a Swedish piece and something exotic in the Anglo-Saxon context. The human faces find their closest analogies in Sweden[41] or in material that may be of Swedish origin.[42] The standard, on the other hand, is a symbol of royal office peculiar I believe to the Anglo-Saxon background and would therefore have a bearing on the nationality and so the identity, of the commemorated or buried man.

Attention has already been drawn to the fact[43] that standards were used by the Saxon Bretwalda (Overlord or High King) and King of Deira, Edwin (A.D. 616–632) as symbols of his power and that there was an intimate connection between Edwin and Raedwald and the East Anglian court.[44] Professor Margaret Deanesly has suggested, independently of the Sutton Hoo object, that Raedwald may have used standards in East Anglia and that Edwin may have learned the use of them there.[45] 'A conscious respect for Roman tradition existed in the early days of the settlement' and the evidence on which Professor Deanesly bases this view belongs particularly to the seventh century. She develops three lines of argument: (i) the probability that the Saxon title Bretwalda meant Ruler of Britain (not of the Britons, still less the Saxons) and that this implies a quasi-Roman claim to territorial rule; (ii) the likelihood that the standards and banners of Edwin of Deira, described by Bede in a passage emphasizing Edwin's dignity and power, were copied from Roman emblems of authority; (iii) the fact that the Saxon moneyers who struck the silver *sceatta* coinage of the eighth century employed in the new designs on the reverses of their coins devices selected from among the age-old emblems of Roman authority, as represented on the reverse of imperial coins.[46]

The Anglo-Saxon silver *sceatta* coinage emerges *c.* A.D. 700,[47] and it should be noted that the standard motif occurs also in the gold coinage that preceded it and that what has been held to be one of the first gold coins struck in England (now in the British Museum), a copy of a gold solidus of Honorius, shows on the reverse the Emperor, standing with his foot on a fallen captive and holding a standard (Fig 2g). This is the well-known coin which bears a runic legend to the right of the Emperor's figure, read as *SCANOMODU*.[47a] This piece seems to be more or less undateable whether by runologists or by numismatic considerations. Nor can it, especially in view of its possibly late date, be localized with any assurance. Dates proposed vary from *c.* 525 to the middle of the eighth century.[48] An early date, before say 650, would be quite likely and, if so, a context is provided for familiarity with royal or imperial standards and insignia in an Anglo-Saxon context at the relevant time. The beginning of the production of gold coins in England for purposes of trade, although some, for example, the Canterbury Coins bearing the *DUROVERNIS CIVITAS* legend, may be earlier, can be assigned to the 630s.[49]

Figure 2 a,b, Constantinian coins showing legionary standards; *c,d,e,f,* Anglo-Saxon silver *sceattas*; *g,* Anglo-Saxon gold solidus; (coins not to scale.) *h,* Standard-bearer from a Roman monument

That the East Anglian royal house, the Wuffingas, shared in the conscious claim to inherit something of the authority of Rome in Britain may be inferred from the fact that (almost certainly at this time), they incorporated the name Caesar in their genealogy after Woden. It appears in the best genealogy, a regnal list dating from the early ninth century (Plate 3 and Fig 3).

Thus we have an historical background into which a royal standard in the Sutton Hoo grave would fit. We must now consider the object itself and see whether its appearance and characteristics are such as we might expect in a barbaric version, possibly derived from the designs of coin reverses, of a Roman standard.

Nerman refers to the suggestion in the British Museum Provisional Guide that this object may be a standard (*fälttecken*) but says that with its horizontal projection it seems impracticable for the purpose.[50] He does not say what he considers the function of a standard to be and the fact is that all Roman standards have horizontal projections of some kind.

The passage in Bede makes it clear that Edwin used no less than three different kinds of standard:

So great was his majesty in his realm that not only were banners carried before

> him in battle but even in time of peace as he rode about among his cities, estates and Kingdoms with his thegns, he always used to be preceded by a standard-bearer. Further when he walked anywhere along the roads there used to be carried before him the type of standard which the Romans call *Tufa* and the English call a *thuf.*[51]

The three types of standard mentioned in this passage are *vexillum*, *signum* and *tufa*. A *vexillum* was a light wooden lance which carried a small flag, pennant or windsock.

Professor Deanesly says of it:

> use of *vexilla* in battle (in the plural) accords with the practice of the Roman army at the end of the 4th century; within each legion the centurions in battle bore the *vexilla* of the units they commanded in order to maintain touch with each other.

Bede was right to use the word in the plural, for the legionary *vexilla* had a tactical, not merely ceremonial use.[52] The light *vexillum* as distinct from the *signum* or *labarum* is not commonly represented on Roman coins of the late Empire and is unlikely to be the prototype of the Sutton Hoo stand. We read, however, that in peace time Edwin was preceded, not by a *vexillarius* but by a *signifer*, and 'this implies the carrying of a copy of some legionary signum'.

> The *signum* of the legion was a wooden lance with a similar sharp metal tip for sticking in the ground, but above the hand-hold it was silver-plated and enriched with a series of discs, fillets and metal ornaments. It was surmounted by a metal eagle and was altogether a much heavier affair than the *vexillum*. Among the discs and fillets and below the eagle there was frequently by the end of the fourth century a metal symbol of the particular legion, sometimes one of the animals of the signs of the Zodiac.[53]

We may also note that there were late forms of standard which sometimes included a small *vexillum* (pennant or banner) beneath the eagle or symbolic animal and that although the eagle became the official legionary *signum*, other legionary symbols and animals continue to appear frequently on coins down to the end of the Roman period.[54]

Research is still needed into the representations of *signa* and *labara*[55] in Roman, Byzantine and Germanic art to see what representations occur that might have given rise to the creation or evolution of the Saxon equivalent resembling the Sutton Hoo object. It is, however, clear that the legionary *signum* was a heavy lance, the height of a man or rather taller (Fig 2h) with an animal or bird crest at the top, cross-bar somewhat lower down, with various elaborations associated with it and a point at the bottom for sticking it into the ground. With such an object the Sutton Hoo stand broadly corresponds in heaviness, in height and

EAST ANGLIAN KINGS

THE WUFFINGAS

(To save space, the descent through WODEN is shown horizontally. Those who came to the throne are shown in black type.)

Frealaf—Woden—Caser—Tyttman—Trygil—Hrothmund—Hrype—Wilhelm—

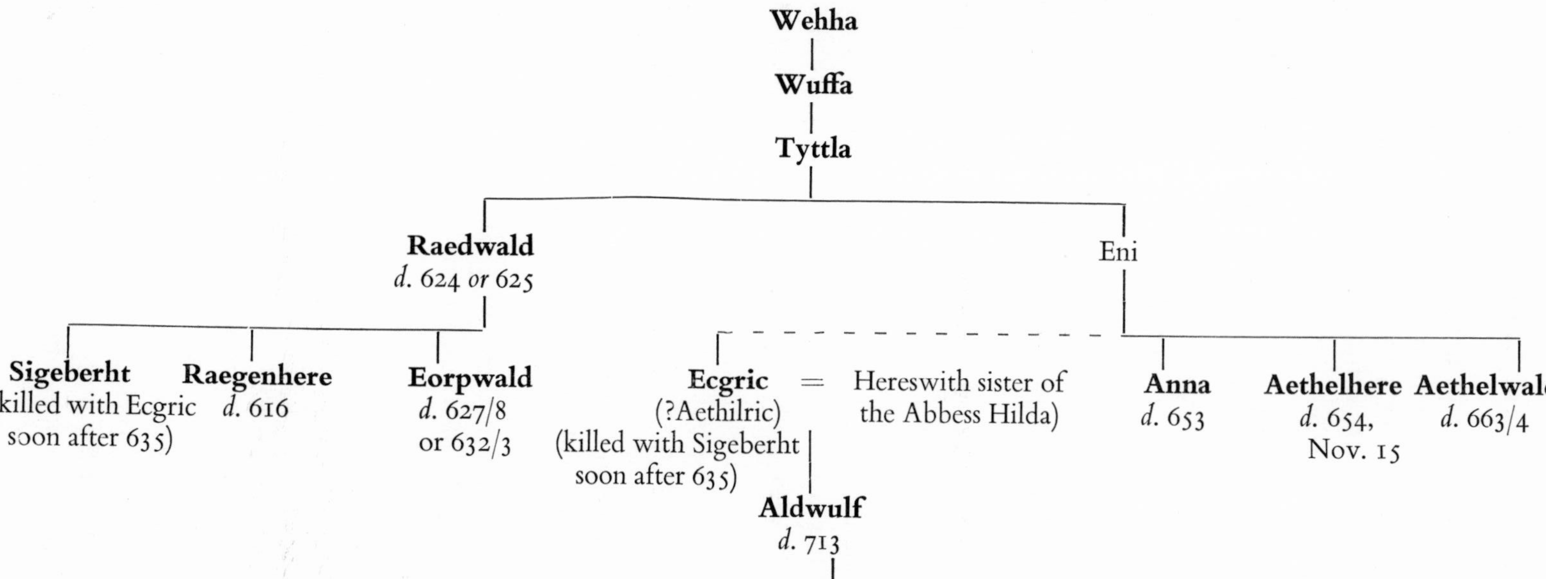

Figure 3 The family tree of the East Anglian Royal House, the Wuffingas. (*Based on Chadwick and Stenton*)

proportion to the human figure, in the spike at the bottom and the cross-bar with complications in between. The stag figure when mounted erroneously on the top of the stand intensified the parallel with a Roman *signum* or analogous creation but this must now be ignored. The characteristic features of the Sutton Hoo stand remain unexplained; the square openwork grid in particular and the short cage of four vertical bars that support it from below (Fig 1). To these and other details in the design of the Sutton Hoo object I do not know of any parallels amongst Roman standards. The important point to remember here is that the Saxon monarchs who we know had standards made for them probably had, if they wished to follow the Roman precedent, no more to go on than oral tradition, miniature representations on coins and possibly in certain places, versions seen in sculptural reliefs. The silver discs, fillets, wreaths, animal figures[56] and symbols, even sometimes a pennant and other niceties that complicated the upper portions of the legionary standard, would probably have been incomprehensible to seventh-century Saxons when depicted on coins and if not understood, could not have been literally incorporated into a piece of Saxon craftsmanship. One would rather expect a translation, or free interpretation of the object seen on the coins in which the general intention and broad characteristics were maintained but the details barbarized, misunderstood or re-adapted to suit the notions of a Germanic king. A similar process may be observed in many items of Germanic equipment derived from Roman prototypes. In this way the aberrant features of the Sutton Hoo standard could, it seems, be explained. The four vertical bars that support the grid seen in profile give a rectangular shape, for they spring from projections that run out horizontally for some little way from the vertical stem. The broad effect of this seen from the side is not unlike that of a *labarum* on a coin, where a flag, often represented by a rectangular outline, appears below the cross-bar of the lance (Fig 2b, g).

Finally we may consider the third type of banner, the *tufa* used by Edwin. Bede calls this a type of *vexillum* ('illud genus vexilli quod Romani *tufam*, Angli appellant thuuf') so that it ought to be comparatively light and the fact that it seems to have accompanied Edwin wherever he went also suggests something of a not very cumbersome or ceremonial kind. It is to this extent perhaps unlikely that the Sutton Hoo object is a *tufa*. We have no real knowledge of the nature of the *tufa* and Professor Deanesly has even argued very plausibly that no such thing existed amongst the Roman military signs, and that the Latin word arose from a textual corruption. Nevertheless, it is clear, however the word may have arisen, that Bede in using it was referring to a specific object that was different from Edwin's *signum* and which, though a kind of *vexillum*, was a special type, different from those used in battle. It also seems clear that the Saxons had a special word for it. The Saxon word *þuf* (tuft) is applied in Anglo-Saxon writers to foliage

(*Þufboere*, leafy; *Þufigum*=frondosus)[57] and it is perhaps worth drawing attention to the feathered extremities of the Sutton Hoo object, the animal's horns on the corners of the grid and the top plate. The Anglo-Saxons of this period did not favour foliate themes in their art but they seem to have done so in their rituals[58] and it is not improbable that the open grid of the Sutton Hoo stand might have been filled with bracken or yew fronds, or carried a wreath or other vegetation. It is not impossible that we may have in the Sutton Hoo stand a standard of the kind 'known to the Angles as Tuuf'. It could have been filled with peacock feathers[59] but philological considerations suggest foliage.

If the object were a standard there might have been banners or pennants hung on the four sides of the grid, perhaps suspended from the bulls' heads and tied off lower down, where the vertical bars below the grid meet the stem and are kept apart by these bars. These are speculations but serve as a reminder that there may have been flags, foliage or other secondary features of a perishable kind, that would alter the appearance of the object and would very likely explain the peculiarities of its design. No textile impressions survive on the iron stand and there is no trace in the burial of gold threads or wires such as are characteristic of Anglo-Saxon gold woven braids.[60]

Finally, it should be noted that the iron stand occurs in the grave alongside (or, if originally erect, near) the sceptre and at the west end of the burial chamber amongst honoured objects – the shield and spears, helmet, lyre, and rare imported bronze and silver bowls (Plate 2).[61] The only humble object at this 'distinguished' end of the burial chamber, was an iron-bound wooden bucket, which was certainly placed there for its contents, whatever they may have been, rather than for its own sake;[62] the most utilitarian appliances, however imposing, like the iron lamp filled with beeswax, the great bronze cauldron with the ornamental suspension gear, those silver dishes, though imposing, that seem to have no particularly personal significance and miscellaneous items, such as the leather bags, combs, shoes, clothes, pottery bottle and so on, were at the east end of the chamber. The siting of the iron stand in the burial alone suggests that it had an honourable significance and was not merely a domestic item.

Research into the designs on silver coins circulating in England may possibly assist in this connection. We have already noted the parallel offered by the unique *SCANOMODU* gold solidus. The silver *sceattas* were 'small, thick . . . clumsily struck coins' and Saxon moneyers often did not get on to them the whole of a *labarum* or standard, but concentrated on recognizable details and significant features.[63] There is, for instance, a coin bearing an enigmatic device[64] (Fig 2f), which might well on the face of it represent, not a classical type of standard but the upper part of the barbaric version of one having the features of our Sutton Hoo object.

The new reconstruction of the stand (1970) as illustrated in Fig 1 recaptures the ornamental and formal characteristics of the original and uses the correct gauge of metal. It stands up by itself perfectly well when struck into soft firm ground but would not carry a heavy overburden without being supported. It is possible that the spike was intended, as Sune Lindqvist has suggested, to fit into a leather frog, so that the object might be carried rather in the manner of modern regimental colours and not struck into the ground. Bede, speaking of Edwin's use of standards, does not connect them with his position as Bretwalda. We cannot say therefore that a 'standard' at Sutton Hoo, if this object in its stag-less form is still thought a possible candidate, must identify the grave with Raedwald, Edwin's host and predecessor as Bretwalda. The use of standards is cited by Bede as evidence, worthy of remark, of Edwin's kingly dignity and style. For this reason as well as for the others adduced, identification of the object as a standard would support the interpretation of the Sutton Hoo ship-burial as the burial of a king and not of any lesser royal personage or guest.

IS THE SUTTON HOO SHIP-BURIAL PAGAN OR CHRISTIAN?

English commentators on the Sutton Hoo ship-burial in the 1950s did not seem at all willing to allow that it could be a Christian burial. In this they were swayed by the late dating then universally accepted. Chadwick, whose knowledge of the period was profound, had said of it: 'It may be doubted greatly whether extravagance on the scale found at Sutton Hoo ever prevailed in the burials of Christian times',[65] and 'We must conclude then, if the funeral took place after 640, that it was due to a deliberate reversion to heathenism.'[66] Kendrick, writing in the *British Museum Quarterly* in 1939,[67] said 'the main case for the identification' (of the grave with Raedwald) 'depends on the view, with which archaeologists must agree, that the burial is pagan. . . .'

In the British Museum's Provisional Guide, I myself wrote: 'There can be little doubt that Sutton Hoo is a pagan burial. It is wholeheartedly, perhaps even ostentatiously so'. Nerman, in his *Fornvännen* article in 1948, said that the Sutton Hoo chief 'was buried in the heathen manner'.[68]

It was thus surprising that Lindqvist, who argued that, on the contrary, the Sutton Hoo ship-burial was 'without doubt Christian, prepared for a convert', went to considerable trouble to demonstrate that the Christian Church did not discourage rich provision of grave-goods in the early stages of the conversion.[69] This is generally accepted. Indeed, the rich furnishing of the graves of Queen Arnegunde at St Denis and of the young prince under Cologne Cathedral (whose grave contained an object loosely identified as a sceptre), both evidently Christian burials, demonstrate the rich furnishing of Christian graves in Christian precincts.[70] Frauke Stein has recently reviewed the deposition of grave-goods in aristocratic burials of the eighth century in Germany, many of them in Christian contexts.[71] Richness of furnishing of the Sutton Hoo grave was not *per se* the reason why English writers felt so confident about the pagan character of the burial.

The fact that richly furnished graves, on the continent at any rate, can be Christian was appreciated from the outset. Chadwick had written in 1940:

> The custom of burying objects of various kinds with the dead did not cease with the introduction of Christianity. Some rich Frankish cemeteries, e.g. at Worms and Mainz, were attached to churches, and in these there have been found a number of graves well-furnished with both weapons and ornaments, and containing grave-stones with Christian inscriptions, which originally no doubt stood or lay above the graves.[72]

The well-known Lombardic graves with gold foil crosses may also be cited. The attitude of modern English archaeology on this point was expressed by Leeds in 1936 in his *Early Anglo-Saxon Art and Archaeology*, and the subject has been further discussed by Lethbridge, who put forward the view (with which I see no particular reason to agree) that the Taplow Barrow, the richest grave known in Saxon archaeology before the discovery of the Sutton Hoo ship-burial, was Christian.[73]

That the Church in England was tolerant of pagan burial customs, in the earlier phases of the conversion at any rate, though not explicitly stated, may be inferred from the accommodating attitude towards pagan practices and thinking expressed in the letter of Pope Gregory the Great to Bishop Mellitus,[74] the text of which is given by Bede, and from the circumstance, also recorded by Bede, that Earconbert of Kent, as late as A.D. 640, 'was the first King of England who of his princely authority commanded that the idols in all his whole realm should be forsaken and destroyed', and fixed punishments for infringements of his edict.[75] Kent had been officially Christian since 597. Compared with worship of idols, deposition of grave-goods was a harmless custom and it must have been practised in Kent by surviving pagans and probably by many Christians also as late as 640, especially in remoter parts, if pagan worship itself was allowed to survive so late. Not a few well-furnished Kentish graves, such as those on Breach Down and Crundale Down, are probably a good deal later than *c.* 640.

On the other hand, though grave-goods continued to be deposited in the early phases of Christianity, there is no evidence in English archaeology, whatever may have been the case in parts of the Continent, that conversion to Christianity *per se* resulted in even a temporary increase in the richness of burials. Lindqvist's view that 'the very fact that such a wealth of grave-goods is not met with in the preceding centuries' shows the Sutton Hoo burial to be Christian[76] cannot be accepted. If the richness of the Sutton Hoo burial has not been met with earlier, this is partly because it is the first royal burial found. It stands at a different social level from all previous discoveries. Even in its own century the difference between a royal grave and any lesser burial would be expected to be marked.[77] It is also because Saxon archaeology in general is richer in the seventh century than in the fifth and sixth centuries, a fact due to the consolidation of the kingdoms of the Heptarchy, the resumption of continental trade and the renewed flow into England of continental gold[78] – and not to the arrival of St Augustine.

The attitude of the Augustinian church towards grave-goods is probably well reflected, as Chadwick has pointed out,[79] in *The Seafarer*:

> Though he will spread with gold the grave of his own brother, and bury with the dead in treasures of various kinds what he wishes to have with him, yet gold, which he has hidden while he is still alive here, will not be able to help a soul which is sinful, in place of the fear of God.[80]

In other words the practice should not be regarded as wrong so much as ineffective. Thus we must expect that with the acceptance of Christianity the custom would in many cases continue, but as a matter of sentiment and tradition and not one of vital importance, and that the grave-goods would assume more and more a token character. This is indeed what happens in English archaeology. Many furnished graves may be late and Christian; but none that may be confidently called Christian is conspicuously rich.[81]

Such considerations must have been in Chadwick's mind when he wrote: 'It may be doubted greatly whether *extravagance* on the scale found at Sutton Hoo ever prevailed in the burials of Christian times.' It seems that the burying of so many rare and intrinsically valuable objects must express a positive feeling and that such lavish provision, if the dead man were a Christian, would represent an improbable sacrifice of many items of costly and rare things to what was now no more than sentiment or tradition.

The most serious objection to Lindqvist's treatment of this subject is that his arguments, however sound in general, can scarcely apply to the particular case of Sutton Hoo. He overlooked the background of the burial in English history, as continental commentators have been apt to do, although it had been carefully and accessibly expounded by Chadwick.[82] Lindqvist, when he wrote, understood the numismatic evidence for the date of the burial to be 'after 650, and most probably not until about 670'.[83] This is now seen to be forty or fifty years too late but the early date suits his argument better.

If I understand him correctly, Lindqvist considers that, in an initial phase, the provision of elaborate grave-goods was encouraged by the Church as an inducement to abandon cremation (which conflicted with the concept of resurrection of the body), as in some sort a compensation for the spectacle and popular celebrations that accompanied important cremations.[84] Even by A.D. 625–40, the likely date limits of the Sutton Hoo burial, cremation, so far as we can tell, had disappeared in Anglo-Saxon England, even in its strongholds.[85]

Again, Lindqvist wrote:

> I have tried to show that the rich grave must be regarded as a typically Christian arrangement, *but only conceivable during a period of transition from paganism which was of very short duration in all parts of England.*[86]

Whether the period of transition was short or long (and there is both historical and archaeological evidence for its gradualness) the dating of 620–625+ certainly brings events closer to the time of the conversion of the royal house and if the burial were Raedwald's, we are exactly in the situation which Lindqvist envisaged.

The reluctance of English archaeologists to see this lavish burial as Christian was based essentially upon the late date (650–660) then accepted for it and Chadwick was correct in saying 'if the funeral took place after 640 it was due to a deliberate reversion to heathenism'. The later one attempts to place the burial after 640, the more compelling does Chadwick's conclusion become.

This is not the end of the matter. Bearing in mind the fact that the new dating of 620–625 for the hoard is only a *terminus post quem* and that, theoretically, the burial could have taken place a good many years after the hoard came together[87] it is necessary to look at the history of Christianity in East Anglia[88] most closely and in particular at the history of Christianity in the East Anglian Royal House (Fig 3).

The story of Christianity in East Anglia begins, some time before A.D. 617, with the conversion of Raedwald on a visit to Kent, although he did not, in the event, give up his pagan practices. Raedwald's son Eorpwald, was persuaded by Edwin of Deira to 'leave off the superstitions of idols, and with his whole realm to receive the faith and sacrament of Christ'.[89] This must have been after Edwin's own conversion (Easter Day, 12 April 627) and before his death in 632. The subsequent history of East Anglian Christianity until the death of Sigeberht (*circa* A.D. 637)[90] is given by Bede in the same chapter.[91]

> But Eorpwald, not long after he had received the faith, was slain by a man, that was a (pagan) named Ricbert, and from that time three years after the province abode in terror, until Sigeberht, brother of the same Eorpwald, took the Kingdom, a man in all points most Christian and learned, who whiles his brother was yet alive, living banished in France was instructed in the mysteries of the faith; of which he went about to make all his realm partake as soon as he began to reign. Whose good endeavour herein the Bishop Felix farthered

> to his great glory, and when Felix came from the coasts of Burgundy,[92] (where he was born and took holy orders) to Honorius the archbishop and had opened his longing to him, the Archbishop sent him to preach the word of life to the aforesaid nation of the East English. Where certes his desire fell not in vain; nay rather this good husbandsman of the spiritual soil found in that nation manifold fruit of people that believed.
>
> For according to the good abodement of his name he brought all that province now delivered from their long iniquity and unhappiness, unto faith and works of justice and the gifts of unending happiness; and he received the see of his bishopric in the city of Domnoc:[93] where when he had ruled the same province seventeen years in that dignity, he ended his life in peace in that same place.[94]

During Sigeberht's reign there came from Ireland direct to East Anglia (not *via* Northumbria, although at about the same moment that St Aidan came to Lindisfarne (A.D. 635)), another missionary figure. This was an Irish ascetic, St Fursey, who 'came through the Britons to the country of the English' with a few brethren.[95] He was received honourably by Sigeberht, made converts and strengthened the hesitant. He built a monastery in the place given by Sigeberht (identified as Burgh Castle, near Yarmouth) 'which afterwards Anna' (d. A.D. 654) 'and all the noble men enriched with buildings of more majesty and with offerings'.

The future of the East Anglian Church was secured by the foundation of a school for which Felix secured teachers 'such as there were in Kent'.[96] Sigeberht himself founded a monastery at Bury[97] and gave up the throne to enter it.

The co-kings Sigeberht and Ecgric, killed together,[98] were succeeded by the good King Anna, an exemplary Christian in every way, founder and benefactor of monasteries, 'all of whose daughters became nuns, and three of them saints.'[99] We have no certain information about the religion[100] of his brother and successor Æthelhere, who reigned only one year but he was almost certainly Christian also: Æthelhere's successor Æthelwald, another brother, we know to have been a Christian and to have stood godfather to the King of Essex, who was baptized at Rendlesham at this time (A.D. 655–664) at the hands of Cedd, Bishop of the East Saxons.[101] Subsequent kings, Aldwulf, who died fifty years after his predecessor Æthwald and who lived in Bede's own day and his son Ælfwald, who died in the middle of the eighth century, may be assumed to have been Christians.

From this survey it is clear that by 640 East Anglia was substantially converted. The course of Christianity there seems furthermore to have been smooth and markedly successful, studded with saints and notable Christian personalities. Before 670 there were at least five monasteries, Felix's at Dunwich, St Fursey's at Burgh Castle, Sigeberht's at Bury, Anna's at Blythburgh; and another presided

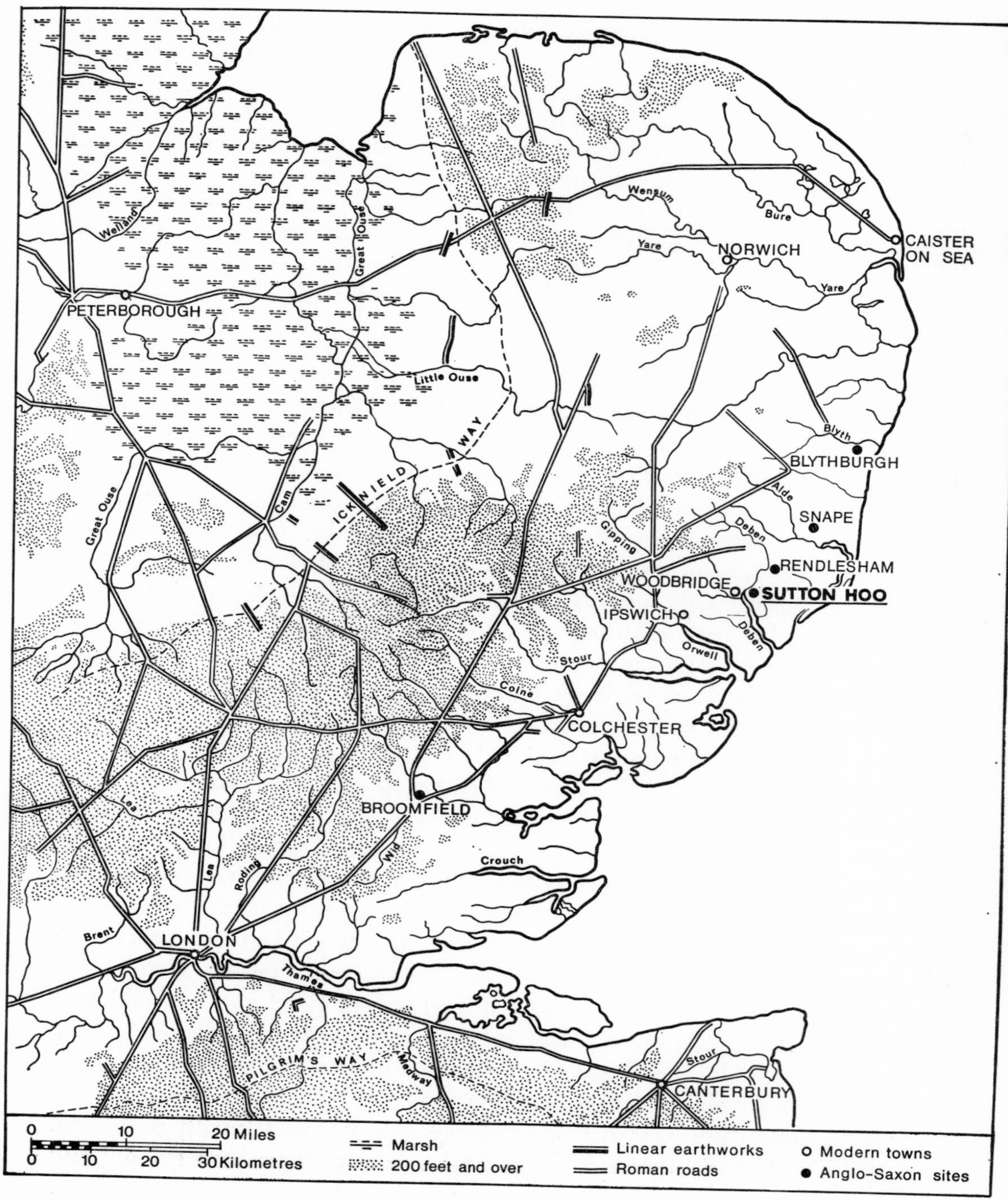

Figure 4 Sketch map of East Anglia, showing some of the places mentioned in this book: based on the Ordnance Survey map of England in the Dark Ages

over by St Botolph at a place called Icanhoh which has been identified with Iken on the Alde[102] (Fig 5) an identification which seems highly probable. So celebrated had this last become that Abbot Coelfrith of Wearmouth journeyed especially to visit it shortly after 669.[103] It seems to have been founded in A.D. 654.[104] Besides monasteries there must have been churches. One of these almost certainly was close to Sutton Hoo at Rendlesham, a church that must have been built for members of the East Anglian royal family and no doubt dated back to Anna's reign, very possibly to Sigeberht's.[105]

It is also necessary to draw a distinction between royalty and converts of lesser standing and especially those in districts remote from Christian centres. It was essential for missionaries to obtain the consent and good will of kings before operating in their territories. If the king and other members of the royal circle could be persuaded to accept Christianity, others would follow and the work of the mission would be given an auspicious start and good prospects of success. Thus we find the efforts of the missionaries everywhere addressed first to kings.

The part played by royalty in the introduction and spread of Christianity was vital, largely through the interconnections by marriage between the different courts, and the royal ability to endow monasteries with land. The way for Augustine in Kent was prepared by the fact that Æthelberht already had a Christian wife, the Frankish princess Bertha, who had with her in Kent before Augustine came, a Christian chaplain, Luidhard, and retinue.[106] Raedwald of East Anglia was converted on a visit to Æthelberht in Kent. Sigeberht of East Anglia became Christian whilst in exile at the Frankish court and when he won back his throne took the vital steps in ensuring the conversion of East Anglia. The first introduction of Christianity to Northumbria was the result of Edwin's marriage with Æthelberht of Kent's daughter Æthelburga, and the fact that Paulinus was sent with her from Kent as her chaplain. After Edwin's death and the return of Paulinus with Æthelburga to Kent, it was at King Oswald's invitation that St Aidan was invited from Iona and settled with his Irish mission at Lindisfarne (A.D. 635). It was Edwin of Northumbria who persuaded Raedwald's son Eorpwald in East Anglia 'to leave off the superstitions of idols and with his whole realm to receive the faith and sacraments of Christ'. It has been said of the policy of the Church towards pagan burials that

> the first effect of the conversion was not so much the discontinuance of grave offerings as a change in the place of burial. People were now taken to churches for burial, and, just as in Iceland in later times, this change probably took place at once.[107]

Nowhere was the Church more insistent, or consistent, in the matter of this change in the place of burial, than with kings and queens and in these cases offerings in the grave, in the pagan manner, seem also to have ceased at once. We can see this change of location in operation on the Continent at an earlier period. Thus, whilst Childeric I, the last pagan king of the Franks, was buried at Tournai in 481 with the richest grave furnishings known in Northern Europe until the Sutton Hoo discovery, his son Clovis, the first Christian king, converted in 496, was buried in the Church of the Apostles at Paris and his descendants seem regularly to have been buried in churches.[108] In Kent, one of Augustine's prime concerns was to build

> a monastery not far from the city (Canterbury) to the eastward, in which by his advice Æthelberht erected from its foundations the church of the blessed apostles Peter and Paul and enriched it with divers gifts; wherein the bodies of the same Augustine and of all the Bishops of Canterbury and of the Kings of Kent might be buried.[109]

Similarly the first act of Edwin of Northumbria after his conversion was to build a stone church at York, in which royal burials from that time onwards took place. He was baptized at York on Easter Day, 12 April 627, in the church of the Apostle Peter 'which in all speed he himself set up of wood in that same place where he was catechized and instructed against his baptism'. As soon as he was christened 'he set to building right in that place a basilica of stone greater and more magnificent'.[110] In this basilica Edwin's two infant children were buried within five or six years of its foundation at most,[111] as was his own head, recovered from the battle of Heathfield (A.D. 632). Chadwick[112] quotes also the burials of Sebbe, first king of the East Saxons to be converted, in St Paul's in London, of Mercian kings at Lichfield, Bardney and other churches, and of members of the royal house of Northumbria in the monastery at Whitby founded in 637 by St Hilda, whose sister Hereswith married the East Anglian King Æthelric.[113] Many of these burials took place within a few years of conversion and there is no indication in Bede that any variation from this rule occurred in any instance of a royal Christian's burial. Whatever may have happened in the countryside at large, in the case of kings and queens, key personalities whose souls must have been directly in the care of bishops, all the evidence indicates that conversions resulted in a clear break with the past both in the place and in the mode of burial.

If we now turn to East Anglia, we cannot say that here in the Wuffinga family this break with the past had been effected by the time of the Sutton Hoo burial, which may have been as early as 625. Raedwald died still attached to the pagan religion. Sigeberht (d. *circa* 637)[114] had left the throne to enter a monastery and we may feel sure that his body, if recovered from battle, was buried in consecrated ground, most probably in the monastery which he had himself founded and entered and from which he was only brought out by force to fight his last battle. We do not know the religion of his co-king Ecgric, killed with him. Anna (d. 654), according to an express statement in the Ely Chronicle, was buried at Blythburgh, his body being still venerated there in the twelfth century. By 654 in East Anglia, any period of transition was over, whereas the need for naïve inducements to abandon cremation by allowing more splendidly furnished inhumations, is something very unlikely ever to have applied in the history of East Anglian Christianity. The burial ground at Sutton Hoo is most unlikely to have been the burial place of a Christian East Anglian king. It certainly had pagan origins and associations, since cremation burials have been found there not only in 1938 in two of the mounds, but again in flat ground in 1967. These pagan roots and associations did not prevent its use as a burial-place continuing into Christian times, indeed as late as the eighth century.[115] As we have seen, the break in the place of burial following conversion was something which applied with particular consistency to kings and queens. We do not of course know that the inhumations found at Sutton Hoo without grave-goods were necessarily Christian, even if of eighth-century date. They could still be burials of obstinate pagans in an era when cremation had been long since abandoned and when social customs had radically changed.

This is the historical background against which the question of the pagan or Christian character of the Sutton Hoo burial must be considered and it explains the view that the great burial, if it took place after *c.* 640, must represent a reversion to paganism, or the accession of an independently-minded king, who had declined to follow the example of earlier kings and other members of his family and had remained faithful to the old gods.

That such an exception might possibly occur is shown by the history of Christianity in the West Saxon royal house. Birinus, first bishop of the West Saxons, found them 'intensely heathen'.[116] He baptized their king Cynegils in 635 and immediately afterwards set up his bishopric at Dorchester-on-Thames. Cynegils's eldest son and grandson soon followed his example but his second son and successor was still heathen in 645 when he was expelled from Wessex.[117] Such a thing could theoretically have occurred in East Anglia, at an earlier date. When the exiled king of Wessex *was* converted, we find that he was converted in East Anglia and under the influence of Anna (d. 654).[118] Nevertheless, in the face of the phenomenon represented by the Sutton Hoo burial the possibility of one or other member of the royal family remaining pagan cannot be ruled out. This is more likely in so well Christianized a milieu than any general relapse and indeed a general relapse in East Anglia would assuredly have been recorded by Bede, who devoted a good deal of space to the East Anglian royalty and who recorded relapses in other kingdoms less distinguished for good works and holy lives.

SIGNS OF CHRISTIANITY IN THE BURIAL

These are positive and striking and seem deliberate. The two silver spoons are marked 'Paul' and 'Saul',[119] that is to say one is marked 'Paul', the other 'Saul' (Fig 5). Kitzinger said of these that there is little doubt that the inscriptions refer

Figure 5 Inscriptions in Greek, 'Saulos' and 'Paulos', from the handles of the pair of Byzantine silver spoons from Sutton Hoo (Scale 1 : 1)

to Paul the Apostle.[120] There surely can be no doubt. The fact that the spoons are a pair and the coupling of the name Saul with that of Paul, seem to put it beyond doubt. Kitzinger also seemed to have some difficulty in explaining the purpose of the spoons and said 'the best solution seems to be to regard them as either as votive gifts to a church or as pilgrims' souvenirs of some sacred place'.[121] This was because he thought that the saint's pre-apostolic name could hardly have appeared on a liturgical object. It would not be appropriate. There is one context in which the use of the saint's pre-apostolic name, in conjunction with his apostolic name, is peculiarly apt. Our spoons make reference not merely to St Paul[122] but to the critical event of his life, the change that came over him on the road to Damascus. We may accept them as a present for a convert – not a Christening gift for an infant but one intended to mark the baptism of an adult convert relinquishing his pagan state and no doubt a royal convert. The pair of silver spoons in the Sutton Hoo ship-burial is thus not vaguely Christian or a tourist's casual souvenir but has a specific significance in the historical context in which they have been found. They might also be supposed to have had special significance for their owner and to be unlikely to have been buried with an active pagan resisting a Christian environment. The set of ten silver bowls with cruciform designs was placed immediately beside the spoons in the burial deposit and away from the rest of the silver.[123] It has already been suggested that the cruciform designs on these bowls may have Christian significance,[124] and their placing beside the spoons and close to the scabbard-bosses which are also charged with Christian symbols,[125] in a spot which must have been, or been taken as representing, the right shoulder or side of the dead man, seems to reinforce this view.

a

b

c

d

Plate 7 a, Detail of framed face in cloisonné work from the bird's leg, Sutton Hoo shield; *b*, Silvered and gilt-bronze bird, Shelford Farm, Sturry, Kent; *c* and *d*, Whetstones with human faces, Church Island, Lough Currane, Ireland and Llandudno, N. Wales
(Scales *a*, Slightly above 2 : 1; *b*, approx. 2 : 1; *c*, 1 : 1; *d*, 1 : 1)

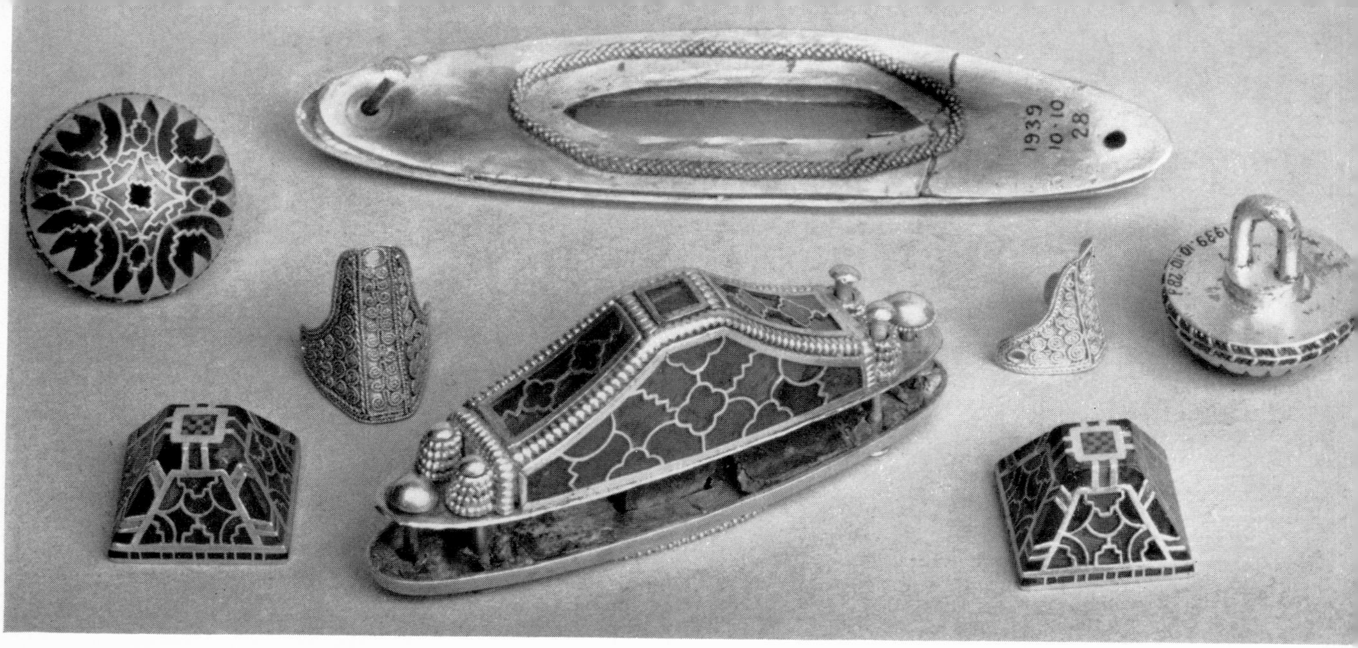

8

9

a

b

c

a

b

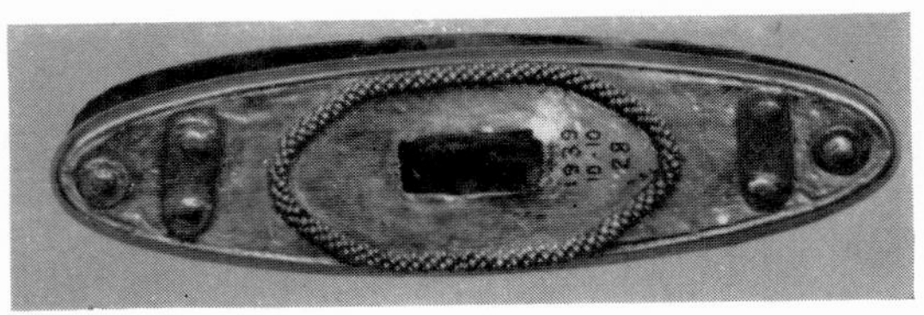

c

d

Plate 10 a, Detail of gold cloisonné composite brooch, Faversham, Kent, showing beaded cloison technique (Scale about 2 : 1); *b*, Rectangular gold cloisonné strap-mount, Sutton Hoo (Scale 1 : 1); *c*, Underside of the upper guard of the sword, Sutton Hoo (Scale 1 : 1); *d*, Part of gold cloisonné pyramid from the west mound (Odenshög), Old Uppsala (Scale 3 : 1)

Plate 8 (opposite page, top) Gold and garnet fittings, Sutton Hoo sword (Scales about 4 : 3)

Plate 9 (opposite page, below) a, The lid of a workbox, Burwell, Suffolk (Scale 1 : 1); *b*, English gold cloisonné brooch, incorporated into one end of a box-shrine (the Egbert reliquary), Trier (Scale 1 : 1); *c*, The Egbert reliquary

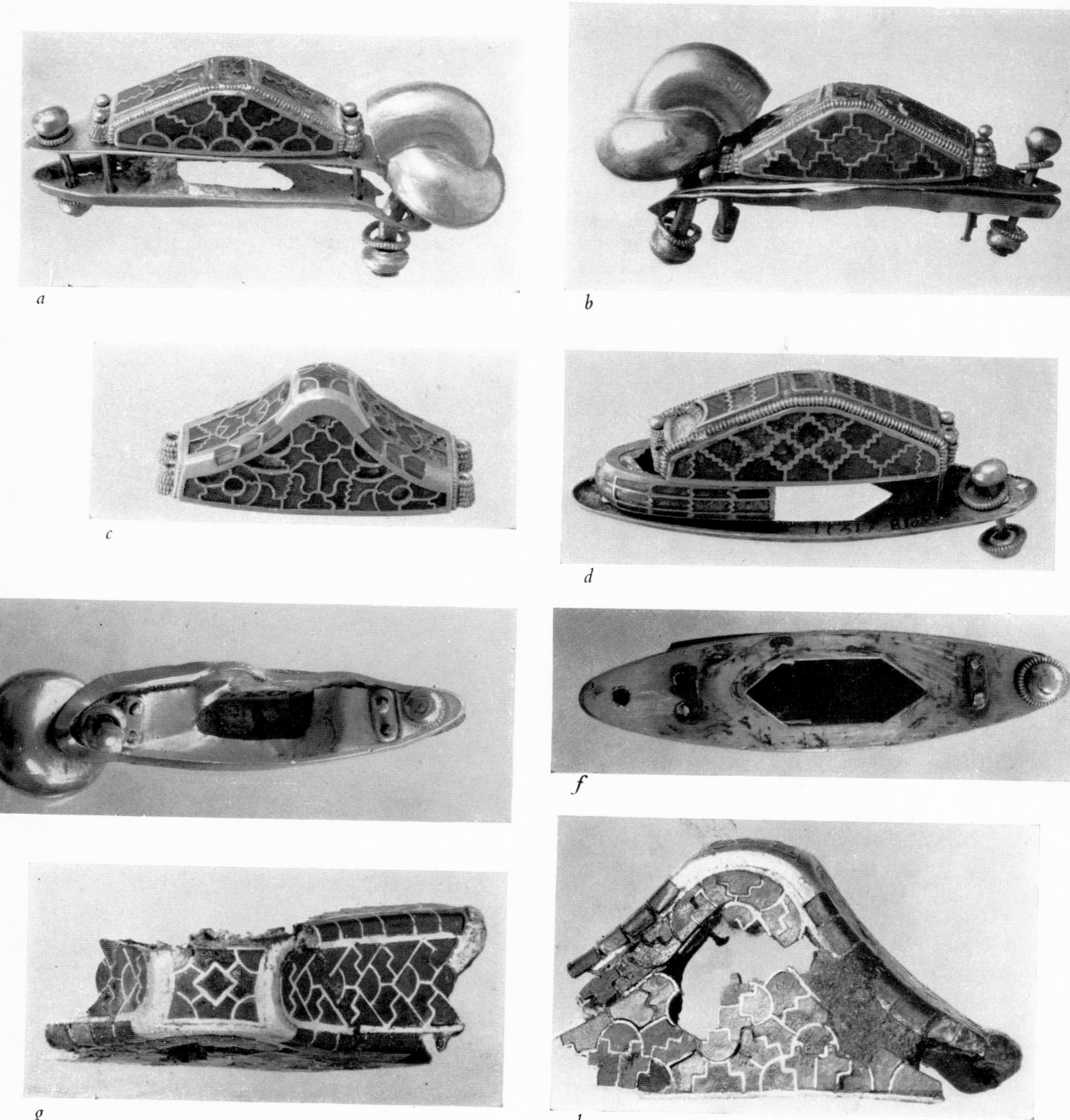

Plate 11 Gold cloisonné sword-pommels found in Sweden: *a,b*, Väsby, Hammarby Parish, Uppland (2 views) (Scale 1 : 1); *c*, Hög Edsten, Kville Parish, Bohushlän (Scale 1 : 1); *d*, Stora Sandviken, Stürkö Parish, Blekinge (Scale 1 : 1); *e, f*, Undersides of the upper guard of the gold sword pommels, Väsby, Uppland and Stora Sandviken, Blekinge (Scales 1 : 1); *g, h*, Gold sword pommel encrusted with garnets, Skrävsta, Botkyrka Parish, Sodermanland (Scales 2 : 1)

Extreme caution is necessary before it can be asserted that a cruciform design or even a specific cross has anything to do with Christianity at this period. I would not claim, for example, that the small crosses which appear with regularity between the rivet-heads on the rivet-shelves at either end of the rectangular plaques that ornamented the Sutton Hoo sword-belt (Plates 4a and 10b) and also in the middle of the garnet-inlaid panels along their edges (Plate 4d) and in similar positions on the unique T-shaped double-hinged mount (Plate 4d) had Christian significance, although it might well be so in this context.[126] The crosses on the scabbard-bosses seem more definite (Plate 5c).

It is true that cruciform designs very similar to those on the scabbard-bosses may be found in early Anglo-Saxon archaeology in a number of instances where there are no grounds for inferring Christian significance. The equal-armed curvilinear cross occurs, for example, on the escutcheons of one of the hanging-bowls from Faversham[127] which belongs to Kendrick's early 'Romanising' group[128] and there seems no reason to assume that it is specifically Christian.[129] Sutherland has pointed out that this form of cross is a fundamental element in the design of some Kentish circular jewelled brooches, for instance the well-known Sarre Brooch[130] and that from Milton, near Abingdon, in the Ashmolean.[131] We may add the Faversham brooch in the Fitzwilliam Museum, Cambridge,[132] and the Dover brooch in the British Museum.[133] Sutherland has also shown how this cruciform design may have evolved naturally in copper coinage of the early Saxon period (attributed by him to the fifth and sixth, and perhaps early seventh centuries out of the square altar with pellets on the reverse of a prominent variety of the common type issued to commemorate the death of Claudius Gothicus in A.D. 270.[134] He also claims that the perfect examples of the 'Celtic' cross that appear on the reverses of certain silver *sceattas* of the London group (Fig 2d) came into being by a similar process of natural evolution from one or other of the two Constantinian types, either the *Virtus Exercit* – VOT. XX (standard and captives) type or the *Beata Tranquillitas* – VOTIS XX (altar) type.[135] Cruciform designs like those on the Sutton Hoo scabbard-bosses cannot therefore automatically be assumed to have Christian significance at this time.

Against this should be said that Sutherland has not been able to demonstrate in the copper coin series the final stage in this pagan evolution of the cross – the emergence of the curvilinear cross of the type that appears on the Sutton Hoo scabbard-bosses. He was not able in the paper quoted to take the development beyond the stage illustrated by the coin in the Black Gate Museum, Newcastle,[136] being obliged to turn to the Kentish brooches (and to a late example at that) to complete the evolution.[137] It may also be claimed that on the Kentish polychrome brooches on which it appears, the 'Celtic' cross may be regarded as little more than an adventitious element, latent in the design of one central and four peripheral roundels and not explicit. Even in simplified line-drawing statements of the designs it appears that the ornamental emphasis rests upon the central and outlying roundels and upon the division of the disc into segments and subsidiary fields[138] rather than upon the cross. This is much more evident when the original specimen is seen, for the roundels are picked out with garnet inlay and prominent decorated shell bosses and the borders, intermediate rings, and the rectilinear pattern often superimposed on the Celtic cross, are accentuated in red by incrustation with garnets and attract attention by the intricacies of their cell work. The clearest unencumbered statement of the cross is to be seen on the Sarre and Dover brooches but even here there is no deliberate accentuation and it can hardly be claimed as anything more than a simplification of the general scheme so well established in the design of this group of brooches.

Nor is the internal evolution of the cross in the *sceatta* series convincing. There is a wide gap between Nos 7 and 8 in Sutherland's series (*op. cit.*, Plate II) and since the *sceatta* series is now held not to have commenced until *c.* 700,[139] the perfect crosses on these coins could very well have been derived directly from outside models, for instance the cruciform pendant series described below (p. 29) or designs like that on the Sutton Hoo scabbard-bosses, or designs derived from the Celtic milieu represented by the Camerton escutcheon, the Wye Down pendant and the Thurnham Cross (Plate 5b).[140] The adoption on coins at this time of fresh designs taken from goldsmith's work (cloisonné jewellery) is illustrated in the *sceatta* series by a coin noted by Baldwin Brown[141] which reproduces a step-pattern design of T-shaped cells, very similar to that which appears, in blue glass paste, on the central disc of the seventh-century Roundway Down pins and chain and which is without doubt imitated from cloisonné jewellery.[142] There need be no connection between the Celtic cross theme of London type *sceattas* and the designs of Roman origin on the reverses of the 'Wolf-standard' group. Indeed had the course of development been as Sutherland suggests, one would expect the cross to appear in the 'Wolf-standard' series, whereas in fact it only appears on the coins with other obverses. The rosettes or annulets between the arms of the 'Celtic' crosses on *sceattas* need not be an original and active element in the evolution of the design but could be no more than conventional fill-ups echoing the familiar patterns of the polychrome brooch series or borrowed from the familiar annulets or rosettes of other types of *sceatta* reverses[143] or from the designs of the copper coinages.

When we come to the cruciform pendants (Plates 5a,b, 94 and 96d,e)[144] the position is quite different from that in the brooches. Here the cross is explicit and the Christian purpose of the pendants cannot be in doubt, for one of them,[145] was worn by St Cuthbert (see Chapter 15) or at least placed on his breast and about his neck in the grave.[146] We may also refer to the obvious Christian character of other pendants of the period, for instance, the gold cross of the Desborough necklace[147] (Plate 6) or the Camerton[148] or Canterbury[149] crosses. For the purpose of the present argument – the significance of the cruciform designs on the Sutton Hoo scabbard-bosses – we are primarily concerned with the gold pendants encrusted with garnets. Two of the three known, those from Ixworth and Wilton (the third being St Cuthbert's cross) were found in East Anglia. That from Wilton, Norfolk, in the British Museum (Plate 96d,e), containing a gold solidus of Heraclius I (610–40) is undoubtedly a product of the workshop that produced the Sutton Hoo jewellery and very probably the work of one of the craftsmen that contributed to the Sutton Hoo regalia. Anyone who handles together the Wilton cross and the Sutton Hoo garnet-encrusted pieces must be impressed by the identity of the metal and the intimate relationship of style, quality of workmanship and finish. The cloisonné work of the pendant is carried out with the absolute regularity and delicacy of the best Sutton Hoo pieces. The garnets used are of the same colour and quality. The closest connection of all is to be found in the repertoire of the cell-types and patterns. On the Wilton pendant there occurs around the central roundel a border of plain rectangular cells, smaller and larger cells alternatively, which is a small-scale version of the border around the lid of the Sutton Hoo purse (Plate 4b). Similar borders of plain rectangular cells but without the alternation of large and small, may be seen on a small buckle and two strap-ends in the Sutton Hoo jewellery[150] and form the spines that run the length of the backs of the boars on the ends of the two shoulder clasps.[151] The distinctive 'mushroom' cell, which, as Kendrick pointed out,[152] is so frequently and prominently employed by the Sutton Hoo jeweller, is used in exactly the form in which it occurs at Sutton Hoo, on the Wilton pendant and we may note that the very unusual[153] herring-bone pattern in cloisonné garnets to be seen on the suspension-limb of the Wilton cross below the barrel-shaped loop, occurs at Sutton Hoo in curved elements that are in effect dummy hinges at either end of the straight frame along the top of the purse-lid (Plate 4b), and again in carved garnets round the edges of the scabbard-bosses (Plate 8). When to these intimate affinities we add the fact that a distinctive cell-pattern theme, much favoured in particular by the goldsmith who made the Sutton Hoo sword-belt fittings[154] (Fig. 6a–c) (Plate 4c) forms the central design of each of the three expanding arms of the Wilton cross (Fig 6e and Plate 96d) it cannot be doubted that this cross came from the workshop of the Sutton Hoo master-goldsmith.

The Christian character of the Wilton pendant should be clear enough and indeed has never been disputed. This seems nevertheless a good moment to resuscitate Reginald Smith's observations that '*the preference given to the cross on the reverse of the coin*, as well as the form of the mount, show that the original owner was a Christian'.[155] There can only be one reason why the maker of the cross set

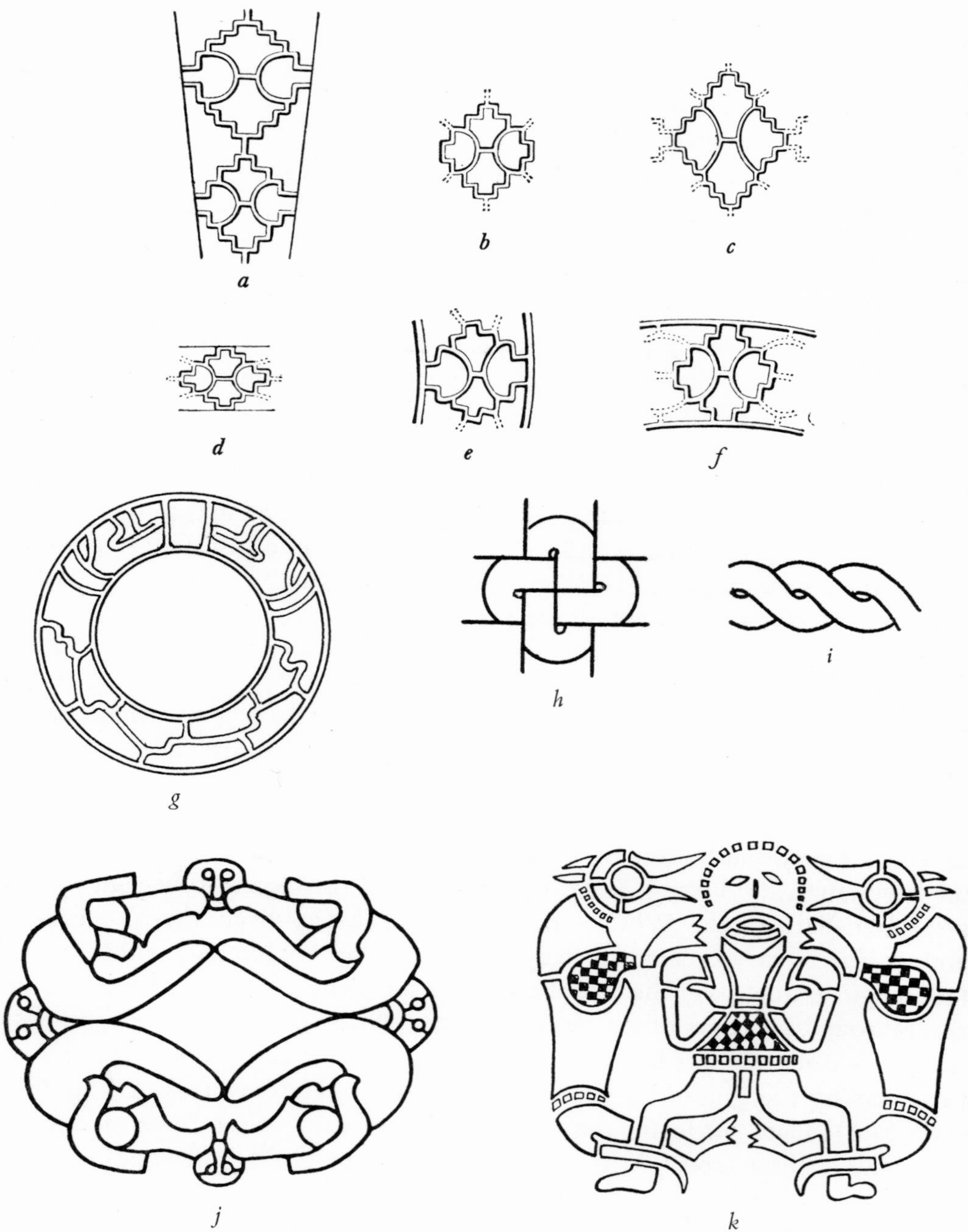

Figure 6 Cell-pattern details from cloisonné jewellery: *a*, Curved dummy buckle, Sutton Hoo; *b*, T-shaped strap-distributor, Sutton Hoo; *c*, Rectangular strap-mount, Sutton Hoo; *d*, Ornament, Tongres, Belgium; *e*, Wilton, Norfolk, pendant; *f*, Egbert shrine, Trier. (Scales *a–f*: all slightly enlarged.) *g*, Detail from composite cloisonné brooch, Faversham, Kent, showing affronted boars' heads (Scale 2 : 1). Interlace motifs in cloisonné work achieved by use of the beaded cloison. *h*, Composite brooch, Faversham, Kent. *i*, Rectangular plaque, Sutton Hoo (both enlarged). *j*, Simplified statement of the 'Daniel in the lion's den' subject, the Reinstrup brooch (Scale: slightly enlarged). *k*, Drawing of scene of man between beasts from a cloisonné plaque from Sutton Hoo (Scale 2 : 1)

the coin in the pendant so that the fine effigies of the Emperor and his son[156] were invisible when it was worn and that is that he was more interested in the cross. That the cross is mounted upside down in no way means that its Christian significance was not appreciated. The cross itself, seen in this way, is equally effective and could be, and evidently was, taken for a pendant cross (like the one in which it was to be set) suspended beneath its own misunderstood steps. The words 'blunder' used by Reginald Smith,[157] and 'unintelligent' by Kendrick,[158] as applied to the employment of the coin, seem quite unjustified. To the goldsmith the coin so set was clearly the right way up, for if he reversed it, the Emperor and his son would then be upside down. He presumably looked at the cross on the reverse the same way up as the portraits on the obverse, and so took it for a pendant cross.

Kendrick in his study of the St Cuthbert, Ixworth and Wilton pendants already referred to, claimed that the Wilton cross was Merovingian work of the mid-sixth century.[159] On this point as on so many others, the Sutton Hoo discoveries throw a flood of new light. We can now recognize the Wilton pendant as local East Anglian work of the second quarter of the seventh century and reinstate it as what it was always supposed to be, a manifestation of seventh-century Anglo-Saxon Christianity.

The general significance of this re-orientation of our gold cloisonné jewellery is great but we must not digress. We may perhaps refer in this connection to Kendrick's rapprochement between the Wilton pendant and the jewel set in the Egbert shrine at Trier (Plate 9b,c and Fig 6f).[160] He points out the occurrence on the Trier brooch of a ring of plain rectangular cells, large and small alternatively and of the distinctive pattern (Fig 6f) which we have already remarked as occurring frequently in the Sutton Hoo jewellery. Both of these elements occur, as we have seen, on the Wilton pendant. We may add as another feature connecting the Trier brooch with the East Anglian milieu, the four simplified animal heads, seen from above, which divide the outer cloisonné zone of the brooch into quadrants. These may well be descended from similarly-seen but more detailed animal heads like those distributed round the Sutton Hoo shield and decorating the extremities of the grip-extensions on the back[161] and a use of similar heads recalling that in the Trier brooch occurs on the lid of the Burwell work-box (Plate 9a).[162] We may well note that two opposite quadrants of the sunk inner zone on the Trier brooch show an incised pattern on the T-shaped fields, the T-motives being alternately the right way up and upside-down. This same arrangement may be seen on the central roundel of the Ixworth cross (Plate 96d).[163] It seems clear that the brooch in the Egbert shrine is an East Anglian product, probably dating from the middle of the seventh century.[164] Standing in intimate relation with the pieces discussed, is another remarkable piece of cloisonné work, discovered by Professor Holger Arbman in the cathedral Treasury at Tongres, in Belgium and undoubtedly emanating from the Sutton Hoo workshop (cf. Ch. 13, Pls 90a–c, 91, Fig 6d).[165]

It seems clear that the goldsmiths who produced the Sutton Hoo scabbard-bosses with cruciform designs were also making, in the same materials and at the same date, Christian pendant crosses. We may certainly assume that the Wilton pendant was not the only one made by this workshop. The cross on the bosses is identical in form with the Christian pendants. It is explicit, an essential element of the design, not latent or adventitious, as is the case with the cross-theme in the polychrome brooch series. It is also accentuated, in that the essential cross, except for the two wedged-shaped garnets at the extremity of each arm, is of a light, brick-red colour, achieved by the employment of thin slices of garnet, allowing the red colour to be modified by the gold foil beneath. Whereas the remaining parts of the design are in deep cells with no foil grounds, the stones having a deep purplish colouring. The identity of the crosses with the pendant series may be further inferred from the elaboration of their cell work at the centre with a concentric rosette-like design. This seems to reflect the central elaboration of the Ixworth or Wilton pendants (Plates 5a, 96d).

It is necessary in considering these points to allow for the possibility that visual effects may have been due to purely technical considerations, imposed by the difficulties of carrying on the design in a raised, almost hemispherical structure. The expansion of the central parts of pendants was no doubt necessary for mechanical strength. There could be no such need for development of the cross on the bosses. On the contrary, expansion of the centre of the cross in the bosses would have complicated a difficult piece of work and tended to obscure, against the background of subsidiary cells, the statement of the cross-theme. The central elaboration of the pendants was retained *ornamentally* in the boss-crosses in a central rosette design that did not break the smooth curves on the cross.

It must also be pointed out that the drawing (Plate 5c) overaccentuates the cross. The extremities are not so clear-cut but lose themselves in the plain gold border and petal-pattern round the edges of the bosses. This submergence of the cross at its extremities is heightened by the fact, already indicated, that the pair of wedge-shaped garnets at the end of each arm have a purplish colour, as well as the form, of the other 'petals' and so differentiate themselves from the brick-red and the differently formed cells of the rest of the cross. This again may be an effect imposed by the internal construction of the bosses.[166]

When all these points are considered, the clear fact remains that chronologically, formally, technically and geographically, the crosses on the scabbard-bosses are very closely related to the gold cloisonné cruciform pendants and it is difficult to avoid the conclusion that they have Christian significance.

If this means that the original owner of the scabbard so fitted out was a Christian, it does not follow that the grave in which they ended up is a Christian's grave. The sword and scabbard could have been won in contest, or received as a gift, or simply inherited from a Christian forbear or relative, by a surviving pagan. The scabbard-bosses, however, do not stand alone in the grave. Close by them were placed the pair of spoons, which we have explained as a present to a convert and the set of silver bowls which also very likely have Christian significance. This combination – and the historical context – are such that we must consider very seriously whether this cannot after all be a Christian monument.

We have now reached the crux of a difficult but fascinating problem. We have seen good reason to believe that the Sutton Hoo ship-burial is that of an East Anglian king, we have seen, from the study of the course of Christianity in East Anglia and from what we know of the dating evidence for the burial, that it must have taken place precisely in the phase of transition between paganism and Christianity. In and close to the 'body space' in the burial chamber is a group of significant Christian objects. These would suggest that the burial is that of a Christian, or they seem to have been grouped and placed with deliberation. Yet it is against every historical probability and the known facts that the body of a Christian Wuffinga king should have been deposited in the pagan fashion in the old pagan burial place when the church was so insistent on the burial of kings in Christian precincts. There is no doubt that these facts suit very well the interpretation of the burial as that of Raedwald (624–5) to whose relapse and subsequent compromise between pagan and Christian practices we have referred.

A second solution is perhaps contained in the words used above, that it seems impossible to suppose that the *body* of a Christian Wuffinga king could have been buried in the pagan grave-field. It remains just possible that there never was a body.[167] The second solution, then, would be that in the Sutton Hoo ship-burial we have a public and traditional monument erected in honour of a distinguished king whose body had received Christian burial elsewhere. Such a phenomenon seems feasible in the peculiar phase of transition between pagan and Christian civilization and in the particular historical circumstances of East Anglia in the second quarter of the seventh century. If so, we should have in the Sutton Hoo ship-burial a monument of the transition comparable with the Franks Casket, with its peculiar mixture of pagan and Christian subjects, the Benty Grange tumulus, sometimes cited as another richly furnished burial of a Christian in the pagan manner,[168] or the Beowulf epic itself, with its blend of pagan and Christian concepts and substance. We may also note, at Jellinge in Denmark, the erection of a royal cenotaph under a great mound in the pagan manner for a convert whose body was actually buried in a church, although in this case only mound and burial chamber were constructed and grave-goods were not deposited.[169]

If this were the case, the only candidate, it seems, for the burial would be Sigeberht the monk, whose body if recovered from the disastrous battle with the Mercians, would have certainly been buried in a monastery or church.

With regard to the cenotaph problem, a full exposition of the evidence is published elsewhere.[170] Clear indications have been found of the original presence on the top of the great silver dish in the burial deposit of a considerable quantity of burnt bone. There is no means of establishing whether this bone-source was animal or human. It is unlikely that it can represent a primary burial. In the first place one would expect the grave-goods (and the ship) to have been burnt with the body and this was so with cremations found at Sutton Hoo in 1938.[171] Secondly, the arrangement of the grave-goods in the chamber shows that those who arranged them were thinking in terms of an inhumed body (Plate 17).[172] Thirdly, the presence of specifically Christian objects is difficult to reconcile with the cremation of their owner. I think that as a result of the fine re-excavation of the surviving monument and of the excavator's dumps in 1967–9, we can be said to have eliminated the real possibility that the cremated bone was intrusive, that is, derived from an earlier cremation, scraped up into the composition of the barrow, which fell on to the Anastasius dish when the chamber collapsed. It remains true that the human character of the original bone source can never be established and even if it were possible to show that the bones had been placed deliberately in a container, we could not say whether they might not represent, for example, the remains of an ox roasted at a funeral feast. What has emerged from an intense and critical study of the conditions in the grave and of the results of chemical tests carried out on soil samples and on the grave-goods themselves is that we can now say that the evidence tends to support, but does not prove, the original presence of an inhumed body in the 'body-space' at the west end of the burial-chamber, where everyone is agreed the primary burial should have been.

Those who wish to go further into the technicalities of an extremely complex scientific and archaeological investigation are referred to Vol. I, Chapter VIII of the definitive publication. It seems reasonable however, all things considered, to regard the burial as a straightforward inhumation. If it is felt that allowance must be made for the one-time presence of cremated bone on the Anastasius dish as possibly human and therefore not to be overlooked in any evaluation of the monument, then the situation becomes extremely complex. Historically, if the monument is a king's, the numismatic evidence permits Raedwald and also enables us to consider, as the only practical alternative, the co-kings, killed together *c.* 637 (Fig 3). Could Ecric have been pagan (the cremation) and Sigeberht notionally present (the body-space, with the phosphate evidence otherwise explained away), his actual burial being in a church or monastery?

To sum up: in the foregoing pages I have argued that the Sutton Hoo burial was that of a reigning king. I have also reached the conclusion that the monument could either be Christian or pagan but that it is not possible to regard it, as Lindqvist claimed, as an orthodox Christian burial containing a body. A final assessment of the evidence now indicates that a body was, in all probability, present.

All these arguments are based on the assumption that the king under consideration was Anglo-Saxon and a Wuffinga King of the East Angles. Since we have dealt with the question of the kingly status of the grave, it remains to consider the question, was this king really East Anglian, or was he Swedish?

THE SWEDISH CONNECTION

Any attempt at the present time to interpret this aspect of the great find (the Swedish connection) must be provisional.

For general interpretation of the find, the greatest importance attaches to the contents of the other burial mounds recognized on the site. The finds from the three excavated in 1938 are published in Vol I, Chapter II of the British Museum definitive publication. The excavation of the others, especially if one or more proves intact, should, with these 1938 finds, make clear many puzzling and obscure points and enable us to see more of the history and sources of the culture that has been revealed in the great ship-burial – which must, I believe, be the latest of the barrow burials. In the meantime, pending further excavation and final definition of all finds so far made, it is necessary to be very cautious in fundamental interpretation. With this proviso constantly in mind, we may proceed to discuss the Swedish connection and comment on the essays in interpretation that have been made. These attempts, even if they prove partly or wholly wrong, have all raised useful points and helped to define and clarify the issues. It is hoped that the present attempt may do the same and furthermore, in the light of our present knowledge of the find, there are some firm conclusions that can be drawn.

Similarities between the Sutton Hoo material and Swedish finds of the Vendel period were noted as soon as the Sutton Hoo pieces were excavated and appeared more striking when the shield and helmet were restored in 1946 and 1947. They have been emphasized still further by the radical reconstruction of these two objects during 1970–73. Some similarities have been noted elsewhere.[173] Before proceeding to draw conclusions from these similarities we must first of all ask whether they really show that a direct link existed between the two areas. The fact is that many parallels that one notices in comparing Sutton Hoo objects with Swedish objects are no more than elements shared in common by the inhabitants of quite extensive areas of Western Europe at that time.

For example, the similarity between the Sutton Hoo sword-pommel (Plate 8 and 10c) and Swedish-found sword-pommels (Plate 11) in the self-same medium (gold and garnets), both in ornamentation and structural design, is obvious. But a very similar gold and garnet pommel has also been found at Nocera Umbra in Northern Italy[174] and recently another in grave 1732 at Krefeld-Gellep (Plate 12a–c).[175] Indeed the hilts of two well-known swords from the Nocera Umbra grave-field, to one of which this pommel belongs[176] both of which carry large rings on their pommels and filigree clips (cf. the two plain gold filigree mounts from either end of the Sutton Hoo sword-grip, Plate 8), closely resemble the distinctive Swedish sword-grips, such as those from Vallstenarum, Gotland and Valsgärde.[177] Again, the figural art of the Sutton Hoo helmet is closely related to that of the Swedish helmets,[178] yet the closest parallel to the scene of the rider and fallen warrior on the Sutton Hoo helmet found, is not in Sweden but in South Germany (Plate 13a, b). Maryon had difficulty when he wrote[179] in finding parallels to the head and leg of the bird on the Sutton Hoo shield.[180] A very similar head and leg on the same scale were found in boat-grave I at Vendel.[181] Whole bird-figures of a similar general character including probably some that are appliqués from shields occur in the Rhineland,[182] in Kent (Plate 7b) and elsewhere.[183] Gold cloisonné work in the style of that at Sutton Hoo, where the whole surface of an object is covered with garnets in a carpet-like spread, had not been regarded as typically Anglo-Saxon prior to the Sutton Hoo discovery, as has been said above.[184] Kendrick regarded a typical example of the style found in England, the Wilton cross, as Merovingian work. The general resemblance between the 'un-Saxon looking' Sutton Hoo jewellery and the Swedish cloisonné work, in the same general style, might at first seem significant but in fact the style of the all-over garnet incrustation, with little or no use of filigree and preserving many distinctive-looking technical devices, is wide-spread, both geographically and in time. The style is characteristic of the gold cloisonné work of the fifth and early sixth centuries on the Continent, for example that from Childeric's grave at Tournai[185] or the treasures of fifth-century date from Aphaida in Roumania[186] which have strong affinities with the Sutton Hoo jewellery;[187] the so-called pectoral of Odovacer at Ravenna,[188] the sword-fittings from Klein Hüningen near Basle in Switzerland[189] and elsewhere. In the seventh century the all-over style still occurred widely, a good instance being the Wittislingen fibula.[190] Indeed, Lindqvist has said of the buckles and strap-mounts at Sutton Hoo: 'everything seems to show that pieces of this type were made by itinerant master-craftsmen, whom great men near and far competed to attach to their courts.'[191] If this is so, identity of pieces of cloisonné work at Sutton Hoo and in Sweden need not imply any sustained political, racial or economic contracts between the two areas but might simply mark two points in the itinerary of a wandering craftsman. Again, on turning over the Sutton Hoo sword-pommel and two of the similar Swedish ones, the very individual-looking trick of making one long oval washer serve the two inner rivets of the three at either end of the pommels (Plate 10c, 11e, f) might seem a significant detail. This device is known, though not on sword pommels (cf. Plate 12b), in the Rhineland. It occurs on sword pommels (though not of cloisonné) in Kent, for example on a sword-pommel from grave 62 in the Bifrons cemetery and on other Kentish pieces. When to this European background we add Lindqvist's warning that

> near prototypes of the shield and helmet forms (found at Sutton Hoo and in Sweden) were in use amongst Germanic peoples along and south of the part of the Roman frontier that followed the line of the Upper Danube, the forms might have spread direct from these people both to England, and to various parts of what is now Swedish territory.[192]

it will be appreciated that particular care must be taken before direct linking of any significant kind between the two areas, Sweden and Suffolk, can be inferred. Our first task then is to enquire whether we can show a genuine, substantial and direct link between these regions, beyond dispute. We shall find that not only are there peculiarly intimate similarities, transcending the more general ones discussed in the foregoing paragraphs, but that these resemblances occur over a broad front and consistently throughout the two cultures, so that we pass beyond the stage of isolated and dispersed parallels, such as may readily be found on the Continent, to individual features of the Sutton Hoo find.

THE DIRECT CONNECTION BETWEEN SUFFOLK AND SWEDEN

A comparison of the scene on the disc-brooch from Pliezhausen with that of the Sutton Hoo helmet may be instructive in helping to form criteria for judging the archaeological evidence (Plate 13a, b). The brooch has been illustrated by Veeck[193] and more recently by Holmqvist.[194] Holmqvist classes its scene with other representations of riders in the art of the Merovingian period,[195] for instance on the Hornhausen grave-slab, Frankish openwork discs and ornaments, the disc-brooches from Oron and Cividale and the helmet from boat-grave No 1 at Vendel, which he regards as Germanic versions or derivatives of the rider scenes that occur in Coptic, Early Christian and late Classical art on textiles, amulets, silverware and in other media. His various illustrations of the rider-theme have points in common. When we insert the Sutton Hoo scene, discovered since Holmqvist wrote, in the series, we see at once that the similarity between it and the disc-brooch is of quite another order than that between these two and any of the many other rider-representations. The subject in both is that of a horseman with shield and lance riding down a fallen mail-clad warrior who stabs the horse in the chest with his sword. Beyond this identity of subject there is a substantial identity both in composition and in detail which shows that they must be copied from a common model, or one from the other, at very few removes, perhaps even directly.[196] Allowing for the fact that the scenes face in opposite directions and omitting as irrelevant to our immediate purpose the appearance above the rider's spear on the disc-brooch of two facing lions, we may note some striking similarities. Compare for instance the position of the fallen warriors, in particular the setting up of their legs; the large heads and small shields of the riders, the horizontal poise of their spears, the treatment of the horses' girths and bridles and the small kneeling figures at the riders' backs, who seem to lend them support by also gripping the spears. The closeness of the relationship between the two scenes is perhaps best to be seen in the close-knit composition of the design around the middle and upper part of the fallen warrior's body, especially about his head. In each representation the blade of the two-edged sword projects to the same degree from the horse's body and the groove down the centre of the blade throughout the exposed length may be noted. A fragment of pattern comprising pellets and some horizontal strokes may be noted (Plate 13a) immediately above the blade of the sword. This is the mail-clad left arm and cuff of the fallen warrior and the position of the cuff (indicated by the horizontal strokes) shows that his arm, in the Sutton Hoo scene, is running outwards to grip the horse's bridle as seen in Plate 13b. Immediately under the blade in both we see the upturned horizontal profile of the head, with falling hair, filling compactly the space between the horse's body and the sword-arm. Lower down we can detect in the Pliezhausen version the edgings, belt and skirt-hem of the warrior's coat (already showing lack of comprehension and the tendency to disintegrate) that can be seen clearly depicted in the Sutton Hoo scene. In both, note also the graphic straddling of the fallen man by the horse's forelegs. One passes conspicuously across the front of the man's body, the other may be seen merging between his shoulder and his belt from behind the man's body. The iconographic correspondence is remarkably close. Against it must be set marked differences in style, technical and artistic ability and detailed comprehension of the subject. The Sutton Hoo version, though more conventionalized and without the élan of the more barbaric Pliezhausen version, is in other respects greatly superior. Every detail is comprehended and stated with perfect clarity. The artist, following a well-established style and convention, is yet working with delicacy. This is particularly noticeable in the sensitive modelling of the fallen warrior's face, hair, bare legs and feet, for instance in the precise and neat, if conventionalized emphasis of the ankle-bones, points not all visible in our photograph but striking on the original. On the

Pliezhausen brooch, on the other hand, the composition does not fit happily into its circular frame, less care has been taken over the making of the die, the whole is appreciably barbarized, and some details, notably the fallen warrior's scabbard, are omitted. The falling away may best be seen by comparing in detail the figures of the fallen warrior in the two scenes, for example in the skirts, skimped and perfunctory in the one, meticulous in the other. In fact although the scenes are to all intents and purposes iconographically identical, nobody would regard them as works of the same school.

We may now consider the second figural scene on the Sutton Hoo helmet, that of twin men with horned hats and spears and its Swedish parallels. Plate 14b shows a reconstruction of the scene as it appeared four times on the Sutton Hoo helmet. It was not at first realized that the scene consisted of two similar figures side by side.

Nerman pointed out the relationship between this figure, who carries two spears and whose head-dress is furnished with flaps or wings and terminates at the top of the horns in birds' heads and the similarly equipped figure on one of the bronze dies (for stamping foil sheets for ornamenting helmets) from Torslunda, Öland (Plate 54c).[197] There are much closer parallels. The *attributes* of the figures in the two scenes are the same but in face, dress (apart from the head-dress), attitude and context, the Torslunda figure bears no very direct artistic relationship to that from Sutton Hoo. In his publication of his restoration of the Sutton Hoo helmet, Maryon described how it had been possible since the publication of the Provisional Guide to reconstruct the whole of the Sutton Hoo scene with the aid of new evidence from Valsgärde.[198] The evidence which enabled us to proceed with the reconstruction of the Sutton Hoo scene occurs on the remarkable helmet from boat-grave 7 at Valsgärde. I am indebted to Dr Greta Arwidsson for allowing me to reproduce for the first time the relevant detail from the Valsgärde 7 helmet and to the Uppsala University Museum of Northern Antiquities for kindly supplying the photograph (Plate 14a). The panel is in poor condition but the wedge-shaped face,[199] horned head-dress and two spears held in the outer hand of the figure on the left can be recognized and the V-shaped neck of the coat, with the lapels quilted or embroidered as on the Sutton Hoo figure but with a different pattern, may be seen. A similar figure stands to the right, his legs and part of the curve of the inner horn of the head-dress can be distinguished on the photograph. On the original it is possible to make out that the inner arms of the two figures cross one another and the hands of these arms are holding hilts of swords, whose blades run vertically alongside the inner horns of the head-dresses. A search amongst the Sutton Hoo helmet remains revealed a fragment showing this central detail of crossed arms and sword hilts (Plate 14b) and with the aid of this key fragment the rest of the panel was built up. The two scenes in fact prove to be iconographically identical, though not from the same stamp. The peculiar behaviour of the legs in the Valsgärde 7 panel should be noted, a convention of Swedish figural art of the Vendel period.[200] The outer leg and foot are trailed so that the heel and sole of the foot face upwards. The outer foot of the left-hand figure (sole uppermost) can be detected immediately below the two spear-points in the Valsgärde panel and a similar attitude is struck in the Sutton Hoo version. Closer still to the Sutton Hoo figure than the panel from Valsgärde 7 is the fragment from the East Mound at Old Uppsala, a Swedish royal cremation (Plate 14c, d). This is almost all that remains of a helmet that may have been very similar to the Sutton Hoo helmet. The figure is not from the identical stamp used for the Sutton Hoo scene (the angles at which the forearms are set, and the angle between the spears, may be contrasted in the two versions) but the relationship is very close indeed. We may note especially the treatment of the cuff, the embroidery of the belt and hem. In the Valsgärde 7 panel and still more in this one, we have the closest possible parallel, not merely of subject and iconography but also of style, detail and function. The Swedish and English representations appear on objects of the same kind (helmets) and also of the same type, the Sutton Hoo helmet being in its general features and many of its constructional details intimately related to the Swedish helmets.[201] With these Swedish parallels in contradistinction to the South German one (the disc-brooch), we are dealing with works of the same school, probably even, in the fragment from the East Mound at Old Uppsala, with dies cut by the same craftsman or at least made in the same workshop.

We may now turn to another group of antiquities, gold cloisonné work. Early in the history of the Sutton Hoo discovery Kendrick drew attention to the connection between a remarkable mutilated composite brooch (now wholly without its garnets or other inlays) from Faversham, Kent,[202] in the British Museum and the Sutton Hoo jewellery. He claimed that the Faversham brooch was made in the Sutton Hoo workshop, in particular because it achieved an interlacing linked-loop device in cloisonné work by means of a technical device – the cloison with the looped or beaded bend (Plate 10a) – also employed by the Sutton Hoo goldsmith in effecting the interlace (*guilloche*) patterns on a pair of rectangular mounts, one of which is illustrated in Plate 10b.[203] Kendrick illustrated this beaded cloisonné device with drawings which are reproduced here (Fig 6h, i). Of interlacing themes in cloisonné work and this 'beaded' elbow cloison Kendrick said:

> There are no other examples of this cloison at all, and no other examples of a cloisonné imitation of interlace; so it is as certain as anything in this world can be that the Faversham brooch and the Sutton Hoo jewellery were made in the same workshop.[204]

The technique of this beaded elbow can be studied in the enlarged detail of the Faversham brooch (Plate 10a), in the linked-loop device to the left and in Fig 6h, i. It will be seen that two vanes or cell walls are involved; one remains straight, while another crosses its end and is then bent round and back to meet it. The little loop so formed is then sealed by fusion or by the addition of a tiny gold lid, in the manner of the highly distinctive, virtually unique, lidded or covered cell technique used on the Sutton Hoo purse-lid and shoulder-clasps.[205] I agree with Kendrick's attribution of the Faversham jewel to the Sutton Hoo workshop. An additional reason is its zoomorphic details – a thing of great rarity in Insular cloisonné work. The central fields of the four small roundels on the Faversham brooch are surrounded by cloisonné belts in each of which a length of geometric cloisonné work terminates in affronted boars' heads separated by a plain keystone cell (Plate 10a and Fig 6g). The only other Insular instances known to me of zoomorphic cloisonné detail of this sort occur on the Sutton Hoo purse-lid and shoulder-clasps, and the only other occurrence of boars' heads in Insular cloisonné is in the interlinked boar figures at the ends of the Sutton Hoo clasps.[206] Many uncommon technical devices employed in the Sutton Hoo jewellery can be paralleled, even if only rarely, in Insular and Continental cloisonné pieces.[207] Kendrick was unable to find another single instance of the ingenious beaded-elbow cloison. After prolonged investigation of European cloisonné work I have managed to discover one other solitary instance of this technique (Plate 10d). Remarkably enough, it comes from the same Swedish group of royal graves at Old Uppsala that produced our closest parallel to the twin warriors scene on the Sutton Hoo helmet. When we also reflect that this tiny but very intricate and skilled piece of gold cloisonné work has the general all-over style characteristic of the Sutton Hoo jewellery, that it renders a zoomorphic design (though distortion in the fire makes it difficult to recover its exact character) and that it is, to judge by its shape and particularly its flat truncated top, in all probability all that has survived the flames of a pyramid[208] like those in Plate 8, it is clear that we have here a parallel of the most striking kind. It is true that in the Old Uppsala fragment the bead is not made by overlapping two separate gold vanes but by bending a single long vane to form a loop in its centre. This may be an adaptation of the idea to suit the peculiarities of the particular design, for the same method is to be seen in the boars' mouths on the Faversham brooch (Plate 10a, Fig 6g), which also has the 'orthodox' beaded cells. The beaded elbow of the Old Uppsala fragment is, in any case, sealed with gold, exactly as at Sutton Hoo and Faversham and the device, that of providing a rounded hub or pivot around which to construct a curved cell to produce a fluent, interlacing effect, radically different from the effect of static geometric cell-work, is identical.

The gold pommel of the Sutton Hoo sword (Plate 8) and the related Swedish gold pommels provide another link between the two areas. All the known Swedish gold pommels with the exception of that from Vallstenarum, Gotland[209] are illustrated in Plate 11. That from Skrävsta (Plate 11g, h) excavated by Dr Greta Arwidsson, is hitherto unpublished and I am indebted to the authorities of the Statens Historiska Museum, Stockholm, for the excellent photographs here reproduced and for permission to publish them. The Skrävsta pommel, from a cremation burial and damaged by fire, and that from Hög Edsten, Kville parish, Bohuslän, have the true 'cocked-hat' form of the Sutton Hoo pommel (with concave upper faces). The Skrävsta pommel, unlike that from Nocera Umbra already referred to,[210] shows the use of the 'mushroom-cell' which is so prominent a feature of the repertoire of the Sutton Hoo workshop and which Kendrick has argued may be 'the hall-mark of an Anglian cloisonné style'.[211] The Hög Edsten piece is, of all these Swedish pieces, the most intimately related to the Sutton Hoo jewellery. It shares with the Sutton Hoo pommel a feature that occurs nowhere else in the Sutton Hoo jewellery, the quatrefoil cell and the half-quatrefoil cell (Plates 8 and 11c). It also has features not present on the Sutton Hoo pommel but characteristic of the other Sutton Hoo jewelled pieces. Particularly distinctive of the Sutton Hoo jewellery is the overloading of the garnet encrustation, whereby garnets are set not only in the main ornamented fields but also on ends, edges and sides, round buckles loops and even functional parts, as in the hinge of the T-shaped mount and rivet-shelves at the ends of the rectangular strap mounts (Plates 4a–c and 8). This florid style can also be seen on the Hög Edsten pommel, in which garnets are set in the upper edges of the pommel replacing the normal beaded or filigree cord. Furthermore, it will be seen that these garnets are not cut flat but are worked in the solid (faceted) and that each of the four garnet bars contain a chevron. The parallel with the edges of the two Sutton Hoo pyramids (Plate 8) is at once apparent. The setting of the faceted garnets in the edges is particularly important, for this is a detail not found in the products of the Childeric period or, so far as I know, anywhere else but on these three pieces and the Skrävsta pommel (Plate 12c, d).[212] To this one may add the engraving of a tabular garnet with a circle which can just be detected in Place 11c – the stone so carved is the topmost one of the pommel, that in the centre of its small convex top – and the rendering of animal heads (seen in the corners of the forward face of the pommel) with large circular cells representing the eyes. These features occur in the early cloisonné work of the late fifth century and both the flat garnets carved with circles (filled in with gold) and the large circular eye-cloisons in zoomorphic heads may be seen in the strike-a-light (*c.* A.D. 500) from Klein Hüningen grave 212.[213] They are also characteristic of the Sutton Hoo jewellery (cf. the eyes of the birds and 'lions' on the lid of the purse) and, combined with the other factors considered, form the strongest link between this pommel and the

Sutton Hoo school. Since in many of these features it stands apart from the other Swedish gold pommels and since it incorporates features characteristic of Sutton Hoo pieces demonstrably of English make,[214] it seems to me possible that this pommel was made in Suffolk. A further point in support of this is the small cruciform design (containing the garnet carved with a circle) in the top compartment of the pommel. As we have already seen,[215] such simple cruciform cell-patterns are not uncommon in English cloisonné work of the period but have not so far been identified in Swedish cloisonné work.

We may now turn to another matter, a question of iconography. On the Sutton Hoo purse-lid a scene appears twice which has been held to represent Daniel in the Lion's Den (Plate 15b).[216] The relationship between this scene and one of the bronze plates from Torslunda, Öland (Plate 15a), was pointed out in the British Museum's original Provisional Guide to Sutton Hoo, and Nerman in his *Fornvännen* paper[217] again referred to the link between these two scenes. I do not now believe that this scene has any connection with Daniel in the Lion's Den, for Miss H. M. Roe has shown that many scenes so classified in the past were nothing of the kind.[218] In Plate 15a–f is given a typical selection of the varieties in which the scenes traditionally identified as Daniel occurs. The scenes on the Bofflens buckle and the Moone cross (Plate 15e and f) (where all the seven lions specified in the Mount Athos Guide for Painters[219] are shown) undoubtedly represent Daniel. The Reinstrup brooch (Plate 15c and Fig 6j) shows the theme in a typically remote and evolved northern form in gold cloisonné work – the same medium as the scene on the Sutton Hoo purse.[220] The piece from Amiens (Plate 15d) is typical of many openwork Frankish ornaments showing similar scenes.[221] Amongst these and indeed all the known Daniel or man-and-monsters or birds-and-vase scenes, no two versions stand in closer relationship than those on the Torslunda plate and the Sutton Hoo purse. There are certain obvious and important differences between them, so that closer analysis is desirable. The grouping and details of the three heads in each version (Plate 15a and b) are particularly alike. In both, the man's head rises slightly higher than those of the beasts and the lips of the animals, curving slightly apart and upwards, are pressed against the side of the man's head, as though the animals were whispering in his ears. In both versions the two small protruding ears and beaded collars of the animals, the alignment across the composition of the four eyes, the large ringed eyes of the animals, the man's rounded face, his moustache and even the beaded treatment of the hair may be noted; at the bottom, similar entanglement of the lower limbs of the three figures and, in the middle, the belts, the breadth across the shoulders of the man and the three-toed paws grasping the upper part of his body. In both, the three figures retain identical proportions and the whole scene is bound into the same close-knit composition. There are nevertheless some marked differences between the three. The stub-tailed bears of the Torslunda plate may be contrasted with the long-tailed, wolf-like creatures of the Sutton Hoo plaques. Again, the man in the Torslunda scene is represented in violent action. The legs and lower part of his body are seen from the back, while the upper part twists right round to face the front. The figure is also armed with sword and dagger and stabs one of the bears in the belly. The Sutton Hoo figure, on the other hand, squats unarmed and apparently uninterested, in Buddha-like detachment. These differences can, I suggest, be to a large extent explained by differences in medium, milieu and style without affecting at all the essential identity of the two scenes. The Torslunda plate is one of a long series of lively naturalistic representations and has the characteristics of the Vendel figural art to which it belongs. The Sutton Hoo scene on the contrary is conventionalized (as may be seen from the spread-eagling of the legs of the man and the placing of his arms and hands)[222] and frozen in a symmetrical design. It is also rendered in a different medium, that of cut stones and inlays in cloisonné work, which does not lend itself to realistic details, such as the bears' pelts in the Torslunda version, as would the wax from which the Swedish version was cast. Again, although the animals are different in the two versions, they are in both instances animals and clearly not, as in the majority of representations of the 'man between monsters', men wrapped or disguised in animal skins.[223] It may be that the artist was illustrating a subject in which monsters of an unspecific physical character were to be represented (as for instance Grendel and his mother in *Beowulf*) and that we have at Sutton Hoo simply a different interpretation of the same subject which nevertheless closely adheres to an established iconography. It seems that at Sutton Hoo we have a conventionalized version suitable for jewellery but still at once recognizable, of a well-known subject, which in the Vendel art milieu and the *pressbleck* medium received a more literal, graphic and naturalistic rendering. At the back of the connection which I believe we have established between these two scenes in different parts of Europe, lies an important physical factor. The connection is not between two pieces in a vacuum. The Torslunda plate is a die from which this scene was impressed onto thin sheets of bronze and used to decorate Vendel-type helmets. It is true that this particular type of plate from Torslunda (like its fellow made by the same hand, showing a man bare to the waist, holding a monster by a rope drawn about its neck) was buried in mint condition and few impressions can have been taken from it;[224] but this is not the only instance of the scene in Vendel art and it must have been quite familiar on Vendel-type helmets. A helmet of just this type was found in the Sutton Hoo grave and no doubt it was not the only helmet of its kind in Suffolk. The next boat-grave to be dug at Sutton Hoo, if intact, might well produce one bearing this very scene. Between the Sutton Hoo and Torslunda scenes there is thus an historical, indeed a physical link, as well as an iconographic one.

It would be possible to go on producing significant parallels between these two archaeologies for a long time. The articles of Nerman, Lindqvist and Maryon already quoted may be referred to for further illustrations. It will suffice here to take two further instances of a distinctive kind that can be briefly dealt with.

First, the Sutton Hoo whetstone (Plate 1). Whetstones occur rarely in graves of the pagan Saxon period. Whetstones, or stones of similar form, carved with faces occur at about this period in Ireland,[225] Wales,[226] and Scotland[227] though none of them are closely datable. Primitive-looking faces carved on pillars or other stones are also characteristic of this period in Ireland.[228] None of the faces of these Insular pieces bears any resemblance to the Sutton Hoo whetstone faces although the Sutton Hoo face is closely paralleled, even its pear-shaped surround, on an Anglo-Saxon silver *sceatta* (Fig 2e), a century or so later in date than the whetstone (Plate 1). On the other hand, Nerman has pointed out not only that whetstones are highly characteristic of Swedish graves (notably the Vendel and Uppsala graves)[229] but also that the faces on the Sutton Hoo whetstone find their closest analogies in contemporary Swedish art. He quotes a number of instances from Gotland.[230] To these we may add some examples closer to Sutton Hoo,[231] namely the pointed faces that appear in the hips of the interlacing animals on the flange of the shield-boss and a rectangular mount from boat-grave 12 at Vendel.[232] The best analogy for the bearded masks on the whetstone seems to me to be the cloisonné face in the hip of the bird on the Sutton Hoo shield (Plate 7a), in which the pointed beard, the moustache and the pear-shaped field of the whetstone, and even the 'stop' or pellet below the point of the beard, are all suggested. This shield is claimed by Nerman as Swedish[233] and it certainly is so.

Lastly we may refer to the solitary gilt-bronze 'sword-ring' found in the Sutton Hoo burial (Fig 7). It never belonged to the Sutton Hoo sword, or to any sword, but to the shield.[234] It is not generally realized that it differs in an important respect from the true sword-ring. The vertically-set element of sword-rings of the solid type (as distinct from the loose functional rings found on some English swords)[235] is always cut away obliquely in an upward direction to fit on to the shoulder of the pommel.[236] Very occasionally, if it is an exceptionally small ring, it may remain unmodified.[237] The Sutton Hoo shield-ring is unmodified and has an absolutely straight undersurface. I know of only one parallel to a ring the size of the Sutton Hoo ring which remains unmodified and that is a 'sword-ring' of similar dimensions excavated in Uppland, at Valsgärde. It does not come from a sword but was mounted on a drinking horn.[238] This unusual ring in the Sutton Hoo grave is closely paralleled in shape and decoration by that on the Vallstenarum sword. Like the shield on which it is mounted it is Swedish and

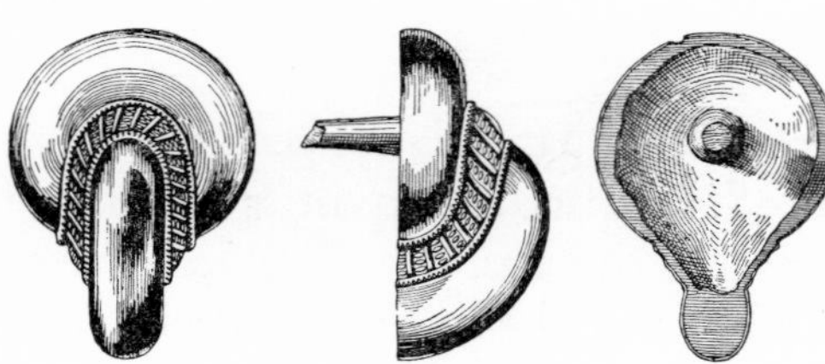

Figure 7 Gilt-bronze 'ring' from the Sutton Hoo shield (Scale 1 : 1)

must be regarded as another distinctive link between the two areas. A further parallel may be claimed, that like the Valsgärde 7 ring of the same type, it was designed for mounting on an object other than a sword.

One more factor of a different but decisive kind must be mentioned – boat-burial. There are only two places in Europe where boat-graves are known to occur in the seventh century – Suffolk and Uppland. This shows, as has already been said,[239] that the two areas share not only distinctive types of object and technical and ornamental details but also distinctive customs. The fact of boat-burial, taken in conjunction with the many close connections to be found in the archaeological materials of the two areas, shows that the link between them is not to be explained solely in terms of gifts or trade, but is something more substantial. Boat-graves do not occur in Suffolk only at Sutton Hoo but more widely.[240]

In contradistinction to the dispersed and often only rather general parallels to be found in the archaeological materials of the Continental mainland and quite remote, even hypothetical, Continental 'prototypes', there are concentrated in our two areas a great abundance of links of the most intimate character covering a broad range of antiquities of different kinds and backed by a common burial-custom of a most distinctive nature. A wandering goldsmith could not suffice to explain the similarities, for they occur in many other things besides goldsmith's work. It seems to me certain that any questions of independent parallel development in Sweden and Suffolk from some supposed common Continental source is completely ruled out. I hope that it will now be accepted by historians, linguists and students of early Northern Literature, as well as by archaeologists – that there existed a direct and substantial connection between East Anglia and Sweden a hundred and fifty years and more before the commencement of Viking raids upon the British Isles. It also seems to me in the present state of knowledge and particularly because of the closeness of the connections with the royal mounds at Old Uppsala, that the connection is between Suffolk and Uppland, that is, with the kingdom of the Svear, rather than of the Geats. There are indications that the bond between the archaeologies of East Anglia and Sweden extends beyond the

Sutton Hoo grave-field and that future discoveries in Suffolk are likely to demonstrate it with increasing force and clarity.[241]

THE INTERPRETATION OF THE SWEDISH CONNECTION

Various attempts have been made to explain the connection with Sweden revealed in the Sutton Hoo ship-burial and these will now be discussed[242] (Fig 8).

Perhaps the most telling consideration against Maryon's view that practically the whole of the Sutton Hoo treasure, including the jewellery, was imported from Sweden, is that no Swedish archaeologist accepts it. 'Maryon's opinion,' writes Nerman, 'can certainly not be accepted by those who know the Swedish material of the Migration and Vendel periods.'[243] Since Nerman, nevertheless, argues that the burial is a Swede's, we may suppose that if it had been possible to say that the majority of the finds were Swedish he would have been the first to say so. A single point breaks down the conception of wholesale importation. The most striking and ambitious pieces in the Sutton Hoo jewellery, purse-lid, shoulder-clasps and the pyramids that presumably decorated the sword-knot, are singled out by the prominent use in their decoration of chequered inlays of millefiori glass.[244] Not a single instance is known of the occurrence of such inlays in Northern or Continental metalwork, and furthermore, the only source from which the millefiori technique can have been derived is Insular. The millefiori technique[245] lived on in the post-Roman world only in Britain, appearing in the sixth and seventh centuries A.D. in the ornamentation of the escutcheons of the thin bronze Celtic hanging-bowls found in Anglo-Saxon graves. The use of millefiori on these Sutton Hoo gold pieces shows beyond doubt that they were made in England.[246] It is furthermore possible, by internal analysis and comparative study of the jewellery, to show that all the other pieces (except the sword pommel) are products, if not of the craftsmen who made the major pieces already referred to, at any rate of the same workshop or milieu.[247] So it is clear that at any rate one major Germanic element in the find – the cloisonné jewellery – is of Insular manufacture.

Nerman has argued at length that the Sutton Hoo ship-burial is the grave of a Swedish chieftain or king. He thinks this Swedish chief or king died in England about A.D. 670 and that he was most probably 'a conqueror who subjected part of the country to his rule'. 'We know so little of East Anglian history at this time that such a possibility cannot be excluded.' The site of the burial, on an arm of the sea, fits admirably with the idea of a foreign intruder of this kind. Nerman also envisages the possibility that, if not a conqueror, the Swede was called in perhaps as a relative, 'to help an East Anglian King in his wars'.[248]

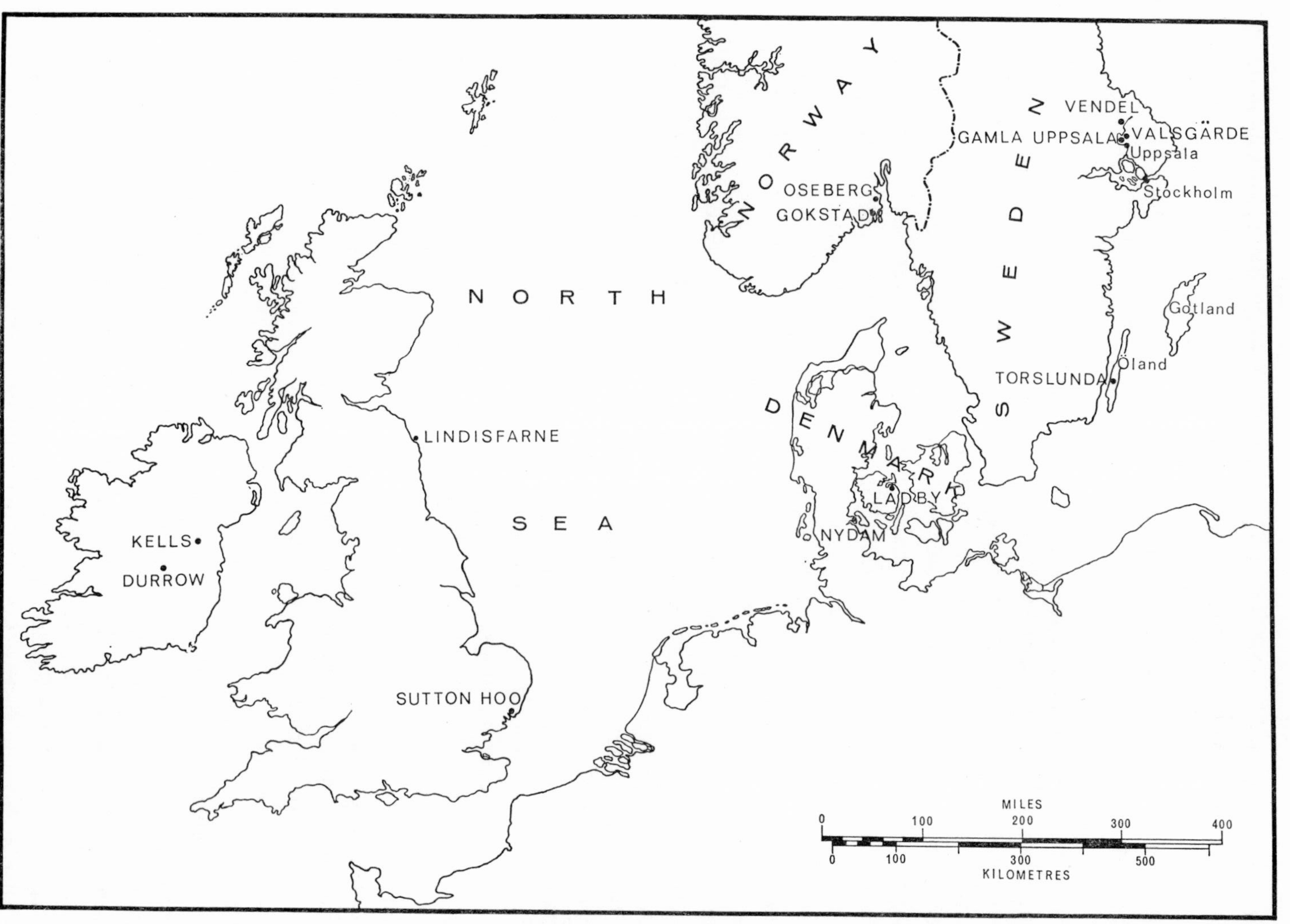

Figure 8 Sketch map of Northern Europe showing the general geographical relationship between Sutton Hoo and the principal related Scandinavian sites

Before considering the supposition upon which this theory rests some general observations may be made.

That a Swedish chief could have been called in to help the Wuffingas in their wars against Mercia is feasible, though we should have to suppose that he arrived in the reign of Sigeberht or Anna, that is before A.D. 654. For Anna's reign saw the last of the early wars of East Anglia, except for Penda's Northumbrian expedition in which Æthelhere took part and met his death and which marked the end of East Anglia's political power. The suggestion of a Swedish conqueror who enforced his rule over parts of the country can, I consider, be completely ruled out.

The fact is that we know much more of the history of East Anglia in the seventh century and in particular its second and third quarters than Nerman supposes; at any rate, enough to decide this issue. We know from Bede and other sources the rulers of East Anglia in unbroken succession. The sequence is confirmed in a good genealogy (Plate 3), written down between A.D. 811 and 814. We know the East Anglian bishops in unbroken succession. Bede, who was well informed about East Anglia in this period, gives no inkling of any such occurrence as the irruption of a pagan conqueror into an area that was at this very time (625–670) the centre of East Anglian Christianity (Fig 4), politically startling and adverse to the developing life of the Church though such a pagan Scandinavian invasion and the resultant counter-operations must have been. The most cogent argument against the notion of a pagan Scandinavian invasion is in the fact of the tranquil progress of East Anglian ecclesiastic and monastic life through this very time,[249] clearly indicated both in the *Ecclesiastical History* and the *Anglo-Saxon Chronicle*. Indeed if the identification of Cloveshoh with Mildenhall is correct (Fig 4),[250] we must suppose that the annual meetings of these important councils of the Church of all England took place in East Anglian territory from 670 onwards. This is hardly compatible with political instability of a pagan régime. Still more cogent is the attested flowering and prosperity of those monasteries – royal foundations or under royal patronage – in the region of Sutton Hoo itself. As for the siting of the barrows on an estuary, it has been said elsewhere that this part of Suffolk was in all probability the core of the East Anglian kingdom,[251] largely because of its easy sea communications with Kent and the Continent. Nothing could be more unsound than to draw a positive inference, such as Nerman draws, from the geographical situation of the burial. The fact that it is only a few miles down-stream from what we may reasonably call one of the more important residences of the East Anglian Royal house at this very date, should counsel caution. Indeed, as Chadwick lost no time in pointing out,[252] we can hardly imagine that the ostentatious treasure-mound (whose reputed wealth must have been widely known)[253] of a foreign invader, set up in the heart of the Wuffingas' domains, would have been allowed to survive intact once the invader had been driven out. It would assuredly have been razed and the treasures confiscated to the royal treasury.

Nerman's view that the burial is a Swede's rests upon the belief that the sword, helmet and shield in the Sutton Hoo grave are Swedish pieces; that the manner of the burial (in a boat, richly furnished with grave-goods and arms and armour, under a low mound) is Swedish and that the burial is pagan. He also supposes the monument to be an ordinary grave and not a cenotaph. It would be possible, as will be indicated below, to accept all these propositions and yet draw a different conclusion. We must however examine the propositions themselves.

IS THE MANNER OF BURIAL SWEDISH?

Nerman writes 'the manner of the burial itself is Swedish. Such richly furnished unburnt warriors' graves in a boat under low mounds or flat ground are known only from Sweden.'[254] However, richly-furnished unburnt warriors' graves, without the boat, are also characteristic of Anglo-Saxon archaeology. We may quote among many, those found at Broomfield, Essex[255] and Taplow in Buckinghamshire,[256] both probably slightly earlier than Sutton Hoo. A plan of Taplow grave is published here for the first time (Plate 16),[257] and attention may be drawn to the sword, angons and two shields. Again, the Sutton Hoo burial was *not* covered by a low mound. It did not have the low flat-topped circular mound, or no mound at all, of the Swedish boat-graves. The Sutton Hoo ship-barrow was a circular mound with a height of eight feet. Such differences are not decisive in themselves but they hardly justify the view that the Sutton Hoo barrow is typically Swedish. The only thing that appears distinctively Swedish about the funeral arrangements is the use of a boat and here we may note that we are not dealing with an isolated phenomenon (such as the burials of a single small group of raiders) since another boat-burial is known from the Sutton Hoo site itself.[258]

Nerman has not sufficiently considered *differences* between Sutton Hoo and the Swedish boat-graves. The concentration of the burial-deposit within a specifically constructed chamber in the centre of the boat is one; but more important is the complete absence of sacrificed animals at Sutton Hoo. Animal sacrifices, often on a lavish scale, are an invariable accompaniment of important Swedish burials. From the royal cremations at Old Uppsala, where we have found the most striking parallels to some of the Sutton Hoo finds (and which illustrate how Swedish kings really were buried), many animal remains were recovered.[259] The East mound from which came the helmet-fragment shown in Plate 14c yielded remains of horses, at least three dogs, sheep or goats and bear. The West mound, which produced the cloisonné fragment (Plate 10d), yielded horse, bird, pig, bear and at least two dogs; the centre mound, cat, dogs, horses, domestic pig, smaller ruminating animals and cattle, fowls and possibly geese. There were similar finds from Ottar's mound in Vendel.[260] From the Vendel boat-inhumations were taken remains of many horses and other animals and species of birds, including falcon, owl and crane.[261] In a Swedish royal grave of the standing of the Sutton Hoo ship-burial we might well expect to find remains of as many as a dozen horses and numbers of other animals. In fact at Sutton Hoo, though ample space was left both inside and outside the burial chamber, there was not a trace of any animal remains. It is inconceivable that every trace of horses' skeletons, with almost indestructible teeth, should disappear, even in the acid sand at Sutton Hoo (pH. 4.5). Equally decisive (though archaeologically regrettable) is the absence of any saddles, bits, bridles, harness mounts or other metal objects such as invariably accompany animal skeletons in Swedish inhumations of the period.

What does the absence of sacrificed animals at Sutton Hoo mean? Animal sacrifices are not characteristic of Anglo-Saxon inhumation graves and it is of course compatible with the view that the grave is Anglo-Saxon. We cannot any longer connect the absence of animals with the absence of a human body, as something due to the peculiarity that the grave was a cenotaph. We have seen that the cenotaph view is very difficult to maintain. Absence of animals would certainly be the proper accompaniment of a Christian burial. At all events, it is clear enough that the Sutton Hoo burial is not typically Swedish but if a Swedish burial at all, one that makes concessions to and is strongly modified by its Insular environment.

ARE SWORD, SHIELD AND HELMET SWEDISH?

They may well be. Anglo-Saxon shields were seldom if ever richly decorated[262] and shield-bosses were seldom large or ornate.[263] No fragment of any shield similar to the Sutton Hoo shield has come from any Anglo-Saxon grave. The heavy, domed overhanging boss, with massive flange rivets, of the Sutton Hoo and Swedish shields, is unknown in England. The type is most closely paralleled in Lombardy and Bavaria. No vestige of a helmet like the Sutton Hoo helmet has come to light in Kentish or other aristocratic warriors' graves. The only authenticated Saxon helmet known, that from the Benty Grange tumulus, is of a quite different character, being constructed with plates of horn over iron strips.[264] Again apart from Sutton Hoo, only one sword, quite possibly later than the Sutton Hoo one, has been found in England with clips on the grip resembling those illustrated on Plate 8[265] and none with a gold cloisonné pommel,[266] or with circular scabbard-bosses such as those found on the Sutton Hoo sword and illustrated on the Vendel XIV helmet.[267] With the possible exception of the sword, I have not been able to find in Anglo-Saxon archaeology any background to suggest that the distinctive forms of the three pieces under discussion could be an original Insular evolution, independent of any Swedish influence, which subsequently came to be transferred to Swedish soil. The uncertainty of the dating of the Swedish royal cremations at Uppsala and the Swedish boat-graves and their related culture makes the matter more complicated but at present I can visualize only two likely explanations of the sword, shield and helmet at Sutton Hoo. Either they were made in Sweden and brought here, or they were made here by craftsmen who must have been fresh from Sweden when they made them.

There are notable differences between the Sutton Hoo shield and the helmet and any Swedish examples yet found, for instance the solid neck-guard and elaborate mask of the Sutton Hoo helmet, as compared with the iron slats and mail curtains of surviving Swedish ones;[268] and the sumptuousness of the bird and dragon mounts of the Sutton Hoo shield. These Sutton Hoo pieces are richer and of better quality than any Swedish examples yet found. These differences may be accounted for by the differences in date and social level. The boat-graves of Vendel and Valsgärde are those of 'yeomen-farmers' or prosperous officials.[269] Contemporary royal inhumations have not been found but the closeness of the parallels already noted in the royal cremations at Uppsala to items in the Sutton Hoo grave (Plates 10d and 14c) suggest that the arms and armour in these and other royal burials may have been closer to the Sutton Hoo examples than those from the Swedish boat-graves. Helmets and shields from the royal graves would presumably have been richer and finer than those from the humbler boat-graves. The divergent elements in the design of the Sutton Hoo shield and helmet, then, when compared with similar Swedish finds at present known, do not support the possibility that they are of non-Swedish origin.

In examining the bases of Nerman's theory of a Swedish intruder or ally, we have reached the conclusion that the manner of the Sutton Hoo burial is not typically Swedish. Indeed we have had seriously to consider whether it is not a Christian monument. As Lindqvist has said,[270] we cannot yet be positive that boat-burial is a Swedish custom in origin and that it could not have been evolved in the East Anglian milieu. We agree that the probability is, as Nerman claims, that the sword, shield and helmet are genuine Swedish pieces, though it is possible that they might have been made here by immigrant Swedish craftsmen. The shield-ring also seems clearly to be Swedish. Whichever is correct, a connection with Sweden is implied and it may be taken as certain that in the Sutton Hoo grave we meet pure Scandinavian elements in the East Anglian milieu, as we meet them in *Beowulf*. How are we to explain this connection, the presence of these Swedish pieces?

The first thing to understand is that the problem is a good deal more complex than Nerman suggested. For instance, the sword in his opinion is 'certainly Swedish'. Hitherto I have agreed without qualification, to avoid introducing complications prematurely, but swords of the period are often composite affairs. For instance, the pommel of the Sutton Hoo sword may have been made in Sweden but the blade was not. It was made in the Rhineland. Radiography shows that it is pattern-welded and there can be little doubt that such blades were manufactured in Rhenish factories. Radiography has not yet been systematically applied to the sword-blades of the period, most of which are coated with rust or concealed within scabbards in which they are inextricably fixed by corrosion. Thus, information about pattern-welded blades and their distribution patterns in time and space is too incomplete for broad inferences to be drawn. Pattern-welded blades are quite as common as plain ones in Saxon England in the fifth to seventh centuries. The swords found in both the Broomfield and Taplow barrows, rich seventh-century graves parallel with Sutton Hoo, have pattern-welded blades and so had the sword from the boat-burial in Mound 2 at Sutton Hoo. The blade of our Sutton Hoo sword may have been imported from the Rhineland into Sweden and the sword made up there but the earliest pattern-welded blade of the Vendel period so far claimed in Sweden dates from the eighth century.[271] On the other hand it is not impossible that a Swedish-made pommel, or a Swedish-type pommel made over here, could have been fitted to a Rhenish blade in England, where such imported blades were common in the sixth and seventh centuries. The filigree clips of the Sutton Hoo sword-grip (Plate 8) find most parallels in shape and general ornamental character (for instance, the use of filigree) in Sweden, though at a later date. The filigree braids, scrolls and hooks on the Sutton Hoo clips are typical of English, especially Kentish work and there is no reason to suppose that the clips were made outside England. The resplendent scabbard-bosses of the Sutton Hoo sword (Plate 8) are certainly English, as has been shown,[272] particularly because of their cruciform designs. The marvellous pyramids that decorated the sword-knot (Plate 8) are English too, as their millefiori glass inlays prove. The design of the scabbard-bosses further suggests, as indicated above,[273] that the man for whom these sword-trappings were made, was a Christian. Almost all the gold pieces found in the Sutton Hoo grave, apart from the purse, belt-buckle and epaulettes were, we believe, made for the leather harness on which the sword was worn and suspended. They are all demonstrably of Insular manufacture and appear to be appreciably later in date than the pommel. The Sutton Hoo sword is thus not a simple import. If it is Swedish at all, it must have been a treasured, ancient, Swedish weapon for which at a much later date, Anglo-Saxon goldsmiths provided a resplendent regal sheath and baldric.

The intimate relationship between the 'man and monsters' scene which appears twice on the Sutton Hoo purse and the Torslunda plate that bears the same scene has been demonstrated (Plate 15a and b).[274] Which is the copy, and which the model? If, as Almgren has argued,[275] and as Lindqvist and Nerman in all probability agree, the Torslunda plates are to be dated to the fifth century, or about the year 500, the Torslunda scene clearly has priority over a seventh-century version in Suffolk. Even if the Torslunda plates are to be dated as late as the first half of the seventh century, the Swedish version must, I think, be the source. The Sutton Hoo purse occurs in a context where strong Swedish influence is otherwise apparent, though this does not mean that influence did not pass in the reverse direction. In addition to this, the Torslunda scene is not an isolated thing but one in a long series of similar representations in the Vendel art of Sweden and is unlikely to have been so completely assimilated into the art cycle to which it belongs as a solitary disconnected element from an outside source. Finally, the mechanical means for its transference from the Swedish to the Anglian milieu are at hand. A Swedish-type helmet, of the kind for whose decoration these plates were designed, has been found in Suffolk.

It is most unlikely to have been the only one to have come across. We must therefore regard the scenes on the Sutton Hoo purse as translations of a Swedish scene into Anglo-Saxon jewellery. The translation, with certain modifications discussed above, is careful and accurate. A specifically Swedish element is thus, it seems, prominently incorporated into the design of 'one of the most sumptuous trappings that a Teutonic grave has ever given to us',[276] made in Suffolk.

Again, the great buckle is without doubt the finest Germanic buckle known. It was the first object in the find in which Swedish characteristics were recognized.[277] The interlace on its lid (it is hollow and opens about a hinge) closely resembles that on certain rectangular plaques from Vendel, grave I,[278] while the animal ornament at the sides of the upper plate forms a surging animal progression like that seen on a long mount from Vendel XII,[279] on which the same spotted inlays in the linear elements of the pattern may be seen and animal heads comparable with the two at the foot of the Sutton Hoo buckle. The spotted interlace and animal heads on the Vendel XII shield-boss[280] also provide an analogy. Yet the buckle is certainly not Swedish. It was disowned by both Nerman[281] and Lindqvist,[282] and Kendrick has correctly said, it was certainly made in England.[283]

Finally, the shield which in all probability is a purely Swedish piece.[284] The shield may have been brought from Sweden just before the burial took place, but it was more likely to have been an heirloom,[285] such as are so frequently referred to in early literary sources and which was taken from the wall and used on the occasion of the great funeral.

The ornamental strips on the Sutton Hoo shield are described incorrectly by

Nerman as gilt bronze.[286] No doubt he visualized them as being the same as on Vendel shields, especially that from Vendel XII. On this shield the ornamentation on one of the strips is virtually identical with that at Sutton Hoo[287] and Nerman has suggested that the bosses of the two shields came from the same workshop.[288] No doubt the original strip on the Sutton Hoo shield *was* of the same character as that on the Vendel XII shield – though at Vendel it was an iron strip, covered with stamped and gilt bronze foil bearing ornament, whereas the strip from the Sutton Hoo shield consisted of an extremely thin stamped sheet of pure gold foil mounted on a piece of wood. This must be considered too fragile an arrangement to have been an original feature of a great war-shield and it strongly suggests that the strip found was a temporary affair.

What picture do we derive from the foregoing examples? It is that the Swedish element at Sutton Hoo is not confined to the presence of certain pieces (sword, helmet, shield) made in Sweden, *but actively permeates the Anglo-Saxon milieu.* A resplendent jewelled harness and fittings are made by East Anglian goldsmiths in honour of an old Swedish sword (if Swedish origin be conceded) and the man for whom the work was done, who carried the sword, may have been a Christian. English-made regalia has Swedish subject-matter and iconography incorporated in its design. English-made metalwork (the belt buckle) bears the impress of Swedish style. A short while ago it was said that the Sutton Hoo funeral arrangements seemed to indicate a Swedish custom modified by the Saxon milieu. Now we seem to see the Saxon milieu in turn modified, indeed powerfully affected, by Swedish influences. It is clear that the Swedish elements present in East Anglia are of a positive, not a negative, kind: that Swedish-trained craftsmen operated in East Anglia; that the man who commissioned the Sutton Hoo jewellery, with its Swedish traits, was a man who could command in Suffolk the services of the finest goldsmith in the whole Germanic world. A foreign raider, or solitary visitor, or any episode, will not explain these phenomena. The Swedish elements in East Anglia seem deeply entrenched and the fact of boat-burial elsewhere than at Sutton Hoo suggests that they were entrenched on a broad front.

CONCLUSION

It has been urged (by Chadwick and by myself) with a bulk of evidence that seems difficult to contravene, that the Sutton Hoo ship-burial is a king's and the question we set out to answer in the latter part of this chapter was – was the king, for whom the monument was made, English or Swedish?

A foreign king who died on a visit, or fighting as an ally, can hardly be visualized as staying long enough, or having power, to modify the arts of the country as we have seen that they were modified, or to commission regalia[289] which must have taken years to make,[290] even if we allow that he might have stayed long enough to alter his own burial concepts and change his religion. A foreign king, visiting or joining in a campaign, would presumably have his own affairs and kingdom to get back to and would not become entrenched. The archaeological evidence reveals an entrenchment of foreign elements. The Snape boat-grave also indicates, if boat-burial is to be taken as a sign of foreign influence, that this influence is not localized to the burial of one individual – a king who happened to be on a visit – or (the other Sutton Hoo barrows included) to the burials of one particular party or group. The foreign influence is on a broader front.

Of the situations visualized by Nerman, the only one that might account for the circumstances we have discussed would be that of a Swedish conqueror who established himself with his followers and ruled as king for a substantial period, commanding the wealth of East Anglia and the finest native craftsmen; becoming to an appreciable extent absorbed in the milieu and accepting Christianity. We have already seen, it is wholly against the substantial body of historical evidence that such a thing could have happened in East Anglia at the relevant time in the seventh century. If there had been such a conqueror he could not have stayed long, for the crown remained in the Wuffinga family (Fig 3 and Plate 3).[291] The hypothetical conqueror's reign could hardly have been more than a violent and precarious interlude, hardly the setting for a great flowering of native craftsmanship. Still less can we imagine any foreigner of lower status – neither a conqueror nor a king – having such an impact on the East Anglian milieu.

Accordingly it seems to me that none of Nerman's explanations fits the complete archaeological picture or is historically plausible.

If we now consider the view that English archaeologists and historians have steadily maintained, that the monument is that of an East Anglian king,[292] we have to account for the presence in this East Anglian king's burial of Swedish objects that were ancient when buried. We have to explain the active Swedish influences seen at work as in the locally-made East Anglian regalia and the following of an exotic usage, apparently Swedish, for the funeral rites of an East Anglian king – if it be allowed, as it must be, that boat-burial may be a Swedish element.

It seems to me that there could be one simple explanation, which would explain everything and is positively suggested by the archaeological evidence as we have it at present. All the phenomena in the Sutton Hoo ship-burial that we have discussed are explicable if we suppose that Nerman's Swedish conqueror established his control over East Anglia not at the period of our burial in the seventh century but a good deal earlier – in fact that he was the man who founded the

East Anglian dynasty in the mid-sixth century. What we find in the burial would then be Swedish heirlooms (sword, helmet, shield) treasured as symbols of the origins or history of the royal house and in things that were made in East Anglia for Wuffinga patrons, traces of Swedish ideas and influences that would naturally spring from such roots. By A.D. 625–635, the time of the Sutton Hoo burial, the dynasty, established for some four generations, would have become absorbed in its Western European milieu, an integral element in Anglo-Saxon civilization. Hence the perfect manner in which the burial as a whole fits into the Insular setting. Once such a family link had been established between East Anglia and Sweden we may suppose that contacts in both directions were renewed from time to time.

The statements in the sagas, of which Nerman has reminded us in connection with the Sutton Hoo burial,[293] and which cannot by any stretch of the imagination be applied to seventh-century England, that the Swedish King Ivar Widefathom conquered a fifth part of England (described as Northumbria),[294] might, if our interpretation is correct, be seen to have some sort of generalized basis in historical fact, even though the achievement might have attached itself to the wrong individual and come to be referred to the wrong part of England.

The theory of Swedish origins outlined above is compatible with what we know of the Wuffingas.[295] The accession dates given in Matthew Paris' *Chronica Majora*[296] (Eorpwald 624, Raedwald 599, Tyttla 577) suggest *c.* 550 as a reasonable date for the establishment in East Anglia of Tyttla's father Wuffa, the probable founder of the dynasty[297] or *c.* 525 for the accession of Wehha, who, if the evidence of Nennius is to be preferred, was the first king 'who reigned in Britain over the East Angles'.[298] Nothing is known of the origins of this ruling family and there is no reason why they should not have come from Sweden.

It must not be forgotten that the Torslunda plates were found in Öland (Plates 57–61); that the pommel from Hög Edsten, for which I have suggested a Suffolk origin, was found in Bohuslän, the province on the west coast of Sweden immediately north of Gothenburg; that Lindqvist considers that the Sutton Hoo shield could have been made on Gotland;[299] and that a boat-grave dating from the sixth century has been found in the extreme south-east of Sweden.[300] It is possible that future excavations may substantially change the present picture of Swedish archaeology in the seventh century. Nevertheless, boat-burial in the sixth-seventh centuries is at present only known in Sweden, where it is well established at the time. The concentration of close parallels in Uppland (suggesting probable Uppland workshops for the Sutton Hoo helmet and shield), in particular the intimacy of the links between the Sutton Hoo graves and the royal mounds of Old Uppsala,[301] strongly suggest that if the Wuffingas came from Sweden, they were an off-shoot of the Royal House of Uppsala, the Scylfings.

Lindqvist has tentatively suggested the possible equation of Wehha with Weohstan,[302] a Scylfing prince and father of Wiglaf, the faithful and heroic companion who went to the aid of Beowulf in his last fight, with the flying dragon. I am not qualified to comment on this tentative suggestion but this seems an appropriate place to publish in facsimile and in a new transcription (Plate 3) the best genealogy of the Wuffingas. This genealogy is included in British Museum Cotton MS. Vespasian B VI, and is part of a document comprising genealogies and lists of bishops and written between A.D. 811 and 814.[303] I am greatly indebted to my friend and colleague Dr C. E. Wright, F.S.A., of the Department of Manuscripts in the British Museum, for help in deciphering the early names in the genealogy which Sweet was unable to read, or read incorrectly.[304] The MS. has been re-scrutinized both in natural and in ultra-violet light and the photograph (Plate 3) is taken by ultra-violet light. That a complete transcription has been possible and in particular the reading of the name *Tyttmaning* is due to Dr Wright. It will be noted that only the direct descent of Ælfwald is given in the genealogy, which must be supplemented by the table in Fig 3 to get the complete picture of the dynasty and of the succession.

The explanation of the Sutton Hoo burial here offered is, it will be noted, the same as that cautiously suggested by Lindqvist in his paper *Sutton Hoo and Beowulf* already referred to but I had reached it independently and have felt able to put it forward less tentatively, on broader grounds and after closer analysis of the Insular setting. Once it is conceded that the burial is that of an East Anglian king, I find it difficult to visualize any other explanation; but, apart from this, the theory receives some direct support if the evidence is considered not in breadth, as it has primarily been in this paper, but as Lindqvist has considered it, in depth.

Earlier on[305] I expressed the view that the great ship-burial must be the latest of fifteen burials so far recognized in the Sutton Hoo grave-field. If it is an Anglo-Saxon burial place and not that of a group of foreigners, this must be so, for it is hardly possible to conceive any burials of this elaborate sort in an old pagan burial place in Christian East Anglia, after *c.* 630–640. One of the other barrows in the Sutton Hoo grave-field contained a boat and the surface indications suggest that some of the others do as well.[306] In the Swedish boat-grave fields boat burials are only accorded to the heads of the family. They are accordingly strung out in time, about a generation apart.[307] If the analogy with the Swedish boat-grave cemeteries is to be pressed, it is likely that if other boat-graves do exist at Sutton Hoo some of them will be appreciably older than the great ship-barrow. If boat-burial is a Swedish custom, its introduction into England would thus have taken place considerably before the 630s.[308] This would imply that the contact with Sweden goes back into an earlier period. The Snape boat-grave (Chapter

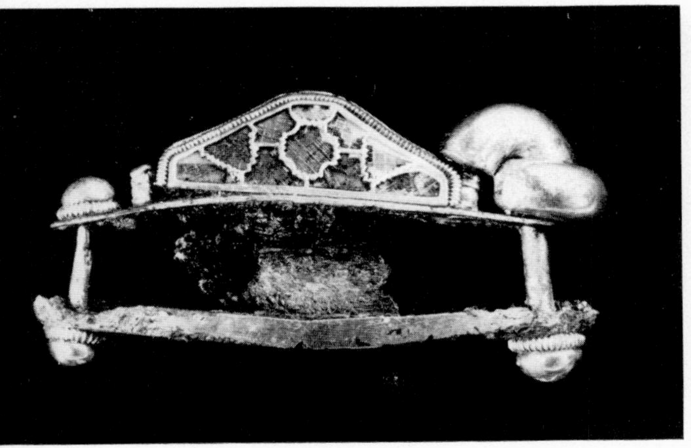

a

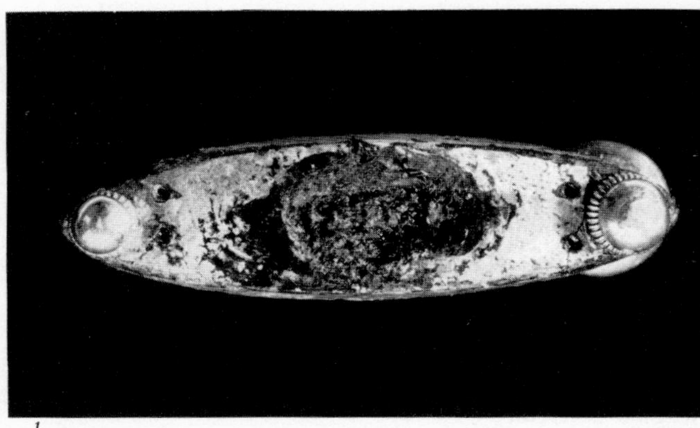

b

Plate 12 a–c, Three views of the gold cloisonné sword pommel set with garnets, from Krefeld-Gellep, grave 1732. (Scale 1 : 1)

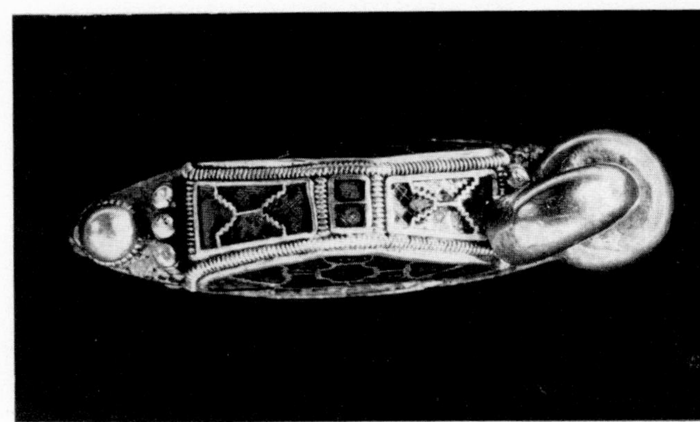

c

a

b

Plate 13 a, Reconstructed drawing of rider and fallen warrior panel, Sutton Hoo helmet (Scale 1 : 1); *b*, Gold disc brooch, Pliezhausen, Wurttemberg (Scale 1 : 1)

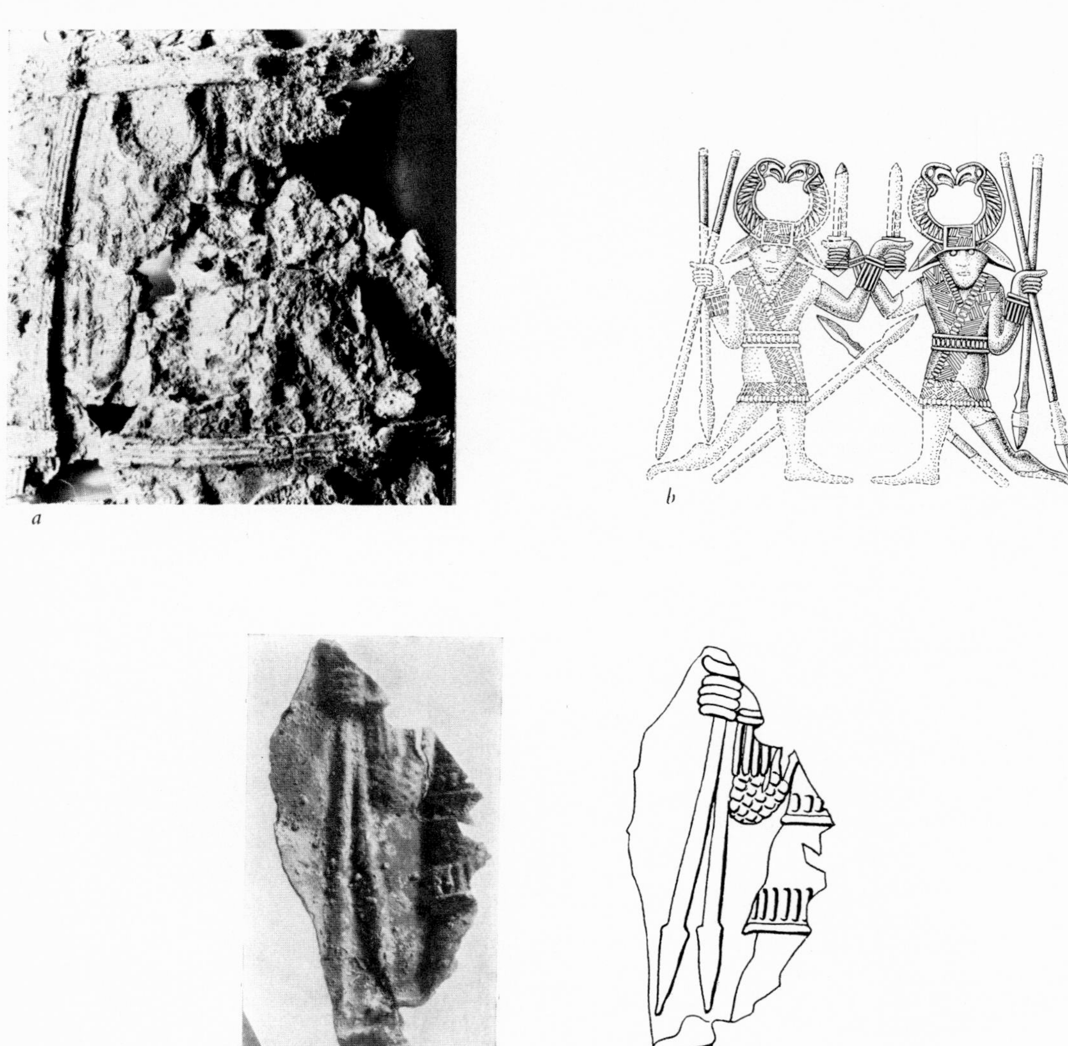

Plate 14 The theme of two dancing warriors with horned hats from Vendel-type helmets; *a*, Panel from the helmet, boat-grave 7, Valsgärde, Uppland (Scale 1 : 1); *b*, Drawing of helmet panel of twin dancing warriors, Sutton Hoo helmet (Scale 1 : 1); *c*, Fragment from a helmet panel, east mound, Old Uppsala, Sweden (Scale 2 : 1); *d*, Drawing of *c* (Scale 2 : 1)

a

b

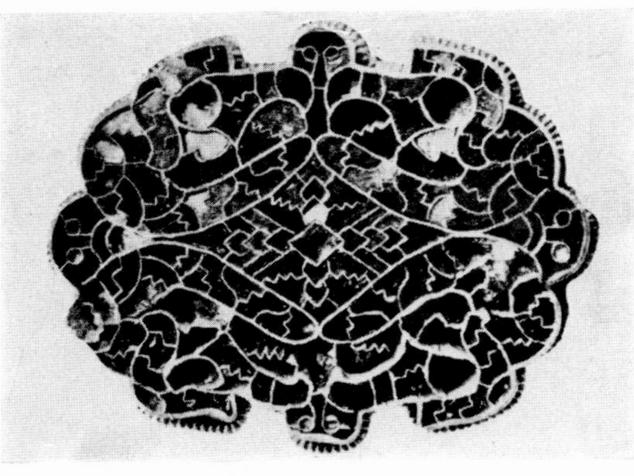

c

d

e

f

Plate 15 a, Drawing of man between beasts from a bronze die, Torslunda, Öland, Sweden (Scale 1 : 1); *b*, Detail of man between beasts, Sutton Hoo purse lid (Scale 1 : 1); *c*, The Reinstrup brooch, Denmark – a cloisonné version of the man between beasts theme (Scale 1 : 1); *d*, Frankish openwork mount from Amiens (Scale 2 : 3); *e*, Ivory buckle from Lavigny, Bofflens, Switzerland (Scale 1 : 1); *f*, Daniel in the lions' den, the Moone cross, Ireland (greatly reduced)

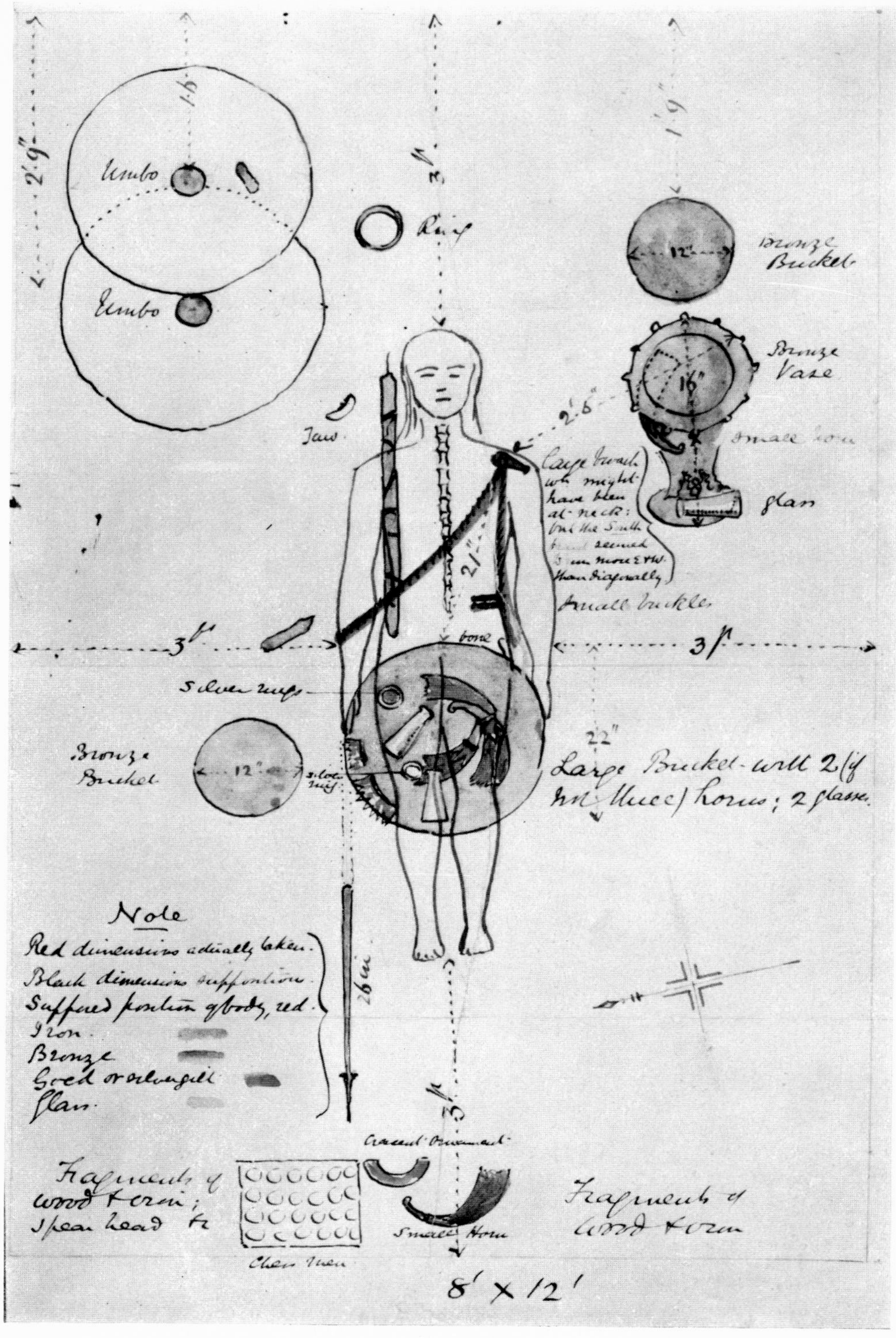

Plate 16 A seventh-century Anglo-Saxon aristocratic burial. A contemporary plan of the Taplow Barrow burial-deposit, excavated in 1882

3) could well be earlier than the 1939 ship-burial, if not as early as Joachim Werner has suggested (pp. 129–31).

A number of the subsidiary gold cloisonné buckles and mounts in the ship-burial were repaired, in some instances extensively and they must have been of some age when buried. If, as analysis suggests, they are all English pieces made or brought together to form a harness for a Swedish sword, this would imply a Swedish cause operating an appreciable time before the Sutton Hoo burial, which we now feel confident took place no earlier than *c.* 625 and no later than A.D. 635–640.

We have already discussed the condition of the shield when buried[309] and I would accept a date earlier than Lindqvist's, of *c.* A.D. 600 or earlier, for its manufacture. The chances are that it fell into disrepair and dilapidation over here. It would hardly have been brought from Sweden in such a condition. If it is Swedish it must then represent Swedish contacts much earlier than the date of its burial.

We may also note in this connection Lindqvist's date for the manufacture of the Sutton Hoo helmet – 'not much later than the Anastasius dish' (A.D. 491–518)[310] – a dating that agrees exactly with Nerman's dating of the East Mound (Odens hög) at Old Uppsala, identified by him as the burial of Aun (d. *c.* 490–500)[311] (see Plate 14c) and receives support from Almgren's dating of the Torslunda plates,[312] although Åberg and others would date all these much later.[313] Whether this very early dating be accepted or not (it must be regarded as no more than a strong body of opinion) it seems to me clear that this helmet (Chapter 8), which certainly stand typologically much closer to late Roman prototypes than any of the Vendel or Valsgärde helmets and which had also suffered some damage and been repaired, must be at any rate at least as old as the date suggested for the shield (*c.* 600 or earlier). If it did not arrive in England earlier, it most likely came with the shield and if so, this again implies Swedish connection at a date much earlier than the Sutton Hoo burial. In these ways the archaeological evidence conveys the impression not only of a pervasive Swedish influence at the highest social level but of such influence extending back into the earlier days of East Anglia and its royal house. From what we know of the dynasty, much the most probable time for the introduction of such an influence would be at its inception.

At this point we must recall the warning given earlier.[314] It is too early to draw final conclusions on the interpretations of the Swedish connection. If I have been definite at the end of this discussion it is partly because a degree of firmness seems justified and partly to invite criticism, which is needed to formulate the final solution. It remains very much to be desired that the implications of the historical situation revealed by the Sutton Hoo burial should be investigated and illuminated now by literary, genealogical and place-name specialists and by general historians and that as many archaeological and other issues as possible should be crystallized and ideas aired in the near future.

Not only will this assist current research on the materials but it will ensure that the excavation of the rest of the Sutton Hoo grave-field, which must not be postponed, is carried out with the maximum sensitivity to the needs and possibilities of the investigation. The need to precipitate such queries is the best justification for what may seem to critical observers in other disciplines somewhat premature theorizing. For this is not a problem condemned to eternal tossing about in a dead academic argument but one very much alive. We are only at the beginning of a process of revelation. As has already been said, even if most or all of the remaining barrows at Sutton Hoo prove to have been robbed, enough information should still be recoverable by sensitive and experienced excavation to reveal the history of the grave-field and to make certain the broad interpretation of the phenomena here discussed, in English history. Further excavations on other sites in East Anglia and also in Sweden are bound to throw increasing light on these problems.

Since the issues raised by the Sutton Hoo ship-burial are of prime importance to Dark Age studies over a broad field, it cannot be overstressed that the story that is emerging is entirely the product of what is, in this country, by far and away the most neglected branch of Dark Age studies. It is an archaeological revelation without a shred of direct documentary support. It is perhaps not the least significant thing about the Sutton Hoo ship-burial that it provides a salutary illustration of the great potential of modern archaeology, not only through its field techniques but equally through its indoor techniques of definition and analysis.

NOTES TO CHAPTER ONE

1 Herbert Maryon, 'The Sutton Hoo Shield', *Antiquity*, XX, 1946, 28.

2 Birger Nerman, *Forvännen*, h, 2–3, 1948, 65–9.

3 *ibid.*, 88.

4 See below, pp. 47–55.

5 A summary of a lecture by myself, entitled 'The problem of the Sutton Hoo cenotaph', which was delivered to the Royal Archaeological Institute in January 1950, appeared in the *Archaeological News Letter*, Vol. 2, No. 10, March 1950, 166–9. Further important results have been obtained from laboratory investigations since that date. The matter is fully dealt with in Vol. 1 of the British Museum's definitive publication, Cambridge, 1974.

6 'Who was he?' *Antiquity* XIV, 1940, 76–7, and Vol. I, Ch. 9 of the British Museum's definitive publication, Cambridge, 1974.

7 See Chapter 2, pp. 75–80 (first printed in *Proceedings of the Suffolk Institute of Archaeo-*

logy and Natural History, XXIV, 1948, 231–4).

8 It was originally thought that there were nine of these bowls (e.g. *Antiquity*, XIV, 52; *Antiquaries Journal*, XX, 166; R. L. S. Bruce-Mitford, British Museum Provisional Guide, *The Sutton Hoo Ship-Burial*, London, 1947, 47.

9 See pp. 26–7 below.

10 See R. L. S. Bruce-Mitford, *The Sutton Hoo Ship-Burial, A Handbook*, London, 1972, 68–9.

11 Bede, *Ecclesiastical History*, Book I, xxxii. *dona in diuersis speciebus perplura* and 'small gifts', (*parua exenia*) given by Gregory the Great to Æthelberht of Kent. The edition of Bede used in this paper is that of Bertram Colgrave and R. A. B. Mynors, *Bede's Ecclesiastical History of the English People*, Oxford, 1969.

12 *ibid*. Book II, x. 'cum ornatura in auro una et lena Anciriana una. . . .' Boniface V to Edwin of Deira.

13 *ibid*. Book II, xi. 'speculum argenteum et pectine eboreum inauratum.' Boniface V to Queen Æthelburgh of Deira.

14 S. Lindqvist, *op. cit.*, *Antiquity*, XXIII, 132–4; *Fornvännen*, 1948, 96–9.

15 T. C. Lethbridge, *Merlin's Island*, London, 1948, 139.

16 J. Werner, *Der Fund von Ittenheim*, Strassburg, 1943.

17 R. Pirling, 'Ein frankisches Fürstengrab aus Krefeld-Gellep', *Germania*, 42, 1964, 188–216.

18 N. Åberg, *The Anglo-Saxons in England*, Uppsala, 1926, 102–6. R. L. S. Bruce-Mitford, *Antiquaries Journal* XXX, 1950, 76–80 (*Review of Nubian Treasure*).

19 Bede, *Ecclesiastical History*, Book III, vi; The Easter Day dinner of King Oswald of Northumbria (633–641) and Bishop Aidan, 'a silver dish was placed on the table before him (the king) full of rich foods'. This dish was afterwards broken up and the pieces distributed to a large number of poor. An interesting account of the same practice is given in Gregory of Tours, *Gesta Francorum*. It seems that the resulting small fragments of silver had a value equivalent to that of coins.

20 'Saxon Rendlesham', Chapter 2, pp. 75–80.

21 H. Munro Chadwick, 'Who was he?', *Antiquity*, XVI, 1940, p. 86.

22 *op. cit.*, 90. 'Möjligen kan man emellertid också tänka sig, att krigaren i Sutton Hoo varit inkallad till hjälp av någon östanglisk konung i dennes strider, kanske i slakt med denne' ('One can also imagine . . . that the Sutton Hoo warrior may have been called in to assist an East Anglian King, perhaps a relation, in his wars').

23 p. 3 above. 'Saxon Rendlesham', Chapter 2, p. 79.

24 'Saxon Rendlesham', Chapter 2, p. 76.

25 For plan of the burial deposit see Plate 17. With hypothetical skeleton drawn in *The Archaeological News Letter*, Vol. 2, No. 10, 1950, p. 167, Fig; *Proceedings of the Royal Institution*, Vol. 34, pt. 3. No. 156 and Vol. I of the British Museum's definitive publication, Cambridge, 1974, Chapter 8.

26 'Saxon Rendlesham', Chapter 2, pp. 76–7.

27 R. L. S. Bruce-Mitford, *The Sutton Hoo Ship-Burial, A Handbook*, London, 1972, pp. 19–23 and Fig 5.

28 *British Museum Quarterly*, XIII, 1939, p. 128.

29 cf. B. Nerman, *op. cit.*, 71–3; e.g. Sune Lindqvist, *Uppsala Högar och Ottarshögen*, Uppsala, 1936, Figs 96, 97 (No. 14), 105; H. Stolpe and T. J. Arne, *La Nécropole de Vendel*, Stockholm, 1927, Pl. VII, Fig. 9. (PL. XI, Fig. 5, PL. XV, Fig. 10 for whetstone in the Viking period graves).

30 B. Nerman, *op. cit.*, 72.

31 S. Lindqvist, *Uppsala Höger, och Ottarshögen*, Uppsala, 1936. Fig. 96, for the East Mound.

31a For the Lough Currane whetstone, *Antiquaries Journal*, XII, 523–4. For that from N. Wales, *Antiquaries Journal*, XXI, 1941, 73.

32 E. Babelon, 'Le tombeau du roi Childeric et les origines de l'orfèvrerie cloisonné', *Mémoires de la Societé Nationale des antiquaires de la France*, 76, 1919–23, Figs. 1–4.

33 *Antiquaries Journal*, XX, 1940, 162–3.

34 At the time the stag was thought to have come from the helmet, *Antiquaries Journal*, XX, 163, 168.

35 The closest parallels to the stag I have been able to find are similar stag figures associated with open-work 'sun-discs' and thought to represent the tops of standards, excavated at Alaça Höyük in Turkey and dating from the Copper Age. (H. P. Kosay: 'Disques solaires mis au jour aux fouilles d'Alaça Höyük', *Annual of the British School at Athens*, XXXVII, 1936–7 (Myres Festschrift), Plates 19, 20, 22. Finds of similar stags are described in the *Illustrated London News*,

21 July, 1945. The resemblances are in some instances quite close and it seems not inconceivable that our stag is an antique of this kind accidentally dug up in the Black Sea area and handed down in a Germanic family. For the Alaça Höyük excavations see also *IPEK*, Jhrg. 1939–40, Bd. 13–14, Berlin, 1941, 23–35. (Remzi Oguz Arik, '*Alaça Höyük – une nouvelle station proto-historique en Anatolie centrale*'). For stags, Plates 4 (nos. 5 and 6) and 6–10. An illustration of one of the Alaca Höyük stags associated with a metal ring and openwork grid, seen as found lying in the ground by the excavator, is also given by Mrs D. E. Martin Clarke in Fig. 12, p. 118 of her paper 'Significant objects at Sutton Hoo' in the Chadwick memorial volume *The Early Cultures of North West Europe*, edited by Sir Cyril Fox and Bruce Dickens, Cambridge, 1950. Mrs Martin Clarke's paper is principally concerned with the Sutton Hoo standard.

36 The value of such negative evidence has been greatly enhanced by the re-excavation of the monument and the meticulous excavation in 1967–8 of the spoil removed from the burial chamber in 1939. (*The Sutton Hoo Ship-Burial*, Vol. I, Ch. 4, Cambridge, 1974.)

37 Unpublished examples in the Reserve collection of the British Museum.

38 cf. also *Beowulf* 1316–7:

Gang ða æfter flore fyrdwyrðe man
mid his handscale -healwudu dynede-

('Then the man distinguished in battle walked across the floor with his little band – the hall-timbers resounded – ').

39 S. Lindqvist, *Uppsala Högar och Ottarshögen*, Uppsala, 1936, 83 (Fig. 60) and 331 (English Summary).

40 J. M. Wallace-Hadrill, 'The Graves of Kings', *Studi Medievali*, Third Series I, Spoleto, 1960, p. 189.

41 Rupert Bruce-Mitford, *Sutton Hoo Handbook*, London, 1972, pp. 24, 80, Pl. 4(b).

42 H. Stolpe and T. J. Arne, *La Nécropole de Vendel*, Stockholm, 1927, Pl. xxxviii, Fig 1 and Pl. xxxiii, Figs 2, 3. See also *Sveagold und Wikingerschmuck*, Ab. 51, Tafel 39; Ella Kivikoski, *Der Eisenzeit Finlands*, Vol. I, Fig. 471.

43 Rupert Bruce-Mitford, *The Sutton Hoo Ship-Burial, A Handbook*, London, 1968, p. 20, and 'Saxon Rendlesham', Chapter 2, p. 76.

44 'Saxon Rendlesham', Chapter 2, pp. 76–7, H. M. Chadwick, *loc. cit.*, 80; Bede, *Ecclesiastical History*, Bk. II, Ch. xii.

45 'Roman traditionalist influence among the Anglo-Saxons', *English Historical Review*, LVIII, 1943, 138. In a footnote on p. 137, Professor Deanesly refers to the Sutton Hoo object. 'It has been suggested that the notable iron "lamp-stand" found at Sutton Hoo (see *Antiquity*, March, 1940, Pl. II) was some kind of a standard but it in no way resembles the *signa* of the legions and a *vexillum* would have perished apart from the metal head of the lance.' Professor Deanesly's impression of this piece was apparently derived from the illustration to which she refers, which presents a foreshortened view. Professor Deanesly has since been kind enough to examine the original object at my invitation in the British Museum and has indicated verbally and in writing that she is now prepared to accept the Sutton Hoo object as a standard.

46 M. Deanesly, *loc. cit.*, 235.

47 The current view. See also C. H. V. Sutherland, *Anglo-Saxon gold coinage in the light of the Crondall hoard*, Ashmolean Museum, 1948, 67.

47*a* *ibid.* 79, no. 22 and Pl. II, 1.

48 See P. Berghaus and Karl Schneider, *Anglo-Freisische Runensolidi in Lichte des Neufunden von Schweindorf*, Münster, 1967. See detailed reviews of the above by R. I. Page, *Numismatic Chronicle*, 1967, 304–6, and Stuart Rigold, *British Numismatic Journal*, 1968, 199–201. I am indebted to my friend and colleague, Dr J. P. C. Kent, for these references and for his comments on the coin.

49 For the whole question of the origins of Anglo-Saxon gold coinage, in the context of the new dating system, see Kent and Rigold in Chapter ix of *The Sutton Hoo Ship-Burial*, Vol. I, 1973 (the British Museum definitive publication).

50 *op. cit.*, 71: 'Denna pjäs, som nedtill har ett par avsatser för att hålla den i lage, om det stötes ned i marken, har tolkats som ett fälttecken, vartill den dock med sina horisontalt anbragta utsprang synes opraktisk.'

51 Bede, *Ecclesiastical History*, Bk. II, Ch. xvi: 'Tantum uero in regno excellentiae habuit, ut non solum in pugna ante illum uexilla gestarentur, sed et tempore pacis equitantem inter ciuitates siue uillas aut prouincias suas cum ministris semper antecedere signifer consuesset; necnon et incedente illo ubilibet per plateas illud genus uexilli, quod Romani tufam, Angli appel-

lant thuuf ante eum ferri solebat.' (ed. Colgrave and Mynors, Oxford, 1969). See also Vegetius, *Flavii Vegettii Renati de re Militari*, Libri Quinque, 1806, 66–7.

52 A recent discovery on the Roman '*limes*' in Germany of a unique instance – a sheet-metal dragon's head with wide-open mouth evidently leading into a textile wind-sleeve, shows the Sutton Hoo object to be different in kind.

53 *ibid.*

54 *ibid.*

55 The *labarum* was a square silken banner bearing the Chi-Rho monogram and suspended from a lance by a silken cord (M. Deanesly, *loc. cit.*, 143). For Roman standards and banners in general see Daremberg et Saglio, *Dictionnaire des Antiquités Grécques et Romaines*, Tom. IV, Pt. 2, under *Signa Militaria*, especially Bibliography and Figs. 6408, 6433, etc.

56 Fr. Klaeber, *Beowulf and the fight at Finnsburg*, 3rd edition with supplement, 1941, p. 129, Note 78, on Hrothgar's hall: ('The hall has been supposed to be named *Heor(o)t* from horns (antlers) fastened to the gables, although the appellation horn = gable (*horn-geap*, 82; *-reced*, 704; *hornas*, Finnsb. 4; *horn-sael*, *-sele* in other poems) seems to be derived merely from "horn shaped projections on the gable-ends" (B-T. cf. Miller, Angl. XXII, 396f). But the name has been primarily symbolical, the hart signifying royalty (A. Bugge, *Zfd Ph.* xli, 375, n.). The name Heorot was explained by Sarrazin from an ancient worship of a "hart-deity", (Angl. XIX, 372, f.) – a claim that has more recently been reinforced by Schutte. . . .

57 M. Deanesly, *op. cit.*, 140, note 2; from Bosworth-Toller.

58 e.g. Bede, *Ecclesiastical History*, Bk. I, Ch. xxx. (The letter to Mellitus); quoted in 'Saxon Rendlesham', Chapter 2, p. 84.

59 Peacocks, common in Mediterranean art in Roman and early Christian times, have been recorded in excavations of eleventh- and twelfth-century sites, in Germanic contexts (information from Dr H. M. Müller, Berlin) and one was buried in the Gokstad ship.

60 See Chapter 12, p. 257 and footnote 17.

61 The mail coat, under The Anastasiv's dish, is the odd man out amongst the war gear.

62 No evidence has survived as to its contents but it may have held wine or mead.

63 M. Deanesly, *op. cit.*, 145.

64 On this coin see G. Baldwin Brown, *The Arts in Early England*, III, 88–9, and Pl. VI, 12.

65 *op. cit.*, 83.

66 *ibid.*, 84.

67 p. 114.

68 *op. cit.*, 89. 'efter hednisk sed'; and p. 93, 'the burial at Sutton Hoo is typically pagan' (English Summary).

69 *Antiquity*, 1948, 133; *Fornvännen*, 1948, 99.

70 A. France-Lanord and M. Fleury, 'Das Grab der Arnegundis in St. Denis', *Germania*, 40, 1962, pp. 34–9. O. Doppelfeld, *Kölner Domblatt*, 18–19, 1960, 85 ff. Joachim Werner, 'Frankish Royal Tombs in the Cathedrals of Cologne and St. Denis', *Antiquity*, XXXVIII, 1964, 201–16, and Pls. XXIV–XXVI.

71 Frauke Stein, *Adelsgräber der 8 Jahrhunderts in Deutschland*, Germanische Denkmalër des Volkwanderungzeit, series A, Band IX, 1967.

72 *op. cit.*, 82, 83.

73 T. C. Lethbridge, *Merlin's Island*, 1948, 139.

74 Bede, Bk. I, Ch. xxx: see also 'Saxon Rendlesham', Chapter 2, p. 84.

75 *ibid.*, Bk. III, Ch. viii.

76 *Antiquity*, 1948, 133: *Fornvännen*, 1948, 99: 'Mot denna bakgrund framstår graven vid Sutton Hoo som utan tvivel kristen, anlagd för en konvertit. Detta redan genom den från föregående sekler ej betygade rikedom på gravgåvor.'

77 See p. 4 above.

78 C. H. V. Sutherland, *op. cit.*, 22, 23.

79 *op. cit.*, 83. The date of the poem is uncertain.

80 The passage is somewhat obscure. *Sweet's Anglo-Saxon Reader*, 1948, gives the text as follows:

þeah þe graef wille
broþor his geborenum
maþum mislicum
ne maeg þaere sawle
gold to geoce
þonne he hit aer hydeð

golde stregan
byrgan be deadum
þaet hine mid wille
þe biþ synna ful
for Godes egsan
þenden her her leofað

81 cf. T. C. Lethbridge, *op. cit.*, 140: 'very few of

the graves at this time had rich associations of grave goods.'

82 *op. cit.*

83 *op. cit.*, 'med all sannolikhet först omkring 670', *Fornvännen*, 1948, 96. Allen said that he had little doubt that the date was 'nearer 670' than 650, which is not quite the same as 'not until about 670'. See *British Museum Provisional Guide to Sutton Hoo*, London, 1947, 42 and Note I on p. 42.

84 *Antiquity*, 1948, 138; *Fornvännen*, 1948, 98–9.

85 For the upper limit in date for cremation in Anglo-Saxon archaeology see E. T. Leeds, *op. cit.*, 33, 35; e.g. 'it is mainly the wide range of brooch-types associated with cremations that serves to establish the persistence of the rite down to the beginning of the seventh century and in a few cases beyond.' cf. R. R. Clarke, 'Norfolk in the Dark Ages', Pt. I, *Proceedings of the Norfolk and Norwich Archaeological Society*, XXVII, 1939, 177: 'Cremation was not general after about 550' (in Norfolk). Probably the latest Anglo-Saxon cremation known is the Asthall Barrow from which part of a Coptic bowl and the remains of a gilt-bronze object ornamented in Style II were recovered, *Antiquaries Journal*, IV, 113–26.

86 *Antiquity*, 1948, 138; *Fornvännen*, 1948, 107.

87 This is fully discussed in Ch. VII, Vol. I, of the definitive publication, Cambridge, 1974.

88 For the conversion of East Anglia see F. M. Stenton, *Anglo-Saxon England*, 1943 (*The Oxford History of England*, Vol. 1), 116–17.

89 Bede, Bk. II, Ch. xv.

90 For the chronology of the East Anglian kings see the British Museum definitive publication, *The Sutton Hoo Ship-Burial*, Vol. I, Chapter x. Sigeberht was killed at the same time as his 'cognatus' and co-king Ecgric in fighting against a Mercian invasion of East Anglia by Penda.

91 Ch. xv.

92 'de Burgundiorum partibus'.

93 Probably Dunwich, in Suffolk, though S. E. Rigold has recently put forward a case for Walton Castle, near Felixstowe, at the mouth of the River Deben.

94 Probably in A.D. 648 or 649. See H. M. Chadwick's calculations, *op. cit.*, 81.

95 Bede, Bk. III, Ch. xvii.

96 F. M. Stenton, *op. cit.*, 116.

97 H. M. Chadwick, *op. cit.*, 81.

98 *ibid.*

99 *ibid.*, 82, note 2.

100 The case for this is given in Vol. I of the British Museum's definitive publication *The Sutton Hoo Ship-Burial*, Vol. I, Cambridge, 1974. The supposed evidence to the contrary based on a misreading of his association with Penda and of his place in the family genealogy has peen disposed of and the Christianity of his parents, brothers and nieces combine with a reference in the Life of St Guthlac to make his Christianity probable.

101 See 'Saxon Rendlesham', Chapter 2, p. 75.

102 *Proceedings of the Suffolk Institute of Archaeology and Natural History*, Vol. 18, 1924, 29–52. (F. S. Stevenson, *St. Botolph and Iken*). I am indebted to Mr Leslie Dow for this reference.

103 F. M. Stenton, *op. cit.*, 117.

104 The Anglo-Saxon Chronicle records under 654 that Anna was slain and Botulph 'began to timber that minster at Ikanhoe'. F. S. Stevenson, *op. cit.*, 29.

105 'Saxon Rendlesham', Chapter 2, pp. 82 ff. Bede refers on a number of occasions to mass baptisms in rivers, the Swale, Glen and Trent for instance. (Bk. II, Chs. xiv, xvi.) These ceremonies were characteristic of rural areas in the early days of the conversion. Thus Bede, explaining the baptism in the Swale at Catterick, says 'for as yet there could not be builded oratories or places of baptism in the very birth of the new church.' Where it was a case of baptizing kings we read of churches set up for the occasion (for example at York and Canterbury) and it must be regarded as in the highest degree improbable that in East Anglia between 655 and 664, a bishop would have conducted the baptism of a visiting king in the river at a royal seat that had belonged to saintly and conspicuously active Christian Kings such as Sigeberht and Anna. It must be regarded as virtually certain that there was a church, even if only of the nature of a private royal chapel, at Rendlesham when this royal baptism took place there between A.D. 655 and 644.

106 R. H. Hodgkin, *History of the Anglo-Saxons*, Vol. I, 264.

107 H. M. Chadwick, *op. cit.*, 83; also footnote on p. 84. 'It may be noted that the (Continental) Old Saxons after their conquest by Charlemagne, in 785 were required to bury Christians in cemeteries of the church and not in "barrows of

the heathens".' cf. G. Baldwin Brown, *Arts in Early England*, I, 260 f.

108 H. M. Chadwick, *op. cit.*, 84.

109 Bede, Bk. I, Ch. xxxiii.

110 Bede, Bk. II, Ch. xiv.

111 H. M. Chadwick, *loc. cit.*

112 *ibid.*

113 F. M. Stenton, 'The East Anglian Kings', in *Anglo-Saxon England* (Studies presented to Bruce Dickins), Cambridge, 1964, first showed that Hereswith did not marry Æthelhoe as formerly supposed.

114 pp. 20–3 above, note 9. 637 is the probable date of Anna's accession.

115 *The Sutton Hoo Ship-Burial*, Vol. I, Cambridge, 1974, Ch. I.

116 F. M. Stenton, *op. cit.*, 117–18.

117 *ibid.*

118 *ibid.*

119 *Antiquity*, 1948, 134; *Fornvännen*, 1948, 99, 'Paulus eller Saulus'.

120 *Antiquity*, XIV, 1940, 59.

121 *ibid.*

122 It may be noted that Augustine built in Canterbury the Church of the Apostles Peter and Paul, and that the first church of the East Saxons in London was St Paul's.

123 See plan of the burial deposit, Pl. 17.

124 Rupert Bruce-Mitford, *British Museum Provisional Guide to Sutton Hoo*, London, 1947, 49.

125 Plate 4b.

126 Similar crosses occupy a central position on the gold cloisonné fittings, probably from a bag or purse, found with the Crondall hoard of gold Saxon and Merovingian coins deposited probably between 660 and 670 (C. H. V. Sutherland, *Anglo-Saxon gold coinage in the light of the Crondall hoard*, Oxford, 1948, 13). See G. Baldwin Brown, *The Arts in Early England*, III, Pl. III, 2; Burlington Fine Arts Club Catalogue, *Arts in the Dark Ages in Europe*, 1930, Pl. XX, M2; N. Åberg, *Anglo-Saxons in England*, Uppsala, 1926, Fig. 290. The coins were purchased by the Ashmolean Museum in 1944 but the gold cloisonné pieces are now lost. (See C. H. V. Sutherland, *op. cit.*, 8).

127 T. D. Kendrick, 'British Hanging Bowls', *Antiquity*, VI, 1932, 176, Pl. III; F. Henry, 'Hanging Bowls', *Journal of the Royal Society of Antiquaries of Ireland*, LXVI, 1939, 227 and Pl. XXVII, 5.

128 *op. cit.*, 170.

129 C. H. V. Sutherland, 'Numismatic parallels to Kentish polychrome brooches', *Archaeological Journal*, XCIV, 1937, 116–27. The fully-developed Celtic cross is seen on one of the Camerton escutcheons (F. Henry, *op. cit.*, PI, XXXIII, 4) but this cemetery is late enough to suggest that this cross may be due to the specific influence of Christian art. On the Camerton cemetery see E. T. Leeds, *op. cit.*, 111–13.

130 *British Museum Guide to Anglo-Saxon Antiquities*, London, 1923, Fig. 60; T. D. Kendrick, 'Polychrome jewellery in Kent', *Antiquity*, VIII, 1933, 440, Pl. IV, 4; N. Åberg, *Anglo-Saxons in England*, Fig. 203 etc.

131 C. H. V. Sutherland, 'Numismatic Parallels', Pl. 1,B.

132 T. D. Kendrick, 'Polychrome Jewellery', Pl. IV, 2; Åberg, *op. cit.*, Fig. 205.

133 T. D. Kendrick, 'Polychrome Jewellery', Pl. I,5. The cross theme does seem to be introduced here in the design of the cloisonné ring of the central roundel, in the form of four short expanding arms proceeding from a large central circle, the general effect being similar to the Wilton pendant. This would seem to be deliberate as distinct from the cruciform pattern formed by the four filigree panels, which may be adventitious.

134 C. H. V. Sutherland, 'Numismatic Parallels', 118.

135 *ibid.*, 121.

136 *ibid.*, 118 and Pl. 1,5.

137 *ibid.*, 120.

138 *ibid.*, Fig. 1 G–H.

139 C. H. V. Sutherland, *Anglo-Saxon Gold Coinage in the light of the Crondall Hoard*, Oxford, 1948, 67.

140 Sutherland's view of the evolution of the 'Celtic Cross' on *sceattas* is repeated and more positively affirmed, in his valuable paper 'Anglo-Saxon sceattas in England: their origin, chronology and distribution', *Numismatic Chronicle*, Sixth series, Vol. II, 1942, pp. 5 and 22–3.

141 G. Baldwin Brown, *Arts in Early England*, III, Pl. VI, p. 85, No. 13.

142 *ibid.*, Pl. LXXXI, p. 371, 2 and 4; and Vol. IV, p. 425.

143 'The lively interplay and merging of types resulted in certain borrowings of type by one

class from another' (C. H. V. Sutherland, 'Anglo-Saxon sceattas', 21).

144 See N. Åberg, *Anglo-Saxons in England*, Uppsala, 1926, 136; T. D. Kendrick, 'St. Cuthbert's Pectoral Cross, and the Wilton and Ixworth Crosses', *Antiquaries Journal*, XVII, 1937, 283–93.

145 T. D. Kendrick, *op. cit.*, 287, 292, regards St Cuthbert's Cross as fifth century and 'a work of the early British Church'. Whilst seriously doubting the validity of this attribution, I agree with Kendrick that St Cuthbert's Cross is strikingly unlike the other cruciform pendants in many ways and presents features at present unparallelable in seventh-century Saxon archaeology. See Chapter 14, pp. 281–302 below.

146 *ibid.*, 284.

147 *British Museum Anglo-Saxon Guide*, London, 1923, Pl. iv, 4; G. Baldwin Brown, *Arts in Early England*, IV, Pl. cii, p. 425, 5.

148 cf. E. T. Leeds, *Early Anglo-Saxon Art and Archaeology*, 111.

149 Burlington Fine Arts Club Catalogue, *Art in the Dark Ages in Europe*, 1930, Pl. iii, A52.

150 Rupert Bruce-Mitford, *The Sutton Hoo Ship-Burial, A Handbook*, London, 1972, Plate 33.

151 *ibid.*, Colour, Pl. F and Fig. 31.

152 *Antiquity*, XIV, 1940, 36.

153 This pattern also occurs in the foot of the Wittislingen fibula (G. Baldwin Brown, *Arts in Early England*, IV, Pl. H, 541. The analogies here cited are much closer than any similarity there may be with the patterns of the Childeric jewellery (cf. T. D. Kendrick in *Antiquity*, XIV, p. 38. For the relevant Childeric pieces, see G. Baldwin Brown, *loc. cit.*, Pl. H) and J. Chiflet, *Anastasis Childerici*, I, etc., Antwerp, MDCLV, *passim*.

154 See *The Sutton Hoo Ship-Burial, A Handbook*, London, 1972, Pl. 32 and Pl. 33.

155 *British Museum Anglo-Saxon Guide*, London, 1923, 61.

156 Plate 94, —; also Kendrick, 'St. Cuthbert's Pectoral Cross', *Antiquaries Journal*, XVII, Pl. LXXVII, B and LXXVIII, C.

157 *loc. cit.*

158 *loc. cit.*, 290.

159 *ibid.* The Wilton pendant (acquired by the British Museum in 1859) was unfortunately a stray find from a chalk-pit, without associations.

160 *op. cit.*, 289–90, Pl. LXXVII and Fig. 3. 'I do not think it is going too far to say that the Wilton pendant and the jewel on this shrine were made in the same workshop, if not by the same man.' For the Trier jewel, see also C. de Linas, *Les Origines de l'orfèvrerie cloisonné*, 1887, Vol. III, Pl. X; H. Rupp, *Die Herkunft der Zelleneilage*, Bonn, 1937, Pl. XXXI, and F. Rademacher in *Trierer Zeitschrift*, II, Jahrgang, etc.

161 *Antiquity*; XX, 1946, 28, Pls. II and III ('The Sutton Hoo Shield', by Herbert Maryon).

162 T. C. Lethbridge, 'Recent Excavations in Anglo-Saxon Cemeteries in Cambridgeshire and Suffolk', *Cambridge Antiquarian Society Quarto Publications*, New Series, No. III, 1931, 48, Pl. III. We may also recall this connection in the zoomorphic catch-plates on the backs of some English brooches, e.g. the Kingston brooch, (T. D. Kendrick, *Anglo-Saxon Art to A.D. 900*, London, 1938, Pl. xxxi, 6), a feature that does not often occur on the back of the garnet-encrusted round brooches of the Rhineland (H. Rupp, *op. cit.*, Plates, *passim*).

163 T. D. Kendrick, *op. cit.*, Pls. lxxvii, c and lxxviii, d. This design occurs also in later Irish metalwork (e.g. the Moylough belt in the National Museum of Antiquities, Dublin), where it must be regarded as derived, along with much else, from Saxon art.

164 It is unwise to express views on such matters without seeing the original pieces but I would very much doubt whether the Trier brooch is the work of the individual who made the Wilton cross. The use of green inlays, such as on the Trier brooch, is not known either in the Sutton Hoo gold jewellery or in the various other pieces of cloisonné work that may be associated with the Sutton Hoo workshop – though in many cases the inlays are missing and we cannot be certain that coloured glass was not used. The unusually irregular cross-section of the Trier brooch and details of the ornament particularly in the inner zone suggest a somewhat later date for this piece than for the Sutton Hoo jewels as a group. Nevertheless, the East Anglian origin of the piece seems certain, especially when it is compared with contemporary Continental material.

165 See Chapter 13, pp. 273–5, and Plates 90 a–c, 91 and Fig. 47*a*.

166 These matters are fully entered into in Volume 2 of the definitive publication of the

Sutton Hoo find in the chapter on the jewellery (in preparation).

167 p. 5, above.

168 G. Baldwin Brown, *Arts in Early England*, Vol. III, 195–6, Pl. xxi, H. M. Chadwick, *Antiquity*, XIV, 84. Chadwick suggests that if this is a genuine Christian burial, it is due to the fact that the burial in Christian precincts was not available at the time, in an officially pagan Mercia.

169 *Antiquity*, 1948, 90 *et seq*; *Frå National museets Arbejdsmark*, 1943, 19–31; *Acta Archaeologica*, XIII, 1942, 65–99.

170 Vol. I of the British Museum definitive publication, Cambridge, 1974, Chapter 8.

171 Definitive publication, Vol. I, Chapter 2, Cambridge, 1974.

172 *Antiquaries Journal*, XX, 1940, 175–6; *The Archaeological News Letter*, Vol. 2, No. 10, March 1950, 167–8.

173 The history of comment on the Swedish connections of the Sutton Hoo ship-burial may be found in these references: T. D. Kendrick in *Antiquity*, XIV, 1940, 38, and *British Museum Quarterly*, Vol. XIII, No. 4, Dec. 1939, 134–5; H. Maryon, 'The Sutton Hoo Shield', *Antiquity*, XX, 1946, 21–30 (especially 28, 29); R. L. S. Bruce-Mitford, 'Sutton Hoo and Sweden', *Archaeological News Letter*, Vol. I, No. 2, May 1948; 'Sutton Hoo och Sverige', *Ord och Bild*, Heft, 3, 1948, 97–104; 'The Sutton Hoo Ship-Burial, a new chapter in Anglo-Sweden relations', *Anglo-Swedish Review*, April 1950. Also B. Nerman, *op. cit.*, and S. Lindqvist, *op. cit.*, especially Nerman's paper for well illustrated comparisons.

174 *Monumenti Antichi*, XXV, Milan, 1918, 159, Fig. 4; Elis Behmer, *Das Zweischneidige Schwert der Germanischen Völkerwanderungszeit*, Stockholm, 1939, Taf. XLI, 7.

175 Renate Pirling, 'Ein frankisches Fürstengrab aus Krefeld-Gellep', *Germania*, 42, 1964, 188–216.

176 *Monumenti Antichi*, XXV, 159 and Fig. 5; E. Behmer, *op. cit.*, Taf. XLI, 6.

177 e.g. E. Behmer, *op. cit.*, Tafs. XLII, 1; XLVIII.

178 For examples of figural art from Swedish helmets of the Vendel period see H. Stolpe and T. J. Arne, *La Nécropole de Vendel*, Stockholm, 1927; also the Torslunda plates, H. Shetelig and H. Falk, *Scandinavian Archaeology*, Oxford University Press, 1937, Pl. 43; K. Stjerna, *Essays on Beowulf*, Viking Club Extra Series, Vol. III, London, 1912, 8, Figs. 2–5; etc.

179 *Antiquity*, XX, 28 (note 2).

180 *ibid.*, Pl. III; Rupert Bruce-Mitford, *The Sutton Hoo Ship-Burial, A Handbook*, London, 1972, Second edition, Pl. 4a,b.

181 H. Stolpe and T. J. Arne, *op. cit.*, Pl. IV.

182 E. T. Leeds, *Early Anglo-Saxon Art and Archaeology*, London, 1936, Pl. XVII (c); Gustav Behrens, Merowingerzeit, Mainz, 1947, Abb. 83, 85; Herman Stoll, *Die Alemannengräber von Hailfingen in Württemberg*, Berlin, 1939, Taf. 21, no. 24, nos. 2(a), (b), (d), (e), and 3(a), (b).

183 Pl. 7b for a bird appliqué from Sturry, Kent, and B. Nerman, *Die Vendelzeit Gotlands*, Stockholm, 1969, Vol. 2, Tafel 13, nos. 108, 109; Tafel 108, nos. 916, 917; Tafel 147, no. 1263.

184 See pp. 31–2.

185 G. Baldwin Brown, *Arts in Early England*, IV, Pl. H. II, p. 541; H. Arbman, 'Les Epées du tombeau de Childeric', *Meddellanden från Lunds Universitets Historiska Museum*, 1948, 97–137.

186 N. Fettich, *La Trouvaille de Apahida*, *Archaeologica Hungarica*, 32, 1953, 145–7, with Pls. 21–27. And also Johannes Hoops, *Reallexikon der Germanischen Altertums-Kunde*, Berlin, 1971, Band I, 336–7 and Pl. 27.

187 See *Antiquity*, XIV, 38.

188 For this piece, now lost, see *Archaeologia*, XLVI, Pt. I, 1880, 237–40 and Plate VII (Count Ferdinand de Lasteyrie, 'Two gold ornaments of the time of Theoderic'). Also S. Lindqvist, 'Some Vendel-time finds from Valsgärde', *Acta Archaeologica*, III, 1932, 35 *et seq.* for the view that these pieces were cheek-ornaments for a helmet.

189 See R. Laur-Belart, 'Ein Alamannische goldgriffspatha aus Kleinhüningen', *Ur-Schweitz*, Jhrg. X, Nr. 4, 1946, 66–73, Fig 50.

190 G. Baldwin Brown, *loc. cit.*, Pl. H.I.

191 *Fornvännen*, 1948, 100, 101; *Antiquity*, 1948, 135.

192 *ibid.*, 105, and *ibid.*, 137.

193 W. Veeck, *Die Alamannen in Württemberg*, Berlin and Leipzig, 1931, Textband, Taf. H:1, (a) and (b) and p. 44 ff.

194 W. Holmqvist, *Kunstprobleme der Merowingerzeit*, Stockholm, 1939, Pl. XXIII, 5 and p. 118.

195 *ibid.*, Pls. XX–XXVII.

196 Designs in stamped foil (*pressbleck*) are 'mass-produced', in the sense that many identical

impressions may be taken from the same stamp and we may assume that identical scenes such as that under discussion were widely distributed, through military operations or other occasions, on the helmets of warriors. The Sutton Hoo helmet (if Swedish) would be an illustration of this dissemination. It could thus be an easy matter for a subject that appeared to be closely imitated at this time in widely separated areas.

197 B. Nerman, *op. cit.*, Figs 17, 19. For Torslunda plates see also Chapter 10, pp. 214–22.

198 H. Maryon, 'The Sutton Hoo helmet', *Antiquity*, XXI, 1947, 139.

199 We have since realized that this was a plaster restoration by Maryon, probably inspired by the sombre faces on the sceptre. The similarity to the Valsgärde 7 helmet faces suggests that Maryon's instinct was sound.

200 cf. Pls. 14a and the Torslunda plate, already referred to, Pl. 57b, with the figure with two spears and horned head-dress.

201 B. Nerman, *op. cit.*, 76–81.

202 *Antiquity*, VII, p. 448, Plate V.

203 See T. D. Kendrick, *Antiquity*, XIV, 1940, 35–6 and Fig. 3; *British Museum Quarterly*, XIII, No. 4, Dec. 1939, 133.

204 *British Museum Quarterly*, *loc. cit.*

205 Rupert Bruce-Mitford, *The Sutton Hoo Ship-Burial, A Handbook*, London, 1972, 70.

206 *ibid.*, Fig. 31, p. 75.

207 See however George Speake in *Mediaeval Archaeology*, XIV, 1970, 1–16. 'A seventh century coin-pendant from Bacton, Norfolk and its ornament', where vestigial affronted boars' heads are recognized on the Bacton pendant.

208 Pyramidal studs are by no means uncommon in the seventh and eighth centuries, occurring in England, in the Rhineland, S. Germany, Italy and Northern Europe. See Chapter 13 section B, pp. 266–8. Its small size suggests that the cloisonné fragment from the Western Mound at Old Uppsala may be the inner field or cloisonné from one face of the pyramid and not the whole side of the pyramid. It is possible that a small fragment of gold cloisonné from the East Mound may represent another pyramid of this sort. (S. Lindqvist, *Uppsala Högar och Ottarshögen*, Uppsala, 1936, 170, Fig. 87).

209 For the Vallstenarum pommel see E. Behmer, *op. cit.*, Pl. XLII, I, or H. Shetelig and H. Falk, *op. cit.*, Plate 42(a).

210 p. 36, above.

211 *British Museum Quarterly*, XIII, 1939, 134.

212 This picture must be modified by the realization that all these technical features occur in the two Aphaida treasures of the late fourth and late fifth centuries found in Rumania. The mount and brooch forms of Aphaida are quite distinctive and no such sword pommel of this kind has come to light in a fifth-century context or a Rumanian one. See *Treasures from Rumania*, Catalogue of the Exhibition of Rumanian treasures, British Museum, 1971.

213 *Ur-Schweiz*, Jhrg. 10, No. 4, 70, Abb. 50.

214 p. 47, below.

215 p. 27, above.

216 *British Museum Quarterly*, 1939, 116; *Antiquity*, XIV, 29, 37; Rupert Bruce-Mitford, *Sutton Hoo Handbook*, London, 1972, p. 73.

217 Nerman, *op. cit.*, pp. 70, 71, footnote.

218 Both W. Holmqvist, *op. cit.*, 141–59, and Miss H. M. Roe ('An interpretation of certain symbolic sculptures of Early Christian Ireland', *Journal of the Royal Society of Antiquaries of Ireland*, LXXV, 1945, 1–23) have discussed the varied representations of Daniel and of the man-and-monsters and birds-and-vase themes in the art of the Merovingian period.

219 H. M. Roe, *op. cit.*

220 It has been said (*Antiquity*, XIV, 38; R. L. S. Bruce-Mitford, *British Museum Provisional Guide to Sutton Hoo*, London, 1947, 56, Note 3) that the Reinstrup brooch is probably English work. Having made a careful examination of it in Copenhagen, I consider that it is quite unlike any English work of the period and it certainly is not of English manufacture.

221 For many further examples of these themes see W. Holmqvist and H. M. Roe, *loc. cit.*

222 Professor Günther Haseloff has suggested that the Sutton Hoo men are depicted in '*orans*' attitude (the hands raised in prayer) and that the scene must accordingly be a version of Daniel in the Lion's Den, as was originally suggested. (*Antiquity*, XIV, 1940, p. 37; *Nordelbingen*, Band 20, pp. 9–20). But this is not the '*orans*' attitude, which is invariably – in Germanic as well as in Coptic and late Roman iconography – with the arms outstretched and the palms of the hands turned upwards. (Plate 15e,f). (See also W. Holmqvist, *op. cit.*, Plates XXXI, 1 and 4; XXXII, 1; XXXIV, 3; XXXV, 2 and 3).

223 cf. H. M. Roe, *op. cit.*, 8. This is a fact which distinguishes the Torslunda and the Sutton Hoo scenes from almost all the representations considered by Miss Roe in her Group I and it is a further point in the establishment of a connection between the two. Our two versions are, for the period to which they belong, in a class apart although close iconographic parallels may be found at a considerably later date, *viz.* the scene on the Kells market cross, with the horned central figure (H. M. Roe, Pl. II, 3) and the capital (twelfth century) from a church in Aisne (W. Holmqvist, *op. cit.*, 147, Abb. 120).

224 See below, Chapter Ten, pp. 215–16.

225 Pl. 7c, and *Antiquaries Journal*, VII, 1927, 323: Reginald Smith suggested a twelfth-century date for this piece.

226 Pl. 7c, and *Antiquaries Journal*, XXI, 1941, 73 and Pl. xvii. The incised interlace at the back of the head suggests a seventh- to eighth-century date.

227 e.g. from Portsoy, Bannffshire (*The British Museum Guide to Anglo-Saxon Antiquities*, London, 1923, 128, Fig. 163), perhaps a trial-piece, and from the Broch of Main, Shetland (*Proceedings of the Society of Antiquaries of Scotland*, LVIII, 1923–4, 17 and Fig. 5).

228 e.g. F. Henry, *La Sculpture Irlandaise*, London, 1933, Vol. II, Plates 7–10.

229 p. 7 above.

230 *op. cit.*, 73.

231 The close relationship between the shield from boat-grave 12 at Vendel and the Sutton Hoo shield has already been commented on by Maryon (*Antiquity*, 1946) and by Lindqvist and Nerman (*Fornvännen*, 1948).

232 H. Stolpe and T. J. Arne, *op. cit.*, Pl. XXXIII, Fig. 2, and Pl. XXXVIII, Fig. 1.

233 *op. cit.*

234 Rupert Bruce-Mitford, *The Sutton Hoo Ship-Burial, A Handbook*, London, 1972, 32–3, Figs. 9, 10.

235 e.g. N. Åberg, *op. cit.*, Fig. 272; E. Behmer, *op. cit.*, Pls. XXXVII, 6a, XXXVIII.

236 e.g. E. Behmer, *op. cit.*, Plates XL, 2; XLI, 6,7; XLII, 2; XLIII, 1–3; XLIV, 4; L, 3,4.

237 As for instance the sword from Sarre, Kent, illustrated by Åberg (*op. cit.*, Fig. 273).

238 Sune Lundqvist, *Från Upplands Forntid* (Kort vägledning genom Uppsala Universitets museum för nordiska fornsaker), Uppsala, 1945, Pl. facing p. 13. Unfortunately there is not adequate evidence as to where in the burial deposit the Sutton Hoo ring lay. (Rupert Bruce-Mitford, *Sutton Hoo Handbook*, second edition, London, 1972, p. 32). I do not think that it can have come from the sword-area, as all the sand from this region was carefully sifted for stray gold coins and loose garnets. A note in the writing of the then Keeper of the Research Laboratory in the British Museum (Dr H. J. Plenderleith, F.S.A.) apparently made after the War (1945 or early 1946) when the fragmentary remains of the shield were unpacked for the first time and the shield was being restored, indicates that the ring came from the shield area.

239 By B. Nerman and S. Lindqvist in *Fornvännen*, 1948, and also in the writer's articles already quoted on Sutton Hoo and Sweden in the *Archaeological News Letter*, *Ord och Bild* and the *Anglo-Swedish Review*.

240 See pp. 50–1, below.

241 As long ago as 1911, Reginald Smith made the suggestion that two bronze scabbard mounts in the Bury St Edmunds Museum (E. T. Leeds, *Early Anglo-Saxon Art and Archaeology*, London, 1936, Pl. XVIIIe) were brought over by a Swedish settler (*Victoria County History*, *Suffolk*, Vol. 1, London, 1911, 338).

242 See pp. 1–2, above.

243 *op. cit.*

244 See Rupert Bruce-Mitford, *The Sutton Hoo Ship-Burial – A Handbook*, second edition, London, 1972, Colour Pls. D and F.

245 For the history of millefiori in Western European archaeology see Dr Françoise Henry, 'Émailleurs d'Occident', *Préhistoire*, II, 1933, 65–146.

246 This statement can be clearly demonstrated by closer analysis of the finds and by technical considerations which are discussed in the Sutton Hoo Catalogue, Vol. 2 (in preparation).

247 See *The Sutton Hoo Ship-Burial*, definitive publication, Vol. II, Ch. 2, 'The jewellery' (forthcoming).

248 *op. cit.*, 90. 'Snarast har han variten erövere, som lagt under sig en del av landet'.

249 See pp. 20–3, above.

250 *East Anglian Notes and Queries*, ii, 69, Claude Morely, 'Cloveso'; *Proceedings of the Suffolk Institute of Archaeology and Natural History*, Vol. 18, 1924, 92–122. I am grateful to Mr Leslie

Dow for drawing my attention to these references.

251 'Saxon Rendlesham', Chapter 2, especially p. 75.

252 *op. cit.*

253 The publicity that must have attended the great burial has already been stressed (*British Museum Provisional Guide to Sutton Hoo*, 41; Lindqvist, *Antiquity*, 1948, 134, and 139, Note 17; *Fornvännen*, 1948, 99 and 107).

254 *op. cit.*, 88–9. '. . . själva gravskiket är svenskt. Sådana rikt ustrustade obrända krigargraver i bat under låga höger eller under flat mark äro endast beckanta irån Sverige.'

255 *Victoria County History of Essex*, Vol. I, London, 1903, 326.

256 *Victoria County History of Buckinghamshire*, Vol. I, London, 1905, 199–204, with colour plate.

257 This drawing is contemporary with the excavation (1883) and is the best of four surviving versions of the grave-plan and the only one that gives any measurements. The original is in the British Museum.

258 I am aware of Professor Nerman's doubts about the Snape boat-grave (*op. cit.*, 89, note 29) but a careful perusal of the contemporary accounts, leaves me with no doubt that this was a genuine burial of the period and that the gold ring and claw-beaker fragments belonged to it, though the whole has evidently been robbed. See Chapter 3, pp. 114–140.

259 S. Lindqvist, *Uppsala Högar och Ottarshögen*, Uppsala, 1936, 342.

260 *ibid.*

261 H. Stolpe and T. J. Arne, *passim*, especially Pls. XLV to LIII.

262 The Caenby, Lincs. mounts (in the British Museum) were elaborate, heavily gilded and decorated with Style II interlace and garnets and mother-of-pearl, but do not come from a shield.

263 That from Bidford-on-Avon, T. D. Kendrick, *Anglo-Saxon Art to A.D. 900*, London, 1938, Pl. XXIX, Fig. 4, is an exception.

264 G. Baldwin Brown, *Arts in Early England*, III, P. XXI, 195–6. See Chapter Eleven, 223–52.

265 From Cumberland, *British Museum Guide to Anglo-Saxon Antiquities*, London, 1923, Pl. VII: E. Behmer, *op. cit.*, Taf. II, 3.

266 Though the existence of a Kentish silver pommel showing imitation step-pattern cloisonné work in niello (N. Åberg, *Anglo-Saxons in England*, Uppsala, 1926, 144, Fig. 274), and parallel with similar continental imitation cloisonné pommels (E. Behmer, *op. cit.*, Pls. XLIV, 3, LX, 1–4 etc.) should be noted.

267 B. Nerman, *op. cit.*, 75, Fig. 12, H. Stolpe and T. J. Arne, *op. cit.*, Pl. XLI, Fig. 4. The gold cloisonné stud from Wickham, Kent (N. Åberg, *op. cit.*, Figs. 270 and p. 141) should not be overlooked. Its form and ornamentation suggest that it might well be a scabbard-boss.

268 S. Lindqvist, 'Vendelhjälmarna i ny rekonstruction', *Fornvännen*, h. 1, 1950, 1–24, Figs. 1–4; p. 9 and 10, note 4. Greta Arwidsson, *Valsgärde 6*, Uppsala, 1942, p. 33, Fig. 127.

269 *Vendel i fynd och forskning* (Ed. Oskar Lundberg), Uppsala, 1938, 78–80.

270 cf. S. Lindqvist, *Fornvännen*, 1948, 106–7; *Antiquity*, 1948, 138.

271 From Valsgärde 6, a burial dated *c.* 750. Greta Arwidsson, *op. cit.*, 47, Figs. 41, 42. I cannot distinguish any signs of pattern-welding on these published photographs.

272 pp. 42–3, above.

273 *ibid.*

274 See Chapter 10, pp. 214–222.

275 Bertil Almgren, 'Romerska drag i nordisk figurekonst från folkvandringstiden' ('Meddelanden från Uppsala universitets museum för nordiska fornsaker', *Tor*, 1948, especially pp. 85–87).

276 T. D. Kendrick, *Antiquity*, XIV, 1940, 29.

277 T. D. Kendrick in *British Museum Quarterly*, XIII, 1939, 135: 'Still more significant is the evidence of the big gold buckle for this, though it is vaguely Frankish in form and bears decoration that might pass as a variant of the South German "Style II" in animal pattern, really finds its closest analogies in Vendel Grave 12, so much that its picture would not seem incongruous if it were inserted among those of the objects found in that famous Swedish ship-burial. Yet this buckle was certainly made in England, for the little animal between the mouths of two beasts at the end of the plate is of an established Anglian type and closely resembles the beasts on a silver mount from Caenby, Lincolnshire' (*British Museum Guide to Anglo-Saxon Antiquities*, London, 1923, Fig. 102). See also R. L. S. Bruce-Mitford, *Provisional Guide to Sutton Hoo*, London, 1947, 53–4 and Fig. 15.

278 H. Stolpe and T. J. Arne, *op. cit.*, Pls. VIII, Figs. 1, 6 and 8; IX, Fig. 12 (border). Fig. 2, etc.

279 *ibid.*, Pl. XXXVII, Fig. 6; *Vendel i fynd och forskning*, Fig. 13, left.

280 *ibid.*, Pl. XXXIII, Fig. 2.

281 *op. cit.*, 70.

282 *Antiquity*, 1948, 135 and note 8; *Fornvännen*, 1984, 100.

283 See note 277 above.

284 For the shield and the problem of its repairs see *The Sutton Hoo Ship-Burial*, Vol. II, Ch. II.

285 On heirlooms see S. Lindqvist, *Antiquity*, 1948, 137; *Fornvännen*, 1948, 105.

286 *op. cit.*, 81.

287 H. Stolpe and T. J. Arne, *op. cit.*, Pl. XXXV, Fig. 1.

288 *loc. cit.*

289 If (as I have argued) the purse and the great buckle show concessions to Swedish taste and interests and most of the rest of the gold jewellery was made as a suspension harness for a Swedish heirloom sword, this would indicate that the gold jewels are not objects of unadulterated Saxon origin given to a foreign visitor, but that they were made for (commissioned by) someone with Swedish tastes and ideas. I have always felt that the jewelled outfit – including the purse, epaulettes and great gold buckle – a complete and elaborate harness transcending anything yet found in a Germanic grave – was not meant for everyday use but must have been an official outfit worn on ceremonial occasions. It may be considered along with the standard and sceptre as demonstrating royal authority, perhaps deriving ultimately from the 'purple belt and gold ornaments' of the Dux Brittaniarum and other high Roman officials and officers and analogous to the gold belt worn by the Welsh prince Cunedda as a symbol of his power and office (M. Deanesly, *op. cit.*, 135). Whether this is so or not, it remains a royal outfit and this and the above considerations explain the description 'regalia'. If this outfit can be accepted as regalia the concessions apparent in the outstanding pieces, to Swedish tradition and taste and the making of most of the rest to honour a Swedish heirloom sword, can hardly fail to be suggestive in the matter of the origins of the dynasty to which these regalia belong.

290 A professional lapidary (gem-cutter) after a close study of the Sutton Hoo jewellery, has estimated that the simplest (flat) garnets would each take one day to cut and finish, using modern equipment; that the more complex ones, for example the facetted stones on the edges and upper corners of the pyramids, would take two or three days each, assuming that the stones did not break whilst being worked (garnets are brittle and the wastage is usually considerable). Over four thousand individual cut garnets were employed in the Sutton Hoo jewellery. This makes it possible to form some estimate of the time taken in making these pieces.

291 In the ninth century genealogy (Pl. 2a, b) Ældwulf is shown as the son of Æthelric. For the equation of Æthelric with Æthelhere and arguments on this point see *Handbook of British Chronology* (ed. F. M. Powicke), 1934, 20 (under Ældwulf).

292 cf. Sune Lindqvist, *Fornvännen*, 1948, 99; *Antiquity*, 1948, 134. 'If we are to look for the owner of the Sutton Hoo grave amongst the East Anglian Royal family, which I too consider natural, but by no means certain. . . .' The case for identification of the burial with an East Anglian royalty strongly made by Chadwick has been developed since Lindqvist wrote (e.g. 'Saxon Rendlesham', Chapter 2, pp. 73–113, and in the present chapter) and, if the grave is not to be a Swede's, I cannot see any doubt on this score. As an argument against the possibility that the burial might commemorate a visiting king from one of the other Saxon kingdoms, or from foreign parts, other than Swedish peninsular, we may now add the use of a boat and the various Swedish elements. These show that the burial is a true expression of the milieu (East Anglia) where the Swedish indications are found concentrated.

293 *op. cit.*, 90, 91.

294 cf. also Birger Nerman, *Sveriges första storhetstid*, Stockholm, 1942, 86, 91; and the same author's *Sveriges rikes uppkomst*, Stockholm, 1941, 195–6.

295 See F. M. Stenton, *Anglo-Saxon England*, 50, and H. M. Chadwick, *op. cit.*, esp. 78–9.

296 H. M. Chadwick, *op. cit.*, 79.

297 F. M. Stenton, *loc. cit.*

298 *ibid.*, also H. M. Chadwick, *loc. cit.*

299 *Antiquity*, 1948, 136; *Fornvännen*, 1948, 102.

300 Birgit Arrhenius, 'Båtgraven från Augerum' in *Tor*, 1960.

301 Allowing for the difference in burial-rite (cremation and inhumation) the connections of the Sutton Hoo burial are in many ways much closer with the royal mounds at Uppsala than with the boat-graves of Vendel and Valsgärde.

302 *Antiquity*, 1948, 139. This suggestion was included in the text submitted for the English translation but does not appear in the Swedish version in *Fornvännen*, 1948.

303 See *The Oldest English Texts*, edited by H. Sweet (Early English Text Society, original series No. 83, London, 1885, Reprinted 1938), 167.

304 *ibid.*, 171.

305 p. 35, above.

306 See S. Lindqvist, *Antiquity*, 1948, 138; *Fornvännen*, 1948, 106 and note 5.

307 *Vendel i fynd och forskning*, 42 and 83.

308 The few objects recovered from the robbed boat-grave excavated in 1938 certainly indicate a seventh-century date for this burial but in my opinion include nothing that necessitates a date for the burial as late as 650. The two other mounds excavated in 1938 did not produce any material upon which reliable conclusions as to the dating of these burials (to within anything less than one hundred years) can be based.

See *Sutton Hoo definitive publication*, Vol. I, Ch. 2, Cambridge, 1974.

309 p. 54, above.

310 *Antiquity*, 1948, 136; *Fornvännen*, 1948, 103.

311 B. Nerman, *Sveriges rikes uppkmost*, Stockholm, 1941, Fig. 34.

312 p. 54, above.

313 For discussion of the divergent views on this subject see N. Åberg, 'Uppsala högars datering', *Fornvännen*, 1947, 257–89, and S. Lindqvist's reply with the same title, *Fornvännen*, 1949, 33–48, and Chapter Ten, pp. 214–22, below; see also *Tiotusen ä Sverige*, Stockholm, 1945, Fig. 185.

314 pp. 34–6, above.

CHAPTER TWO

Saxon Rendlesham

ROYAL ASSOCIATIONS OF RENDLESHAM IN SAXON TIMES

The discovery at Sutton Hoo, near Woodbridge, in 1939 of the great ship-burial of the seventh century A.D., dating from *c.* 620–*c.* 635 and very likely the monument of the High King or *bretwalda* Raedwald, has focused archaeological attention on the quiet, sparsely-populated Deben parish of Rendlesham. This parish lies, like the Sutton Hoo burial-ground, on the east bank of the river and is four miles north of the burial-ground. The river between Woodbridge and Rendlesham runs fairly straight. The distance by water is about four and a quarter miles.

Rendlesham has long been recognized as a place with early royal connections and it has been constantly associated with Raedwald who was the greatest of the early East Anglian kings and the only one to attain the eminence of *bretwalda*, or overlord, with some power over the other kingdoms of the Saxon heptarchy. Raedwald seems to have died about A.D. 624–5. The East Anglian kings were known as the Wuffingas (descendants of Wuffa or Uffa).[1]

A typical illustration of this customary connection of Rendlesham with Raedwald is provided by Wodderspoon's *Historic Sites of Suffolk*.[2]

> At Rendlesham in this county it is recorded that Raedwald, a King of the East Angles, built a magnificent palace for the residence of himself and court, and occupied the building as his seat of government.

John Weever, in his *Ancient Funeral Monuments*, says of Rendlesham that 'by supposition' Raedwald, 'as also Swidelme lye buried at this place'.[2a]

Practically every Suffolk historian says something similar. W. G. Arnott, in his *Place Names of the Deben Valley*, is the most recent writer to refer to 'Raedwald at Rendlesham'.[3]

It seems that the ultimate source of all these writers must be Camden's *Britannia*, in the first edition of which (the octavo Latin version of 1596) and in all the subsequent English versions, the following matter occurs:[4]

> . . . Rendelisham, ubi Redwaldus, Orientalium Anglorum rex, primus ex sua gente Baptismatis fonte Christo renatus erat: qui tamen postea ab uxore seductus in eodem fano et altare, ut inquit Beda,[5] ad Christi religionem et arulam ad Daemoniorum victimas habuit.

This passage is rendered in Philemon Holland's translation of 1610, the first English translation of Camden, as follows:

> . . . Rendelisham, where Redwald King of the East Saxons (*sic*) kept usually his court, who was the first of all his nation that was baptised, and received Christianity; but afterwards seduced by his wife, he had in the self-same church, as saith Beda, one altar for Christ's religion and another for sacrifices unto devils.[6]

The phrase 'kept usually his court', to which the later English versions adhere, has no basis in the Latin. Raedwald's baptism, as Bede tells us in the same passage, took place in Kent.

Camden gives no evidence for the statement that Raedwald 'kept his court' in Rendlesham. Indeed I have not been able to discover any evidence for associating Raedwald with Rendlesham at all.[7]

It would be surprising if no attempt had been made to derive the name Rendlesham from Raedwald and in fact this has been done. The Rev. Francis Blomefield, the Norfolk topographer, in his *Topographical History of the County of Norfolk*[8] in discussing Raedwald and his supposed palace at Rendlesham says 'which place' (Rendlesham) 'if we may credit history, received its present name from his'. Davy[9] quotes from the Hawes MS., pp. 555–60, 'Rendlesham, or Redwalsham, so called from Redwald, a Saxon king of the E. Angles, who usually kept his court there.' Bede, who wrote only a hundred years after Raedwald's death and who went to the trouble of explaining the name, paraphrased it, not as having any connection with Raedwald (Redwaldus), but as '*mansio . . . Rendili . . .*', 'in the royal village called Rendlesham, that is, the residence of Rendil'.[10] Bede had already referred at some length to Raedwald (Redwaldus) in four earlier chapters[11] but he did not suggest that the name of this royal residence, Rendlesham, was connected with him. No reputable historian makes this claim and in fact the derivation of Rendlesham from Raedwald is philologically hardly possible.[12] Who then was the unknown Rendil? Our knowledge of East Anglian personalities in the seventh century, in spite of references in Bede, is very slight and in the sixth century and the period of the first settlements, apart from the first few names in the genealogy of the Wuffingas, nil. Bede was in all probability simply rendering the Anglo-Saxon name into Latin without any actual knowledge

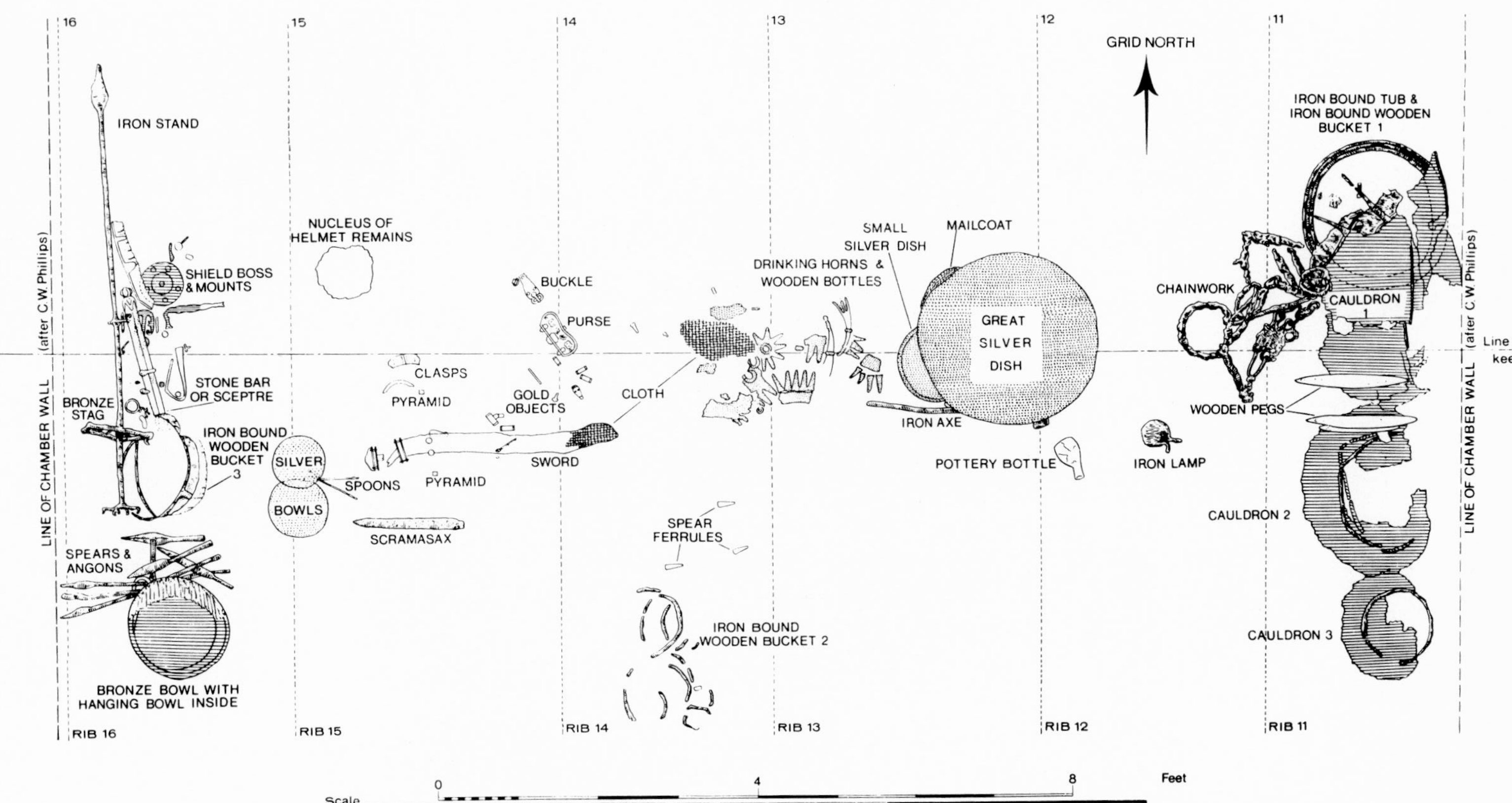

Plate 17 Plan of the Sutton Hoo burial-deposit, based on 1939 field drawings by Stuart Piggott, with the keel-line and rib-positions added

18

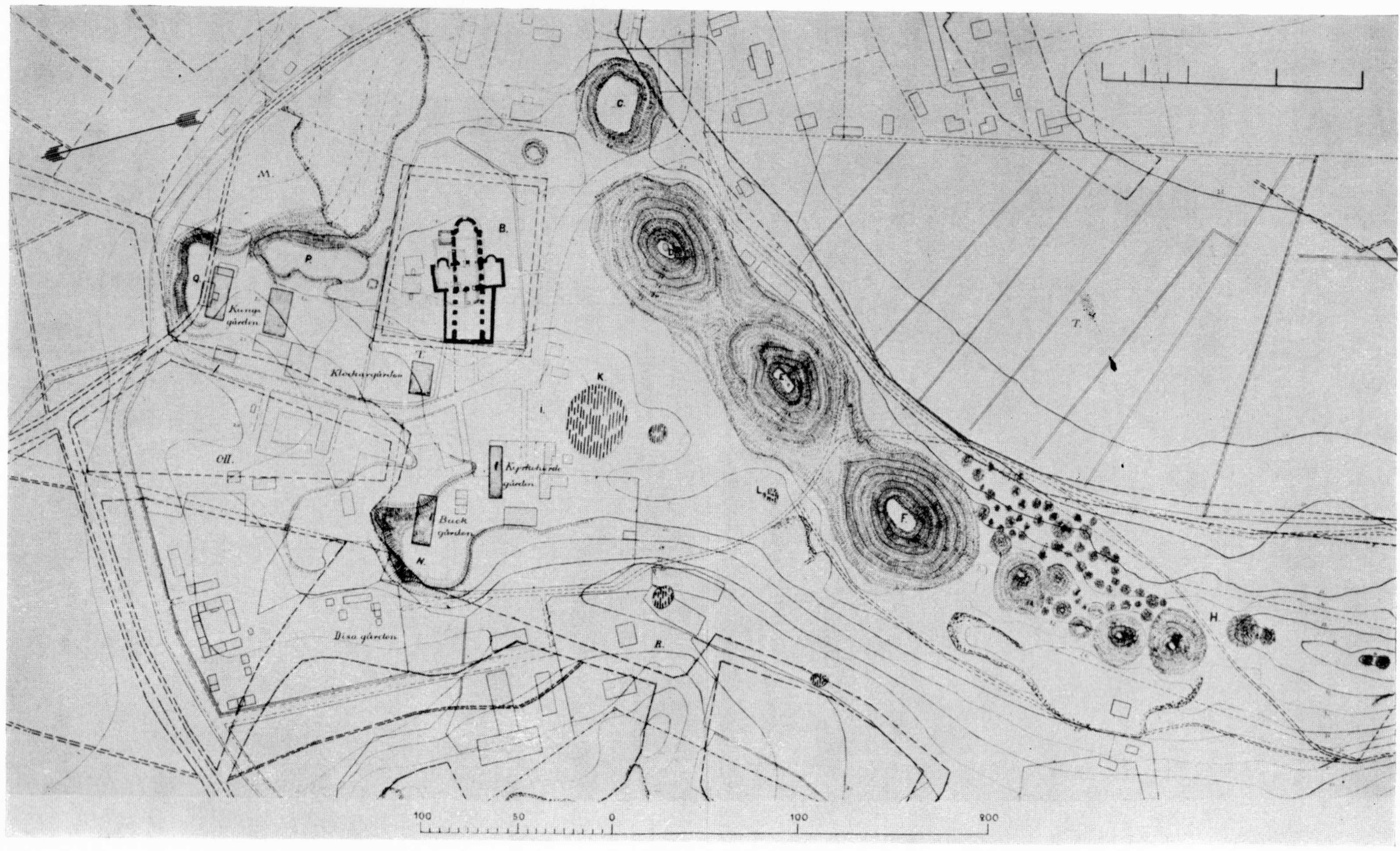

Plate 18 Temple and royal hall sites at Old Uppsala, Sweden: P,Q. Artificial terraces, probably the sites of royal halls of the Viking Age. N. Artificial terrace, probably the site of a Vendel period royal hall. The rectangular plan, supposedly of the pagan temple may just be seen faintly outlined beneath the choir crossing and north transept of the mediaeval cathedral (see detail, Fig 11). The great mounds are to the right, the flat-topped '*Domarhög*' (C) is at the top and small burial mounds, mostly of the Viking period, below and to the right (*after Lindqvist*)

Rendlesham

In a piece of the Glebe Land of the parish, known by the name of the How, or Haw Hill Piece, containing about 2 acres, there have for several years been dug up numerous pieces of Roman urns, but all so brittle, that none were ever taken up whole, nor even nearly so, till the present Year 1837, when one with nothing broken off but the rim of the mouth, was procured with great care, which I saw, July 7th at the Parsonage House, in the possession of the Rector, Lord Thomas Hay; it is of a coarse brown earth, of good shape, & more than half filled with fragments of bones & ashes: the height of it, with the rim broken off is near 8 inches, & the breadth in the middle about 6. The following rough sketch was taken at the time, & may give some idea of its make & shape.

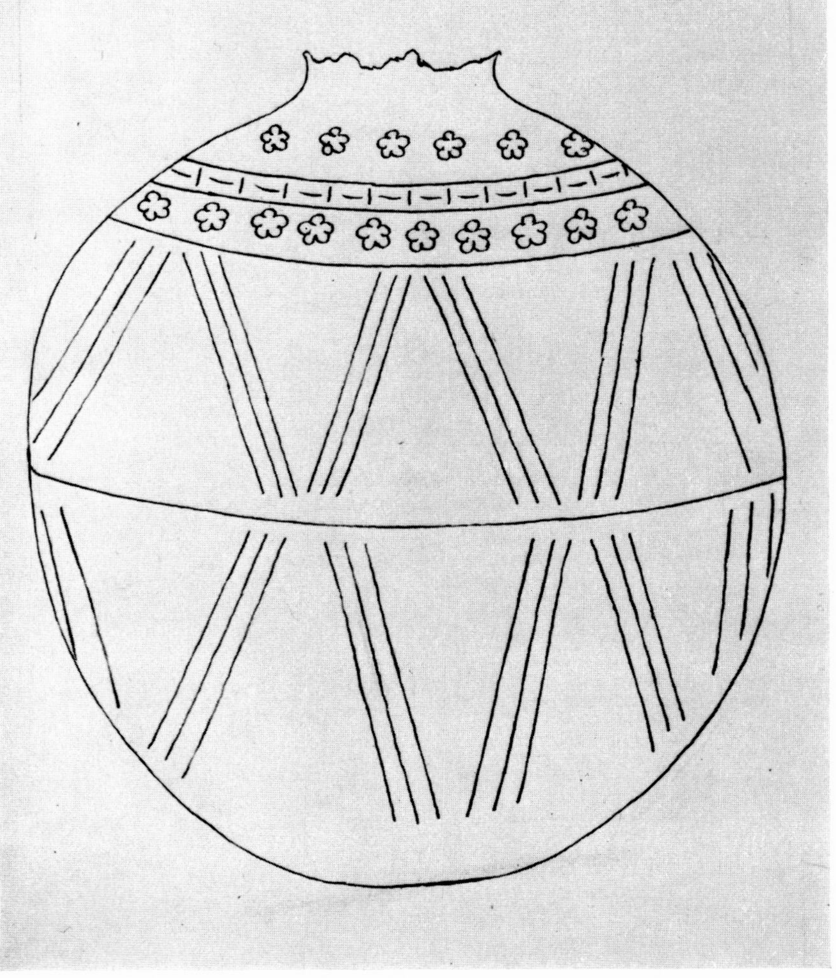

Plate 19 Saxon cremation urn found at Rendlesham, Suffolk, in 1887 (from the Davy papers)

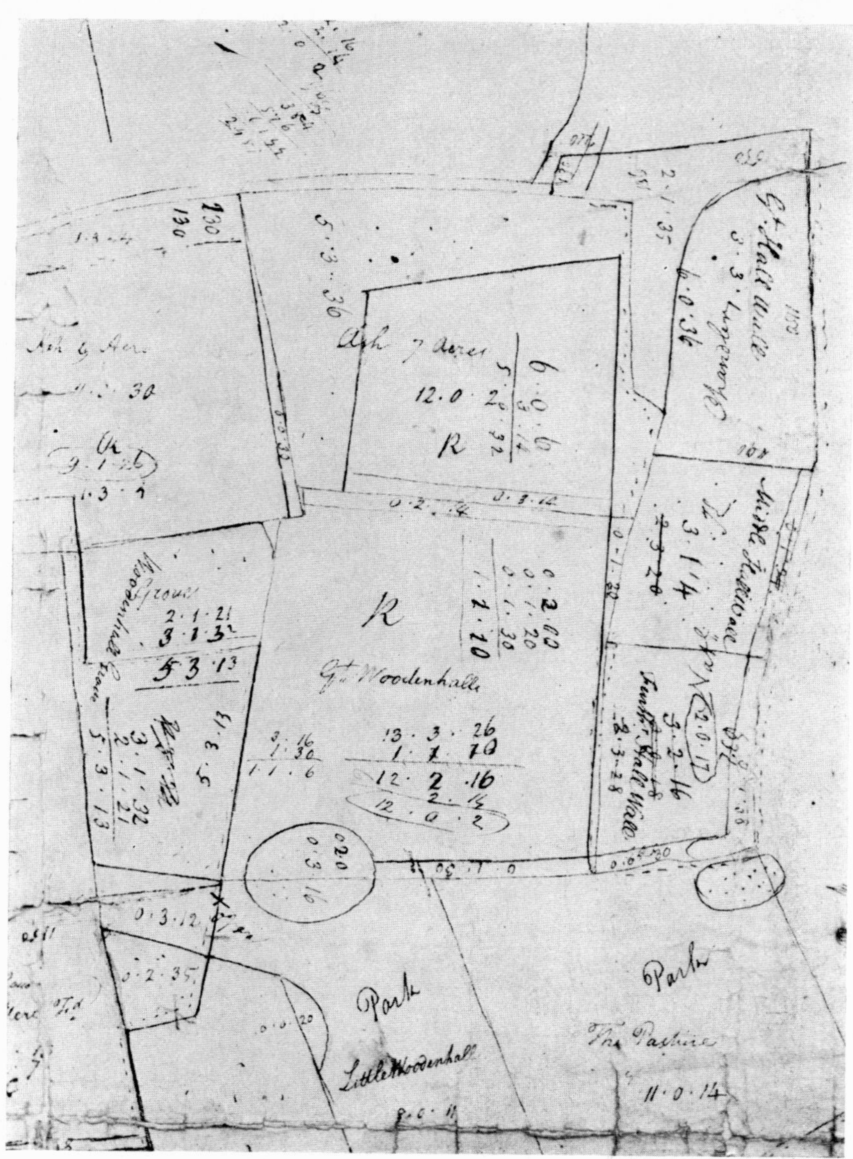

Plate 20 Detail from a sketch map of Rendlesham entitled 'Park Lands 1828', showing 'Woodenhall' field names

of an individual of the name of Rendilus. The name may go back to a period of early settlement before the association of the Wuffingas with Rendlesham began.

Apart from Raedwald, the royal character of Rendlesham in the seventh century is clear from the one passage in Bede in which it is mentioned:[13]

> Swithhelm, the son of Seaxbald,[14] was successor to Sigeberht; he was baptised by Cedd in East Anglia, in the royal village called Rendlesham, that is, the residence of Rendil. King Aethelwald of East Anglia, the brother of King Anna, the previous King of the East Angles, was his sponsor.[15]

This passage tells us three things about Rendlesham. First that Rendlesham was during Æthelwald's reign (655–664) a *vicus regius* of the East Anglian kings. Secondly, that there was most probably a church there at the time and thirdly, that this was a *vicus regius* of some consequence if, as the passage seems to imply, it included what must have been one of the earliest churches in East Anglia, since Bishop Cedd was operating there and since the reception of the East Saxon king and the solemnization of his baptism took place there.

It seems that Wodderspoon's 'magnificent palace' must be reduced to Bede's non-committal expression *vicus regius*, to which little more force can be given than 'a royal residence' or 'a royal seat'. Nevertheless it remains clear from the passage quoted, that some thirty years after the Sutton Hoo burial took place (*c.* A.D. 625) Rendlesham was playing an active part as a royal residence of some importance. No doubt it had begun to play this rôle earlier, if the derivation of Ufford (Uffa's ford) is to be taken into account. Uffa, or Wuffa, from whom the Wuffingas took their names, was Raedwald's grandfather.

RENDLESHAM AND SUTTON HOO

In the first sentence of this chapter it is stated that the discovery of the Sutton Hoo ship-burial has focused attention on Rendlesham. Why is this? The reason is that the great ship-burial is regarded as the grave or memorial of one of the East Anglian kings and consequently the group of some fifteen or more barrows at Sutton Hoo as the burial-place of the dynasty, corresponding with their known use of Rendlesham as a *vicus regius*. If this is correct, then both the finds already made at Sutton Hoo and the results of further exploration of the site may throw valuable light on Rendlesham and on the Wuffingas. Rendlesham in its turn may throw light on Sutton Hoo. Archaeologically speaking, the Rendlesham *vicus regius* would be the habitation site corresponding to the Sutton Hoo burial-ground. The location and excavation of the 'palace' and other buildings there, together with the further excavation of the Sutton Hoo grave-field, should yield, in a unique way, a comprehensive picture of the life and progress of a Saxon dynasty, in one of the most fascinating phases of English history. This should make a remarkable study were it ever to materialize, for the Sutton Hoo grave is not just any chieftain's tomb but a phenomenon of the first magnitude even against the European background. It has implications in many fields.

Before linking Sutton Hoo with Rendlesham in this way, we must first be satisfied that the great ship-burial really is the grave, not of some lesser dignitary or a foreign adventurer[16] but of an East Anglian king.

That the great ship-burial was the grave or monument of an East Anglian king was the conclusion of the late Professor Chadwick who, shortly after the discovery, discussed at length the question of whose grave (or cenotaph) it was, in a classic essay.[17] There is no point in repeating here his arguments which are in general convincing.[18] Those interested in this point may now refer to the more detailed chapter, under the same title ('Who was he?') in Vol. I of the British Museum's definitive publication, which incorporates Chadwick's arguments and brings them up to date.

It is worth referring here to points which have emerged since Chadwick wrote which seem to clinch the matter. One and perhaps two objects in the grave are now recognized as in all probability symbols of authority such as at this period can, it seems, only have been attributes of a king. Both were placed amongst the prestigious material against the west wall of the burial chamber, the stone bar (Fig 9) standing vertically, as it appears, on the central axis, in line with what must have been, or if it were a cenotaph[19] have been deemed to be, the position of the body, along the keel-line. The first is the unique portable wrought-iron stand (Fig 1) 1·65m in height, which, whatever may have been the exact use and purpose of its curious grille,[20] could be in its size and shape and its spike at the bottom, some sort of barbaric version of the late Roman *signum*.[21] Bede describes the use of what may be such an object by a Saxon *bretwalda*, Edwin of Northumbria, who died in 633:

> So great was his majesty in his realm that not only were banners carried before him in battle, but even in time of peace, as he rode about among his cities, estates and kingdoms with his thegns, he always used to be preceded by a standard-bearer. Further, when he walked anywhere along the roads, there used to be carried before him the type of standard which the Romans call a '*tufa*' and the English call a '*Thuf*'.[22]

Edwin's immediate predecessor as *bretwalda* (Overlord or High King) was Raedwald. It was Raedwald who placed Edwin, then an exile, on the Northumbrian throne, after the Battle of the Idle (A.D. 616). Edwin's final years of exile had been spent in Raedwald's court. It would not be surprising to find that Edwin, who, so far as we know his history from Bede, was unacquainted with continental courts, had gleaned some of his ideas as to the kind of pomp with which a great king should surround himself from Raedwald's ceremonial in Suffolk. The presence of such an object as a 'tufa', or standard, in the grave of one of the Wuffinga kings of *c.* A.D. 625 and more especially if it was Raedwald's, would not be at all surprising. It may be that in this Sutton Hoo piece we have such an object. The matter is discussed in Chapter One.

The second object, also unique, is the great elaborate stone bar, two feet nine and a half inches long with its terminal fittings, and with them weighing over 7lbs (Plate I and Fig 9). There can be no doubt that this is a ceremonial piece. Apart from a very gentle smoothing or polish of its sharp edges such as would result from handling, the stone is without the faintest trace of wear and although made in the semblance of a whetstone it has never been used to sharpen anything. It is impractical as a sharpener since it is too heavy to carry about and the painted knobs at either end, with the bronze saucer-fitting at one end and the stag mounted on its iron ring held by a bronze pedestal on the other, would not be only superfluous to the operation of sharpening, but in the way. The saucer-fitting is too fragile to be gripped with the strength necessary to wield so heavy and cumbersome an object or even to bear its weight, if one end of it were to be rested horizontally on a support. The only way in which one could perhaps envisage the use of the stone for sharpening would be if it were lying flat on a table but even in this position weight falls directly upon the bronze cages that clasp the knobs and they could not have stood up to it, or to any additional pressure, for long. Sir Thomas Kendrick referred to the object before its full nature was known, that is, before the stag and its ring were known to have been mounted on one end thus:

> It is a unique, savage thing; and inexplicable, except perhaps as a symbol proper to the King himself, of the divinity and the mystery which surrounded the smith and his tools in the northern world.[23]

There could still be some such significance attached to the choice of a fine-grained whetstone-type stone for the object even if it is unrelated to any practical form of whetstone in its design. Now, in its new reconstruction (Plate I) it has a top and a bottom, the saucer on the lower end being shaped to fit the knee-cap. It seems impossible to see this piece as anything other than a sceptre, that is, a symbol of royal power and authority.

A third point is the richness of the burial. This alone led Chadwick to conclude that it was royal. It is worth stressing here how far Sutton Hoo does stand apart in elaboration and splendour from any other Saxon grave. A simple comparison between its grave-inventory and that of the richest Anglo-Saxon grave previously found, that of the chieftain Taeppa at Taplow[24] in Bucks, would make this clear

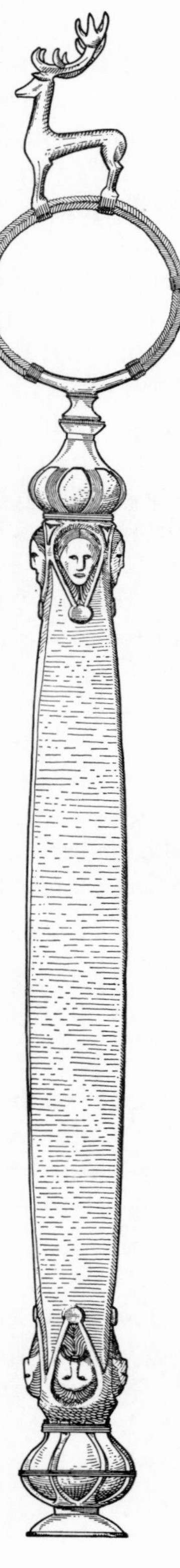

Figure 9 The sceptre, Sutton Hoo (Scale 1 : 4)

(Plate 16). Without going into detail over this comparison, which is very revealing, some outstanding differences are the presence at Sutton Hoo of symbols of authority already mentioned; of the great sea-going ship, greater in length than the longest surviving vessel of the later Viking age; the elaborate gold 'regalia' of supreme workmanship set with over four thousand cut garnets; the large treasure of foreign silver and the regal sword to which, with its baldric, most of the lesser jewelled pieces belonged. The Sutton Hoo burial strikingly agrees with the descriptions of the royal funerals of Scyld and of Beowulf in the Beowulf epic[25] and in so far as royal burials, as distinct from those of chieftains, are known to archaeology, we can at least say that the Sutton Hoo finds are strictly comparable, if not superior in quality, to what we know of the furnishings of the rich grave of Childeric 1st (d. 481), King of the Franks and father of Clovis, and that they show intimate links with the cremated scraps from the Swedish royal mounds at Old Uppsala.[26]

Finally, without attempting to argue the case for the royalty of the burial in full,[27] there is the proximity to the Sutton Hoo burial ground of the royal seat of the Wuffingas at Rendlesham. There seems no room for doubt that the great Sutton Hoo burial is royal.

It may be thought that if the Wuffingas lived at Rendlesham, they would have buried their kings there and it is true that at Old Uppsala the royal burial mounds are close to the sites of what are thought to be the halls of the royal seat (Plate 18). However, in *Beowulf*, which may be equally relevant to Sutton Hoo, Scyld's funeral boat was set adrift and Beowulf himself was buried not near his royal hall but on Whale's point, where his burial-mound stood as a landmark:

Geworhton ða   Wedra lēode
hlæw on hliðe   sē waes hēah ond brād
wæglīðendum   wīde gesyne   *Beowulf* (lines 3156–8)

('Then the people of the Wederas construction a barrow on the headland – it was high and broad, visible from far to all seafarers').

It would not be unnatural for the Wuffingas to choose for their burial ground a spot more central than Rendlesham to the settlements in the Deben valley, on a bare ridge visible to the traffic moving up and down the water thoroughfare and passed on the way up the estuary to Rendlesham itself.[28]

All the foregoing considerations enable us to accept the great seventh-century Sutton Hoo grave with complete confidence as the burial of an important East Anglian king[29] and so to associate directly the Sutton Hoo burial ground with the *vicus regius* at Rendlesham. If so, no doubt the funeral cortège, escorting the great ship, set out from Rendlesham by water and moved down at high tide to the mouth of the coombe below the ridge at Sutton. The patches on the hull of the ship show that it was a boat of some age and use, and not a vessel built on the spot expressly for the funeral.

THE STATUS OF THE *VICUS REGIUS* AT RENDLESHAM

There are factors that suggest that the south-eastern area of Suffolk roughly delimited by the valleys of the Deben and Alde may have been the political heart of the East Anglian kingdom. It is suitably remote from the troubled frontier with Mercia and protected from the west by the north-south line of the Deben valley. It is separated from the frontiers of the east Saxons[30] by the successive barriers of the Stour, the Orwell and the Deben and is itself fed by three estuaries (the Ore, the Deben and the Butley River). There is no indication here of dense and early settlement, such as can be inferred from the numerous urn-fields and cemeteries of north-west Suffolk (the area between Freckenham and Redgrave), or of a number of regions of Norfolk. Nor is the area central to the East Anglian kingdom. On the other hand, the Deben valley abounds in royal associations and in signs of activity and prosperity in the seventh century. Place-names such as Kingston and Ufford indicate royal connections and Melton, two miles downstream from Rendlesham, was an ancient royal demesne and was given with Kingston to Ely Cathedral by King Edgar.[31]

The highly distinctive and aristocratic custom of boat-burial is so far known in Anglo-Saxon England from three instances only (two at Sutton Hoo, one at Snape). All are from this corner of Suffolk and one at least, if the foregoing arguments are accepted, a royal burial. Above all, there is the testimony of this royal burial.

The extraordinary range of rich and exotic pieces in the great Sutton Hoo boat-grave was, we now see, to some extent already foreshadowed by earlier finds of Saxon antiquities in the Deben valley area. Reginald Smith has pointed out the concentration of early Saxon finds in the eight miles or so of the Deben valley that runs more or less parallel with the sea.[32] To the sites he mentions, from which Anglo-Saxon finds have come, others such as Sutton Hoo, Rendlesham itself, Martlesham[33] and apparently Woodbridge[34] can now be added. Norman Scarfe has recently assembled archaeological and other evidence to suggest that the port of Ipswich originated in the seventh century and owed its foundation and development to the patronage of the Wuffingas.[35]

What is interesting about the finds mentioned by Reginald Smith is not so much their comparatively large number (considering that most are loose finds) but the evidence they afford, apart from the ship-burial, of prosperity in this part of Suffolk and of intercourse with the Continent. They include antiquities not normally associated with Anglian areas; a circular gold cloisonné disc-brooch,[36] remains of imported blue glass vessels[37] and a jewelled buckle of Kentish type[38] with embossed gold foil covering the upper plate of the buckle. The silver-gilt radiate brooch, set with garnets, described in the *Victoria County History* (Vol. I, p. 330), no doubt came from this part of Suffolk. A 'Coptic' bronze bowl of Egyptian origin has been found at Wickham Market, a little north of Rendlesham.[39]

If to all this we add the discoveries at Sutton Hoo in 1938 and 1939 and consider the potential of the Sutton Hoo grave-field of barrow-burials, it appears that the Deben valley became, in the sixth and seventh centuries, a gateway of Suffolk to trade and civilizing influences from the south and east. These considerations, together with its strategic advantages, make it a not unreasonable location for the political headquarters of East Anglia.

In this connection we must note the reputed discovery in Rendlesham about the year 1690 of a silver crown weighing sixty ounces. This is first mentioned, so far as I have been able to discover, in the 1722 edition of Camden's *Britannia* (Vol. I, Cols. 445, 446). In the course of a reference to Rendlesham in column 445, Bishop Gibson, the editor, inserts the following in parenthesis:

> It is said that in digging here about thirty years since there was found an ancient crown weighing about 60 ounces, which was thought to have belonged to Redwald, or some other king of the East Angles. But it was sold and melted down.

Gibson does not say as later writers have done[40] that the crown was of silver but presumably if it was sold and melted down it was either of silver or of gold. 'About thirty years since' would place the year of the discovery in the early 1690s.[41] It is only at the time of the Wuffingas that we know of royal occupation of Rendlesham and the reported discovering of the crown may perhaps reinforce its royal associations in the pre-Danish period, although so far as we know true crowns were not first worn as part of a royal regalia until some centuries after the ship-burial (the first representation being the well-known miniature of King Edgar in the tenth-century Winchester manuscript known as the Newminster Charter, B.M. Add. MS., x). The supposed crown might have been a massive gold or electrum torc, like those found in East Anglia at Snettisham and Ipswich but taken to be some sort of diadem.

Discoveries of a considerable number of pieces of imported glass and of Frankish and Kentish antiquities in the Ipswich cemetery[42] on the Orwell estuary and of a claw-beaker amongst the scanty remains fron the once rich Snape boat-burial on the Alde,[43] further emphasize the geographical advantages of the south-eastern corner of Suffolk. The few finds from cremations or robbed graves at Sutton Hoo in 1938 include unusual and exotic pieces.[44] There is also evidence at this date of royal religious foundations in the area. St Fursey was established at Burgh Castle, Anna was buried at Blythburgh and the brothers Æthelhere and Æthelwald, according to a twelfth-century life of St Botolf, were concerned in the founding of the important house of Icanhoe, almost certainly Iken, near Snape, which achieved a great reputation for its good organization.[45]

All these considerations seem, in the general context of East Anglian archaeology of the time, to contribute to a picture of Rendlesham as an important centre of the Wuffingas, possibly even the principal one,[46] in the seventh century. We may think that it was more than just the one of many country seats of the Wuffingas which happened to get a mention in Bede. If this is so, it had certainly already begun to play this rôle in the period of Raedwald's High-Kingship and it might well have been the place in which, on his return from Kent, he set up his Christian altar in the pagan temple. Certainly if the ship-burial is to be regarded as the latest of the barrow-burials in this field of tumuli, as I think it must, the character of the place as a principal burial ground for the dynasty will have been already established in the sixth century.

CHURCH AND TEMPLE AT RENDLESHAM

It has been inferred from the passage in Bede already quoted, about the baptism of Swidhelm of Essex, and from other evidence, that between 656[47] and the year 664 (when both Bishop Cedd and the East Anglian King Æthelwald died) and no doubt earlier, there were at Rendlesham the buildings of an important royal seat or manor (*vicus regius*) and that these included a church.

We cannot be certain that the event described by Bede implies the presence of a church but it is in the highest degree probable that there was one.

By the time this royal baptism of the king of another Saxon kingdom took place at Rendlesham, East Anglia had become widely if not completely Christianized. Bishop Felix had set up his see at Walton, the Saxon Shore fort now off the coast of Felixstowe, near the mouth of the Deben,[48] in the early 630s and monasteries and schools had been founded.[49] The East Anglian King, Sigeberht, who became a monk, and his successor Anna (d. 654) were not merely devout but active Christians. All Anna's daughters became nuns and three of them Saints.[50] Æthelhere (d. 655), Anna's brother and successor, is said in the twelfth-century *Life of St. Botolf*, as we have seen,[51] to have been concerned in the foundation of the monastery at Icanhoe, most probably Iken on the River Alde near Snape,[52] with his brother Æthelwald. Earlier acquaintance of members of the East Anglian royal house with Christianity is reflected in the Sutton Hoo burial (regarded as a royal burial), whether it be itself the burial of a pagan or not.

It is seen particularly in the pair of silver spoons inscribed '*Saulos*' and '*Paulos*' in Greek letters and the set of ten silver bowls inscribed with large crosses, both very likely gifts of Pope or Bishop to converts in the East Anglian royal family and if so brought to Sutton Hoo from Rendlesham. When we consider further the probable status of this *vicus regius* argued above, how the Augustinian mission concentrated first of all on kings and royal personages, the importance attached to the early provision of churches, as indicated by the letter to Mellitus (below) and the comparatively numerous seventh-century church foundations in Kent, Essex and elsewhere, the days when a royal baptism must have had to take place in the river were evidently passed. We may feel sure that the Rendlesham ceremony of 655–664 took place, as that at Dorchester no doubt did, in a church. Even if for some special reason the ceremony might have been held in the river, it is hard to believe that a popular centre of a royal family that had already produced some exemplary Christians, where yet another Wuffinga king was standing godfather to the King of Essex in a ceremony performed by Bishop Cedd, could have been without a church and baptistry of some kind at this date.

The only reference to a building connected with the Wuffingas is the passage in Bede's eulogy of Edwin of Northumbria which mentions Raedwald's notorious temple in which he erected the altar to Christ alongside another for sacrifices to devils:

> So great was Edwin's devotion to the true worship, that he also persuaded Eorpwald, son of Redwald and King of the East Angles, to abandon his idolatrous superstitions and together with his kingdom, accept the Christian faith and sacraments. Indeed his father Redwald had long before been initiated into the mysteries of the Christian faith in Kent, but in vain: for on his return home, he was seduced by his wife and by certain evil teachers and perverted from the sincerity of his faith, so that his last state was worse than his first. After the manner of the ancient Samaritans he seemed to be serving both Christ and the gods whom he had previously served; in the same temple he had one altar for the Christian sacrifice and another smaller altar on which to offer victims to devils. Ealdwulf, who was ruler of the kingdom up to our time, used to declare that the temple lasted until his time, and he saw it when he was a boy.[53]

The conversion of Eorpwald and his kingdom must have taken place before Edwin's death in 633 and we know from Aldwulf's statement that this temple (*fanum*) survived for some considerable time the introduction of a general and more organized Christianity. Bede says that Aldwulf (Ealdwulf) who reigned from 664–713, remembered seeing it as a boy. This suggests that it must have remained substantially intact until about 650, or later. There is no evidence that this temple was at Rendlesham, nor do we know that, apart from its association with the royal house, it was a temple of any great importance. It is clear from Bede's words that it was the temple itself and not the shrines or altars set up to Christ and the devil that survived. Possibly this is suggestive.

Temples, it is implied, might be substantial, well-constructed buildings and such edifices were not to be lightly cast away. The instruction received by St Augustine's mission in this matter is made clear by Pope Gregory the Great's letter to Bishop Mellitus:[54]

> However, when Almighty God has brought you to our most reverend brother Bishop Augustine, tell him that which I have decided after long deliberation about the English people, namely that the idol temples of that race should by no means be destroyed, but only the idols in them. Take holy water and sprinkle it in these shrines, build altars and place relics in them. For if the shrines are well built, it is essential that they should be changed from the worship of devils to the service of the true God. When this people see that their shrines are not destroyed they will be able to banish error from their hearts and be more ready to come to the places they are familiar with, but now recognising and worshipping the true God. And because they are in the habit of slaughtering much cattle as sacrifices to devils, some solemnity ought to be given to them in exchange for this. So on the day of the dedication or the festivals of the holy martyrs, whose relics are deposited there, let them make themselves huts from the branches of trees around the churches which have been converted out of shrines, and let them celebrate the solemnity with religious feasts. Do not let them sacrifice animals to the devil, but let them slaughter animals for their own food to the praise of God, and let them give thanks to the Giver of all things for this bountiful provision.

It may be that the reason why the fabric of Raedwald's temple, the scene of so disgraceful a compromise survived, was that it had been turned into a Christian church and it is not impossible that, if the temple of Raedwald were at Rendlesham, Swidhelm's baptism might have taken place in it. If a new church of specifically Christian character had replaced it by 664, this would quite likely be on the same spot or close by.

In this connection we may note the relationship thought to have existed in the royal capital at Old Uppsala in Sweden between the temple, the royal halls and the first Christian church. This parallel seems remote but in the event it may prove to be the most relevant of all. There are indications in the Sutton Hoo ship-burial and elsewhere in East Anglian archaeology to suggest that the Wuffingas may have come originally (about the middle of the sixth century) from the Uppland region of Sweden and that they subsequently maintained these family connections.[55]

Plate 18 shows the relevant part of the layout of the monuments of Old

Uppsala[56] which was the religious as well as the political centre of the ancient Swedish kingdom. At the top right of the plate, marked with the letter C, is the flat-topped '*domarhögen*' or 'Mound of Justice', the site of the 'thing', on which judgments were pronounced and councils held. Below this can be seen the contour lines of the northern edge of the great East Mound, one of the line of three great burial-mounds erected over the remains of royal cremations of between *c.* A.D. 500–650. P and Q which, surprisingly enough, have not yet been excavated (1973), are built-up terraces, demonstrated by trial holes to be artificial. They are about one hundred and sixty feet in length. They are thought to be platforms built for the reception of large wooden halls of the Viking period. The area N towards the bottom of the plate is a similar artificial platform but belonging to an earlier period, since burial mounds of Viking date were later erected here and there upon it. Soundings in this terrace revealed a stone pavement which was presumed to be the floor of a large building. This earlier hall was no doubt contemporary with the construction of the great mounds, that is, it belonged to the period fifth to seventh century. The point to notice here is the relationship between these halls and the temple, a famous shrine known throughout the North and graphically described in the eleventh century by Adam of Bremen. Post-holes belonging to the ground plan of what has been taken to be this temple can be seen indicated in light shading beneath the choir and north transept of the early mediaeval Romanesque cathedral, which was built about 1150 (Fig 10). The choir of this

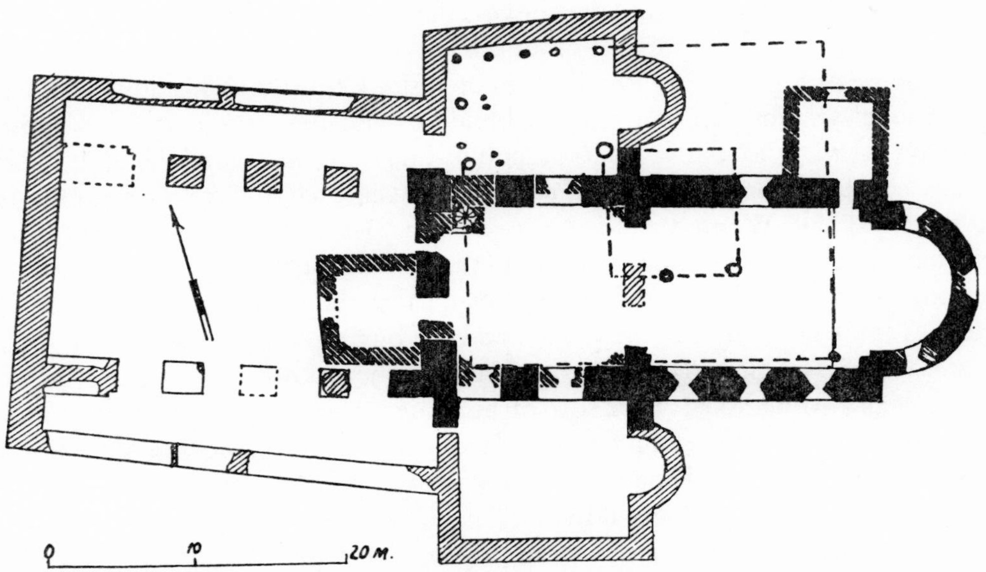

Figure 10 Gamla Uppsala: Detail (based on Plate 18) showing, beneath the choir and north transept of the mediaeval cathedral, the suggested plan of the pagan temple

early cathedral forms the present-day parish church and beneath the floor of this, Professor Sune Lindqvist excavated in 1926 a number of the presumptive temple's post-holes (Fig 11).[57] If his identification is correct (the location of the cathedral

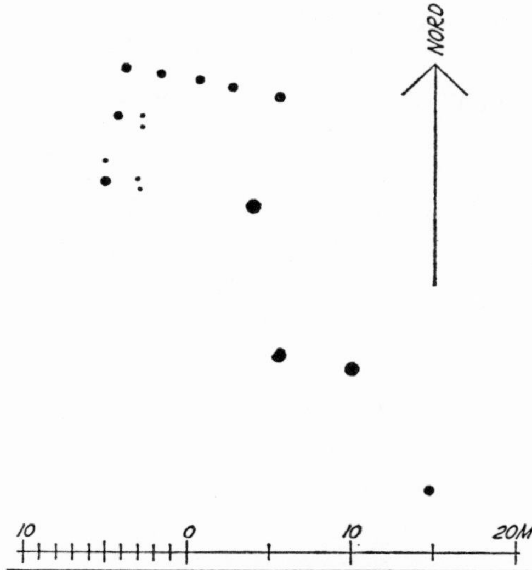

Figure 11 Post-holes, supposedly of the pagan temple at Gamla Uppsala, Sweden

above it might suggest a continuity of sacred sites) then the temple at Old Uppsala was immediately adjacent to the royal halls.

If the Wuffingas are eventually shown, through the study of the 1939 Sutton Hoo excavation and the excavation of other barrows there, to be a branch of the royal house of Uppsala and Rendlesham opposite Ufford their headquarters, then the general relationship of the royal buildings and the temple at Old Uppsala may be relevant to the lay-out of public buildings in Rendlesham. It might in any case be thought a matter of practical convenience to have the temple close to the royal hall. We may note at Yeavering in Bernicia (Fig 12), the north half of the Northumbrian kingdom, how the moot (or local equivalent of the Scandinavian '*thing*'), the successive royal halls, the building believed by Dr Hope-Taylor to have been the church and the burial place of what is referred to as a *vicus regius* by Bede, lay close together as a coherent group.

It remains to be asked what sort of building or structure Raedwald's temple might have been. One would suppose from the letter to Mellitus that Anglo-Saxon temples were well-built structures which could be easily adapted for use as churches. Gregory may, however, have only been propounding general principles and not writing from knowledge of the types of buildings actually in use. Equally it may not have been all, but only some, of the temples ('*fana idolorum*') that were of a kind that would be suitable for conversion. Gregory

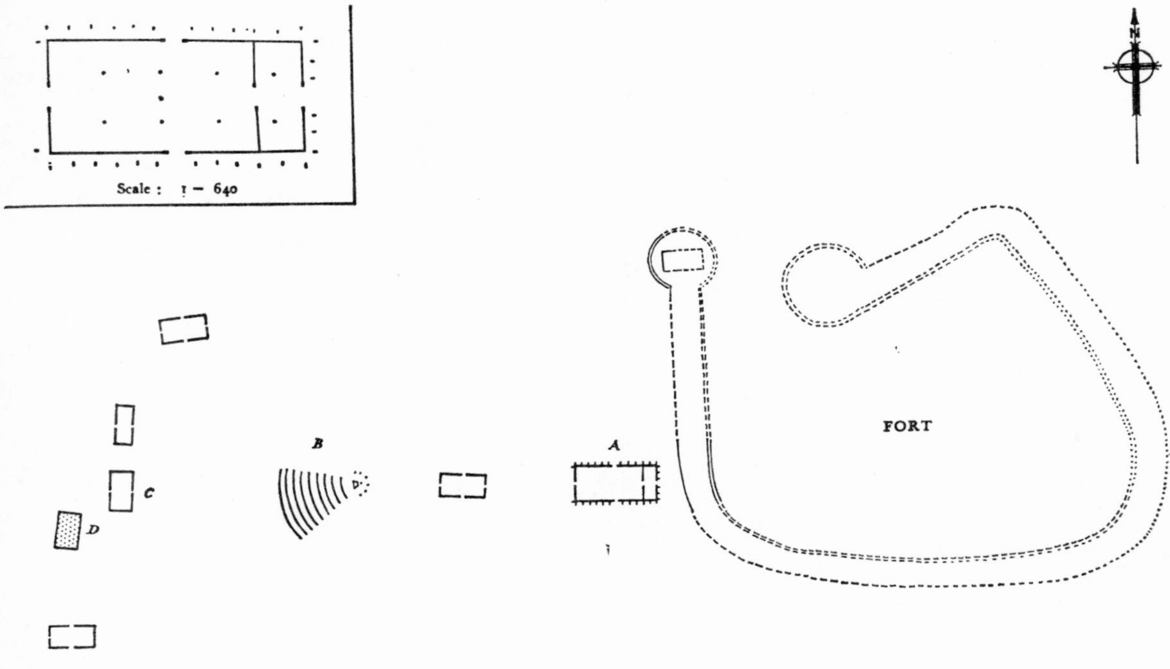

Figure 12 Yeavering, Northumberland. Plan of the *vicus regius* at the time of King Edwin (*c.* A.D. 616–632) (after Hope-Taylor). Many burials were found within the fort and near Hall A.

A. Hall
B. Timber moot
C. Possible temple converted to Christian use
D. Building with a sunken floor

The inset shows the timber hall (A) to a larger scale

wrote 'if' not 'since' or 'as', the temples are well-built ('*si fana bene constructa sunt*'). This may have referred to their condition rather than their type but it is also possible that more than one type of temple existed in Anglo-Saxon England, some suitable for conversion and others not. As we have postulated a possible dynastic connection between the Wuffingas and the Swedish royal house, we should also ask what sort of structure the temple of the Swedish kings at Old Uppsala may have been.

TEMPLES AND SACRED PLACES

The subject of Germanic places of worship, their nature and the relationship between these sites and the first Christian churches, has been bedevilled by almost unparalleled volumes of speculation, loose thinking, dubious philology and misuse of literary sources; and by the inadequacy and misinterpretation of archaeological evidence.

The Danish mediaevalist and archaeologist, Professor Olaf Olsen, has in recent studies effectively swept away most of this[58] and laid the foundations for fresh progress.

A great deal of recent excavation has been carried out in Denmark on the sites of early parish churches in which traces of wooden churches underneath have been sought. In more than twenty such excavations, no evidence of earlier religious use of the site has been forthcoming. Towards the end of these investigations, however, some evidence began to emerge to suggest that this continuity did exist in special cases. Olsen found, in collating the Danish results since 1947, that only very few and then only scattered traces of use of the sites in earlier periods had been discovered. This did not prove, however, that the early churches were not built on pagan religious sites, since the nature of such pagan sites was unknown.

Olsen's analysis of literary, philological and archaeological evidence has led him to define two types of site characteristic of pagan religion. One was the ordinary farm building in which special feasts of a religious kind could be held, rather in the way that a Christmas feast with friends and relations might be held at home, or else feasts of a more formal kind. The building could belong to a large or a small farm, acting as centres of larger or smaller communities. The other type of site is the outdoor one, which need be no more than the idols or sacred features themselves, which might in the course of time come to be protected by a tent or other temporary cover. The holy place could be an image or effigy standing in a cairn of stones. Perhaps the holy place might be fenced. The farm building where feasts might be held was called '*hof*', the covered or tented shrine or idol was called '*høgr*'. That this kind of shrine was known in the Roman Iron Age is clear from a number of finds.[59] For early Germanic times, *Beowulf* may be cited. The inmates of Hrothgar's hall reverted to pagan gods and sacrifices '*aet hoergtrafum*' (in the *hørgr-tent*) in the hope of getting rid of Grendel:

Hwīlum hīe gehēton   æt hærgtrafum
wīgweorþunga   (*Beowulf* 175–6)
('At times they offered sacrifices to the idols in their pagan tabernacles . . .').

The first type of building or sacred place (the *hof*), as Olsen points out, is not to be distinguished by the excavation process from an ordinary farm. The second cannot be distinguished at all – or only exceptionally. Thus, continuity of pagan and Christian sites is not necessarily disproved by the drawing of apparent archaeological blanks from the modern excavations beneath parish churches. Both the open-air *hørgr* and the *hørgr* with a shelter still existed, as Olsen shows, in Viking times.

THE TEMPLE AT OLD UPPSALA

Where Sutton Hoo and Rendlesham are concerned, apart from the *Beowulf* reference, we are naturally drawn, in the search for relevant parallels, to the famous temple at Old Uppsala, described by Adam of Bremen. The fact is that we really have no certain knowledge of it at all in an architectural sense. The cult-place was probably an ancient sacred grove (perhaps surrounding the sacrificial well). It may have become a '*hørgr*', that is, have developed as a tent or shelter for the idols. Olsen's summary of what we know of the Uppsala temple can be presented thus:

(i) In about A.D. 1070 a famed temple existed at Uppsala.

(ii) It contained idols, said to be of Thor and Odin and Freyr.

(iii) Gruesome sacrifices took place in the holy grove in the precincts.

(iv) The temple is not mentioned in connection with these sacrifices but only the grove and its sacred well.

(v) In spite of the gruesome sacrifices in the grove, the cult at Uppsala was clearly centred on the images (idols), and the temple building is best interpreted as a shelter for them (*hørgr*) (we do not know the Norse word that was applied to the Uppsala religious structure, only the Latin (*fanum*) of Adam of Bremen).

(vi) As to the actual remains at Gamla Uppsala, in 1926, Sune Lindqvist found under the twelfth-century church traces of earlier occupation or use in at least three strata; but what he found is insufficient to allow a reconstruction of a timber building associated with the intermediate phase.

(vii) Lindqvist's attempt to make such a reconstruction was dependent on the Wendic temple plans of Schuchardt from the site of Arkona and elsewhere on the south shores of the Baltic (that is, on Schuchardt's reconstructions of the Wendic temples).[60] Olsen maintains that Schuchardt's plans of what would be in any case a 'temple' of a later period in a different cultural milieu are so hypothetical as to be wholly unreliable.

(viii) Olsen then sets out to analyse the Gamla Uppsala post-holes in themselves without reference to the Wendic temples (Fig 13).

(ix) His conclusion is that the features under the twelfth-century stone church do seem to indicate that it stands on the very spot of the old sanctuary, perhaps even on the site of the temple itself but that we cannot say whether the temple should relate to the second occupation stratum, which contained Lindqvist's post-holes, or to the lowest one, represented by traces of cobbles and burning.

(x) We cannot say that Lindqvist's post-holes represent not the temple but a first, pre-stone, wooden Church within an enclosure.

(xi) Whether the recorded post-holes represent a pagan or Christian building, there are too few of them in too big an area and they are consequently too tenuously interrelated to allow any valid reconstruction to be based on them. Indeed, Olsen bids fair to have reduced the exercise to absurdity by illustrating on one page (here Fig 13) eight different interpretations put forward so far of this same set of post-holes, which may be thought sufficient to discourage further attempts at reconstructing from them Adam of Bremen's temple.

(xii) Olsen eliminates also the 'parallel' to the Uppsala site, found by Gerda Boethius at Saebol in Iceland (*Dyraffofur*) (more probably a mediaeval farm-chapel, if not a stable).

The recent work in Denmark has established that two wooden churches frequently preceded a Romanesque stone church on the same site. The early wooden buildings at the Danish royal burial place of Jellinge and at Gamla Uppsala in Sweden might well be of this type; in fact that at Jellinge has been shown to be so. There is not enough evidence to justify the view that the earlier Danish churches were erected on pagan cult-places. In Anglo-Saxon England the position would seem to be somewhat different. We have seen that Gregory's advice to the Church was initially to make use of temple buildings if they were well built and to turn them into churches. This is a policy which would favour continuity. An example from Northumbria (its southern part, the kingdom of Deira) seems to show the use there of a *hørgr* type of shrine as the principle sanctuary of the realm. The episode described by Bede (Book II, Chapter 13) follows his account of the conversion of King Edwin by Paulinus in A.D. 627, that is, the precise period of the Sutton Hoo burial. The episode introduces us to the interesting personality of the Northumbrian high priest, Coifi.[61] Bede's account is as follows:

> Coifi added that he would like to listen still more carefully to what Paulinus himself had to say about God. The king ordered Paulinus to speak, and when he had said his say, Coifi exclaimed, 'For a long time now I have realized that our religion is worthless; for the more diligently I sought the truth in our cult, the less I found it. Now I confess openly that the truth shines out clearly in this teaching which can bestow on us the gift of life, salvation, and eternal happiness. Therefore I advise your Majesty that we should promptly abandon and commit to the flames the temples and the altars which we have held sacred without reaping any benefit.' Why need I say more? The king publicly

accepted the gospel which Paulinus preached, renounced idolatry, and confessed his faith in Christ. When he asked the high priest of their religion which of them should be the first to profane the altars and the shrines of the idols, together with their precincts, Coifi answered, 'I will; for through the wisdom the true God has given me no one can more suitably destroy those things which I once foolishly worshipped, and so set an example to all.' And at once, casting aside his vain superstitions, he asked the king to provide him with arms and a stallion; and mounting it he set out to destroy the idols. Now a high priest of their religion was not allowed to carry arms or to ride except on a mare. So, girded with a sword, he took a spear in his hand and mounting the king's stallion he set off to where the idols were. The common people who saw him thought he was mad. But as soon as he approached the shrine, without any hesitation he profaned it by casting the spear which he held into it; and greatly rejoicing in the knowledge of the worship of the true God, he ordered his companions to destroy and set fire to the shrine and all the enclosures. The place where the idols once stood is still shown, not far from York, to the east, over the river Derwent. Today it is called Goodmanham, the place where the high priest, through the inspiration of the true God, profaned and destroyed the altars which he himself had consecrated.[62]

This passage would suggest that the principal shrine of the kingdom of Deira, not far from York, was of the *hørgr* type – idols under cover within a fenced enclosure, not a hall or barn-like building (*hof*). Since there is evidence, as Olsen points out, that the south Germanic peoples, influenced perhaps by prolonged contacts with the Roman world, were familiar with other types of temple, it need not follow that if the Anglian national shrine at Goodmanham were of the *hørgr* type, all Anglo-Saxon temples must be the same. The Anglo-Saxon settlers in Britain being of different stocks and origins may have brought different types of temple with them. There is nothing definite that we can say about the sort of structure to expect for Raedwald's temple, scene of his disgraceful compromise. The excavation of temple sites is among the most important objectives of Anglo-Saxon archaeology and our lack of knowledge on this subject – the pagan religion, its structures, observances and social rôle – is the most striking *lacuna* in our knowledge of early Anglo-Saxon life. The approximate location of several such sites is known. They ought not to be impossible to find.

As far as Goodmanham is concerned, Bede's account may be thought to suggest that the site of the temple is not likely to be that of the present early Norman church. The enclosures and other structures of the temple were evidently not converted for Christian use but burnt down and destroyed. The site was still shown to visitors in Bede's own day, which may also be thought to indicate that it had not been taken over for use as a Christian burial ground with a new building (a Christian church) erected in its midst. The whole tenor of Bede's story suggests abandonment. It is evident from Bede's text that King Edwin had a *vicus regius* or royal seat in the vicinity. This was far enough off to cause Coefi to ride to the temple, i.e. the relationship between royal hall and temple was not the very close one which the evidence seems to suggest at Uppsala and which may have existed also at Yeavering. The fact that the temple was burnt should make it easy to recognize and to excavate, should traces of it come to light. Both temple and *vicus regius* may have owed their location to some extent to the presence of the Roman road, providing ready access, which ran across the low ground below Goodmanham, at the base of the wolds. A hasty reconnaissance of the area offers no clue, beyond suggesting that the immediate site of the church, from which the ground falls away, seems too restricted. There is no local record of archaeological finds or of any other indications. The dramatically broken ground in a field two hundred yards due south of the church suggests open-cast quarrying or other industrial activity. The earthworks are too incoherent to represent an archaeological site.

Olsen has shown that the post-holes found beneath and outside the Romanesque stone cathedral at Old Uppsala are inadequate for reconstruction of the building or structures to which they belonged; and, further, that we cannot even be sure that the post-holes belong to the temple of Adam of Bremen's account and not to earlier wooden church structures which may have preceded the stone cathedral. None the less, it remains possible that the post-holes do represent the temple structure. We should therefore note their ambitious character.

They were of various diameters according to their position and function. Those in the central area attained 80 cms in diameter (2ft 8ins) whilst the smallest, round the periphery of the temple area, were 40 cms (1ft 4ins).[63] Although the diameter of the posts themselves cannot be precisely calculated, they must have been very substantial. The great posts of the central area must have carried a superstructure of very considerable height (cf. Fig 13, where these factors have been taken into account in the reconstruction attempts). It is to be hoped that the opportunity may arise for more extensive excavation at Old Uppsala beneath and around the cathedral, the surviving chancel of which now serves as a parish church.

Finally, another class of monument which should be mentioned is recognized in Denmark, the V-shaped 'shrines' or sanctuaries at Jellinge, Tibirke and Tingsted, brought into the discussion by Eijner Dyggve. These are of uncertain interpretation and appear to be related to burial mounds at their open end. Certainly the large V-shaped enclosure of set stones at Jellinge is linked to the royal barrow at its open north end, in this case the north barrow (Queen Thyra's). Olsen regards the 'V' at Jellinge as primarily a monument to the dead, not a cult place, shrine or temple-precinct.

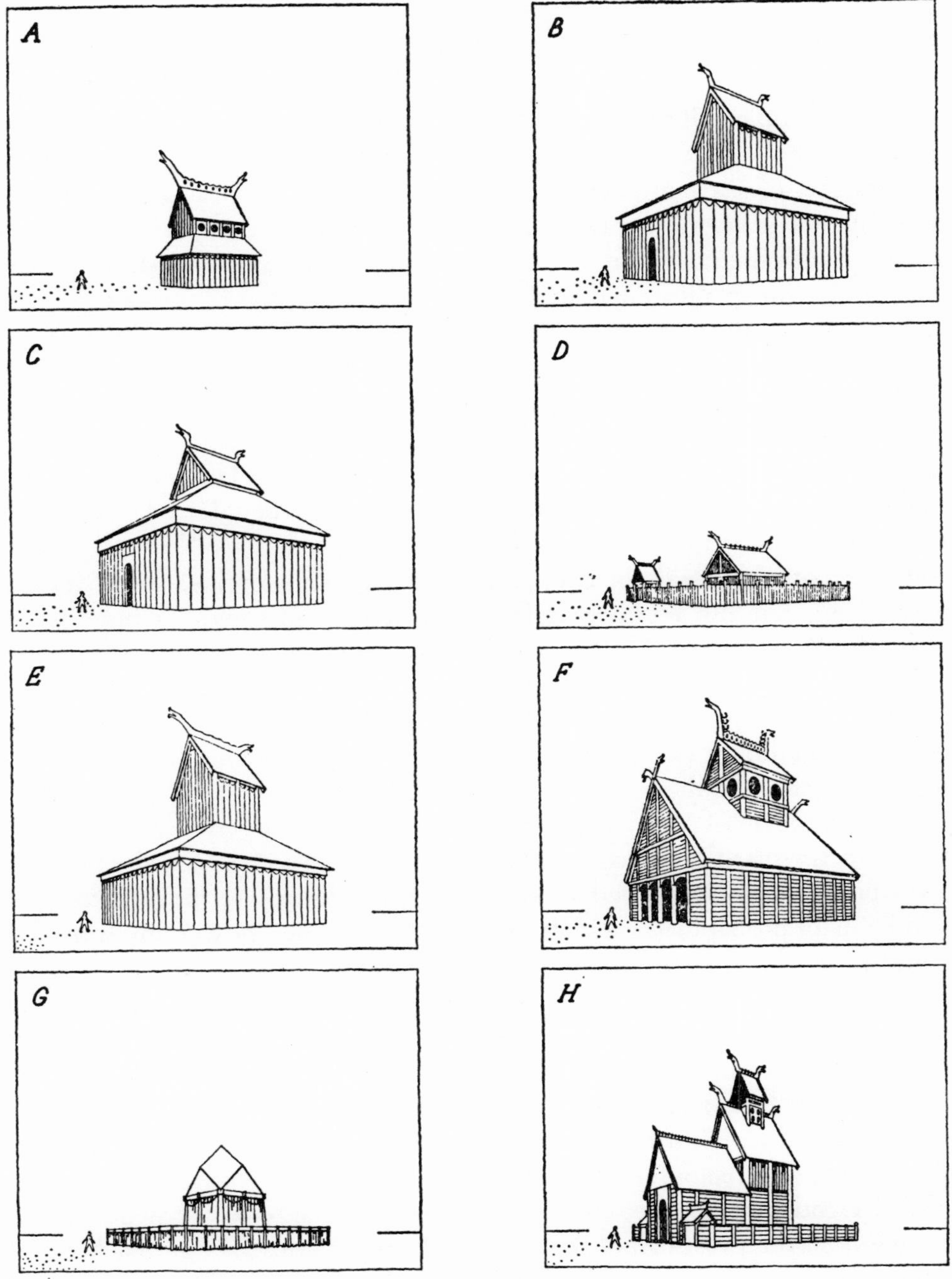

Figure 13 Eight proposed reconstructions of the temple at Uppsala, all based on the post-hole plan shown in Figure 11

THE PHYSICAL CHARACTER OF THE *VICUS REGIUS*

Church and temple at Rendlesham, if probable, are presumptive, but we can be sure that the main building of an important *vicus regius* would be a large wooden hall.

The features of a seventh-century Saxon royal hall have become known to us to some extent from the excavation of the *vicus regius* at Yeavering, a site contemporary with the use of the sites at Rendlesham and Sutton Hoo. The general layout of the site is illustrated in Fig 12.[64] The complex of structures, which included several halls of different periods, is fully discussed in Dr Hope-Taylor's report.[65] Our knowledge of Germanic timber buildings has dramatically increased in the last twenty-five years.[66] Yeavering remains the unique exposition of the layout of an Anglo-Saxon *vicus regius* and one which can be precisely dated and documented from Bede's *Ecclesiastical History*. The habitation layers had all gone. The uses of the various buildings can only be inferred. It is a layout of the deeper foundations and post-holes.

Some idea of what might be expected of the hall of an Anglo-Saxon Bretwalda or High King can also be inferred from the literary analogies. A principal hall used by the Wuffingas or by Raedwald, to judge by the degree of royal dignity and sophistication revealed at Sutton Hoo, might well have been a structure not unlike Heorot, Hrothgar's renowned hall, described in *Beowulf*. It would be a large timber building, reminiscent of a mediaeval barn but no doubt hung with figured tapestries like those of Overhögdal or Oseberg, with narrative scenes in the vernacular style of Vendel art or the Franks Casket, a genre from which the Bayeux tapestry itself is descended. The walls would also be decked with shields and weapons, the gables carved and decorated. In addition to the hall itself there would be in all probability a withdrawing room or ladies' bower and some lesser buildings.

Of Hrothgar's palace we read (*Beowulf*, lines 68–83) that 'tribes without number even to the ends of the earth were given orders to deck the hall', that it was called Heorot ('Hart'), perhaps because of stags' heads fixed to the gables, that 'it towered high lofty and wide-gabled'. Later on, it is spoken of as 'the great hall Heorot, adorned with horns' (line 780). With regard to outbuildings or subsidiary rooms, we are told that after the reception of Beowulf by Hrothgar . . . 'the court rises' . . . Hrothgar gave Beowulf 'good luck, and charge of the wine hall'. . . . 'have and hold this great hall of the Danes'. Hrothgar himself 'went back with his troop out of the hall . . . to seek his wife, his Queen abed'. The other buildings here implied may have been in this case *ad hoc* arrangements, since Grendel had for some years past rendered the hall untenable. When he was slain, 'all slept in hall again, as in former years . . . but Hrothgar went within to rest in his own chamber'. As for his troop, 'bolsters and beds were spread on the benches' . . . 'the Ring-Danes slept around the hall'. At the same time 'Beowulf was not at hand, for after the treasure-giving, other room was given to the famous Geat'. Besides a withdrawing room and one or two out-buildings of a reasonably dignified character, we might also expect at Rendlesham to have the workshops of royal craftsmen, perhaps of the goldsmith who made the Sutton Hoo jewellery and of the royal armourer, as well as wooden outhouses and sheds for different purposes. To a great extent the building materials available locally would determine the size and character of such structures but for a royal hall of this class special materials may have been procured from some distance. The general proportions of such a building may be inferred from the one hundred and sixty feet platforms of Old Uppsala, or the one hundred feet tenth-century timber barrack-buildings of the Danish camps at Trelleborg and Fyrkat,[67] or more relevantly, the halls at Yeavering with their subsidiary buildings.

To revert to ecclesiastical buildings, the presumed church where Swidhelm was baptized, if not the same building as Raedwald's temple, would have probably been a considerably smaller construction, no doubt also built of timber (since building stone does not occur in the area) perhaps resembling the timber church at Greenstead, Essex, or the early churches of the seventh-century missionaries.[68]

Any group of structures of the general character of those described, should it be wholly or partly in arable land and given favourable conditions of crops and subsoil, might be expected to respond well to aerial photography.

The discovery of the crown at Rendlesham (p. 81), if this can be related to the Wuffingas, is also suggestive. Crowns in the normal course of events are not lost by accident or buried. If the story is to be taken seriously and the object in reality were some sort of diadem or circlet of the seventh or eighth century, this might suggest that the 'palace' at Rendlesham was sacked or burnt. A habitation site put to an end in this way is more likely to yield small finds and general information than one which has been abandoned with deliberation.

THE GENERAL IMPORTANCE OF THE SITE

We need hardly stress the desirability, both as a parallel study and background to the excavation of the Sutton Hoo burial ground and for Anglo-Saxon studies at large, of locating and excavating the royal complex, which we may suppose to have existed at Rendlesham in the seventh century. We have in recent years progressed beyond the idea that 'the poverty and architectural squalor of pagan village sites'[69] represents the best domestic amenities to which pagan Saxons could aspire. Rectangular timber-framed buildings, smaller and larger, have come to light on sites without the royal associations of Yeavering or Cheddar.[70] Any fresh hall structure or complex, especially one with known dates and a known historical context,[71] will be likely to add significantly to our knowledge, perhaps producing the kind of information, from habitation strata, that has been lost at Yeavering. We may note J. N. L. Myres' comment of many years ago in the Council for British Archaeology's *Survey and Policy of Field Research in the Archaeology of Great Britain*:

> There must have been 'halls', no doubt mainly of timber like that of Hrothgar in *Beowulf*, at every royal or aristocratic centre, but no such structures have ever been located. The obvious sites on which to seek them would be those known from early literary evidence as *villae regales*, of which a considerable number are mentioned by Bede, or in early land-charters. Place names may also provide clues in this line of enquiry: for example, the numerous 'Kingstons' (itself merely a translation in some instances of *villa regalis*) and other compounds with King, some of which, as Kingston-on-Soar (Notts) or Kingsdown (Kent) are the sites of pagan cemeteries.

One such Kingston, as we have seen above (p. 80), lies on the Deben estuary, almost opposite Sutton Hoo, at the mouth of Martlesham creek. To quote further from Myres on the subject of temples:

> It has already been mentioned that no sites of pagan temples or ceremonial structures have hitherto been recognised, and practically nothing is known archaeologically about the material surroundings of pagan worship. But literary and place-name evidence points to a number of localities where such structures seem to have existed. . . . In some cases, names of heathen holy places are preserved in the boundary marks of Anglo-Saxon estates described in land-charters or have survived as medieval and later field names: this may make it possible to identify a site very closely. It is much to be hoped that by following such clues it may one day be possible to pinpoint and excavate an Anglo-Saxon temple.

What hope is there then of locating on the ground the buildings of the Saxon *vicus regius* at Rendlesham?

The following section is as written in 1948, with minor alterations. The parish has experienced major changes since 1948, particularly the demolition of Rendlesham Hall and the digging up of the parklands for agricultural purposes and the incursions of the American air-force base, its runway cut out of Rendlesham forest to the south, although these are well away from what seem to be the likely areas. A general watch has been maintained through the Cambridge University Committee for Aerial Photography by Dr St Joseph. In spite of such developments I have kept the text which follows virtually unaltered, since it gives accurately the state of things when my field-work in search of the site of the *vicus regius* was carried out. It is expected that a further survey will be published before long by David Sherlock, recording observations of his recent survey of the parish. This was undertaken on foot and completed over Easter 1972. Allowing for his results, it can still be said today, as when I wrote this section initially, that thorough reconnaissance of the parish on foot has shown that there are no surface indications and that there is a total lack of local lore or stray archaeological finds, apart from early mediaeval pottery recorded by the Ipswich Museum from four sites. There is no hope here of quick results, unless air photography may in the future dramatically solve the problem for us.

The parish (Fig 14) has never been extensively built on and contains no village. It is largely arable land and the greater part of the parkland of Rendlesham Hall was brought under plough for the first time in memory in 1948. The area might thus be considered promising from the point of view of yielding its archaeological secrets to a systematic air survey. On the other hand, the subsoil is in general sand, which does not usually yield good crop-marks and there are some areas of heath and woodland. The Saxon buildings may also have been, as some local historians have claimed, without giving any evidence, on the site of the Tudor and nineteenth-century Rendlesham Halls and have been obliterated in this way. There are also R.A.F. hut camps, erected in the 1939–45 war, cavalry lines of the 1914–18 war and small-scale gravel and marl workings.

The present-day church has an early dedication (St Gregory the Great) and there was an earlier church presumably on this site at the time of the Domesday Survey. No fragments of Norman or Saxon sculpture or masonry appear to be incorporated in the present church fabric which dates from the fifteenth century. The site of the seventh-century (wooden?) church, if we are right in interpreting the Rendlesham baptism described by Bede as implying the existence of such a building, as we almost certainly are, may be covered by the Saxon and mediaeval churches.

Since the name Rendlesham goes back at least to the early eighth century, the '*ham*' which gave the area its name has probably always been the nucleus of the development of the parish and no doubt lies within its present-day boundaries. Bede describes the *vicus regius* as in this '*ham*'.

There is nothing to indicate that there has ever been any revision of the parish boundary of Rendlesham[72] nor does there seem any reason for such a change, since the region is so sparsely populated. We should be safe in looking for the *vicus regius* within the boundaries of the modern parish. On the other hand, the church now lies very close to the parish boundary and the area immediately to the south and south-west of it in Eyke parish must also be scrutinized. The parish with this extension is a formidable area. What can be done to reduce the field of search?

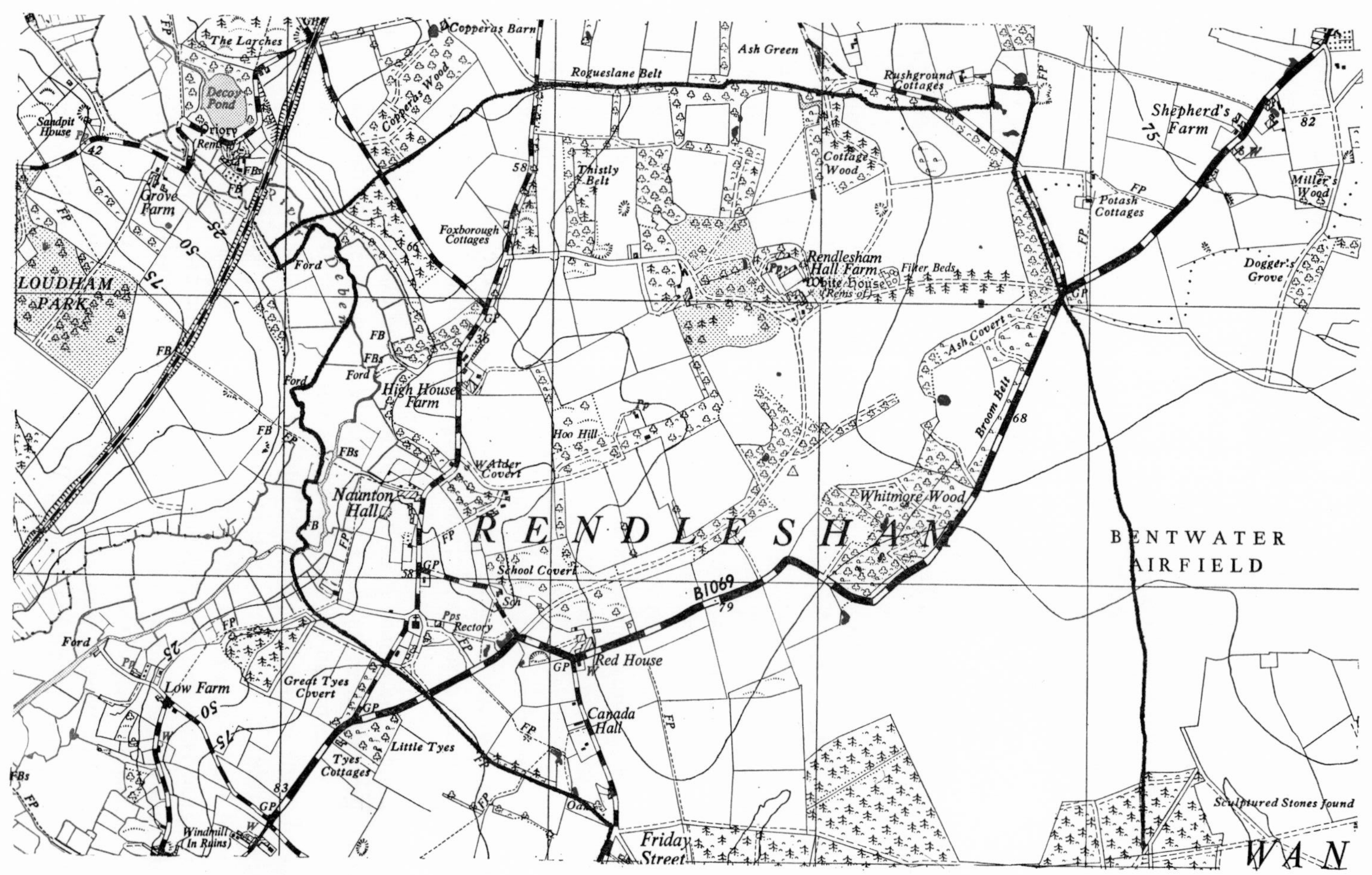

Figure 14 Rendlesham parish showing the frontage on the river Deben. The parish boundary is outlined in black. A belt about six hundred yards in depth at the extreme south of the parish is not shown. A little below the limits of this map the boundary runs east and west again (Scale: $2\frac{1}{2}$ ins to 1 mile)

From the map (Fig 14) it will be seen that the parish has a very short frontage, only two-thirds of a mile, on the Deben whereas further east the parish measures more than two miles from north to south. The parish thus narrows from north and south towards the river frontage. Across the middle of the parish runs, from west to east, the road from Eyke to Tunstall. South of this road except for a few cottages at Friday Street, the parish is virtually uninhabited, consisting today of arable land and heath. North of the road the greater part of the area is occupied by the Rendlesham estate, comprising parklands, wooded belts and some arable fields. The old western limit of this estate is marked by the line of Silvestor's Belt (the line of trees along the east side of the road that runs north from High House Farm past Foxborough Cottages (Fig 14) and the fence that runs south-east from the road fork above Crag Pit past Hoo Hill towards Red House (Fig 15).

Today Rendlesham belongs to the line of hamlets along the east bank of the Deben (Bromeswell, Eyke, Campsey Ash), linked by the road that runs along the east bank of the river. Such village life as there is centres on the parish church, the manor house of Naunton Hall and the school (Fig 15). In mediaeval times this area was also clearly the focus of interest in the parish. To the finds of 'a large quantity of bones in different places' in an area which appears to lie between the Church and Naunton Hall and was then an open green,[73] the Davy MSS.[74] in the British Museum adds an illustration of a mediaeval jug from this same area.

That the settlement equally belonged to the Deben valley in early Saxon times is clear. The river was the great thoroughfare, round which the pattern of early settlement took shape and what has already been said of the royal sites and Saxon finds in the Deben valley makes it clear that the royal *vicus* would have been sited with relation to the river. It seems reasonable to look in the area of the river frontage and its hinterland north of the Eyke-Tunstall road and as far east as Rendlesham Hall for the site of the early Saxon church and 'palace'.

We must now see what the lie of the land in this part of the parish has to tell us which may help in closer definition of the area in which the site may lie.

It will be seen from Fig 14 that at Rendlesham the River Deben makes a sharp bend to the east. It is just this eastward bend which is covered by the short parish frontage to the river. The behaviour of the fifty-foot contour line should next be studied in Fig 15. It shows that here in the bend the river bank takes the form of three spurs between which two flat-bottomed coombes run inland (both marked Alder Covert on the map, Fig 15). Of these, the southern coombe leads directly into the heart of the parish (Fig 14). The northern coombe tends to run out of it. We may note that on the prominent southern spur stands the church of St Gregory the Great, almost on the Parish boundary, and the manor house of Naunton Hall. This southern coombe itself forks at its southern end. The northern arm of the fork develops into a gentle valley leading to Rendlesham

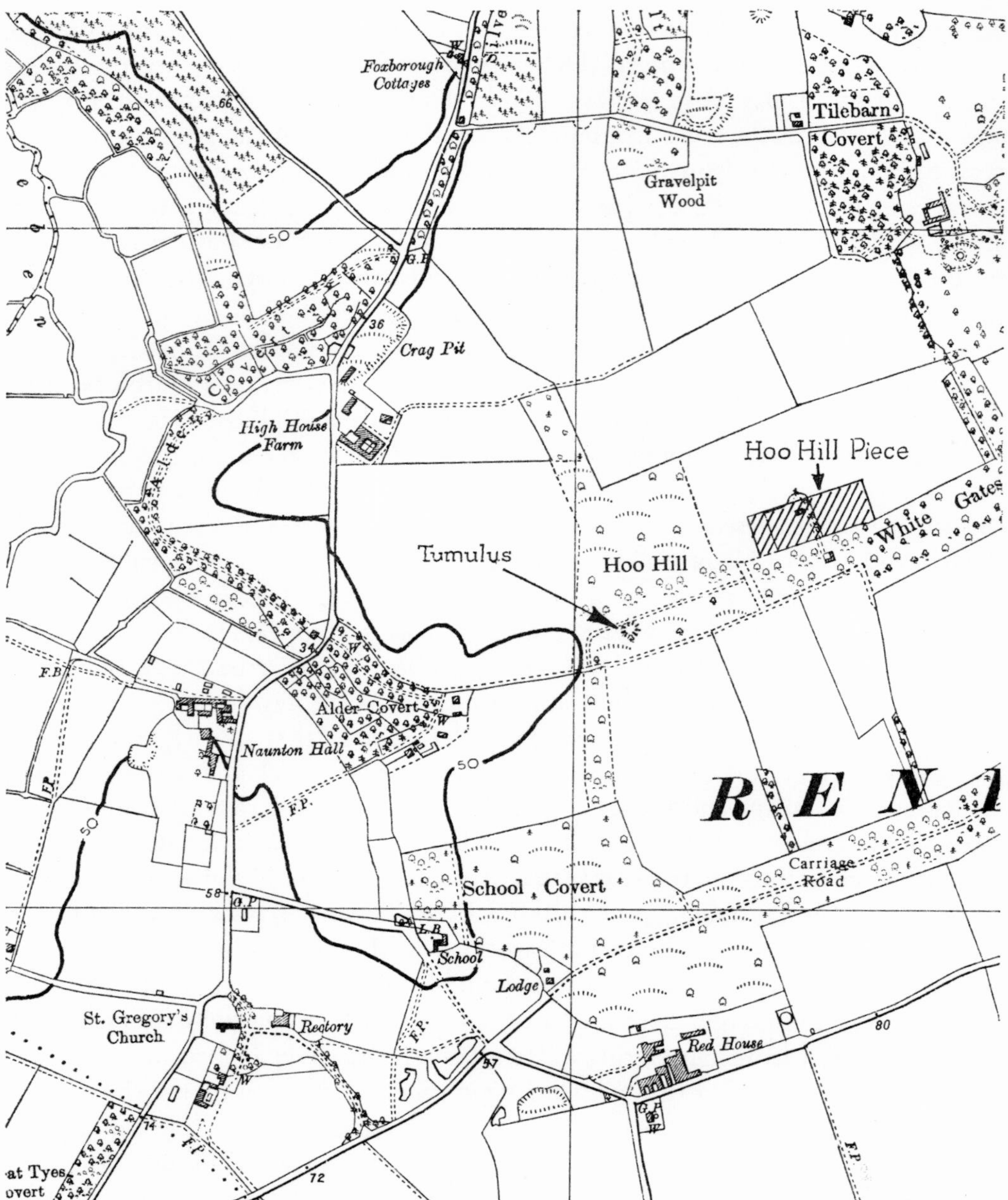

Figure 15. Part of the parish frontage on the river Deben, showing Hoo Hill piece (the hatched area to the right of the printed name Hoo Hill) with the newly observed barrow marked (Scale 6 in to 1 mile). *Sheet no. TM 35 SW*

Hall and to the north of it runs high ground bearing the suggestive name, Hoo Hill.[75]

To anyone approaching, as our Saxon forebears must be conceived as having approached, by water, the spurs at Rendlesham appear prominent and the coombes lead invitingly between them into the hinterland. I think it can be assumed that in Saxon times, before the construction of the bridge and its cause-ways of approach at Melton or development of the innumerable drainage dykes and banks that have turned the floor of the valley into pasture (Fig 14), the Deben was here a broad tidal stream. It is said that the building stone for the present (fifteenth century) church at Rendlesham was brought by barge to the foot of the lane that runs steeply westward from the church into the valley bottom. Similarly, J. N. L. Myres and J. B. Ward Perkins uncovered at Butley Priory a mediaeval wharf showing that the tide must formerly have run right up to the Priory which now stands high and dry.[76] This being so, we may visualize these flat-bottomed coombes in Saxon times as providing sheltered bays into which, at high tide, keels could be rowed.[77] On this reasoning one might expect the early settlement and royal Hall to be sited with relation to this approach and this in turn suggests as a likely site either the spur on which the church is built and round the back (or eastern side) of which the southern fork of this coombe runs or the long elevated ridge of Hoo Hill, which along the north side of Alder Covert forms a steep bank above the coombe bed and would have provided easy and dry access to the deepest water (Fig 15).

If one considers the more exposed northern coombe, one might regard as likely sites the high ground to the north, lying in the fork of the roads, while to the south and east of this coombe once more lies the broad area of Hoo Hill and the comparatively elevated flat ground where the successive Rendlesham Halls of more modern times were sited.

On the whole, the spur where the church now stands may be considered as perhaps too exposed and somewhat too confined a site for the royal 'palace'. The Hoo Hill region in its broadest sense, including the area to the north of the position in which the name is printed (Fig 15), is more central to the area and a little more sheltered from the river approaches and yet commands a fairly extensive prospect south over the coombe and towards the river valley.

THE SITE OF THE EARLY CHURCH AND A PAGAN CEMETERY ON HOO HILL

The first Christian missionaries concentrated their attention on the royal courts, kings were the first converts and the first churches are recorded as having been built for the use of royalty. It is thus likely that the early church where Swidhelm was baptized was close to, or at any rate in the same general area as, the Wuffingas 'palace'. If it were possible to locate the site of this early church, this would help us to check the general correctness of our topographical calculations and very likely provide a clue to the whereabouts of the major site.

The site of the seventh-century church is either that of the present church, or it is not. If it is, there is no prospect of discovering it at the present time but the fact would reinforce our selection of the area of the parish towards the river as that of the early Saxon occupation. If, on the other hand, the site was somewhere else in the parish, how might this be detected? In reply to this question, Miss Lilian Redstone suggested that parish records should be scrutinized in order to find out whether there existed in the parish, but away from the present church and its glebe land, any outlying or isolated area of glebe. Such an outlying piece of glebe might be the site of an earlier church which had consequently come down as ecclesiastical land from ancient times. Mr W. G. Arnott of Woodbridge, in consequence of this suggestion, kindly examined a number of early records. For the tithe award of 1840, now in the custody of Messrs Garrod and Turner at Ipswich, Mr Arnott found that just such a piece of outlying glebe existed. The remaining glebe is nucleated round the church and parsonage. The isolated strip (measuring 2 acres, 1 pole, 20 perches) was on Hoo Hill.

In the earlier part of the nineteenth century, David Elisha Davy collected valuable material for a parish history of Suffolk. His manuscripts, bound into fifty large volumes, are now in the British Museum. Following upon Mr Arnott's discovery I went through Davy's sections devoted to Rendlesham (Add. MS. 19097, folios 253–304). On folio 303r there is a drawing of a cinerary urn (Plate 19) above which appears the following text:

> In a piece of glebe land of the parish, known by the name of How or Haw hill piece, containing about 2 acres, there have for several years past been dug up numerous pieces of Roman urns, but all so brittle that none were ever taken up whole, nor even nearly so, till the present year, 1837, when one with nothing broken-off but the rim of the mouth, was procured with great care, which I saw, July 7th, at the Parsonage House, in the possession of the Rector, Lord Thomas Hay; it is of a coarse brown earth, of good shape, and more than half filled, with fragments of bones and ashes; the height of it, with the rim broken-off, is near eight inches and the breadth in the middle about 6. The following rough sketch was taken at the time and may give some idea of its make and shape.

The urn is of course not Roman but Anglo-Saxon and the urns indicate a cemetery of the pre-Christian period.

This discovery is an interesting one. If the urn-field is not the burial place of earlier settlers of a period before the royal association with Rendlesham began, it is no doubt the burial place of the people of the *vicus regius*. The apparent absence of *tumuli* in the area may be explained if the members of the royal family had their own place of burial elsewhere (at Sutton Hoo), the site on Hoo Hill being the urn field of a village community amongst or close to whom the *villa regalis* had been established. We should also note that at Easter 1972, in the course of his exploration in the parish, David Sherlock has located on Hoo Hill, though not in the glebe strip, what he considers to be very likely a burial mound. He describes it in his notes which he has kindly put at my disposal (the site has been added in Fig 15):

> Near the SE corner of the wood, before the ground begins to fall, is a broad low mound (with 2 oaks near its centre). About 2 feet high and 65 feet in diameter. Very likely a flattened tumulus. The dimensions are not dissimilar to those of some of the less conspicuous mounds in the Sutton Hoo site, but we cannot be sure without excavation whether it is a genuine barrow or if it is of Saxon date.

The location on Hoo Hill of a pagan cemetery confirms our supposition that the early Saxon settlement is likely to have been in this portion of the parish. It is furthermore an interesting fact that this isolated strip of outlying glebe should mark the site of a pagan burial place. Can this be pure coincidence? It may be. On the other hand it is possible that this piece of land may have been given to the Church in the earliest times because of its religious significance as the burial place of members of the settlement and forebears who had died before Christianity came to Rendlesham. It may be that the occurrence of cremation burials in the glebe strip is incidental or accidental and that the strip is glebe land because it was, as we had hoped it might be, the site of the first Christian church.

Early documents relating to the parish and the glebe lands do not, so far as I have yet been able to discover, throw any light on the origin of Hoo Hill Piece. The earliest reference to it known to me is a document copied by Davy,[78] entitled 'A terrier of all the houses and landes belonging to the psonage of Rendlesham, XVIII Maye 1633'. The last entry in this is as follows:

> 12. Item tooe acres of land lyinge in a close of Mr. Mawes called Hoo Hill, the one end abbutinge upon a close of Mr. Robt. Spencers on the north, the other end on Mr. Mawe's on the south.

This document shows that Hoo Hill Piece was glebe in 1633.

We know nothing of the relationship between temples and burial places in pagan Saxon times. At Old Uppsala innumerable burials lie around the west end of the line of the three great mounds and may be said to be in the vicinity of the temple. We may perhaps also note that at Frilford in Berkshire the mixed Romano-British and Anglo-Saxon cemetery lay about two hundred yards away from the Romano-Celtic temple.[79] If there were a temple at Rendlesham the location of the pagan cemetery might thus indicate its general whereabouts.

If the isolated glebe strip were, as has been suggested, the site of a seventh-century church, this might also indicate that the temple was in this area, since in England some of the earliest Christian churches were very possibly purified temples and we have noted the possibility that this may have been the case with Raedwald's temple which may have been at Rendlesham, although there is no evidence that this was so. The location of a cremation cemetery on Hoo Hill and perhaps the presence there of this isolated strip of glebe, confirm in a general way the impression already formed as a result of the study of the local topography, that the seventh-century *vicus regius* probably lay in the Hoo Hill area or, at any rate, in that part of the parish between Rendlesham Hall and the river valley.

The presence of a cremation cemetery at Rendlesham is a matter of some interest, since apart from the mixed cemetery at Ipswich where about one hundred and sixty burials were examined[80] and scattered groups of tumuli such as those at Martlesham, Sutton Hoo and Snape, a solitary urn, now in the British Museum, from Waldringfield[81] and another from Kesgrave,[82] no cemetery has come to light and no early Saxon pottery exists in this area of Suffolk to offset the mass of finds and the numerous cemeteries of the north-west of the County.[83] Furthermore the area within which the cremation urns were found in the 1820s and 30s is specified. They were from within the glebe strip and the boundaries of this can be fixed with complete accuracy (Fig 15). The boundaries are shown and their positions fixed by measurements, in a number of documents relating to the Rendlesham glebe and parklands. Unfortunately, a number of short trial cuttings dug by the writer in June 1949 in various parts of Hoo Hill Piece, failed to produce a single sherd of Saxon pottery or fragment of burnt bone and it may be that the whole of the urn-field has been swept away by surface workings for sand, gravel or marl. Traces of such workings are visible in various places of Hoo Hill Piece. Nevertheless, the entry in the Davy MSS. is sufficiently precise to be accepted without hesitation. It is certain that there was a cremation cemetery of the pagan Saxon period either coterminous with Hoo Hill Piece, or impinging on it.

Advertisements in the East Anglian press and a note in the *Archaeological News Letter*,[84] as well as enquiries at the Ipswich and Bury St Edmunds Museums, have failed to bring to light any pottery or other finds from Rendlesham and it may be that no more pottery from the site will come to light.

A trace from the drawing in the Davy MSS. was submitted to Dr J. N. L. Myres, already at that time our leading authority on pagan Saxon pottery. His comments (16.1.49) were as follows:

> I am afraid I have not been able to find the original of your drawing of the A.S. pot from Rendlesham. But it is rather interesting that the closest parallel

> to it known to me is an urn in the Acton Collection at Bury St. Edmunds Museum, from an unknown site, presumably in Suffolk. This is also globular, with a narrow neck, $8\frac{1}{2}$ inches high, with the same sort of 'two decker' linear ornament separated by a group of horizontal lines on the maximum diameter. . . . It has no stamps, is in brown, gritty, smooth ware, and the linear ornament is very lightly drawn. The parallel is not exact, but this kind of thing is sufficiently uncommon to make it an interesting coincidence. I wonder if there is any chance of discovering where the pots in the Acton Collection came from. Apart from this, the nearest parallels to this variety of 'two decker' ornament that I know come from Sancton, Yorks, now at Hull. One is fairly close, a very much restored pot. . . . It has two stamps, filling some of the triangles made by the groups of chevrons. . . .

The Rendlesham urn, to judge by Davy's careful drawing (Plate 19) has in addition to two zones of chevron ornament of lightly incised lines on the body and a band of incised ornament on the neck, two lines of stamps in the form of a small five-lobed rosette. The pot is unusual as Dr Myres makes clear but it does not seem to possess any obviously early features. It was referred again to Dr Myres in August 1971, who commented as follows:

> Some further parallels, perhaps closer than those I mentioned in 1948, have turned up since. The closest is a pot found in 1955 in Pagham churchyard, Sussex, now in the Chichester Museum, which has the same tall globular shape with narrow neck and similar two-decker chevron decoration, but is much more elaborately stamped, with two different circular stamps all over the surface. Chichester Museum has a sherd from another pot of this kind (no. 1926) with the same large circular stamp, and there is a third example, apparently from the same workshop, in the Portsmouth Museum from N. Hayling (no. 66.59). In addition to the parallels I noted from Sancton, Yorks. (nos. 3 and 188 A in the Hull Museum), there is a rather similar one from Heworth, York, (no. 8 in the Yorkshire Museum) but this has a wider mouth. Another from Earsham, Norfolk, is in the National Museum of Antiquities, Edinburgh.
>
> I think the Rendlesham pot[85] and the Sussex ones are probably well into the seventh century, and form the end of a series with this type of 'two-decker' chevron decoration, of which the earlier examples running right through the sixth century are of more normal biconical or sub-biconical forms. One of the earlier sub-biconical examples, Loveden Hill, Lincs., 58/137, now at Lincoln, is conveniently dated by a Group II cruciform brooch.
>
> You ask about the Waldringfield pot in the B.M. I know of no others from Waldringfield, but it may be of interest in connection with the 'continuity' argument of the 1948 paper that this one came from the churchyard. It is of course a much earlier urn than the Rendlesham one.

CONCLUSION

It has, I think, been found possible to concentrate the search for the *vicus regius* into a fairly well-defined and manageable area, consisting largely of arable land which it should not be impracticable to keep under archaeological scrutiny from the air. In spite of the unfavourable subsoil a complex of structures such as we have visualized, if it was in the arable areas, could hardly fail, given suitable conditions, to yield some sort of indication to air observation. A programme of air survey spread over three years, so that each field could be studied under a suitable crop, might well reveal the site. If it did not, the negative evidence from the fields should serve to concentrate the ground search to the comparatively few and small plausible areas of woodland, heath and pasture. The worst prospect is that the site has been lost under the later halls and their gardens. It seems unlikely that such a group of structures as one might expect in the *vicus regius* would have been destroyed in any of the comparatively recent gravel workings, which have not been on a large scale, without some record having survived.

Documentary sources may also yield more information. Might it prove possible to relate the discovery of the precious metal crown 'about the year 1690', with some record of development that was being carried out at that time and so to discover where the supposed crown was found?[86]

TAILPIECE

On Fig 14 the printed name Thistly Belt may be seen some distance to the north of Hoo Hill Piece. To the east of this is a wood, at the south-east corner of which is a curious, roughly circular projection of trees into the arable and pasture, indicated by an arrow on the map. The wood is called Bush Covert. To the east of Bush Covert is a field. To the east of this field again is a small wood which bears the name of Hall Walls. Anyone studying the modern Ordnance Survey 6in map would naturally associate this name with the successive Rendlesham Halls that lie a little to the south. However, the name seems to have a different origin. There exists a sketch map of Rendlesham Park entitled 'Park Lands, 1828'.[87] This map Miss Redstone says 'looks like the work of Isaac Johnson of Woodbridge, one of the best known of our 18–19th century surveyors in Suffolk'.

A detail of this map is reproduced in Plate 20. This shows that the old name of Bush Covert was Woodenhall Grove. The field to the east of it was called Great Woodenhalls. The wood to the east of this again (Hall Walls on the

Ordnance map) is divided into Further Hall Wall and Middle Hall Wall and a field to the north is called Great Hall Wall. A piece of pasture to the south is called Little Woodenhall. These names seem to centre about the projecting circle of trees at the south-east corner of Bush Covert. It has been remarked above how names indicating, for example, Saxon heathen holy places, can survive as mediaeval or later field names, 'sometimes preserved in the boundary marks of estates described in land charters'. When one reflects that a great wooden hall and possibly a smaller one is what we hoped to find in our *vicus regius* and that the memory of a royal hall might well be expected to linger, this cluster of lost field names in a likely place, seems an odd coincidence. It is difficult to see how these names could have arisen in connection with the Tudor or later halls which were of brick or stone, or how they could very well have been applied to anything like a barn. The manorial history of Rendlesham[88] gives no suggestion that this was the site of a mediaeval manor house. The name might also possibly derive from Woden and have a pagan significance.

The probability is of course that the names are recent corruptions and no more than an instance of popular etymology. They cannot be traced further back in documents. The place-name specialists, Margaret Gelling and Kenneth Cameron, have given me their opinion. They feel that the name Woodenhall recorded at Rendlesham is likely to be a variant of Wood Hall or Woodhall, a rather common minor name in Norfolk, Suffolk, Hertfordshire, Lincolnshire and Yorkshire. The meaning of the compound does not seem to have been carefully considered by place-name workers. The reference books tend to prefer meanings such as 'hall in a wood' or 'hall for a forest court'. Some of the Woodhall place-names in eastern England must refer to ancient buildings since they are recorded in the mediaeval period. A case might be made out for *wudu-hall* being a technical term for a kind of wooden building but detailed studies of the whole group of such names would have to be made before it could be put forward. The form 'Woodenhall' does not seem to occur elsewhere as a place-name. This area and the projecting circle of trees (detached from Bush Covert in the 1828 map) should not be overlooked in any field work or air survey of the area. The ring is defined by a shallow ditch and another shallow ditch divides it centrally along its east-west axis into two parts. It may prove to be nothing more than an ornamental ring of trees such as exist elsewhere in the parkland. It is, however, at the back of the later halls close to the cultivated areas of the estate and the map shows that in 1828 it was not then a detached ring but a development at the end of a belt of trees that joined it to what is now Hall Walls. The names may prove not to have any significance for our purposes but at least they serve to make the point, at the conclusion of this survey, that apart from survey from the air, the best hope of finding the site, there is more investigation to be done both amongst documents and in the field. If a wooden hall were by any chance to be revealed in the fields bearing these names the name should be reviewed afresh in the context of all the other Woodhall, Wood Hall names in eastern England.

POSTSCRIPT

At the time of going to press, in 1973, no further clue has come to light as to the location of the *vicus regius*. It is important that the parish should be kept under observation and its few inhabitants made aware of the possibilities, for many changes are taking place. As has been mentioned, Mr David Sherlock has been keeping an eye on it. A trial excavation would still be worth attempting in the Wood Hall area, at the point suggested. Meanwhile a watch is also being kept on the parish from the air by Dr St Joseph, as occasion permits. Flying schedules are complicated by the presence of the American Air Force base.

NOTES TO CHAPTER TWO

1 For further details of Raedwald and the family tree of the Wuffingas, see Chapter One. The fullest account is in Vol. I of the definitive publication, Cambridge, 1974.

2 John Wodderspoon, *Historic sites of Suffolk*, Ipswich, 1839 and 1841, p. 115. I am indebted to Mr Leslie Dow for this reference.

2a London, 1631, p. 777. I am indebted to Miss Lilian Redstone, M.B.E., F.S.A., of Woodbridge, for this reference. In the Davy MSS. in the British Museum, referred to more fully below, it is said that there was a local tradition to this effect and that the then Rector, the Rev. Samuel Henley, D.D., F.S.A., 'this eminently learned orientalist' as Davy calls him, conducted a search in the parish church for the supposed royal remains. The suspected tomb proved to be mediaeval. Davy describes the episode as follows (*Add MS.* 19097, fol. 282r, 282v):

> Weever's authority and the prevailing tradition of the place, that two kings were buried here, induced Mr. Henley the Rector to examine in 1785 what appeared to have been the place of their interment. The spot was covered with two coarse flat stones, which being raised, proved to be slabs of two very fine figures of a Knight and his Lady . . . from the arms, which are Ufford and Valoines, I conceive this to be the monument of Robert de Ufford, 2nd of that name. . . . at a considerable depth under these slabs was found something like the dust of a human body.

3 Ipswich, 1946, 1. Mr Arnott's survey, unfortunately, stops short of Rendlesham.

4 Vol. I, 258.

5 Bede, Bk. II, Ch. xv. 'ab uxore sua et quibusdam peruersis doctoribus seductus est, atque a sinceritate fidei deprauatus habuit posteriora peiora prioribus ita ut in morem antiquorum Samaritanorum et Christo seruire uideretur et diis quibus antea seruiebat, atque in eodem fano et altare haberet ad sacrificium Christi et arulam ad uictimas daemoniorum.'

6 Camden does not say, any more than does Bede, that the temple was at Rendlesham, though his words may perhaps have given rise to that impression.

7 Richard Gough, in Vol. II of his 1789 edition of

Britannia, p. 86, realizing the absence of any foundation for these statements, reduces the Rendlesham entry to one sentence: 'At Rendlesham Suidhelm, King of the East Angles, was baptised by Cedda: but Bede nowhere says that Redwald kept his court here'. Suidhelm was in fact king of the East Saxons, not of the East Angles. Gough is here transmitting a mistake that occurs as early as Philemon Holland's translation.

8 1805 edition, Vol. II, p. 18. The first edition of this work, which was in five volumes, appeared between 1739 and 1775.

9 *loc. cit.*, fol. 271r.

10 Bede, Bk. III, Ch. xxii. 'In uico regio dicitur Rendlaesham, id est mansio Rendili'.

11 Bede, Bk. II, Chs. v, xxii, xv; Bk. III, Ch. xviii.

12 E. Ekwall in his *Oxford Dictionary of English Place Names*, 1936, has the following under Rendlesham:
'Rendel's HAM: Rendel must be a short form of names in Rand. Such names are not well evidenced in O.E. but are common in Scandinavia and on the Continent.' Bede may well have been paraphrasing.

13 Bede, Bk. III, Ch. xxii.

14 'Successit autem Sigbercto in regnum Suidhelm, filius Sexbaldi, qui baptizatus est ab ipso Cedde prouincia Orientalium Anglorum, in uico regio qui dicitur Rendlaesham, id est mansio Rendili; suscepitque eum ascendentem de fonte sancto Aediluald, rex ipsius gentis Orientalium Anglorum, frater Anna regis eorundem.' In other words, the East Anglian King, Æthelwald, acted as godfather to the King of Essex, in the same manner that Oswald of Northumbria had acted for Cynegils of Wessex at his baptism by Bishop Birinus at Dorchester.
(The English translation of Bede used in this book is that of Bertram Colgrave and R. A. B. Mynors, *Bede's Ecclesiastical History of the English People*, Oxford, 1969.)

15 It is doubtful whether the words *susceptique eum ascendentem de fonte sancto* can be held to imply the presence of a baptistry, or even of a font, which would in turn imply the presence of a church. The phrase may be no more than a conventional formula used by Bede to mean 'stand sponsor'.

16 See *Antiquity*, XX, 1946, 28, 30; *Fornvännen*, h. 2–3, 1948, 'Sutton Hoo: en svensk kunga eller hövdinggrav?' by Birger Nerman (with English summary).

17 H. Munro Chadwick, 'Who was he?', *Antiquity*, XIV, 1940, pp. 76–87.

18 For arguments against the view that the burial is of a foreigner see H. M. Chadwick, *loc. cit.*, 77; also R. L. S. Bruce-Mitford, *British Museum Provisional Guide to Sutton Hoo*, London, 1947, 42; 'Sutton Hoo and Sweden', R. L. S. Bruce-Mitford, *Archaeological News Letter*, Vol. I, No. 2, March 1948, 5–7; and Sune Lindqvist, 'Sutton Hoo and Beowulf', *Antiquity*, XXII, 1948. See Vol. I of the British Museum's definitive publication, *The Sutton Hoo Ship-Burial* by Rupert Bruce-Mitford, Cambridge, 1974, Ch. X, 'Who was he?', where the same ground is covered and Chadwick is brought up to date.

19 For the cenotaph problem see Vol. I, Chapter 8, of the British Museum's definitive publication, Cambridge, 1974, Summary and conclusions. There now seems only a bare possibility that the monument may have been a cenotaph.

20 See Rupert Bruce-Mitford, *The Sutton Hoo Ship-Burial, A Handbook*, London, 1972, pp. 19–21.

21 See Professor Margaret Deanesly, 'Roman traditionalist influence among the Anglo-Saxons', *English Historical Review*, LVII, 1943, 129–46.

22 Bede, Bk. II, Ch. xvi. 'Tantum uero in regno excellentiae habuit, ut non solum in pugna ante illum uexilla gestarentur sed et tempore pacis equitantem inter ciuitas siue uillas aut provincias suas cum ministris semper antecedere signifer consuesset, necnon et incedente illo ubilibet per plateas illud genus, uexilli, quod Romani tufam, Angli appellant thuuf, ante eum ferri solebat.'

23 T. D. Kendrick, *British Museum Quarterly*, XIII, 1939, 128.

24 See *Victoria County History, Buckinghamshire*, Vol. I, 1905, pp. 199–204; N. Åberg, *The Anglo-Saxons in England*, Uppsala, 1926, pp. 10, 11; *British Museum Guide to Anglo-Saxon Antiquities*, London, 1923, pp. 63–8; R. H. Hodgkin, *History of the Anglo-Saxons*, I, Frontispiece and Colour Plate II (buckle).

25 R. L. S. Bruce-Mitford, *British Museum Provisional Guide to Sutton Hoo*, London, 1947, 40, 41; S. Lindqvist, *loc. cit.*

26 No one doubts that these are royal burials and

they are particularly relevant to Sutton Hoo. The grave goods must have been subjected to intense heat on the pyre and hardly anything survives. Included in the fragments that do survive, are, from the West Mound, part of a gold cloisonné pyramid very similar to those found at Sutton Hoo but smaller (Pl. 10b) (Sune Lindqvist, *Uppsala Högar och Ottarshögen*, Uppsala, 1936, 179, Fig. 101) and from the East Mound, part apparently of a similar pyramid (*loc. cit.*, 170, Fig. 87) and a fragment of thin bronze sheeting from a helmet, stamped with a figure holding two spears (*loc. cit.*, 171, Fig. 89a). The details of this latter are so similar to those of the identical scene on the Sutton Hoo helmet as almost to suggest (Plate 14b–d) that the two may have been struck from the same stamp.

27 See Vol. I, Chapter X, of the British Museum's definitive publication, Cambridge, 1974, 'Who was he?'. Also J. Wallace Hadrill, 1971, pp. 69–71, which modifies the scepticism as to the royalty of the burial expressed in his Spoleto lecture, 'The Graves of Kings; an historical note on some archaeological evidence', *Studi Medievali*, 3rd series, I, 1960, 177–94.

28 G. F. Dimbleby's environmental study at the Sutton Hoo site has shown that the area was open heathland at the time of the burial and the site of the ship-mound itself under cereal crop. The slopes were bare. The English translation of *Beowulf* used is that of Kevin Crossley-Holland, Macmillan, 1968.

29 If it is accepted that the burial is royal, we need not doubt that the king in question belonged to the East Anglian dynasty. Bede's reference in connection with the baptism of Swidhelm, quoted above (note 14), makes it clear that the East bank of the Deben was East Anglian territory at the time. Chadwick (*loc. cit.*, 77) has further arguments to support the view that the burial was that of one of the Wuffingas and this receives strong support, in ways which cannot be elaborated here, from the study of the burial itself.

30 H. M. Chadwick, *loc. cit.*, pp. 77, 78: 'There is no evidence that the Kingdom (of Essex) ever extended beyond the mouth of the Stour'. It was certainly East Anglian territory in the seventh century, as Bede's reference, quoted above, and the other historical factors, already discussed, make clear.

31 I am indebted to Miss Lilian Redstone for this reference to Melton.

32 *Victoria County History, Suffolk*, Vol. I, London, 1911, p. 329.

33 See 'The removal of a tumulus on Martlesham Heath, Suffolk' by G. Maynard and H. E. P. Spencer: *Proceedings of the Suffolk Institute of Archaeology and Natural History*, 1947, pp. 3–24. The group of mounds on Martlesham Heath belongs to the Saxon period. (See also G. Arnott, *op. cit.*, 3). The only feature found in the excavation described in this report that might suggest this was the sand concretion reminiscent of the clay pans found at Sutton Hoo in 1939 and also apparently in 1938. (For the 1939 clay pan, see *Antiquaries Journal*, XX, p. 159 and Pl. XVII (a)). One of this group of barrows was earlier excavated by Mr J. Reid Moir, F.R.S., and proved to be Saxon in date. It contained a bone comb and iron rivets. Three others were investigated at this time. All were apparently of pagan Saxon date. The occurrence of Bronze Age sherds in the make-up of the tumuli at Martlesham and Brightwell Heaths puts these sites into line with the mounds at Snape and Sutton Hoo, where the same thing occurred. I am indebted to Mr Basil Brown for this information.

34 W. G. Arnott, *op. cit.*, 3.

35 N. Scarfe, *The Suffolk Landscape*, 1972, 98–102.

36 *Victoria County History, Suffolk*, Vol. I, London, 1911, Fig. 5.

37 Sutton Hoo, 1938 excavations, finds now in the Ipswich Museum. *Antiquaries Journal*, XX, 1940, 152, 3, and Sutton Hoo definitive publication, Vol. I, Ch. 2, Cambridge, 1974.

38 Illustrated in colour, *Victoria County History, Suffolk*, Vol. I, London, 1911, frontispiece, Fig. 1.

39 Ipswich Museum. See N. Åberg, *The Anglo-Saxons in England*, Uppsala, 1925, p. 103 and Table III, No. 118, p. 207. A bowl of this class was also found at Sutton Hoo in 1939.

40 Cf. also H. M. Chadwick, *loc. cit.*, 77.

41 I have not been able to discover the evidence upon which Professor Chadwick based his precise statement (*loc. cit.*, 77) that the crown was dug up in 1687.

42 *Victoria County History, Suffolk*, Vol. I, London, 1911, 332, frontispiece, and Pl. II (Figs. 2, 3 and 5).

43 See Chapter 3 and Pl. 23.

44 See *The Sutton Hoo Ship-Burial*, Cambridge, 1974, Vol. I, Ch. 2.

45 See Vol. I of the definitive publication, Cambridge, 1974, Chapter X, 'Who was he?', for a fuller treatment.

46 The Rev. Francis Blomefield, who was Rector of Fersfield in Norfolk, states that the capital of the Wuffingas was at Thetford (*loc. cit.*, 17, 18, and *History of Thetford*, 1739, 21). Thus (Topographical History) 'Uffa took the Government of the East Angles, in 575, and settled at Sitomagus [Thetford], the prosperity and grandeur of which city is allowed by all authors to be owing to the Saxon Kings making it the metropolis of their kingdom'. And later 'Redwald, the greatest of the E. Anglian Kings . . . made Thetford not only the seat of his government, but the metropolis of all the Saxon government'. Blomefield's statement has from time to time been repeated by later writers. It appears to be totally without foundation. Blomefield gives no authority for it and the most casual perusal of his books makes it clear that he freely used the most suspect sources quite uncritically to suit his own purposes. A little later he expresses his conviction that the Synod of 664 (the Synod of Whitby) was held in Thetford, again giving no authority. His main sources for this period seem to have been John Brame (first denounced by Sir Henry Spelman in the seventeenth century as a fabulous writer), Sammes (*Britannia Antiqua*), Fabian and Holinshed.

47 Æthelhere, Æthelwald's predecessor, was killed on November 15, 655, and it can be assumed that an international event such as Swidhelm's baptism would not have been arranged before the new year. (R. L. S. Bruce-Mitford, *British Museum Provisional Guide to Sutton Hoo*, London, 1947, 43, note 5.)

48 S. E. Rigold, 'The Supposed See of Dunwich', *Journal of the British Archaeological Association*, XXIV, 1961, 55–9. I am indebted to Mr David Sherlock for this reference.

49 Bede, Bk. III, Ch. xviii, says of Sigeberht, 'intraret monasterium, quod sibi fecerat'.

50 H. M. Chadwick, *loc. cit.*, 82.

51 Note 45 above. *Vita Sancti Botolfi Abbatis Ikenhoensis*; Mabillon (ed.), *Acta Sanctorum Ordinis S. Benedicti*, III (i), 1734.

52 In spite of the case made out by E. O. Blake in his edition of the *Liber Eliensis* (p. 222, note 1) for supposing it to have been Hadstock in Essex, Ralegh Radford, following Blake in preferring Hadstock, saw in the existing eleventh-century Hadstock church-plan, the vestiges of a much earlier Minster. The case for Iken is made by F. S. Stevenson in his paper, 'St. Botolph and Iken' in *Proceedings of the Suffolk Institute of Archaeology*, XVIII, 1924, 29–52. There are no grounds whatever for supposing Icenhoe to have been in Lincolnshire. Bede's account of Ceolfrith's visit makes it clear that the monastery was in East Anglia. I am grateful to Mr David Sherlock for information about Dr Ralegh Radford's arguments, put forward in a lecture.

53 Bede, Bk. II, Ch. xv: 'Tantum autem deuotionis Eduini erga cultum ueritatis habuit, ut etiam regi Orientalium Anglorum Earpualdo filio Radualdi persuaderet relictis idolorum superstitionibus fidem et sacramenta Christi cum sua prouincia suscipere et quidem pater eius Redwald iamdudum in Cantia sacramentis Christianae fidei inbutus est, sed frustra; nam rediens domum ab uxore sua et quibusdam peruersis doctoribus seductus est, atque a sinceritate fidei deprauatus habuit posteriora peiora prioribus, ita ut in morem antiquorum samaritanorum et Christo seruire uideretur et diis quibus antea seruiebat, atque in eodem fano et altare haberet ad sacrificium Christi et arulam ad uictimas daemoniorum. Quod uidelicet fanum rex eiusdem prouinciae, Alduuf, qui nostra aetate fuit, usque ad suum tempus perdurasse et se in pueritia uidisse testabatur.'

54 Bede, Bk. I, Ch. xxx: 'Cum ergo Deus omnipotens uos ad reuerentissimum uirum fratrem nostrum Augustinum episcopum perduxerit, dicite ei quid diu mecum de causa Anglorum cogitans tractaui; uidilicet quia fana idolorum destrui in eadem gente minime debeant, sed ipsa quae in eis sunt idola destruantur, aqua benedicta fiat, in eisdem fanis aspergatura, altaria construantur, reliquiae ponantur. Quia, si fana eadem bene constructa sunt, necesse est ut a cultu daemonum in obsequio ueri. Dei debeant commutari, ut dum gens ipsa eadem fana sua non uidet destrui, de corde errorum deponat et Deum uerum cognoscens ac adorans, ad loca quae consueuit familiarius concurrat. Et quia boues solent in sacrificio daemonum multos occidere debet eis etiam hac de re aliqua sollemnitas immutari; ut dedicationis uel natalicii

sanctorum martyrum, quorum illic reliquiae ponuntur, tabernacula sibi circa easdem ecclesias, quae ex fanis commutatae sunt, de ramis arborum faciant et religiosis conuiuiis sollemnitatem celebrent, nec diabolo iam animalia immolent, et ad laudem dei in esu, suo animalia occidant et donatori omnium de satietate sua gratia referant. . . .'

55 See Professor Lindqvist, *op. cit.* This interpretation of the Swedish connection at Sutton Hoo had long been under consideration by English scholars when Professor Lindqvist wrote. At the present state in our knowledge of the Sutton Hoo finds, it appears to fit our observations very well. See also 'Sutton Hoo and Sweden', by R. L. S. Bruce-Mitford, *Archaeological News Letter*, Vol. I, No. 2, March 1948, 5–7.

56 This illustration is taken from Professor Sune Lindqvist's great work on the monuments of Old Uppsala, *Uppsala Högar och Ottarshögen*, Stockholm, 1936, to which reference should be made for the full particulars. There is an exceptionally full summary in English.

57 See Sune Lundqvist, 'Uppsala hednatempel,' *Ord och Bild*, 1927, 641–54.

58 Olaf Olsen, 'Vorchristliche Heiligtumer in Nordeuropa und opferplätze in Mittel und Nordeuropa', *Symposium in Reinhausen bei Göttingen*, October 1968; Olaf Olsen: *Hørg, hov og Kirke*, København, 1969, Ch. IV, 116–66.

59 For such sites in the Scandinavian Iron Age see P. V. Glob, *The Bog People*, London, 1969, Ch. VI, 180 *et seq.*

60 Kyell Kumlien, 'Bishop Karl av Västoräs och Uppsala ärkesates flyttning', *Historiskt Archiv* 14, Stockholm, 1967.

Sune Lindqvist, Uppsala hedna-tempel och första Katedral, *Nordisk tidskrift*, 1967, 236–42.

Hans-Emile Lidén, 'From Pagan Sanctuary to Christian Church, *Norwegian Archaeological Review*, 2, 1969, 3 ff., with commentary by Olaf Olsen, 25 ff.

Eijnar Dyggve, *Mindesmaerkerne i Jelling*; *Form og tydning*, København, 1964.

The evidence of the Arkona Wendic temples reconstructed by Carl Schuchardt after excavation in 1921, Carl Schuchardt, *Arkona, Rethra, Vineta: Ortsuntersuchungen und Ausgrabungen*, Berlin, 1926.

Margaret Gelling, 'Place names and Anglo-Saxon paganism', *Univ. of Birmingham Historical Journal.*

61 The date of the Sutton Hoo ship-burial is exhaustively dealt with in Chapter IX, Vol. I, of the definitive publication, Cambridge, 1974.

62 Bede, Bk. II, Ch. xiii: 'Adiecit autem Coifi, quia uellet ipsum Paulinum diligentius audire de Deo quem praedicabat uerbum facientem. Quod cum iubente rege faceret, exclamauit auditis eius sermonibus diecens: "Iam olim intellexeram nihil esse, quod colebamus, quia uidelicet quanto studiosius in eo cultu ueritatem quaerebam, tanto minus inueniebam. Nunc autem aperte profiteor, quia in hac praedicatione ueritas claret illa, quae nobis uitae salutis et beatitudinis aeternae dona ualet tribuere. Vnde suggero, rex, ut templa et altaria, quae sine fructu utilitatis sacrauimus, ocius anathemati et igni contradamus." Quid plura? Praebuit palam adsensum euvangelizanti beato Paulino rex, et abrenuntiata idolatria fidem se Christi suscipere confessus est. Cumque a praefato pontifice sacrorum suorum quaereret, quis aras et fana idolorum cum septis quibus erant circumdata primus profanare deberet, ille respondit: "Ego: quis enim ea, quae per stultitiam colui, nunc ad exempium omnium aptius quam ipse per sapientiam mihi a Deo uero donatam destruam?" Statimque, abiecta superstitione uanitatis, rogauit sibi regem arma dare et equum emissarium, quem ascendens ad idola destruenda ueniret. Nonenim licuerat pontificem sacrorum uel arma ferre uel praeter in equa equitare. Accinctus ergo gladio accepit lanceam in manu, et ascendens emissarium regis pergebat ad idola. Quod aspiciens uulgus aestimabat insanire. Nec distulit ille, mox ut adpropiabat ad fanum, profanare illud, iniecta in co lancea quam tenebat, multumque gauisus de agnitione ueri. Dei cultus, iussit sociis destruere ac succendere fanum cum omnibus septis suis. Ostenditur autem locus ille quondam idolorum non longe ab Eburaco ad orientem ultra amnem Deruuentionem, et uocatur hodie Godmunddingaham, ubi pontifex ipse inspirante Deo uero polluit ac destruxit eas, quas ipse sacrauerat aras.'

63 *Ord och Bild*, Stockholm, 1927.

64 From *The History of the Kings Works*, Vol. I, 1963, Her Majesty's Stationery Office, pp. 2–4.

65 B. Hope Taylor, *Yeavering*, Her Majesty's Stationery Office, forthcoming.

66 *cf.* examples at Cheddar, Yeavering and the Viking camps of Trelleborg-type.

67 For Trelleborg and Fyrkat, see *Recent Archaeo-*

logical Excavations in Europe, London, 1974, Chapter VII (Olaf Olsen, 'Viking Fortresses in Denmark').

68 See A. W. Clapham, *English Romanesque Architecture*, London, 1930, Vol. I, Before the Conquest: Ch. II ('Church building under the heptarchy'). For the Greenstead timber church, see A. W. Clapham, p. 106, and *Royal Comm. on Hist. Mons*, Essex, ii, 112.

69 *Roman Britain and the English Settlements*, R. G. Collingwood and J. N. L. Myres, Oxford, 1936.

70 Yeavering and Cheddar, *op. cit.*

71 Such as Mucking; see *Recent Archaeological Excavations in Europe*, ed. Rupert Bruce-Mitford, London, 1974, Chapter Eleven.

72 I am grateful for Miss Redstone's advice on this point.

73 Quoted by W. A. Copinger, *Manors of Suffolk*, Vol. II, 1901, 322.

74 See below, p. 102.

75 Mrs Margaret Gelling tells me that the name Hoo does not indicate a burial mound or suggest a burial place and that the sense likely to suit the circumstances at Rendlesham is a low projecting piece of land in the bend of a river or 'in more level ground'. Would not the name Hoo Hill then be hard to account for? The archaeological site at Sutton Hoo is on an escarpment, it is true, but is a re-entrant rather than a projection. The name Hoo may have been attached to the spar which runs out a little to the north-west above Little Sutton Hoo Farm. But on the Norden survey of 1601, the name Hoo seems rather to be attached to the cluster of tumuli, which carry against them the name 'Mathershoe'.

76 The Butley River comes in from the east to rise at the south-east corner of Rendlesham parish. See J. B. Ward Perkins, 'The Priory Wharf or Landing Stage', 'Butley Priory, Suffolk', by J. N. L. Myres, W. D. Caroe and J. B. Ward Perkins, *Archaeological Journal*, XC, 1933, 260 *et seq.* Before the beginning of the nineteenth century, when the sea wall was built up the Butley River, the tide must have run right up to the Priory; in the Middle Ages, at Butley as elsewhere in East Anglia, there is evidence of great incursions by the sea and the Priory Grounds then abutted straight upon tidal marshes.

77 Sir Charles Bunbury, Bt., the owner of Naunton Hall, has observed a low but clearly defined causeway which crosses the southern angle of the meadow north-west of Naunton Hall, bounded on the west by the stream. This appears to run eastwards and to lead towards the mouth of the southernmost coombe. I have not had the opportunity of examining this construction, to which Sir Charles had kindly drawn my attention.

78 *loc. cit.*, fol. 294r. Davy copies it from 'An old book communicated by the Rev. Cuthbert Henley, Rector' in 1818. In this terrier the areas of the glebe lands are given to the nearest acre.

79 *Cp.* J. S. P. Bradford and R. G. Goodchild, 'Excavations at Frilford, Berks.', *Oxoniensia*, IV, 1939, 1–71.

80 By Miss Nina Layard. The finds are in the Ipswich Museum. *Archaeologia*, IX, 325–52; *Proceedings of the Society of Antiquaries*, XXI, 241 and 242–7. See also *Victoria County History, Suffolk*, Vol. I, London, 1911, 330–4. *Proceedings of the Suffolk Institute of Archaeology*, XIII, 1–19.

81 *East Anglian Notes and Queries*, I, 347.

82 *Collectanea Antiqua*, II, 233, Pl. XIV, Fig. 4 (now in the Ipswich Museum).

83 See R. G. Collingwood and J. N. L. Myres, *Roman Britain and the English Settlements*, Oxford, 1936, Map VII.

84 Vol. I, No. 10, 16.

85 A reference to the Rendlesham urn is to be found in J. N. L. Myres, *Anglo-Saxon Pottery and the Settlement of England*, Oxford, 1969, 41, note 1.

86 Camden's *Britannia* (Vol. I, Cols 445, 446).

87 I am indebted to Miss Lilian Redstone for bringing this map to my attention.

88 W. A. Copinger, *Manors of Suffolk*, 1909, Vol. IV.

CHAPTER THREE

The Snape Boat-Grave

Snape is an East Suffolk village on the north bank of the tidal estuary of the Alde, about five miles due west of the small coastal town of Aldeburgh (Fig 4). Here in 1862 and 1863 a pagan burial-ground was partially excavated.[1] It lay exactly half a mile due east of Snape church, immediately west of the point at which a minor road, running north and south past Snape Priory, crosses the west–east road from Snape to Aldeburgh (O.S. map reference 403593) (Fig 16).

The burials excavated in 1862 and 1863 were immediately north of the Snape–Aldeburgh road and their site would seem to be largely contained today by the enclosure marked on the Ordnance maps as 'St. Margaret's' – a private house – which lies in the north-west angle of the cross-roads. South of the road on older editions of the Ordnance Survey 2½ and 6in maps, two tumuli were marked opposite St Margaret's (Fig 16). This agrees with the contemporary accounts which state that the Snape–Aldeburgh road was driven 'between five or six[2] large barrows which stand on either side of the road'

> a matter of wonderment to the simple peasant – who in these latitudes is remarkably simple indeed – and by reason of the large size of some of them, to the more educated traveller who may wend that way . . . the road had run so close that it had cut off a considerable slice of one of them.[3]

The two south of the road were not excavated by the 1862–3 diggers but are said by them to have been opened, together with the three that lay north of the road, some twenty or thirty years since 'by some gentlemen who were supposed by the inhabitants to have come from London'. Of the waggon-load of vases and other things then said to have been taken away, nothing can now be traced. It may be that this earlier excavation came about in connection with the construction of the road, which besides separating the five barrows, must have disturbed a considerable number of cremation urns in the flat ground between.[4] The field on the south of the road was ploughed for the first time within memory in 1951. The easternmost of the two barrows, the one at the cross-roads, remains untouched and the other has disappeared, though when I visited the site in May,

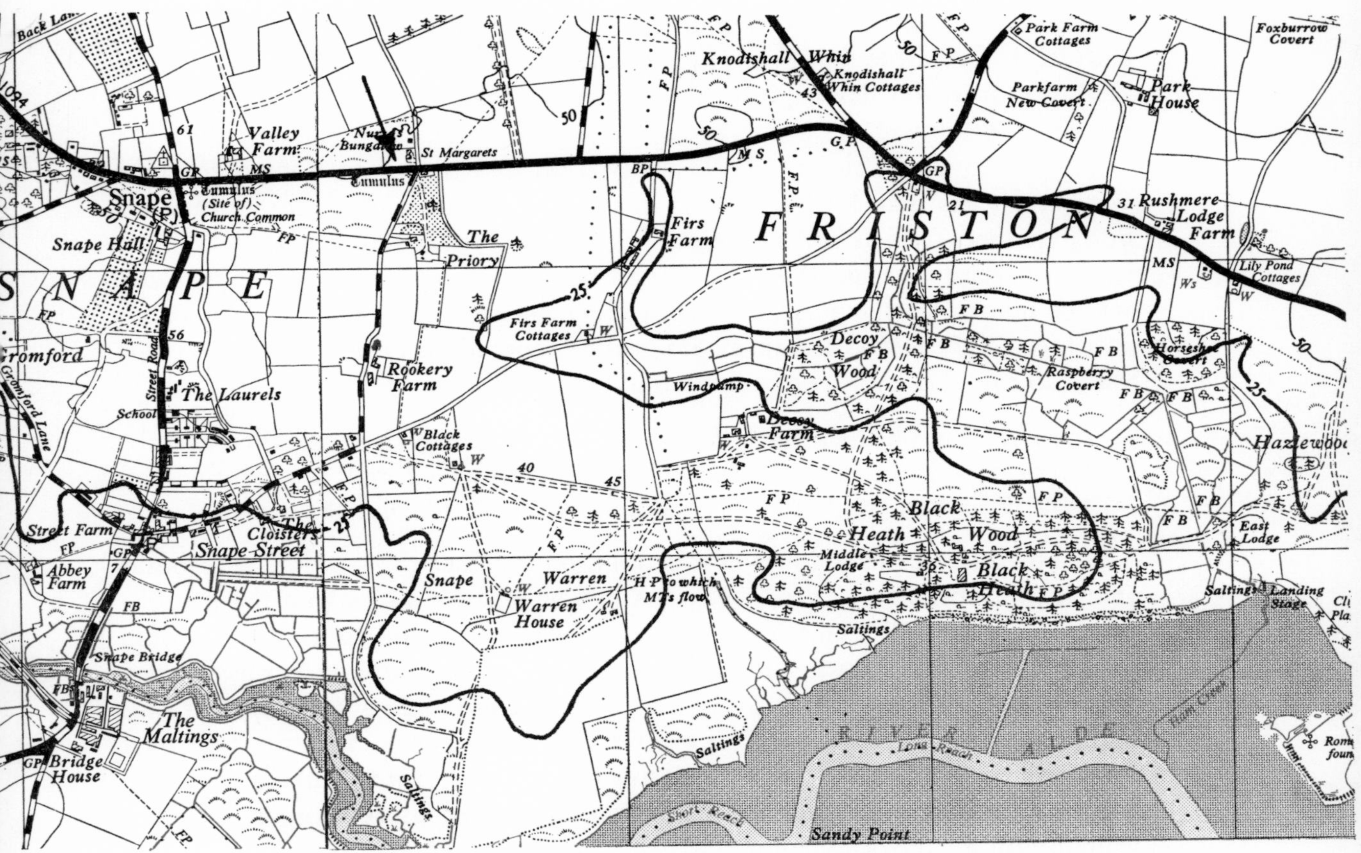

Figure 16 Map of Snape and the Alde Estuary showing the position of the Saxon burial ground (indicated by an arrow). The 25-ft contour line is thickened to emphasize the coombe by which the boat was no doubt brought to the place of the burial (Scale: $2\frac{1}{2}$ ins to 1 mile)

1951, it was still just possible to recognize the place of it in the ploughed soil some fifty yards to the west of the surviving mound. I was unable to find any recognizable remains of the three barrows to the north of the road, either in the garden of St Margaret's or the adjacent ground to the west.

Reginald Smith in the *Victoria County History*, repeating earlier accounts, says that the site lies 'halfway between Snape and Aldeburgh but rather nearer Snape'. It is in fact quite close to Snape, at the spot where the barrows referred to were shown on the map (Fig 16). Its proximity to Snape Priory has been confirmed by a number of letters to the writer from local residents and from members of the Swinburne family who lived in the Priory, where the finds, with the exception of the gold ring, remained until they were presented to the Museum of the Aldeburgh Literary Society at Aldeburgh apparently about the year 1911.[5] The site is on the fifty-foot contour-line and the cemetery comprised an urn-field in which stood at least five tumuli.[6] Beneath one of these, already robbed, the excavators found the first boat-grave of the Anglo-Saxon period to be recorded in England. In this lies the immediate interest of the site and the reason for its present re-examination.

The estuary winds along the vale below at distances from the mounds nowhere very much less than a mile at high tide but as in the case of the Sutton Hoo burial ground (which lies only nine miles to the south-west, Fig 4), a coombe runs in towards the site (Fig 16). Francis Francis, whose contemporary account will be quoted later, evidently thought it peculiar that so large a boat (its length was forty-eight feet as traced in the ground) should be buried so far from the water, for he says by way of explanation,

> there is no doubt that the Alde, which is navigable to smacks and colliers for a considerable distance higher up, did at one time, before it was confined by river walls etc., run within probably some one-third mile of the spot.

This is broadly correct, although it is doubtful whether the sea-level hereabouts at that time rose higher than today.[7] Allowing for this and taking the coombe into account, it still seems impossible that in pagan Saxon times a boat could have been brought by water at all close to the burial ground. It might have come as far up the coombe as the present site of Firs Farm Cottage (Fig 16), that is to within eight hundred yards of it, even if one could assume that the tide then rose as high as the present day twenty-five feet contour, that would come only to within about seven hundred yards. A very considerable effort of organized man-handling must have been required to get the boat to its place of burial.

THE DISCOVERY

Of the various accounts of the excavation listed in footnote 1, Reginald Smith's in the *Victoria County History* is a careful and judicious condensation of the rather confused earlier accounts and its substance need not be repeated here. Professor Birger Nerman, the Director of the National Historical Museum in Stockholm, has cast doubts upon the association of the ring, claw-beaker and other finds with the boat[8] and so upon the existence of a boat-grave at Snape at all and these doubts must be disposed of by reference to the original accounts.

In the summer of 1862, excavations had been taking place in all three mounds north of the road and quantities of cremation pottery, mostly sherds, had been found in the mounds. Mr Francis Francis's account in the *Field* goes on (the italics are mine):

> The remains being found all over the mounds, and at all levels, Mr. Davidson was induced to try lower yet, and go completely under *one of the mounds* and into the virgin, and as was supposed, undisturbed soil. Accordingly they trenched down deeply below *one of the mounds*: the soil here *lost all appearance of the black burnt strata* or the peaty colour and consisted of a *pure bright-yellow or golden sand. While digging in this* they came upon the remains of some woodwork. The wood was of course perfectly decayed though retaining its form and fibre. *Carrying the excavation further, the woodwork seemed to form a flooring of some kind.* Proceeding with the greatest care and caution they came upon a few fragments of glass, and close by it, a mass of human hair, about the covering for one head. It was dark dirty red. This hair, or the head upon which it formerly grew, (but of which no trace had been found) had been wrapped up in a cloth of some kind, for though the fabric had been entirely destroyed by decay, its texture and the warp and woof could be distinctly seen; about four feet from it was found another, but smaller mass of hair. No bones or traces of bones, as far as I could discover, were found. . . .
>
> The fragments of glass were all carefully collected, and, upon examination, proved to be the remains of a small vase of some kind; and while throwing out the sand a magnificent antique gold ring slipped out of the sand, and was pounced upon by my friend C.
>
> The body of the vase itself was of corrugated glass, while the glass itself was of the commonest known, being similar to our pale green bottle-glass. These things, the hair, and vase and the ring, with a small fragment or two said to be of jasper, lay apparently in the middle of the woodwork, which appeared so far to be the flooring of some wooden sarcophagus. *All around at equal distances lay small masses of iron* coated with sand and entirely oxidised.

The mass of 'dirty red' 'human hair', 'wrapped in a cloth of some kind', is worthy of note. Precisely similar finds occurred in both the Sutton Hoo ship-burial of 1939, and in the Broomfield, Essex, barrow.[9] The Sutton Hoo red hair has been identified by the Wool Industries Research Association as 'animal fibre, i.e. probably wool, dyed a dark brown' and it is clear, especially from the fairly well-preserved Broomfield remains, that these finds represent the remains of shaggy cloaks in which long matted tufts of animal hair or fur were inserted into a cloth base, in some cases during the weaving process and in others, after it. A detailed study of these remains of 'fur coats' will be given by Mrs G. M. Crowfoot and Miss E. G. Crowfoot in the account of the textiles in *The Sutton Hoo Ship-burial*, Volume 3.[10]

Francis Francis had been helping with the excavations for some time but happened to be away when the boat was discovered. His main account of it was written from verbal reports of his friend 'Mr. C.' who has been referred to already as 'pouncing upon the gold ring' and who was a principal in its excavation.

The day after the excavation 'Mr. C.' wrote a letter to Francis Francis giving further particulars and this is quoted in the *Field* account.

> We traced the pieces of iron *from one end of the trench to the other, without removing the pieces*; the result was this: I think we have most clearly and satisfactorily established that the pieces of iron were large rivets. On either side of the trench there were *six rows exactly corresponding, having the appearance of so many steps*; in fact they were the ribs of a boat, for the wood between them had all gone to decay. The rivets were all horizontal. Proceeding with our investigations, we came to the *flooring, where the rivets were vertical*, and also to the ends . . . the clear outlines of a vessel were apparent, *in the centre of which it was that we found the ring and the hair and the débris of the glass vase.* The boat was from 46 to 48ft. long and about 9ft. 9ins. or 10ft amidships. The woodwork at the bottom, although quite rotten, was sufficiently well-defined to show clearly what it had been.

Francis Francis adds 'subsequently the spot was visited by a naval gentleman, who quite confirmed all that remained doubtful as to the woodwork being that of a vessel'. The ring and the glass vessel are illustrated in Plates 21a–d and 23.

The glass, gold ring and other remains were thus found on the bottom of the boat ('on the wooden flooring') and 'in the centre of the boat'. It is not clear whether this latter expression means 'amidships', or 'on the centre-line', or 'keel-line'. Septimus Davidson refers to the finds as having been made 'in the boat, at one end'. His account is much less detailed on this aspect of the excavation, and much less of a narrative than that given by Francis Francis. The precise location of the finds need not be of any great significance, for the burial had been robbed and so disturbed. In the comparable and contemporary Swedish boat-graves, where the deposit is not concentrated in a central chamber as was the case in the Sutton Hoo ship-burial, the grave-goods are spread out over a longer length of boat. The general context is perfectly clear. They were found '*on the wooden flooring*', and '*all around at equal distances lay small masses of iron*', i.e. the boat-rivets. It may further be noted that the excavators were working in '*bright yellow sand*' well below the level of cremations and the black and sticky soil associated with them. In other words, their finds were insulated from the layers containing cremation material and they were not mixed up with the remains of other burials. The fact that they did not come from a cremation is in any case clear from their condition. As the illustrations show, the glass and the gold ring had never been through a fire, however imperfectly, and the presence of hair and of cloth vestiges again shows that the grave-goods had not been burnt. Since the boat had not been burnt either, then presumably being under a barrow and in the middle of a grave-field, it must represent a boat-inhumation and one would naturally assume that the remains of unburnt grave-goods found on its floor belonged to it. No other inhumations at all were encountered in the course of extensive trenching in the surroundings by the excavators. Thus it cannot be doubted that the finds belong to the boat and date the boat-burial.

The excavations were naturally carried out in a manner which leaves something to be desired by present-day standards and parts of Francis Francis's racy and entertaining account now seem hair-raising. 'We came on an urn,' he writes, 'and crush went the spade through a portion of it, fracturing the rim seriously.' His account of the method used to excavate a barrow shows that, as one might expect, neither the significance of the physical relationship of the various remains to each other in the ground, nor their stratigraphy, was realized.

'We worked from the centre towards the outside,' he writes, 'conducting the digging with the greatest caution, and rather under-digging and mining so as to let the upper mass of the earth, in which the remains might be supposed to lie, to fall in.' Nevertheless, it is quite clear that the work was carried out by careful and intelligent men in a scientific spirit. In view of the earlier history of excavations and rifling, they began their investigations 'with little expectation of gathering any results'.[11] They were as interested in the boat as in the conventional 'finds' and the accounts abound with interesting and intelligent observations, some of a stratigraphical nature, which illuminate the structure of the mounds and the character of the site as a whole. In particular we may be thankful for the excavation and record of the boat, a considerable task, which might so easily have been bungled by digging out the rivets as they were seen, or left incomplete and in a state of uncertainty. The work was carried out with great care, the excavators 'scraping and sweeping with the hands only between the rows of rivets'. We may be thankful also for the trouble taken by the excavators to collect almost every fragment of the shattered claw-beaker.

The original account also allows us to clear up a point with regard to the boat. In discussing it (*Antiquaries Journal*, XX, 1940, p. 191) C. W. Phillips refers to accounts which say that it had only six strakes a side, though he pointed out that if this were so the plan of the clench nails in the original publication (Fig 17) must be incorrect. 'Mr. C.'s' letter speaks of six strakes on either side *of the trench*, in which the rivets were all horizontal and *in between* a floor in which the rivets were vertical. Since the sides of the boat were roughly vertical (rivets horizontal), or 'at an obtuse angle from the floor upwards', as Septimus Davidson has it (Fig 17), and the gunwales were 9ft 9ins or 10ft apart amidships, the floor (that is, the flattening or flattened bottom of the settled boat) must have been of appreciable width – certainly more than one plank (the keel plank) – and this implies an additional two or three strakes a side for the boat.

The contemporary plan and section, not professionally surveyed but probably accurate in general,[12] shows an odd number of alignments of rivets, seventeen.

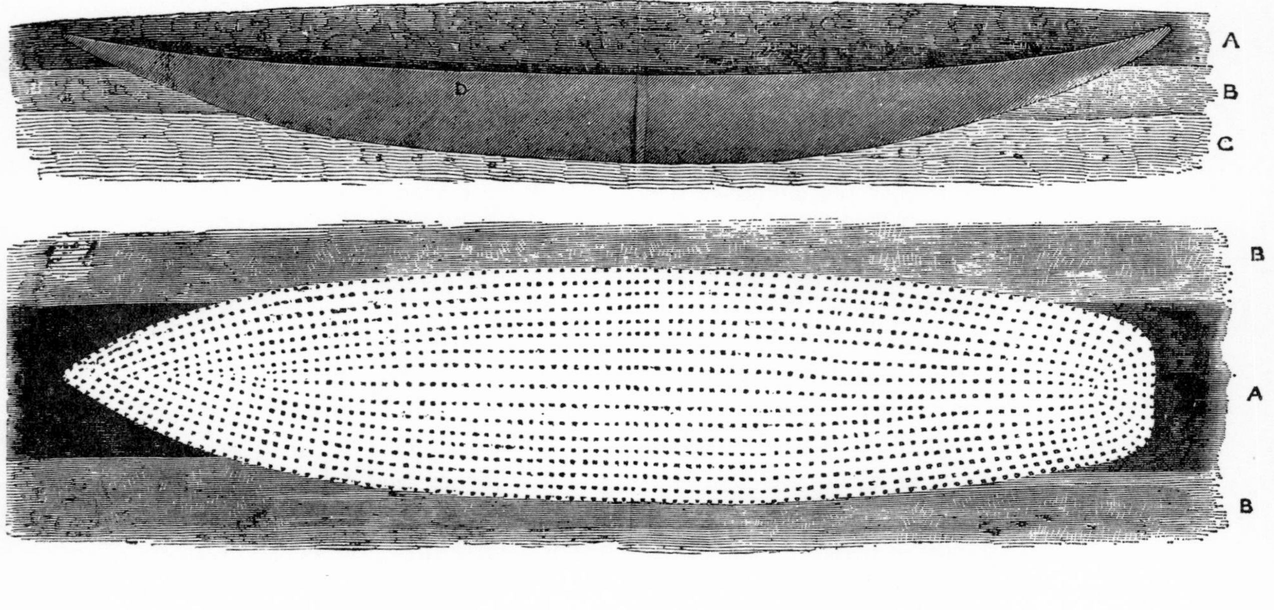

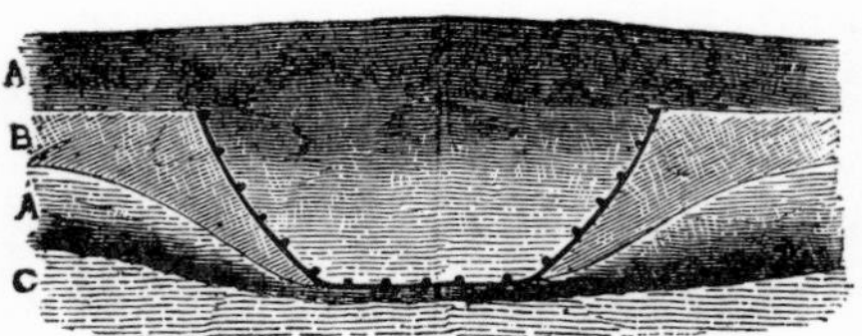

Figure 17 Plan and sections of the Snape boat: A, Black and white sand; B, reddish sand; C, yellow sand. (After Hele, *Notes on Aldeburgh*) (Scale: a little under 1 in to 8 ft)

The Sutton Hoo ship of 1939 had an even number, eighteen, and this would allow a narrow keel plank coming between the ninth and tenth alignments, counting from either side, these being the lines of rivets that would fix the lowest strakes on either side (garboard strakes) to the keel plank. The odd number seventeen, shown for the Snape boat, can hardly be correct since the halves of the boat must balance. The probability is that there were eighteen alignments in the Snape boat, not seventeen, and that its construction was the same in this respect as that of the Sutton Hoo ship but it is safest to say that the boat had either eight or nine strakes a side.

Septimus Davidson himself, in the account as given in *Proceedings of the Society of Antiquaries*, 2 Series, Vol. II, p. 177 *et seq.*, says that the rows were six in number on either side and four or five in the bottom of the boat. The probability is that the rivet pattern had been confused by repairing or patching, or by the appearance of heads of scarf-bolts, joining stem and stern to keel, in the middle of the keel plank fore and aft. The keel region in the Sutton Hoo ship, when re-excavated in 1967–8, was confused by repairs and accumulated stones and it was often difficult to identify the keel plank. The Science Museum plan, made before the ship lost its upper strakes through wartime damage, making it sometimes difficult to locate positions precisely, nevertheless contains inconsistencies.

In discussing the boat, it may be noted that its peculiar feature, the blunt stern as shown in the plan, is not referred to in the contemporary accounts. Two other observations by Septimus Davidson may also be noted. 'In each row of rivets, seven were included within a distance of 3 ft.' and 'All the rows terminated in two bolts lying parallel with each other, one at the stem, the other at the stern'.

In spite of the lack of any express statement on the point and the confusing accounts of the work, it is possible to deduce under which of the mounds the boat-grave was found. It lay under the westernmost and largest of the three on the north side of the road. There are various reasons for thinking this. First, there is nothing to indicate that it was under the smallest, easternmost mound, whose excavation is dismissed in a few sentences by Francis Francis and not even mentioned by the others. Secondly, it can hardly have been under the central mound, 60–70ft across, and 4ft 6ins high, which was the first to be opened. In this mound 'a wide and deep central excavation extending to a depth of several feet below the base of the mound' had already been made in which 'nothing was found' and 'it was obvious that the natural soil had not been disturbed'. The observant Dr Hele, who was present, says that the excavations were 'carried down to a depth of about 10-ft.' and that they then stopped, 'being satisfied the soil we were working had never before been disturbed, being red and yellow sand'. The depth of the boat was four feet as excavated, and its bottom is shown on the sections (Fig 17), which are drawn to scale, as six feet below the crest of the mound. It can thus hardly have been in a mound which had already been excavated to a depth of ten feet or thereabouts and into the natural soil. It is clear that the Bronze Age urn, the urn with batches of vertical grooves and swastikas and at least one other Saxon urn as well as the two iron spearheads which were found near the Bronze Age urn, all came from the westernmost mound. Septimus Davidson's account speaks of the deepening of the excavations, which resulted in the discovery of the boat, as following directly upon these discoveries. The western mound (like the central one) had a broad cutting right through it from margin to margin. As a large slice of mound on the south side had been cut off by the road, we can assume that this margin-to-margin cutting ran east and west, parallel with the road. This would also be the natural way to site a cutting, so that the spoil could be carried out freely from either end without encroaching on the highway. Such a long trench would be a necessary preliminary to the exposure of a forty-eight feet boat throughout its length. Dr Hele tells us that the boat lay east and west. For all these reasons there is no occasion to doubt that the boat was under the westernmost of the three mounds.

The dimensions of this mound are given by Septimus Davidson as 72 ft in diameter and 4 ft 6 ins in height. This is somewhat bigger than mounds 4, 6, 8, 9 and 11 at Sutton Hoo but smaller than 3, 5, 7 and 10, and of course No. 1, the ship-barrow.[13]

Of the finds mentioned in these accounts, the 'red hair', coarse sail-cloth, 'jasper fragments' and the two spear-heads said to have been found in one of the mounds are now missing. A considerable number of heavily-rusted iron boat-rivets, the fragments of the glass beaker and a good deal of cremation pottery comprising nine or ten complete or restored urns (some being from the 1863 excavation), and fragments of numbers of others, are now in the Ipswich Museum.

Nothing was known of the whereabouts of the ring, when the present re-scrutiny of the Snape discoveries was in progress. It was not among the Snape items given to the Aldeburgh Museum. It was a piece of considerable interest. Classical intaglios like that with which the Snape ring was set are otherwise unknown in pagan-Saxon archaeology. Three classical cameos and a plaque with a figural scene in late antique style, occurred in the West Mound at Old Uppsala in Uppland, Sweden.[14] When we remember that part of a plaque with a classical figure of a Winged Victory was found in the 1938 boat-grave at Sutton Hoo, there is a suggestion here that we have another curious parallel between the archaeologies of Suffolk and Uppland. In any case, the ring was obviously a fine piece, to judge by the engraving published by Septimus Davidson, and the details of its filigree work seemed to offer the best evidence for allotting a fairly precise date to the burial.

Another point of interest has made the ring a subject of international discussion. One of many reasons for supposing the Sutton Hoo ship-burial of 1939 to have been a cenotaph is the absence of any intimately personal objects from the burial deposit and the absence of a finger-ring had been given as an example.[15] Nerman claimed that this had no bearing on the presence or absence of a body at Sutton Hoo, since finger-rings never occurred in any of the related Swedish boat or other graves in the Vendel period (later sixth to eighth century) in spite of the fact that finger-rings were a distinctive feature of Scandinavian archaeology in both the preceding and succeeding periods.[16] To this it was replied that even if finger-rings were conspicuously absent in Vendel-period archaeology in Scandinavia, they were quite common in the Anglo-Saxon graves of that time in England and had in fact occurred in an East Suffolk boat-grave, since the Snape burial had certainly contained a gold ring, which was also a particularly fine specimen.[17]

Nerman was not to be persuaded by this since he doubted whether the Snape objects were found in the boat or whether the Snape discoveries represented a boat-grave at all. The Snape ring was thus from many points of view an object of great interest and since a piece of such obvious and intrinsic value was unlikely to have been lost, the writer made strenuous efforts to trace it. Letters were written to the Ipswich Museum, the Aldeburgh authorities, the Vicar of the parish and other local residents and clues provided were followed up. But the descendants of the excavators could not be traced and the search had reached a dead end when the following letter, addressed to the Secretary of the British Museum and dated 24th November, 1950, appeared on the writer's desk:

21 Addison Gardens, W.14.

Dear Sir,

My father, the late Hugh Morgan Davidson, had in his possession an antique ring found during the opening of a burial mound at Snape in Suffolk. It was always his wish that you should accept this ring for your collections after his death.

An account of the finding of the ring, I believe a photograph of it, appears in a book of notes on Aldeburgh by Dr. Hele. My grandfather Septimus Davidson was present at the opening of the mound, and was I believe the finder of the ring.

If you would be so kind as to give me an appointment I shall have great pleasure in bringing it to you.

Yours faithfully,

(Mrs.) W. M. Christie.

It was pure coincidence. It need hardly be said that an appointment was made with alacrity and that the ring is now in the British Museum (1950, 12–6, 1), so that a detailed publication with photographs is now possible. The National Collections are indebted to Mrs H. M. Davidson, into whose ownership the ring had passed, for the gift in accordance with her late husband's wish. 'I should like this to be presented to the British Museum, as it is in my opinion a National treasure.' No further information was forthcoming from Septimus Davidson's descendants about the jasper fragments or other missing items.

THE FINDS

1. *Large gold ring* (Plate 21a–d), weight 14 grammes; diameter of hoop (internal) 9/10ths inch or 2·2 cms; width of bezel (outside measurement giving maximum width of ring) 9/10ths inch or 2·2 cms. The central raised setting for the gem is surrounded by a beaded gold wire and contains a late antique onyx (nicolo)

intaglio, with bevelled edges, bearing on the flat central portion a nude male figure personifying BONVS EVENTVS (a happy outcome) holding two ears of corn in his right hand and a libation bowl (showing faint horizontal flutings, possibly unintentional) in his left. The hair is dressed in a roll. The stone is primarily black and this is the colour of the bevelled edge. The flat central part in which the figure is carved is a pale milky blue. The oval gem is set with its long axis at right angles to the hoop, not as usual with classical rings, in the same alignment. This gives the bezel unusual width. The broad shoulders thus provided are richly embellished with filigree scrolls, comprising on each shoulder an elongated 'hook' motive of hook-and-eye type, the 'hook' separating two opposed S-scrolls, which have a single gold granule in each terminal. The filigree scrolls, executed in twisted wire, are set about with granules, most but not all of which were surrounded by individual beaded-wire collars. The bezel and both ornamented shoulders are included within another outer beaded-wire border. The '*äquator-schnitt*' (a cut across each bead along its maximum diameter) is nowhere present. The hoop of the ring is broad and flat and carried a milled or barred central moulding flanked on either side by two raised lines. At either end of the hoop, where the shoulders begin to develop, and outside the beaded-wire border that encloses the filigree-work, is a transverse line of four collared granules (one missing) giving the impression of rivet-heads. The internal diameter of the ring is unusually large. It must have been worn by a man, either on the thumb or forefinger.

The fields that contain the filigree work on the shoulder of the ring show a matt, unfinished surface which no doubt made it easier for the solder, by which the filigree is affixed, to grip. The remaining gold surfaces are smooth and polished. The shoulders, 'dummy rivet-heads' and the bars and beads on the hoops show clear signs of wear and suggest that the ring had been in use for an appreciable period of time before it was buried.

The ring was previously known from the engraving published by Septimus Davidson, *loc. cit.*, p. 181, and repeated in Hele's *Notes about Aldeburgh*, and by Reginald Smith in the *Victoria County History*.

2. *Glass claw-beaker*, in many fragments, including seven claws and most of the rim, the foot missing (Plate 23). Above the claws the wall is practically straight. The rim leans outwards and is slightly thickened at the lip. The metal is bubbly, olive green in colour, rather like that of the Taplow Barrow vases but duskier and with wisps of rich brown pigment conspicuous in the claws. There were eight broad-lobed claws with lobes and shafts well inflated and hooked out completely *à jour*. The claws are arranged in two tiers. Each claw has a vertical overtrail covering the central hook-channel, six of these are notch-tooled, the

seventh is plain. The shafts of the claws in the upper tier are drawn well down the vase between the claws of the lower tier. The claw shown in Plate 23 had an overall length of at least three and a half inches. The vase has a distinct waist between the two tiers, the lobes of the lower claws resting on a bulge of the vessel. The upper trail extends to 2·7 ins below the rim and is of twenty-six or twenty-seven close-set lines. The lower trail is clear of the lobes of the lower tier and is of fine execution, with thin fully rounded lines thickening (as is usual) towards the bottom of the vase. Wall-thickness, 1 mm or under, is practically uniform except where features (cf. claws, rim) develop.

Estimated diameter of mouth: 9 cms (3·6 ins).

Estimated height: 18·5 cms ($7\frac{1}{4}$ ins).

3. Numerous *iron boat-rivets* (Plate 24), much corroded, among which the following appear to be represented: (i) Rivets with circular domed heads and diamond-shaped roves, heads and roves *c.* 1·2 ins apart (Plate 24d,k,m). (ii) Rivets of the same form, heads and roves *c.* 1·75 ins apart (represented by Plate 24f). (iii) Rib-bolts: a 2·5 ins length preserved, of something more massive and longer than the clench nails (Plate 24h). (iv) Portions of iron strip, of uncertain original length and purpose, through which iron bolts are fixed (Plate 24i,j). Of three bolts associated with such strips, one shows a length of 1·75 ins, one 1·5 ins and the third 1 in between the rove and the inner face of the iron strip.

The iron objects are much corroded and incrusted with sand and radiography yields no further information, beyond providing a nice illustration of the typical rivet form with diamond rove and domed circular head (Plate 24l, m).

Some of the rivets illustrated have been subjected to cleaning by mechanical means (picking and scraping) and the shapes and dimensions of the shafts are not necessarily those of the original rivets. The radiograph probably gives a truer impression of the original, in this case a plank-joint pin.

FINDS NOT PRESERVED

The following, mentioned in the accounts of the excavation, are not now preserved:

4. A mass of dingy-red hair, with a smaller mass found four feet away.
5. Coarse 'sail cloth', in which the hair was wrapped.
6. Some fragments described as jasper.
7. Part of a second glass vessel. In describing the glass that was collected, Francis Francis says: 'One small fragment alone however differed from the rest, and

belonged evidently to some other vessel which was not present.' Later he adds to this description as follows:

> The solitary other piece of glass found amongst the fragments of the glass itself is also a point of consideration as it differs entirely from all the other fragments, being more of an opaque blue, and being a thicker glass and of better manufacture, more in fact like a fragment of Roman glass. (*The Field*, January 24th, 1963, p. 75).

8. Two iron spear-heads, found near the Bronze Age urn, that is, over the boat-grave in the westernmost mound. One spear-head remained attached to a portion of its wooden shaft. These spears were no doubt derived from the primary inhumation, that is, from the boat-grave, which had been ransacked.

Nos. 4 and 5 may be treated as a unity as discussed on page 117 above.

ARCHAEOLOGICAL COMMENT AND THE DATE OF THE BOAT-GRAVE

The Snape finger-ring is the finest ring of the pagan Saxon period yet found and is of the highest quality. The nicolo intaglio evidently came from a Roman finger-ring and very possibly from a Romano-British one. Such onyx (nicolo) intaglios, in which the design, usually a single figure, is cut in the bluish-white layer on the darker background, were very common in Roman Britain[18] and the style of engraving of the Snape intaglio agrees closely with that of numerous Romano-British nicolo-intaglio finger-rings in the British Museum collections. The gold ring and setting is Germanic work, built and designed to take this particular intaglio gem. Where was the ring made and when? In the early post-Roman period or in the sixth or seventh century? It is the only item that survives from the burial which may permit of the fixing of its chronological horizon with some precision and any hopes of attempting to date the burial must look principally to it. Since my original publication of it, Joachim Werner has argued that the Snape ring is of continental manufacture[19] and this point and its chronological implications must be considered separately. The ring may also be considered as Anglo-Saxon and, adopting this assumption for the time being, we may consider how it fits in with the background of Anglo-Saxon archaeology from the point of view of its date.

From this point of view, two features of the ring are distinctive if it is considered as native work: the 'hook-and-eye' filigree motive and the granulation. The S-scrolls of the Snape ring, which occur in Romano-British gold work, for example on the New Grange ring,[20] are common in Anglo-Saxon gold jewellery of the later sixth and seventh century. The hook-and-eye motive on the other hand is extremely rare in Anglo-Saxon work. The only occurrences known to me amongst the English-found material are on the two gold clips fitted to the hilt of the Sutton Hoo sword (Plate 25d,e); on each of the three gold bracteates found together at Milton Regis near Sittingbourne, Kent, in 1915 or 1916 and now in the British Museum (Plate 25a–c) and on an unusual gold ornament, certainly imported, from Faversham, Kent, also in the British Museum (Plate 25f). This latter is an early piece and probably of the late fifth century. The bracteate-pendants were said to have been found with six silver *sceatta* coins and, if so, could hardly have been deposited much before *c.* A.D. 700, the now accepted date for the emergence of the silver *sceatta* currency. The association however is suspect.[21] One of the three pendants (Plate 25f) has an unusual design and on it gold granules appear as eyes for small filigree zoomorphic heads. In some ways, in particular in the use of collared granules and the open, rather bitty filigree, the closest parallel to this piece is a rather similar bracteate, no doubt of English origin, in the heterogeneous treasure found at Hon in Norway,[22] deposited in the ninth century. On the whole the general complexion of these pendants, quite apart from any connection with the *sceattas*, is very late in the pagan period, or even well into Christian times. The closest parallels in the execution of the hook-and-eye device to the Snape ring are on the Sutton Hoo sword-clips (Plate 25d,e). The Faversham ornament is a parallel for the hook-and-eye device but a Frankish import is not a guide to the dating of Anglo-Saxon work. The two little gold fittings of the sword-grip are of different sizes and made to fit onto opposite sides of the grip, which was evidently asymmetrical. It seems clear that they were made for the Sutton Hoo sword, not transferred from some other weapon, and they should be no older than the sword itself, the sword having been buried with the other treasures as we now think *circa* A.D. 625. The Krefeld-Gellep grave 1782 suggests that the sword of itself could well be of mid-sixth-century date (pp. 129–31 below and *cf.* Plate 12).

The other distinctive feature of the filigree-work that helps us to date it, if the ring belongs to the Anglo-Saxon context, is the use of granulation. The closest parallels to the granulation on the Snape ring are the late pendant of pale gold from Breach Down, Kent (Plate 25g),[23] with Celtic cross design; the ornamental pin from Wingham, Kent (Plate 25h),[24] which had a bird's head design in cloisonné garnets, with cabochon garnets for eyes and the remarkable and highly distinctive buckle of silver and pale gold from Crundale Down, Kent (Plate 25i),[25] all in the British Museum and all quite possibly dating to the second half of the seventh century. While granulation is of early occurrence in Scandinavia, for example on Norwegian scabbard-mounts such as those from Egge, Opland and Etne, Hordaland,[26] and still earlier on the great gold collars and other objects of the Migration period,[27] it appears as a late development in West Europe and typical of the ninth century and of the Carolingian, Ottonian and Viking periods.[28] In Anglo-Saxon archaeology, pieces such as the eighth- and ninth-century rings from Meux Abbey, Garrick Street, London and Stockbridge, Hampshire (Ehlla's ring),[29] or the Kirkoswald trefoil brooch[30] and the animal-snout of the Alfred Jewel in the ninth century and the openwork border of the tenth-century cloisonné enamel Dowgate Hill Brooch,[31] may be quoted as examples of increasing use and development of granulation in later Saxon times. In Anglo-Saxon jewellery the fashion may be seen beginning in a small way on quite a number of well-known pieces in the earlier part of the seventh century.

For example, the eyes of the bird's heads in filigree on the back of the Kingston brooch (Plate 26a)[32] and on a remarkable little gold buckle with zoomorphic filigree from Faversham in Kent (Plate 26b)[33] are individual gold balls in collars and small individual gold pellets each in a wire annulet are set in and between the heart-shaped filigree scrolls in the outer-zone of decoration of the gold pendant from Faversham, Kent, which has three birds' heads in triquetra arrangement in cloisonné step-pattern garnet work (Plate 26c).[34] A line of collared granules appears round the toe of the belt-buckle in the Taplow Barrow (Plate 26d).[35] The Snape ring, Wingham pin-head, Breach Down pendant and Crundale buckle, all show granulation liberally used and well established. These are the closest parallels, on which individual granules are set about in the terminals of the filigree S-scrolls as on the Snape ring and the Wingham pin-head, whereas on the Snape ring some of the granules set about in the field are with collars and some deliberately without. The Crundale buckle, with its running knot interlace in the borders terminating in snakes'-heads seen from above, its unique cloisonné scale-pattern on the tongue-shield reminiscent of the bird's wings of the Lindisfarne Gospels, its Book of Durrow style animal sketch on the back plate (Fig 18)[36]

Figure 18 Unfinished sketch of an animal in Book of Durrow style, from the back of the Crundale Down Buckle (Scale 2 : 1)

and its developed use of granulation, can hardly be any earlier than A.D. 650 at the earliest. Finally, granulation is used on one of the Sutton Hoo shoulder-clasps in the fields between the legs of the intersecting boars at either end of the clasp (Plate 26e). The clasps, though not in mint condition, give the impression of being almost the latest pieces of cloisonné jewellery in that dated find. They can scarcely be earlier than *c.* A.D. 600 and I would regard them as quite possibly part of a regalia made for Raedwald *c.* A.D. 615.

In view of these parallels, I find it difficult to assign the manufacture of the Snape ring, if it is Anglo-Saxon work, with its combination of hook-and-eye filigree, granulation using large granules with and without collars and S-scrolls with a granule in each terminal, to a date much earlier than *c.* A.D. 600 and its burial consequently to any date much before around A.D. 615 since there are signs of wear on the shoulders which show that it must have been worn for some little while before burial. On the evidence of the ring then, if this is Anglo-Saxon, the Snape boat-grave can, I suggest, be safely placed no earlier than the first quarter of the seventh century.

The claw-beaker cannot be dated with anything approaching the weight of evidence that bears on the ring. One can only say that it belongs to the middle phase of claw-beaker evolution. In the spacing and dove-tailing of the claws, with the shafts of the upper tier drawn well down between the claws of the lower tier, in the concentration of the claw-lobes into a narrow zone at the middle of the vase; in the rim form, the character and extent of the two horizontal trails, the shape of the claws and the character of their notch-tooled overtrails, especially the narrow, lightly nicked rods on the lower claws and even in the general colouring of the glass, though greener than most, the vase belongs with the vases of the Newport Pagnell, Howletts, Fairford and Westbere group.[37] The Westbere vase is particularly close. Yet the Snape beaker with its waisting and greater height, its fullness of claw and general fine quality, also shows affinities with the vessels of the Reculver type;[38] and in its tendency for the elongation of the claws, seen in those of the upper tier which attain a length of at least three and a half inches, suggests a movement towards the tall Taplow-type beakers with prolonged claws, of the seventh century.[39] On the whole it may be attributed to the latter part of the sixth century.

The solitary small fragment of thick blue glass is of great interest. It almost certainly, from its thickness and colour, represents a squat bowl of the small Cuddesdon-Broomfield group, a further example of which was found in the small boat-grave at Sutton Hoo in 1938.[40] This type of bowl is late in the pagan-period glass series (seventh century) and is probably the product of a Kentish glasshouse.

We must now consider the argument brought forward by Joachim Werner[40a] to the effect that the Snape boat-grave dates from the first half of the sixth century, at the latest from around A.D. 550. His case for this early dating rests upon two factors, first, that the Snape ring is of Continental, not Anglo-Saxon, manufacture and finds a close counterpart in the princely grave from Krefeld-Gellep, No. 1782,[41] a grave which has been dated to *c.* A.D. 550; and, secondly, that the claw-beaker, which is agreed to be Continental, belongs to the earlier type found in various Continental grave groups of the second half of the fifth century or the first half of the sixth. On the strength of the early date he assigns to these two pieces, Werner assigns the burial also to *c.* 550 at the latest. This is clearly a matter of the greatest importance since the Snape boat-grave, if dated to the first half of the sixth century, would become the earliest boat-grave in Europe, going back, apparently as an established form of burial (p. 132 below), to a period before the earliest boat-burial hitherto claimed, that at Augerum, in south-east Sweden, rehabilitated by Birgit Arrhenius. It would raise the possibility that boat inhumation, in the form known to us from Vendel and Valsgärde, originated in south-east England, probably in East Anglia; and it would raise also the whole question of the priority of England or Sweden as the source of elements in the rich and distinctive Vendel culture of Sweden, which appear to indicate a direct connection between the two areas. It would also, as Werner pointed out, affect the question of the period at which the Wuffingas came to be established in East Anglia and the origins of the dynasty. It should be said firstly that of course it is risky to date any burial on the strength of two solitary items that happen to have survived, out of what must have been a very rich inventory. If one of the items so to survive had a firm date, as for example the gold solidus of Anastasius (A.D. 491–518) in the Krefeld-Gellep *fürstengrab*, this would provide a precise *terminus post quem* (post A.D. 491). The two items in the Snape burial give us only a vague *terminus post quem* – after the date of their manufacture, whenever that may be. If both the ring and glass are themselves early, it does not of course necessarily follow that we have to accept a correspondingly early *terminus ad quem* for the burial.

A burial has to be dated from the latest object in it. Who can say what later items the Snape deposit might not have contained? In the case of Krefeld-Gellep, grave 1782, this was an intact deposit and from the wide range of objects, none of which need be later than *c.* A.D. 550, a consistent picture emerges. To take the two surviving items from the Snape boat-grave severally; the finger-ring is a classic candidate for the heirloom category which we must always be alert for amongst the grave-goods of the period. A very fine and costly ring of this kind could easily remain in use for a couple of centuries before burial. The Snape ring shows considerable wear, as has been said, and beyond providing a *terminus post quem* is of no use in dating the burial. It certainly cannot be used to provide a *terminus ad quem*.

It might be supposed that the glass claw-beaker would be of more value for purposes of dating, since glass vessels are fragile and, *a priori*, unlikely to survive. Yet in the Krefeld-Gellep grave 1782, it is precisely this fragile glassware that proves to be the oldest element in the grave, both the engraved bowl and the

a

b

c

d

Plate 21 The Snape Ring: *a*, Side view; *b*, Back view; *c*, Front view; *d*, Detail with a plaster cast from the antique central moss-agate intaglio, showing the figure of *Bonus eventus* (Scales 3 : 1)

a

b

c

Plate 22 a–c, Three views of the gold ring from Krefeld-Gellep (grave 1732) (Scales *a*,*b*, 2 : 1; *c*, 4 : 1)

Plate 23 Fragmentary glass claw-beaker, Snape boat-grave (reduced)

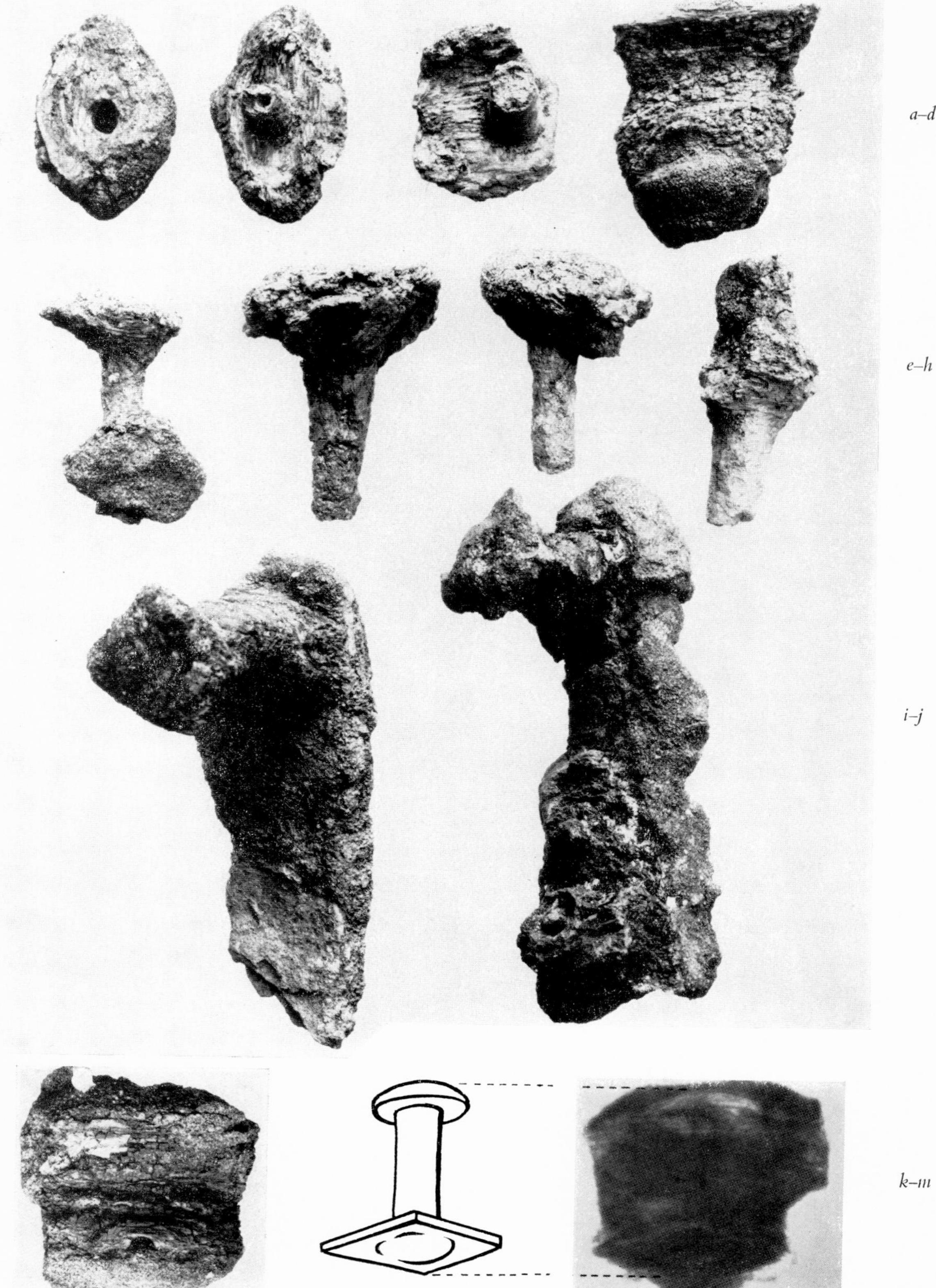

Plate 24 a–j, Iron rivets, bolts and cleats from the Snape boat;, *l*, sketch of a plank-joint pin (*k*), based on the radiograph (*m*) (Scales 1 : 1)

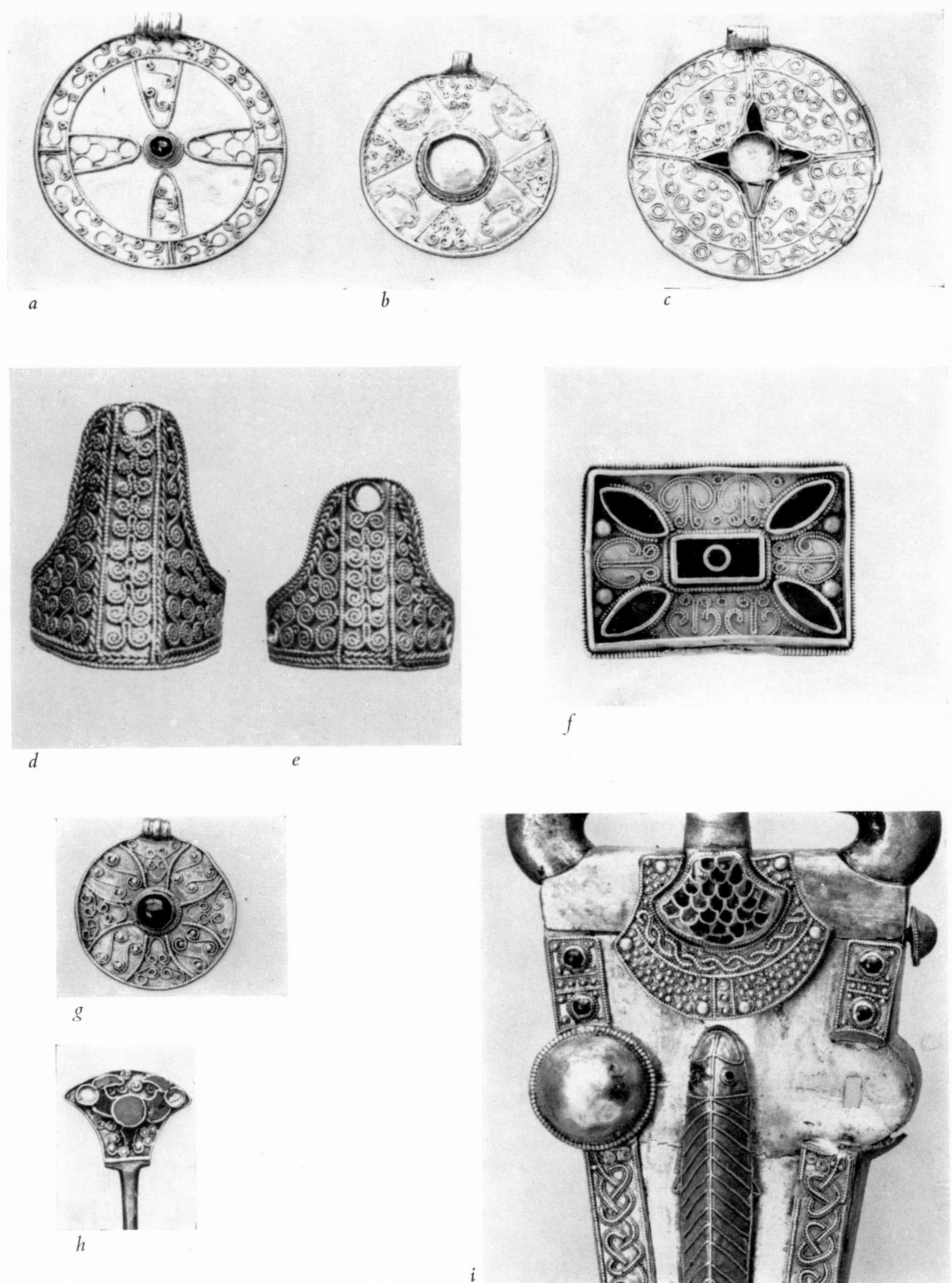

a *b* *c*

d *e* *f*

g *h* *i*

Plate 25 Examples of gold filigree work: *a–c*, Three gold bracteates, Milton Regis, Kent; *d,e*, Gold clips with filigree decoration, the sword grip, Sutton Hoo, Suffolk; *f*, Gold ornament, Faversham, Kent; *g*, Pendant of pale gold, Breach Down, Kent; *h*, Head silver and gold pin, Wingham, Kent; *i*, Detail of silver and gold buckle, Crundale Down, Kent (Scales *a–c*, *f–i*, 1 : 1; *d,e*, 2 : 1)

a

b

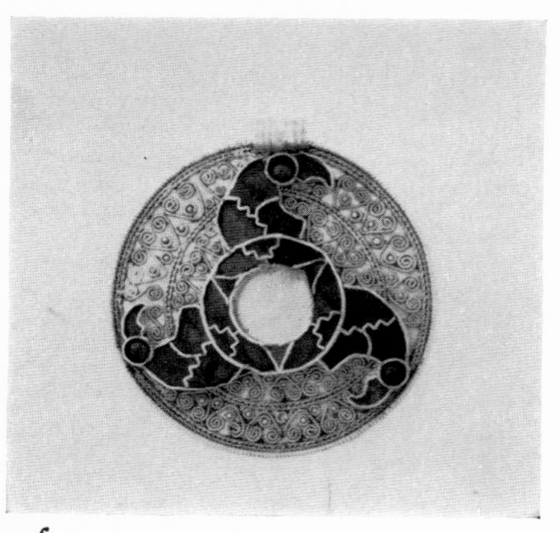

c

d

e

Plate 26 a, Kingston Brooch back view, Kent; *b*, Gold buckle, Faversham, Kent; *c*, Gold pendant with triquetra design of bird's heads, Faversham, Kent; *d*, Gold buckle detail, Taplow Barrow, Bucks; *e*, Detail from one of the pair of gold shoulder clasps, Sutton Hoo, Suffolk (Scales *a–d*, 1 : 1, *e*, enlarged)

Plate 27 Basil Brown in 1939, standing in the Sutton Hoo ship impression

Plate 28 The Sutton Hoo ship re-excavated, 1967

handled jug being fourth-century pieces and some two centuries old before they came to be buried in the Germanic *fürstengrab*.[42] Thus even if we accept Werner's dating of the glass vessel and the ring, they cannot help us to assess with any assurance the date of the particular boat-grave in which they occur.

The finger-ring and that from Krefeld-Gellep 1782 are of the same kind – similar classical intaglios similarly mounted in gold hoops with shoulders heavily decorated with filigree. They are by no means identical. In the Snape ring the scrolls and hook-and-eye themes and the collars in filigree are made from lengths of wire that are not beaded as in the Krefeld grave, but twisted. The area of filigree on the shoulders of the Snape ring is demarcated by a wire border and inside this border the surface of the gold is left rough to offer a better purchase for the solder. Annulets, common in the Krefeld-Gellep grave 1782 gold-work, do not occur on the Snape ring and the S-shaped scrolls of Snape do not occur on the Krefeld-Gellep ring. If we accept the ring as Frankish, Krefeld requires a possible horizon for its manufacture in the second quarter or the middle of the sixth century. If it is Anglo-Saxon, the Anglo-Saxon parallels to the filigree seem rather to indicate a late sixth- or seventh-century date.

With regard to the claw-beaker, this belongs to a large class of vessel which Dr Harden has described as one of the most difficult both to study and to date.[43] The fifty-odd examples known do not lend themselves to any clear typology. Werner says that the Snape beaker belongs to the 'earlier group' found on the Continent in grave-groups of the second half of the fifth or the first half of the sixth century. This category, as listed in his distribution map, covers several variants in form. Typologically, the Snape vase seems to belong to Harden's type Ci, the Fairford type, and this type he assigns to the full sixth century and the Taplow phase to the seventh century. As is said above in discussing its features, the Snape vase belongs to the middle phase of the claw-beaker development and seems to show tendencies towards the Taplow development. There seems no need to date it earlier than A.D. 550–575.

We should not overlook the lost blue glass fragment found in the Snape boat-grave, described in detail by Francis Francis and further discussed below. This we have supposed to belong to the Cuddesdon/Aylesford squat jar type found in seventh-century contexts.

Indeed Harden, in his discussion of these square jars (*op. cit.*, p. 141) says that 'dark or iron-blue glass in Saxon graves is normally late and probably not before the seventh century'.

Werner's verdict of before A.D. 550 at the latest, on the strength of ring and claw-beaker, seems an over-simplification of the situation. The ring and glass together may be thought quite compatible with a date of *c.* 600, or even later, for the boat-burial itself.

GENERAL OBSERVATIONS

Various points of interest emerge from the foregoing study and from the original accounts. First, the ring and the claw-beaker and the other remains undoubtedly belong to the buried boat. The whole represents a robbed boat-grave which may be attributed to the period *c.* A.D. 600. There is no reason whatever to suppose, as Nerman claimed, that the objects do not represent a boat-grave especially since we know from Sutton Hoo that boat-graves occur in this part of Suffolk at this date. A boat of Saxon character under a barrow in the middle of an Anglo-Saxon cremation cemetery can hardly represent anything other than an Anglo-Saxon boat-grave, especially when unburnt grave-goods of the period, left behind from the robbery of the mound, were found lying on the bottom of the boat.

Secondly, the fifty feet long boat (if one may make some small addition to the recorded length for the stem and stern posts) was manhandled to the site over half a mile at least of mild gradient. Why was all this trouble taken? Why was one of the convenient bluffs or spurs nearer the water or overlooking the estuary not chosen but instead the boat pulled well inland and quite out of sight of the water? The answer is clear; so that it might be buried in the pre-existing grave-field and near the settlement this served. There must have been a well-established settlement nearby and it was probably near the present church.

Furthermore, the trouble taken suggests that boat-burial must have been a well-established custom of real significance in the life of the community. The probability is that the other boats are buried there, presumably under others of the mounds.

One would only expect in an English boat-grave cemetery of the period few, perhaps very few, boat-graves. The rite is always exceptional but while in Swedish boat-grave fields it continues without interruption through the Viking period, in England, and more particularly in Suffolk, it must have died out along with pagan burial in general by *c.* A.D. 650, at the latest *c.* A.D. 675, with permanent and general establishment of Christianity. For Suffolk the earlier date must be accepted.

We may safely say that the Snape boat-grave does not represent a temporary settlement of (?Swedish) raiders or the temporary occupation of a riverine or coastal foothold. The boat-burial was the act of an established community, as the organized effort of dragging up the boat to a site a mile inland and invisible from the main estuary (but marked by the pre-existence of a sizeable urn field) shows. They were a settled group, boasting a certain wealth and distinction at the top, to whom boat-inhumation of their leading figure meant much. The proximity of their burial ground to the mediaeval church and village of Snape suggests that the community lived on in the same place and has flourished ever since.

It is unwise to apply Swedish analogies too rigidly to the very different milieu of East Anglia.[44] If Snape were a boat-grave cemetery in Sweden its boat-graves (we have suggested that there may be several) would represent the special treatment by inhumation, in a boat, of the successive male heads of the dominant family, in a community in which all other dead were cremated.[45] At first sight the Snape cemetery appears to run true to this pattern, for only cremations have been found there, apart from the boat-grave. Is the Snape boat-inhumation and urn-field a true parallel to the Swedish practice, or does the boat-inhumation, as inhumation, merely indicate that the community as a whole was abandoning cremation? Are any of the cremations round the boat contemporary with, or later than it? Or do they belong to a distinct and earlier period in the settlement's history?

We must remember that in England, unlike Scandinavia, a 'flight from cremation' (less fashionable now than it used to be)[46] had been in steady progress from the time of the invasions.[47]

In East Anglia and other 'strongholds' cremation certainly persisted in some localities into the seventh century and even to the eve of conversion, that is, overlapping with Christian burial elsewhere, though this is exceptional. At Lackford in the north-west of Suffolk, a Lark valley site that really belongs to the Cambridge fens, there is good evidence that cremations took place in the seventh century but only very exceptionally does evidence suggest a really late cremation, that might be after say A.D. 630. The only reason for supposing that cremation persisted without dilution at Lackford until the conversion (*c.* A.D. 650) is that no trace whatever of the inhumation rite has been found in excavations and agricultural activity that all told must have yielded remains of some six hundred urns. If the unexcavated portions[48] adjacent to the main excavated areas run to form one might consider this true of an area containing a thousand urns. Yet this by no means exhausts the site and it is not impossible that a large community abandoning cremation with some rapidity might utilize free ground on the fringes of the great urn-field for this fresh start. Meaney and Hawkes have discussed examples of this practice of abandoning the pagan grave-field for a new site, on the conversion of the community.[49] There may be inhumations still to be discovered at Lackford and the same remains true of Snape.

We must also reflect that south-east Suffolk is not an area in which cremations might be expected to persist to any unusual degree. It is the part of Suffolk most open to civilizing and southern influences and most sensitive to the influences and example of a Christian royal house[50] and the mixed cemetery at Ipswich, the Coptic bowl from Wickham Market, near Rendlesham, and other finds, show that cremation had given ground here well before the end of the pagan period.

Can it be that Snape is an exception and that here boat-inhumation and cremation are contemporaneously practised by the same community?

It is not at all easy to obtain from the first-hand accounts (Septimus Davidson, Francis Francis and Hele) a clear picture of the stratigraphy at Snape and it is not surprising that Reginald Smith's summary in the *Victoria County History* does not clear up the ambiguities and seems in fact to be misleading in some respects. After studying all the accounts with the greatest care I think the circumstances were as follows:

A trench, probably some sixty feet long, fourteen feet wide and six or seven feet deep, was dug in the midst of a fairly dense urn-field, in which Bronze Age urns occurred alongside Anglo-Saxon ones, and the boat was placed in the trench. The funeral deposit having been laid out in the boat, it was either covered across with planks, as in Sweden, or else, if the deposit was concentrated into a central chamber, as in the Sutton Hoo ship, bows and stern on either side of the chamber were filled up flush with the excavated sand. The perimeter of a circular barrow was marked out around the boat and turves and soil scraped up from the surrounding heath[51] and thrown up into the middle to construct the mound. Sherds of broken urns from the surrounding ground may be expected to have become incorporated into the mound at all levels as a result of this process. The scraping caused a general lowering of the ground surface around the barrows and denuded the urns buried there so that they were later to come to light 'with the removal of the first sod'. The building of the mound, on the contrary, covered those urns that happened to lie within its circumference with a greater depth of soil, the mound being built up on the original undenuded ground surface that concealed them.

The surprise of the excavators in 1863, when they found many urns *between* the barrows and 'in the flat ground *clear of their margins*', shows that they were unaware of the existence of such a feature as an urn-field. They set out to excavate the barrows and when they found urns supposed them to be part and parcel of the barrows, not realizing that they came from a flat cemetery which underlay the mounds. The situation may have been still more complex, for not only had all the mounds been dug into deeply at the centre by previous searchers (which presumably added further broken sherds to their upper levels), but it is possible that some intact urns encountered and displaced by the early Anglo-Saxons in the digging of boat-trenches or primary burial pits, or in scraping the adjacent heath, were deliberately re-interred by them in the barrows as these were being built up. It is not surprising that the original accounts make somewhat bewildering reading.

Francis Francis's account gives the impression that whole urns full of bones occurred in the mounds like currants in a bun, the remains (but note *remains* not specifically *urns*) occurring all over the mounds and at all levels and 'at depths varying from one to three feet' (but no datum given). In instances, he adds, the urns were so placed as to suggest that they had been placed *on* the ground surface and covered over with soil. It also appears that some urns at least were encountered in the six to eight feet wide trench which Septimus Davidson cut through the largest seventy-two feet westernmost mound from edge to edge, a cutting which had been 'kept to the level of the natural soil on which the tumulus was raised'. Reginald Smith, after studying these accounts, was clearly left with the idea that the urns were discovered *in* and not *under* the mounds and this is the impression one gets from his summary in the *Victoria County History*.

Dr Hele here comes to the rescue. This part of his account is written in the first person with an assurance evidently based on precise first-hand observation, so that one feels able to accept his version when it is at variance with the others. It was also written after the other accounts, with which he must have been quite familiar. He quotes Davidson's description of the boat and uses his blocks but on other points, writing as an eye-witness, he deliberately amends him and here I feel his account can be accepted.

'The first urn we encountered,' he says, 'was found three or four inches below the surface of the ground, the latter in the immediate vicinity being of a peculiarly unctuous character' – presumably the black sticky layers noted elsewhere under and outside the barrows. The second urn found (an Anglo-Frisian type of pot with batches of vertical grooves separated by swastikas, *R.B-M.*)[52] was found 'just below the surface, as the former'. One of the urns found (and none of the accounts differentiates between its placing and that of the other urns) was a large collared urn of the Late Bronze Age. This was upside down (a normal position for such Bronze Age burials) and intact and therefore presumably undisturbed. Hele describes it as being found 'in precisely the same circumstances as the others' (that is, three or four inches below the surface of the ground) 'but upside down'. Whereas the other accounts disagree as to its contents, Septimus Davidson saying that it was, he believed, almost empty, Hele, who was a surgeon and who was present, says specifically, 'It contained as in the other examples, human bone, the femur or thighbone and part of the pelvis being perfect'.[53] From Hele's account it seems clear that these three urns, at least, were undisturbed burials in the flat ground immediately beneath the mound. The other urns found within the circumferences of the barrows were probably so also but some may have been encountered by the burial parties and later placed with reverence on the ground surface (perhaps over the top of the boat) and covered over again as the barrow was raised. It is not necessary to regard the six or more whole urns found as being secondary burials, inserted in the tumuli, as is implied by Reginald Smith's account.

This is a point of importance, for it also seems clear that the majority of the urns so encountered were found in the western mound, that which contained the boat. If this mound was erected as we have suggested *c.* A.D. 600–625, and the urns were intrusive secondary burials, this would be proof of a wholly unexpected persistence of cremation in this corner of Suffolk right up to the Christian period. Secondary urn-burials in the mound would yield the picture of boat-burials as a special custom reserved for the leaders of an otherwise cremating community, as in Sweden. Secondary urn-burials might have borne directly upon an important and mysterious problem, the one-time presence of a quantity of burnt bone on the Anastasius dish in the Sutton Hoo ship-burial; in other words on the problem of the Sutton Hoo cenotaph.[54] They would at least have shown us that cremation existed contemporaneously with the Sutton Hoo ship-burial in this area. These are not problems that would have worried Reginald Smith, for he regarded the Snape ring, both gem and setting as Roman, the vase as early and the whole burial as belonging to the sixth century – a time when intrusive cremations need cause no particular comment. In fact we need not hesitate to regard the boat-burial as later than the cremations, possibly appreciably later, since it was dug into the thickest part of the urn-field ('the urns were particularly thick in the region of the boat'). The urns that survive from Snape have not been studied in detail but inspection suggests that there is nothing abnormal or especially late about them.

The Snape burial-ground naturally invites comparison with that at Sutton Hoo. Like the Swedish boat-graves and also the great royal mounds at Old Uppsala, the Snape tumuli are part of a much larger grave-field containing ordinary burials. At present there is no sign of this at Sutton Hoo. Although abundant prehistoric pottery, chiefly of the Neolithic Bronze Age, overlapping with many Beaker sherds, has been found in the Sutton Hoo excavations up to 1970 and one Saxon urn-burial has also been found in flat ground to the north of the ship-barrow, there has been no indication of a Saxon habitation site in the vicinity of the mounds or any normal cemetery whether of cremation or inhumation burials. Three extended skeletons without grave-goods have also been found. Nonetheless, the Sutton Hoo grave-field still seems a thing apart, a place reserved for the burials of the royal family and its retainers, while the sizeable urn-field found at Rendlesham[55] presumably represents the burial place of the community associated with the royal seat there. Great interest attaches to the complete excavation of the flat ground around and under the barrows at Sutton Hoo, as well as to the exploration of the primary burials in the mounds as yet unexcavated and of the mounds themselves, which may perhaps contain features of a ritual or structural kind. Fairly substantial investigation so far does not suggest a situation corresponding with that at Snape.[56]

A few final points may be noted. The boat mound was not under the largest barrow of the group. The largest barrow, measured by Francis Francis and given as eighty-five feet across and seven or eight feet high, was on the south side of the road. It was not touched in 1862 or 1863 and may have been the one whose site has been lost, through ploughing.

The quality of the ring and the presence of gold, wholly absent from the contemporary burials of the Vendel and Valsgärde boat-grave cemeteries of Sweden and also the large size of the boat suggest that in the Anglo-Saxon milieu our second-class (as compared with Sutton Hoo, non-royal) boat-graves are likely to be wealthier and more luxuriously furnished than the Swedish ones.

The ring, 'pieces of jasper' and glass vessels amongst the vestiges from the Snape boat are all items absent from the Sutton Hoo ship-burial and tend to emphasize the variety we may expect from these burials.

Lastly, while it is always dangerous to argue from negative evidence, the apparent total absence of bone in the Snape boat, together with the absence of any of the horse trappings, saddle studs and other metal objects associated with animals, again suggests that the burial is not 'pure Swedish', as Professor Nerman considered the Sutton Hoo ship-burial to be, but is a boat-grave at least modified or coloured by its English milieu. Swedish boat-graves are well-furnished with such animal remains and furniture. These are normally laid outside the concentration of grave-goods, in or outside the bows or stern of the boat and so might be expected to have been missed by the grave robbers who dug in the centre of the mounds. Their absence from the excavators' accounts at Snape, where the boat was cleared from end to end must, it seems, represent a genuine absence from the original burial.

ADDENDUM

In the autumn of 1972, a sewer trench was dug along the north side of the Snape–Aldeburgh road, running just inside the hedge. To the east of St Margaret's (Fig 16), at the junction of the Snape–Aldeburgh road with the narrow unmetalled road running north on the east side of St Margaret's, the trench cut obliquely through the hedge into the road and continued westwards within its line, close to the hedge which marks the southern boundary of St Margaret's. Some thirty yards west of the St Margaret's enclosure, the trench again cut back obliquely northwards into the field, running along inside the hedge for another two hundred and fifty yards. It then again cut through the hedge obliquely across the road and across the corner of the big field south of the road, in a south-westerly direction. Along some fifty yards of the trench, south of St Margaret's, seven or eight Saxon cremation urns were encountered at depths varying between seven inches and three feet below the road-metalling. There was also a shallow bronze bowl or pan containing cremated bones. The bowl has some good textile impressions or remains both on its inner and its outer surfaces. Its rim-diameter is about twelve inches. The sides have a shallow inward curve. The bowl had no escutcheons and was not a hanging-bowl. There were no lugs or ears upstanding from the rim, a fairly common Anglo-Saxon form; the rim is thickened but shows no other development. Adhering to the bronze were well preserved sections of oak board, 0·8 cm thick, suggesting that the bowl had been placed on a wooden tray, like that underlying the deposit in Mound 3 at Sutton Hoo (p. 145 below). The finds are in the Ipswich Museum, and these notes are written with kind permission of Miss Elisabeth Owles, F.S.A., who is to publish the finds in the *Proceedings of the Suffolk Institute of Archaeology*.

NOTES TO CHAPTER THREE

1 The primary accounts of the 1862 excavations are those of Francis Francis in *The Field, the Country Gentleman's Newspaper*, January 17th, 1863, 61–2, and January 24th, 1863, 74–5; Septimus Davison, *Proceedings of the Society of Antiquaries*, Second Series, Vol. II, January 8th, 1863, 177–82, and Dr N. F. Hele, *Notes About Aldeburgh*, 1870, 24–9. Secondary accounts based on these, are those of the Rev. H. M. Scarth in *Archaeological Journal*, XX, 1863, pp. 188–91, and Reginald Smith in the *Victoria County History, Suffolk*, Vol. I, London, 1911, 325–9. The further excavations of 1863 in the flat ground around the barrows, which produced remains of forty urns, are described by Francis Francis in *Archaeological Journal*, XX, 1863, 373–4. The cemetery is recorded in R. G. Collingwood and J. N. L. Myres, *Roman Britain and the English Settlements*, Oxford, 1936, Vol. I, Map VII and p. 390.

2 Septimus Davidson, the owner of the land and leader of the excavators, speaks of 'at least eight or ten tumuli on Snape Common' but later comments that 'some of these are not exceeding six or seven feet in diameter', *Proceedings of the Society of Antiquaries*, 2 Ser., II, 177.

3 Francis Francis in *The Field*, January 17th, 1863.

4 The majority of the urns excavated to the north of the road in 1863 are said to have been 'within a short distance of the hedge to Southward', that is to say, close to the road, which seems to have passed through the middle of the grave-field.

5 The Snape finds are in the custody of the Ipswich Museum. The gold ring is in the British Museum.

6 See note 2 above.

7 For a discussion of the water-level in the Suffolk estuaries in early times see Chapter Two, pp. 99–101.

This should be modified in the light of Dr Everard's account in Vol. I, Ch. I, of *The Sutton Hoo Ship-Burial*, Cambridge, 1974.

8 B. Nerman, 'Sutton Hoo-en svensk kunga – eller hövdinggrav?' *Fornvännen*, 1948, p. 89 and note 29. He speaks of 'a rather uncertain boat-grave' and in the footnote adds 'men det kan, bl. a.på grund av fyndets egendomliga sammansättning och föremålens lage i båten, knappast anses säkert att föremålen verkligen hört till båten.' ('but because, amongst other things, of the peculiar circumstances of the find and the position of the objects in the boat, it can hardly be considered certain that they really belong to it').

9 The Broomfield discoveries are described in *Victoria County History, Essex*, Vol. I, London, 1903, pp. 320–5, and in *Proceedings of the Society of Antiquaries*, XV, pp. 250–5. The pile textiles are not referred to in the printed accounts but exist in some quantity amongst the materials from the site in the British Museum.

10 *The Sutton Hoo Ship-Burial*, definitive publication, Vol. III, in preparation.

11 cf. Septimus Davison, *loc. cit.*, p. 177.

12 'The plan, not having been made by a professional surveyor, may not be minutely accurate, especially as to the exact position of the rivets at the smaller end', Septimus Davison, *loc. cit.*, p. 181.

13 *Antiquaries Journal*, XX, 1940, 152.

14 Sune Lundqvist, *Uppsala Högar och Ottarshögen*, Stockholm, 1936, p. 184. Figs 106, 107 and 185.

15 *Antiquaries Journal*, XX, 1940, 176, R. L. S. Bruce-Mitford, *The Sutton Hoo Ship-Burial, A Provisional Guide*, London, 1947, 32.

16 'Sutton Hoo-en svensk kunga – eller hövdinggrav?', *Fornvännen*, h. 2–3, 1948, 84–7.

17 *Archaeological News Letter*, Vol. II, no. 10, March, 1950, 166–9. But see Greta Arwidsson, 'Valsgärde – Fullerö' in *Tor*, I – two gold finger-rings – one with a stone.

18 cf. *Antiquities of Roman Britain*, British Museum, London, 1951, Fig 13, 1, 2, 3, and 5.

19 In a paper read before the VII International Congress of Prehistoric and Protohistoric Sciences in Prague, 1966. (See *Actes du VII Congrès*, Prague, 1970, published by the Czechoslovak Institute of Archaeology, pp. 997–8; J. Werner, *Zur zeitstellung des Bootgrabes von Snape, Suffolk* (Zusammenfassung).

20 T. D. Kendrick, *Anglo-Saxon Art to A.D. 900*, London, 1938, Pl. XXXII, 4.

21 Sonia Chadwick Hawkes and L. R. A. Grove, 'Finds from a Seventh-Century Anglo-Saxon Cemetery at Milton Regis', *Archaeologia Cantiana*, Vol. LXXVIII, 1963, 22–38.

22 Sigurd Grieg, 'Vikingetidens Skattefund', *Universitetets Oldsaksamlings Skrifter*, Bind II, Oslo, 1929, 182–98; Fig. 22, 189.

23 N. Åberg, *Anglo-Saxons in England*, Uppsala, 1926, Fig. 240.

24 N. Åberg, *op. cit.*, Fig. 267; R. F. Jessup, *Anglo-Saxon Jewellery*, London, 1950. Pl. IX and p. 102, No. 7; *British Museum Guide to Anglo-Saxon Antiquities*, London, 1923, Fig. 63.

25 N. Åberg, *op. cit.*, Fig. 222; G. Baldwin Brown, *The Arts in Early England*, III, Pt. 73: I.

26 Bjørn Hougen, *The Migration Style in Norway*, Oslo, 1936, Nos. 62–64.

27 cf. B. Salin, *Altgermanische Thierornametik*, 212–3, esp. Fig. 499, e, f, g; *Tiotusen År i Sverige*, Statens Historiska Museum, Stockholm, 1945, Figs. 175–6, and 177, top left.

28 cf. Holger Arbman, *Schweden und das Karolingische Reich*, Pls. 54–64; and numerous examples in the ninth-century Hon find.

29 These three things are all illustrated in R. F. Jessup, *op. cit.*, Pl. XXXVI (Nos. 7, 8 and 10).

30 T. D. Kendrick, *op. cit.*, Pl. LXXVIII, 3; *British Museum Guide to Anglo-Saxon Antiquities*, London, 1923, Fig. 122.

31 R. F. Jessup, *op. cit.*, Pl. XXXII, (1).

32 T. D. Kendrick, *op. cit.*, Pl. XXXI, 6.

33 *British Museum Guide to Anglo-Saxon Antiquities*, London, 1923, Pls. 1, 3.

34 N. Åberg, Fig. 243; *British Museum Guide*, Pl. 1, 4.

35 N. Åberg, Fig. 220; *British Museum Guide*, Pl. V, 2; T. D. Kendrick, *Anglo-Saxon Art to A.D. 900*, London, 1938, Pl. XXIV, 5. I cannot agree with Sir Thomas Kendrick's early dating (beginning of the sixth century) of the Taplow Barrow, which I would be inclined to attribute to the period A.D. 625–630, in general agreement with long-standing orthodox opinion.

36 *IPEK*, IX, 1934, Tf. 28, 12.

37 W. A. Thorpe, *English Glass*, London, 1935, Pls. X (e), XI (a).

38 *ibid.*, Pl. XI (c).

39 *ibid.*, Pl. XIII (c).

40 G. Baldwin Brown, *Arts in Early England*, Vol. IV, Pl. CXXXVI, 2.

40*a* J. Werner, Zur Zeitstellung des Bootgrabes von Snape, *Proceedings of the Seventh Congress of the International Union of Prehistoric and Protohistoric Sciences*, Prague, 1967, 183–4.

41 Renate Pirling, 'Ein Fränkisches Fürstengrab aus Krefeld Gellep', *Germania* 42, 1964, 188 ff.

42 R. Pirling, *op. cit.*, 213.

43 D. B. Harden, 'Glass Vessels in Britain, A.D. 400–1000', *Dark Age Britain*. Ed. D. B. Harden, London, 1956, 139.

44 See Chapter 1, pp. 50–1; also some salutary remarks by T. C. Lethbridge, *A cemetery at Lackford, Suffolk*, 1951, p. 11, first paragraph.

45 cf. *Vendel i fynd och forskning*, Uppsala, 1938, 79, 80 – speculations subsequently confirmed in the excavation of the cemetery at Valsgärde.

46 T. C. Lethbridge, *op. cit.*, p. 3.

47 cf. R. G. Collingwood and J. N. L. Myres, *Roman Britain and the English Settlements*, 448–9.

48 T. C. Lethbridge, *op. cit.*, Plan II (p. 2).

49 Audrey L. Meaney and Sonia Chadwick Hawkes, *Two Anglo-Saxon Cemeteries at Winnall, near Winchester, Hampshire*, Society for Mediaeval Archaeology, monograph series, No. 4, London, 1970.

50 See Chapter 2, p. 82.

51 For evidence of this procedure in the construction of the mound of the Sutton Hoo ship-burial, see *Antiquaries Journal*, XX, 1940, 202, and *Sutton Hoo*, Vol. I, Cambridge, 1974, Chapter IV.

52 A pot of similar form and decoration was found at Bifrons in Kent and is in private ownership, being with the early group of grave-goods formerly at Bifrons House. On this urn the swastikas and vertical grooves are very faintly incised.

53 *op. cit.*, 26.

54 Chapter 1, p. 5.

55 Chapter 2, pp. 104–5.

56 For details of the Sutton Hoo site up to the present time see the British Museum's definitive publication, Vol. I, Ch. 1 and 4, Cambridge, 1974.

CHAPTER FOUR

Basil Brown's Diary of the Excavations at Sutton Hoo in 1938–39

Introductory Note

A personal account of an historic excavation is always relevant. In the case of the Sutton Hoo ship-burial nothing has been heard from the man who began the excavation and whose experience and sound instinct was responsible for the preservation of the tenuous structure of the ship. Basil Brown (Plate 27), now in his eighties, is a self-taught local archaeologist with great experience of Suffolk sites and soils. The field techniques he used in 1939 were rudimentary by contemporary standards but he has 'green fingers'. Hardly any archaeological work has been published under his name. The Ipswich Museum, for whom most of his excavations were undertaken, edited or summarized his accounts and results as best they could. He has been responsible for a great deal of rescue work in the county and for the recovery of a great deal of material which came into the Ipswich Museum's collections. Brown kept his own private records and these have been of value in reconstructing the early activity on the Sutton Hoo site before Phillips took over. Brown's log of these events is moreover a personal record which I feel should be in print somewhere, both as a tribute to an unique Suffolk character and as an essential part of the story of the most remarkable single find in British archaeology. I have added occasional comments in the form of footnotes but have not interfered with his text. A full account of the discoveries in the three mounds opened by Brown in 1938 appears in Vol. I of the British Museum's definitive publication, The Sutton Hoo Ship-burial (1974)*. Brown's services to archaeology were recognized in the award to him in 1968 of a Civil List pension.*

1938 EXCAVATIONS

The first reference to proposed excavations came to me in a communication from Mr. Guy Maynard, Curator of Ipswich Museum, asking if I would be willing to undertake the exploration of some supposed burial mounds in another part of the County (I was then at Stanton Roman Villa). No location was given and I had no idea where.

Later I had a further short letter from Mr. Maynard telling me that the mounds were on the estate of Mrs. Frank Pretty, Sutton Hoo, near Woodbridge, who wished to know if the mounds were really burial mounds or not. I said I should be willing.

17 June 1938 Mr. Maynard came to Stanton on Friday June 17th, 1938 and I discussed the position with him re remuneration. I was at the time getting 30/– per week, and he had, he told me, informed Mrs. Pretty that I should be satisfied with such amount if accommodation was provided.

On Saturday June 18th, I asked various questions re mounds, their period, and size, so that I should have an idea as to what literature to take *etc.* As to their size Mr. Maynard only gave me a vague idea, and as to height, said about that of the hut we had at Stanton, *viz.* approx. 10 feet, and stated that they might be of any period but were possibly Danish. Regarding the procedure to be adopted he informed me that I should use my own judgment when I got there and consult Mrs. Pretty as to which mound she wanted opened up, etc. I also asked about things found and was then informed that anything found would be Mrs. Pretty's to dispose of to any museum, but Mr. Maynard said he hoped that I would suggest and recommend Ipswich Museum, and before clearing get them photographed in situ, and asked me to telephone the Ipswich Museum and Cullum (an assistant at the Museum) would take photographs.

I then went to the nearest telephone, Mr. George Adams, Builder, Stanton, to ring up Sutton Hoo, paying for call myself. I was answered by Mr. Grately, the Butler, who told me that Mrs. Pretty was not at home and asked my business. I replied that Mr. Maynard had told me that Mrs. Pretty wanted some Tumuli explored and that I would arrive at Sutton Hoo on Monday, and he told me the way after reaching Melton station via the Lodge gates.

On Sunday I got various things ready, selected appropriate literature, as far as I was able to judge, on Bronze Age, early Iron Age, Roman and Anglo-Saxon periods, and some suitable excavation reports.

Monday 20 June I arrived at Sutton Hoo at 11 a.m. and shortly afterwards had an interview with Mrs. Pretty, and who I found had kindly arranged lodgings for me with her chauffeur Mr. Lyons, at White Cottage, Bromeswell, about half a mile distant. Mrs. Pretty then took me to see the mounds, which were much hidden by bracken, and was rather alarmed by their sizes which were I found on examination far larger than Mr. Maynard had led me to expect (he afterwards told me that he had made no individual survey as they were so much bracken-covered when he visited the site). Mrs. Pretty at first thought of opening the largest barrow of the group (Tumulus I)[1] but I drew attention to the signs of much disturbance on the western side where many tons of soil had been removed, so much so as to alter the whole contour and give the mound a hog back appearance.[2] I then selected a well shaped barrow (Tumulus A)[3] for exploration purposes and Mrs. Pretty agreed after suggesting a trial on the top of Tumulus I with a long probing iron she had had made.

The two workmen, Bert Fuller of Bromswell and Tom Sawyer of Sutton, labourers on the Sutton Hoo estate, arrived with equipment for excavating, and I went to see the gardener Mr. Steward for other tools required. Meantime the prodding iron had been pushed down on the top of Tumulus I and had reached a hard substance. A small excavation was then made to determine this to a depth of 6 feet and it was found to be a stone of no particular significance. This trial did, however, give me some data regarding the soil composition of the mound, which came in useful when excavation was undertaken.

Mrs. Pretty then said she wished all the excavated soil to be put ready for filling in by the side of any trenches made into the mounds so as to be easy to fill in as she wanted the mounds to be filled up so their original appearance was unaltered.[4]

At no time either in talks or correspondence with Mr. Maynard or in my interview with Mrs. Pretty was the question of Museum supervision raised and I regarded myself as having a free hand subject only to the wishes and instructions of Mrs. Pretty who actually became my employer with Ipswich Museum helping and advising as Mrs. Pretty at any time wished, the dig being solely hers. I therefore decided that all reports would be made to Mrs. Pretty and not to any other quarter, and she would communicate them to whom she wished. The first mound to be explored[5] was suggested by me for the following reasons: (i) It was of medium size. (ii) It was practically circular and no material seemed to have been at any time removed. (iii) The top of the mound showed little disturbance other than rabbits and even rabbit holes were not numerous. (iv) The mound was marked on the Ordnance Survey map (Suffolk East) sheet LXXVI N.E.

The group of which it is a member is situated on the high land on the south bank of the river Deben and called locally Sutton Hills.

There is also a nickname, i.e. 'Little Egypt'. From one of the mounds a fine view of the town of Woodbridge on the opposite side of the river may be obtained.

I then made a rough drawing showing the several mounds of the group, those shown on the O.S. and others added from which much of the mound content may have been removed and subject to question (12 in all).[6]

Tuesday 21 June After clearing the mound of bracken, taking compass readings, I measured it and prepared for driving a trench 4 feet wide through the mound in direction West-East down to the plain level or old ground surface. The work of cutting the trench was commenced with the help of the two estate labourers Fuller and Sawyer and good progress made by evening.

Wednesday 22 June It should be noted that the exploration should be quick, i.e. take about a fortnight, the idea being to prove if the mounds did or did not contain any remains. I therefore adopted similar tactics to those adopted by the Norfolk Research Committee in their excavation of Charborough Hill, Stiffkey, Norfolk (*Norfolk & Norwich Arch. Soc. Vol. XXV*, pp. 408–428) where also time was limited.

Carried on with the trench carefully examining soils, in fact anything which can be regarded as possible clues. I am leaving nothing to chance, as the small things often count.

Thursday 23 June Making progress in clearing out the trench towards the centre of the mound and 2 feet below the surface soil with its many bracken roots a distinct difference in the strata was noted and from this the existence of a pit was deduced. Cross trenches were then commenced to determine the nature of the pit, its area and whether due to subsidence or other causes (see plans for position of these exploratory trenches, also small field note book). The main trench was from E. to W. (per compass alignments).[7]

Friday 24 June Work continued to main and cross trenches and some revision of the idea of putting the spoil heaps along the main trench. This was moved aside and sufficient room was obtained for both cross trenches and spoil heaps. A few hours were, however, taken up in getting the matter suitably adjusted.

Saturday 25 June Determined pit at least to my own satisfaction. In fact I considered that there was sufficient evidence produced by the appearance and contours of the strata as seen in the main and cross trenches to regard the matter settled. In the afternoon I made further general inspection of the soils and the Tumuli to see what had been brought up by rabbits. The finds were several worked flints and a few small fragments of Bronze Age pottery.

Sunday 26 June Continued my explorations and took some photographs.

Monday 27 June Continued work with the trenches and trouble began with landslides. What appears to happen is that the soil content of the mound is very liable to slip and unless the whole area of the pit is completely cleared, that the soil left will slip in, leaving the shape of the pit. The actual significance of the pit is at present unknown, or how deep it goes. Still as a pit or grave exists it is O.K.

Tuesday 28 June It was rather an uncomfortable time at this stage. I had challenged Museum people that we should find [the burial] in a certain place, i.e. beneath the depression and its black earth layers, which I believed to be the residue of a fire, and also had not been helped by the Museum in getting the sample of the black matter analysed quick as I wanted. And I had also informed the men where I expected to find [the burial]: the central portion of the mound at the junction of trenches A.B. and C. was being cut away, an area 12 feet square, and we were digging down into yellow sand. All black layers had now disappeared and still no result. Then I was expected to destroy the pit by cutting through it.

Wednesday 29 June Work continued; reached 8 feet below the top of the mound with no change except the pit continued.

Thursday 30 June Results became almost certain for when we had reached a depth of 9 feet, Mr. Lyons, the chauffeur, who was watching, saw two or three small fragments of bone in the sand, which looked hopeful, and later I saw what seemed to be wood.

Friday 1 July The looked-for result at last, wood was found but not cleared. It may be a box or part of a boat.[8] Reported the find to Mrs. Pretty and a description was also given to Mrs. Pretty by myself by telephone.

Saturday 2 July Further clearing revealed the timber found was the west end of what appeared to be a dug-out, or wood tray, on which were the following objects: fragments of bone inlay probably from a trinket-box or casket, one having a female figure on part of a medallion; bronze object, possibly from a hanging bowl or lamp; bones (calcined), a sherd of Anglo-Saxon pottery (part of a burial urn), fragment of thin bronze, a mass of corroded iron (afterwards found to be a battle axe).

It is probable that grave robbers had disturbed this burial very soon after it took place and any valuable objects removed. The collapse of a chamber of turves could hardly account for the fragmentary state of the objects and disappearance of missing portions which would not have decayed.[9] In spite of the soil being well sifted nothing else was found. It is possible that the bone objects came from a Frankish casket.[10] The objects were later handed over to Ipswich, for treatment, by Mrs. Pretty.

Tuesday 26 July THE CONTROVERSY The events which led to this are obscure. I had gone to undertake exploratory excavations at Sutton Hoo, prepared to take instructions from Mrs. E. M. Pretty who initiated the dig on her estate, the expense being borne by her. The Ipswich Corporation Museum I regarded as occupying an advisory capacity; as also I did Mr. Vincent B. Redstone, F.S.A., and the Misses Redstone of Seckford Street, Woodbridge. The first interference was the arrival of an assistant from the Museum, who said that I should not have been there at all and said he had been told by the Museum authorities to supervise. What he told Mrs. Pretty I do not know, but he was invited to lunch, introduced to Miss Price, the governess-companion, etc.

Mr. Maynard was at this time over at Stanton[11] a good deal, but I preferred to write no letter to anyone except my wife regarding the dispute, and go straight ahead unless of course Mrs. Pretty had asked me to go. The assistant from the Museum told me that I did not know about the soils in that part of the county, and I strongly objected to this statement for the following reasons: I have had a lifetime's experience with soils both practical and theoretical, and have studied geology from age of 15 when I received a certificate (for an examination paper) signed by Arthur Mee, stating in the opinion of the examiner I had a reliable knowledge of the undermentioned subjects:

'GEOGRAPHY, GEOLOGY AND ASTRONOMY'

I also devoted some space in my work on Astronomical Cartography published by Search Publishing Co. at 18/–, 1932. Also I was born at Bucklesham a few miles from Sutton where my parents lived for some years, where soils are very similar. Also every evening after my arrival I cycled around the locality examining every pit where the strata could be well observed, and those I had no means of getting to on private property I observed through field glasses I bought from Sawyer.[12]

Anyway as I wrote in my note on June 25th, I felt convinced in the existence of a pit and Mrs. Pretty invited Mr. Vincent Redstone and fetched him in her car to look. Mr. Redstone however accepted the existence of a pit but said it must have been a dew pond. However, this helped, and work proceeded. I allowed the men to dig a hole into, I considered, undisturbed sand for the assistant from the Museum until 6 feet down Fuller and Sawyer were nearly buried, and on the second occasion he had to dig a hole himself as I told the two workmen to go and cut bracken and dig no more holes. Mr. Reid Moir was also over and eventually told the assistant from the Museum that he could come over and look, but his visits practically ceased and there was no further hindrance. I can say that the men would almost certainly have refused to do anything if there had been and asked Mrs. Pretty if she would let them go to work on the farm instead of the mounds. The only definite attempt to upset my calculations re pit by influencing Mrs. Pretty was on June 26th, and the following note from Mrs. Pretty brought to me by the butler:

> Dear Mr. Brown,
> Mr. Moir will call on Tuesday afternoon, Mr. Spencer on Tuesday morning.
> Mr. Moir would like you to cut a trench through at the level of the ditch.[13]
> E. M. Pretty.

With a little diplomacy I got out of bother and the pit survived and finds followed on the Thursday.

Sunday 3 July At home discussed the dig and finds with my friend Mr. R. W. Whitmore, M.A., and his daughter and Mr. Cornwell took me over to the Stanton Roman Villa where Mr. Thomas is in charge and we had a talk with him. They then took me back to Sutton Hoo with my bicycle, to save me cycling back on Monday morning.

Monday 4 July Heard from Mrs. Pretty that the figure on the bone disc was minus its head, that portion had been broken. Did a most intensive search but the only thing found was one very small fragment of the bone inlay. I later saw the object and the figure appeared complete, and one of the men said, "We might well look"; I also cut further back to prove to Mr. Moir the limits of the grave.

Tuesday 5 July Incidental work, the dug-out or tray was covered with a large piece of hessian and made safe. I removed it to show visitors. Mr. Maynard, Mr. Reid Moir, Mr. Pigot and Mr. Spencer were also over at the weekend and removed the battle axe which I had left in situ.

MOUND NO 2

Wednesday 6 July As Mrs. Pretty had thought of exploring another mound and was not particular which one was opened I proposed to attack Tumulus D, a large mound and the most easterly[14] of the group, which had to be cleaned of bracken and preparations made for driving a trench 6 feet wide across the mound along the old ground surface. This I decided should be from East to West and as nearly as possible in the alignment of the boat, tray or dug-out found in Tumulus A. This mound had been much disturbed by rabbits, and there may have been other disturbances at various times, as there was a depression across the top of the mound and which may have been due to a trench filled in by explorers.[15]

I was also told by Sawyer about digging into the mounds, and that this had been done in the time the property was owned by Mr. Lomax, by a Mr. Harvey now living at Sutton. Mr. Harvey informed me that such had been the case. Also that material had been taken from the mounds for a private golf course.

Thursday 7 July Work of cutting the 6 feet trench was carried on, but it was obvious that there was a chaotic condition of the material constituting the mound due to disturbances. Some pieces of iron were found. One was certainly the remnant of a ship rivet, much corroded. On this day an interesting find was made in a patch of black earth almost certainly due to burning. There were associated with this many small sherds of Bronze Age pottery and I decided to sieve all this layer. In this process Fuller saw a small blue object among the stones and bits of pottery in the sieve. I examined this and found it to be a Bronze Age faience bead of a turquoise blue colour and probably the only one, or as far as I know the only one, to be found in Suffolk. I reported this to Mrs. Pretty and lent her the B.M. Guide to the Bronze Age after handing over the find. The description and dating of these segmented beads being given on pp 88 and 89. Mrs. Pretty was very interested.

Friday 8 July Work continued. We are getting the trench down but up to the present there is no stratification to speak of above the old ground level, as in Tumulus A.

Saturday 9 July Ditto. Nothing of moment to report.

Sunday 10 July Went to Bawdsy, very interesting re fossils.

Monday 11 July On the old ground surface we found evidence of a fire, but whether it belongs to Bronze Age or Anglo-Saxon is uncertain. Above this a few loose ship rivets were found. This is interesting. Spencer has been over, also Cullum[16] who took photographs of the first boat, tray or dug-out (Cullum is quite nice and does not bother). I have also asked the Museum to forward me particulars of the Snape ship, and Mrs. Pretty talks of sending Lyons and me to Aldeburgh Museum to examine the finds made in the Snape ship and have written to the curator to make an appointment, as this Museum is only open on Wednesday afternoons.

Tuesday 12 July Work continued, nothing of moment to report. Mrs. Pretty allowed me to see Norden's Plan of 1601, re mounds.[17]

Wednesday, 13 July Ditto. There has been no interference from Spencer or any of the Museum officials. I have found the pit or grave dug into the undisturbed soil beneath the old ground surface which coincides with plain level, and have put up datum post. There should be no risk of floating as each mound opened is marked on the O.S. maps, so is a definite fixed area and can be detailed as such. Mr. Reid Moir has been over and walked down to the excavation with Mrs. Pretty, and saw me preparing to clear down in the pit area. Apparently he does not yet believe in the pits or graves beneath the mounds for he shouted out to me, "That's not the way to do it, Brown", but Mrs. Pretty made no remark and provided Mrs. Pretty gives no special directions, I will take advice or help only if it is useful from the Museum officials or anyone else, but I've decided I will go home rather than be dictated to, if I am certain of being right re graves beneath the mounds.

Thursday 14 July Carried on and we found a piece of human femur[18] but above the grave and some beautiful pieces of blue glass definitely Anglo-Saxon. Took the glass to Mrs. Pretty who appeared pleased and gave me boxes and cotton wool. There had, up to now, been no stratifications of soils in the mound proper, until the old ground surface is reached, but as we excavate the pit grave there is a line of dark soil with an occasional ship rivet at the sides of the pit graves, so the deduction is that it has contained a small ship or a large boat, but these remains have certainly been subjected to disturbances other than those definitely due to rabbits.

Friday 15 July Received the following useful letter from Mr. Guy Maynard – and acted on his suggestions.

July 14th 1938

Dear Basil,

I send herewith a tracing of the Snape Boat from N. F. Hele's Notes about Aldeburgh 1870. Hele notes that the centre of each of the tumuli on Snape Common have been removed years before so that none represent their original height. The boat was 48ft. in length, 9ft. 9in. in width, 4ft. in depth. Seven rivets in each row within (a length of 3ft.). He means apparently 3ft. measured longitudinally fore and aft. Six rows of rivets on each side and four rows or five along the bottom of the boat. At the side the rivets rested horizontally. At the bottom they stood vertically in the sand. Within the breadth of the ship near one end were found some auburn coloured hair, two pieces of cloth each about 1 inch square, a ring (gold) and some pieces of light orange coloured glass once forming a tall vessel with pendant ornaments on the exterior, some remains of weapons where a mass of iron much corroded has a central space containing some fragments of wood, ? battle-axe. Many dark marks in the soil running in perpendicular direction and varying from a few inches to a few feet in width. Soil where marks occurred of a greasy consistency. No pottery recorded in the boat. Hele records pottery as discovered in quantities. More than 40 boxes between the two largest tumuli, much outside the base of either. No ordered arrangements in the placing of the vases, some solitary others in groups.

As the Museum Assistant seems to have been given a packet of too rapid plates he may have to retake the first site again. In any case clear back at the end as I told you and cover up with the sack. Mr. Moir quite agrees to all this. Also I think you had better put in a few stakes around the first boat and cord it in so that the enclosed area shall not be trodden on during work in cutting back etc. (Note below on this – see Saturday July 16th and 18th Monday).

The note above re urn outside the barrows is interesting and a little surface trenching might be tried some day after the bigger job.

I told Moss that you were clearing so as to get the middle of the second boat exposed and you should do all you can to preserve the internal figure of shape of the inside of the ship. Look out for falls of course so it would be wise to reduce the top load to somewhere near the beginning of the evidence of the ship.

Lord and Lady Boston came with Mr. Reid Moir.

Saturday 16 July Mr. Lyons brought stakes and ropes and we corded round the first site at which Lyons put a notice DANGER LIVE BOMBS to keep people away.[18a]

Sunday and Monday 17 and 18 July At home, Mrs. Pretty saying I could have Monday.

Tuesday 19 July Cut trench from the end of the tray or dug-out in Tumulus A to the east joining the large central excavation with Trench D to suit Mr. Reid Moir, but there was nothing at all or sign of any objects. This, however, proved the eastern limit of the grave to everyone's satisfaction I believe on this day, July 19th. I had Mr. J. Reid Moir, Mr. Pigot and Mr. Baden Powell in this afternoon. Afterwards we went on with the interrupted work at Tumulus D and found some more pieces of the nice blue Anglo-Saxon glass.

Wednesday 20 July Held up by a rather bad landslide. In the evening Mr. Lyons took me over to Aldeburgh on appointment with the curator Mr. Gilcrist to examine the relics and rivets of the Snape ship 1870.[19] The large showcases contained many Bronze Age urns and are quite an interesting display, and in the small ones were the ship relics, many rivets, some pieces of iron possibly from weapons, a sword-hilt encased in wax, so that I was unable to get an absolutely clear idea to define it, although it seemed to be an Anglo-Saxon type. There was also a piece of bronze said to be part of helmet, a comb, a lock of hair but not now auburn. However all the objects were badly in need of treatment. No glass or the gold ring. The rivets were very like those at Sutton Hoo, so it will be advisable to keep these finds in mind as the only ones of the Anglo-Saxon period in Suffolk, the rivets to be smaller due to rust from being untreated. The description labels were apparently in the handwriting of Dr. Hele. I later purchased Dr. Hele's work.

Thursday 21 July Work continued at Tumulus D in clearing out the ship. Several formless black patches were noticed in the sand and these were apparently the remains of decayed timbers. In this case there were small pieces broken and there were no indications of cross pieces of any length. Mr. Redstone visited the site. As the bottom of the ship approached interesting finds began to increase. A few small fragments from the blue glass vessel, cracked apparently by the effects of fire. Then a bronze brooch (long), probably bronze gilt, set apparently with stones;[20] thin bronze (gilt) from perhaps a belt, some fragments; Bronze Buckle, iron hasp possibly from bucket, other undefined iron objects and many loose ship rivets, and at the east end of the ship was an iron band marking the extremity of the vessel. By this and the dark coloured sand at sides and the size of the pit grave cut in the undisturbed hard yellow sand it could be seen that the vessel was of comparatively small size and of similar build to the Snape ship and this was further confirmed by a few positional rivets. Also the black at the bottom and its area could be well studied.

Friday 22 July A landslide held up matters for a time and upset calculations. It was, however, not serious and was cleared up by noon, and a start was then made with the work of clearing the ship towards the western extremity to find further burial objects and determine the length of the vessel. The soil removed was being put through the sieve, when Sawyer who was doing this found a bronze disc.

I was able to deduce the spot from which it had come to my plan. Here was a most interesting object and I was able to get some ideas of the date (and that of the other bronze gilt ornament) for it was very similar in the design interlacing etc. to that found in the barrow explored by the Rev. Edmund Jarvis at Caenby (Lincs.) (*British Museum Guide to Anglo-Saxon Antiquities* pp 86 & 87) and I again lent the book to Mrs. Pretty. Other books were also lent me by Mrs. and the Misses Redstone (including the work on the Snape ship, Hele's *History of Aldeburgh*) who were kept informed of events right through the dig and who helped me in every possible way.

Saturday 23 July Probably the large disc was the centre ornament of the warrior's shield as at Caenby. A small bronze gilt stud was also found as we continued on towards the bow of the ship.
(*Note*: My notes at this time give a provisional dating of A.D. 450–560 for the objects from both mounds but the date of the burials is certainly much later)

Sunday 24 July At home.

Monday 25 July Work continued. Nothing of moment to report. Had Inspector of Police for my statement re witness.

Tuesday 26 July Clearing along bottom of ship and sieving all but nothing found. The bottom of the ship as seen by the thin wood (or what was once wood) appears to be flat, but this may be due to the pressure of the mound above and not its original form. There is no sign of a keel however.

Wednesday 27 July Getting towards the end of the ship and certainly the black lines on each side of the pit are curving to bow shape. The pit itself is also following this form without any question, i.e. boat shape.

Thursday 28 July Away owing to being a witness in a case at Woodbridge Court House. Mr. Maynard, however, came over and helped the men to finish the bow of the ship. They had some landslides when I went up to the site in the late afternoon and Mr. M. asked how I described myself in Police Statement – Archaeologist in the employ of Mrs. Pretty.

Friday 29 July Finished Mound D, took some photographs as did Miss Price, the Governess-Companion, and prepared to excavate one of the small barrows, (Tumulus E), as Mrs. Pretty wanted three done.

MOUND 4

Saturday 30 July Cleared Tumulus E of bracken and proposed to excavate a trench 4 feet wide from east to west to reach burial in expected alignment.

Monday 1 August August Bank Holiday. Visited Wymondham and its Church as was at home doing write-up etc.

Tuesday 2 August Excavating Tumulus E by cutting a 4 feet wide trench across the mound from outside the ditch to locate the grave pit. (The ditches are so called but are not well defined).

Wednesday 3 August Continued work, good progress made, but unlike the two other mounds, the soil of the Tumulus E contains no fragments of Bronze Age pottery. It is also smaller than A and D and lies probably outside area of Bronze Age settlement or hutments.

Thursday 4 August Located the black earth pit grave and began to widen out to 12 feet to enable the grave to be cleared. Nothing found.

Friday 5 August Clearing the grave pit below the old ground surface. This is found to be very shallow and the indications are that this burial is not of great importance. Only 2 feet below the old ground surface on plain level. The grave was then cleared down to the hard yellow sand. At the east end a rabbit had caused much disturbance but whether the condition of the burial is due to this or other causes one is unable to say. The burial pit contained many fragments of thin bronze evidently belonging to a vessel of thin bronze which had been smashed. It had most likely contained the bones from a cremation burial. These may have been wrapped in a linen cloth or textile of some kind for we found pieces of textile were adhering to the fragments of the bronze vessel. The calcined bones appeared to be those of a young man.[21] No ornaments were found although all the sand content of the grave was sifted. Mr. Maynard was over and helped.

Saturday 6 August Work continued in the morning. Only meagre finds (a few small bronze fragments from the smashed bronze vessel) obtained by sieving. Every fragment was kept.

Monday 8 August Got up at sunrise and took photographs of the mounds, grave-pits etc. Explored the small rise marked [?] on plan to the east[22] of Tumulus E and black earth, so it is possible there is a burial below. Heard from Mrs. Pretty that Mr. Reid Moir etc. had telephoned three times to ask for me to go to Stanton, who said as they wanted me so badly I'd better go.

Tuesday 9 August General rush to get finished. Mrs. Pretty sent the car to fetch Mr. Needs the photographer from Woodbridge. I showed him what I could and he took various photographs. The negatives of these are still in his possession.[23] Returned home late in the evening, Mr. Bigg, our Newsagent, coming also and picking me up. This was lucky as I had missed the last train. Mrs. Pretty thought they wanted me back at Stanton.

Wednesday 10 August Arrived at Stanton Villa. Saw Maynard and found there were no reasons for hurrying me back before week-end. Note: Regarding the tray or dug-out in Tumulus A. It was proposed to remove this bodily to Ipswich Museum and timber was sent over. One of the assistants from the Museum came over while I was there to do this job, but I sent Fuller to help him if required, while I was excavating Tumulus D. The tray was, however, broken through while Mrs. Pretty was watching. I had considered that it would have to be made solid before moving and experiments with water glues etc. this year showed that it might have been done. Anyway I reconstructed the tray where broken and visitors were able to see it for some time, until the Assistant came again and removed the best part with plaster of Paris. I believe he also removed the iron band from the ship or large boat in Tumulus D (after I left) to the Museum, as I observed this object in the show case in the Museum vestibule. Regarding its removal etc. I obtained particulars from Spooner, the gamekeeper. *Plans*: In addition to the various small plans in my field notebook etc. I have the following large scale plans: 1. Tumulus A and Details (A); 2. Tumulus D and Details (B); 3. Tumulus E and Details (C).

Extract from letter from Mr. Guy Maynard, Aug. 23rd 1938

> We should like to have your report on the details of the Sutton excavations as early as convenient. It need not be long but should give the essential details as to dimensions of the mounds (if you have them) and a note as to composition, i.e. material, and any evidence as to the method of erection, any observation on the method originally employed in depositing the remains, position of the deposits in relation to surrounding surface level, and a list of objects recovered or disclosed in each, also any general observations. The British Museum people want the objects to be reported in the *Antiquaries Journal* but this would not prevent your report, together with their observations on the finds, being used in the Suffolk Institute. Also we want the report for reference purposes in arranging the exhibition of the relics here. The B.M. people are going to clean the gold-plated bronze objects for us, and no doubt will be down if any other mounds are opened, which I should think is likely, so that you will have a chance to make their acquaintance if the job proceeds as before.[24]

1939 EXCAVATIONS (INTRODUCTION)

The following note on Tumulus I which is to be excavated, that is if Mrs. Pretty thinks she would like me to explore it, is given as preliminary.

It is the largest of the group, probably originally nearly circular, but as many tons of material have been removed from the western side and the whole aspect of the barrow has been changed it is difficult to say definitely what the original form of the barrow was, but with the concave instead of the normal convex outline from the west, it has a hog back appearance. (We refer to Ordnance 6in Sheet, Suffolk East, LXXVI NE.).

[The attached photograph][25] is a view of the largest mound which we have denoted Tumulus I from the east on this side a few tons only material had been removed apparently for the bunker in the private golf course constructed either by Mr. Lomax or Lady D'Arcy.

The barrow in spite of disturbances and soil removal still remained the largest of the group which have been known for years as The Mounds. Its diameter was approximated 104ft from North–South, and if a circular original outline, is presumed 102ft from East–West. It rises 12ft above plain level.

Proposed excavations in 1939, Sutton Hoo

On November 24th, 1938, Mr. Maynard wrote, in letter re Stanton: 'Perhaps we can get Mrs. Pretty to start again before May, so that our Stanton work shall not be interrupted.'

The 1939 Excavations: Tumulus I and its Ship Burial at Sutton Hoo

Letter from Mr. Guy Maynard (April 14th 1939)

> Dear Basil,
>
> If you would like another spell at Sutton Hoo, Mrs. Pretty is willing to resume work on the barrows. She has not got the two men at present but thinks she can get them. If anything looks like preventing it she will let me know otherwise I thought you might be available after the end of next week? I don't know if this suits you or not, so you must decide and let me know. I found your book of photos all right.

24 April 1939 Mr. Maynard wrote: 'Mrs. Pretty will be away for some days and has suggested a commencement at Sutton Hoo in a fortnight's time, if this would suit you.' (This was actually due to Mrs. Lyons being away.)

4 May 1939 '. . . will get into touch with Mrs. Pretty tomorrow and see whether all is in order for you to come next week, so that you may know.'

6 May 1939 Mr. Maynard wired as follows: 'Start Sutton Hoo work on Monday. Maynard.'

Monday 8 May 1939 Arrived at Sutton Hoo and after leaving my luggage at Mr. Lyon's house where I lodged in 1938 interviewed Mrs. Pretty who accompanied me to the mounds. I asked which one she would like opened and she pointed to I, the largest barrow of the group, and said "What about this?" and I replied that it would be quite all right for me. Mrs. Pretty informed me that she had not the two men Fuller and Sawyer that worked last year, but she suggested two others, William Spooner her gamekeeper, and John Jacobs the gardener at Little Sutton. Did it matter? And I replied "Not in the least as men who were not used soon got interested and learned quickly." I then said I would start the work. Spooner was ready to begin but Jacobs was in the garden and not able to come till the following morning. No reference was made to Ipswich Museum or supervision, so I regarded the position as similar to that in 1938. I then made a survey.

Tuesday 9 May I with Spooner and Jacobs continued the digging of the six feet wide trench into the mound from East to West by compass reading and had made good progress with the upper layers by evening.

Wednesday 10 May Work was continued with the initial trench which was driven towards the west on the old ground surface and in view of the data assimilated last year a most careful note of the strata was made, in fact anything which could be of use as possible clues came in for study. The workmen were particularly instructed to keep the exact old ground surface and do no levelling. If there was a slight rise or ridge it was left; if a slight depression it was carefully cleared out. In this way I was able to get a fairly good idea as to what had happened before the mound builders began to erect the Barrow.

Thursday 11 May I was able to deduce with certainty the existence of a pit or trench below the old ground surface, and I proceeded to widen the trial trench to enable exploration to be undertaken. Also meanwhile keeping a look out for ship rivets. About mid-day Jacobs, who by the way had never seen a ship rivet before and being for the first time engaged in excavation work, called out he had found a piece of iron, afterwards found to be a loose one at the end of a ship. I immediately stopped the work and carefully explored the area with a small trowel and uncovered five rivets in position on what turned out to be the extreme end prow or stern of a ship.

Friday 12 May Continued the widening of the trial trench and carefully explored to admit of following the upper line of rivets by the red spots in the sand which denoted the underlying rivet and found spacing of approx. 5 inches between each rivet showing a resemblance in spacing which was noted by Hele in the ship found in a large mound on Snape Common in 1870 (Hele's *History of Aldeburgh*) also *Victoria History of Suffolk*. Informed Mrs. Pretty and in the evening consulted Mr. Vincent Redstone and the Misses Redstone[26] and who lent me various books on Viking Ship Burials as we thought it was a Viking ship burial.

Saturday 13 May Being the half day, work proceeded in the morning in widening trench in preparation for clearing the end of the ship and finding out its condition or if any traces of wood existed together with the rivets or only as black sand as was found in the small ship in Tumulus D (1938). A few isolated pieces of timber like charcoal were found near the end and left in situ in a test block or section until it can be carefully examined and recorded.

Monday 15 May The widening of the trench was now sufficient to admit of clearing out and finding out if it would be possible to make a successful job of excavating the ship (which appeared to be a small one at the time). The ship is in a slanting position which if it continues will bring it to a depth of some 20 feet below the summit of the barrow. The rivets are in lines about 7 rivets to 3 feet, lines at side are horizontal, at bottom vertical, the angle at which the ship lies makes it very difficult to clear, and there is the necessity of preventing landslides. Whether the ship contains much or not the ship itself is of great interest as ship burials in this country are rare, as Isle of Man, Snape (near Aldeburgh) and the one I found last year seem to be the only ones noted. The Isle of Man ship seems to be Viking.

Tuesday 16 May Progress being made with the ship in spite of bother from landslides and the cutting through the mound has to be widened. This is a big job but must be done before excavation can proceed in safety.

Wednesday 17 May Continuation of work of yesterday. Nothing of special interest to report, but conditions are safer.

Thursday 18 May Clearing ship with small tools and hands as much as possible owing to the head of each individual rivet has to be found and cleared. As I continue the ship widens as it goes deeper. Am unable to let the men do this work owing to the risk of damage and they are getting on with the widening of the trench. Mrs. Pretty seems to be greatly interested.

Work continued and the ship begins to look like one. The rivets show up extremely well towards sunset. Am taking special precautions in case if they did we should have headlines with Viking War Ship found etc. etc. I expect many visitors.

Friday 19 May This is a tremendous job. The cutting has now been widened to 24 feet and even that is not sufficient to prevent landslides owing to the nature of the soil. Have been working lately from 5.00 a.m. (when soils can be best studied) until late at night.

Mr. Guy Maynard came over and agreed that such a find is unique in this country. Ship Burials have of course been found but not so good as this. He took photographs and made drawings of the part excavated.

Saturday 20 May Very busy. A friend, Mr. Prentice of Diss, came over. Worked late. (Eric Payne took photographs.)

Sunday 21 May Taking photographs as the work progresses in case of anything going wrong. To push things on worked today and Spooner also helped. Mrs. Pretty came and watched in the afternoon.

Monday 22 May The work is getting interesting. Technical notes are being made in my field note book and rough plans in preparation for the large detail plans. The widening of the cutting through the mound to allow clearance of the ship and its trench grave is progressing while I am continuing the slow excavation work of the ship itself carefully creeping along rivet by rivet. It is now evident however that we are up against a far larger thing than anyone suspected.

Tuesday 23 May Work continued as before, working early and late paying visits when possible to the Redstone's to keep them informed of progress. They are getting me any books I require from Seckford Library etc. and anything relating or having a bearing on the ship in the way of literature I am sending to Mrs. Pretty who is very nice – and interested in the progress made in view of reaching the chief's burial amidships in all probability. Mr. J. Reid Moir has visited the site but no interference whatever from any quarter. I have also more timber for preventing landslides and am making the excavation much safer. Fragments of Bronze Age pottery continue to turn up as mentioned in my field book and one small piece was found in the ship itself.

The trench graves for the ship has been dug through a Bronze Age site (Hill Top Village) and the hearths or fire pits of hutments can be clearly seen. Mr. Maynard came.

Wednesday 24 May Mrs. Pretty is keen on reaching the Burial and I hope to be well advanced by Saturday. It is a big find and as we go on the ship gets wider and we are certain of a length of at least 50 feet, but the clearance of such a huge thing takes time owing to the depth at which it lies, and this, as we approach amidships, is approximately 20 feet below the top of the mound. We must now be approaching the cabin amidships.

Thursday 25 May Work continued, but further cut-backs are required. The ship is still gradually widening, and more planks are advisable. It will therefore be impossible to reach the Burial before Whitsuntide.

Friday 26 May Mrs. Pretty came down and decided to order another load of planks which, owing to the holidays, would not be able to reach us before Tuesday next.

Saturday 27 May Prepared everything in the morning and cleared up spoil heaps etc., and left for home in the afternoon, Spooner being in charge of the site re possible visitors or trespassers.

Whit Monday Visited the site with Mr. J. B. Watson[27] to see if things were in order.

Tuesday 30 May Planks arrived and were placed in position and sides of the cutting well sloped as it is evident that these must be kept back to allow a good clearance away from the ship grave or pit, otherwise any overhanging soil will slip into the ship as it is excavated, and this is dangerous, and I only escaped being buried by a large landslide of 10 tons or more, missing me by a few minutes. Signs of medieval disturbance found and sherds of jug (the treasure seeker's hearth).

Wednesday 31 May Continued work of excavation, it being now evident that the ship is broadening though there is a tendency to flatten out. 33 feet clear.

Thursday 1 June The cutting will have to be made at least 40 feet wide to clear and for safety and to enable the ship to be excavated in view of its huge size so we got on with this work. The work was then held up by a heavy landslide which prevented all chance of the burial being reached for a few days at least. Asked Mrs. Pretty if I could have another man to help and suggested Bert Fuller, one of the two men I had last year. The ship varies from the usual type of Viking war vessel which invaded this country. Received letter from Mr. Brander Worthem asking me to ask for planks re falls.

Friday 2 June Very busy early to late. Mrs. Pretty is anxious to get to the burial. The ship has widened out to something approaching 15 feet, and its appearance exceeds all estimated proportions and expectation. All concerned want to get to the burial, but I am afraid everyone will have to wait a few days longer before they know what the ship contains. Certainly now we have beaten the record for ships found in burial mounds in the British Isles and one might put either the Snape or the Isle of Man ships inside this easily. Mr. J. Reid Moir and Mr. Pigot (Financial Secretary to the Suffolk Institute of Archaeology and Natural History) arrived. They were pleased with what they saw and Mr. Reid Moir came down in the ship to see exactly its size, appearance of wood decomposition etc., which one is not able to see from above. He agreed with me that further widening is necessary before carrying on to reach the burial and advised me to inform Mrs. Pretty.

Saturday 3 June Continued the widening and taking off the top soil preparatory to excavating another section of the ship and other parts of the medieval jug came to light.

Sunday 4 June Some work on this day to get the work forward. The jug fragments were handed to Mrs. Pretty.

Monday 5 June Continuation of work. The whole excavation is beginning to look safe. A fine sherd of beaker pottery found.

Tuesday 6 June Work continued until near lunch time when Mr. Guy Maynard arrived accompanied by Mr. C. W. Phillips, M.A., F.S.A., (Hon. Sec. Prehistoric Society) of Cambridge. Things then became a bit animated. Mr. Phillips declared himself surprised and that the ship was on a scale comparable with the big ships found in Scandinavia, and that the ship was likely to extend far outside the mound, and it was a find of national importance. In further conversation he acknowledged my excavation had been perfect and could not have been better done. In any case, even if the Office of Works do not take control or place a representative to keep in touch with work on the dig, we shall be certain of having numerous distinguished people visiting the site in the near future. I hope however the newspapers won't get hold of anything concerning the find before an announcement is made later on.

Wednesday 7 June Work of clearing the ship continued and removal of further surface soil towards the west side of mound where many tons of soil content had been removed at some period unknown so as to alter the whole original appearance or contour of the barrow from a probable circular mound to an oval with a hogback appearance. Some of the soil may have been removed by treasure seekers, or taken in more recent times for filling in farm yards. Traces of attempts by treasure seekers were clearly shown by a filled in hole which could be traced downwards to 10 feet from the apex or summit of the barrow. At the side of this was what was thought to be the base of a burnt off post. It existed with a central core of black matter surrounded by a red ash band. This material was kept and submitted to examination by Mr. C. W. Phillips. The feature was then clearly proved to have been the remains of a hearth evidently that of a fire lighted by treasure seekers. This feature was allowed to remain and nicknamed "The Lighthouse" by Jacobs, but it later collapsed, when the soil near it was being removed. I was in consultation with Mr. V. B. Redstone, F.S.A. about treasure hunters and the jug being found near the bottom of the hole which had been dug into the Barrow, and was informed that traditional and other evidence was in existence as follows:

> King Henry VIII dug for treasure in a mound at Sutton Hough but nothing was found, and John Dee, the Court Astrologer, was commissioned to search for treasure along the coast by Queen Elizabeth, and apparently came to Sutton.

Thursday 8 June Work progressed chiefly taking off the top layers, the additional man making a good deal of difference. Also there seemed to be nothing further we could do to make the dig as perfect as possible as was pointed out by Mr. Megaw (Douglas Museum, I.O.M.) and Mrs. Megaw who visited the site with Mrs. Pretty. I had a most interesting talk with this gentleman regarding the ship burial in the Isle of Man, as he was associated with it. He remarked to Mrs. Pretty that he wished theirs had been excavated like this, and he then gave me an account of the Isle of Man dig and that too much reliance could not be placed on the plan given in *Archaeology in England and Wales, 1914–1931*, Kendrick and Hawkes, p. 336, as the excavator, Mr. Kermode, really expected Bronze Age remains, and a hole was dug right through the ship before the significance was seen. I asked him if the burial was really amidships and he said even that was uncertain.

Friday 9 June Heard from Mrs. Pretty that various people were coming to see the ship from the Office of Works, The British Museum, etc., and discuss matters, so not much excavation work could be got on with till they arrived.

The first was Mr. C. W. Phillips accompanied by Dr. Clark, who arrived about noon from Cambridge, followed later by Mr. Baillie Reynolds (Office of Works), Mr. C. F. C. Hawkes (British Museum), Mr. J. Reid Moir, Mr. Guy Maynard and Mr. C. B. Pigot. A discussion took place at the site with Mrs. Pretty followed by another at her residence. Mr. Baillie Reynolds came down in the excavated part of the ship and examined the condition of the wood, that exists not as wood proper but as ash or black dust due to decomposition of the ship timbers throughout the many centuries. Everyone appeared satisfied, and were quite complimentary to me regarding the way this portion of the ship had been cleared, but of course I have put in a lot of time and used great care, and at the commencement it was still more difficult because no Viking ship had been excavated so much in this country and it was only by careful experiments and reasoning that I found it really was possible. Of course at this stage it is not so difficult for one knows exactly what to do and how it must be done. The decision eventually arrived at was to cover the portion excavated with Hessian etc., and fill it in with sand until a shed could be put over it, and the excavation of the other part of the ship to continue as before.

Mr. Maynard had brought over several large pieces of Hessian which had been used in the Museum and we put what we could (Mr. Maynard and I) with the aid of nails etc., Mrs. Pretty had already obtained. This work was done after the men had gone home.

Saturday 10 June Mrs. Pretty purchased more Hessian and I finished the job of covering the sides and bottom of the ship as far as excavated and then put in sand obtained from the next section being excavated while the men removed the top layers from a further section (well above the ship).

Have just heard that the Office of Works Commission wanted Mrs. Pretty to wait until the shed was built over the cleared part of the ship before going on with the examination and this would have meant a suspension of work until about October. I am glad to write that this matter was satisfactorily adjusted and there will be no interference. The shed would be expensive as the ship must be about 80 feet long and a shed would have to be about 100 feet in length.

Sunday 11 June Did various checking and went over the whole data concerning the ship and problems entailed, especially so as Mrs. Pretty has asked me if I could reach the burial as her sister was coming next week. I have replied that I would do my best to reach it by Wednesday afternoon or late on Thursday morning (rather difficult to carry out even if one knows how long each section takes to clear). Mrs. Pretty would like her sister to be present when the burial is reached I expect.

Regarding data I expect the following: A ship about 80 feet in length and a burial amidships. I believe the treasure chamber to be intact in spite of attempts at various times to dig down to it. Henry the Eighth's workmen tried and most likely John Dee for most pieces of a jug of this period were found 10 feet down. However in discussing the burial with Mr. Reginald Smith[28] and Mr. J. Reid Moir who have just come over to see the ship, I said "If any of the treasure hunters ever got down we should find their bones at the bottom of the hole, as the soil below is extremely treacherous and would slip in without warning", and that only a big excavation with careful timbering would be likely to succeed.

This is the second visit this year of Mr. Reginald Smith who is fond of using the Sideric Pendulum and the divining rod for finding treasure, but the position is much the same as last year and I don't know what success he has had. I think too much reliance must not be placed in these things. He got as before reaction for gold and silver in certain positions (so do I, but not in his positions but shall mark his and await results by the spade). We get few visitors except archaeologists and friends of Mrs. Pretty.

Monday 12 June Carrying on, the men taking off the upper layers to just above the ship while I am working below clearing slowly along each rivet separately and leaving plenty of sand on each rib (which are in fact only a black powder). Worked very late.

Tuesday 13 June Work as yesterday, making progress but no sign yet of the burial.

Wednesday 14 June Work proceeded as before. No signs yet of the burial but a large rib or timber where a rib should be has come to light with some long vertical rivets. Cleaned this as the ribs had been done and left plenty of surrounding sand as before for safety and it was 5 o'clock (time for tea).

After tea I came back alone and worked hard, and then came the first find, a large iron ring[29] and what appeared to be a smaller one close by and with my hands I carefully cleared away the sand above using a soft brush which Mrs. Pretty had sent down some days before. Then green of bronze bands, or what appeared to be bands, showed up and what was undoubtedly wood which gave out a hollow sound.[30] At this time Spooner arrived and helped me. I conclude that the bronze objects have been crushed by the great weight of soil breaking in the cabin, and perhaps the iron object may be the anchor which fell from above in the collapse. We carefully covered the objects over with Hessian and sand as it was now dusk, and I went to report to Mrs. Pretty. I saw the footman who took my message to her that I had found the burial and its condition, and I went to my lodgings very tired. I then made a drawing of the objects and noted them.

Thursday 15 June Showed Fuller and Jacobs the objects when I recovered them with paper, then Hessian, and lastly sand, and we then all went on with the task of removing the upper layers preparatory to clearing the next section (i.e. an excavating section, the same as carried on from the start of excavation, 6 feet in length).

Mrs. Pretty came down with Mr. Maynard who seemed inclined to want the men to slow up things. Mrs. Pretty said to me that her sister was not coming now, and Maynard said we should most likely be having visitors from Scandinavia. If I can get this ship cleared satisfactorily I quite expect we shall have all the chief archaeologists in the British Isles to see it.

Friday 16 June We carried on with the top layers, pushed back spoil heaps and generally tidied up the excavations.

Saturday 17 June Carried on this work in the morning.

Sunday 18 June At home.

Monday 19 June Heard that further excavation is to be suspended until a shed is up over the part we have done already, i.e. from what is assumed to be the stern to the beginning of the burial amidships, also that Mr. Phillips[31] is being sent over to Denmark to find out the best methods for preserving the ship. The British Museum are arranging this instead of Ipswich Museum. As far as I can find out I shall continue and there is a lot of work at the present time cutting back ready for the proposed shed which is to have glass in roof (skylights etc). This find has certainly caused a big stir everywhere in the antiquarian world and is of the greatest importance. This day was very wet and little work was possible.

Tuesday 20 June This and succeeding day were devoted to widening the cutting and Spooner and Jacobs went back to their usual work while Fuller assisted me.

Wednesday 21 June Ditto. Cutting back south west side of the excavation. Visited Snape.

Thursday 22 June Making progress although the work is naturally slower.

Friday 23 June Continued. Uneventful except for the finding of further Bronze Age hearths and fragments of pottery.

Saturday 24 June Ditto (morning). In afternoon visited Snape.

Sunday 25 June Mr. Maynard came over and Eric Payne arrived from Harrow-on-the-Hill. Payne took photographs of the Bronze Age hearths etc. Maynard informed me that Mr. Bushe-Fox of the Office of Works had asked him about my capabilities. Perhaps we may be able to get on with the burial in a few days if Phillips can get over to see or represent the Office of Works.
Extra note: Abridged B.P. visit to Snape Common. Saw friend of Captain Wentworth R.N. who owns the property from Aldeburgh to Snape Bridge. Had a talk re estate records etc.

Monday 26 June Work continued. Mrs. Pretty with Mr. Fairweather, the proprietor and editor of the Woodbridge Reporter. Mr. Fairweather was quite nice and realised the position – that we did not want people here yet. He was shown everything and told various things regarding the ship. Mrs. Pretty has promised him the first story when the Press can be allowed to know. He is certainly a reliable man and will certainly keep his word.

Tuesday 27 June Work progressing. We are continuing excavation by clearing along the line of the grave trench which is the only way as I am prevented from carrying out the original plan of creeping along section by section. In this way I shall be able to find the end of the ship when the end of the grave trench is reached. It is more difficult but the same result must come.

Wednesday 28 June Work going on well. Mr. Maynard arrived in the evening and we then proceeded to draw up plan of the ship (i.e. of the part excavated so this will be ready to hand over to Mr. Phillips when he comes. He also brought over a field book so I can copy the plans and notes from my private notes and keep this at the dig for inspection of visitors etc.*
[*MS. Note added*] *1964* *No opportunity of doing this and no place at the dig to keep anything. Mrs. Pretty's residence being fairly near and everything went there she asked for.

Thursday 29 June Work progressing. I have now found the rivets at the west end of the ship. It is not so much pointed as the other but a little may have been cut off when the field was ploughed, which was up to 1882. The end comes quite to the surface outside the mound and a furrow had been ploughed right over the end of the ship. Only one loose rivet was found near. All are in situ. Roughly the ship measurements are approximately 82 ft. long with 15 feet beam. A ship of this size must have been that of a king or a person of very great importance and it is the find of a lifetime. The ship however will take a lot of clearing out yet. Mr. Maynard came.

Friday 30 June Work continued. The form of the ship now begins to show. It can now be divided into three parts, the bow, amidships, stern. These may now be roughly estimated as 30′ – 20′ – 30′, making 80 feet in length.

Saturday 1 July Work continued, everything satisfactory. Just received a long letter from Mr. Maynard dealing with plans and also he was sending over the work on the Oseberg ship for me to study. Said that Mr. Bushe-Fox was afraid of thunderstorms, and proposed sending over tarpaulins to cover over the ship, gave some hints but said he must leave my ingenuity to find a way, and wrote, "for goodness sake don't go far down inside the ship once the western half is established. Let Phillips & Co. take the onus and play for safety."

Sunday 2 July Mr. Cullum and Mr. Pigot brought over the book and took measurements for tarpaulins.

Monday 3 July Work continued and cleared the clay deposit amidships exactly above the place where I expect the chief lies. Covered this with Hessian etc., but we want to get on.

Tuesday 4 July Expect we shall now get a move on as Phillips is expected on the 7th or 8th. Work continued; am studying the large book and am lending it to Mrs. Pretty for a day.

Wednesday 5 July Work continued but nothing of importance transpired although things are now moving to allow us to be getting on per Mrs. Pretty.

Thursday 6 July Working at cut back etc. I have of course only had one man to help for some days, i.e. Fuller. We have however managed to get much useful work done. Have been studying the Oseberg ship excavation reports, the large work Mr. Maynard sent over for me. The excavation of the big Scandinavian ship said to have been the Queen's burial ship must have been a very interesting job. In it were beds, carts and a sleigh all jumbled together. Treasure hunters however had looted the valuables by cutting a hole in the chamber in early times. I don't think grave robbers have ever got down to the burial in the Sutton Hoo ship, but we must await the time when the burial will be cleared. I hear Mr. Phillips is coming tomorrow, so Mrs. Pretty has now definitely moved things so it won't be very long.

Friday 7 July Work continued. Nothing of moment to report. Phillips has not arrived – is said to have had an accident and have a badly cut thumb.

Saturday 8 July Mr. Phillips arrived at last in the afternoon. Is not staying at the mansion but at an hotel in Woodbridge. He had he believed not been let know (apparently by Ipswich Museum and did not seem to be pleased about it. His attitude was a bit bellicose).

Sunday 9 July Went home and went over my plans and notes as I am discussing the matter of the ship and various business connected with the dig with Mr. Phillips on Monday.

Monday 10 July We have made a start in clearing down in the ship above the burial. Phillips will apparently act as representative of the Office of Works here so he will keep his own log. Anyway I shall not have so much bother and responsibility now in case anything went wrong. I think we shall be able to co-operate all right, at least I hope so. For the future I shall confine my log to brief notes as I think advisable. Commander Hutchison, the authority on ancient ships from the Science Museum, London, is expected tomorrow. He will be in control of all matters (technical) relating to the ship and its details. My status now is, after consultation with the Office of Works and Mrs. Pretty it was decided to place the supervision of the excavation under Mr. C. W. Phillips and I am to be his assistant, but still in the employ of Mrs. Pretty.

Tuesday 11 July Work carried on getting ready for Commander Hutchison and clearing down in the ship. Spooner is now helping again and Jacobs is coming in a few days. The Museum Office apparently put off Commander Hutchison coming in the afternoon. There was a heated discussion between Maynard and Phillips and Phillips said "From now on Maynard I'm in control here". This apparently terminated any interference by Ipswich Museum or its officials, and leaves only Mrs. Pretty and the Office of Works. I have decided to be neutral in all disputes but as the employee of Mrs. Pretty I should carry out any suggestions or orders she might express, even if I should differ with or obstruct anyone, but I do not think that any difference or bother is likely to arise through Mrs. Pretty.

Basil Brown's log concludes with a copy of his evidence before the treasure trove Inquest, which is reproduced in Chapter XI of Vol. I of the British Museum definitive publication. There follows an entry 'August 27th – September 2nd – War. Ship filled with bracken'; a note 'Death of Mrs. Frank Pretty – Woodbridge Reporter, December 17th, 1942'; a record of a visit to the site paid by Brown on April 27, 1947; and finally a letter of receipt from the Bury St Edmunds Solicitors, Bankes Ashton & Co., dated 26th February, 1964, of the originals of his log book and plans of the 1939 excavations. More recently

Mr Brown has visited the site every year during our re-excavations of 1965–70, and has been a welcome and honoured visitor at the British Museum, where he has seen the new developments in conservation and restoration of the Sutton Hoo material and the new displays in the galleries.

NOTES TO CHAPTER FOUR

1 This refers to a rough plan made by Brown on that day, a copy of which is in the Department of Medieval and Later Antiquities in the British Museum.

2 This was Brown's first sight of the mounds.

3 Brown's rough plan, made on June 20th, shows these to have been mounds Nos. 1 and 3 respectively.

4 Presumably Brown followed the same procedure in 1939; this explains how the contours of the ship-barrow came to be altered. The trench Brown put down was initially forty feet long, running up onto the mound. He dumped topsoil and barrow material initially to either side of it and this was later shifted further back as the trench was widened.

5 His tumulus A, that is Mound No. 3 in our general site plan, *c.f. The Sutton Hoo Ship-Burial, a Handbook*, London, 1972, Fig. 2.

6 Brown was the first to have recorded more than the nine mounds shown on the Ordnance Survey Maps. In his rough plan of 20th June 1938, the mounds are not very precisely sited in relation to each other but the additional three mounds he recorded appear to be those seen again and recorded in the 1965–6–7 survey and appearing in the general site plan as Nos. 5, 13, and 15. His plan is dated 21 June 1938 and in fact shows thirteen mounds, three of which are marked with queries.

7 Fair copies of these plans are published and discussed in Chapter II of Vol. I of the definitive account of the Sutton Hoo ship-burial, Cambridge, 1974.

8 It is interesting to see Brown considering this possibility before he came upon a boat in Mound 2.

9 The condition of the objects was apparently due to cremation. The burial does not appear to have been robbed. See *The Sutton Hoo Ship-burial*, Vol. I, Cambridge, 1974, Chapter II.

10 A photo of the excavation was here appended to Brown's log. It shows little detail but is reproduced as fig. 59 in Chapter II of *The Sutton Hoo Ship-Burial*, Vol. I, Cambridge, 1974.

11 Where the Ipswich Museum were excavating a Roman Villa.

12 A photo was here annexed in Brown's log; captioned 'My birthplace, Bucklesham, near Woodbridge'.

13 H. E. P. Spencer was the geologist at the Ipswich Museum. J. Reid Moir, F.R.S., F.S.A., Chairman of the Ipswich Museum Committee, was famous at that time as a palaeolithic pioneer and the discoverer of 'eoliths'.

14 Northerly, in fact, as marked on his plan.

15 This is an important observation suggesting that the external appearance of the boat-grave tumulus was similar to that of Mounds 7 and 10 and also like that of the Välsgärde boat-graves.

16 An assistant at the Ipswich Museum.

17 The mound-like shapes which dominate the area in this map are only Norden's convention for rough heath-land; the tumuli are represented by a smaller tightly-knit cluster on the south edge of the map labelled 'Mathershoe'. The Norden map is reproduced in Chapter I of Volume I of the British Museum's definitive publication, Cambridge, 1974.

18 This supposed piece of bone did not survive and is unlikely if correctly identified as bone or as human to have belonged to the primary burial.

18a This somewhat tasteless joke proved prophetic, since no less than three live mortar bombs were found in the mound when the barrow was re-excavated in 1965–70.

19 This is the date of Dr Hele's book *Notes on Aldeburgh*. The excavation of the ship was in 1863. For a full account see Chapter Three in this volume.

20 This was a damaged fragment which, after careful enquiry and investigation, is thought to be part of a mount from a shield. It is illustrated with the other finds in Chapter II of Vol. I of the definitive publication, *The Sutton Hoo Ship-Burial*, Cambridge, 1974.

21 For identifications of these cremated bones which included those of a deaf horse, see Vol. 1 of the definitive publication, Ch. II, Appendices.

22 Brown's compass bearing on his plan of 21st June is incorrect and explains his use of east instead of north here. The site is mound 13 on the plan, Rupert Bruce-Mitford, *Sutton Hoo Handbook*, London, 1972, Fig. 2.

23 Subsequently acquired by the British Museum.

24 It is of interest that Maynard had got into touch with the British Museum about Sutton Hoo finds before the dig in 1939 was begun, when the ship-burial was discovered.

25 One of the only two surviving pictures of the mound before excavation, both of which, with a detail of the ordnance survey six-inch map referred to by Brown, are published in Volume I of the British Museum definitive publication, *The Sutton Hoo Ship-Burial*, Cambridge, 1974, Figs. 31, 94 and 98.

26 V. B. Redstone was a master at Woodbridge School and a Fellow of the Society of Antiquaries. He had three scholarly daughters who ran the Seckford Library in Seckford Street, Woodbridge. The youngest, Lilian Redstone, M.B.E., became known as a local historian and genealogist and wrote a number of books.

27 A personal friend of Brown's from his own village of Diss, Mr Watson ran the local potteries and subsequently became involved in the excavation of Roman kilns that had used the same clay supplies and in experiments, in which the British Museum took part, in the building and firing of Roman-type kilns.

28 Keeper of British and Mediaeval Antiquities at the British Museum and Director of the Society of Antiquaries.

29 This was the large ring at the top of the cauldron-chain.

30 The iron-bound tub and bronze cauldron No. 1.

31 In fact not Phillips but Dr H. J. Plenderleith, Keeper of the British Museum Research Laboratory.

CHAPTER FIVE

Excavations at Sutton Hoo, 1965–69

It was decided in 1965 to return to the site of the ship-burial, to uncover the ship again and to investigate the remains of the tumulus. We did not know what the original shape of the tumulus was – whether oval or circular – what its height had been before excavation, whether it was surrounded by a ditch, or what structural or ritual features it might possess. We also planned to gain more information about the burial-ground as a whole by cutting grass and bracken and making a new and sensitive survey of its surface features. In the process the number of barrows recognizable rose from eleven to sixteen. It was also planned to sound the flat ground between and near the barrows to see whether ordinary burials, whether cremation or inhumation, could be located and to establish the nature of the Neolithic-Bronze Age occupation plentifully attested on the site by stray finds. It had already produced a segmented faience bead (an Egyptian import) and duly yielded, apart from structures, fine Beaker pottery, good flints and loom weights.

Work on the barrow was directed by Paul Ashbee, F.S.A., who also supervised the new survey of the site. His team located, in the 1939 dumps, the stratum of spoil carried out from the burial chamber while the grave-goods were being excavated. The stratum was located in the 1967 season and almost at once by highly organized and disciplined trowelling, fragments of helmet and of the large hanging bowl – including parts of the decorated frames surrounding the escutcheons and the missing third boar's head – as well as fragments of shield ornaments and a tine from the stag were found. Also found, adhering to a piece of wood and intact to its full length, was one of the wrought-iron animal horns from a corner of the grille of the iron stand, and various iron fragments, portions of cleats, nails, etc. A bucket handle with bird's head finial ornaments was found still *in situ* on the side of the ship in my own re-excavation of the ship (Plates 28 and 29).

It should be remembered that the 1939 excavations were essentially a 'rescue dig', improvised and carried through under the threat of war. Many of the grave-

Plate 29 Taking a plaster cast of the Sutton Hoo ship, 1967. The roof is of polythene sheeting reinforced with nylon net

Plate 30 The plastering operation at various stages: *a*, Applying the paper towelling. The rivets have been covered with clay; *b*, Applying plaster to a section outlined with 'sausages'; *c*, A number of completed casts made in a few days. The sections show handles for convenient lifting; *d*, Raising a cast. The paper came away with the plaster, as did the clay cups covering the rivets

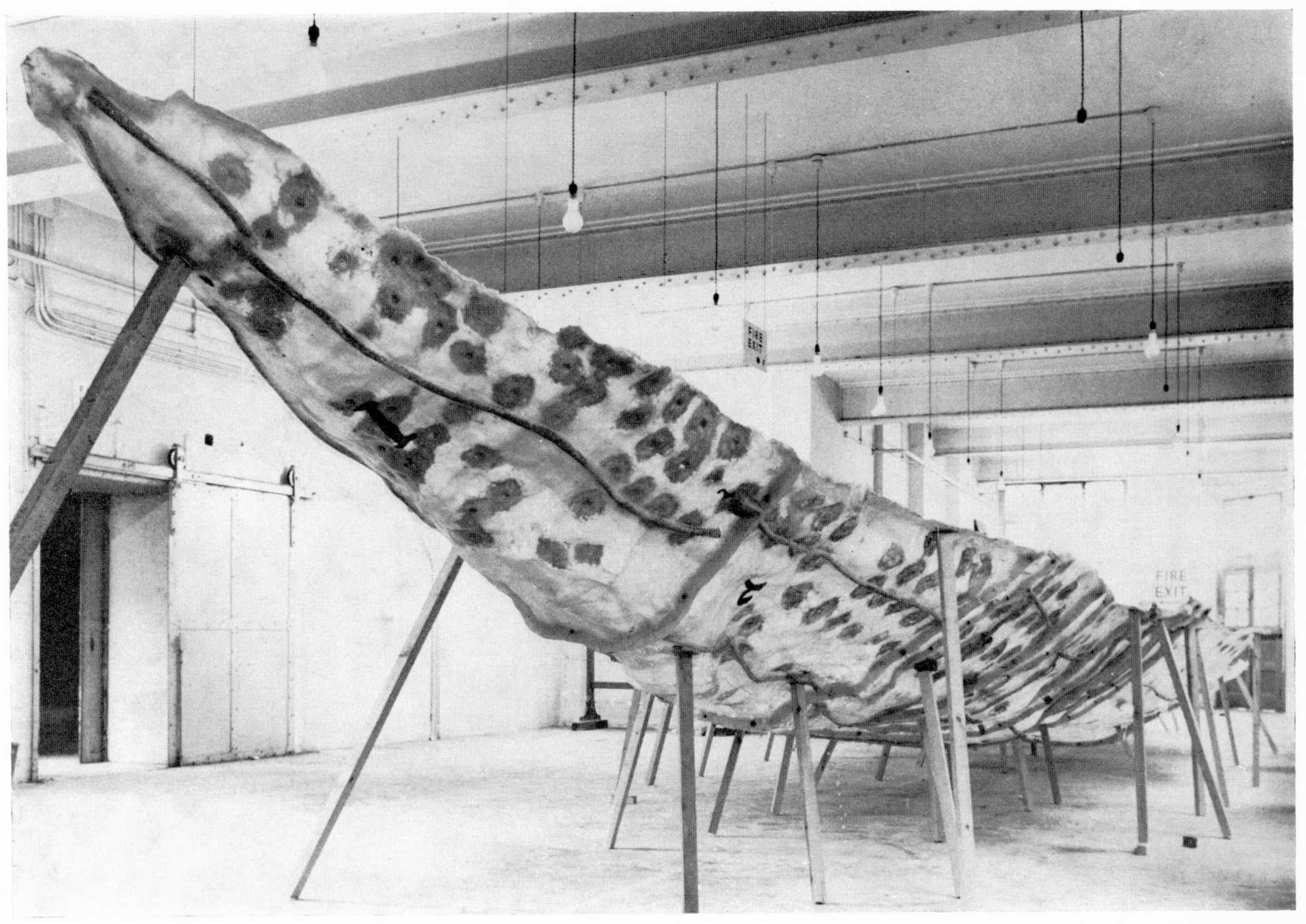

Plate 31 Fibre glass reproduction of the form of the Sutton ship as it survived in 1967, made from the plaster moulds taken in 1967

32

Plate 32 Detail of ship's figure-head from Appels, Belgium (reduced)

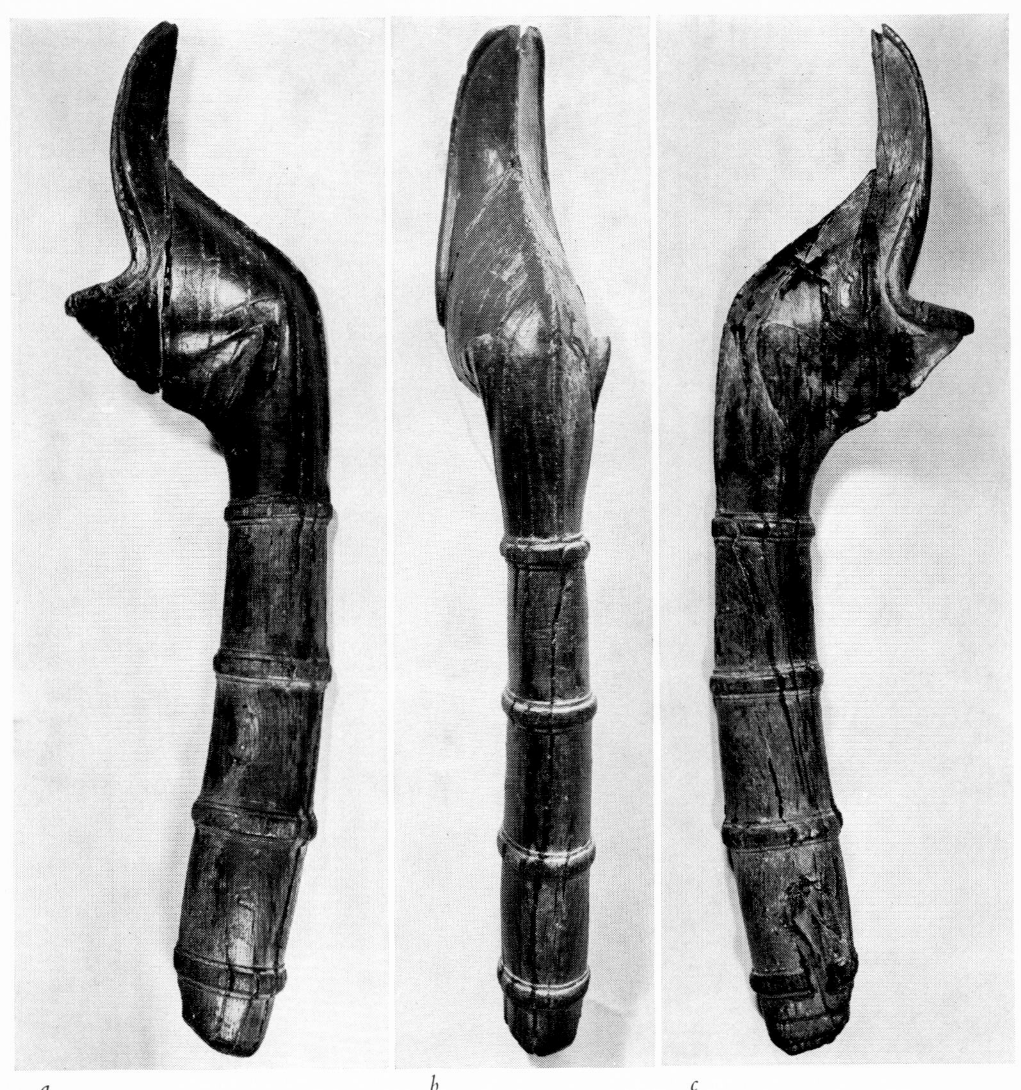

a b c

Plate 33 Ship's figure-head from the River Scheldt between Moerzeke and Mariekerke, Belgium. General views (Scales 1 : 7)

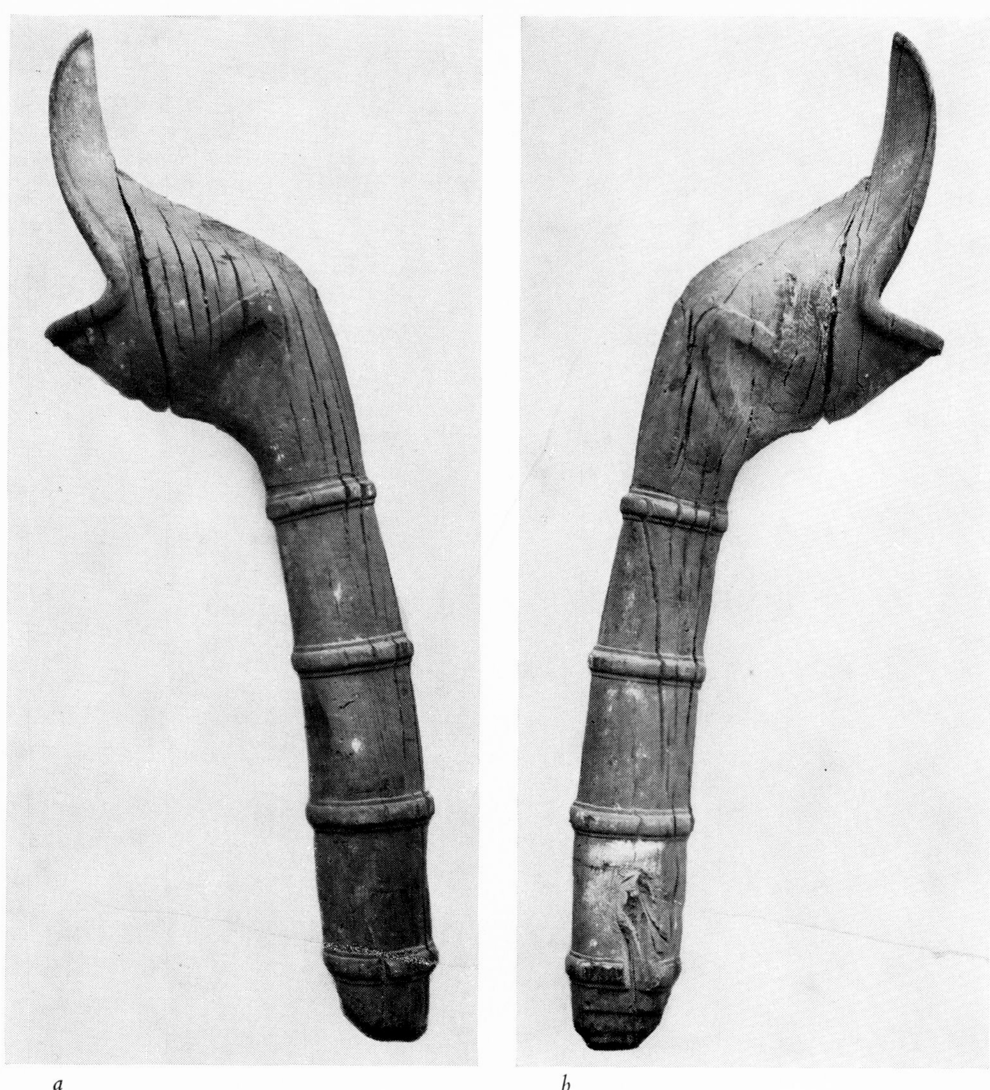

a b

Plate 34 Moerzeke-Mariekerke head. Photographs taken in 1941–2 (Scales 1 : 7)

Plate 35 a, b, Moerzeke-Mariekerke head. Detail of head, back and front; (reduced)

Plate 36 Zele head (reduced)

goods were in a highly fragmentary state, so that the incorporation of some of the fragments in spoil carried out from the chamber is not surprising. The systematic excavation of the 1939 dumps was a serious archaeological exercise, in which both negative and positive evidence were sought for specific ends.

In my own re-excavation of the ship and its trench, the objectives were to uncover the hull, which had not been backfilled in 1939 but had silted up, and to ascertain how much of it remained undisturbed and whether there was any point in attempting to preserve what might remain for posterity. The next objective was to record additional information about the hull and its construction, which it was thought should be recoverable through close and specialized scrutiny, in which answers to specific questions might be sought. For example, whether caulking (probably animal hair) could be located where the strakes had overlapped; whether traces of tar from the surface of the wood were detectable; whether the ribs were of rounded or square cross-section; the number and distribution of plank-joints; the cross-sections of the keel at intervals along the hull and a number of other technical details of the ship's construction.

It was also hoped to seek within the burial chamber area traces of phosphate which might have a bearing on the original presence of a body from the burial deposit.

It was found that the hull, with the exception of the top two or three strakes on either side, at least ten feet of the bows and part of the stern, was substantially intact and still capable of yielding a great deal of information (Plate 28). The remains, although sadly inferior to the magnificent and sensitive record of the ship at its full extent visible as a result of skilful excavation in 1939, were still an extremely impressive sight and it was thought wise to obtain a consensus of opinion before the ship, a sight unparalleled in this country, was dug up and destroyed for good. Consequently, the Ancient Monuments Board for England were invited to visit the site and indeed discussed the whole question in some detail. It was eventually decided that preservation would not be practicable. Indeed the full range of information which the remains in the ground might supply could not be recovered without sacrificing the impression that was left. The need to excavate beneath the boat, in order to be sure that nothing had been missed and that the story was complete, also meant the destruction of the ghost of the ship itself.

In retrospect this was clearly the right decision, for when all the rivets, some two thousand in number, were lifted, a considerable variation in size and in the angles between head and rove were seen. These differences could not have been observed had the rivets been left in the ground. The three-dimensional method of recording that had been followed enables us, in considering the individual characteristics of each bolt and rivet, to say exactly the point on the hull from which it had come. Analysis of the individual characteristics of the bolts and rivets yielded information about the constructional details of the ship which could not otherwise have been recovered.

Once the decision to dig up and destroy the remains of the ship had been taken it was first necessary to ensure that they were completely recorded. In addition to the existing 1939 records, the 1966 rivet plan and additional photographic and other records and to the lifting of certain portions of the structure for removal to the Museum, it was thought desirable to make a cast of the entire inside of the hull. Such an operation had never before been undertaken in British archaeology. Over six and a half tons of plaster were used in making a record of this seventy-six feet shape in the soil (Plates 30a–d).

The problem was to make a cast without destroying the surface or the details of the ship, for these must be scientifically excavated and parts were suitable for preservation *en bloc* and removal to the Museum. As the surface from which the cast had to be taken consisted only of sand, it was necessary to prevent the wet plaster from adhering and simply pulling away the surface when an attempt was made to lift the set plaster. It was essential that the plaster should come away cleanly. Consolidation of the surface only made matters worse, for the hardened surface only came away the more readily from its loose sand backing. Some sort of insulation had to be devised and experiments had to be carried out. A further problem was posed by the rivets. These were only rust, yet they projected in the shape of rivets from the skin of the ship inwards, each one terminating in a diamond-shape flattened rove. Clearly these projecting roves and shanks would become embedded in the plaster and would be torn away when an attempt was made to lift the casts. In the event it was decided to cover each individual rivet with a little cap of clay, which gave the effect of studding the inside of the ship with a whole lot of regularly distributed limpets. In between these clay 'limpets' stretched the flat sand surface of the boat. The technique eventually adopted was to use tissue paper as an insulating medium. Various forms of polythene or latex sheet were tried but all were insensitive and tended to wrinkle under the application of the liquid plaster. In the event lengths of Scotch towelling torn off a roll were used. These were dipped in water and laid on the side of the ship and over the 'limpets' (Plate 30a). The wet paper adhered to the surface and was made to fit exactly by being tapped everywhere into position with a soft paint-brush. Upon this wet paper ground, within a rectangular area marked out by sand-filled polythene 'sausages', liquid plaster was sloshed in (Plate 30b). This was reinforced at intervals by lengths of scrim to prevent cracking. As the depth of the plaster was built up, handles made from bent conduit tubing, the ends wrapped round with scrim soaked in plaster, were inserted (Plate 30c). These set like welded joints. The whole of the operation had to be completed in eight minutes, for that was the period of time it took the plaster, once mixed, to solidify.

The sand ribs which transversed the hull every 3 ft 6 ins or so were the subject of separate castings because of their irregularity and often undercut shapes. The moulding process was much more complicated. The edges of the rib-pieces and of each section of the cast were coated with French polish so that they could be detached from one another without sticking. The size of the individual sections of the cast varied from about 5 ft square to about 3 ft square and a pulley and ratchet had to be rigged up from the scaffold poles which held the polythene and nylon roof that spanned the whole of the excavations. With the pulley and chain the heavier sections could be lifted and swung to the cat-walk on either side of the boat and so carried out.

The casting operation proved completely successful. As each section of the cast was lifted it came away cleanly (Plate 30d). If nailed copper tags (stamped with the individual numbers allotted to each rivet) came away with the plaster, an immediate scrutiny identified them and enabled them to be replaced alongside the rivet from which they had been derived. If any rivets came away with the clay 'limpets', these could similarly be replaced at once before the plaster-cast was removed and after it had been raised from the surface of the boat. When the entire cast had been removed the hull was seen to be to all intents and purposes intact and undamaged, apart from the occasional small splashes of plaster left adhering to the sand.

The sections of the plaster-cast were transported by lorry to the British Museum, where an impression in fibreglass has been taken from them (Plate 31). This is light and indestructible and the sections can be easily stacked and stored. In the impressions, the position of each rivet is marked by a protuberance representing the clay 'limpet'. If it were ever desired to build a full-scale replica of the ship in the British Museum or elsewhere, as it was in 1967, the fibreglass sections could simply be run together to build up the complete shape of the hull as it then was. The technique can now be profitably applied to new finds of ships in their undamaged state.

After the remains of the ship had been lifted, the trench that had contained it was completely excavated. Traces of two split logs were found, one at the stern and one at the bow, lying slightly obliquely at right-angles across the keel line and parallel with one another. They seemed to be timbers put down to facilitate the manoeuvring of the boat into position in its trench. Nothing else was found beneath the ship.

The casting operation lasted three weeks and was carried out by four men, including Mr P. Langhorn, the Senior Technician in charge of the plasterers' shop at the British Museum, and the Senior Conservation Officer in the Department of Medieval and Later Antiquities, Mr P. Van Geersdaele.[1] In addition, the plastering team was helped by two or three assistants who swept out the cast before sections were lifted, mixed and carried plaster, applied French polish and made polythene sand-sausages. In the lifting one of the excavators checked each cast with the correspondingly numbered rivet plan already made, to ensure that any detached rivets (very few) or copper tags were correctly replaced.

Soil samples were taken from immediately beneath each of the two thousand odd rivets (which were almost completely corroded to iron oxide) in the hope of finding phosphate remains in the form of iron phosphate, which is insoluble and it was thought might be expected to remain trapped in these positions. In addition, soil samples were taken throughout the burial chamber area, where in the bottom of the boat the rivet-pattern had not survived, on a grid at one foot intervals. A good deal of solid cream-coloured phosphatic matter was also found in the burial chamber area, particularly in the region where the shield and sword had lain, probably derived from a set of ivory gaming-pieces. This evidence has been duly assimilated into the study of the cenotaph problem in the British Museum's definitive publication of the ship-burial.[2]

NOTES TO CHAPTER FIVE

1 P. van Geersdaele, 'Moulding the Impression of the Sutton Hoo Ship', *Studies in Conservation*, 14/4, Nov. 1969, 177–82.
P. van Geersdaele, 'Making the fibreglass replica of the Sutton Hoo Ship Impression', *Studies in Conservation*, 15/3, Aug. 1970, 215–20.

2 *The Sutton Hoo Ship-Burial*, Vol. I, Ch. 8, 'The Cenotaph Problem', Cambridge, 1974.

CHAPTER SIX

Ships' Figure-Heads of the Migration Period

I A NEW WOODEN SHIP'S FIGURE-HEAD FOUND IN THE SCHELDT, AT MOERZEKE-MARIEKERKE

The oak figure-head which is the subject of this chapter (Plates 33–37, Fig 19a–c) was formerly the property of Mr Sylvio Galardi who kindly gave me permission to publish it and offered every co-operation in its study. I am very grateful for his assistance. The figure-head is now in the British Museum.

The figure-head is of oak, made of a single piece of wood. It is incomplete, the lower end having at some time been chopped off (Plates 36a and Fig 19a–c). In its present state it weighs 9 lbs 12 ozs and has an overall length of forty inches (one metre). The oak post is fashioned from a natural branch expanded at its junction with the trunk, providing the rounded swelling which is utilized to form the animal's head. This carved head is dolphin-like with open mouth, the upper lip curved upwards and backwards and elongated, the under lip being shorter and straight. Both jaws are slightly pointed. Central carinations run down from beneath the thick lip of the lower jaw to what might be described as the Adam's apple of the creature under the chin, where it ceases, and above, from the tip of the upper lip over the back of the head, like an inconspicuous crest and down as far as the uppermost of the four raised lateral mouldings round the shaft. These carinations of head and chin are pronounced. The animal-head has no carved eye, worn down or otherwise, no trace of any attachment for an eye in material other than wood, nor any trace of a painted eye.

A thick moulding, which is up to $\frac{4}{5}$ inches (over 2 cms) wide at the side of the lower jaw but tapers to the points of the jaws, outlines the mouth, representing the lips. It shows a particularly graceful sweep in the elongated upper jaw. The ears are triangular, projecting at the point and thinning below to merge into the surface of the head. When the post is held vertical, the upper edges of the ears dip slightly downwards in the direction of the mouth. When seen from the back they project clearly on either side of the head. The sides of the ears are slightly convex. The floor of the open mouth is sunken and flat and there are no teeth.

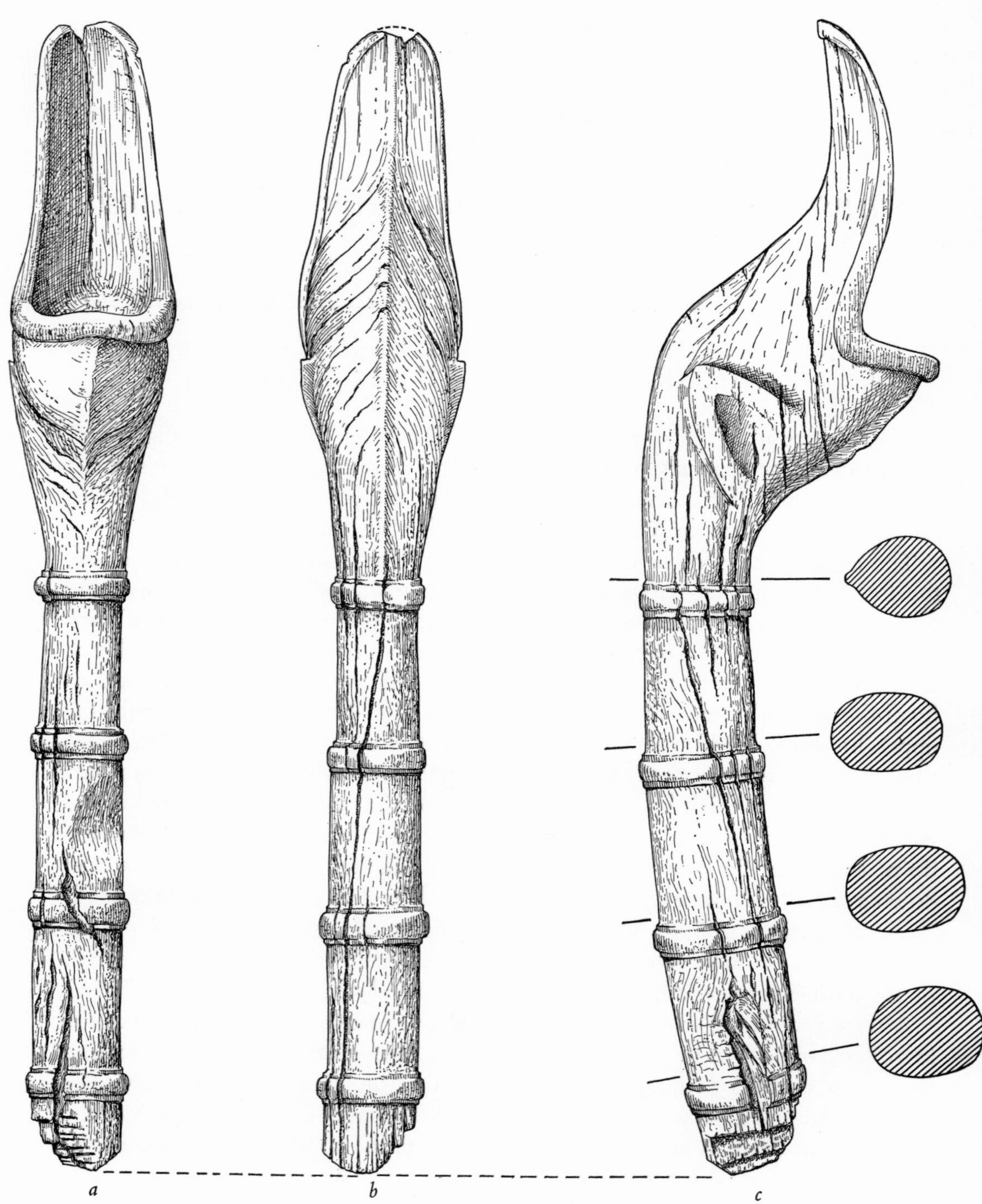

Figure 19 Three views of the oak figure-head from Moerzeke-Mariekerke, Belgium (length 1 metre)

A sizeable piece of wood comprising the mouth and part of the lower jaw has split off from the rest and is now held in position by two screws. The neck narrows to three inches maximum diameter immediately above the uppermost lateral band. The post then expands to a maximum width, at and including the third band down, of $4\frac{5}{8}$ inches (12 cms) and thins again slightly by a quarter of an inch at the lowest band. At this point and between the lowest band and the next one above it is a knot or blemish.

The oak of the post has split badly along the grain in many places (Fig 19a–c), particularly in the head (Plates 34, 35a, 37), and the cracks have been plugged with bitumen and glue. The whole of one side of the head is covered with bitumen (Plate 33a). A rounded slice has been chipped off on the inner face of the post between the middle two lateral mouldings (Plates 33a, 34a and Fig 19a) as though by an axe or weapon and there are signs of mild battering or wear and tear in places. Below the lowest lateral ring the posts have been cut off apparently by an axe, the chopping marks being quite distinct (Plate 34b and Fig 19a–c). The post is slightly curved, the profile facing the direction in which the head points being slightly concave. The curvature seems to become intensified at the lower end of the post. The cross-section of the post is a slightly flattened oval, measuring $3\frac{1}{2} \times 2\frac{1}{2}$ inches just below the topmost lateral moulding and 4×3 inches just below the second moulding down. Its long axis lies in the direction faced by the animal head.

I have taken pains to try to trace the history of this find and have discussed the matter personally in London with its second owner M. René Van de Broek, a well-known Brussels dealer, whose establishment is at 9a Bd. de Waterloo (Porte de Namur) Brussels 1, with whom I have also corresponded. M. Van de Broek acquired the post in 1942. I have also corresponded with its first owner, M. Philip H. Duprez, of Holdaal 8, Ghent, Belgium.

At some time the figure-head was sold to the Rexist, M. Léon Degrelle, who took it with him when he fled in 1945 to Spain, where it was eventually acquired by Mr Galardi.

According to M. Philip Duprez, it was brought up by a dredger operated by the firm Entrepreneur de Wilde of Baasrode in 1939 or 1940 near Moerzeke-Mariekerke, on the Scheldt – some fifteen or so kilometres downstream from Appels, near Termonde, where the well-known figure-head, now in the British Museum, was found.[1]

With the post were found, M. Duprez states, 'several pieces of the hull-planks of a ship. They were fixed together with "red copper nails". These nails also "ran through thin copper tubes". An axe was also found at the same time and place.' The fate of these associated finds is not known. They were not acquired by M. Duprez. The descriptions of them must be taken with every reserve, for the

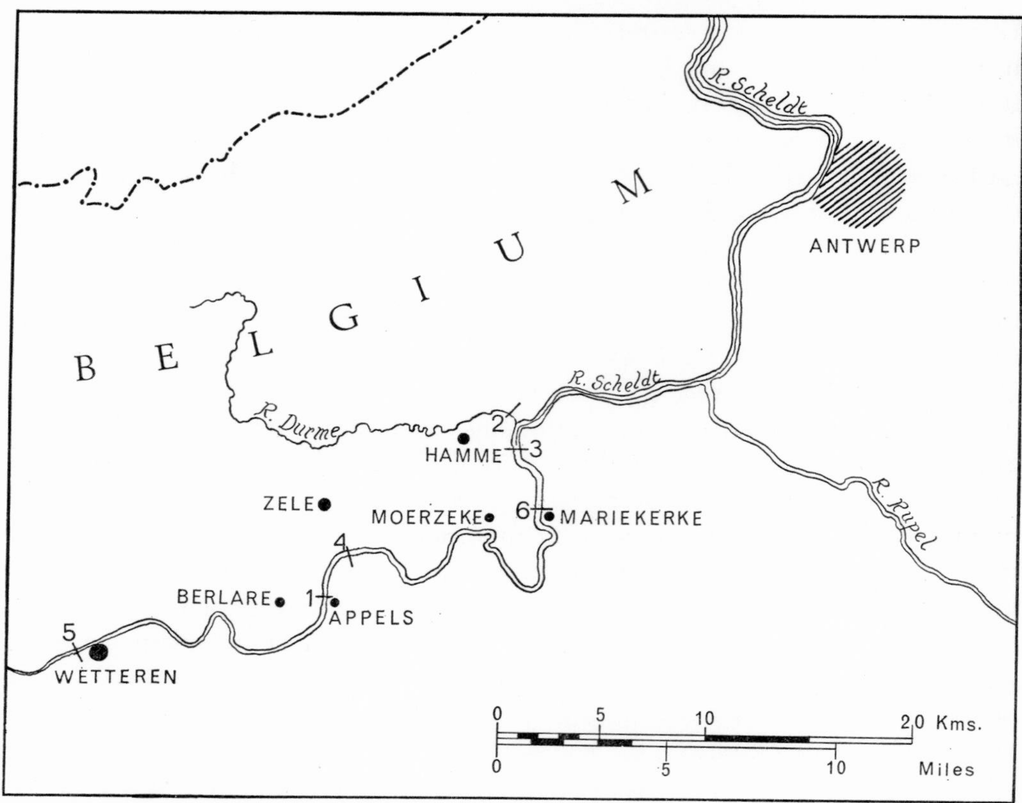

Figure 20 Map showing find spots of wooden animal-heads found in the River Scheldt

true nature of such finds is often only ascertained through laboratory examination and study by specialists.

The post is said by M. Duprez to have come out of the river mud and to have been 'wet but in good condition' when he acquired it. M. Van de Broek bought it from M. Duprez a year later and has provided me with photographs taken for him in 1942, which show it in very much the same condition as it is today (Plates 34a,b).

The date of the discovery may be taken as definite. This is an important point in establishing the authenticity of the new figure-head. As will be demonstrated, it shares certain distinctive features with the Zele head to be referred to below, now in the National Maritime Museum (Museum Steen) at Antwerp.[2]

All the evidence agrees that the Zele head was found in 1951. The new head, the subject of this paper, which was found in 1939 or 1940, cannot be explained as copying features already known from the Zele find, since this had not then been made.

The new Moerzeke-Mariekerke post, as described above, is cut off at the bottom

(Plate 38a) just at the point where a tang or some development in profile might have shown what the post was, how it was attached and to what it was attached. It seems clear from the light concavity facing forward, which seems to be slightly intensified at the bottom (a feature exactly paralleled in the British Museum Appels figure-head) and from the size and shape (rounded oval cross-section), that this piece is from a ship or boat and is not a carved post or part of some piece of furniture. The lack of any grooving or slotting for lateral connections supports this. If this is correct, the figure-head while not so complete, large, ambitious or impressive as the British Museum piece, nevertheless ranks as a most important find. It is only the second ship's figure-head to have survived from this era, since it is very doubtful whether any of the other posts with zoomorphic finials described by de Laet in the paper cited are ships' stem- or stern-posts. That from Zele certainly is not. Even though recovered from rivers, they seem in most cases more likely to have belonged to household or ships' furniture. They appear to lack the scale or formal characteristics natural for ships' stem- or stern-posts, particularly the delicate curves which echo and complete the lines of the ship and the rounded, streamlined surfaces. Holmqvist, in his study of the animal-headed board from Välo,[3] illustrates high-backed thrones or seats with animal-headed posts, depicted in early manuscripts and sculptures.

When the new stem-post was examined in the British Museum Research Laboratory no suspicious feature was found. The wood has an ancient appearance to the expert eye, as have the cuts on the base of the post and the surface abrasions. The surface is glossy and polished all over, a feature compatible with long exposure under running water to the movements of sand and silt and suggestive of appreciable age. This polish covers the cut surfaces at the bottom of the post, indicating that the cutting is not recent, or at least that it had taken place before the post assumed its position in the bed of the river. There is evidence of clayey deposit ingrained in the wood. The heavy splitting, a feature characteristic also of the British Museum Appels stem-post and of some of the wooden zoomorphic posts from the Scheldt published by de Laet, is consistent with shrinkage after being taken out of the water. The double-headed oak piece from Wetteren, now in the Maritime Museum, Antwerp (G. Hasse Collection, de Laet, *op. cit.*, pp. 133–5, Fig. 10) is described as having 'deep and wide desiccation cracks', an appearance which must seem very similar to that of the Moerzeke-Mariekerke post. Radiography of the Moerzeke-Mariekerke post revealed nothing abnormal. Visual examination of a split in the bottom of the post revealed a trace of iron, apparently the tip of a thin spike or nail, probably modern and perhaps to do with mounting the stem-post on a block at some time.

It was hoped to settle the antiquity of the piece, as has been successfully done by Holmqvist in the case of the dragon-headed board in the Valö find and by the Antwerp Museum in the case of the Zele head, by a Carbon 14 determination. The detachable piece of oak comprising the jaw and mouth was removed in the British Museum by removing the wooden screws that hold it and the interior of the head thus exposed was examined with a view to making a boring for a sample. The splits in the wood were many and deep and the bitumen, wax and glue had been forced into the cracks. Bitumen is usually applied when hot under pressure and penetrates the pores of the wood. This gave rise to risks of contamination of the sample. The cost of eliminating the contamination would have been great and the margin of error unpredictable and it was at first decided in this case by the British Museum Laboratory that a Carbon 14 determination would not be practicable. However, a sample of wood free from risk of contamination was eventually obtained, as described in Part Two of this chapter, where the resultant dating is published. It will be profitable to examine the authenticity of the figure-head from other angles. There are, as we have seen, no technical reasons for doubting the authenticity and age of the oak figure-head and on the other hand some positive indications of age and of prolonged immersion in moving silt. The Scheldt is a well-known source for such objects of interest, the British Museum stem-post being a sensational precedent, and Viking activity in the region offers a plausible background for any bogus 'find' of this nature which might be put on the market.[4] Will the figure-head stand the test of stylistic and formal study?

If it is compared with known parallels, it at once attaches itself to the two most striking previous finds (Plates 32, 36, Fig 21). It shares with the British Museum stem-post a similar choice by the carver of a branch with a swollen junction with the trunk. It also has in common the oval cross-section, the slight forward concavity, intensifying towards the bottom and the thick moulding defining the lips of the animal head. It shares with the Zele head the very distinctive triangular ears, the absence of any eyes and, again, the thick moulding defining the lips. The new figure-head has two features not found in these parallels. It lacks teeth, which both the others show in emphatic fashion and it shows a distinctive treatment of the lines of the mouth, with an elongated and curled back upper lip. The spaced lateral bands on the stem may seem contrary to the concept of a fluent line continuing the sweep of the stem or stern, as seen in the British Museum figure-head from Appels. Such lateral mouldings on stern- and stem-posts are to be seen on ships in the Bayeux tapestry, notably in the English ships rather than the Norman.[5] One might expect teeth on wooden animal-heads of the Merovingian or early Viking periods, like those recently found at Stettin in Poland with the planks of a ship and probably the head of a tiller, the athwartship lever attached to the steering oar,[6] and in Norway at Midtvåge, Tisnes, Hordaland,[7] and in the dragon-head on the Valö plank published by Holmqvist. Another feature links

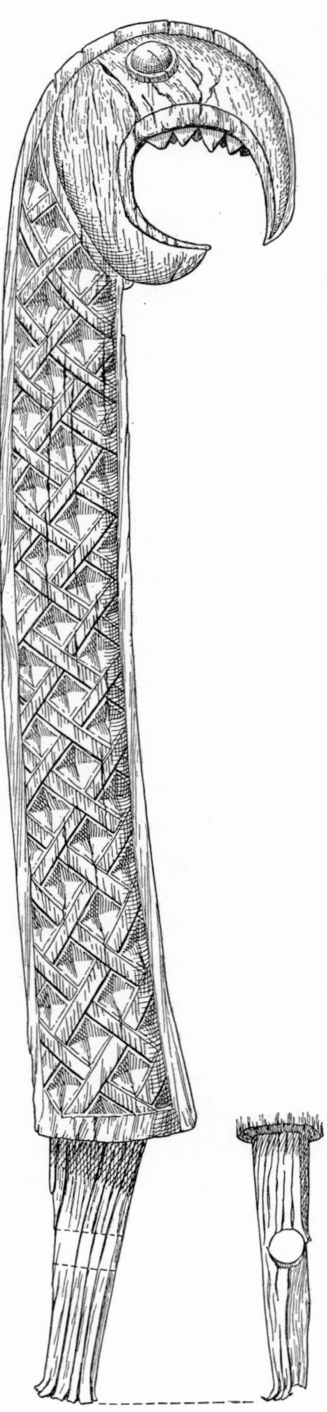

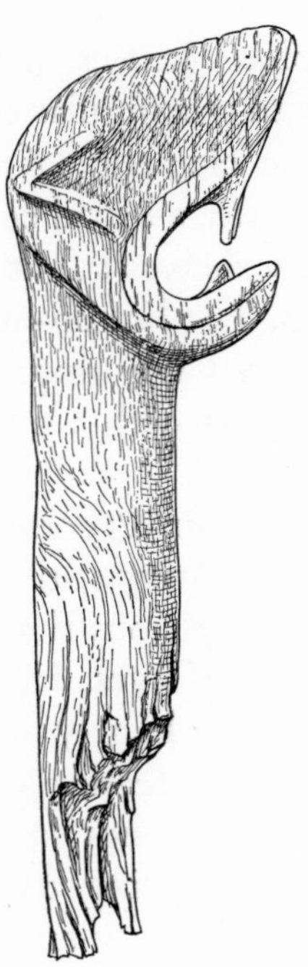

Figure 21 (*left*) The Appels animal-headed post (Scale 1 : 8); (*above*) The Zele animal-headed post (Scale 1 : 8)

the new post with the British Museum example. The spaced lateral mouldings on the posts are not paralleled in any of the other surviving wooden animal-headed posts. The manner of the cutting of these mouldings is that seen on the British Museum piece. In this, the post is covered with a lattice pattern of interlacing ribbons, with rectangular counter-sinkings excavated in a chip-carving technique between the elements of the interlace. The ribbons themselves consist of an inch-wide band, a broad central strip of which is raised and very lightly rounded, with narrow shelves left at the lower level running along both sides of the raised central strip. The button-eye of the British Museum figure-head is also carved in a similar way. The rings on the new prow from Moerzeke-Mariekerke are similarly carved with a raised, lightly rounded, central strip and lower 'shelves' to either side.

Mr O. Crumlin-Pedersen, to whom photographs of the new head were sent, noting the similarity of the triangular ears on the new prow to those on the Zele head, felt it suspicious that the new head sharing the ears of the Zele head also shares its lack of eyes. He thought that the Zele head probably originally had eyes which were largely worn away by the action of water. Eyes, he suggested, were an essential feature of ships' figure-heads, which sometimes have painted eyes where they do not have carved ones and which must be thought of as 'seeing' where the ship is going, to guide it on its path.

I do not know how much weight to attach to this. It seems that the Zele head in fact never had eyes. There is no apparent indication on photographs and de Laet in his account of the Zele head says that there is 'no indication of any eyes'. On the other hand, there is no reason to consider the Zele head to be a figure-head from a ship, so the theory of eyes as something 'obligatory' for ships' figure-heads would not be invalidated by their absence from the Zele head. Secondly, there may be something haphazard about the inclusion of such features, for the beautifully carved British Museum head from Appels lacks ears.

The most novel aspect of the new figure-head is the treatment of the mouth, with the upward swing of the elongated upper lip and the lack of teeth, giving the head a serpentine or dolphinesque appearance, rather than a dragonesque one in the Germanic tradition. This may perhaps explain the lack of emphasis on eyes. It is to the sub-Roman or Merovingian period that one might be inclined to allot the figure-head. It lacks elements that are recognizably of Viking style or date. The broad analogies for the style of the head, with the curve of the upper jaw and mouth, are to be found in the Thorsberg chapes (fifth century), the Faversham hanging-bowl escutcheons (sixth century), the wolf-like figures on the Sutton Hoo purse (seventh century) (though these last have prominent eyes), and one of the chapes in the eighth-century treasure[8] from St Ninian's Isle, Shetland.

I do not believe that any forger would produce an object so ravaged as this was before its cracks were plugged, or one which was mutilated at a crucial place (the junction with whatever it fitted onto or into).

Such defects would reduce its interest and saleability. The stylistic features which the new figure-head shares with the British Museum and the Zele pieces seem to be genuine period features and the departures from the known possible models – the lack of teeth, the curled treatment of the upper jaw, the spaced lateral mouldings on the stem, the absence of eyes – seem as much in favour of genuineness as the sharing of features with other pieces from the Scheldt might be against it. A final point already alluded to seems strongly in favour of the authenticity of the new piece. On the evidence of M. Van de Broek it was already in his possession ten years before the Zele head came to light in 1951. If this is so, the newly produced head cannot derive any of its distinctive features, particularly the triangular ears or lack of eyes, from the Zele head, since it was found before that. That it was found in 1951 (the year of the Zele find) is in any case clear from its having come at some time after M. Van de Broek's ownership into the possession of M. Léon Degrelle. This no doubt explains the appearance of the new figure-head in Spain where M. Galardi acquired it.

My conclusion is that the new figure-head must be accepted as a genuine find from the Scheldt (Fig 20) dredged up in the period 1938–40 and that it is from a small ship, of which it was probably the stem-post. It may date from as early as the fifth or sixth century A.D. but might be as late as the end of the eighth century. It seems to lack any mediaeval (post-Viking) characteristics. It seems to be only the second ship's figure-head of the pre-mediaeval era to survive. If this assessment of date is correct, it is the earliest one known from the northern world, though the British Museum Appels head may be earlier than the date of *c.* 800 suggested for it by Kendrick and Nerman.

The indication of the antiquity of the Zele head by Carbon 14 methods implies equally the antiquity of the new head since this, as has been stressed, was found earlier than the Zele head and yet shows features, especially the ears, which have a very distinctive character and are not known from any other object. It seems to give it a chronological position broadly equivalent with the Zele head and the British Museum figure-head from Appels. Probably the bracket sixth to eighth century would safely include it.[9]

The figure-head was auctioned at Messrs Sotheby & Co. in London on June 12th 1967 and illustrated in their sale catalogue of that date. It was bought in at the sale but has been acquired by the British Museum.

II A NOTE ON SHIP'S FIGURE-HEADS IN THE MIGRATION PERIOD AND EARLY MIDDLE AGES

Figs 19 and 21 illustrate three animal-headed posts all from the River Scheldt, for which recent C14 datings have been obtained. Figs 19 and 21 (left) are both thought to be stem-posts and from vessels of some size; Fig 21a could have come from a 60-ft (*c.* 18m) boat to judge by its proportions. It is worth noticing that it was fastened by a cylindrical tree-nail and was detachable. There is a reference in the Landnámabók to an old heathen law requiring dragon-heads to be removed from ships on approaching unfamiliar shores, to avoid alarming the spirits of the place. There is nothing to suggest that Fig 21 (above) is from a ship.[1] It might be the top of a rudder (steering oar). It cannot be the end of an athwartship tiller, inboard from the steering oar, like that of *c.* A.D. 800 found recently at Stettin,[2] to which Mr O. Crumlin-Pedersen has drawn my attention, in connection with animal heads and ships. It is too thick and clumsy for the purpose. It may have come from a piece of furniture, perhaps a high-seat pillar. It is in the Leyden Museum and has been published by de Laet.[3] Figs 19 and 21 (left) are in the British Museum, purchased in 1967 and 1938 respectively. Fig 19 is described and discussed in Part One of this chapter. Both pieces in Fig 21 are also featured in Part One where attention is drawn to the very distinctive stylistic features shared by the three heads. The post from the river at Appels (Fig 21, left) has been universally taken to be of the Viking period but it has always seemed to me more likely to be pre-Viking. It has none of the stylistic traits characteristic of Viking art and seems restrained and primitive when compared with the representations known to us of figure-heads of Viking ships. The C14 datings show both British Museum posts to belong in fact to the Migration period. The C14 results for the three heads are as follows:

1. *The Appels Head* (Museum number 1938, 2–2, I) BM 476: 1550 ± 150 BP (*c.* A.D. 400).
2. *The Moerzeke-Mariekerke post* (Museum number 1967, 10–1, 1) BM 372: 1598 ± 70 BP (*c.* A.D. 350).

The deep desiccation cracks in this oak post had been plugged by restorers in about 1940 with pitch which had been forced into the cracks when it was hot. It was at first not thought possible by the British Museum C14 Laboratory to get a worth while result, free from the risk of contamination. Samples have since been taken from an unaffected spot in the interior of the post, revealed by removing the piece of wood comprising the jaws and lips. The reduced margin of error with the Moerzeke-Mariekerke post is notable.

These results were obtained in the British Museum C14 Laboratory and each date is the mean of two determinations which were in good agreement.

3. *The Zele Post.* IRPA–23 1259 ± 180 BP (*c.* A.D. 690)[4] *Radiocarbon* 1968, 34 (work carried out in Amsterdam).

I am grateful to Mde J. Lambrechts-Douillez of the Vleeshuis Museum, Antwerp, for drawing my attention to this result.

Wood carvings of the Migration period are practically unknown.[5] There is nothing in wood with which these heads may be compared. The Moerzeke-Mariekerke head has stylistic affinities with sub-Roman metalwork and the stylistic traits of these three heads which are the expression of a wood-carving technique (chip-carving, two-tier carving, the handling of the mouldings, a breadth and simplicity of treatment) are interesting to see.

The C14 method does not date the artefact but the oak from which it was cut. This might have been, for example, a seasoned beam from the ruins of a considerably older hall. In this trio of results we have three subjects sharing distinctive stylistic features and yielding closely similar C14 dates. The chances that old timber was used in all three cases is perhaps not so great. The probability is that the C14 dates do really date the artefacts (that is, they seem likely to have been made from wood freshly cut for the purpose).

The importance of these results, apart from revealing for the first time something of wood-carvers' style and technique in the Migration period, lies in establishing that dragon-heads or serpentine stem-posts, well known later from the Oseberg Ship,[6] the Gotlandic Stones,[7] the Bayeux Tapestry,[8] trial-pieces[9] and moulds[10] were already established in the barbarian north in the fourth and fifth centuries A.D. No doubt they were confined to the more important ships. We may visualize the chiefs of the invaders of Britain, at the time of the *Adventus Saxonum*, appearing at times in ships so provided. We may suppose that some such stem-post but larger and more imposing in its treatment presided over the Sutton Hoo ship, a vessel probably built in the latter part of the sixth century A.D. As is usually the case with buried ships, any trace of any stem- or stern-post which, if the ship was buried with these still attached, would have risen visibly from the ground or protruded well up into the tumulus above the old ground level, had disappeared.

Zoomorphic figure-heads on Scandinavian ships can be traced back into prehistoric times but have hitherto been unrecorded between the Early Iron Age and the Viking period. I am grateful to Mr Ole Crumlin-Pedersen for references to prehistoric occurrences.

NOTES TO CHAPTER SIX

PART I

1 British Museum Reg. No. 1939, 2–2, 1. Professor S. J. de Laet ('Wooden Animal heads of Carolingian times found in the River Scheldt (Belgium)', *Acta Archaeologica*, XXVII, 129 and n. 2) gives a more loosely defined location for the discovery ('between Schoonaarde and the mouth of the Durme at Hamme' but 'most probably between Appels and Moerzeke' – distances of some 32 and 16 Km of the river). The Museum register is more precise 'in the vicinity of Appels, near Termonde'. A map marked by M. Philip Duprez, the first owner also of this figure-head, from his recollections, arrows a particular point in the river a little upstream from Appels, opposite Bac. For this piece see *British Museum Quarterly*, XII, 1939, 73–4 and Pl. XXVI; *Fornvännen*, 1942, 64–6 (B. Nerman); *Germanien*, 1939, 385 ff. (P. Paulsen) and *Acta Archaeologica*, XXVII, 1956, 129, Fig. 2 (S. J. de Laet). The intention of the map included with this chapter (Fig. 20) is to clarify the distribution of the wooden animal-heads which have been found in the River Scheldt, concentrated in a stretch of the river between Antwerp and Ghent. The basic principle has been to revise the original map published by Prof. de Laet in *Acta Archaeologica*, XXVII, 1956, marking the actual findspots of the heads as far as they can be ascertained both from the text of Prof. de Laet's paper and from fresh information obtained during the search for material relevant to the Moerzeke head.

Apart from the importance of showing the Moerzeke head in its over-all context, it was thought worthwhile to prepare a new map, as the original map in *Acta Archaeologica*, XXVII, while giving the impression of being a straightforward distribution of findspots, was in reality a map of the towns near which the Scheldt heads were found. This resulted in some apparent discrepancies between Prof. de Laet's map and text – Schoonaarde, for example, was not a findspot in the strictest sense. It is mentioned merely to define that stretch of the river where the so-called Appels figure-head was found, while Moerzeke, referred to in a similar context, is not shown on the map. Equally, Hamme is shown as a single findspot while the text states that two heads were found in the neighbourhood of Hamme – one (de Laet No. 2) in the River Durme near its confluence with the River Scheldt, the second (de Laet No. 3) in the River Scheldt near the confluence of the River Durme. It was appreciated that the purpose of the original map was to give the nearest town or village to the findspot of each head and thus give it geographical identity, but it was felt not only that this was misleading but also that the impact of the unusual concentration of wooden heads in this locality was lost. For the revision of the map I am indebted to Miss A. C. Evans, Research Assistant in the Department of Mediaeval and Later Antiquities in the British Museum.

2 It was transferred to the Maritime Museum (Museum Steen) from the Antwerp Archaeological Museum (Butcher's Hall) in 1958.

3 W. Holmqvist, *Valöfyndet: Antikvariskt Arkiv* 4, Kungl. Vitterhets Historie och Antikvitetakademien, Stockholm, 1956.

4 Referred to by S. J. de Laet, *op. cit.*, 136, note 19.

5 *The Bayeux Tapestry, a comprehensive Survey*. Edited by Sir Frank Stenton, London, Phaidon Press, 1957, Pls 5, 6 and 7.

6 S. Wesotowski, *Odkrycie lodzi Slowianskiej na podgrodziuw Szczocinie, Z Otchtani Wieków. Kwartalnik Popularnonaukowy Polskiego lowarzystwa Archaelogieznego*, XXIX, 4, Warszawa-Poznań, 1953, 254–8.

7 As yet unpublished, I am indebted for the reference to the Stettin ship and the Midtvåge find to Mr Crumlin-Pederson, and to Mr Arne-Emil Christensen for kindly sending drawings of the latter.

8 'The St. Ninian's Isle Silver Hoard', *Antiquity* XXXIII, 1959, Pl. XXXII, a–e.

9 A recent paper, the substance of which has not been assimilated into this chapter, should be consulted. It is H. E. F. Vierck, 'The origin and date of the ship's figure-head from Moerzeke-Mariekerke, Antwerp', *Helinium* X, 1970, 139–149.

PART II

1 A. W. Brøgger and H. Shetelig, *The Viking Ships*, 139–40, Oslo, 1947.

2 S. Wesotowski, *Odkrycie lodzi Slowianskiej na podgrodziuw Szczocinie, Z Otchtani Wieków. Kwartalnik Popularnonaukowy Polskiego lowarzystwa Archaeologicznego*, XXIX, 1953, 4, 254–8 (Warszawa-Poznań).

3 S. de Laet, 'The wooden animal-heads of Carolingian times found in the River Scheldt, Belgium', *Acta Archaeologica*, 1956, XXVII, 127–137.

4 Chapter Six, Part I, p. 183.

5 P. Schmidt, 'Die Holzplastik aus der Wurt Hessens in Kulturbild des 7 nachchristlichen Jahrhunderts', *Nachrichten aus Niedersachsens Urgeschichte* 24, 1955, esp. Abb 32 and Taf. 2.

6 F. Johannessen, 'Osebergskibets stavner', *Universitetets Oldsaksamlingens Årbok*, Oslo, 1928, 31–8.

7 S. Lindqvist, *Gotlands Bildsteine*, I, 1941, Figs. 79, 80, 81, 85, 97 etc.

8 Sir F. H. Stenton (ed.) and others, *The Bayeux Tapestry*, London, 1957, pls. 42–5.

9 J. R. C. Hamilton, *Excavations at Jarlshof, Shetland*, 1956, pl. XXI, 4.

10 K. Thorvildsen, *Ladbyskibet*, Copenhagen, 1957, Fig. 24. (A stone mould from the Black Earth (town site) at Birka.)

CHAPTER SEVEN

The Sutton Hoo Lyre, 'Beowulf' and the Origins of the Frame Harp

by Myrtle and Rupert Bruce-Mitford

The six-stringed musical instrument found in the Sutton Hoo ship-burial was first reconstructed, in 1948, as a small quadrangular harp some 15 inches high (Plate 39). Doubts were cast on the authenticity of this version by the subsequent discovery of additional fragments of maple-wood belonging to the instrument. These fragments had been thought by the excavators in 1939 to be connected with the wood from the roof of the burial chamber and had been collected and boxed accordingly and so lost their connection with the instrument. When the Coptic bowl complex was separately excavated in the British Museum Research Laboratory it was assumed that its contents had been left intact and that the wood remains found during this investigation were all that remained of the instrument; the 1948 reconstruction was therefore based on these fragments only.

Fresh appraisal of the fragments together with the rediscovered additional material (Plates 41 and 42) led eventually to a new reconstruction of the instrument in the form of a round lyre of Germanic type. Though the resonator, or soundbox, is still missing it was found that contrary to what had previously been supposed most of the rest had survived.

The reconstruction process was complicated by the fact that varying conditions had caused some parts of the instrument to shrink by as much as 25 per cent, while others retained their original proportions. It has been possible to calculate the original shape and dimensions of the crucial fragments with a much greater degree of accuracy than before, and the new version can be accepted as correct in most of its detail.[1] A full explanation of every stage of the reconstruction process will be provided in volume 3 of the British Museum's definitive publication on the ship burial, now in hand.

The reconstructed lyre (Plate 40), like its predecessor, is of field maple (*acer campestre*) with six pegs of poplar or willow. In its new form the instrument consists of three sections: the partially hollow arms and the soundbox, which are made from a single piece of wood; a thin soundboard covering the hollowed area; and the symmetrical yoke, or peg-arm, which is secured to the main body of the lyre by tenon-and-mortice joints (Plate 41). The joints are held in place by gilt-bronze bird-headed escutcheons and by their attached rivets, which are burred over washers at the back. The soundboard is fixed to the soundbox by headless bronze pins; apparently these were sufficient for the purpose, since no trace of glue was found on the wood fragments.

The new reconstruction measures 29¼ ins (742 mm) in length and its width, uniform from top to bottom, is 8¼ ins (209 mm). Its depth, also uniform throughout, is ⅞ in (22 mm), and the soundboard is ⅛ in (3 mm) thick. Of these measurements only the length is conjectural; the other dimensions can be accurately calculated from the surviving fragments.

The validity of the reconstruction is supported by comparison both with fragments of lyres of slightly later date found in Germany and with contemporary manuscript illustrations. The hollow arms are similar to those of lyres from Oberflacht and Cologne, and the bridge on our replica is a copy of the earliest known bridge, from Broa i Halle, Gotland (see also Fig 23). There are no sound holes in any of the surviving German instruments, and none (that I know of) shown in any manuscript representations of *plucked* lyres until the thirteenth century, so that although the soundbox of the Sutton Hoo instrument did not survive we can be fairly certain that it, too, was without sound holes. The tailpiece on the reconstruction is of deliberately simple design, in the absence of any positive evidence as to its original shape. The small knob at the bottom, to which it is attached, is copied from a similar feature on two of the instruments mentioned above. Lyres are depicted with tailpieces in some of the more detailed manuscript illustrations, and it is clear that this was a standard method of securing the strings of instruments of this type.

As the strings are all more or less the same length (slight variations being imposed by the curvature of the peg-arm) the difference in pitch is dependent upon their thickness and tension and on the material used. The model has been strung with gut; metal was ruled out by the softness of the pegs, though horsehair remains a possibility. There is no record of the tuning of Saxon instruments, so the reconstruction has been tuned to a pentatonic scale, characteristic of early folk music. Despite the shallowness of the resonator and the absence of sound holes, the tone is vibrant and surprisingly robust. Professor Donald K. Fry of the State University of New York has informed me that during a recent experimental hearing a copy of our replica was easily audible at the back of a large hall with rather poor acoustics.

The positioning of the bridge must be largely a matter for conjecture, since no evidence survives. As Plate 39 shows, the tailpiece on the first lyre replica was fairly long and ended a little way above the bottom of the instrument, so that the bridge had to be placed slightly higher than the centre of the soundbox. A second model, made for experimental purposes, was equipped with a smaller tailpiece fixed right at the bottom, thus allowing the bridge to be moved down the box to give a vibrating length of some 23 ins (584 mm). This string length was found to produce in every way a more satisfactory sound, not only lower in pitch but fuller in tone. When the instrument is tuned to a pentatonic scale its compass now lies comfortably within the tenor register.

M. B-M.

The 1948 reconstruction (Plate 39) of the Sutton Hoo musical instrument, which I based on preliminary work done in the British Museum's Research Laboratory, caused a gratifying stir in circles interested in such matters. My paper reconstruction was given body in the Dolmetsch workshops at Haslemere, and the resultant maple-wood instrument was played to the Society of Antiquaries at Burlington House by Mrs Arnold Dolmetsch, who spoke of its small range but said that an illusion of playing in different keys could be produced, and the compass increased, by the use of harmonics (though we do not necessarily suggest that it was played in this way).[2] Sir Cyril Fox, the President, announced that 'we were having an evening of surpassing interest'. He was a great believer in the value of physical reconstructions and in a presidential address had produced and expatiated on his model reconstruction of the Iron Age chariot found at Llyn Cerrig Bach, in Anglesey. A third leader appeared in *The Times* under the heading 'The harp that once . . .'. The instrument was recorded by the B.B.C. and, in replica, by American broadcasting companies. Students of *Beowulf* seized on its potentialities. Professor J. C. Pope's *Rhythm of Beowulf*[3] had claimed that a harp conditioned the rhythmic organization of Old English poetry; now here at Sutton Hoo (just where it should have been) was, it seemed, the very harp. The reconstruction was published, placed on exhibition in the British Museum and discussed by musicologists, archaeologists and students of Old English.[4]

This sort of publicity made the subsequent discovery of additional fragments of the instrument and its eventual transformation into a Germanic lyre something of an embarrassment. The 1948 reconstruction was nevertheless a reasoned piece of work, accepted by those who knew the arguments for it. It was not based on preconceptions but was an honest attempt to make sense of the fragments as we then knew and assessed them. It remains significant that the old reconstruction as read (or misread) from the fragments is supported by graphic representations in manuscripts (albeit of later date) such as the eleventh-century psalter in St John's College, Cambridge, and the twelfth-century ivory cover of Queen Melissenda's psalter in the British Museum[5] (Plates 44c and d), as well as on Irish stone crosses, for example at Carndonagh and Castledermot. Since an instrument resembling a small quadrangular harp did apparently exist, the 1948 reconstruction retains a distinct musicological interest of its own even though it does not represent the instrument in the Sutton Hoo ship-burial.

The Sutton Hoo instrument is now seen to be not a harp but a lyre. These are instruments of different classes (Fig 22),[6] the basic difference being that in the harp the strings are attached to and rise from the sound-board, whereas in the lyre they pass horizontally over it, their vibrations being transmitted to the sound-box by means of a bridge. The harp is asymmetrical, triangular or sub-triangular. Its triangular frame in the developed instrument, though not in any early quad-rangular versions, imposes variation in the length of strings, allows of more strings and permits their number to increase with the size of the instrument. The lyre, on the other hand, is symmetrically designed and the strings are usually few in number and of equal lengths, rising to a yoke held between supporting arms.

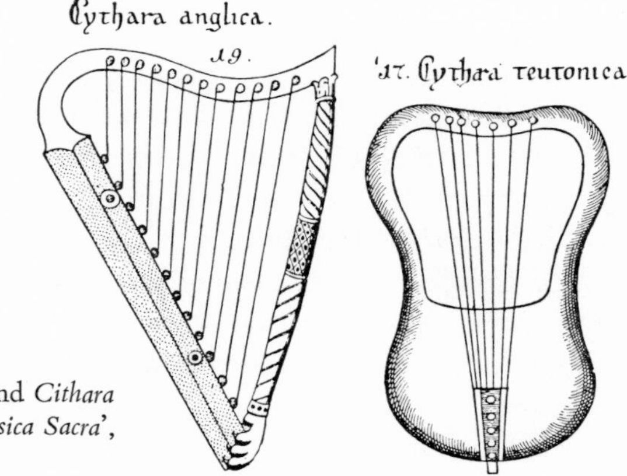

Figure 22 Harp and lyre (*Cithara anglica* and *Cithara teutonica*) from Gerbert '*De Cantu et Musica Sacra*', reproducing a lost twelfth-century MS.

The musical properties and possibilities of the new reconstruction, as distinct from its shape and dimensions, are not markedly different from those of the old. What students will at once ask is, can its general form be relied upon and, if so, how much of its detail is valid?

The answer is that we believe the new reconstruction, once the instrument is accepted as belonging to the lyre class, can be relied upon in almost all its detail. We know what the Germanic lyre was like at this period not only from slightly later manuscript illustrations but from three actual examples found partially or substantially preserved in Germany.[7] The remains at Sutton Hoo correspond with these very closely. The width across the top of the instruments is the same. As for the length of the Sutton Hoo lyre, this is determined by the fact that the reconstruction of one of its two arms is now possible, with the help of the newly-found fragments, up to the point where the arms were fractured over the edges of the two nested bronze bowls (the Coptic bowl with the biggest of the hanging-bowls inside it) into which those parts of the instrument which survive had happily fallen. By this point the soundbox had not begun to develop, so that we are given a minimum length for the arms and for the open space between them. The resonator cannot afford to be much larger than it has been made in the reconstruction if due proportion with the upper part of the instrument is to be observed and if the instrument is to be played on the knee, as it is seen to be in various manuscript illustrations (Plate 45). The evidence of the surviving Sutton Hoo fragments indicates a flat, straight-sided soundbox. The bridge and tailpiece are based on near-contemporary analogies. There is nothing amongst the Sutton Hoo remains, or in any of the comparative material, to suggest that plucked stringed instruments of the period had sound holes; indeed, there is ample evidence to the contrary (p. 189). We may, then, accept the new Sutton Hoo reconstruction with a confidence which the old one, referred to by us as 'provisional', did not everywhere enjoy.

The Sutton Hoo instrument has proved not to be musicologically a harp. This does not make it any the less important, for several reasons. First, it is demonstrably of Anglo-Saxon manufacture and not imported. This can be inferred from the gilt-bronze bird's-head escutcheons (Plate 44a) that fastened its joints (not found with any of the Continental examples) and from their ornamental style. Secondly, it is closely datable to not later than the first quarter of the seventh century A.D. Thirdly, we can assume that it was in the front rank of its kind, since it is from a royal grave, the richest grave to have survived in Europe. Fourthly, another contemporary Anglo-Saxon instrument, previously unrecognized as such, can be classified with it – that from the well-known seventh-century barrow at Taplow, Buckinghamshire. At the time of excavation in 1882, the metal mounts and the few associated wood fragments were described as a 'crescentic ornament'. They were not correctly identified until work on the Sutton Hoo instrument was under way, when the close similarity of the two sets of fragments and escutcheons (Plates 44a and b) was remarked (both instruments also proved to be of maplewood). So little of the Taplow instrument survives that without comparative evidence, that of Sutton Hoo in particular, correct identification would have been very difficult. Now one can say with certainty that if the Sutton Hoo instrument is a lyre, then the Taplow instrument is too. It follows that the native lyre found

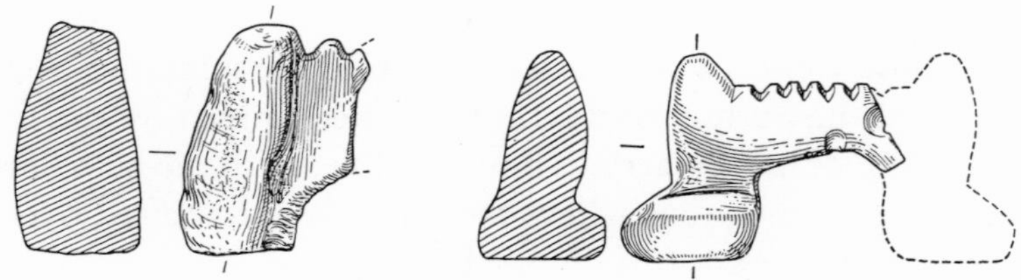

Figure 23 Two amber bridges found at Elisenhof, Schleswig, in 1967 (Scale 1 : 1)

in the two richest Anglo-Saxon graves yet excavated should be the instrument commonly in use in aristocratic Anglo-Saxon circles.

Now that the Sutton Hoo instrument and that from the Taplow Barrow can be identified as lyres, the picture of early Germanic stringed instruments is clarified. Counting lyre-bridges (in amber (Fig 23), bronze or bone), actual fragments of wooden instruments, and two graphic representations of the early, pre-Christian period (e.g. Plate 43b, Figs 24 and 25) no fewer than fifteen lyres are known from before the Viking period and just into it (i.e. up to, say, the early ninth century).

Figure 24 Representation of a lyre-player perhaps carrying a tuning key or plectrum from a patch on a bronze bowl with beaded rim, from Gilton, Kent, sixth century A.D.

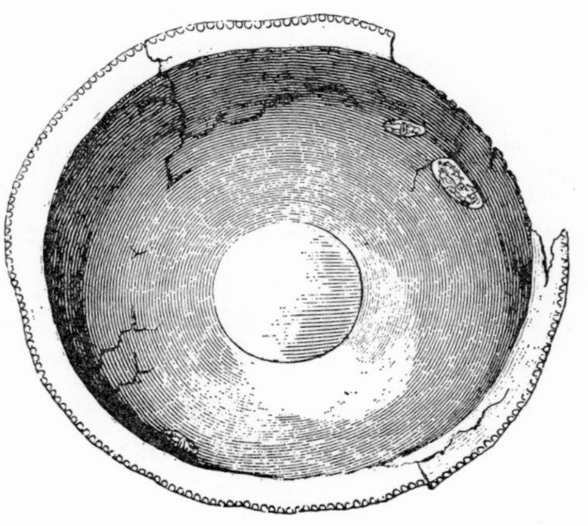

Figure 25 Bronze bead-rim bowl, from Gilton, Kent, showing patches

Since the earliest, the English example from Abingdon, Berkshire[8] (Plate 43a), is from a fifth-century immigrant's grave[9] and since the type is so widespread on the Continent this, the round lyre, must surely be the typical early Germanic stringed instrument. Two manuscript illustrations from the north and south of England of the early eighth century (the period of the majority of the German-found lyres and bridges), the British Museum Vespasian Psalter (Plate 45), a product of Canterbury, and the Durham Cathedral Library copy of Cassiodorus's *Commentary on the Psalms*, perhaps written at Lindisfarne or Melrose, add to the picture of the universality of the lyre in these early centuries. Both show King David playing a native round lyre of the Sutton Hoo type. There is no trace of a harp throughout this early period, in the British Isles or elsewhere in Europe.

The fact is that the study of very early musical instruments in northern Europe is bedevilled by philological confusion. When the sixth-century poet, Venantius Fortunatus, names the instruments characteristic of the different peoples (or, perhaps, gives the different names given by these people to instruments of the same basic type):

> Romanusque *lyra*, plaudat tibi barbarus *harpa*,
> Graecus *Achilliaca*, *Chrotta Britanna* canat

– that harp, which he cites as the typical Barbarian instrument was, we must conclude, in reality the round lyre. The instrument which charmed the courtly society of Beowulf and at the approach of which (passed from hand to hand) the shy cow-herd Caedmon, our first English poet, used to leave the table, was also a round lyre. The quest for a second, different Germanic instrument of harp type seems a futile one. The harp of *Beowulf* in musicological terms, we may now conclude from the archaeological evidence, did not exist.

This need not worry students of Old English, for it is no more than a matter of terminology. They should now have a new confidence in pursuing the subject of the possible effect of stringed accompaniment on the performance of Old English poetry and (in so far as this took shape in an oral tradition) even on its composition. For it seems clear that the instrument which was used in the singing of this poetry was the Germanic round lyre. That the king's instrument of music at Sutton Hoo is a round lyre supports the view that this is the instrument called *hearpe* in *Beowulf*. C. L. Wrenn called the discovery of the Sutton Hoo ship-burial 'perhaps the most important happening in *Beowulf* studies since the Icelander Jón Grímur Thorkelin made his transcripts of the *Beowulf* MS. and from them published the first edition of the poem'.[10] Whether this is accepted or not, no archaeological context, it will be agreed, is more relevant to *Beowulf* than Sutton Hoo.

This instrument, the *hearpe* of *Beowulf*, is now rebuilt in a form which, we believe, leaves only little margin of error. How it was played and how used with the performance of poetry is a matter for experiment and discussion, now possible on a sound basis.

We are left with the question, what of the frame-harp, i.e. the harp with a fore-pillar, ancestor of the pillared harp of the modern orchestra? The problem of its origin is one of the most baffling and important in early musicology. There seems to be agreement that the frame-harp was invented, or evolved, in the British Isles. The discovery of what (in the old reconstruction) we believed to be an actual harp, typologically primitive, in the English royal grave at Sutton Hoo, pre-dating the earliest harp-pictures by nearly three centuries, seemed to clinch the theory of origin in the British Isles and to make this origin more specifically Anglo-Saxon and not Celtic. Its rectangular form also seemed to indicate the process (coalescence of the resonator with the back of the frame) by which the triangular form developed. This may indeed be the way in which the true

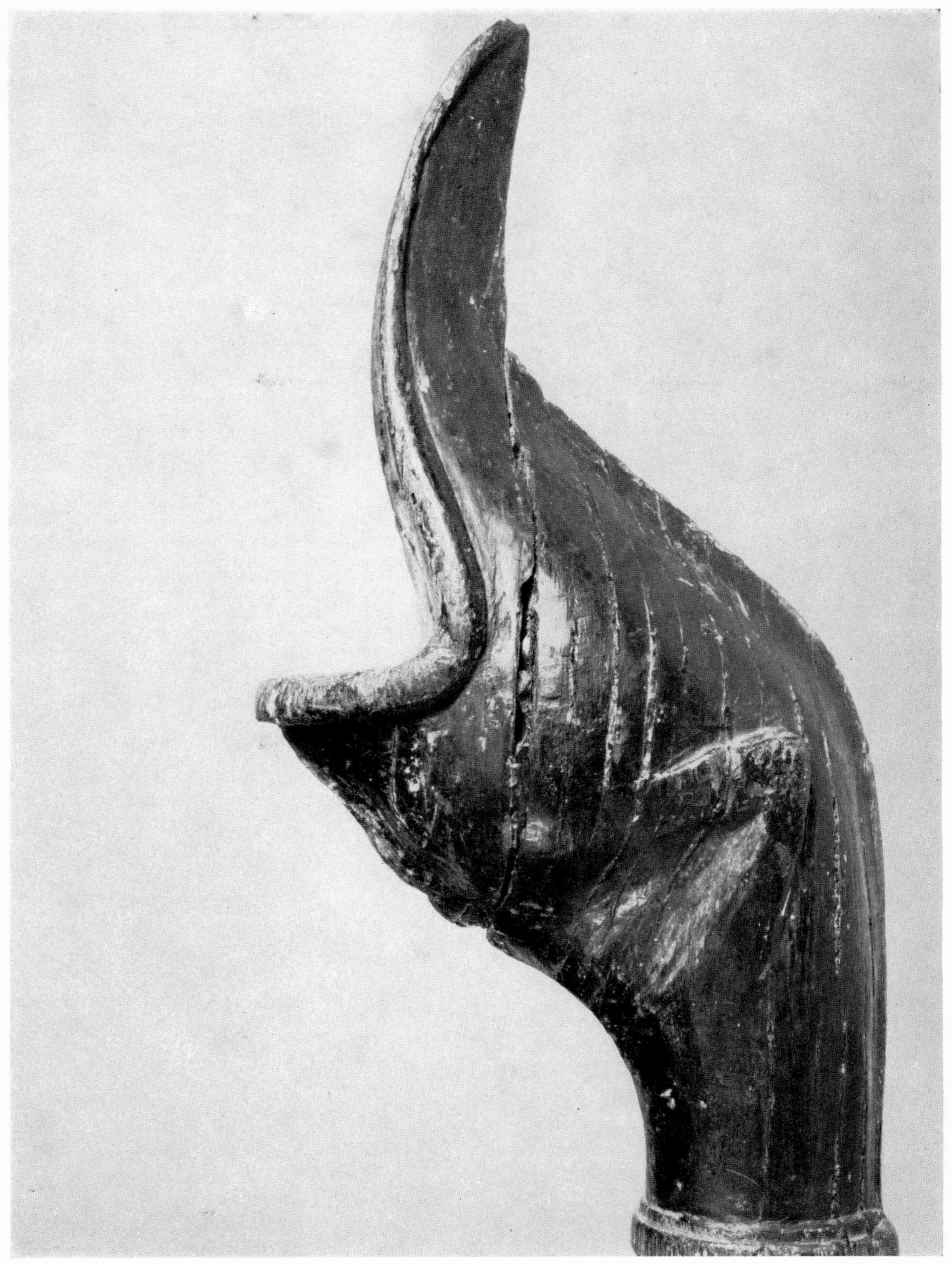

Plate 37 Moerzeke-Mariekerke head (reduced)

38

Plate 38 Moerzeke-Mariekerke head. Detail of lower end (reduced)

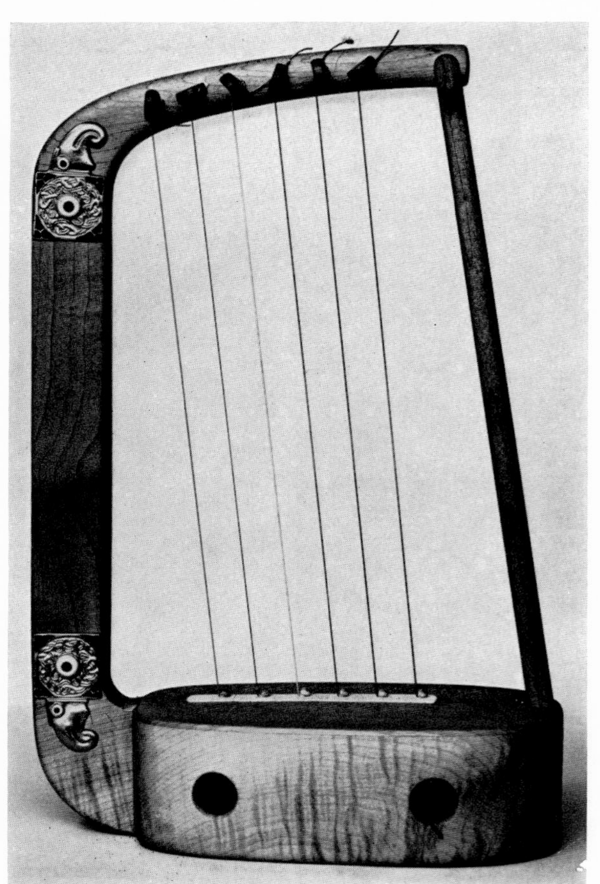

Plate 39 The superceded reconstruction of the Sutton Hoo musical instrument as a small rectangular harp (Scale a little under 1 : 4)

Plate 40 (*opposite*) The new reconstruction of the Sutton Hoo musical instrument as a round lyre (Scale a little under 1 : 3)

39

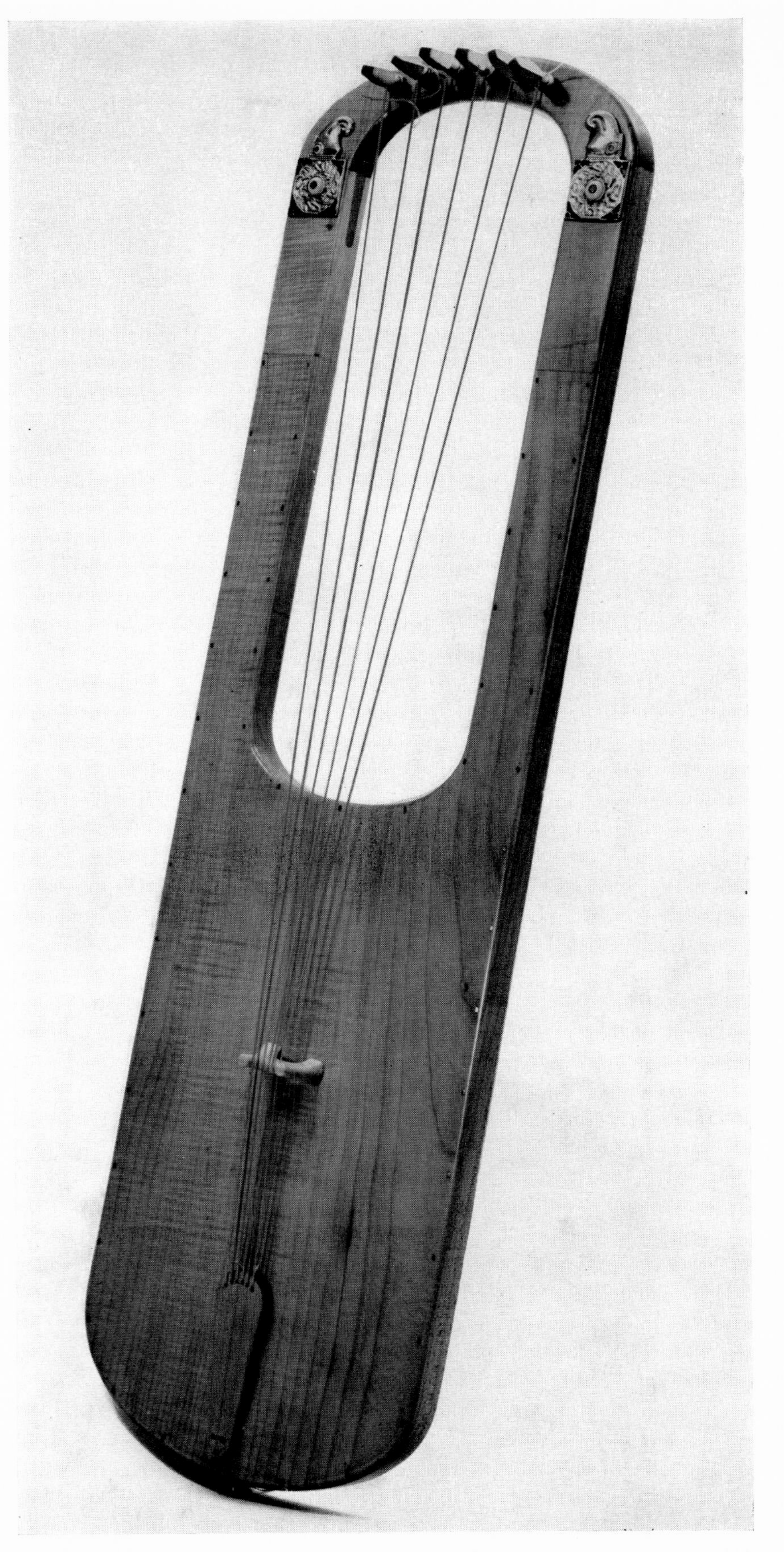

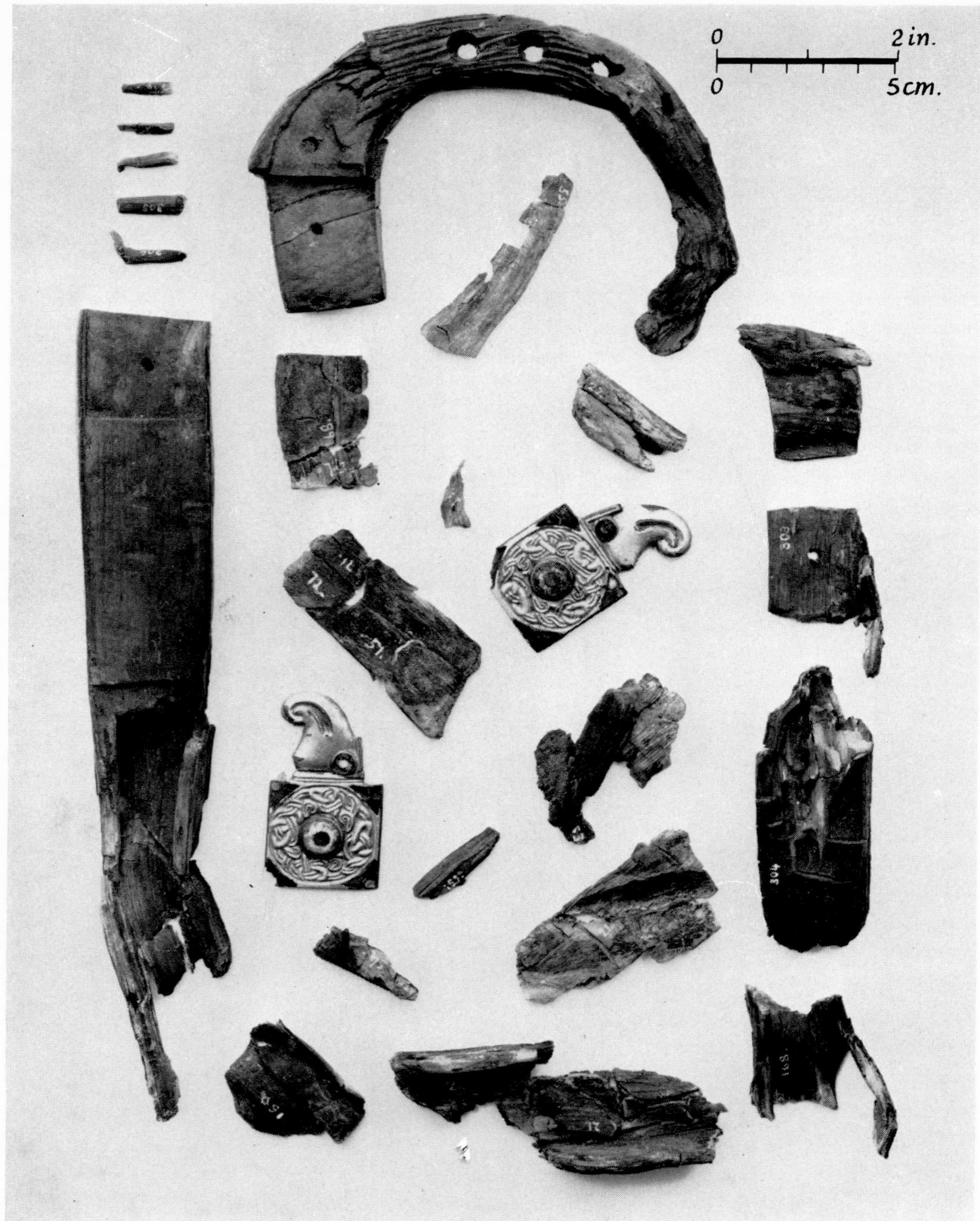

Plate 41 Metal fittings, maple-wood fragments and remains of poplar or willow pegs of the Sutton Hoo lyre, before assembly (Scale a little under 1 : 2)

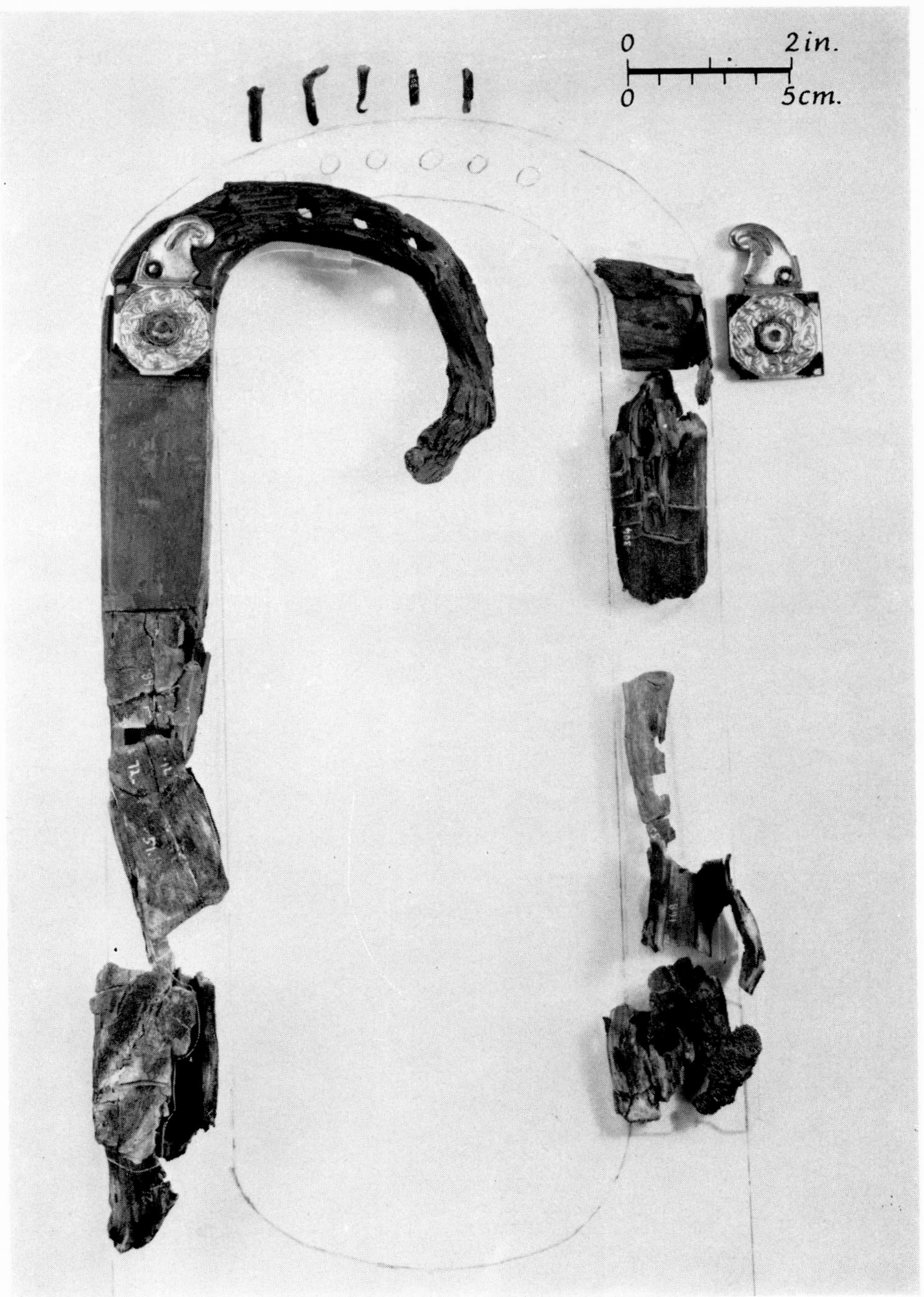

Plate 42 Surviving fragments of the Sutton Hoo lyre assembled (Scale a little under 1 : 2)

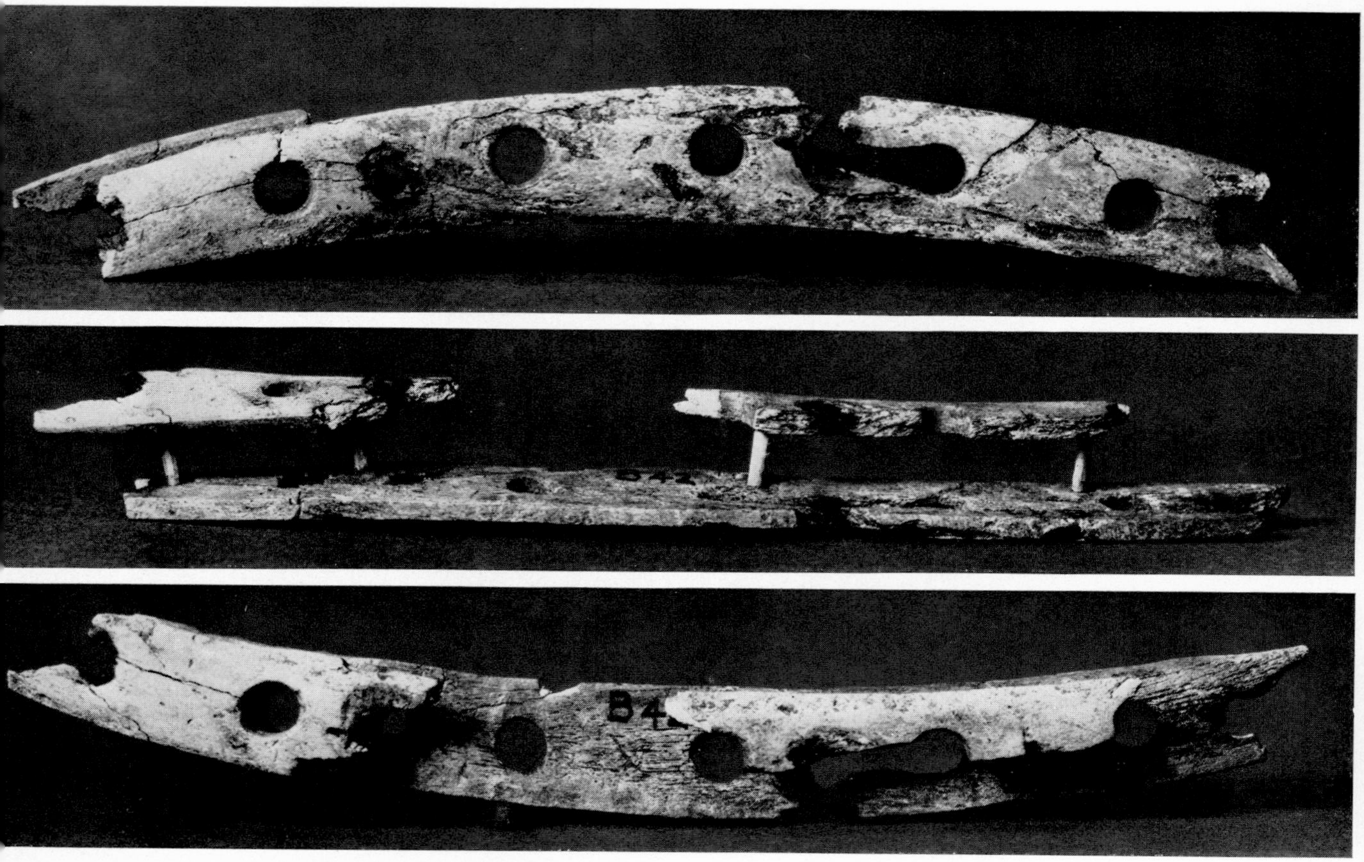

a

b

Plate 43 a, Bone facings from the peg-arm of a lyre from a grave, Abingdon, Berks (fifth century A.D.) (Scale 1 : 1); *b*, Carving of a lyre from a Gotlandic standing stone (sixth century)

Plate 44 Pairs of bird's head escutcheons from *a*, The Sutton Hoo and *b*, the Taplow lyres (Scale 1 : 1); *c*, Detail from the ivory cover of Queen Melissenda's Psalter, twelfth century A.D., showing the tuning of what seems to be a small quadrangular harp, with a boat-shaped resonator; *d*, Sacred instruments of music from a twelfth century MS in St John's College, Cambridge, showing a quadrangular harp-type of instrument being played

Plate 45 King David playing the 'harp' (a Germanic round lyre), with musicians and dancers. A Canterbury manuscript of the early eighth century (British Museum Cotton Vespasian B I, fol. I*v*)

frame-harp developed from the quadrangular versions which seem to have existed but the Sutton Hoo evidence for it, and for placing the quadrangular type in a seventh-century Anglo-Saxon setting, has gone.

The theory that the frame-harp originated in the British Isles is based on two pieces of evidence which have nothing to do with the Sutton Hoo instrument. One is an illustration in a copy by Gerbert of the twelfth-century treatise *De Cantu et Musica Sacra* (the original was destroyed by fire), in which the harp is labelled *Cithara anglica*, while the round lyre is labelled *Cithara teutonica*[11] (Fig 22). The other is the fact that all the earliest pictures of true harps, and also of a range of harp-like primitive forms, come from the British Isles. Once evolved, the true harp seems rapidly to have displaced the round lyre, though the latter survived at least into the twelfth century and continued thereafter in bowed form, to yield descendants like the Welsh *crwth*.

The earliest pictures of the true harp are from the ninth to tenth century. It is depicted in developed form, resting on the ground and as tall as the player, on standing stones thought to be of this date in Scotland, at Nigg in Ross-shire and Dupplin in Perthshire. The small form held on the knees is depicted in many Anglo-Saxon manuscripts, one of the earliest representations, in which the instrument is given a sub-quadrangular form by its bent fore-pillar, being in the Bodleian Caedmon manuscript Junius XI (late tenth century). As the harp seems to develop early in size in the north and since the Irish stones and crosses show a range of hybrid forms, perhaps the place of origin was Northumbria, where diverse influences met. It was to become an instrument equally common with Saxons and Celts.

If the Northumbrians invented the harp they must have done so in the ninth to tenth centuries. It became the Anglo-Saxon plucked instrument *par excellence* and, we suggest, took the name (*hearpe*) which had already been applied to what we call the round lyre (also a plucked instrument). For a transitional period the name may have been applied to both.

It is a sad minor example of the waste of war that of the actual lyres that were partially preserved, two of the three in Germany were destroyed some time between 1939 and 1946. The St Severin's Church lyre and its records were bombed in Cologne. In Berlin, where the complete lyre from Oberflacht (it had no sound holes) was preserved in a tank of alcohol, Russian soldiers drank the alcohol, so liquidating the bits of wood. The sixth-century bronze bowl from Gilton in Kent with its silver patch depicting a lyre-player[12] (Figs 24 and 25) was destroyed by bombing in Liverpool. Only one of the German lyres survives, at Stuttgart, incomplete and in fragments. So the Sutton Hoo and Taplow remains are of outstanding importance. We may with luck one day unearth another musical instrument but the grave will have to be one in which soil conditions and local factors permit organic matter to survive and where the surviving organic matter happens to include a musical instrument. Had some part of the Sutton Hoo lyre not fallen into a bronze bowl, this instrument placed amongst the grave goods would have vanished; and had the Anglo-Saxon version of the instrument not developed metal joint-plates it would have vanished without trace.

R. B-M.

NOTES TO CHAPTER SEVEN

1 We are indebted to many specialists for help. The woods were identified by Dr C. R. Metcalfe and Dr David Cutler of the Jodrell Laboratory, Kew, and Dr Cutler conducted the tests which determined the degree of shrinkage and distortion of the fragments. Beaver hairs surviving as dark patches on the outside of the frame of the Sutton Hoo instrument show that it was kept, and buried, in a beaver-skin bag, with the fur inwards. The hairs were identified by Dr Mary Dempsey, of the British Leather Manufacturers' Research Association, and by Dr J. L. Stoves. The new reconstruction was made, from detailed drawings supplied by the British Museum, in the Arnold Dolmetsch workshop at Haslemere, under the direction of Mr G. H. Carley. The cost was met from a grant made by the National Geographic Society of America. In the complex work on the fragments and the working out of the new reconstruction Mrs. C. Fenwick contributed valuable ideas and Mrs. G. Keiller did much useful work on the recording and restoration of the hundreds of wooden pieces, both those that were part of the instrument and others associated with them.

2 R. L. S. Bruce-Mitford, *Archaeological Newsletter*, 1948.

3 J. C. Pope, *The Rhythm of Beowulf*, Yale University Press, 1942, 88 ff.

4 J. Werner, 'Leier und Harfe im Germanischen Frühmittelalter', in (eds.) H. Büttner, O. Feger, B. Meyer, *Aus Verfassungs und Landesgeschichte* (Festschrift für Theodore Mayer), 1954, I, 9–15.
J. B. Bessinger, 'Beowulf and the Harp at Sutton Hoo', *University of Toronto Quarterly*, 1958, XXVII, 148–68.
G. Hayes, in (ed.) J. Westrup, *New Oxford History of Music*, Oxford, 1960, III, Ch. xiii.
H. Steger, *David Rex et Propheta*, Nürmberg, 1961, 53.
C. L. Wrenn, 'Two Anglo-Saxon Harps', *Comparative Literature*, XIV, 118–28, 1963. 'Sutton Hoo and Beowulf', in (ed.) L. E. Nicholson, *An Anthology of Beowulf Criticism*, 321–5, University of Notre Dame Press, reprinted from *Mélanges de Linguistique et de Philologie* (Fernard Mossé in Memoriam), Paris, 1959, 495–507.

5 R. L. S. Bruce-Mitford, 'The Sutton Hoo Ship-Burial', *Proceedings of the Royal Institution of Great Britain*, XXXIV, 1949, 3, No. 156, 10, 448, Pl. 2.

6 For early harps and hybrid instruments, see F. W. Galpin, *Old English Instruments of Music*, London, 1910, Ch. 2, and Hortense Panum, *Stringed Instruments of the Middle Ages*, London, 1921, 102 and 117.

7 One of the Oberflacht lyres is illustrated by F. W. Galpin, *Old English Instruments of Music*, London, 1910, Pl. 9; both by W. Veeck, *Die Alemannen in Württemberg*, Berlin and Leipzig, 1931, Pls. 4b9 (tafel.) and A.4 (text). See also J. V. Megaw in (eds.) J. M. Coles and D. D. A. Simpson, *Studies in Ancient Europe*, Leicester University Press, 1968, 352 and Pl. xvi. For the St Severin Church lyre see F. Fremersdorf, 'Zwei Wichtige Frankengräber aus Köln', IPEK, 1943, 124.

8 E. T. Leeds and D. B. Harden, *The Anglo-Saxon Cemetery at Abingdon, Berkshire*, Oxford, 1936, pl. ix (b).
V. I. Evison, *The Fifth-Century Invasions South of the Thames*, London, 1964, III, Fig. 22.
R. L. S. Bruce-Mitford, review of Evison, 1964, *Archaeological Journal*, 1965, CXXII, 247–9.

9 The grave (B 42) contained an early fifth-century sword and is considered one of the

earliest in the cemetery, quite possibly before A.D. 450. J. N. L. Myres, *The Early History of Abingdon and its Abbey*, in M. Biddle, Mrs H. T. Lambrick and J. N. L. Myres, 'II, The Anglo-Saxon Cemetery', *Medieval Archaeology*, 1968, XII, 35–41. The original bone fragments can be seen in the Museum at Abingdon.

10 R. W. Chambers, *Beowulf, An Introduction to the Study of the Poem*, 3rd edition with supplement by C. L. Wrenn; Cambridge University Press, 1967, 509.

11 Martin Gerbert, *De Cantu et Musica Sacra*, 1774, Tom. II, Tab. VI (T. II T. XXXII).

12 B. Fausett, *Inventorium Sepulchrale*, London, 1856.
C. Roach Smith, 'Account of some Antiquities found in the neighbourhood of Sandwich, in the County of Kent', *Archaeologia*, 1843, XXX, 132–6.

CHAPTER EIGHT

The Sutton Hoo Helmet – a new Reconstruction

One of the most important objects found in 1939 in the funeral deposit contained in the Sutton Hoo ship was the helmet. When found it consisted of a great many fragments of corroded iron, amongst which there stood out some better preserved and recognizable pieces in cast bronze – a modelled nose and mouth with tooth-brush moustache and a pair of eyebrows. The iron had completely oxidized before the wooden burial chamber amidships collapsed. This was a good thing because the egg-like helmet simply shattered and clean fractures offered the hope of restoration to the original shape. Had the helmet merely squashed, as would have been the case if the chamber had fallen too soon, it would not have been possible to examine it with such freedom or to restore the shape. It was reconstructed in 1945 (Plates 46a,b and 49a). Unfortunately no photographs had been taken of the remains in the ground and no plan had been made to record the relative positions of the fragments. The task of restoration was reduced to a jigsaw puzzle without any sort of picture on the lid of the box.

A curious feature which emerged from the 1945 reconstruction was that so much was missing. Over half the surface area of the original substance is not there, nor is it represented by any fragmentary material that might possibly fill the *lacunae*. This is still more clearly seen on the 1972 reconstruction (Plates 47a,b, 48 and 49b). Why the pieces that were recovered, though wholly oxidized, are relatively well-preserved and yet no trace survives amongst the excavated material of the rest, is inexplicable.

The helmet is a great rarity. Only one other authentic helmet find is known from the British Isles of the early post-Roman Germanic era – indeed, in the six and a half centuries between the departure of the Romans and the Norman Conquest. That found at Benty Grange in Derbyshire[1] (Plates 63 et seq.) is of a different type, lacking the elaborate decoration of the Sutton Hoo example and with its cap constructed largely from plates of horn. The Sutton Hoo helmet moreover is not Anglo-Saxon at all but Swedish. As such, it is a key-piece in the important new picture which has emerged from the analysis of the Sutton Hoo ship-burial of intimate links with Scandinavia long before the Viking age and of a likely Swedish origin for the East Anglian royal house, the Wuffingas.[2]

The restoration of 1945 has always seemed unsatisfactory in a number of respects and it was soon criticized, though not in print, by Swedish scholars and others. As the backs of the fragments had not been recorded – including those of the bronze castings – the evidence could not be checked. The restorer was our friend and colleague, Herbert Maryon, O.B.E., F.S.A., an authority on early metallurgy and also a sculptor, who had been especially engaged by the Trustees, in his retirement, to work on the restoration of the Sutton Hoo finds under the direction of Dr Plenderleith in the Research Laboratory. Maryon did the best he could with the fragments and the result represented six months' full-time skilled and patient work. The restored helmet was widely published[3] and has been on exhibition for twenty-five years. It has been much cited and discussed, particularly (for reasons which will become apparent) by students of Old English language and literature. Much of Maryon's work was valid – that is to say, the general character of the helmet was made plain. The following features became known:

The helmet was made of sheet-iron and consisted of a cap to which were attached, hanging below the level of the cap, a neck guard, two cheek guards and a face mask. The iron of all these elements had been originally covered externally by sheets of bronze, parts of which had survived in very fragmentary form. These bronze sheets had carried decorative and symbolic subjects stamped into them by dies. There were two distinct dies of interlacing animal patterns, one larger in scale and of rectangular shape measuring 5 × 5·3 cms (Fig 26), the other smaller in scale and long and narrow in form. There were also two dies with figural scenes.

Figure 26 The larger interlace pattern, Sutton Hoo helmet (Scale 3 : 2)

The four designs are identified by numbers as follows:

1. Figural scene: dancing warriors.
2. Figural scene: rider and fallen warrior.
3. Large interlace.
4. Small interlace.

One of these was later reconstructed, after Maryon's work had been completed, as showing twin male figures engaged in a ritual dance (Plate 14b). Each man carried two spears, point downwards, in his outer hand, while the inner arms of the figures crossed and each inner hand held a naked sword, pointing upwards. Both figures were identically dressed in a kind of knee-length belted coat with quilted or embroidered edgings and in hats of cocked hat shape, worn across the head in Napoleonic fashion and crowned by a pair of tall inward-curving horns ending in affronted birds' heads. The second figural scene showed an armed rider on horseback, carrying shield and spear, riding down a mail-clad enemy who, as he lies on the ground, is shown stabbing the horse in the chest with a sword. On the horse's rump a little man is seen kneeling, apparently guiding the rider's spear. Only parts of this scene could be reconstructed, although it has been possible to build up that of the twin dancing warriors almost in its entirety (Plate 14b).

A panel, carrying a single small leg, firmly placed by Maryon at the bottom of the cap of the helmet against the crest at the back, apparently represented a third figural scene. The rest of this scene was lost, the bronze sheet carrying the design having been torn off the surface of the iron by the point of a spear which was said to have been thrust through the helmet from the inside. This has been cited as an example of ritual 'killing' of the object before burial[4] – a pagan practice supposed to release its spirit, a function also of fire in the cremation rite, described in the Old English epic, *Beowulf*. It was evident that the helmet did not carry a boar crest such as is encountered in the pictorial art of the Swedish Vendel period. The bronze eyebrows inlaid with silver wires and picked out along the outer edge with a line of square garnets, terminated, however, in gilded boars' heads (cf. *Beowulf*, 303–4):

Eoforlic scionon
ofer hlēorbergan gehroden golde
(above the cheek guards shone boar images adorned with gold).

and cf. lines 1448–50:

. . . *se hwita helm since geweorðad*
(the white helmet enhanced by treasure)

The helmet also had the silver look referred to in the poem as the surfaces of its decorative bronze plates were tinned. The details of the helmet design, for example its size, the lay-out of the ornament, the shape of the crown, the shape of the cheek-pieces, neck-guard and face-mask, were not clearly established.

To check the evidence for the 1945 reconstruction on these points was impossible without dismantling it. Maryon had sculpted a man's head in solid plaster and had sunk into it those surviving fragments whose positioning seemed fixed or could reasonably be guessed. A box of bits was left over, mostly small fragments, in one case crucial, and with these, lumps of rust, deposited or developed externally on the bronze sheets, in which impressions from the stamped ornament remained in reverse. Casts had been taken by Maryon from these and the ornamental details represented so recovered. So, although Maryon's work had gone far to recover and describe the features of the helmet, many of the key points were conjectural. He did not have the opportunity of travelling to Sweden to examine the comparative material. The total disintegration of the old reconstruction required (Plate 50) could not be undertaken until a combination of facilities and time for joint work by conservation and archaeological specialists could guarantee uninterrupted progress and final enquiry into every point, together with full recording of every stage of the work and every scrap of evidence; followed by a rebuilding of the helmet into what was hoped would be a more intelligible and authentic form. This operation was completed in 1972. It took eighteen months in all and, interspersed with other work at stages where some waiting was necessary, occupied a full year's work by Mr Nigel Williams, Conservation Officer in the Department of Medieval and Later Antiquities, whose achievement merits the highest praise.

In order to appreciate the problems posed and to understand the plan of campaign to which the work of restoration was addressed, we need to look at the old reconstruction (Plates 46a,b and 49a). The side view (Plate 49a) is instructive. The jaw is almost wholly unprotected, the so-called cheek-pieces acting as little more than ear muffs. The cut-away shape at the front of the cheek-pieces serves only to expose more of the cheek. This is the opposite to normal in late Roman helmets where the cutting away of the cheek-pieces generally occurs at the rear. It may be seen in Plate 49a that the face-mask is pushed out in order to clear the nose. The concavity at the back of the nose, although two holes below act as nostrils, allowing the air in, is too small to accommodate a real nose – a point remarked by Her Majesty the Queen when she was shown the Sutton Hoo treasure on the occasion of the party given by the Trustees to mark the Museum's two-hundredth anniversary. This pushing out of the face would entail bending the sheet metal, since no hinges existed at its three points of junction with the cap of the helmet (Plate 46a). Eyebrows and top of nose meet in a rigid assembly as Maryon had said and as the central point of connection was not hinged the

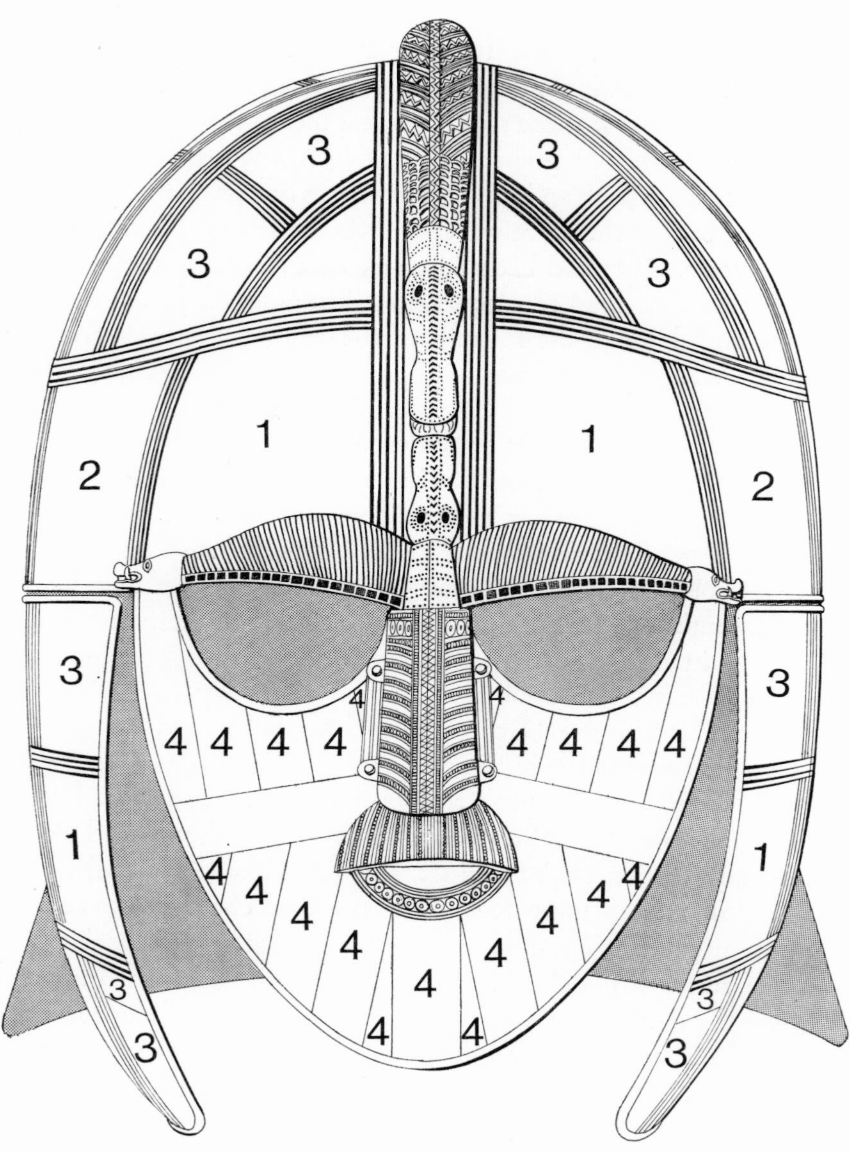

Figure 27 Schematic drawing of the front, Sutton Hoo helmet showing the layout of designs (Scale: about 1 : 2)

a

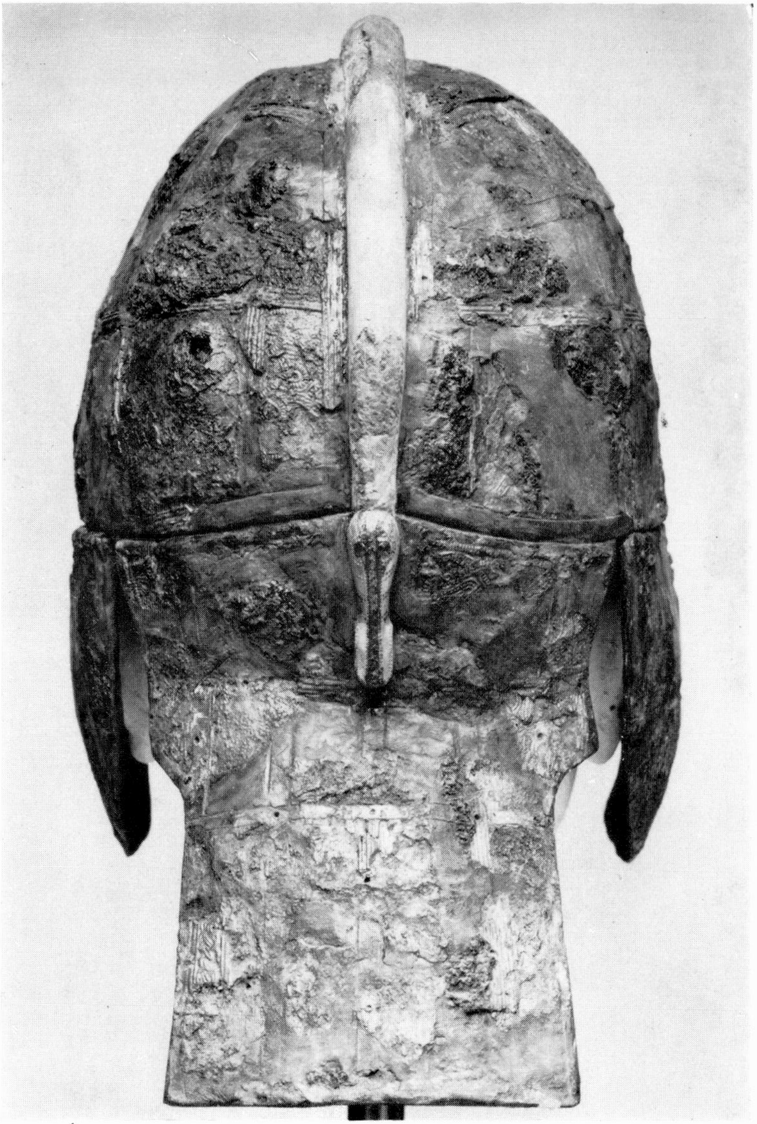

b

Plate 46 Sutton Hoo helmet, 1945 reconstruction: *a*, front view; *b*, back view

a

b

Plate 47 Sutton Hoo helmet 1972 reconstruction: *a*, front view; *b*, back view

Plate 48 Sutton Hoo helmet, 1971 reconstruction seen from above (reduced)

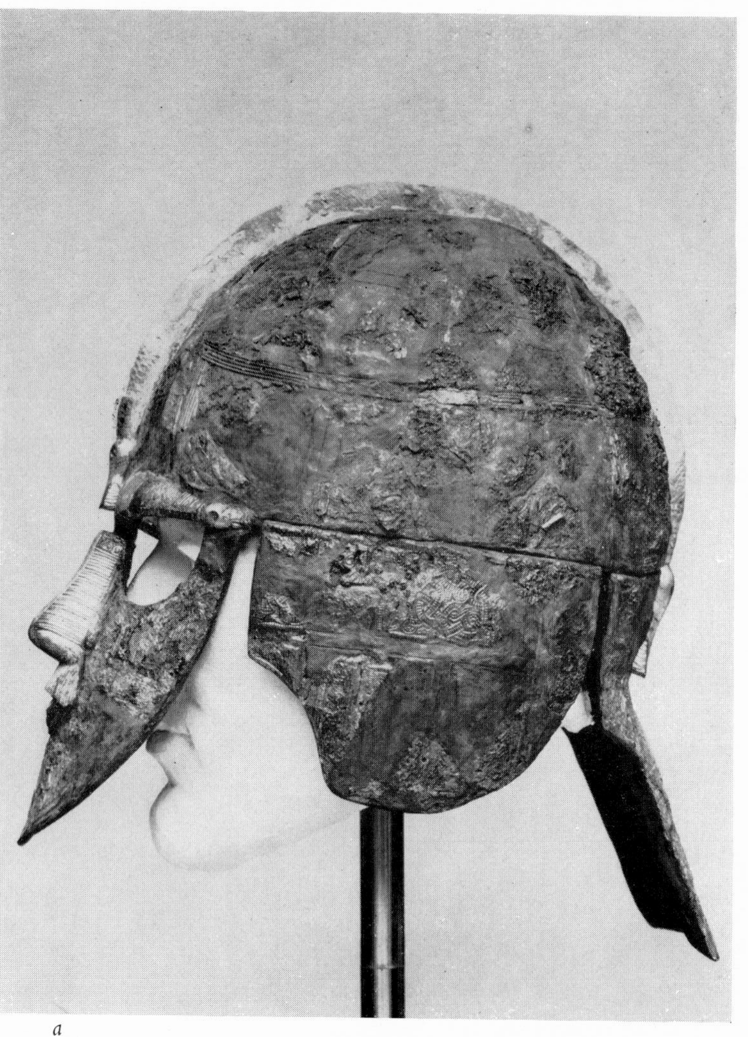

a

b

Plate 49 Sutton Hoo helmet, 1945 and 1972 reconstructions: side views compared: *a*, 1945, *b*, 1972

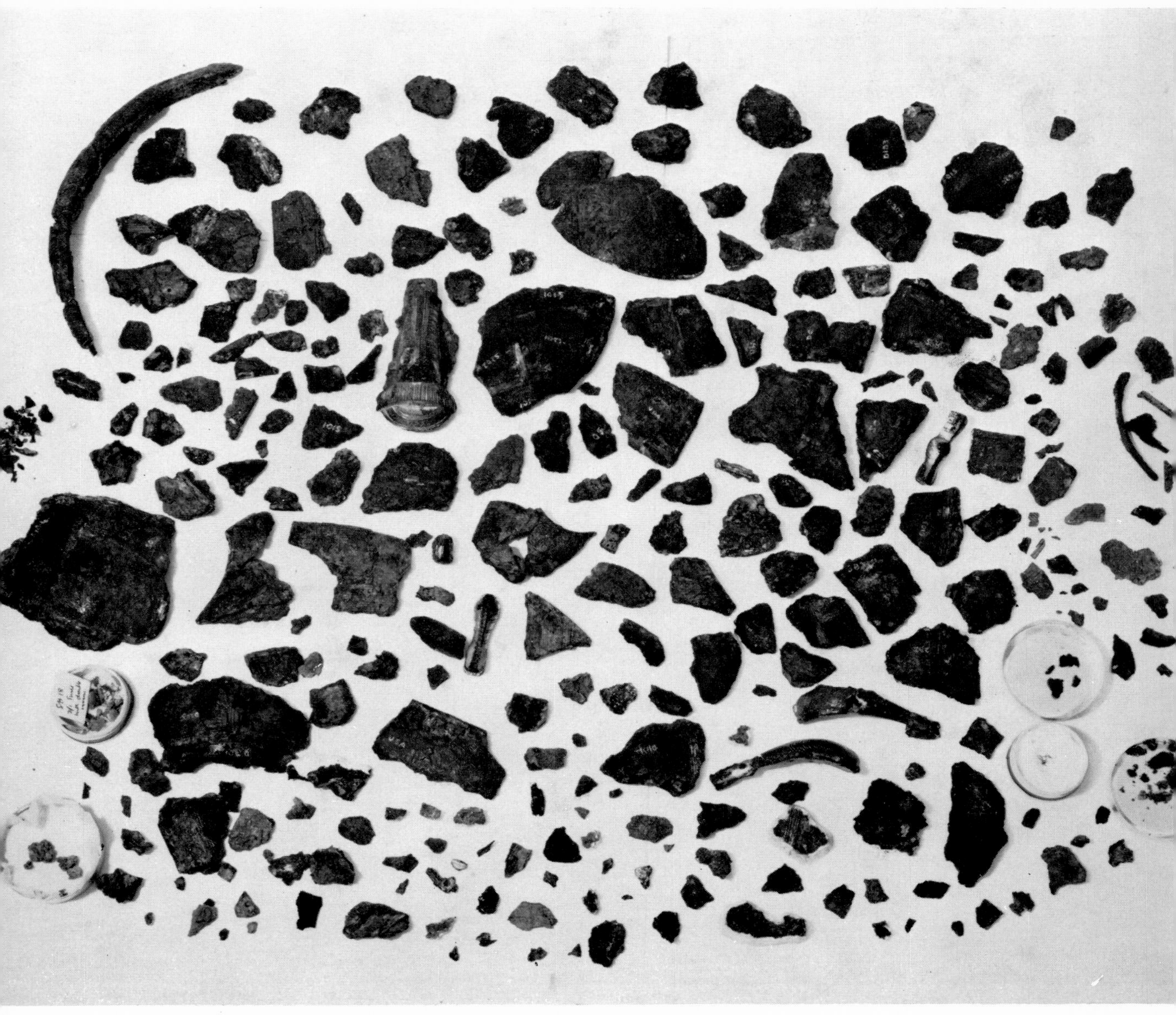

Plate 50 Remains of the Sutton Hoo helmet assembled prior to the commencement of work on the new reconstruction in 1971 (reduced)

51

Plate 51 Underside of the crest and the backs of adjoining fragments showing short but accurate joins with the crest. The corrosion patterns should be noted (Slightly reduced)

Plate 52 Interior view of the crown of the Sutton Hoo helmet (reduced)

52

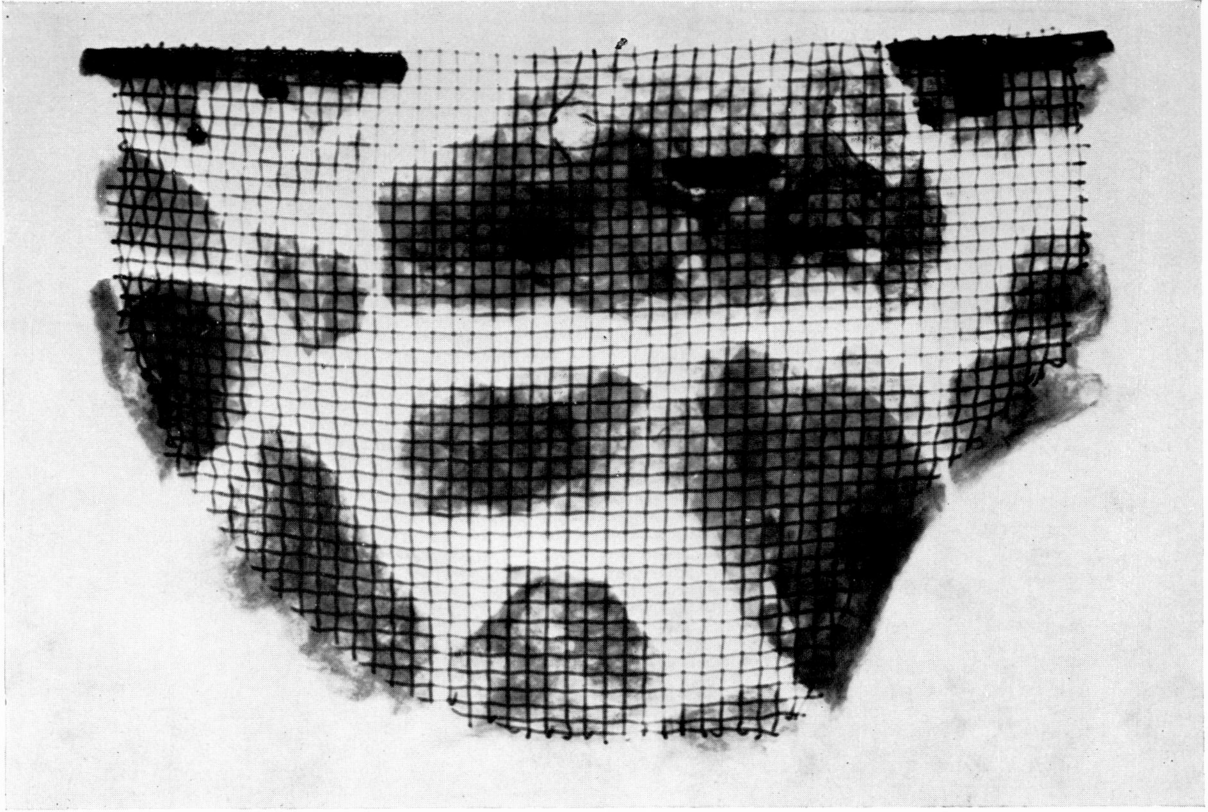

a

Plate 53 a, Sutton Hoo helmet. Radiograph of a cheek-piece of the old reconstruction picking out the original fragments from their plaster bed and showing their steel wire mesh backing (Scale 1 : 1)

Plate 53 b, Finglesham buckle (Scale 1 : 1); *c, d*, Dover pin or stylus – front and side views (Scale 2 : 1)

b

c

d

a

b

c

Plate 54 a, Ekhammar appliqué (Scale 1 : 1); *b*, Drawing from a fragment of bronze foil, the Anglo-Saxon barrow at Caenby, Lincolonshire (Scale 2 : 1); *c* Torslunda die stamp (detail much enlarged)

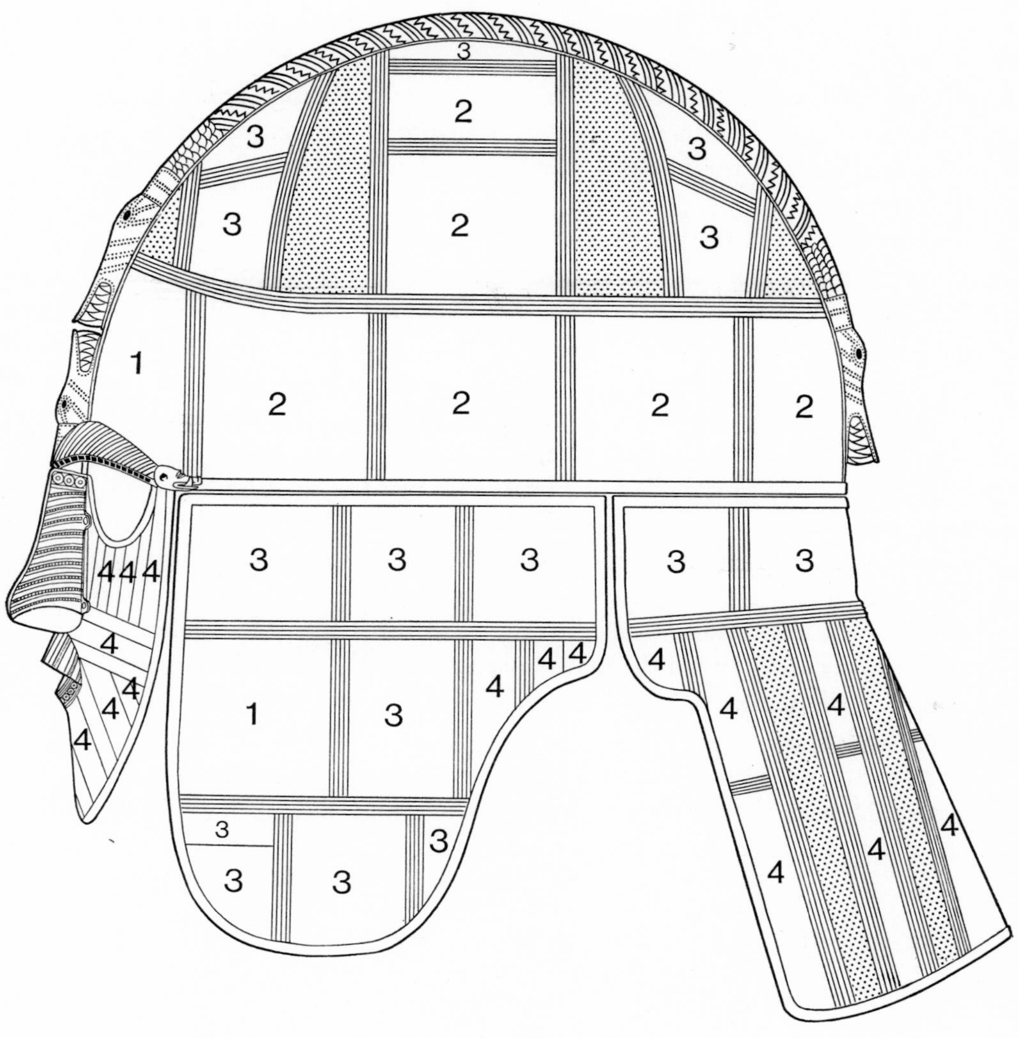

Figure 28 Schematic drawing of the side, Sutton Hoo helmet showing the layout of designs (Scale: about 1 : 2)

other two could not have been hinged either. This bending out of the sheet-iron seemed an unlikely proceeding for a good craftsman. Had the forehead of the cap been built out a little, the mask could instead have come down vertically, clearing the nose. A basic fault of the old reconstruction was Maryon's decision to build it up on an average-sized man's head which he had sculpted in plaster. The fragments were fitted to this predetermined size by being sunk into the plaster instead of letting the fragments themselves dictate the shape. Insufficient allowance had also been made for internal padding or lining or for the mass of hair no doubt worn.

A further problem related to the crest (Plates 46a,b, 49a and 51a). This fitted over the crown and terminated at front and back in a cast-bronze gilded dragon's head. In Maryon's reconstruction the rear dragon head was placed off the cap, on the neck-guard. Since there is no suggestion of a hinge at the end of the crest and none of the related Swedish helmet crests are hinged here, this could only mean that the neck-guard must be rigid. If it were so, apart from any difficulty in the wearing that this might cause, one would expect it and the cap to have been beaten out of a single sheet of metal. This was not the case, since just enough original metal survived both along the back edge of the cap and the upper edge of the neck-guard (Plate 46b) to show that each was separately finished, having its own bronze edge-binding. Furthermore, in order to place the dragon-head on the neck-guard (where according to Maryon it agreed in length with the depth of the vertical zone of the neck-guard, before this turned outwards), a good three inches of plaster had had to be inserted in the crest towards the front (Plates 46a,b).

There seems no reason for this. The crest is made of solid D-sectioned iron tubing inlaid with silver wires, whose presence may have helped to preserve it. It is a striking instance of the type of helmet-crest described in *Beowulf* (1030–1):

> *Ymb ðaes helmes hrōf hēafodbeorge*
> *wīrum bewunden wala ūtan hēold*
> Round the helmet's roof a comb (or 'an external
> ridge') bound with wires protected the head

and indeed has enabled the meaning of the unique word '*wala*' to be established precisely for the first time.[5] If there were really another four inches of the crest to complete the length as shown in Maryon's reconstruction, where is it? There is no reason why it should not have been found by the excavators. Finally, Plates 46a,b and 49a may give an idea of the incoherence in the old reconstruction of the decorative design. It had not been found possible to work this out at all.

If we consider the front view of the old reconstruction (Plate 46a), the eye-openings seem unduly large and vulnerable. The chin is long and projects downwards, so that if one compares the front and side views, there is no link in design between the face-guard and the cheek-guards. They drift apart. The lower part of the face-guard carries narrow panels of interlace ornament set vertically (Plate 46a). The solitary warrior-figure holding spears in his outer hand and with horned head-dress may be seen above the wearer's right eyebrow. Finally, a curious gap exists immediately above the nose, where its top and the inner ends of the eyebrows abut. This seemed a weakness at the focal point of the design of the front of the helmet. No good Germanic craftsman, considering the *horror vacui* evident in Germanic ornament and the stylistic instincts of the time, would have tolerated it. In one Swedish helmet, that from boat-grave no. 1 in the Vendel cemetery, this gap is filled by a human head. No helmet of the period, other than that from Sutton Hoo, has a face-mask. The Vendel 1 helmet has a bird-shaped nose-protector above which the human head is set. It was noted by Williams that the flat top of the nose of the Sutton Hoo mask was gilded as though intended to be seen. The gilding stopped halfway back along the flat top of the nose, suggesting that the rear part, exposed in the Maryon reconstruction, was intended to be covered.

A final point about the old reconstruction. Amongst the helmet remains gathered up from the burial-chamber was part of a third gilt dragon-head, showing the jaws and teeth. Maryon had found no place for this and had consequently omitted it from his reconstruction. He made no mention of it in his publication of the helmet in *Antiquity*, XIV, 1946. He was no doubt influenced by the fact that it was not of cast bronze, like the two other dragon-heads, the eyebrows and the nose and mouth, but of plaster over which gold leaf had been laid. One objective of the new attempt at reconstruction was to account for this third dragon's head.

A clear-cut campaign with a long list of specific questions requiring to be answered was prepared before the old reconstruction was touched. Once it was started there was no going back or stopping. Plates 47a,b, 48 and 49b illustrate the new reconstruction and we will first of all list its new features and then outline the evidence for them. With these plates go Figs 27 and 28 which show the decorative design of the helmet, now established for the first time. The front view (Plate 47a) shows much reduced eye-openings and a vertically set and considerably shorter face-mask. Above the nose, resting on its flat top, is one of the cast bronze dragon-heads, *facing upwards*. In this position it becomes the head and shoulders of a winged dragon – having found, so to say, its body (Fig 29). The eyebrows are the spread wings, the nose, the body, the moustache and mouth a fantail. The winged dragon confronts head-on another dragon-head fitted on the front end of the crest (Fig 29). It can be seen that the neck-guards are now longer than the face-mask. Indeed, when they are drawn onto it they are found to fit flush to its curved profile. They were evidently fastened in position by means

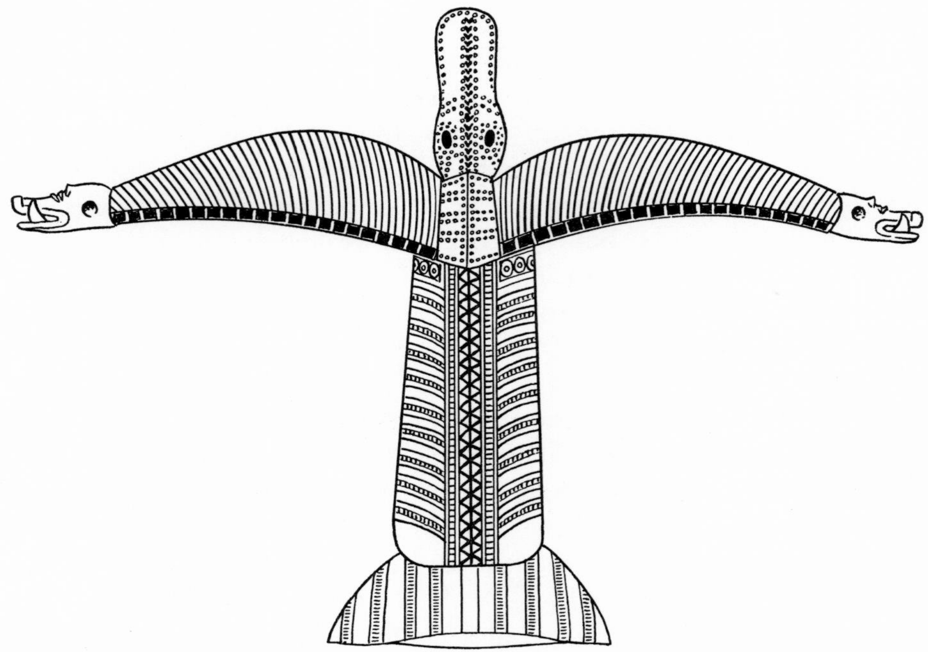

Figure 29 Features of the front of the Sutton Hoo helmet, isolated to show the suggested flying dragon (Scale 3 : 4)

of tapes sewn to the lining of the helmet and tied under the chin.[6] The side view (Plate 49b) shows the newly designed cheek-pieces. They are cut away at the back instead of at the front. It will be seen that this cut-away shape corresponds with the cut-away edge profiles of the neck-guards. Experience in wearing the new reconstruction shows that the shaped space thus created allows free movement of the shoulders and so of the arms. The rest of the head is totally protected. The vertical set of the face-mask can be seen, and the shortened crest. Finally (Plate 47b) the broad fan of the new neck-guard may be compared with the old (Plate 46b). In establishing (on internal evidence) this new breadth for the neck-guard we find that we have ended up with the broad guard seen in certain representations in Swedish Vendel-period art (Plate 58b) not hitherto matched in the archaeological material. The upstanding collar of the neck-guard has been reduced in depth, the new depth, incidentally, being too short to accommodate the longer dragon-head. The helmet is reconstructed as a light shell, with the back of every fragment fully visible, the fragments being suspended in a filling layer of fibrous impregnated resin (Plate 52). It may be said at once that many of the problems posed by the helmet were solved by the process of finding new joins. Almost all of these Williams recognized from study of the corrosion patterns on the inside of the helmet. This corrosion, of a unique blackened, rippled and bubbly nature, almost grained in parts (Plate 51), was distinctive and we explain it as a disintegrated leather lining permeated with iron oxide. Some of the joins were only a few millimetres long but nevertheless clear and definite beyond argument (Plate 51). This result in itself involved a crude minor achievement in the field of archaeological surgery. Fragments had to be dug out of the plaster skull and the mask, neck-guards and cheek-pieces were sawn up with a hacksaw. Radiographs of these latter parts of the helmet before work started revealed that Maryon had mounted the original fragments on a strong steel-wire mesh, bedded in plaster (Plate 53a).

Each original fragment as seen on the radiographs had to be sawn out separately and plaster dissolved from its back and sides, the steel grid removed and the fragment then cleaned without sustaining the slightest damage to its surfaces or edges. New joins effected between the loose fragments showed that the interlace patterns in the lower part of the face mask ran obliquely instead of vertically, reduced the size and altered the shape of the mask and shrunk the eye-openings. New joins also established the occurrence of the scene with twin dancing warriors, formerly thought to have been confined to the cap of the helmet, as is the other figural scene (the fallen warrior, Plate 13a), on the front edge of each cheek-piece. The establishment of firm joins against the top centre of the crest (Plate 51) following upon correct continuous assembly of the crest fragments themselves moved the solitary small leg, supposed to represent a third scene, from the bottom edge of the cap at the rear up to a position against the crest at top centre. Thus positioned, the leg has to be read horizontally rather than vertically and is seen to be the missing rear leg of the small figure that kneels on the horse's rump in the rider panel. The supposed third scene is thus eliminated. In these ways the decorative scheme shown in Figs 27 and 28 was established.

The position of the dragon-head with a bronze neck or collar facing upwards as shown in Fig 29 was established partly by the fact that, so positioned, its collar covered up the non-gilt area of the top of the nose and also because the curious curve of its collar (Fig 30) fitted exactly, in length and curvature, to the convex surface of the inner ends of the eyebrows. In this position it also filled up the awkward gap seen at the focal point of the front of the Maryon reconstruction.

The meaning of the explicitly drawn scenes, rich in detail, encountered in the wide repertoire of Swedish Vendel art, to which our two scenes (Plates 13a and 14b) belong, and the identity of the figure depicted has been much discussed[7] without any agreed and full solutions. The scenes are evidently of significance and hold, if they could be fully understood, a key to the world of ideas that enriched the illiterate early Germanic societies. No doubt they were chosen advisedly, as evoking heroic history and divine protection and as suited to the enhancement of battle and ceremonial helmets.

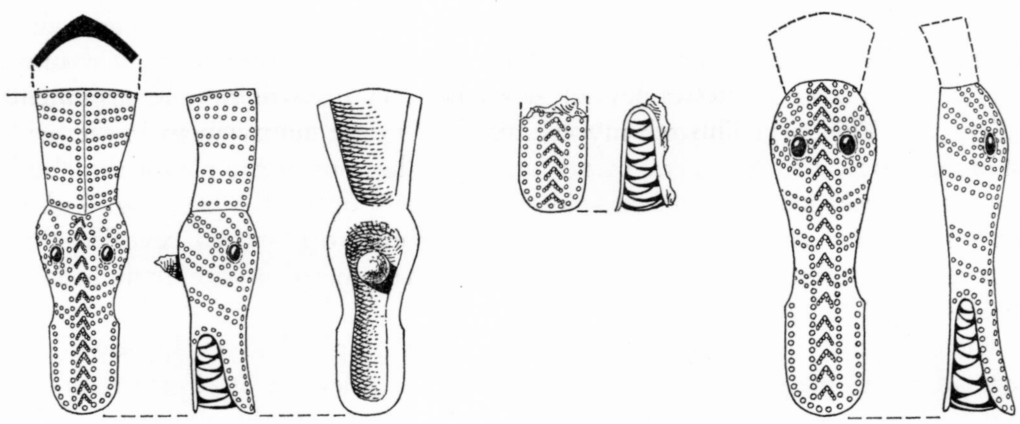

Figure 30 Details of all three dragons' heads, Sutton Hoo helmet (Scale 1 : 1)

The twin figures depicted performing a dance (the soles of the feet of their outer legs are turned upwards) may represent men or priests engaged in rituals associated with the cult of Odin, the war-god. The figure seen alone with the same attributes (helmet with eagle-head terminations to its horns, spears, magic belt (Plate 53a) has been thought to be Odin himself, supposedly identified by the fact that, in one version, a helmet die from Öland, Sweden (Plate 54c), he is depicted as having one eye. However, as Miss Evison has pointed out, the figure occurs in non-military contexts such as the woman's grave, No. 161 of the Dover cemetery,[8] on what may be the handle of a miniature steel for sharpening knives and on buckles[9] and appliqués[10] (Plates 53b–d, 54a). No doubt it was known also in textiles and wood. These scenes on the Sutton Hoo helmet introduce into England Vendel illustrative art, a northern development not tied to classical models but capable of free formulation of new subject matter. Its entry into native Anglo-Saxon art may be seen on the Sutton Hoo purse-lid, a local creation in which figural scenes derived from Vendel art are seen rendered in the less fluent techniques of goldsmith and gem-cutter. It is a living vernacular tradition which later makes its contribution to the Franks Casket (British Museum), to certain stone crosses which illustrate legendary subjects and ultimately to the Bayeux Tapestry, woven by Anglo-Saxon ladies.

Plate 54b shows a new occurrence of the theme of the dancing warrior with bird's head horned hat and carrying sword and spears. It was discovered by my colleague Mrs Leslie Webster in examining fragmentary material from the Anglian tumulus at Caenby, Lincolnshire, in the British Museum. I am grateful to her for allowing me to publish a drawing here.

NOTES TO CHAPTER EIGHT

1 R. L. S. Bruce-Mitford, *Annual Report of the City Museum at Sheffield*, 1955–6, 13, and Chapter Eleven in this volume.

2 Chapter 1, pp. 55–60.

3 Herbert Maryon, 'The Sutton Hoo Helmet', *Antiquity*, XXI, 1947, 137–44.

4 L. V. Grinsell, 'The Breaking of Objects as a Funerary Rite', *Folklore*, 72, 1961, 475–91.

5 See Chapter Nine in this volume, pp. 210–13.

6 Traces of fine linen tape with fifty-six warp threads to the centimetre were found in the vicinity of the helmet. Details of linen tapes in the ship-burial are given in Vol. 1 of the definitive publication, Cambridge, 1974.

7 e.g. by Karl Hauck, 'Germanische Bilddenkmaler des Frühen Mittelalters', *Deutsche Vierteljahresschrift für Literaturwissenschaft und Geistes-Geschichte*, XXXI, 1957, and 'Herrschaftzeichen eines Wodanistischen Königtums', *Jahrbüch für Frankische Landesforschung* 14, 1957, 41. Also see summary in H. Beck, 'Einige Vendelzeitlichen Bilddenkmaler und die literasche Uberlieferung', *Baverische Akad.d.Wissenschaften* (Phil. Hist. Klasse) 6, 1964, 7 ff.

8 V. I. Evison, 'The Dover, Breach Down and Birka Men', *Antiquity*, 1965, 215, Fig. 1.

9 S. C. Hawkes, 'The Finglesham Man', *Antiquity*, XXXIX, 1965, 17–32, pl. 4a.

10 Per-Olof Ringquist, 'Två vikingatida uppländska människofigurer i brons', *Fornvännen*, 64, 1969, 287–96, Fig. 1.

CHAPTER NINE

A Note on the Word Wala *in 'Beowulf'*

Ymb þaes helmes hrōf   hēafodbeorge
wīrum bewunden   wala ūtan hēold
þaet him fēla lāf   frēcne ne meahte
scūrheard sceþfan,   þonne scyldfreca
ongēan gramum   gangan scolde.

Beowulf (1030–4)

Around the helmet's crown a projecting rim, surrounded with bands, guarded the head above, that the sword wrought by files, hard in the storm of battle, might not sorely injure it, when the shielded warrior must go forth against foes. (Clark Hall's prose translation).

In his note on line 1031, Klaeber[1] says that the exact nature of a '*wala*' is not known and follows this with a confusing reference to Stjerna, whom he misunderstood. Stjerna's view on the meaning of '*wala*' is clear from his reference to the detached comb found with the helmet in boat-grave 1 at Vendel (Fig 31).[2] The evidence of the Sutton Hoo helmet seems to put this identification beyond doubt. First of all we may note that the raised ridge or comb which runs over the top of the Sutton Hoo helmet from front to back (Plate 48) would perform exactly the function attributed to '*wala*', that is, to protect the head from severe injury through sword-cuts. It consists of a strong tube of iron, D-shaped in cross-section which attains a height of ¾ inch at its middle point on the top of the helmet. This tube would have tended to prevent the cleaving of the crown by the sword that must often have befallen helmets not so protected, such as that from grave 14 at Vendel (Plate 55). A quick turn of the head as the blow fell would enable the wearer to take it across the 'comb' and avoid its falling parallel with the comb and splitting the cap. Secondly, this feature on the Sutton Hoo helmet provides a clear and unexceptionable illustration of the phrase '*wīrum bewunden*'. The outer surface of the iron tube is elaborately inlaid with ornamental silver wires.[3] The effect of this and the force of the description '*wīrum bewunden*', 'wound about with wires',

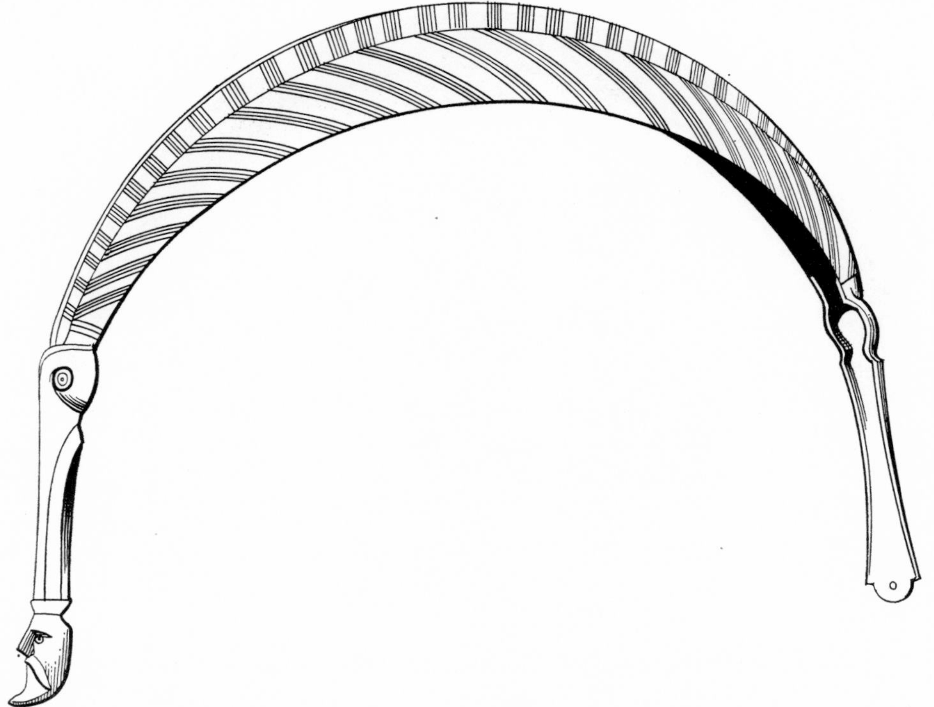

Figure 31 Crest and eyebrows from the helmet, grave I, Vendel, Uppland, Sweden (Scale: approx. 1 : 2)

may be best imagined from Fig 32 and from the simpler version of silver wire inlay seen in the eyebrows of the Sutton Hoo helmet (Fig 29). In case it should be thought that we are trying to dictate an explanation of the text based on a solitary archaeological find which may be a freak, it should be said that inlay of silver wires in iron is a standard technique of the time and that we may suppose that it occurred on the crests of other rich helmets of the period. This is implied by the number of examples known of Vendel-type helmet-crests in which such wire-inlay patterns are imitated in casting or engraving. We should also remember that there is not at present any archaeological context more relevant to the poem than the Sutton Hoo ship-burial.

Stjerna made heavy weather of his attempt to explain '*wīrum bewunden*' for he did not know that the cast chevron patterns on the comb of the Vendel 1 helmet were reminiscences or imitations of actual wire inlays on earlier or richer helmets. His gauche attempts to explain the phrase seem to have misled some translators and to be the source of such renderings of it as 'a rib to which plates were made fast' and 'surrounded with bands'. The explanation offered here does not involve an unorthodox use of the word '*ymb*'. As Stjerna said, 'the form of the helmet and

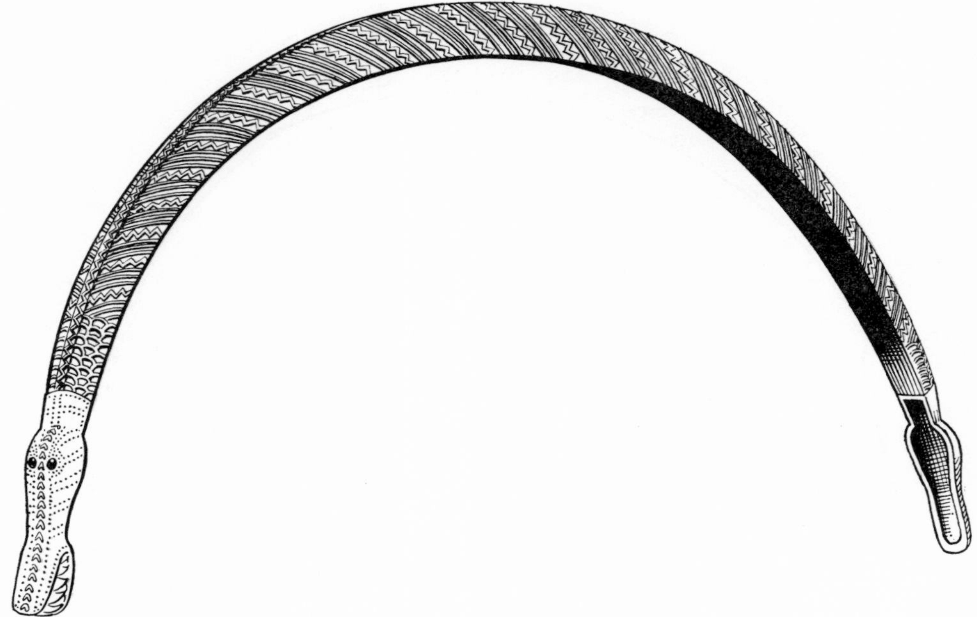

Figure 32 Silver wire inlays on the crest, Sutton Hoo helmet (Scale 1 : 2)

its comb show clearly what a graphic and correct expression "around the crown" ("*hrōf*") was in reference to the "*walu*".'[4] The side view of the Sutton Hoo helmet (Plate 49b) should make this clear. There is no reason why the term '*ymb*' should not be applied to the vertical as well as to the horizontal axis of a rounded object. It is possible that the tendency to think that '*ymb*' in this passage implies some feature set horizontally is due to the attaching of insufficient weight to the word '*hrōf*', which would seem to refer not to the cap of the helmet (as distinct from its cheek, face-, or neck-guards) so much as to the topmost part of the cap. The expression '*heaþosteap*', 'towering in battle', as applied to helmets, may reflect this emphasis on the high top of the helmet (its '*hrōf*'), as distinct from the cap in general. The new reconstruction of the helmet (1971) is considerably larger and taller than the old one (1945) (Plate 49a and b).

It is difficult to make any sense out of the passage we are discussing unless the '*walan*' of the manuscript is emended to a nominative singular form '*wala*' or '*walu*', and taken as the subject of the sentence. This emendation, which is generally accepted,[5] makes perfect sense of the passage in the light of the new archaeological evidence.

In connection with this identification of '*wala*' with the ridge or comb that runs over the top of Vendel-type helmets from front to back, it is interesting to note the use of '*waele*', '*wael*' in Middle High German, to mean the 'contrivance on a helmet by which the plume is fastened.[6]' We may also note that the Sutton Hoo helmet consists of a sheet-iron cap, made in one piece, inside which we can infer a substantial padded lining. The whole of this protective structure is internal and concealed from view by the tinned-bronze sheeting and tinned strips that form the outer surface of the helmet. The 'comb', however, is an external addition, fixed on over the top of the cap. As compared with the concealed iron cap it provides head-protection (*heafodbeorge*)'*utan*', 'from without', externally to the cap of the helmet.

In every way this identification of '*wala*' fits and clarifies the text, for which the following literal translation might be offered: 'Around the helmet's top a wire-bound ridge protected the head from without, that the sword . . . might not sorely injure it . . .' The small textual point we have discussed illustrates the intimacy of the relationship between the archaeological material in the Sutton Hoo grave and the *Beowulf* poem.

NOTES TO CHAPTER NINE

1 F. Klaeber, *Beowulf and the Fight at Finnsburg*, London, 1922, 169.

2 K. Stjerna, 'Essays on Beowulf', *Viking Club Extra Series*, Vol. III, London, 1912, ed. and trans. by J. R. Clark-Hall, 14.

3 The description of the 'comb' or crest of the Sutton Hoo helmet given in *Antiquity*, XXI, 141, is incorrect.

4 *op. cit.*, 14.

5 R. W. Chambers, *Beowulf with the Finnsburg Fragment*, ed. by A. J. Wyatt, 53, second ed., Cambridge, 1920. Note on lines 1031ff.

6 *Vorrichtung am Helme wodurch der Helmsbusch befestigt wird*; M. Lexer, *Mittelhoch-deutches Handwörterbuch*. I am indebted to Miss V. I. Evison for this reference.

CHAPTER TEN

Fresh Observations on the Torslunda Plates

The four much published 'plates' from Torslunda, Öland (Plates 57–60), found in 1870,[1] are dies cast in bronze. From them, impressions were struck in sheet bronze. Many identical impressions may be taken from a die in the course of its useful life. As in the case of coins, such impressions will reflect the condition of the dies, that is, the degree of wear or damage sustained by them. It should be possible to distinguish at times between later and earlier impressions from the same die.

The impressed bronze sheets struck from these Torslunda dies were, we know, designed to be mounted on helmets. Since dies of this size, shape and character appear to have been used exclusively in the manufacture of helmets, their discovery on Öland might suggest the presence there of a workshop either specializing in the production of helmets, or perhaps producing other items of military equipment as well.

However, the site was not investigated at the time of the discovery. The plaques, for all we knew, might have come not from a workshop but from a grave – that of the helmet-maker. Even so (that is, even if the site were not a workshop), this might suggest that helmets of the types so decorated, familiar to us from the more northerly territory of the Svear, north of Lake Mälaren at Vendel, Valsgärde, and Gamla Uppsala in particular,[2] were being produced by a craftsman working a long way to the south on Öland in the Baltic, in territory associated with the Geats and not with the Svear. The question must arise, did both peoples use exactly the same type of helmets (if such helmets were made on Öland) or are all the helmets of this type found north of Mälaren battle-trophies won by the Swedes from their Geat enemies to the south? This site, which Ulf Erik Hagberg and I recently identified and inspected together, has now, at my suggestion, been investigated. It is clear that the 'plates' did not come from a grave. The site is a settlement of the fifth to sixth century. A preliminary note on the excavations, by courtesy of Dr Hagberg and Miss Kristina Rosell, is given later (pp. 219–220).

Meanwhile, I propose to look at these all-too-familiar objects from a different point of view, the technical.

The four bronze plates were found together, by two different men, at one place and under the same prevailing soil conditions.

The plates may be designated individually as follows:

A Man between bears.
B Man with axe holding roped animal.
C Walking warriors carrying spears.
D Dancing man in horned head-dress and man with spear wearing wolfskin.

Recently, for exhibition purposes, they were cleaned and all now present a similar surface appearance, as far as colour goes. My careful notes made before this cleaning took place referring to D and C (Plate 59a,b) read as follows:

> There is a clear difference in colour between D and C. D is more patchy, not so dark, shows much more positive green and is of a much more bronze-like metal, i.e. of a more yellowish hue. C has also reddish tones seen on the back, while D, seen from the back, is much greener. These differences should be due to differences in the metal, and not merely differences in patination of an identical alloy, since all the plates were found buried together in the same soil. C and D, however, are in spite of the differences, alike in thickness and weight and general technical features and in size of figure-subjects and treatment of borders. They differ from A and B.

Comparing them with A and B (Plate 58b,a) my notes make it clear that before cleaning, these latter had a 'leaden' look and a bluish tone. The bronze of A (Plate 58b) was described as an 'almost black bronze showing gold tones where wear can be observed on the high lights. A slightly leaden appearance'. B was virtually identical in appearance to A.

There are, in fact, clear distinctions in design as well as in colour between the four plates, particularly between A and B taken together and C and D taken together. But also, to a lesser extent, between C and D themselves.

The differences can best be seen in comparing B and D (Plate 57a,b). They are very different in size and shape. B is in mint condition, D is very heavily worn. B is meticulously finished, with sharp, clean edges to the die, D is ragged-edged, the casting poorly cleaned up and the casting-jet left in the bottom right-hand corner. The surface is blemished and rough. There is also a considerable variation in the level of relief to which the figures and the different parts of them stand out in D. In B there are more or less two planes only, a background and a flat general level of the raised surface of the design. The flat-chestedness of the human figure holding the animal by a rope round its neck is in strong contrast to the convexity and on top of this again the projecting ring-sword hilt on the chest of the human figure in D. The figures on B are more compactly composed and fill the plate up to its edges.

The differences in colour and patination observed before cleaning have already been mentioned. A and B were evidently both designed by the same person and made together as a pair by the same person. Not only do they seem technically and stylistically identical but B fits on top of A, both tapering slightly upwards together (Plate 58a,b). B is evidently intended to ornament an upper zone of the helmet and A to fit below it, in a lower ornamental zone.

If we turn to C and D (Plate 59a,b) these two are very close in general features, especially when compared with A and B. Both show ragged outlines, feeble borders, roughnesses, and the casting jet left in the corner and had to some degree a similar general appearance of the metal before they were cleaned; yet these two are distinctly different. D is much more worn than C, there is a difference in the colour and patination of the metal and, most notably, a difference in the style and competence of the figure-drawing. The two men with boar-crested helmets on C are somewhat flatter in relief and less irregular in surface treatment than the figures on D.

A further point of interest emerges from the study of the backs of the plates (Plate 60). The backs of A and B are quite smooth. Those of C and D are rough and marked with small irregularities and with excrescences of metal. This difference reveals a different technique of employment. In A and B, the thin bronze sheets were laid on a bed presumably of bitumen or wax and the dies hammered into the sheet from the back, that is, by laying the dies pattern downwards on the foil and hammering their backs. This may in part account for the immaculate condition of their faces. In the case of C and D, the backs of the dies were not hammered, as their roughnesses show, but evidently the bronze sheets were hammered or driven directly onto the *front* of the die which carried the figures. This may in some degree account for their worn surface condition.

It seemed essential to see whether or not these impressions from superficial observation would be supported by chemical analysis.

With the ready permission of the Statens Historiska Museum the opportunity was taken when the plates were in the British Museum for the Exhibition of Swedish Gold in 1966 to take small carefully recorded and controlled drillings for analysis. Some part of each sample taken was retained for a later more accurate result by refined methods which it was hoped would become possible shortly, when new apparatus would be available. In the meantime, two tables are here published giving firstly the dimensions and weights and secondly the spectrographic analyses of the four plates.

The larger area but smaller weight of the thinner plates C and D stand out clearly. The following are provisional Laboratory notes by the British Museum Research Laboratory on the spectrographic results obtained:

1. An experimental or methodological error of ±20% of the quantities given is possible.

2. The spectrographic analyses show virtual identity between A and B. The only difference is a marked one in iron content. This could be accidental, that is, due to the accidental inclusion of iron traces or a small iron scrap in the casting. The marked difference in iron content would call for a slight difference in the height of the melting temperature of the alloy with 0·3% iron as against that with 0·4% iron.

3. The metal or scrap used for C is or was 'very much like gilding metal'. This was a favourite metal used by the Romans as a cheap substitute for gold, where glitter rather than intrinsic value was called for, for example in gladiator's helmets,

TABLE 1

TORSLUNDA PLATES
Dimensions (cms)

	Top	*Bottom*	*Left side*	*Right side*
A	4·5	4·75	4·5	4·6
B	4	4·5	4·5	4·6
C	5·5	5·5	4·7	4·7
D	5·6	5·6	4·8	4·8

	Thickness (mm) (approx.)	*Weights* (Gms)
A	4–4·5	62·52
B	3·5–4	57·1
C	2–2·5	32·52
D	2·5–3	38

TABLE 2

TORSLUNDA PLATES
Spectrographic Analysis (1967)
(percentages)

	Tin	*Zinc*	*Lead*	*Silver*	*Iron*	*Nickel Gold Antimony*	*Copper*
A	3	4	3	3	4	0·2–	82·8
B	4	4	3	3	0·3	0·2–	85·5
C	2	7	1	1	0·6	0·2–	89·2
D	8	0·1	4	0·3	3	0·2–	85·5

A = Man between bears
B = Man with axe leading animal
C = Walking warriors with spears
D = Men with horned helmet and in wolfskin

for jugs, bowls, and so on. Gilding metal is not applied as a surface, like gilding, but is an alloy, usually about 50% gilding metal and 50% of 5% or low tin bronze (i.e. gilding metal is a natural alloy from ore containing zinc and copper and is produced by mixing equal quantities of gilding metal and low tin bronze).

4. The differences between C and D are significant since they are not only pronounced but also outside the range of error of spectrographic analysis.

The statistics provided clearly indicate that the four plates fall into three distinct 'strata'.

A and B, in mint condition, technically sophisticated and highly finished, and with patterns whose freshness is probably in part preserved by the technique of hammering on the back and not on the face of the die, seem to be appreciably later than C and D and are certainly the work of one man at one time. Of C and D, D is older than C, though perhaps only a somewhat earlier, less sophisticated effort by the same craftsman. It is considerably more worn than C and shows less experience in die design.

As we have said, two plates each were found by two different men. We do not know which were found together, or whether they were found in the pairs into which they now seem to fall.

The analyses were carried out by Dr Michael Hughes.

Since the first set of results were published the promised second set, from the portions of sample which had been reserved pending the availability of new apparatus, have been obtained. The latest analyses have been done by atomic absorption spectrometry and polarography and the result is as follows:

TABLE 3

TORSLUNDA PLATES

Second Analysis (1972) from reserved portions of samples taken in 1967.
(The figures obtained from the first analysis of the same samples are given in brackets following the new figure)

	A		B		C		D	
Copper	88	[*82·8*]	89	[*85·5*]	88	[*89·2*]	*88*	[*85·5*]
Tin	3·4	[*3*]	3·6	[*4*]	1·4	[*2*]	7·6	[*8*]
Lead	2·1	[*3*]	1·9	[*3*]	0·9	[*1*]	3·2	[*4*]
Zinc	2·7	[*4*]	4·1	[*4*]	8·8	[*7*]	0·8	[*0·1*]
Iron	2·8	[*4*]	0·3	[*0·3*]	0·5	[*0·6*]	0·1	[*3*]
Silver	0·7	[*3*]	0·8	[*3*]	0·4	[*1*]	0·1	[*0·3*]
Gold	0·09		0·095		0·16		0·03	
Antimony	0·14	[*0·2–*]	0·10	[*0·2–*]	0·10	[*0·2–*]	0·11	[*0·2–*]
Nickel	0·04		0·043		0·05		0·04	
TOTALS	99·97		99·93		100·31		99·98	

These results confirm the general picture obtained from the earlier series, but

Plate 55 Vendel 14 helmet

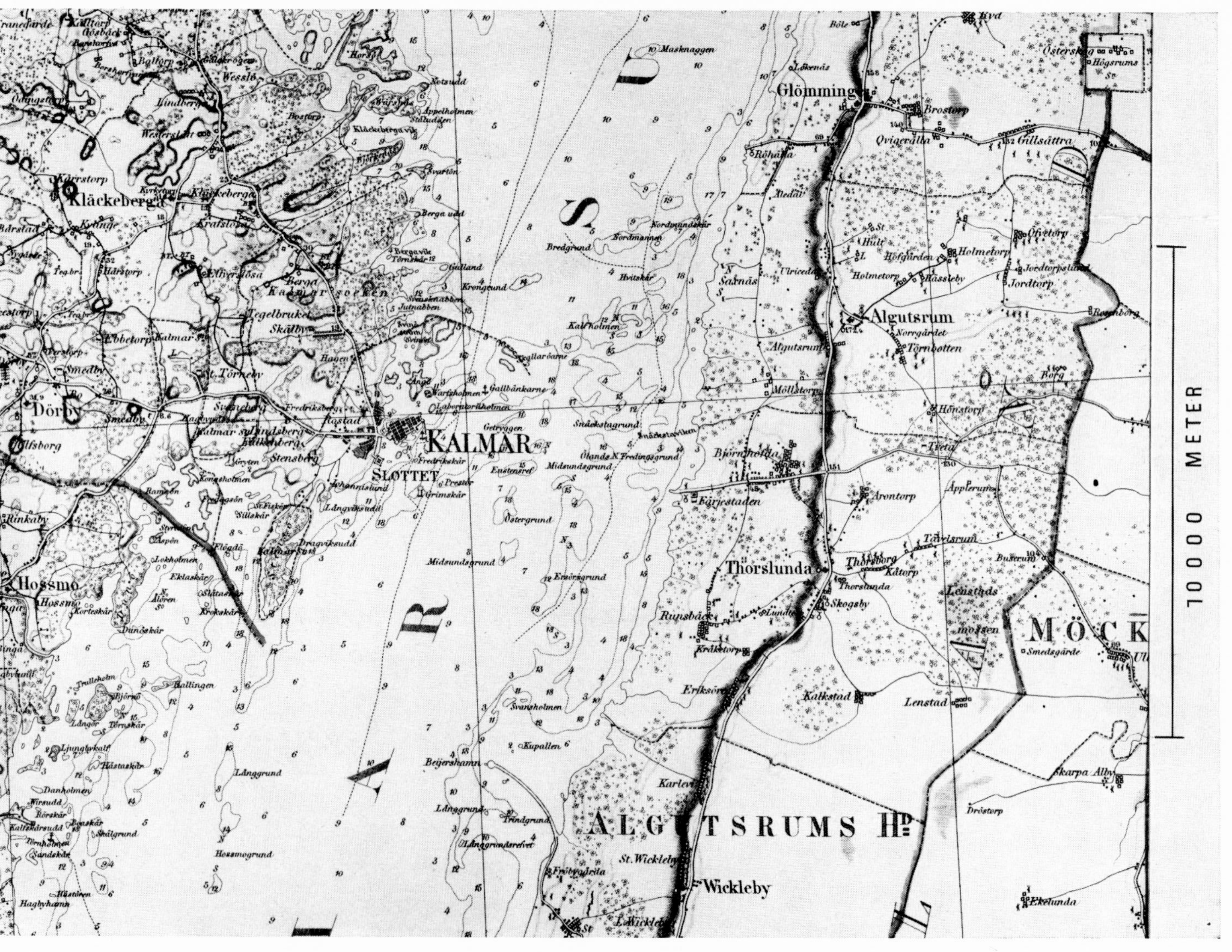

Plate 56 Map of part of Öland and the Swedish mainland to the west. The bronze dies were found in a field immediately to the east of the road between Torslunda and Algutsrum, some two hundred metres north of the Björnhovda cross roads

a

b

Plate 57 a,b, Torslunda plates, Dies B and D compared (Scales 2 : 1)

a

b

Plate 58 a,b, Torslunda plates, Dies B and A compared (Scales 2 : 1)

a

b

Plate 59 a,b, Torslunda plates, Dies D and C compared (Scales 2 : 1)

Plate 60 The backs of the Torslunda plates (Scales 1 : 1)

Plate 61 Post-hole plan of the first house uncovered at Torslunda, seen from the air

a, b

c d e

Plate 62 Benty Grange. Original fittings of the wooden cup with silver cruciform mounts; *above a,b*, Rim with the cross-mount inside it; *below c–e*, three surviving double cruciform mounts (Scales 1 : 1)

Plate 63 The Benty Grange helmet restored on a perspex mount (reduced)

64

a

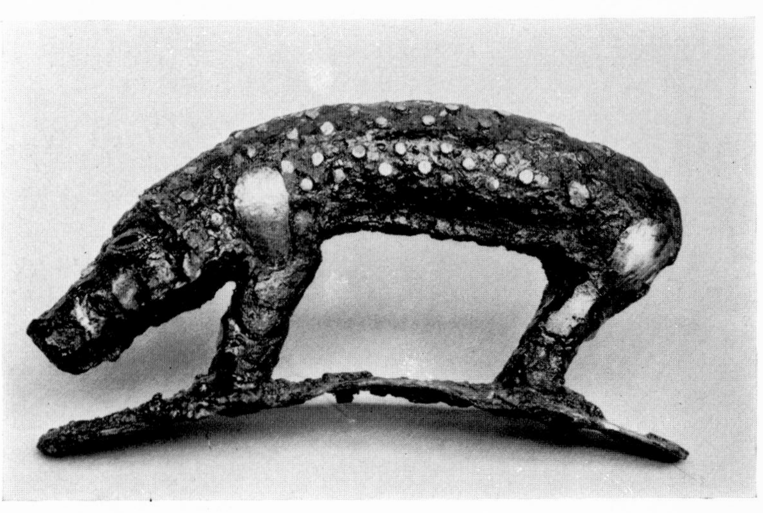

b

65

a

b

Plates 64 and 65 Benty Grange boar before and after removal of iron oxide concretions (Scales 1 : 1)

a

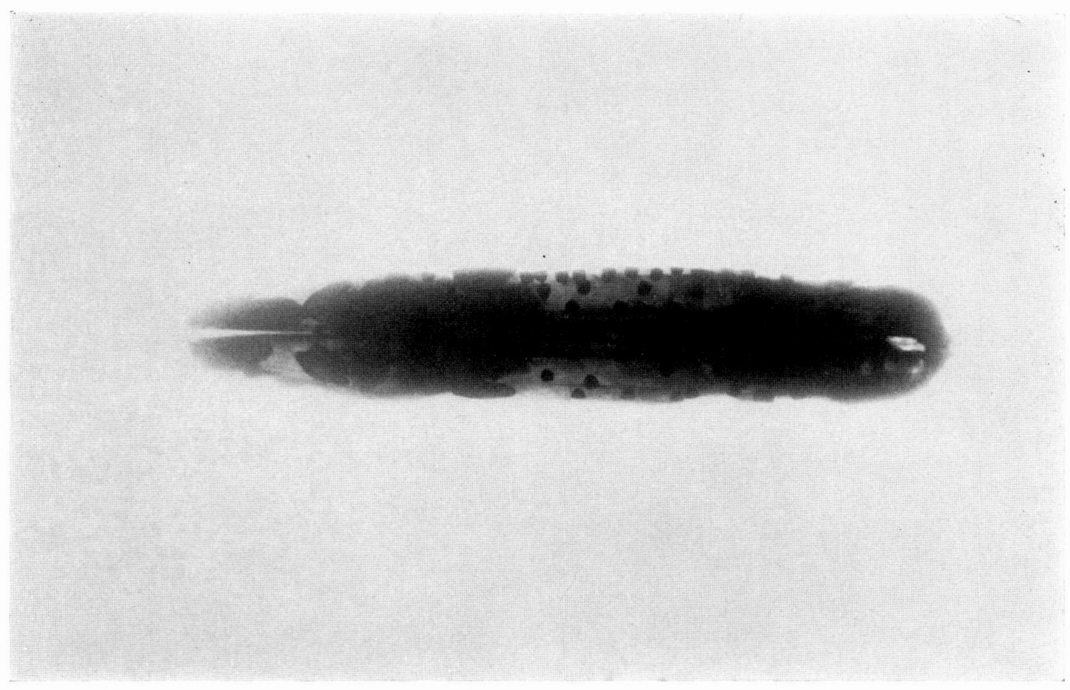

b

Plate 66 Radiographs of the Benty Grange boar after repair, *a*, from side; *b*, from top (Scales 1 : 1) (modern reinforcing-wires can be seen)

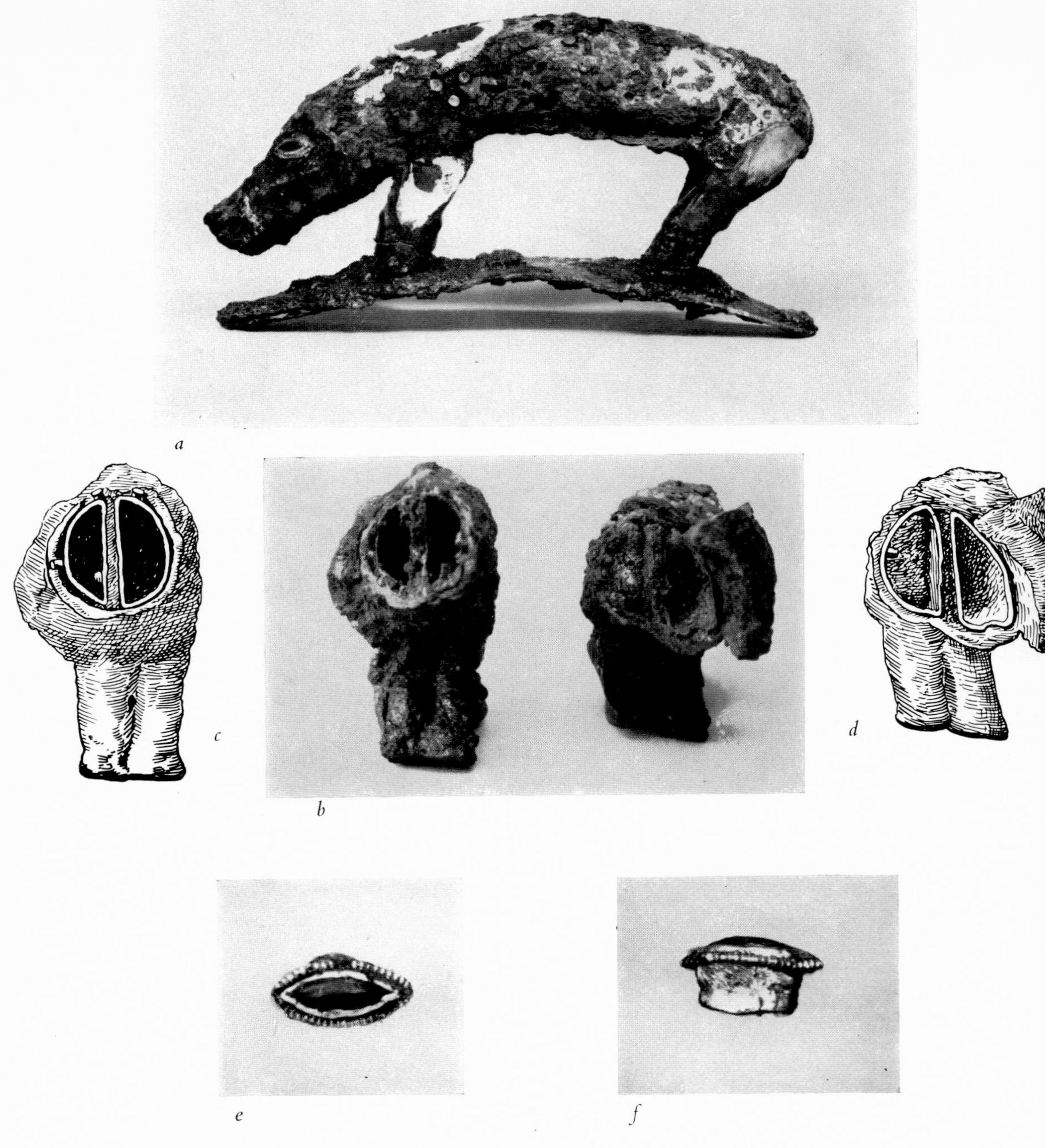

Plate 67 a, Benty Grange boar during repair work after fracture (Scale 1 : 1); *b*, Section across broken body of Benty Grange boar (Scale 1 : 1); *c,d*, Drawing of section across broken body of Benty Grange boar (Scale 3 : 2); *e,f*, The eye of the Benty Grange boar (enlarged)

the variations in the two sets of readings are to be noted. The following comment is supplied by the Research Laboratory:

The most significant differences between the second and the first sets of results are the lower content of silver found in plates A and B, the lower content of iron found in plate D, and the higher content of zinc found in plate D. The composition of plates A and B is quite similar, except that plate A is characterized by a higher content of iron and contains less zinc. It should be noted that no cobalt was found in any of the plates; also the consistency in the amount of copper is noteworthy (in previous analysis copper was not determined directly, but by difference). It is interesting to note that, although plates C and D contain similar amounts of copper, the alloying elements are present in significantly differing amounts. The metal of plate C is nearer to a brass (copper/zinc alloy) whereas the metal of plate D is a bronze (copper/tin alloy) containing some lead.

EXCAVATIONS AT TORSLUNDA IN 1968 AND 1969

The site at which the Torslunda plates were found is recorded in the Riksantikvarieämbete on Sheet 4G6 of the Economic Map of Sweden (printed 1942) (1 : 10,000) (Kalmar Län, Färjestaden). A rough sketch taken by me from the map in the Riksantikvarieämbete is reproduced here (Fig 33). The find-spot is marked with a cross and allotted the serial number 40^a. It is on a strip of land (5^5A) in the present ownership of Evald Sturesson. The strip to the south is numbered 5^{16}, and is in the present ownership of Lage Engström. The site 40^a is marked on the map as 175m north of the permanent landmark, a monument consisting of a ring of five standing stones (perhaps of Viking date) with the number 40; hence the allocation of the number 40^a to the find-spot of the bronze plates, 175m to the north. The entry as written on the map reads 40^a: *fyndplatsen för figurprydde bronsmatrisen* with an added reference *Våren 1870 uti en stenrör* ('find-spot of four bronze dies decorated with figures' and 'Spring 1870, from a heap of stones').

The site of the discovery is beside the road which runs north/south along the edge of the *landborg* (the escarpment facing Kalmar Sound) which runs the length of the island. From the cross-roads six hundred metres south of the site a road to the west drops down past Björnhövda village (Bear's head, a significant-sounding name) to Färjestaden, the point from which the ferry to Kalmar plies, where the famous gold collar was discovered.[3] The original location on the *landborg* has produced also a remarkable concentration of stray finds of gold *solidi*, no less than thirty-six in all, evidently once contained in a purse and scattered; and eight other gold *solidi* are recorded as single finds from other sites in Torslunda parish.[4]

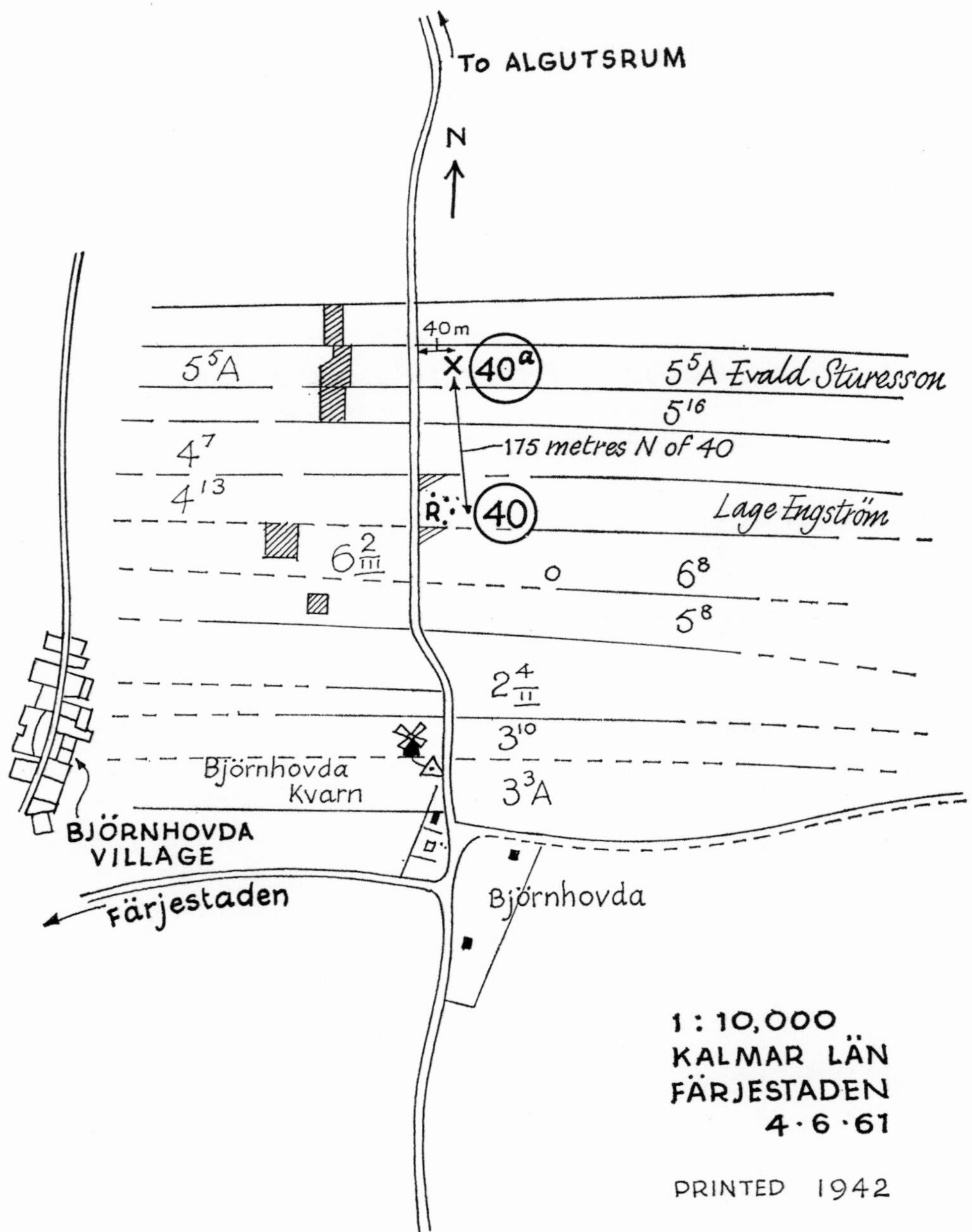

Figure 33 Sketch map of the Torslunda area

The place-name Björnhovda (Bear's head) was attached to the cross-roads south of the windmill (known as Björnhovda mill) but has since been transferred to a modern village on the coastal strip below. A phosphate survey of the whole

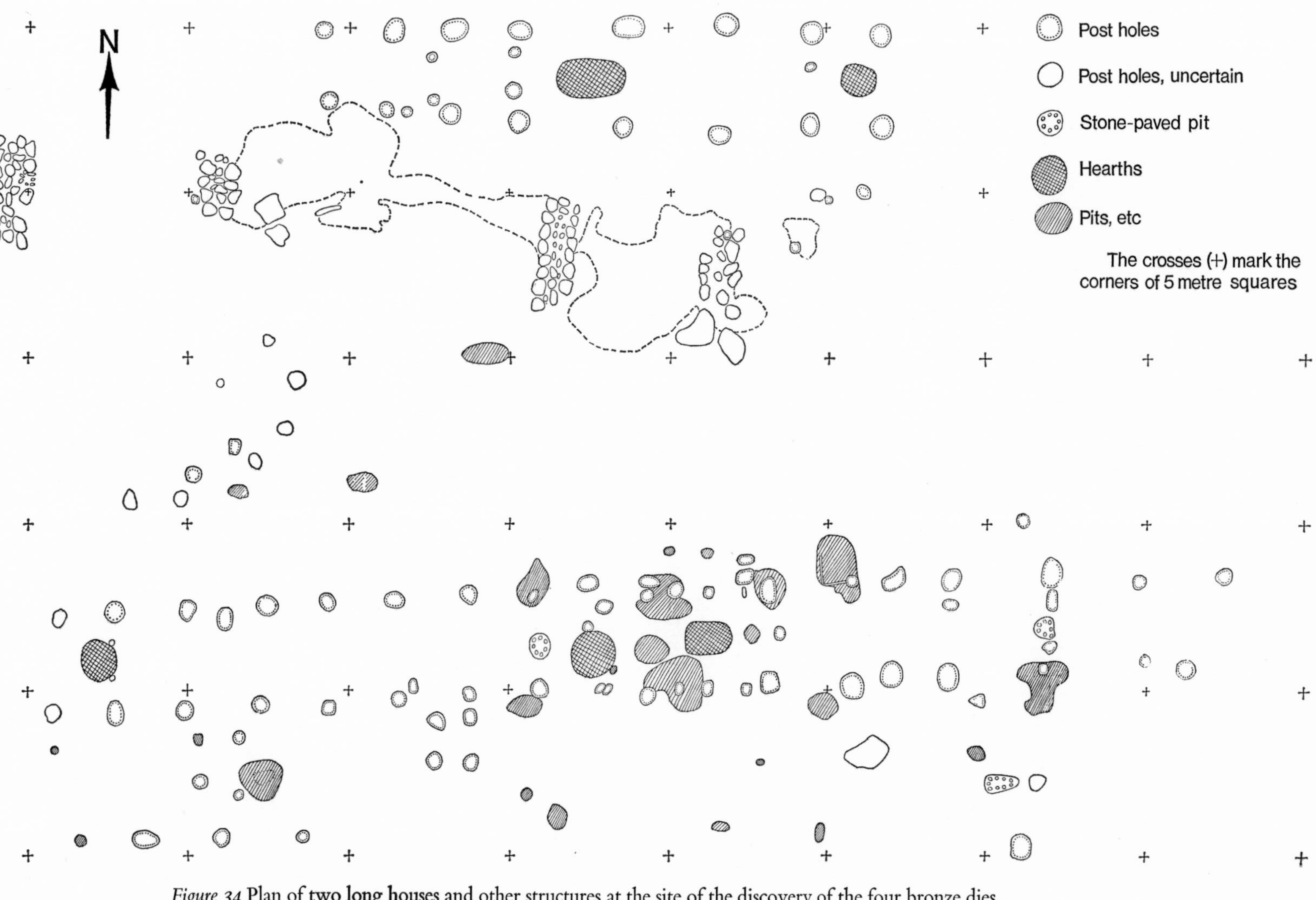

Figure 34 Plan of two long houses and other structures at the site of the discovery of the four bronze dies, Torslunda, Öland, 1972

parish carried out separately by S. Göransson, shows the highest phosphate concentration in the area on the *landborg* around the cross-roads.

In the spring of 1968 and summer of 1969, two seasons of excavation were carried out on the site of the discovery. They were directed by Dr Ulf Erik Hagberg and supervised in the field by Fil-Kand Kristina Rosell. The excavations revealed a settlement site. Three long-houses with east/west orientation were located. The roofs were supported by two alignments of posts. No definite evidence of an actual workshop in the form of scraps or slag or extensive burnt layers or of furnaces was encountered. It is at all events clear that the plates were not found in a grave. No graves were encountered during the excavations. The house-types are unlike the normal 'giants' grave-houses' (*Jättergravs-husen*) of Öland but are paralleled in east Öland, that for example at Sörby Tall in Gärdslösa excavated by Ulf Erik Hagberg and Margarete Beskow.[5]

Fig 34 and Plate 61 give an impression of the settlement-remains from which the Torslunda plates came. More extensive excavation should yield more specific information.

The finds include a handled comb of the Migration period, which is probably fifth-century and is the best dated of the finds; a large lump of amber and shards of green glass. There was a hearth in one of the houses of unusual type with very black and sooty earth and some good slag.

I am greatly indebted to Dr Hagberg and Miss Kristina Rosell for supplying me with this information and for the plan and photographs of the house-plan of their excavations. Their work is to be published elsewhere, and they have shown great generosity in allowing me to anticipate it in this way.[6]

NOTES TO CHAPTER TEN

1 For the Torslunda plates see H. Arbman, 'Några guldsmedmatriser från vikingatid och äldre medeltid', *Fornvännen*, 1933, 341.
Mårten Stenberger, *Det forntida Sverige*, Uppsala, 1964, 125, 172, 198, and map p. 97.
A. Oldeborg, *Metalteknik i Forhistorisk Tid*, Stockholm, 1965, Vol. 2, 70.
Tiotusen År i Sverige, Stockholm, 1945, Fig. 185.
For a recent study of dies for stamping foil see Torsten Capelle and Hayo Vierck, 'Modeln der Merowinger- und Wikingerzeit', *Frühmittelalterliche Studien*, Munster, 1971, 42–100.

2 It has not been established whether the fourteen or more helmets represented by fragmentary material from Gotland were so embellished; Birger Nerman, *Die Volkerwanderungzeit Gotlands*, II, Tafeln, also H. Stolpe and T. J. Arne, *La Nécropole de Vendel*, Stockholm, 1927, Pl. 5, Figs. 1 and 2, Pl. VI, Figs. 1, 2, 3, 6, 7.

3 For the Färjestaden collar, see *Tiotusen År i Sverige*, Stockholm, 1945, 161, and Fig. 174, also H. Shetelig and H. Falk, *Scandinavian Archaeology*, Oxford, 1937, Pl. 43.

4 Joan M. Fagerlie, *Late Roman and Byzantine solidi found in Sweden and Denmark*, American Numismatic Society, New York, 1967, 194–195, Cat. nos. 115–119.

5 Ulf Erik Hagberg, *The Archaeology of Skedemosse*, I, Stockholm, 1967, Fig. 3, pp. 8, 9 note.

6 For general background in Öland see M. Stenberger, *Öland under Äldre Jarnaldern*, Stockholm, 1933.

CHAPTER ELEVEN

1: *The Benty Grange Helmet*

by Rupert Bruce-Mitford and Marilyn R. Luscombe

DISCOVERY

A grave was found by Thomas Bateman at Benty Grange near Monyash, Derbyshire on May 3rd 1848, under one of a group of tumuli. The barrow, according to Bateman,[1] was 'on a farm called Benty Grange, a high and bleak situation, to the right of the road from Ashburn to Buxton' (Fig 35). He describes the barrow as 'not of considerable elevation, perhaps not more than two feet at the highest point: but spread over a pretty large area, and surrounded by a small fosse or trench.'[2]

The body had originally been laid in a central position under the barrow on the natural ground surface. Bateman noted that nothing remained of the body except for the 'hair' (probably fur, cowhide or similar material) (Plate 73d). Near the 'hair', in a position inferred from the presence of 'hair' to have once been near the head, was 'a curious assemblage of ornaments' some of which Bateman drew and some of which his helper, Llewellyn Jewitt, painted in water-colour in his own notebook, though not to scale (Plates 72–75 and Figs 36, 37, 41). Bateman remarked that the hardness of the soil prevented the removal of these objects with any degree of success. Bateman described the 'silver edging and ornaments of a leathern cup' of approximately three inches diameter at the mouth, which was 'decorated by 4 wheel-shaped ornaments and two crosses of thin silver, affixed by pins of the same metal, clenched inside'. This he illustrated in *Ten Years' Diggings* and it is reproduced here as Plate 73c and Fig 41. Only the metal ornaments of this 'leathern cup' now remain. In the Bateman catalogue[3] the remnants as received at the Sheffield Museum in 1876 were described by Howarth as follows:

> Silver border from a leather cup – with two projections cracked and corroded. 3 ins. diameter. Found in a low mound, surrounded by a slight rampart of earth, at Benty Grange near Monyash, Derbyshire, May 3rd 1848.
> One cross $1\frac{1}{4}'' \times 1''$. – three wheel-shaped ornaments – all silver, being part of the decorations of a leather cup.[4]

In the same position near the 'head' were found what Bateman describes as

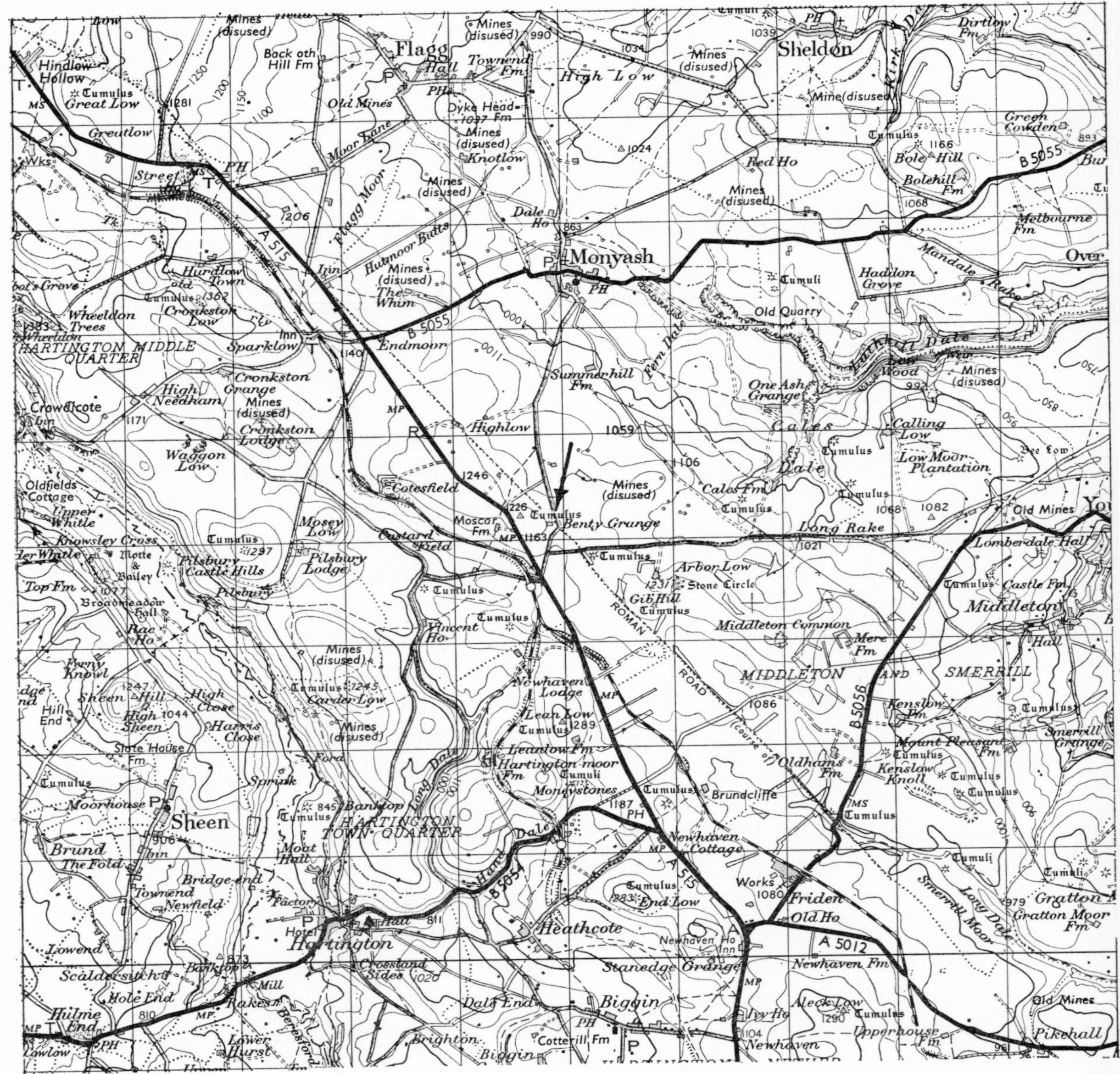

Figure 35 Map showing the topography of the Benty Grange barrow (arrowed, centre) with other antiquities, including the Arbor Low stone circle. (Scale 1 in : 1 mile)

'personal ornaments'. These consisted of 'two circular enamels upon copper $1\frac{3}{4}$ diameter, in narrow silver frames, and a third, which was so far decomposed as to be irrecoverable' (Plates 73a,b,e,g, and Plate 76a). They were enamelled with a 'yellow interlaced dracontine pattern', intermingled with a 'peculiar scroll design' which Bateman shrewdly linked with the decoration of the initial letters in

Figure 36 Bateman's published drawing of the Benty Grange helmet and other fragments he associated with it (not to scale)

seventh-century manuscripts. Bateman drew these enamels but not accurately, for they were obscured by corrosion, in *Ten Years' Diggings* (Fig 37). He describes the three enamels as some sort of brooch or plaque to be attached to clothing. They are in fact hanging-bowl escutcheons. Two fragments, belonging to different escutcheons, survive and are now in the Weston Park Museum, Sheffield, and in the Ashmolean Museum, Oxford (Plate 76).[5] A new reconstruction drawing of the original design is given in Plate 76b.

Figure 37 Bateman's published drawings of the Benty Grange escutcheon fragments (not to scale)

With these enamels, Bateman noted 'a knot of very fine wire and a quantity of thin bone variously ornamented with lozenges etc. (Plate 73g and Fig 37) which was mostly too decayed to bear removal'. It appeared to have been attached to some garment of silk, as the glossy fibre of such a fabric was very perceptible when they were first uncovered though 'it shortly vanished when exposed to the air'. None of this remains now. The quantity of thin bone may have either been attached to the 'silk' or may have rested on it or been compressed against it and subsequently become attached. What the material was, which Bateman found, is uncertain and the nature of the garment, if any, cannot be determined.

The most important find in the grave, apart from the hanging-bowl escutcheons, was found 'westward from the head for about six feet'. Bateman writes 'we arrived at a large mass of oxidised iron, which, being removed with the utmost care and having been since repaired, was unavoidably broken; now presents a mass of chainwork[6] (Plate 75) and the frame of a helmet (Plates 63, 72 and Figs 36, 38)'. The chainwork and the helmet fragments appear to have been found in a confused mass. Plate 74 illustrates a six-pronged object which Batemen describes as follows:

> Amongst the chainwork is a very curious six-pronged instrument of iron in shape much like an ordinary hayfork, with the difference of the tang which in the latter is driven into the shaft, being in this instrument flattened and doubled over so as to form a small loop for suspension: whether it belonged to the helmet or to the corselet, is uncertain. . . .

These circumstances probably explain why parts of the iron helmet frame and, in particular, the boar, were encrusted with excessive accumulations of iron oxide. The corrosion of the extensive chainwork could well have led to the deposition of iron oxide on the objects under or involved with it.

Bateman has the following remarks to make:

> The iron chainwork . . . consists of a large number of links of two kinds, attached to each other by small rings half an inch in diameter: one kind are flat and lozenge-shaped about an inch and a half long; the others are all of one kind, but of different lengths, varying from 4 to 10 inches. They are simply lengths of square rod iron with perforated ends, through which pass the rings connecting them with the diamond-shaped links: they all show the impression of cloth over a considerable part of the surface, and it is therefore no improbable conjecture that they would originally constitute a kind of quilted cuirass by being sewn up within or upon a doublet of strong cloth.

Textile impressions are apt to remain on corroded iron (replaced in iron oxide but retaining their form) and the connection could be purely incidental, i.e. the impressions could have been derived from cloth which had been placed over the chainwork.

The ironwork was evidently created with an eye for intricate design and decorative effect; the links are too complex and diverse in shape and size to be exclusively functional.[7]

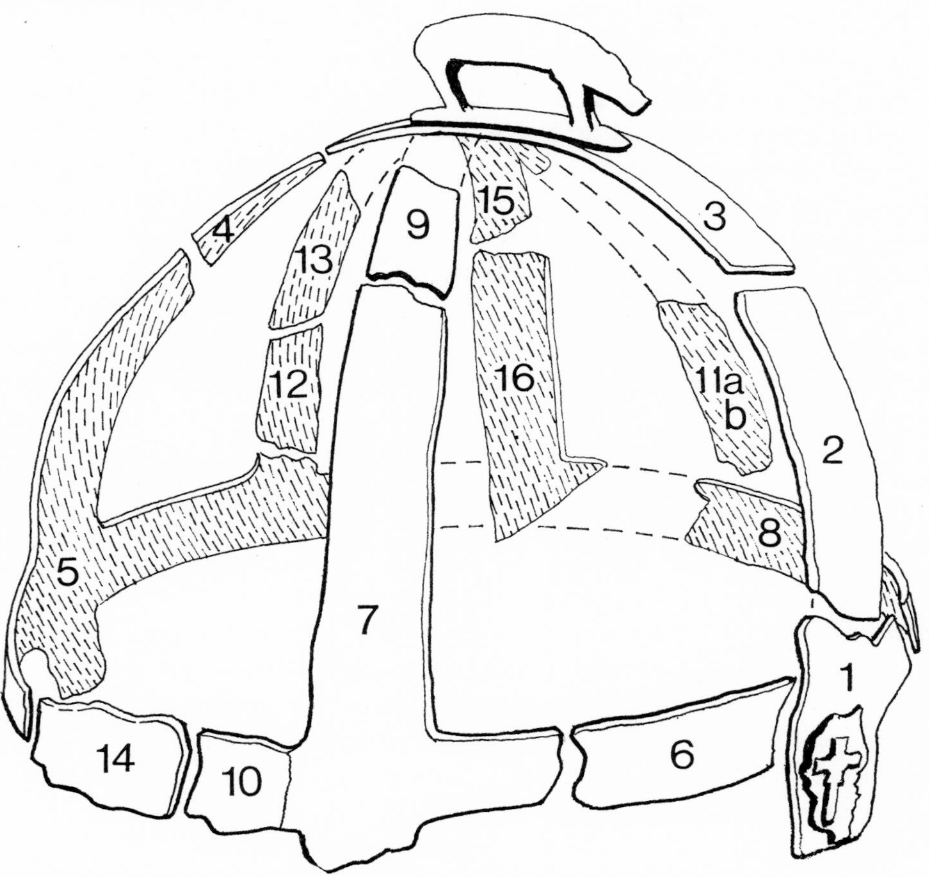

Figure 38 Schematic diagram to show the present disposition of the fragments of the Benty Grange helmet

The helmet (Figs 36, 38, Plates 63, 72) Bateman described thus:

> The helmet consists of a skeleton formed of iron bands, radiating from the crown of the head, and riveted to a circle of the same metal, which encompassed the brow; from the impression on the metal (Plate 77) it is evident that the outside was covered with plates of horn disposed diagonally so as to produce a herring-bone pattern: the ends of these plates were secured beneath with strips of horn corresponding with the iron framework, and attached to it by ornamental silver rivets (Fig 36, Plates 72c, 80) at intervals

> of about an inch and a half from each other; on the bottom of the front rib, which projects so as to form a nasal, is a small silver cross (Figs 36, 38, 40b, Plates 70 a–c, 72a) slightly ornamented round the edges by a beaded moulding and on the crown of the helmet is a elliptical bronze plate supporting the figure of an animal carved in iron (Fig 36, Plates 63, 71, 72) with bronze eyes, now much corroded, but perfectly distinct as the representation of a hog.

This description is important as the only first-hand account of the helmet as it came from the ground. In many details Bateman has been proved correct by subsequent examination but as he had no means of scientific investigation some details naturally eluded him. The boar, for example, was not really carved in iron although it may have had iron in its make-up. He correctly observed the method of construction of the iron frame and the evidence for the original horn plate covering, held down to the iron framework by added horn strips fastened by rivets with ornamental heads.

The beaded moulding of the nasal cross (Fig 36, Bateman's drawing) has proved to be a misreading of the corrosion present. The cross had in fact plain straight sides (Fig 40b).

The boar figure he notes as iron ('carved in iron') and 'with bronze eyes'. It has proved to be of very different construction and character. The boar figure was not merely corroded in the way Bateman supposed, that is to say, from within, by its own corrosion. It carried a thick superficial pad or encrustation of iron oxide (Plates 65a, 72 and Fig 36). Removal of these accumulations in the British Museum Research Laboratory in 1948 (p. 230 below) revealed that under these superficial lumps the boar was in a reasonable state of preservation and its original profile recoverable (Plate 64b). Bateman's published drawing (Fig 36) had none of the authentic features of a boar, which the revealed figure possesses – snout, tusks, lowered head and swine-like stance. The boar's tail in Bateman's drawing was not recognizable when the boar was investigated and the drawing is probably not a true reflection of any original feature here, although the tail area of the boar is incomplete (Plate 69b).

Bateman ended his helmet description, following on from the passage already quoted:

> There are, too, many fragments, some more or less ornamented with silver, which have been riveted to some part of the helmet in a manner not to be explained or even understood [They are now explained below, p. 232] there are also some small buckles (Plate 72 f,g and Fig 36) of iron which probably served to fasten it upon the head.

The buckles which he suggested were for helmet-fastening may or may not have been for this purpose. Similar buckles found in Sweden in the Vendel and

Valsgärde boat-graves (for example, Valsgärde 7) were associated with mail-shirts and not with helmets,[8] though the idea of buckles to fasten the helmet cannot be dismissed.

A further object apparently bone (Fig 36 and Plate 72e), unfortunately no longer extant, is enigmatic. It has the appearance of an oblong plate with rounded corners and concave sides, broken at one end, having a lattice pattern all over its surfaces and five remaining 'depressions', each with a 'collar', which could originally have been matrices, or single cells, perhaps for garnets. The object has no known parallels and it looks extraordinary. Bateman gave no dimensions and the drawings are not to scale. It seems unlikely that the object was connected with the helmet, although evidently found and drawn with it.

Bateman summed up by remarking that the 'peculiarly indurated and corrosive nature of the soil in this barrow, is a point of some interest'. He remarks that this is a feature common in Saxon tumuli in Derbyshire – he considered that the earth had been mixed with some corrosive liquid, 'the result of which is the presence of thin ochry veins in the earth, and the decomposition of nearly the whole of the human remains'.

The disappearance of human remains may be due to the soil conditions observed by Bateman. The process of disintegration was no doubt advanced by the robbing of the grave. The objects found must be regarded as only the broken remains of a very incomplete part of a rich grave inventory. Evidently from the helmet, a unique find, it was a man's grave and a warrior's grave, yet there was no trace of sword, shield or of other weapons or of armour and only small indications of containers and vessels. This must imply that the bulk of the deposit had been removed or broken up and scattered. The fact that what was left was found in two areas with nothing in the intervening six-foot space, may again suggest removal of the central core of the burial deposit. No signs of disturbance were noted by Bateman, but we should none the less regard this as a robbed inhumation.

THE HELMET

In 1947, impelled by the desire to investigate more closely the only Anglo-Saxon helmet known, for purposes of comparison with that from the Sutton Hoo ship-burial, the writer spent some time in Sheffield examining the Benty Grange remains. It seemed clear that laboratory study would yield new information and the writer accordingly obtained permission from N. J. W. Baggeley, the Curator, and the Trustees of the Weston Park Museum for the transfer of the helmet to the British Museum for study and cleaning. The laboratory work was carried out in response to the writer's queries under the direction of Dr H. J. Plenderleith, the Keeper of the Research Laboratory, and in part, particularly the mechanical work on the boar, with his own hands.

When the helmet came to the British Museum (April 1948) the boar figure (Plates 64a, 65a) was almost wholly obscured by massive and extremely hard superficial deposits of iron corrosion products. It bore no apparent resemblance to the impressive boar-crested helmets of Germanic literature, which we may suppose to have resembled those familiar from representations amongst the figural scenes of Vendel art. No details of either the helmet frame or the boar were legible at all and only brief and unsatisfying accounts of it existed in the literature. There was no trace of the 'bronze eyes' of the boar to which Bateman had referred. The ornamental silver rivets (Plates 80, 72c and Fig 36) on the framework strips, mentioned in the 1899 Bateman catalogue as being one and a half inches apart, were also wholly invisible. Only the faintest suggestion of the cross drawn by Bateman (Fig 36) could be detected on the nasal, if this was carefully scrutinized (Plate 70a). The boar itself was a featureless lump (Plates 64a, 65a) with two thick supports, the oxidized and iron-encrusted front and rear legs. The animal was not recognizable as a boar.

The Research Laboratory at this time did not possess X-ray apparatus sufficiently powerful to penetrate the iron deposits covering the boar. The only way to elucidate the object was to remove the encrustations mechanically, chipping and picking at the substance, which as has been said was very hard – a process itself hampered by the fact that radiography was not possible. The hollow interior structure of the boar subsequently found (Plate 67b–d) was unsuspected. At intervals over a period of time, Dr Plenderleith worked off the hard superficial substance with a strong needle. A perfectly life-like boar-image eventually emerged, unique in construction and character (Plates 64b, 65b). It naturally lacks its original brilliance but enough emerged to give an indication of this and to yield information as to its nature and construction. The boar, however, is technically enigmatic in spite of the most prolonged and thoroughgoing studies on this and subsequent return visits to the Research Laboratory for further elucidation.

THE HELMET AFTER CLEANING AND EXAMINATION IN 1949 AND SUBSEQUENTLY

Leaving aside the boar-crest, the remains of the helmet consist of sixteen fragments of corroded iron strip (Fig 38). These fit together to comprise a framework of iron bands (Plate 63), originally between 1 and 2 mm in thickness, constructed as follows:

(i) A horizontal band 65 cms long, and 2·5 cms (one inch) broad, encircled the head at brow-level. All the other fragments of strip belonged to vertical bands which form the inner structure of the crown of the helmet and rise from the horizontal band. They consisted of:

(ii) Two strips, also 2·5 cms wide, which crossed at right angles above the top of the head. One of them, 40 cms long, which ran from front to back, projected at both ends below the horizontal circle. The projection is *c.* 4·75 cms in front and 3·8 cms at the back. The projection in the front was straight, dropping vertically from the horizontal band and it carried an applied silver cross of elongated form (Plate 70, Fig. 40b). The projection at the back apparently curved in to fit the nape of the neck (Plates 63, 72, 79). The other main vertical strip ran over the top of the head from ear to ear crossing the front-to-back strip at the apex on top of the crown. The ends of this second strip also extended down over the ears below the horizontal circle, these extensions presumably being connected with some form of ear or cheek protection. Both are broken off close to the lower edge of the horizontal band. This strip passed outside the nose-to-nape strip at the top of the crown, *inside* the horizontal band on the left side of the helmet and *outside* the horizontal band on the helmet's right side. Between the intersecting strips were four large open quadrants. These spaces were originally subdivided by four narrower subsidiary strips of iron. Each of these subsidiary strips rose from outside the 'brow' band at an angle of 70°, the strips each beginning at a point 7 cms out from the centre of the ear-to-ear strip. From this point, where it was 22 mm wide, this strip tapered to a width of 15 mm and overlapped the ear-to-ear strip just below the crest, making an angle of 50° with it. Only one of the four original subsidiary strips survives. The end of a second strip is attached to the horizontal band and there is a loose portion 6 cms long.

Unlike the case of the Germanic 'Spangenhelme' group, this iron framework (Plate 63) was not visible in the completed helmet. The strips were presumably necessary for the support of the cap of the helmet proper, which was probably of leather or cloth inside but wholly covered externally with horn plates. The use of horn plates for the structure of a helmet is only paralleled in the small *spangenhelm* found in the young prince's grave under Cologne Cathedral.[9] At Benty Grange the horn is completely mineralized and survives only on the outer surfaces of the iron strips, projecting a little beyond them here and there. The horn can be recognized as a pattern of many close-set fine parallel lines, showing like grain in the iron oxide which coats the whole of the surviving metal (Plates 77–79). The grain of the horn ran obliquely, being roughly at right angles, in adjacent plates, to form a chevron pattern where adjacent plates join along the centre line of the main struts, as can be clearly seen on some of the extant iron fragments (Plates, 77, 79_3).

The horn was cut to fit over the eight spaces, of unequal size, between the horizontal and vertical iron strips and was trimmed so that the edges of the horn plates abutted along the centre lines of the iron framework strips. The horn was presumably softened and bent to the required shape. A small ridge is visible down the centre line of each iron band, where corrosion products have worked up through the junction between the horn plates (*e.g.* Plate 78).

The junctions of the horn plates along the centre lines of the iron strips were sealed by further strips of horn, cut to the width of the iron bands beneath. These upper strips of horn were held down, and the whole assembly clamped together, by a succession of longer rivets with ornamental heads of double-headed axe-shape (Plate 72c) coated in, or made of, silver, some of which survive in position (Plate 80) under the rust. They are evenly spaced at four centimetre intervals and sited in between the underlying pairs of iron rivets which held major horn plates to the frame. They were set along the central axes of the strips and their shanks passed through the middle of the upper horn strip, between the abutting plates beneath, and through the iron frame.

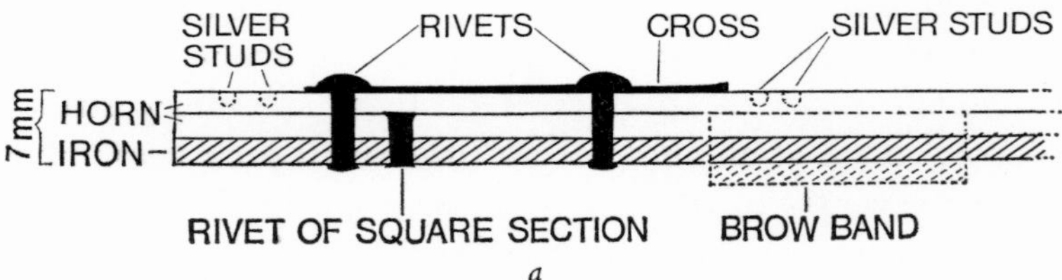

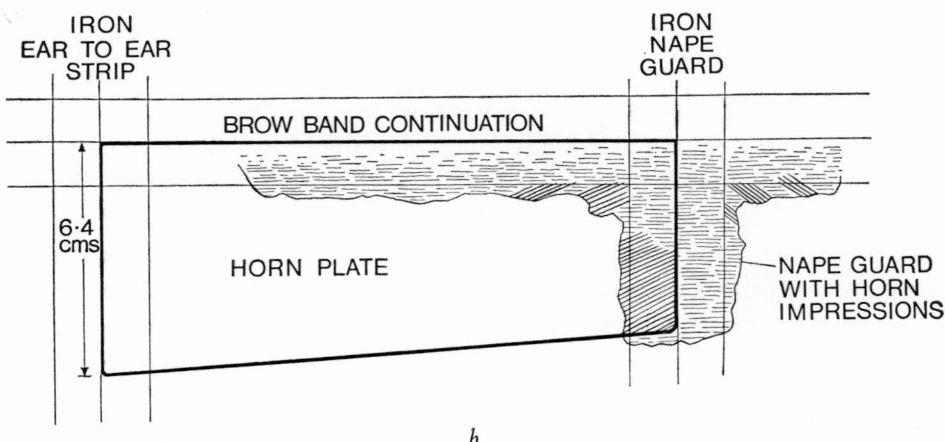

Figure 39 a, Diagram of the nasal of the Benty Grange helmet and *b*, Conjectural shape of the horn plate below the helmet in the sinister near quadrant. Based on drawings by Mrs V. H. Fenwick

The horn traces surviving on the helmet were examined at the National History Museum by the Keeper of Zoology, Dr F. C. Fraser, and experiments were carried out by softening and spreading a horn from a shorthorn breed. It was clear that a much bigger horned breed of cattle must have been involved in the construction of the helmet. This was presumably *bos longifrons*; and there is no need to postulate aurochs. Horn is of fibrous structure and as a protective substance has the advantage of being light and tough. Whalebone (baleen) was ruled out as the substance employed on the helmet.

The ornamental silver rivets were positioned with their long axes vertical on the horizontal band, horizontal on the vertical strips and at an angle of about 65° on the subsidiary strips.

THE NAPE PROJECTION, NECK-GUARD AND EAR-FLAPS

The fragment from the back of the helmet showing the intersection of the horizontal and vertical iron strips is the largest and the best preserved portion of the framework to survive (Plate 80). Four decorative rivet heads, covered by rust, remain in position and two layers of horn are visible in the graining. The lower layer appears to project beyond the edge of the iron strip to which it is fixed. This would appear to indicate that horn plates formed a protective covering for the back of the neck below the level of the horizontal band (Fig 39b). The graining of these horn plates is visible against the median ridge of the horizontal band at an angle of 20° from the horizontal. At a point on the nape extension 5 cms lower than the median ridge of the horizontal band the remains of the plate on the left side of the helmet terminate. The line of the edge is seen to be clean and does not coincide with the grain of the horn, as would be expected if this were a broken edge. It makes an angle of 5° with the median ridge of the headband. If the line is extended it meets the centre line of the ear-to-ear strip at a point 6·4 cms below the centre of the horizontal band.

Unfortunately on both sides of the helmet the strip which projected down over the ears is damaged (Fig 38, frags. 7, 16 and Plate 63) and no oblique grain is visible on what remains. However, oblique grain can be detected on the lower edge of fragments 14 and 10, showing that the horn plate extended as far as the ear-flaps. No trace of oblique grain can be found on any of the fragments forming the front half of the helmet which suggests that horn plates below the horizontal band did not continue in front of the ears, to form a visor or cheekguard. The neck-protecting feature appears to have been finished off at the ears.

THE CROSS

Bateman in *Ten Years' Diggings* described the cross as 'A small silver cross, slightly ornamented round the edges by a beaded moulding', and he illustrated it with a drawing (Fig 36). Its position is on the nasal of the helmet below the headband (Fig 36, Plate 72). The cross is 3·9 cms in length and measures 2 cms across its arms. When the helmet was examined at Sheffield in 1947, no clear trace of this feature was to be seen. The horn layer which held the cross was detached from the underlying iron strip in the British Museum Laboratory (Plate 70a). It was radiographed and the back was excavated in order to expose the cross (Plate 70b). The substance on which the cross was mounted was evidently horn. The probing from the back was taken as far as was considered safe, in view of the risk that the cross might break up and crumble into pieces. The cross itself was not revealed but the two long rivets which fastened it to its backing were exposed (Plate 70b) along with some silver studs which surrounded the cross, the existence of which was not previously suspected. None of these studs was extracted but chemical analysis of a small fragment taken from one of them identified the metal as silver. The studs are not identical with those on the flanks of the boar (Plate 68a). They have the same diameter and circular section but are rather more like brads or pins, one being pointed and no less than 4·5 mm in length.

Radiography revealed that the cross is of the type that expands into a circle at the intersection of the arms (Plate 70c and Fig 40b) and the short arms themselves have expanding ends. Study of the radiograph (Plate 70c) reveals that the cross is a composite affair. It evidently consisted of an equal-armed cross, presumably originally mounted on a cup, garment, or other object. A separate strip of silver had been added to the back of the cross to lengthen one of its arms, making it more like a processional type of cross and giving it a long shape adapted to the iron nasal. The profiles of the cross are plain and straight (not 'framed by a beaded moulding' as Bateman supposed) (Fig 36). The lower limb of the cross, longer than the others, comes to a rounded point and terminates in a rivet. The lower limb expands like the other limbs until it is 6 mm wide at a point 2 cms from the top of the cross; then the sides shrink inwards, so that the rest of the limb is 4·5 mm wide with parallel sides. Two substantial rivets hold the cross in position (Fig 39a). The central rivet at the intersection of the arms extends for 7 mm from the undersurface of the cross, where it appears to have an irregular, possibly a broken, end (the rest of it presumably being buried in fragment 1). The rivet at the lower end of the cross is longer, about 9 mm. It is likely then, that the minimum thickness for a strip of horn on the nasal would be 6 or 7 mm, allowing for the thickness of the iron band. This suggests that there was a double thickness

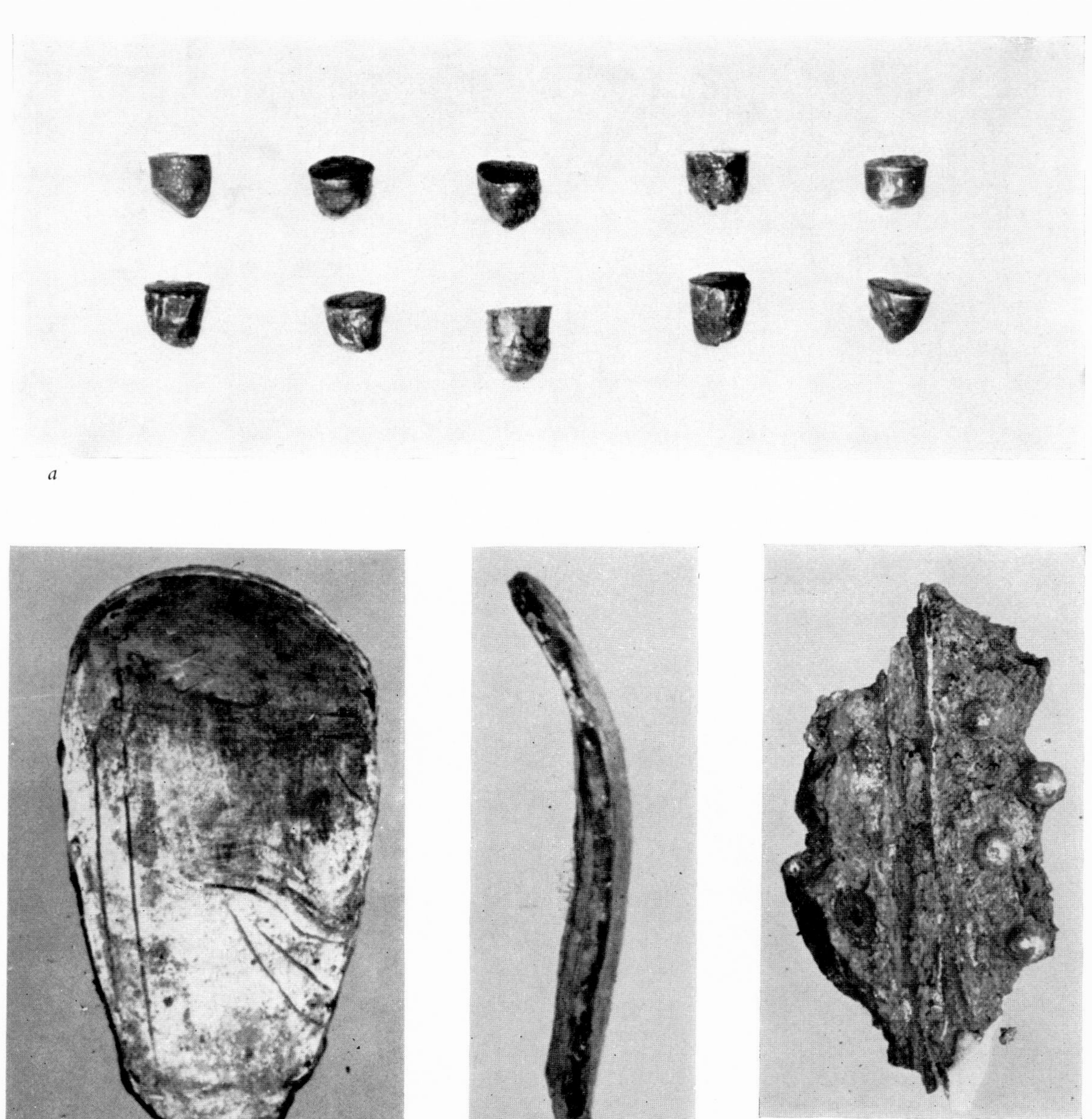

Plate 68 *a*, Ten silver studs from the body of the Benty Grange boar (Scale 5 : 1); *b*, Reverse of silver hip plate showing part of a classical design, Benty Grange boar (Scale 4 : 1); *c*, Side view of silver hip plate, Benty Grange boar (Scale 4 : 1); *d*, Reverse of fragment of broken Benty Grange boar (Scale 3 : 1)

Plate 69 a, View of silver hip plate and silver studs in position on Benty Grange boar, showing marks of filing (Much enlarged); *b*, Detail of back view of Benty Grange boar (Scale 2 : 1); *c*, Radiograph of back view of Benty Grange boar (Scale 2 : 1)

Plate 70 opposite a, Benty Grange, front view of fragment carrying the cross on the helmet nasal (Scale 2 : 1); *b*, Benty Grange, back view of fragment, bearing cross, dug away, exposing studs and rivets (Scale 2 : 1); *c*, Radiograph of cross fragment from nasal (Scale 2 : 1)

a

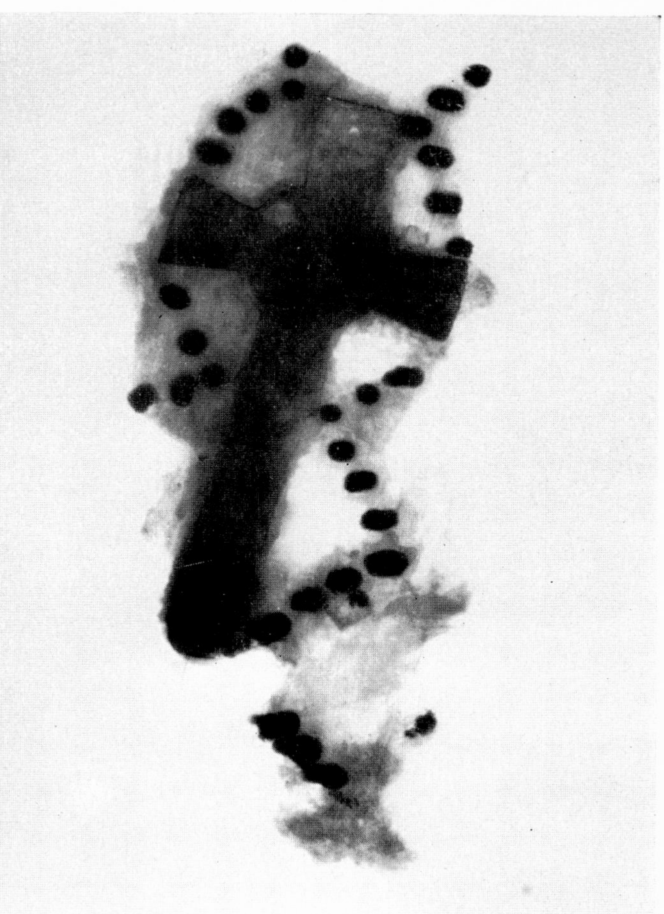

c

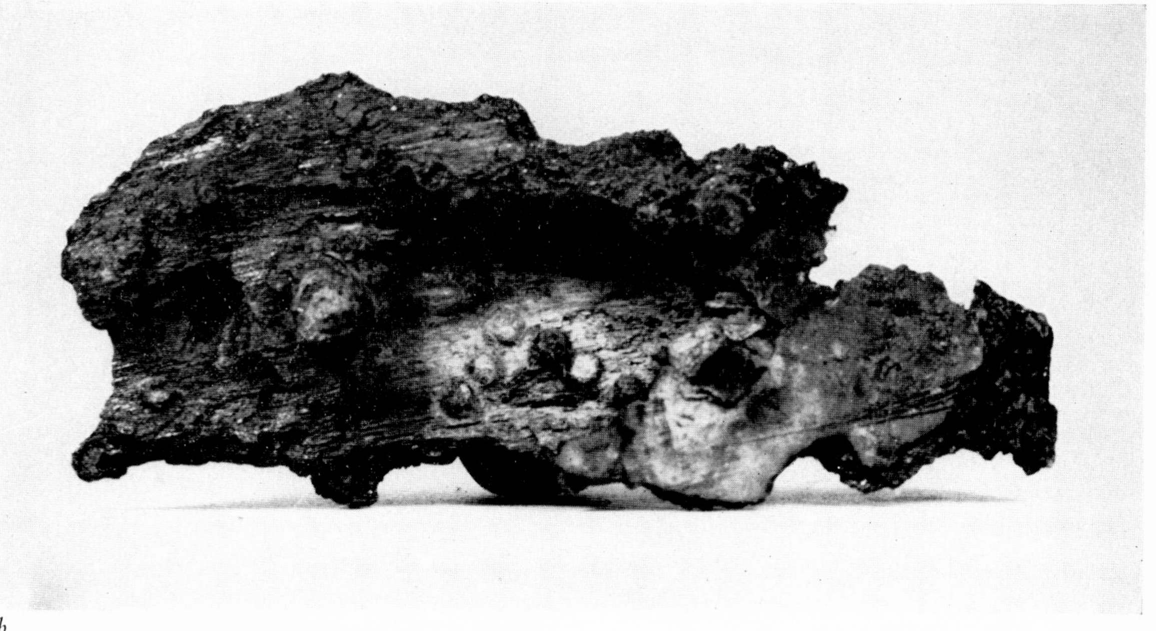

b

Plate 71 Three-quarter view of Benty Grange boar as crest of helmet (enlarged)

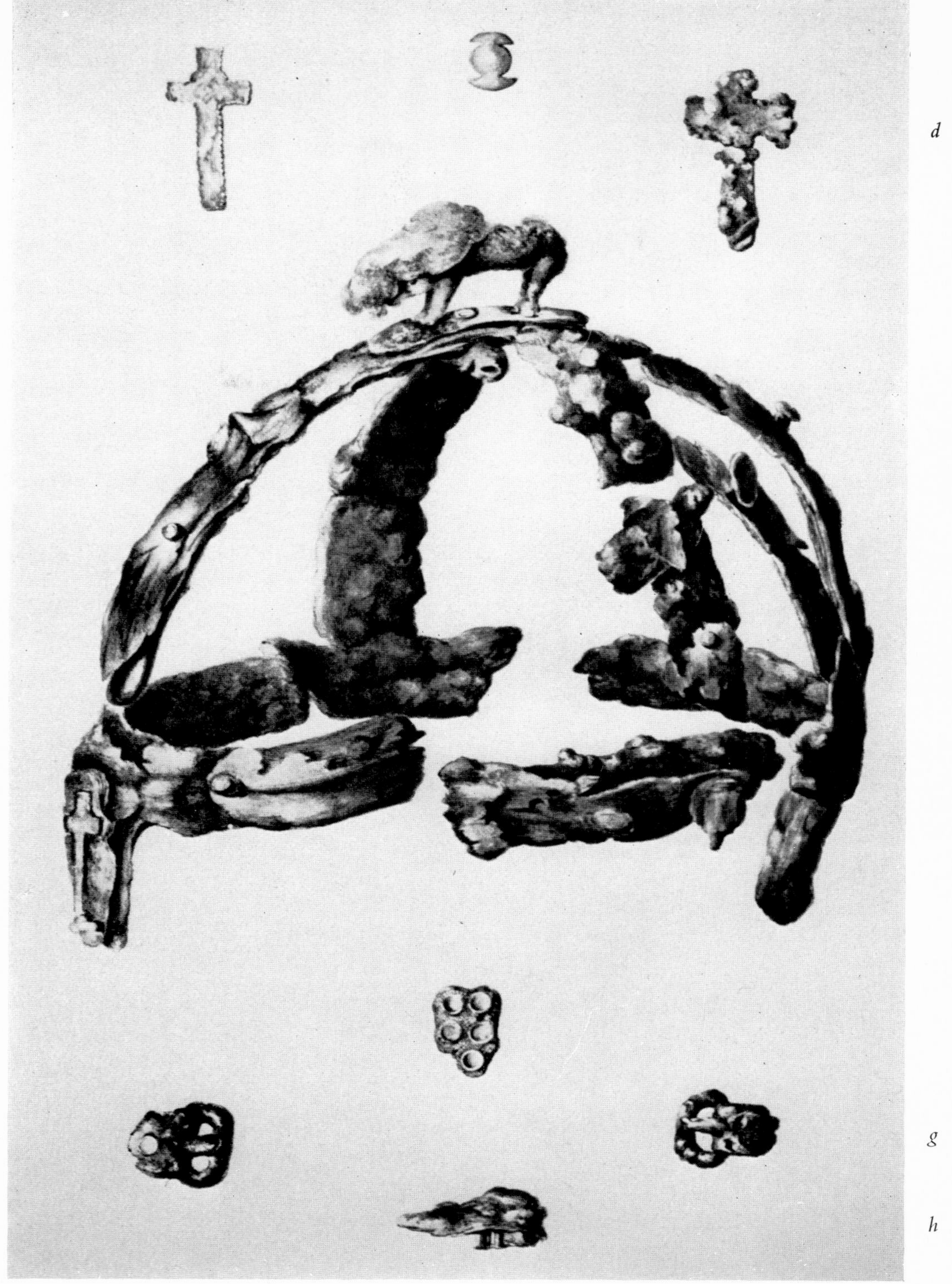

Plate 72 Watercolour from the Benty Grange notebook of Llewellyn Jewitt, showing: *a*, the Benty Grange helmet; *b*, *d*, details of the silver cross from the nasal of the helmet; *c*, a double headed silver rivet from the helmet; *e*, bone fragment with empty cloisons; *f*, *g*, small buckles, possibly from the chinstrap of the helmet; *h*, unidentified fragment (Not to scale)

Plate 73 Watercolour from the Benty Grange notebook of Llewellyn Jewitt, showing: *a*, *b*, hanging-bowl escutcheon fragments; *c*, cup with silver rim and cross-mounts; *d*, 'hair', probably pile from a cloak; *e*, *f*, escutcheon fragments; *g*, bone fragment with incised design (Not to scale)

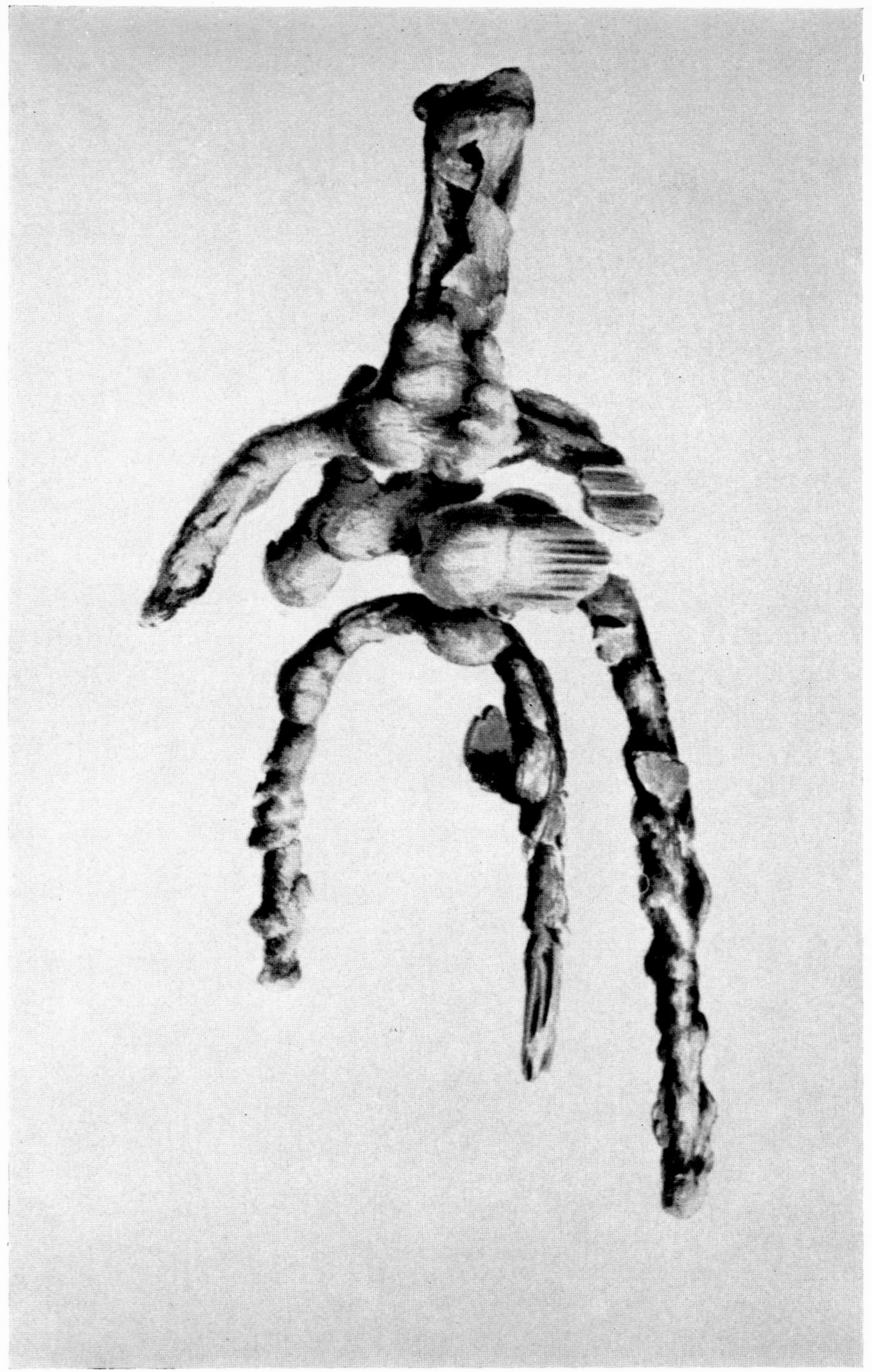

Plate 74 Watercolour from the Benty Grange notebook of Llewellyn Jewitt, showing the 'six pronged iron fork' (p. 226) (Not to scale)

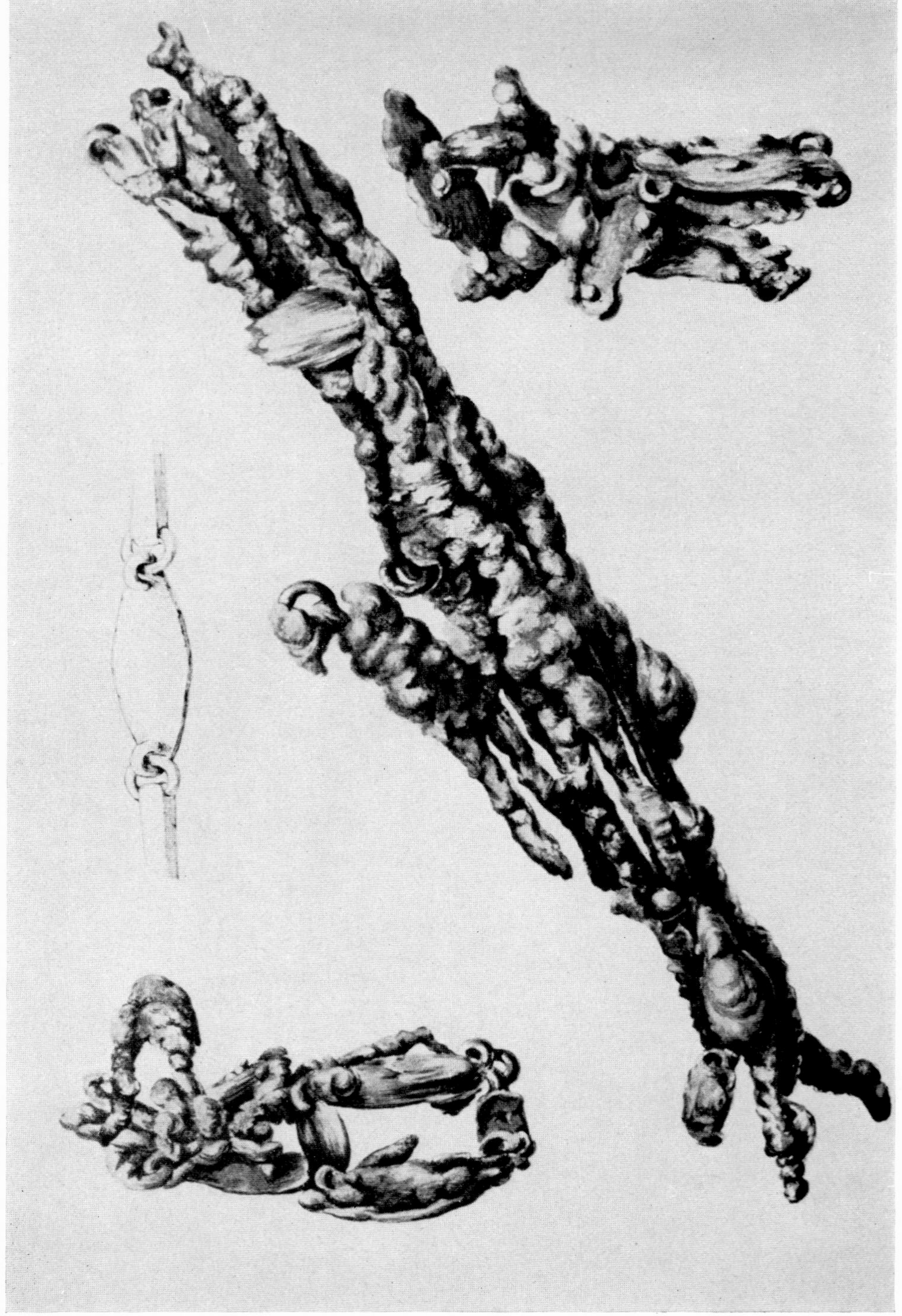

Plate 75 Watercolour from the Benty Grange notebook of Llewellyn Jewitt, showing masses of corroded chainwork, with an elucidatory sketch (Not to scale)

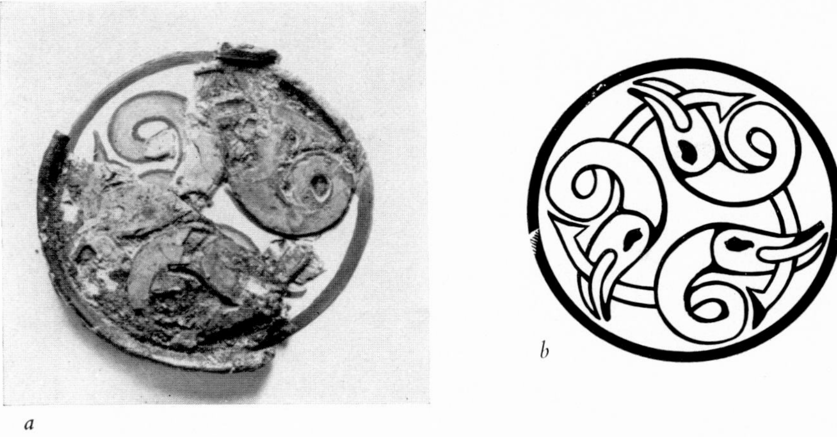

a

b

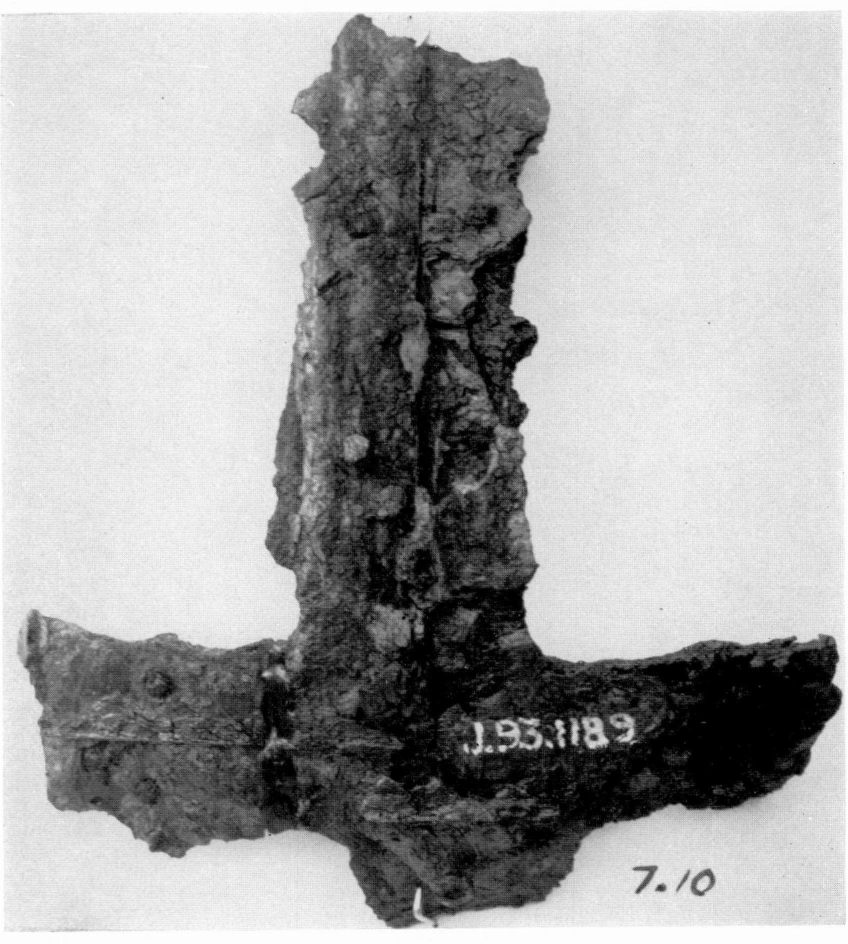

c

Plate 76 a, An attempt to relate two portions of hanging-bowl escutcheon from Benty Grange (lower fragment now in Sheffield Museum; upper fragment now in Ashmolean Museum, Oxford: with *b*, a reconstruction of the escutcheon design (Scales 1 : 1); *c*, Fragments 7 and 10 of the helmet frame (Scale 1 : 1)

Plate 77 Fragment 3 of the Benty Grange helmet from the crown of the frame showing (top) the junction of four horn plates with grain in different directions (Scale nearly 3 : 1)

Plate 78 Eight fragments of the Benty Grange helmet frame, showing graining and median ridges (Scales 1 : 1)

Plates 79 Six fragments of the Benty Grange helmet frame, notably fragments 5, with the nape-guard extension, and 1, the nasal, with rust flakes containg cross, detached (Scales 1 : 1)

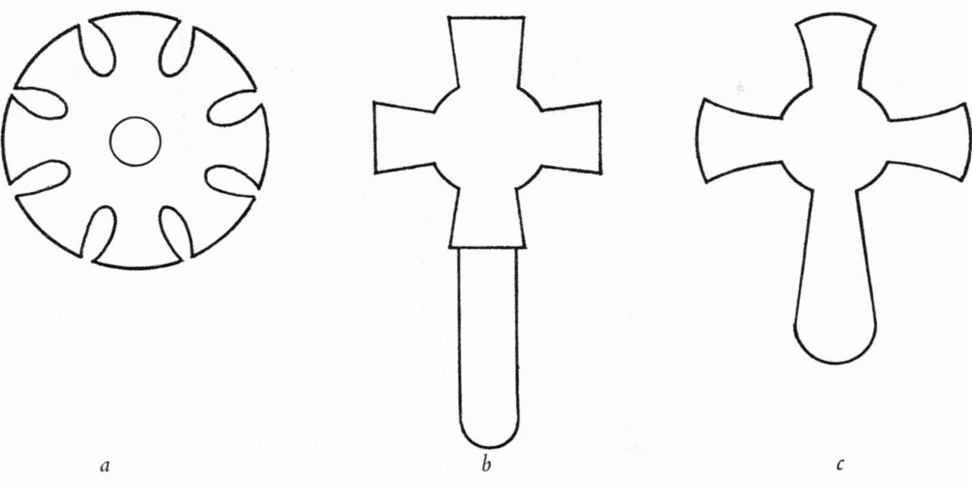

Figure 40 a–c, Crosses from Benty Grange (Scale 2 : 1) and *d*, *e*, Winster Moor (Scale 3 : 1)

of horn here, as on the other iron strips of the framework. In this case, however, the grain throughout is uniformly aligned along the nasal. There is no trace of oblique or lateral graining, such as might suggest horn plates coming in towards the nasal from either side.

Twenty-nine silver studs survive on the nasal (Plate 70c) and from these an original symmetrical pattern of forty studs can be reconstructed. The two spaces between the upper limb and the arms of the cross were each filled by a line of four studs. The spaces between the arms and the lower limb were bordered by a zigzag pattern of studs, which extends in a diagonal line both above and below the limits of the cross.

The studs would appear simply to have been tapped into small holes drilled or bored in the horn layer. The only other applied crosses of this form, that is with elongated lower limb, known in Anglo-Saxon archaeology also occur at Benty Grange. Two silver crosses which decorated the drinking cups are figured by Bateman but badly drawn (Fig 41). The shapes he published are no more precise than was his drawing of the cross on the nasal. One original survives (Plate 62b) and the true shape is given in Fig 40a. The subsidiary circular appliqués on the drinking cups are corroded but their basic form may be taken to be that of two equal-armed crosses with central expansion superimposed to form a wheel-device (Plate 62c–e, Fig 40).

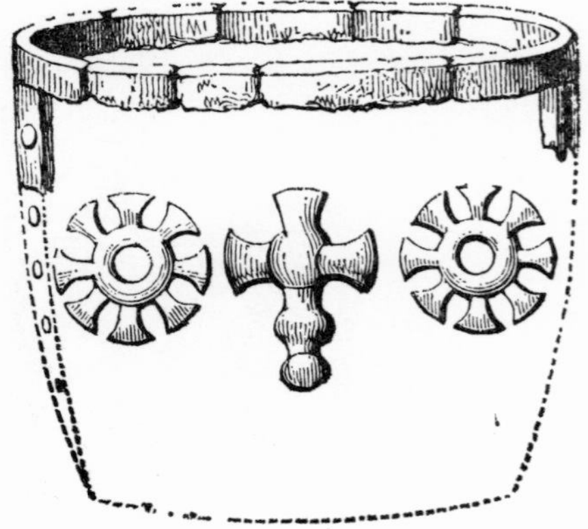

Figure 41 Bateman's published drawing of the cup with silver cross-mounts, Benty Grange (Not to scale)

THE BOAR

The crown of the helmet at the intersection of the iron framework is surmounted by the figure of a boar with lowered head, about $3\frac{1}{2}$ ins long (Plates 63, 71). It is this feature which originally brought the Benty Grange helmet to pre-eminence, since it is not only the sole extant Anglo-Saxon helmet but the only actual helmet so far found anywhere with a free standing boar-figure as a crest – a feature often alluded to in Northern literature and depicted in Vendel figural art. Until the discovery of Benty Grange these pictures and the verbal descriptions were not supported by concrete evidence. The Benty Grange boar crest is, however, much smaller and less dominant than those depicted in Vendel art.

The mechanical removal of the heavy rust concretions in the British Museum Research Laboratory revealed a complex construction and unsuspected decorative and technical features (Plate 64b). In the course of prising off the iron concretions (Plate 67a) the figure (fortunately) fractured and its cross-section was revealed (Plate 67b,c). The body was seen to be made up from two hollow bronze tubes of D-shaped cross-section, assembled back to back, the flat surfaces juxtaposed. Between the juxtaposed backs of the tubes was a uniform space about 2 mm. This extra space fills out the shape and results in a body which is truly circular in cross-section, the D-shaped tubes in themselves being fractionally less than semi-circles. The space left between the tubes was an integral part of the design and seems to have accommodated as a central element a flat sheet of some substance which projected to form a central spine or crest along the boar's back. The filling, however, whether horn or metal, had disintegrated and the residues could not be identified.

The central element was certainly not of solid bronze. The boar was thus made in two halves longitudinally. These halves and the 2 mm thick element or vane between them had to be fastened together. The assembly was in fact clamped together by four long silver rivets, two at the rear of the boar and two at the front, held at either end by large curved silver-gilt plates shaped in the form of the boar's hips (Plate 68b,c). The rivets were in pairs one above the other (Plate 69b) and passed through the whole assembly from side to side, being welded at both ends to the external silver plates. No traces of solder could be detected, such as might have supplemented the riveting. Some adhesive could have been used, but no trace would be expected to remain.

The massive encrustations of iron which covered the boar-figure (Plates 64a, 65a) probably derived from the corrosion of the iron chainwork which was in close proximity to it (Plates 74, 75). If the boar were indeed not of iron, as Bateman supposed, but of bronze, then the iron oxide deposits can only have been derived from an external source. But even if the boar was partly of iron, the external corrosion was much too bulky (Plates 64a, 65a) to have been due to the corrosion of this alone.

The surface of the boar's body is closely dotted with solid silver studs with round or roughly pointed bases and flat tops (Plate 68a,d). Investigation suggested they had been tapped into holes drilled or punched in the bronze tubes and then that their tops had been filed down to a uniform level regardless of their exact stance (i.e. whether they had been set in quite vertically or somewhat obliquely) (Plate 69a). This presupposes that the studs, when their tops were filed, were already embedded in a hard ground of some substance by which they were firmly supported; otherwise the filing down operation would have pulled them from their holes. The studs had been cut from a silver rod or thick wire of circular section, about 1·5 mm in diameter, and resemble pieces of thick pencil lead (Plate 68a). A few are roughly facetted at the points (probably the result of the holes having been punched rather than drilled, leaving jagged edges which scored the silver). The upper filed surfaces are sharp-cornered, showing no sign of wear at the edges; this tends to support the theory that they were bedded or countersunk in some substance. This in turn implies that their present free-standing appearance is not as originally designed. It had at first been supposed that the studs were free-standing, perhaps representing conventionalized bristles. The god Freyr in Northern mythology owned a boar *Gullinborsti*, 'golden-bristled', which may have a bearing on the design of the Benty Grange boar, especially since the exposed surfaces of the silver studs were gilded.[10] With the studs embedded, an effect of gold spots would be given but the intention could well have been to suggest golden bristles.

If one presumes a 'field' of hard or firm material, what could it have been? Since the body of the boar was bronze, it seemed unlikely that a second metal should have been used. Traces of a dark red substance said by Dr Plenderleith to show a 'vitreous texture' were found between the silver gilt studs in several places. The Laboratory view at the time was that the studs were 'loose' and floating in a vitreous sticky bed, probably enamel. (This was prior to the additional work which showed independently that the studs had not been loose.) Red enamel would have provided a suitable background against which the gold studs would have shown, the red and gold combination being familiar in Germanic jewellery. The use of enamel would be a matter of great archaeological interest, since the eyes of the boar were in a typically Germanic gold, garnet and filigree technique; whereas enamelling is, of course, Celtic. Could this be, in a geographically plausible Midland area, the first manifestation of the live fusion of Germanic and Celtic crafts and techniques, which led to the development of Hiberno-Saxon art?

The idea of red enamel (as distinct from any other possible bedding for the studs) was based on purely visual observation of the red pigment. The identification was challenged in correspondence and discussion in the Laboratory by Dr Françoise Henry, who argued that enamelling on a curved surface was not technically possible at this time. Her scepticism, although not necessarily her argument, was justified, for examination of the red substance by spectrographic analysis subsequently identified it as not enamel but cuprite (cuprous oxide), a decomposition product of bronze (Plate 81). In the opinion of the Research

Laboratory, even heavy contamination by iron oxide would not have disguised the original presence of the corrosion products of enamel under the spectrographic analysis, and none was identified. Enamel as a possible bedding for the studs, if this is so, can be ruled out. Evidence for the use of niello as a possible bed for the studs (giving the visual effect of gold on black) was also considered to have been ruled out by spectrography.

It is worth considering the technical difficulties that would be involved in the employment of red enamel and its application to curved surfaces such as the flanks of the boar, considered by Dr Henry not to be possible. It seems that the studs, apart from their decorative purpose, could have served to make this practicable. *Red* enamel, as distinct from enamelling in other colours, has to be applied in a semi-solid, putty-like condition. It is almost impossible to stick onto metal in this semi-solid state. It will not even stick to itself. In this situation, the (numerous, close-set) studs might have been a device to key a red enamel which could not otherwise be made to adhere long enough for the fixing operation.

Although we must accept that an enamel or niello coating for the boar is in fact ruled out by spectrographic analysis, the evidence of the filed-down, not too securely held studs (Plates 68a, 69a) clearly requires a bedding for the studs of some kind. A partial answer to the mass of iron oxide which enveloped the boar (Plates 64a, 65a) might be provided had the studs been originally embedded in iron sheet. Such iron plates could well have 'exploded' into a cauliflower of corrosion products, a process familiar to us from the uncovered panels of the Sutton Hoo helmet (i.e. those not covered by bronze sheeting). The characterization of the red remains as 'vitreous and sticky' would fit the physical appearance of ferric chloride, which would certainly be present in corroding iron.

Artistically, the effect obtainable with iron flanks might not have been unlike that with nielloed flanks, that is, gold spots on black, or blue-black. We should remember that inlay of silver in iron is a standard Germanic technique of the period, the Sutton Hoo helmet crest (iron inlaid with silver wire) being an example. The thinnish sheets of iron envisaged, however, would not of themselves account for the bulk of iron corrosion built up on top of the boar (Plates 64a, 65a).

It has already been noted that the basic D-shaped tubes were of bronze. A tubular bronze lining for an iron-flanked boar seems both unnecessary and irrational. If iron was being used externally it would surely have made a stronger and more efficient internal structure as well. A reason for making the body at least in part of iron might possibly have been tradition (*eofer irenheard*, *Beowulf* line 1112); if so this might explain why an iron surface was presented to the onlooker, although the object was not primarily of iron.

It was suggested by Herbert Maryon that the bronze inner lining might have served to indicate to the craftsman when the holes cut in the supposed outer iron layer for the studs were sufficiently deep; this would be indicated by a change in colour in the products of the drill. The holes, on this view, would not actually penetrate the bronze lining but would be 'blind'. The surviving studs vary in length from 1 mm to 1·75 mm and are not of the uniform length one would expect in this case (Plate 68a). Furthermore, a photograph of the inside of the tube (Plate 68d) shows the studs seen from the back and suggests that most of them did in fact penetrate the bronze tubing.

The evidence on balance seems to suggest that the boar's flanks consisted of outer sheets of iron into which the silver studs were inserted, mounted on an inner lining and shaped of bronze. The complex and somewhat flimsy construction visualized is not paralleled elsewhere. The only other free-standing animal figure of the early (pagan) Anglo-Saxon period – the bronze stag on the Sutton Hoo sceptre (Plate 1) – is cast in bronze.

The hips of the boar were represented by pear-shaped plates of gilded silver (Plate 68b,c). These were presumably also bedded in the same surface material as the silver studs with which the tops of the plates were flush (Plate 69a). One was removed during the cleaning of the boar, when it became apparent that these plates had been cut and filed down from Roman silver. This plate, the front left one, had on its reverse part of a naturalistic leaf design within a narrow border of two parallel engraved lines (Plate 68b). On the outer surface, file marks are visible through the gilding. The four plates all appear to be of different sizes, being between 12·5 mm and 17·5 mm long and between 6 mm and 10 mm wide as exposed. The plates are held together in pairs through the hollow body of the boar by means of strong silver rivets (Plate 69b), and were both decorative and functional. Decoratively, they serve to define the hip-joints in a manner typical of the animal-style of the seventh century (Plate 64b) (cf. the hips of the boars at the ends of the Sutton Hoo clasps, those of the birds on the Sutton Hoo purse-lid, the hips of the animals on the Crundale Down sword-pommel, or the processional animals on the carpet-page f.124 of the *Book of Durrow*, etc.). The silver shanks joining the two rear plates are welded to their extreme edges, not to their centres as one would expect.

A fragment of bronze appears to be attached to the lower rivet at the rear of the boar and retains gilding (Plate 69b). It may represent the remains of the tail. A small socket is present which could have held a tail and the fact that it was apparently made separately and then attached to the body is in keeping with the treatment of other details of the boar, such as the ears and the eyes. It is not clear whether the tail was a continuation of the 'spine' or central plate or whether it was separately attached. The gap left by the missing tail at the rear of the boar reveals clearly the D-shaped tubes backing on to each other inside the body (Plate 69b). The rear legs of the boar were X-rayed, to obtain evidence of their structure

(Plate 69c). The resulting radiography showed that the legs were hollow. They also proved to be magnetic, indicating that metallic iron was present. It may be inferred that the legs were originally solid, the iron, in the process of corrosion, having migrated outwards, leaving an empty centre, a familiar occurrence. This had happened for example to all the rivets of the Sutton Hoo ship which, when fractured, proved to be hollow. It may also be inferred that the legs were originally much more spindly since corrosion will have thickened them. Their hollow interior dimension probably represents their true original diameter. There does not appear to be any trace of bronze in connection with the legs. Artistically, the legs were not very realistic. The animal has been given two sets of 'front' legs (see photo prior to treatment) (Plate 64a). That is to say, the back legs have 'knees' in front instead of at the back.

The head of the boar (Plate 71) is the most complex part of the animal. The outstanding feature is the eyes. The eyeballs are pointed oval garnets 5mm long (Plate 67e,f), set in gold sockets edged with filigree wire (8 mm × 3·5 mm) and having hollow gold shanks (Plate 67f) 8 mm long, which were sunk into a hole in the hollow (?sheet-bronze) head. The garnet eye was held up inside the shank by a plug of beeswax. The edge of the gold setting was burred over to hold in the garnet.

The use of garnet, gold and filigree is a standard combination of Germanic jewellery. Their use in combination with iron, silver and bronze as in the Benty Grange boar would be unique. The Sutton Hoo helmet has an iron crest inlaid with silver wires (which parallel the postulated sheets of iron inset with silver-gilt studs in the boar) and garnet-inlaid bronze eyebrows which also have silver wire inlays; but the combination of all these techniques, with gold, on one object of an ornamental kind, as seems to have been the case at Benty Grange, in the case of the boar, is unparalleled.

Most of the silver features – the hip- and shoulder-plates, the silver studs – were gilded after they had been filed down (the file marks show through the gilding). The remains of the tail, the tusks, the ears and the spine were all mercury-gilded. The gilding would provide a visual contrast against an iron field, since the colours would then be gold on dark blue-grey. The gilding was presumably the penultimate process, having been effected by firing a small quantity of mercury flux to the top of each stud and to the other features which were not attached separately. This must have been done before the insertion of the eyes, since although mercury gilding requires only a relatively low temperature of 360°C., the eyes were fixed with wax which would not have withstood any heat.

Little trace remains of the ears (Plate 71 and 65b) but they seem to have been separately cast, mercury gilded and then attached, by means not apparent, to the head. Traces of gilt bronze can be seen to run continuously between the ears over the head at this point (Plates 66a, 71). There is little remaining of the muzzle, the tusks and jaw (Plate 64b, 67a). The inlays forming the muzzle and jaw have unfortunately been damaged. Radiographs seem to indicate that they were more extensive than they now appear (Plate 66). The muzzle was formed from gilt-bronze sheeting. All that is now visible is part of the upper jaw and tusk (Plate 64b), on the left side, seen as two narrow strips forming a right angle and having broken projections where the jaw continues.

It is not possible to distinguish quite where the iron inlay of the body ended and the gilt-bronze inlays of the head began.

The boar stands on an oval bronze plate (Plates 63, 64), 9 cms long and with a maximum width of 1·9 cms. It is 1 mm thick and curved to fit the top of the helmet (Plate 71). It has eight small holes in it, two pairs are associated with fixing the legs of the boar to the plate, plus a large rivet-hole to the rear of centre. Three more rivet holes served to secure the plate to the helmet. The plate was positioned slightly to the front, to judge by corresponding rivet traces on the helmet's frame. This would bring the boar-figure into a horizontal position when the helmet was being worn (Plate 71). This slightly forward positioning of the boar can be seen on one of the helmet dies from Öland (Plate 59b) and also on the Gundestrup cauldron.

Thus, an ungilt bronze plate was used to rivet to the horn surface of the helmet, through its concealed iron structure, a boar with iron legs and applied iron flanks, over a hollow tubular sheet bronze body made in two equal halves, and set with cast bronze ears, a gold eye, silver gilt studded flanks and silver gilt hip plates and gilt-bronze details (tail, tusks, jaw line etc.). The mixture of techniques appears utterly irrational.

The use of a cabochon garnet eye with beaded filigree collar and the ornamental exploitation of the pear-shape of the hips (picked out in gold) would all be compatible with a seventh-century date, and if the cross on the nasal is an original feature, as the evidence indicates, and not added later this again, in a Germanic context, would indicate a seventh-century date for the helmet,[11] suggesting indeed a date not earlier than about the middle of the century. It was therefore not an antique, but more likely one of the most recent objects in the grave.

II. OTHER 'HELMETS' FOUND IN BRITAIN

Rupert Bruce-Mitford and Marilyn R. Luscombe

A few objects found in Britain, apparently rather similar in construction to the Benty Grange helmet, have in the past been described and published as helmets, and some have been assigned to the Saxon period. The evidence for both the dating and the true nature of these objects seems in most cases to be unsupported by any evidence. The objects found at Leckhampton, near Cheltenham, Gloucestershire,[1] Souldern, Oxfordshire,[2] and Hamworthy, Dorset,[3] will be examined, with a view to establishing whether or not they can be regarded as representing Anglo-Saxon helmets.

I: THE LECKHAMPTON HILL 'HELMET'

This was found in 1844. The first reference to it and to the barrow at Leckhampton in which it was found reads as follows:

> A few weeks since, some labourers, in digging for gravel on the hill above the manor-house of Leckhampton, about two miles from Cheltenham, suddenly came upon a skeleton in a bank at the side of the high-road leading from Cheltenham to Bath. It was lying doubled up, about 3′ under the surface. On the skull, fitting as closely as if moulded to it, was the frame of a cap, consisting of a circular hoop, with two curved bars crossing each other in a knob at the top of the head; this knob, finishing in a ring, seems to have been intended for a feather or some such military ensign. The rim at the base is nearly a perfect circle and the bars are made apparently of some mixed metal, brass fused with a purer one; they are thin and pliable, and grooved: the knob and ring are brass, covered with verdigris, while the bars are smooth and free from rust. When first found, there was a complete chin chain, of this only 3 links remain, those next the cap very much worn. The skull is tinged at the top with green from the pressure of the metal, and in other parts blackened as though the main material of the cap had been felt and the bars added to stiffen it. They are hardly calculated from their slightness to resist a sword cut, but the furrowed surface gives them a finish and proves that they must have been outside the felt. Nothing else whatever was found. A black line was distinctly traceable all round the earth in which the body lay. A Roman camp rises immediately over the spot where this relic was found and large traces of Roman interment are found within a hundred yards of it.[4]

The excavator, W. H. Gomonde, supposed the skeleton to be Saxon, an opinion later followed by both Stjerna and Baldwin Brown.[5] Sketches of the object were published by Roach Smith[6] and Gomonde (Fig 42a,b). Saxon antiquities associated with Gloucestershire are comparatively rare.

The burial was isolated and without associations, and there is no evidence, beyond pottery vaguely associated with the find, itself of uncertain date, and now lost, for assigning it to the Saxon period. It was apparently assumed to be Saxon because the assembled strips superficially resembled the remains of the helmet of known Saxon date from Benty Grange (Plate 63). The object itself does not appear to have survived. Clark Hall in 1912, editing Stjerna in English translation, states in a footnote that he had no success in tracing the remains of the object[7] and nothing is now known of it at the museums of Cheltenham or Bristol.

The structure of the 'helmet' from Leckhampton Hill, as shown by Roach Smith[8] consisted of four main vertical strips and a circular horizontal band, similar in general appearance to the Benty Grange helmet.

The strips were described by their excavator as having been made of thin bronze, and 'hardly calculated from their slightness to resist a sword-cut', ill-suited for protective purposes. All Dark Age helmets whether of Swedish type or *spangenhelme* are basically iron caps, or have a framework of iron bands. Any bronze attachments are decorative. The circumstantial evidence that the Leckhampton object was found on the head of the skeleton cannot be gainsaid, so that we should probably regard the thin bronze strips as embellishments for a padded cap of a ceremonial or religious rather than military character. The ring at the top and the supposed neck-chain seem to be compatible with this. Although

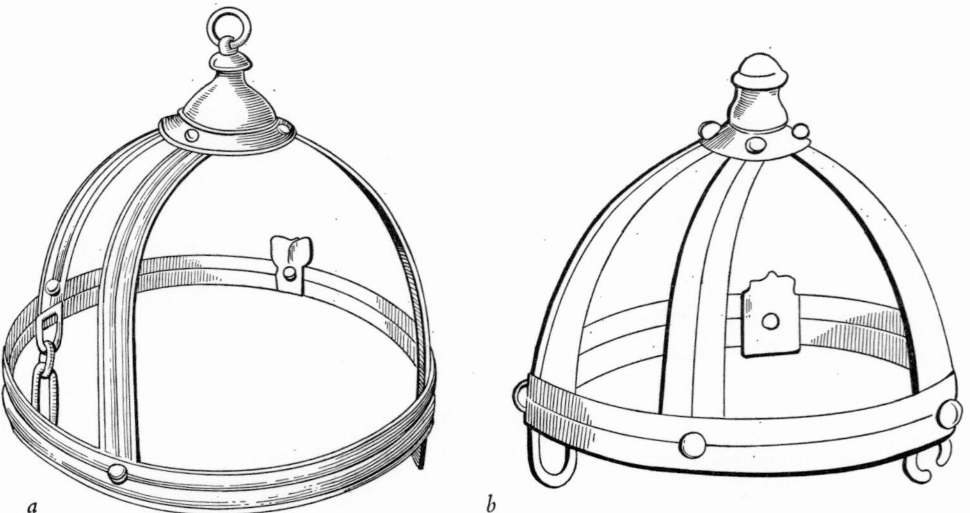

Figure 42 a,b, Leckhampton Hill, Cheltenham helmet, early drawings by Gomonde (1846) (in *Arch. Journal*, Vol. III) and Roach Smith (1852) (in *Collectanea Antiqua*, Vol. II) (Not to scale)

the chain cannot be paralleled, the Leckhampton object evidently belonged to a type of Romano-British priestly headgear represented by a relatively large number of recent finds, amongst which are the Hockwold crowns in the British Museum.[8a] The distinctive colour and quality of the metal, as carefully described by Gomonde in the passage cited above, corresponds with that of the Hockwold crowns.

The Leckhampton fragments should be firmly deleted from the list of Dark Age helmets given by Stjerna[9] and more recently cited by Sigurd Grieg.[10] It was evidently a Romano-British diadem or headgear of priestly use.

II. THE SOULDERN 'HELMET'

In 1844, while digging for stone in a garden near the main street at Souldern, Oxfordshire, workmen discovered a skeleton lying three feet deep in a grave, hollowed out of the limestone rock. Sir Henry Dryden recorded the following particulars regarding this interment:

> On the right side of its head lay a pair of bone ornaments two inches long, in shape four-sided cones, having on each side nine small engraved circles. At the small end of each is inserted an iron rivet, which is probably the remains of a hook for suspension, perhaps from the ear, by another brass ring. About the head were many fragments of thin brass (one part tin to seven parts copper) which when collected and put together form parts of two bands, the first of which is seven inches long and three-fourths wide, and had encircled the lower part of a leathern skull-cap. The edges of the leather and of this brass band were held together by a thin concave brass binding, in the hollow of which fragments of leather are still to be seen. On each side of the helmet, attached to the brass band, was an ornamental hinge for a chin-strap. Of the other band about 1 ft. 5 inches are existing the whole of which is equal width, and one eighth narrower than the first. It was probably the binding of the edge of the helmet, where there would be a seam, or intended to encircle the helmet close above the other binding. On both these bands are rivets, which show that the leather riveted was three sixteenths thick. Nothing else according to my informants, was found with the skeleton.[11]

Baldwin Brown satisfactorily disposed of this 'helmet'. He referred to it with an illustration, in 1915, in the following terms:

> The side piece and handle hinge of a bucket from Souldern, Oxon, in Mr. S. G. Fenton's collection, has on it a rudely formed head, for which . . . the Aylesford bucket provides a prototype. The many Saxon urns found in the vicinity would support the Saxon date were any such support necessary.

The remains are now in the Museum of Archaeology and Ethnology at Cambridge.[12] Pottery found with the fragments and noted in William Wing's subsequent account[13] may support a Saxon date for the find but it is obvious in any case from Baldwin Brown's illustration[14] that the fragments are from a bucket rim and handle, and Anglo-Saxon.

III. THE HAMWORTHY 'HELMET'

The third dubious example of a helmet came from Hamworthy, Dorset, a relatively recent find (1932) which was published and illustrated soon after its discovery (in colour) in the *Proceedings of the Dorset Natural History and Archaeological Society*, LIV, 1932, pp. 1–4, where the discovery was described as follows:

> This extraordinarily interesting and spectacular find – the remains of a leathern helmet, strengthened with metal bands, and studded by way of adornment, with cornelians, was made last summer at Hamworthy by two allotment holders. . . . The relics were unearthed on two distinct dates, the first discovery being a bronze plate, backed with iron and showing fragments of leather still attached to it, and twelve oval or circular jewels in their bronze settings.
>
> About a month later, a second allotment holder unearthed two additional bronze plates, another fifteen jewels and one empty setting and quite a spadeful of leather dust.

The Hamworthy finds consisted of twenty-seven large flat-cut cornelians, up to one inch across, round or oval, and one of rectangular shape, all in metal settings. One setting was found empty. Remains of leather showed in places, where it could be seen that as many as three thicknesses had been riveted together. Some lengths of bronze sheeting and traces of iron backing were also found. The rectangular cornelian was found fixed centrally to an openwork bronze plate. Plate 82 illustrates part of the Hamworthy find, with the exception of the openwork bronze plate, some of the cornelian settings and the leather.

The finds were submitted to the British Museum, where reputable authorities (C. F. C. Hawkes and Reginald Smith) suggested, guardedly, that the fragments might have formed part of an ornamental parade helmet of late Roman date. They were careful to state that they found difficulty in relating the find to any existing Romano-British parallel. The finds were subsequently exhibited, at the London Museum, to the first International Congress of Prehistoric and Protohistoric Sciences, in August 1932 where, in general, they were internationally accepted as fragments of a helmet. The general theory then was that the closest parallels were 'Merovingian Frankish helmets of sixth century date', though it is difficult to imagine what was meant. The find was published as such in the Dorset *Proceedings* with a conjectural reconstruction based on helmets published by Lindenschmidt.[15]

The late Roman attribution, expressed with due caution by the British Museum authorities, was reasonable. The practice of setting large flat-cut stones in metal collars is well established in Roman jewellery. One may cite the bracelet found at Rhayader, Radnorshire (Plate 84a), in 1899.[16] Here large oval, rectangular and more or less round cornelians were fixed with metal collars onto a series of rectangular gold plates. The corners of the rectangular gold plates have lentoid settings which must have originally contained cabochon stones which would have corresponded in general effect to the prominent domed rivets that occupied the corners of the Hamworthy plate. A peculiar type of gold filigree used, a free-standing haze of curled gold wires arranged around the large central cornelian, gave the impression of openwork. When it is remembered that the rectangular cornelian found at Hamworthy (Plate 83, top left) was found fixed onto the openwork bronze plate with large domed rivets at the corners, it was reasonable to consider the Hamworthy bronze pieces as a version of the same ornamental scheme. We know moreover that some Roman parade helmets were ornamented in this style. The Budapest helmet, now in the Hungarian National Museum[17] (Plate 84b) shows large cornelians and other stones in collar-settings studded about the crown and cheek guards. This helmet is late Roman in type, according to Alfoldi. Both Byzantine coins and Trajan's Column[18] depict helmets, or at least head gear, in which large oval stones are set round the brow and in strips over the head, as in the Hamworthy reconstruction. Some of these caps would certainly have been of leather with metal fittings. There is nothing in the Dark Age repertoire of either Vendel type or of *spangenhelme* that in any way suggests the Hamworthy fragments.[19]

Some years after the publication of the Hamworthy helmet, T. D. Kendrick happened to see, on a trolley moving through the British Museum, the object illustrated in Plate 82, and at once realized what the Hamworthy 'helmet' really was. The object is studded with a large number of cornelians, mostly oval, some circular but one or two rectangular. The crudely pierced openwork plates with roughly incised wavy-line borders and large domed rivet heads at the corners (Plate 82) are identical to the one from Hamworthy (not illustrated). There is no point in further stressing the resemblances, for what the allotment holders at Hamworthy found in 1932 was the remains of a Montenegran bride's belt. The fact that only one of the metal plates was found at Hamworthy makes it clear that the find consisted of only parts of the half of the belt containing the stone settings.

The British Museum belt is a massive affair, 58 ins (4 ft 10 ins) long, and $2\frac{7}{8}$ to $3\frac{3}{4}$ ins in width and it averages $\frac{5}{8}$ in to half an inch thick. It is made of leather, consisting of one extremely long strip of hide folded and doubled back along itself. It is ornamented with forty-two large cornelians and fourteen pierced openwork plates (Plate 82). The fold where this long strip of hide is bent back on itself forms one end of the belt. Extra thickness is obtained by filling in with a number of shorter lengths of leather between the two portions of the main length. The ends of these filling-up lengths are sliced away obliquely and made to overlap with the next pieces. At such an overlap the section of the belt shows four separate thicknesses of leather. These leather lengths are riveted together at the edges by innumerable small iron shanks with round slightly convex sequin-like heads (Plate 82).

Other features of the construction are best seen by studying the end of the belt formed by the fold-back of the long leather strip not seen in Plate 82. On top of the folded-back leather, between the leather and the cornelians in their settings, the ends of two metal sheets can be seen. The inner is iron, the outer bronze (note the Hamworthy find, where the first discovery was a bronze plate backed with iron). The iron strip runs the whole length of the belt between the borders of small rivets. It is visible through the pierced openings of the bronze plates (Plate 82), as well as through the openings of the bronze strip of different character which lies behind the cornelians. The bronze strip on which the cornelians are mounted is ornamented more or less uniformly throughout its length, with vertical lines of holes separated by a band of lightly impressed vertical herring bone, which can be seen in Plate 83a. Plate 83b shows that the belt widens at the front, where it bears a triple row of cornelians, the biggest stone of all occupying the central position (Plate 83a). The openwork plates decorate the back of the belt. A rectangular cornelian is set between four rosettes in the middle of an openwork disc, to which a fastening hook and three pendant links are attached. Similarly, another rectangular cornelian is fixed above the openwork pendant at the opposite side of the belt (Plate 82b). When worn, this massive, heavy object goes almost twice around the wearer and must have imprisoned the luckless Montenegran bride of the last century, in keeping with her impregnable veiling and servile status.

The belt described above was given to the British Museum in 1914 by Miss M. E. Durham, the well-known Balkan authority and anthropologist. Attached to it is a label in her writing written between 1903 and 1914 which reads '*Herzegovnian belt bought in Ragusa in 1903*'.

Miss Durham describes the elaborate preliminaries of a Montenegran wedding:

> *Svatori* (men who come to fetch the bride) go to the bride's home and join in a feast. After the feast the two *Djervi* (bride-leaders, usually uncle or brother of the bridegroom) went into the room where the bride was and gave her a new pair of sandals which she put on. The women of the house veiled her face and put a woman's belt on her (leather, set with cornelians or silver

> filigree. Her hair was plaited in two long tails). The *djervi* then escort the bride to the bridegroom's home usually at some distance (the Balkan tribes being exogamous), and the marriage ceremony takes place there.[20]

Miss Durham stresses the antiquity of many of the marriage ceremonies of the Balkan tribes. Of mountain weddings she says:

> In Klementi, the bride, coming to her husband's home, must throw an apple over the roof and is given some 'corn'. This recalls the *confarreatio* of the Romans.

And again of Albanian bridal ceremonies in general:

> Much of the ceremony resembles Roman practice. The distaff, the casket of household implements, the throwing of sweets, the sprinkling of water, *epithalamia* and *patria potestas* also.

Elsewhere she suggests the derivation of tattoo devices regarded as signs of good breeding amongst Albanian tribes from motifs on Byzantine coinage and suggests that some modern Balkan ornaments descend directly from prehistoric ornaments, the form of which have totemic or other esoteric significance as sun symbols and so on. A study on the same theme is that of the Swedish archaeologist Holmqvist who has traced ornamental themes popular with modern Lapps back to the seventh and eighth century Vendel art of Southern Scandinavia, dispersed through Viking trade. The significance of the Hamworthy belt, consisting as it does of Balkan peasant ornamentation of large gems in collar-settings, is that it represents a similar illustration of survival from Roman times in the peasant art and folk-life of these conservative mountain tribes of Albania.

In conclusion, with these three finds which have appeared in the literature all dismissed as possible helmets, that from Benty Grange which is evidently Anglo-Saxon, and the Sutton Hoo helmet, held to be a Swedish import, stand alone as the only helmets to survive in England in the nine hundred and fifty years between the departure of the Romans and the mid-fourteenth century.

NOTES TO CHAPTER ELEVEN

PART I

1 *Ten Years' Diggings in Celtic and Saxon Grave Hills in the Counties of Derby, Stafford and York from 1848 to 1858*, London and Derby, 1861, 28–33.

2 *Catalogue of the Bateman Collection of Antiquities in the Sheffield Public Museum*, London, 1899, prepared by E. Howarth, 242–3, Benty Grange: Howarth reproduces Bateman *verbatim* including the description of the barrow as 'surrounded by a small fosse or trench'. The Howarth introductory remarks state it was a 'low mound surrounded by a slight rampart of earth'; Reginald Smith in *Victoria County History, Staffordshire*, London, 1908, adheres to Bateman's description saying that the mound is surrounded by a 'slight ditch'.

3 *Catalogue of the Bateman Collection of Antiquities in the Sheffield Public Museum*, London, 1899. Prepared by E. Howarth, 245.

4 This cup was no doubt of wood as all other such small vessels from Saxon graves seem to be. The appearance of the damp wood of such vessels is not unlike leather. Those from Sutton Hoo were taken as gourds but proved to be of walnut burr-wood. The silver edging of the Benty Grange cup is paralleled amongst the burr-wood bottles from Sutton Hoo. Most of these have gilt-bronze rims. One however had a silver rim, and silver rims are well known on drinking horns, e.g. in the Taplow Barrow and the Sutton Hoo horns.

5 Bateman describes the enamelling of the escutcheons thus:

> 'The pattern was first cut in the metal, threads of it being left to show the design, by which means cells were formed in which the enamel was placed before fusion. The whole being then polished became what is known as champlevé enamel.'

The curious fish-like animals, as can be seen from the extant fragments, were drawn in outline and the background cut away to receive the enamel. The bodies of the fish and the background were both of yellow enamel. Françoise Henry describes the discs incorrectly as 'enamelled in yellow on a red field' and adds that the bronze has also been 'plated with silver', *Journal of the Royal Society of Antiquaries of Ireland*, LXVI, 1936, 236, Fig 9f. Kendrick described them as 'silvered bronze and yellow enamel', *Antiquity*, VI, 1932, 'Hanging Bowls', 178, Fig 10b. Bateman does not mention either the silvering or the presence of red enamel and he calls the discs 'copper'. Françoise Henry correctly drew comparisons with the Faversham zoomorphic escutcheon, the cast disc found with the Lullingstone bowl, the disc from Leke, Germany, and a silver disc from Kent, now in the Mayer collection, Liverpool Museum.

The design of the escutcheons is unique. The three animals are fish-like, resembling dolphins biting each other's tails, and must be of late antique, sub-Roman or early Christian origin. The most significant parallel is in the manuscript field. The lateral stroke of the N in the IN monogram from St John in the Durham Gospel fragment MS A II 10 is built of two similar fish motifs. The MS dates from about A.D. 650. A third bronze fragment drawn by Bateman (reproduced here as Fig 40) has a scroll design. This fragment is reputed to have disintegrated after its arrival at the Sheffield Museum in the 1870s. This was apparently a third escutcheon with a different design—perhaps the 'print' from the base of the bowl—since a small segment of the rim can be seen on Bateman's drawing (Fig 40).

The two surviving fragments of enamels with 'dolphin' design belong to two separate escutcheons, as the designs overlap.

6 The chainwork described by Bateman is much too heavy to have been related to the hanging bowl, or to have been part of a cuirass as Bateman suggested. The Sutton Hoo cauldron was suspended by a long and elaborate chain and it is possible that a further example of such a complex cauldron-chain occurred at Benty Grange, although there is no similarity between any of the elements of the Sutton Hoo chain and the drawing of links of chain from Benty Grange published by Bateman.

7 Bateman's conjecture that the chain-mass was a cuirass is only based on the evidence of textile

Plate 80 Fragment 5 of the Benty Grange helmet frame, enlarged nearly three times, showing the nape-guard extension, and the crossing of the vertical and horizontal strips. Four silver rivet-heads of double axe form remain in position, two of them (*top and left*) arrowed. The straight grain of the nose-to-nape outer horn strip can be seen overlying the oblique grain of the neck-guard (below lowest arrow). Cf. Fig 39 *b*

81

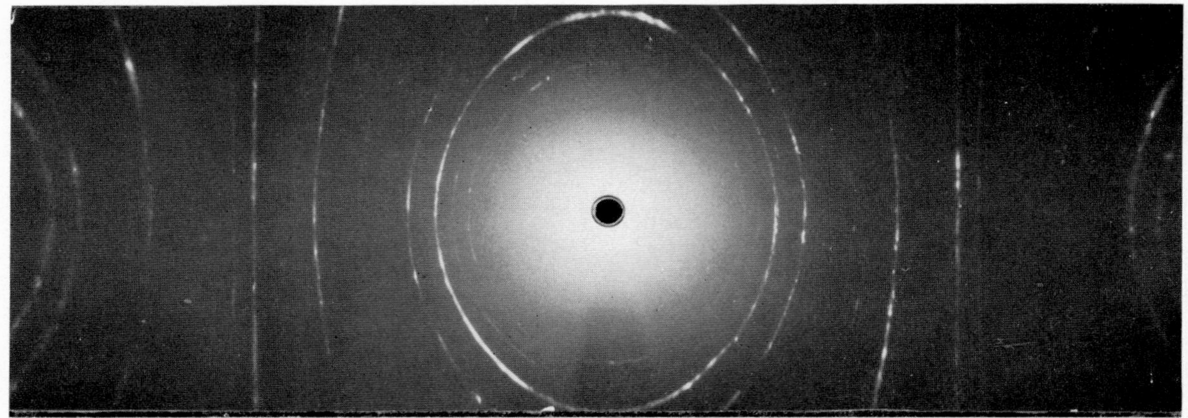

Plate 81 X-ray powder photograph of an 'enamel' sample from the Benty Grange boar, showing lines due to cuprite (p. 238)

a

b

82

Plate 82 A Montenegran bride's belt (Scale 1 : 2)

Plate 83 Fragments of the Hamworthy 'helmet' as found (Scale approx. 3 : 5) An openwork plate similar to those seen in Plate 82 was also found. Note in both cases the one stone of rectangular shape.

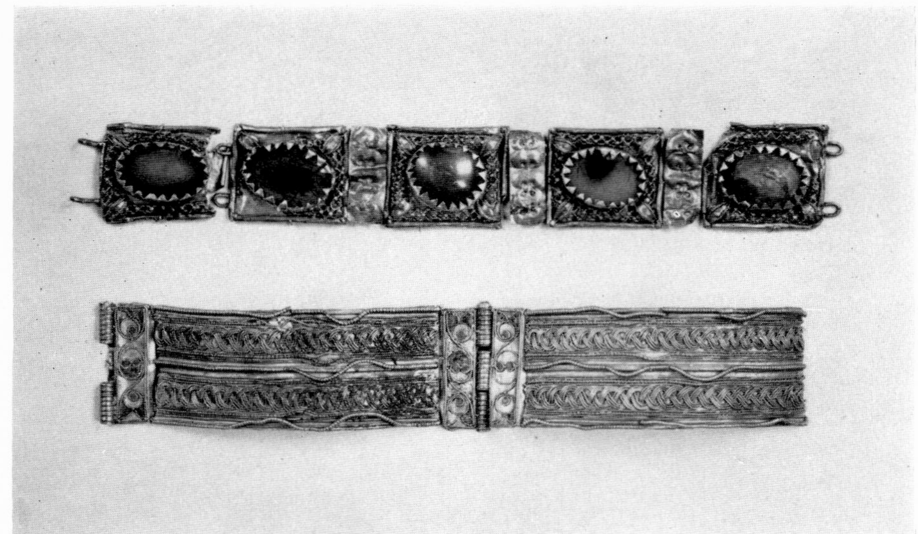

a

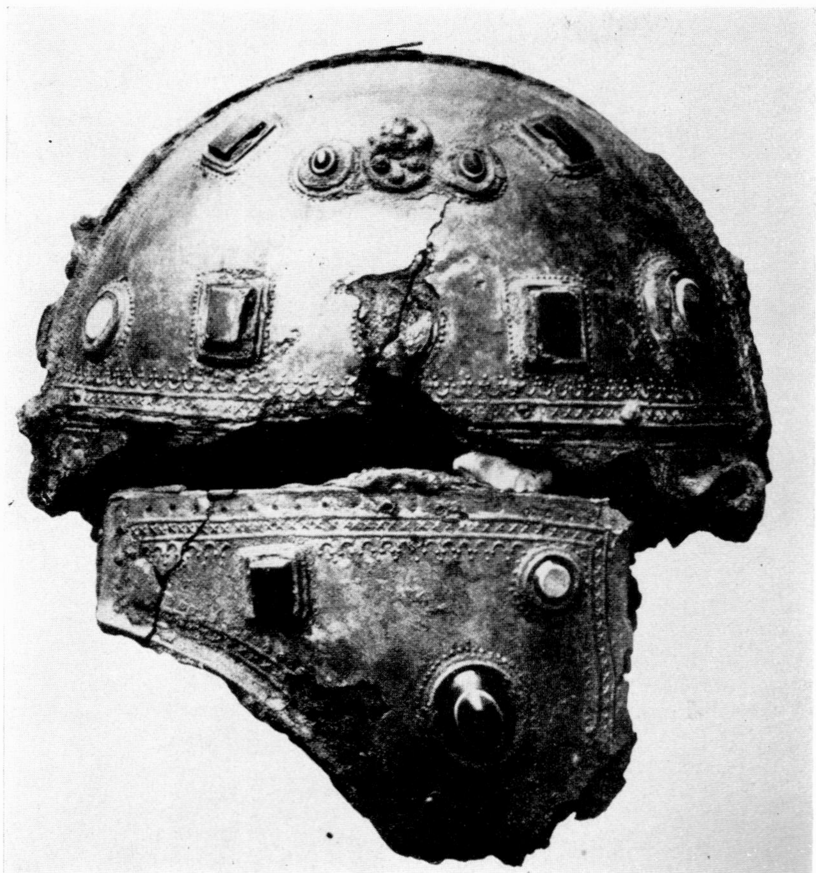

b

Plate 84 *a*, Bracelet from Rhayader, Wales (Scale 1 : 1); *b*, The Budapest helmet (reduced)

impressions on them. He notes that the straight links are between four and ten inches in length. This bears no relation to the chain mail – i.e. the normal mail from late Roman and Merovingian times. Nor are these strips of the flat kind reconstructed by Greta Arwidsson as body armour in the boat-grave Valsgärde 8, but shown by Paul Post to be a form of leg-armour.

8 Valsgärde 7 is not yet published. For the Vendel finds see H. Stolpe and T. J. Arne, *La Nécropole de Vendel*, Stockholm, 1927.

9 O. Doppelfeld, *Germania* 42, 1964, 1–45.

10 By mercury gilding, which can be seen in several cases. I am indebted to Mrs. Hilda Davidson for the reference to Freyr's bow.

11 Another case of a cross on the front of a helmet of comparable date is on a *spangenhelme* from the Battle of Tolbiacum, A.D. 496, now in the Städtisches Altertumsmuseum, Mainz. The cross is however on the helmet casque and not on a nasal. See H. Russell Robinson, *Oriental Armour*, London, 1967, 59, Fig. 32. An example of a nasal cross on a helmet is now in the Library at Grenoble, found at Vézeronce near Vienne on the Rhône and supposed to have been lost there during a battle between the Franks and Burgundians in A.D. 524.

For other Dark Age helmets of both the Romanesque and Vendel types, see footnotes 9, 15, 17, 18, 19 associated with Part II of this chapter.

PART II

1 *Journal of the British Archaeological Association*, Vol. I, 1845, *Report of the Proceedings for 9 October 1844*.

In the *Archaeological Journal*, Vol. III, 1847, 352 under 'Archaeological Intelligence' are particulars sent by W. H. Gomonde of the 'very curious object' found on the skull of a skeleton exhumed at Leckhampton Hill in Autumn 1844, near the site of a Roman camp. On p. 353 of the same volume, is a report by Mr Gomonde of another interment, and it is stated 'that the clay surrounding the skull, which was full of iron studs, sufficiently indicating that the head had been protected by a cap of singular construction having been covered all over with these iron studs.'

Journal of the British Archaeological Association, Vol. I, 1846: 43. *Proceedings of the Central Committee*, 11 Dec. 1844: Mr Wright communicated a letter from Mr W. H. Gomonde of Cheltenham, giving some additional information on the discovery of the interments near the camp on Leckhampton Hill, as the result of further excavation there, a horse's bit, ring for attaching reins, spearhead and a curved iron implement were found. Fragments of urns were discovered; some with small perforated handles (pierced lugs?) for suspension: 'the colour of the ware is a deep glossy black and some pieces are of fine quality'. Gomonde also states 'the bronze helmet found at Leckhampton and exhibited to your society, has been pronounced by Sir S. R. Meyrick to be British, of that kind called *penfesdon*, or "skull cap" '.

An illustration of the head-piece found at Leckhampton Hill forms part of the ornamental border to W. H. Gomonde's *Notes on Cheltenham: Ancient and Medieval*, printed for private distribution, 1849. There is no information as to the helmet. A mere reference to the illustration is given in the 'explanation of Frontispiece' on p. 20.

Archaeological Journal, Vol. XI, 1854, 291–3: *Proceedings of the Institute*, (2–6–1854): Mr Jabez Allies communicated particulars of 'ancient reliques' near Cheltenham, including details (p. 293) of the bronze helmet found in 1844 at Leckhampton. The helmet was exhibited at a meeting of the Institute on No. 3, 1854, *Journal*, XI, 413.

Archaeological Journal, Vol. XII, March 1855, pp. 9–21: 'Notice of a Bronze Relique, assigned to the later Roman or the Saxon Age, discovered at Leckhampton, Gloucestershire', by Albert Way, with illustration facing p. 9. He says: 'several Urns were disinterred . . . of the black pottery showing the peculiar scored and impressed ornament which characterizes the fictile ware of the Saxon Age.'

He gives no source for this statement. In this paper, he also compares other head-coverings with the Leckhampton example. The headpiece was exhibited at the Meeting of the Archaeological Institute held at Gloucester in 1860 and is described on page 7 of *Catalogue of the Museum formed at Gloucester during the Meeting* as the property of Captain Henry Bell, of Chalfont Lodge, Cheltenham. The 'helmet' appears more recently in *Transactions of the Bristol and Gloucestershire Archaeological Society*, Vol. 59, 1937, 324–7, Pl. p. 328 where the published accounts of it up to that date are summarized, and in the *Transactions of Bristol and Gloucester Archaeological Society*, LVIII, 1936, 167ff. and LIX, 1937, 324–326.

2 William Wing: *Antiquities of Steeple Aston*, Deddington, 1845, (Sir H. Dryden) pp. 72–4.
Archaeological Journal, III, 1844, 352–3.
Oxford Archaeological Society Publication, XXII, 1887, 3–5.
J. C. Blomfield: *History of the Deanery of Bicester*, 1882, p. 21.
G. Baldwin Brown: *The Arts in Early England*, 1915, IV: p. 658, 464, Plate CXIII.

3 H. P. Smith and Colonel Drew in *Proceedings of the Dorset Natural History and Archaeological Society*, LIV, 1932, 1.

4 *Journal of the British Archaeological Association*, Vol. I, 386–7: Report of the Proceedings for 9 October 1844.

5 The Cheltenham helmet was said by its excavator to be Saxon in date, and this view was followed by Stjerna, *Essays on Beowulf*, Viking Club Extra Series, p. 11 and footnote, Vol. III, 1912, and G. Baldwin Brown, *Arts in Early England*, Vol. III, London, 1915, 195–6.

6 A sketch and brief account is given by Roach Smith, *Collectanea Antiqua*, Vol. III, 1852, 238ff.

7 Knut Stjerna, *Essays on Beowulf*, Viking Club, Extra Series, Vol. III, London, 1912, footnote, p. 12.

8 *op. cit.*, footnote 6.

8a For the Hockwold crowns see *British Museum Guide to the Antiquities of Roman Britain*, London 1964, p. 62 and Plate XXV, and K. S. Painter in *Antiquaries Journal*, LI, 1971, 319–21.

9 Knut Stjerna, *op. cit.*, list of helmets, pp. 10–11. See also Sigurd Grieg, 'Gjermund bufunnet', *Norske Oldfunn* VIII, 1947, 37–8, Fig. 14, 15, where the Leckhampton Hill and Benty Grange helmets are discussed and illustrated. For other segmented helmets, related to the Sarmatians and found in graves and carved on stone figures from Kertsh, Crimea, dating from fifth to sixth centuries, see H. Russell Robinson, *Oriental Armour*, London, 1967, 55, Fig. 29A, (from grave) and 54, Fig. 28 (stone figures).

10 Sigurd Grieg, 'Gjermunbufunnet', *Norske Oldfunn*, VIII, Oslo, 1947, 37–8, Fig. 15.

11 *Archaeological Journal*, Vol. III, 1846, Archaeological Intelligence, 352–3.

12 Audrey Meaney, *A Gazeteer of Early Anglo-Saxon burial sites*, London, 1964, 212.

13 William Wing, *op. cit.*, footnote 2.

14 G. Baldwin Brown, *The Arts in Early England*, Vol. IV, London, 1915, p. 464, and Pl. CXIII, Fig. 4.

15 *Die Altertumer unserer Heidnischen Vorzeit*, Band V, Mainz, 1911, Tafel 35 (helmet from Baldenheim), and Tafel 11, (find from Gültlingen).

16 For the Rhayader bracelet, see *British Museum Guide to Roman Britain*, London, 1900, Pl. III, p. 64; and *Archaeologia Cambrensis*, 1899, 259.

17 For the Budapest helmet, see Andreas Alfoldi, *Acta Archaeologica*, 1934, 99ff. 'Eine spätromische Helmeform und ihre schicksale im Germanische-Romanischen mittelalter', esp. Pl. III, IV, V, 144.

18 For helmets on Byzantine coins and Trajan's Column, see Andreas Alfoldi, *op. cit.*, footnote 17, p. 107, and also Andreas Alfoldi in *Journal of Roman Studies*, 1922.

19 For Vendel type helmets see H. J. Stolpe and T. J. Arne, *La Nécropole de Vendel*, Stockholm, 1927. The helmet from grave 14 at Vendel is the best preserved, the rest are fragmentary.
Valsgärde 6, Greta Arwidsson, Uppsala, 1942, Pls. 1–5.
Valsgärde 8, Greta Arwidsson, Uppsala, 1954, Pls. 1–6.
Valsgärde 7, helmets at present unpublished.
Sune Lindqvist, *Uppsala Högar och Ottarshögen*, Stockholm, 1936 – the helmets from Gamla Uppsala are greatly damaged by cremation.
'Vendelhjälmarnas Ursprung', *Fornvännen*, 1925, 181–207. 'Norske Hjelmer fra folkevandringstiden', *Bergens Museums Aarbok*, 1922–1923, 1–12.

20 M. E. Durham, *Tribal Origins, Laws and Customs of the Balkans*, London, 1928, 207.

CHAPTER TWELVE

Sutton Hoo and the Background of 'Beowulf'

Archaeology is the sole branch of Dark Age studies (to use a convenient term) in which the documents are being continually augmented – by the discovery of new antiquities and structures. This is true especially of the pagan centuries of the Germanic peoples, when things were placed in the grave to accompany the dead – centuries for which other kinds of documents scarcely exist. Standards in Germanic archaeology have also in recent years become more critical. Technological advances in the research laboratory and the conservation workshop have provided new means of appraising old finds and new. Since 1935, when Ritchie Girvan published his lectures, *Beowulf and the Seventh Century*, the archaeological picture of the relevant centuries has in consequence become a good deal clearer. So far as *Beowulf* is concerned this new clarity is being created above all by the Sutton Hoo ship-burial, discovered near Woodbridge, in Suffolk, in 1939 – only four years after Girvan's book appeared.

It is the purpose of this chapter to show how Girvan's discussion of the background of the poem has been affected by the Sutton Hoo discovery. The chapter does not set out to give a balanced treatment of *Beowulf* and archaeology, nor to take up a position upon the difficult, perhaps insoluble, questions of the poem's date and provenance, although it naturally stresses the possible significance of Sutton Hoo in these connections.

In considering the relevance of Sutton Hoo to *Beowulf* we need, in the first place, to be clear as to the date at which the burial took place. The purse in the burial-deposit held thirty-seven Merovingian gold coins. These always seemed to offer the best hope of dating the burial, but it is only recently that fundamental advances in the field of Merovingian numismatics have enabled us to reach a firm conclusion. The coins, it can now be said, were almost certainly assembled no later than *c.* A.D. 620–625.[1] The coins, it is true, only provide a *terminus post quem*. The assemblage might have been kept intact for any length of time before it came to be buried. But the burial can hardly be much later, on historical grounds. Because of the establishment of Christianity in the East Anglian royal house a king's burial (as this must be) in a pagan grave-field is very unlikely after *c.* A.D. 635. The ship-burial may, after all, as was originally suggested, be that of the greatest of the East Anglian kings, Raedwald, who seems to have died in A.D. 625 or 626.[2]

The date favoured by Girvan for the making of *Beowulf* was not earlier than 670 and most probably A.D. 680–700. If this were correct, it could mean that the poem had been composed within living memory of the Sutton Hoo ship-burial.[3]

Girvan's dating was based essentially on the conviction that the only suitable place of origin for so sophisticated and civilized a poem was Northumbria of the 'golden age'.

In his review of the archaeology of the poem Girvan is especially concerned to counter the view that it reflects the customs and manners of the Migration period (*c.* A.D. 350–550). In *Beowulf* practices and objects are described which Girvan supposed to belong to this early age – or at least to be contemporary with the historical events alluded to in the poem, that is of the early sixth century. He argued that these early elements were not evidence for a date of composition earlier than that which he favoured because they were covered at best in vague language, lacking the familiar touch of personal knowledge. 'I shall endeavour to show that little or no trustworthy evidence of life and manners in the Migration period, as distinct from later times, can be derived from the poem.'

The Sutton Hoo burial supports Girvan's attempt to detach *Beowulf* from the later Migration period (though not his arguments for doing so) by demonstrating that what he took to be archaic elements in a late seventh-century poem are not archaic. They are consistent with the century to which he would like to attribute the poem, the seventh.

Corrections to Girvan in this respect may be quickly made. Thus of Scyld's funeral he wrote:

> It is impossible that the poet had personal knowledge or direct information ... it ought not to be forgotten that ship-burial was obsolete long before the sixth century. The ancient founder of the house of the Scyldings was buried in an obsolete way.

It is true that Scyld's funeral-ship was not buried but abandoned to the sea, a practice which, if it ever existed in fact, has naturally left no trace. In the poem it may be seen as a mythical or literary element, Scyld's departure made as mysterious as his arrival. At all events the distinction between being buried and set adrift is not made by Girvan, who speaks of Scyld's funeral simply as a ship-burial. It represents in effect the ship-burial idea, the dead man being placed in his vessel for his last journey and richly provided with belongings and symbols of his status. The Sutton Hoo burial shows at any rate that ship-inhumation with provision of grave-goods similar to that of Scyld was being practised in an Anglo-Saxon setting, in a royal context and on a scale comparable with Scyld's funeral, as late as the second quarter of the seventh century; that is to say, within reach of the period to which Girvan would attribute the composition of the poem.

Again, Girvan refers to 'the damascened swords, no longer made'. We now know from the application of radiography to oxidized iron that these resilient pattern-welded blades continued to be made regularly down to the tenth century. The two swords so far represented at Sutton Hoo both had blades of this type.[4]

Also in the Sutton Hoo burial was one of the rarest of Anglo-Saxon grave-goods, a corselet, or coat of mail. It survives only as a folded mass of rusted links. There is no justification for Girvan's comment 'the corselet of chain in *Beowulf* must have been a survival'. He was influenced in saying this by the many corselets supposedly of provincial Roman origin now in the Schloss Gottorp Museum, Schleswig. These are from the Nydam and Thorsberg bog-finds, showing this type of body-armour to be typical of the fourth century; but evidently such corselets, with the same alternating rows of welded and riveted links, continued in use in aristocratic Germanic circles. The Sutton Hoo example is matched by chain-mail in Swedish seventh- and eighth-century boat-graves, including mail curtains attached to the caps of helmets as neck-protectors and explaining, as Rosemary Cramp has established, the phrase *befongen frēawrāsnum* (circled with noble chains) as applied to a helmet.[5]

There is no reason to suppose that the use of corselets like that at Sutton Hoo did not continue to the Norman Conquest. Here, as with much else, the Sutton Hoo find demonstrates that the poet's knowledge need be sought no further afield and no earlier than seventh-century England. Another point that struck Girvan was that in the account of the burials of both Scyld and Beowulf, nothing is said 'of horse, hawk or hound[6] or wife or slaves, male or female'.

Such Scandinavian ship-burials as that of the Russ (or Swedish Viking) chieftain cremated on the Volga or the Queen's ship-inhumation at Oseberg in Norway, or that of an early Norse settler in the Isle of Man,[7] show that slaves were sacrificed to accompany the dead. In the Viking ship-burial at Ladby in Denmark, the earlier Vendel-age boat-graves in Sweden – at Vendel itself and at the more scientifically investigated Valsgärde – a wide range of animals including bulls, saddle horses, leashes of dogs, falcons, an eagle, owl and a tame crane have been identified.[8] This solemn and colourful sacrifice of living things in the provision for the dead was regular Scandinavian practice from early times, both with inhumation and cremation burials.

It is a peculiarity in the poem, as Girvan saw, that there is no reference to any such practices in its accounts of what purport to be important Scandinavian burials. Girvan suggested that this, along with other omissions, was part of a 'policy of deliberate suppression by the poet of all that is shocking to Christian sentiment'. It is perhaps more likely to be a reflection of the funeral rites of late pagan times in the milieu in which the poem took shape, for absence of human and animal sacrifice was characteristic of rich Anglo-Saxon and Continental Germanic inhumations in the sixth and seventh centuries. What is of interest is that at Sutton Hoo we find this absence in the Anglo-Saxon milieu, in a royal ship-burial of an east-Scandinavian type containing Swedish elements.[9] Girvan thought that the failure in the poem to mention the firing of Scyld's vessel showed lack of direct knowledge. In literary accounts from later saga sources collected by Stjerna of funeral ships abandoned to the sea, the ships were fired.[10]

As has been said, there is archaeological record of this practice. Stjerna pointed out long ago[11] that there are plenty of examples of unburnt ship-burials of the pre-Viking age in Scandinavia. The Sutton Hoo burial (with the only two other known examples of pre-Viking ship-burial from the British Isles, both from the same corner of Suffolk, that recognized at Sutton Hoo in 1939 and another found at Snape in 1862[12] shows that unburnt ship-burials were known to the Anglo-Saxons in the early seventh century.

These features discussed by Girvan may be taken then as reflecting Anglo-Saxon society of the early seventh century, rather than as implying ignorance, remoteness or any distaste for pagan practices on the part of the poet or his audience. The poem is reinforced as to its plausibility, consistency, artistic integrity and setting.

Archaeologists must not claim too much for their discoveries, lest they mislead colleagues in other fields of study, or worse, cause the evidence itself to be underestimated. Equally, literary and linguistic scholars must be careful not to get carried away by enthusiasm in finding in archaeological evidence interpretations of detail in the poem, when archaeologists themselves are aware of the deficiencies of that evidence. An example, not meant with disrespect, may be taken from a distinguished contributor to *Beowulf* studies, the late Professor C. L. Wrenn, who wrote:

> Indeed the royal standard, though of course the gold embroidery of the Sutton Hoo exemplar has left no trace, with all its complicated ritual symbolising victory, protection, death, etc., as it waved over the King's treasure in death as in life, is a marked feature alike in Sutton Hoo and in *Beowulf*. Both in the cenotaph and in the poem it always implies royalty and treasure.

and:

> If we may judge of the exquisite delicacy and beauty of the gold and inlaid purse frame of the Sutton Hoo cenotaph, the purse itself must have been made of wondrously embroidered cloth of gold, as must also the standard, whose iron frame alone survives.[13]

It is perhaps unfair in me to point out how many questions this passage begs. Is the object certainly a standard? If so, does not Bede suggest the knowledge of three different types (*signum*, *vexillum*, *tufa*), all evidently used by Anglo-Saxon royalty?[14] This top-heavy iron affair with volutes to either side of its point for driving it into the ground is not the kind of thing that one would expect to find attached to the mast, *heah ofer heafod*.[15] Again, is the object, or the grave, certainly royal?[16] Is the monument really a cenotaph?

Without answering these questions there is one thing that we can be sure about in connection with the Sutton Hoo iron stand. Whatever the explanation of its unique design may be, there never was any gold embroidery associated with it, nor was there with the purse. The gold threads of Anglo-Saxon embroideries invariably survive in all soil conditions and in a properly conducted excavation are always found.[17] Indeed the rusted iron stand is conspicuously free from textile impressions of any sort. No gold embroidery hung above the Sutton Hoo hoard.

Yet, when Wrenn claimed for the Sutton Hoo discovery that 'it may well seem the most important happening' (in *Beowulf* studies) 'since the Icelander Jón Grímur Thorkelin made his transcripts of the Beowulf MS. and from them published the first edition of the poem'[18] it would not be surprising if time did not show him to be right. This we will return to shortly.

The correspondence between the provisions for the dead at Sutton Hoo and that for Scyld described in the poem – the ship itself, the weapons and armour, the gold, the symbols of tribal power or office (*ðeodgestreon*, *ðeodenmaðmas*) the treasures from afar – need not of itself be of special significance. Similar provision occurs in non-royal Scandinavian boat-graves of the seventh and eighth centuries A.D. and no doubt occurred in the royal burials of the time. Even the specific nature of certain correspondences, for example between helmets described in the poem and the Sutton Hoo helmet, need not mean anything special. Isolated parallels can always occur and are to be found in other Germanic graves. The only surviving helmet with a boar-crest, for example (though itself not of the Swedish helmet-type described in *Beowulf* and found at Sutton Hoo), occurs in the Benty Grange tumulus, in Derbyshire; one of two known sword-pommels with runic inscription occurs in a grave at Gilton, in Kent, to choose Anglo-Saxon examples.[19] What seems significant is the hitherto unlooked-for concentration of such parallels, including reflections of Christianity[20] and lack of funeral sacrifice, in a royal ship-burial of Scandinavian type in a civilized Anglo-Saxon setting. Two of the Sutton Hoo finds may be singled out here as having a special interest.

Since Professor J. C. Pope published in 1942 his theory of the use of the harp to fill initial rests and provide a regular beat in Old English Poetry to organize its rhythm, interest has attached to the kind of instrument this was and to the sort of accompaniment it might have provided. When Pope wrote he felt it necessary to say 'we may never know, and perhaps can never even conjecture, just what the musical accompaniment was like'. He speculated a little on how 'the small harp then in use' may have been used. Now the Sutton Hoo burial contained the remains of a six-stringed instrument of music which has recently been, it seems, validly reconstructed.[21] We seem justified in claiming it as the instrument called in *Beowulf* '*hearpe*', although it is not technically a harp but a round lyre. The recovery from the Sutton Hoo burial of the instrument used to accompany the performance and even to assist or condition the composition of early Anglo-Saxon poetry, even if we do not know how it was tuned and no note of music survives from this era, should enable practical experiments to be carried out on a valid basis. It becomes possible to demonstrate the capacities of the instrument and allow of sounder thoughts on its possible relevance to the problems of Old English prosody and its role in Anglo-Saxon courtly life.

Secondly, the Sutton Hoo helmet provides the closest analogy yet with those described in *Beowulf*. It is the self-same type and of Swedish make. It is the only Germanic masked helmet. It is shining and silver-coloured (*hwit*), its surface being tinned. Boar-images are set over the cheek-pieces and it provides an unexceptionable explanation of the word *walu*,[22] as referring to the thick external iron crest which runs over the top of the helmet from front to back (Fig 32). Even if the Sutton Hoo helmet may be old – an heirloom, perhaps an historic battle-trophy – its presence in the Sutton Hoo burial shows that the type was known to courtly circles in East Anglia in the seventh century.[23]

The potential of the Sutton Hoo discoveries for *Beowulf* studies may be found to rest not so much on such analogies in themselves as on the clue that the ship-burial as a whole may provide to the poem's place of composition and to the transmission of its Scandinavian themes to the Anglo-Saxon milieu – two of the major problems to do with the poem which are still unsolved. The excavation of the remaining burial-mounds at Sutton Hoo may well yield discoveries that will strengthen the case for a possible East Anglian origin of the poem, a possible origin which must now be given serious consideration.

Sutton Hoo has revealed a level of sophistication and material culture at the East Anglian court not suspected hitherto. It was a milieu capable of producing the finest gold jewellery of its era to survive in Europe, having wide contacts (treasures from afar – Frankish coins, Byzantine silver, Coptic and Celtic bowls, etc.) and Scandinavian links so strong, it seems, as to indicate very plausibly for the Wuffingas (the East Anglian royal house) dynastic origins in Sweden.[24]

It seems therefore that an archaeological context has appeared with a particular relevance not matched elsewhere. With this should be taken into account certain evidence from place-names and the royal genealogy.[25]

We have no knowledge of East Anglian culture at this later time to set beside what we know of the achievement of Northumbria or Mercia but the Christian monastic foundations continued to prosper[26] and the Wuffinga dynasty survived through a period of irreversible political decline.

There is scope in East Anglian history for pride in lineage and for a nostalgic looking-back in decline to days of greatness, qualities of *Beowulf* which Girvan thought particularly appropriate to the Northumbria of the end of the seventh century.

Schücking's attempt to date *Beowulf* to the end of the ninth century[27] and to find a setting for the poem in the court of an Anglo-Danish king in the Danelaw was stimulated by the need to find a substantial motive for 'the very remarkable interest taken in matters Scandinavian'.[28]

'This', Klaeber said, 'still calls for an adequate explanation. It is something that has ever haunted scholars since the days of Thorkelin and Thorpe.' Earlier Klaeber wrote of the ubiquitous Scandinavian elements in the Old English poem, 'it is not their mere presence that has to be accounted for but their curiously historical character'. He quoted Morsbach's speculation:

> The most satisfying explanation offered by way of a hypothesis is that there may have existed close relations perhaps through marriage between an Anglian court and the Kingdom of Denmark, whereby a special interest in Scandinavian traditions was fostered among the English nobility.

If the East Anglia royal house, the Wuffingas, were of direct Swedish or Geatish origin, would this not supply the required motive? And is this not reinforced by the nature of the evidence which enables us to suggest it, viz. the discovery in Suffolk of a royal ship-burial – very likely that of the greatest of the dynasty – containing objects of Swedish origin virtually identical (where we can check) with objects described in the poem?

When we have a single long poem that deals with royal and secular society in the pre-Viking age and a single royal grave (as we suppose) of the pre-Viking period, we must be careful not to force the obvious relevance of the one to the other into a dual reflection of the same milieu. But it may well seem that at Sutton Hoo that is just what it is. It is the unique nature of the Swedish connection revealed at Sutton Hoo that seems to open up the possibility of a direct connection between the poem and the burial.

NOTES TO CHAPTER TWELVE

1 A detailed exposition of the new dating is given in the British Museum's definitive publication, *The Sutton Hoo Ship-Burial*, Vol. I, Cambridge, 1974.

2 H. M. Chadwick, 'Who was he?' *Antiquity*, XIV, 1940, Section VIII.

3 An eighth-century date for *Beowulf* is now generally advocated and is best argued in Dorothy Whitelock's *The Audience of Beowulf.*

4 The tip of a sword-blade was found in the boat-grave excavated in 1938. See *The Sutton Hoo Ship-Burial*, Vol. I, Chap. 2, Cambridge, 1974.

5 Rosemary Cramp, 'Beowulf and Archaeology', in *Medieval Archaeology*, Vol. I, 1957, 57–77 and reprinted in Donald K. Fry, *The Beowulf Poet*, 1968, 114–40.

6 Dorothy Whitelock has noted the fondness of the Anglo-Saxon upper classes for hunting and fowling and alluded to the references in *Beowulf* to stag and boar hunting and hawking, (*The Audience of Beowulf*, 1964, 92–3).

7 Gerhard Bersu and D. M. Wilson, *Viking burials in the Isle of Man*, Society for Medieval Archaeology Monographs, No. 1, 55–61.

8 H. Stolpe and T. J. Arne, *La Nécropole de Vendel*, Stockholm, 1927, 8–9.

9 Shield, helmet, sword (but not scabbard), are all of Swedish make. At Sutton Hoo the soil conditions were such that inhumed bone might have disappeared without trace. Nevertheless, the absence of any metal elements from animal harness, or fittings or equipment that might have been associated with a second person, as well as negative chemical evidence derived from the grave-goods, justify a firm conclusion that no remains of inhumed animals were present, certainly not on a scale commensurate with the rest of the grave furniture. A slight possibility that the Sutton Hoo burial was a cenotaph and therefore abnormal, remains. This would hardly of itself explain the absence of sacrificial animals or humans, when it was nevertheless thought fit to sacrifice so much treasure.

10 K. Stjerna, *Essays on Beowulf*, trs. J. R. Clark Hall, London, 1912, 112.

11 *Op. cit.*, 126–7. Stjerna's chronological sequence of types of funeral practice associated with ships, is invalid.

12 See Chapter Three in this volume.

13 *Mélanges de Linguistique et de Philologie*; Fernand Mossé *In Memoriam* 'Sutton Hoo and Beowulf', 489–9: reprinted in Lewis E. Nicholson, *An Anthology of Beowulf Criticism*, University of Notre Dame Press, 1963, 311–30.

14 Bk. II, Chapter 16.

15 'There remains the question of the mast, which comes in twice, supporting the body, and carrying the golden standard 'high over his head'; cf. Stjerna, *op. cit.*, 130, on the *segn* in Scyld's funeral ship: 'It was fastened to a long pole . . . probably made fast to the mast also' (Klaeber, Third Edition, with supplement, 1941, 127, note 47).

16 J. M. Wallace-Hadrill, 'The Graves of Kings', *Studi Medievali* 3 Ser. I, i, Spoleto, 1960 (Centro Italiano di Studi sull' alto medioevo).

17 Elisabeth Crowfoot and Sonia Chadwick Hawkes, 'Early Anglo-Saxon Gold Braids', *Medieval Archaeology*, XI, 1967, 42–86. Quantities of gold thread from braids can be seen with the Taplow Barrow finds in the British Museum.

18 C. L. Wrenn, in his supplement 'Sutton Hoo and Beowulf' to the Third Edition of R. W. Chambers, *Beowulf – An Introduction to the Study of the Poem*, 1967, 508 *et seq.*

19 See H. E. Davidson in Garmonsway and Simpson, *Beowulf and Its Analogues*, London, 1968, 354–6.

20 The spoons, silver bowls with cruciform designs, crosses in the scabbard bosses etc.

21 See Chapter 7 in this volume, pp. 188–97.

22 See Chapter 9 in this volume, pp. 210–13.

23 For a detailed discussion of helmets, see Rosemary Cramp, 'Beowulf and Archaeology' in *Medieval Archaeology*, I, 1957, reprinted in Donald K. Fry, *The Beowulf Poet*, Prentice-Hall Inc. 1968, 119–25.

24 Cf. R. H. Hodgkin, *A History of the Anglo-Saxons*, 3rd Edition, 1952, 719–24, Wrenn, *loc. cit.*, 521–13. J. L. N. O'Loughlin, 'Sutton Hoo – the evidence of the documents', *Medieval Archaeology*, Vol. 8, 1964, 1–19. Rupert Bruce-Mitford, *The Sutton Hoo Ship-Burial, A Hand-*

book, British Museum, Second Edition, 1972, 80–3, S. Lindqvist, 'Sutton Hoo and Beowulf', *Antiquity*, XX, 1948, 131–40.

25 G. Sarrazin as long ago as 1899 suggested that Norfolk and Suffolk were settled by a branch of the northern tribe known as Wylfings (O'Loughlin, *op. cit.*, 5, Lindqvist, *op. cit.*).

26 As at Ely, St Botulph's monastery at Icanhoe (Iken, near Snape, is a very probable location) the foundation of which in 654 involved both Æthelhere and Æthelwald, according to one source and obtained a reputation for organization and efficiency such that it was specially visited by Coelfrith (the future Abbot of Monkwearmouth and Jarrow) shortly after A.D. 669 (F. M. Stenton, *Anglo-Saxon England*, p. 117), before the Jarrow-Wearmouth venture was launched.

27 'Wann entstand der Beowulf'? Glossen, Zweifel und Fragen, *Beiträger zur Geschichte der Deutschen Sprache*, X/ii, 1917, 347–410. Apparently, still taken seriously by some authorities, although I can see nothing at all to recommend it.

28 F. Klaeber, *Beowulf and the Fight at Finnsburg* (1942 edition), Introduction cxxiii, cxv, etc.

CHAPTER THIRTEEN

Six Interesting Pieces of Cloisonné Jewellery

I. THE GOLD PLATE FROM A DISC-BROOCH FROM THE PARISH OF SUTTON, SUFFOLK

The only Anglo-Saxon antiquity known to have come from the Suffolk parish of Sutton, near Woodbridge, apart from material from the well-known burial-ground of Anglo-Saxon tumuli, is the gold front plate of a circular disc-brooch of Leeds, Class II Type[1] (Plates 85a,b and Figs 43, 44, 45). It is a piece of some importance in the present phase of our knowledge of Anglo-Saxon cloisonné work and of the inter-relationships between its various and distinctive manifestations, since although found at Sutton, it is quite unlike the gold cloisonné jewellery so abundantly represented in the ship-burial, both in type and, essentially, in style or design. It is at first sight an orthodox Kentish piece and shows that orthodox Kentish-type Anglo-Saxon jewellery was known to East Anglian goldsmiths and in use in the same local milieu that knew and produced the Sutton Hoo jewellery.[2] It is a brooch such as would be worn by a woman, whereas the Sutton Hoo jewellery is of a different kind, namely regalia and sword-trappings of a king. The disc does bear a feature which links it with the Sutton Hoo jewellery, namely, as Charles Green pointed out,[3] 'the use of the "mushroom" cell', once described by Sir Thomas Kendrick (after the discovery of the Sutton Hoo ship-burial) as 'the hall-mark of an Anglian cloisonné style'[4] and as being a cell-type 'so frequent at Sutton Hoo, so rare elsewhere'.[5]

Kendrick's statement about the uncommonness of the mushroom cell in Anglo-Saxon gold cloisonné jewellery outside Sutton Hoo, or at least outside the East Anglian area, remains valid enough today.[6] It appears to occur in Kentish-found material only in the composite brooch from Gilton, Grave 42 (Plate 85e)[7] and there in a somewhat minor and ambiguous rôle (the eight instances of this cell-type seem to hover uncertainly between curved and angled tops). Other examples outside East Anglia, excepting Faversham, are the unusual jewel from Forest Gate in the Ashmolean Museum, an Essex find[8] (Plate 85c,d) and the gold pyramid virtually identical with the Sutton Hoo gold pyramids, found at Dorchester-on-Thames (Plate 86a, Fig 45a). Amongst material from Faversham, a *vicus regius* and probably in the seventh century a port, having connections with one newly established at Ipswich,[9] apart from the two pendants and the top plate of a composite brooch with empty cloisons cited by Kendrick, it occurs in a 'pure' form, that is, as a mushroom-shape more or less in isolation, in a disc-brooch of Leeds Class II.[10]

The top plate of a composite brooch from Faversham with empty cloisons seems attributable to the Sutton Hoo workshop, combining as it does the mushroom cell with the 'beaded cloison', or cell with a gold lid, used to provide a pivot to a twisting or rotating pattern, and with the execution of an animal head (in a fairly naturalistic phase of the development of such themes in cloisonné work) in cloisonné inlay (see pp. 40–1 and Fig 6g).[11]

If the Faversham composite-brooch top with inlays missing was a product of the Sutton Hoo workshop, it illustrates the manufacture in that workshop of jewellery of a more characteristically Anglo-Saxon aspect and adds to the possibility that the Sutton brooch which is the subject of our discussion was also made there.

The Sutton disc is in a very damaged condition. The inlays have been gouged or broken out of their cells and nothing of the rest of the brooch has survived, apart from this upper plate.

The circular plate is of thin gold and measures 45 mm in diameter. It is the base-plate upon which were erected and soldered the cloison rings and circular settings for studs and to which in the spaces between the cloisonné elements, the decorative scroll-devices in gold filigree were soldered. A large circular hole at the centre of the disc held a separate circular setting, now missing. There are four peripheral and smaller circular settings, being circular cloisons of large size erected on the base-plate, each showing a hole more or less centrally placed which held the shank that fastened a contained stud, now missing. These four peripheral circular settings are marked A, B, C and D on the drawing (Fig 43). Bisecting the spaces between the four circular settings and given express form by pairs of parallel gold walls radiating outwards across the middlemost of the zones of decoration is a basic cruciform pattern which divides up the disc into quadrants, each quadrant containing one of the peripheral circular settings. The cruciform theme is finished off by four outward-pointing triangular settings which intrude into the outermost filigree zone. The general design is typically Kentish.

The brooch was found in about the year 1835 'by a ploughman in the parish of Sutton, Suffolk'. The assumption is that he found it in the course of ploughing, although this is not explicitly stated. The ploughman extracted and threw away the coloured inlays or settings and sold the gold. The plate with its empty cell work passed into the Fitch Collection and with that Collection in 1894 into the Norwich Castle Museum. Under a recent exchange of material between the two Museums the disc has now been transferred permanently to the Ipswich Museum, where it bears the registration number 962 . 140. The former Norwich Castle Museum registration number was 618 . 7694.

Evidently, although no single inlay survives, there were inlays other than red garnets and the usual white bosses of cuttlefish bone.

The Victoria County History[12] records the statement of the ploughman to the effect that the brooch had 'studs of precious stones or glass, red at the centre, and others blue, while the small spaces' (cloisons) 'were filled with green and other colours'. This can be taken as a clear indication of polychromy and indeed of polychromy of an unusual kind, since Kentish or Anglo-Saxon composite brooches do not in any other example contain green or other coloured inlays, except blue. The introduction of green and other colours (ochre or orange?) suggests a link with the Kentish silver disc-brooches or with the polychrome Swedish cloisonné work in bronze cells on the Sutton Hoo shield. We do not know whether the Faversham composite brooch with inlays missing contained inlays of colours other than red, white or blue. It is not impossible if these brooches were products of the Sutton Hoo workshop that *millefiori* chequers might have been used.

A number of points of special interest arise from the Sutton disc. Firstly, it should be said that the presumption that the brooch was turned up in the course of ploughing has been taken to mean that it cannot have come from the site of the tumuli. However, recent investigation of the Sutton Hoo site has produced evidence of ploughing in relatively recent times, over the area of Mound 5 and

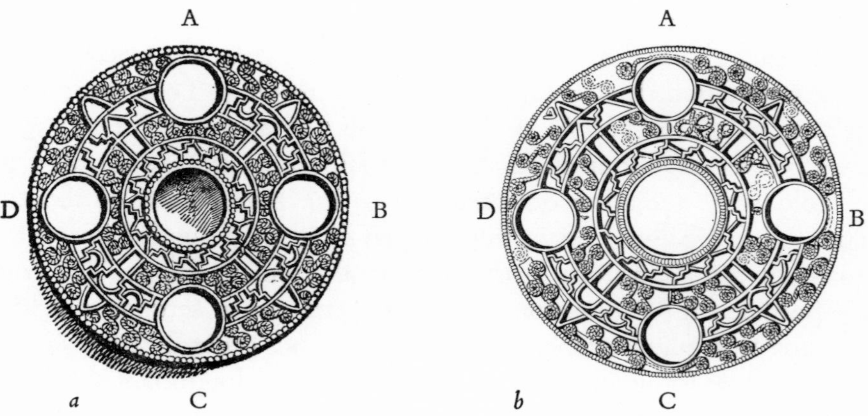

Figure 43 a, Sutton Brooch: a drawing published in the Victoria County History of Suffolk, 1911
b, Reconstruction drawing of the design of the Sutton disc-brooch (Scales 1 : 1)

ploughing certainly took place over part of Mound 12.[13] Derivation from the site of the Tumuli seems possible.

Two drawings have been published of this brooch and both call for some correction. Charles Green's is generally more sensitive and accurate[14] than that in the *Victoria County History* but is itself incorrect in certain details. Fig 43b attempts a more definitive rendering, although the reconstruction of the original design which it seeks to achieve is made difficult by the damage which the cloisons have sustained.

The four peripheral roundels in Fig 43a are lettered A–D. The *Victoria County History* drawing of 1911 shows separate elements in the filigree design under each roundel. These are wholly omitted by Green in his drawing. In case it should be thought that the Victoria County History drawing made fifty years earlier shows the brooch in a more authentic state, it should be said that it cannot possibly have been correct. Some of the spirals shown in the *Victoria County History* drawing are in the same general positions and there is no room for the extra detail as fitted in on the *Victoria County History* drawing. The position under roundel C makes this clear. While the Victoria County History shows the design as in Fig 44a, the actual position of the filigree in this position is as shown in Fig 44b.

The base of the gold cell-wall running transversely across the zone remains and to the left of it a smaller S-scroll. This could never have slipped into the position shown in Fig 44a and in any case the illustrator has drawn an element of a different shape. On the other hand the *Victoria County History* drawing is more accurate than Green's in showing the gaps between the roundels and the beaded rim, and in rendering the four cells which intrude into the outermost filigree zone as sharply-pointed triangles rather than as cells with rounded tops. The large circular hole at the centre of the disc contains a separate tall collar of a different metal of paler colour, perhaps silver. This is splayed out and soldered to the back of the disc, the collar having been cut in ten or eleven places and fanned out. The beaded gold wire which surrounds this central collar is also of a different alloy from the disc. It must have been added at the time of the insertion of the (?)silver collar for the central setting. The innermost cloisonné zone has a circular inner wall and the beaded wire is soldered or otherwise fixed on top of the cloisonné wall and against the outer face of the collar. The outer beaded border shows considerable wear. A gold-foil underlay with a strictly rectilinear small-scale pattern survives in the triangular cell in the outermost filigree zone between B and C (Fig 43). A curious feature of the disc, shown in Green's drawing and in our Fig 44b, is that in the inner filigree zone the filigree changes character between A and B. The wire elements are thinner, more heavily worn and with less pronounced beading. Moreover, whereas elsewhere S-scrolls or half S-scrolls are employed, the filigree wires here were evidently twisted into figure-of-eight

Figure 44 Above, details of filigree in a drawing of the Sutton brooch made in 1911 (enlarged) Below, correct versions as seen at the present time (enlarged)

shapes. Short hook-like straight lengths also occur, though it is not clear whether these are displaced portions of broken wires (Plate 85a).

Straight elements or walls are shown in Fig 43 joining the outer wall of the inner cloisonné zone to the four roundels. Part of one such wall is clearly seen at C and traces of another at A; at B a double feature is visible in Plate 35a but both elements appear beaded and it seems that these are lengths of displaced filigree. The cloisonné work in general shows some irregularity. Most of the apparent inconsistency in cell-shapes is due to the effect of the ploughman's prising out of the inlays but there is a definite change of design in the outer cloisonné zone between D and A, perhaps due to faulty spacing out, and a mistake in the same zone between C and D, where the central curved cell faces the same way as the two that flank it instead of facing in the opposite direction, with its ends resting on the cloisonné steps. In other respects the cloisonnage is even, solid and competent. The number of complete S-scrolls in the individual sections of the outer filigree zone varies from two to three and in most instances the space was filled out by half-scrolls, the tails of which fitted the spaces between the peripheral roundels and the filigree border.

There seems no justification for Green's suggestion that the mushroom cells in this brooch may have been accidentally produced and that it may be the origin of the mushroom-cell theme, which was then deliberately exploited by the Sutton Hoo master-goldsmith, spreading subsequently from England to the Continent.

II. TWO PIECES OF EARLY ANGLO-SAXON CLOISONNE JEWELLERY

Plate 86a illustrates in an eighteenth-century sketch an entirely unambiguous example of a gold cloisonné pyramid now lost but evidently closely similar to the

Plate 85 a,b, Front and back of a gold plate from a disc-brooch, Sutton, Suffolk (Scale 3 : 2); *c,d*, The Forest Gate jewel (Scale 1 : 1); *e*, Disc-brooch, Gilton, Kent, grave 42 (Scale 3 : 2)

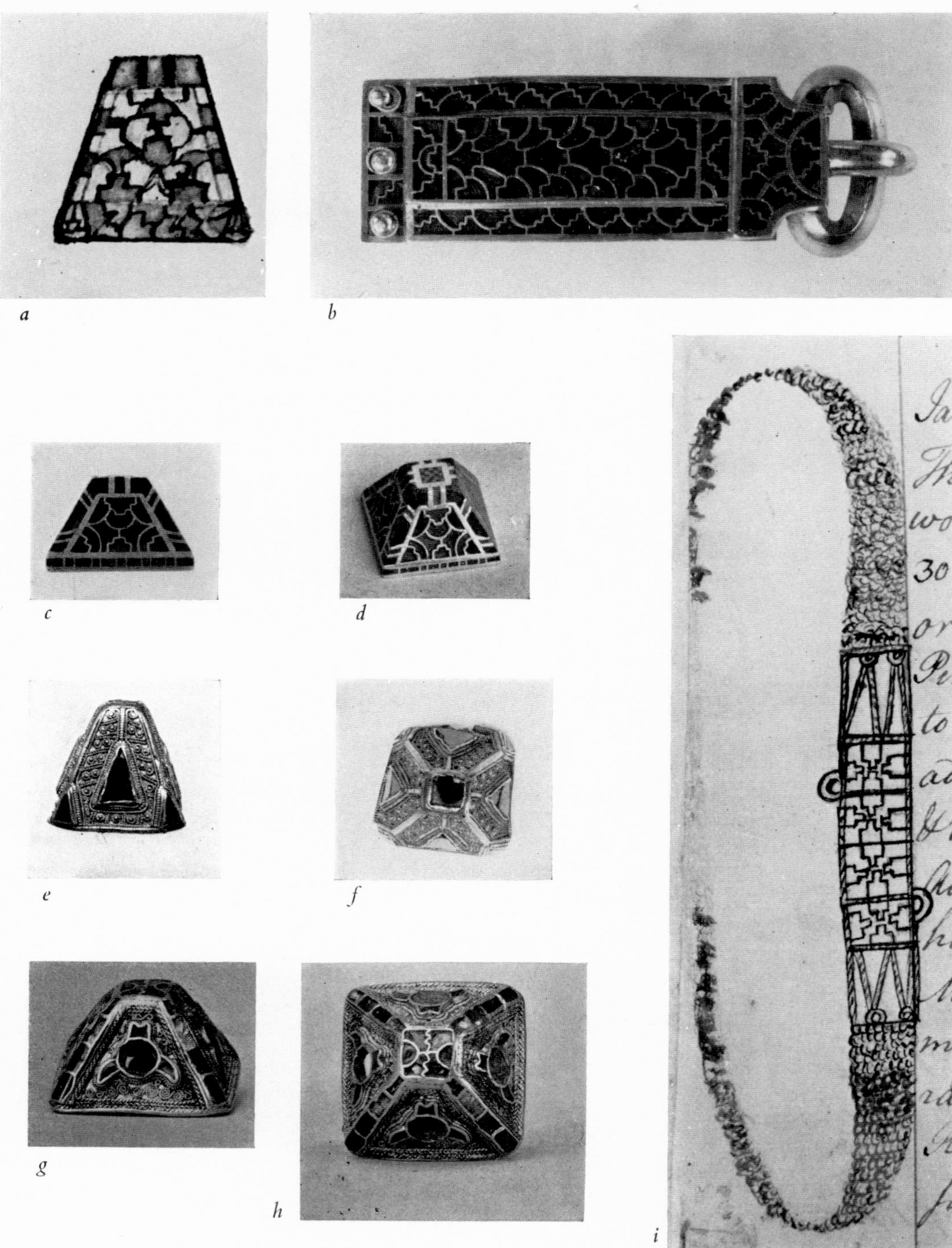

Plate 86 a, Gold cloisonné pyramid, Dorchester-on-Thames, Oxfordshire (Scale 3 : 2); *b*, Gold rectangular buckle, Sutton Hoo (Scale 1 : 1); *c,d*, Gold and cloisonné garnet pyramid, Sutton Hoo (Scale 1 : 1); *e,f*, Gold pyramid, Dalmeny, Roxburghshire (Scale 1 : 1): *g,h*, Pyramid, Ezinge terp, Holland (Scale 1 : 1); *i*, Bracelet, Shortgrove, Essex (Scale about 1 : 1) (pp. 267–70)

a

b

Plate 87 a, b, Gold and garnet pyramid, Dalmeny, Roxburghshire. Two views (Scale 5 : 1)

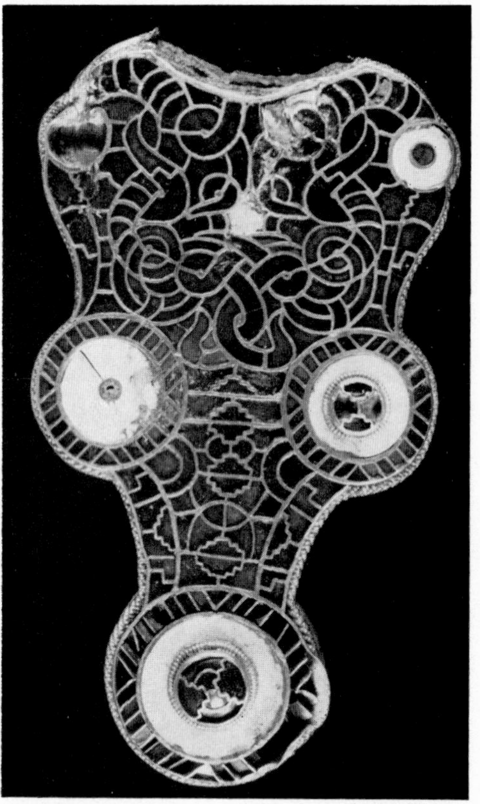

a

b

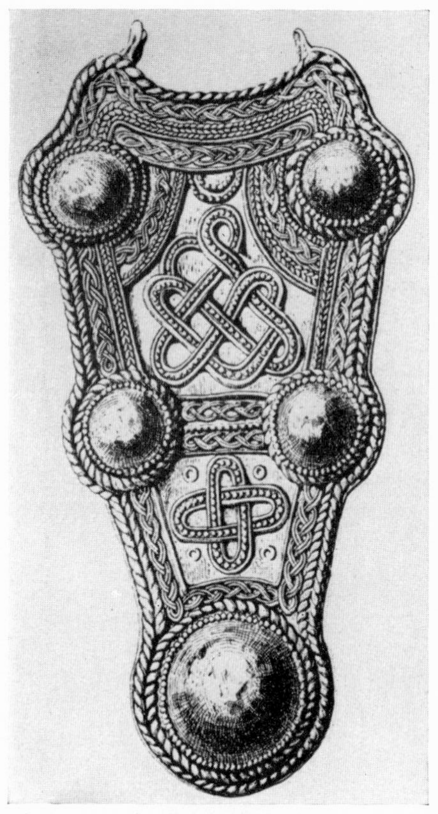

c

Plate 88 a,b, Gold and silver buckle-plate with cloisonné garnet decoration, Wynaldum, Harlingen, Friesland, front and back (Scales 1 : 1); *c*, Buckle-plate from Wienwerd, Friesland (Scale 1 : 1)

a

b

c

e

d

Plate 89 *a*,*b*, Details from the purse-lid, Sutton Hoo (Scales 1 : 1); *c*, The Great gold buckle, Sutton Hoo (Scale 1 : 1); *d*, T-mount, Sutton Hoo (slightly enlarged); *e*, Detail from a shoulder-clasp, Sutton Hoo (Enlarged)

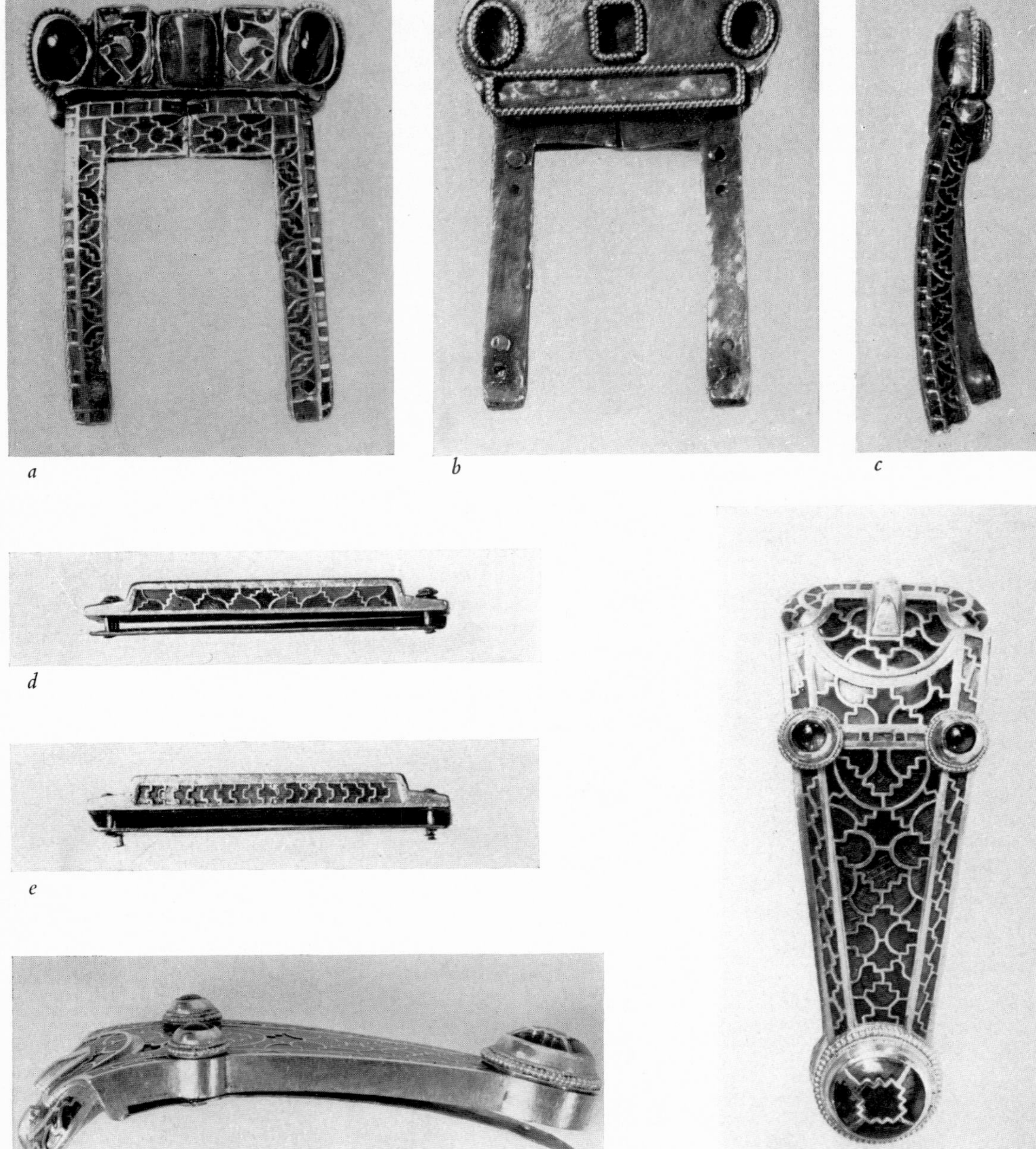

Plate 90 a,b,c, Tongres mount, front, back and side views; *d*, Sutton Hoo, rectangular mount, side; *e*, Sutton Hoo, rectangular mount from a different pair, side; *f,g*, Sutton Hoo, curved mount, front and side views (Scales all 1 : 1)

Plate 91 Tongres mount, enlarged detail

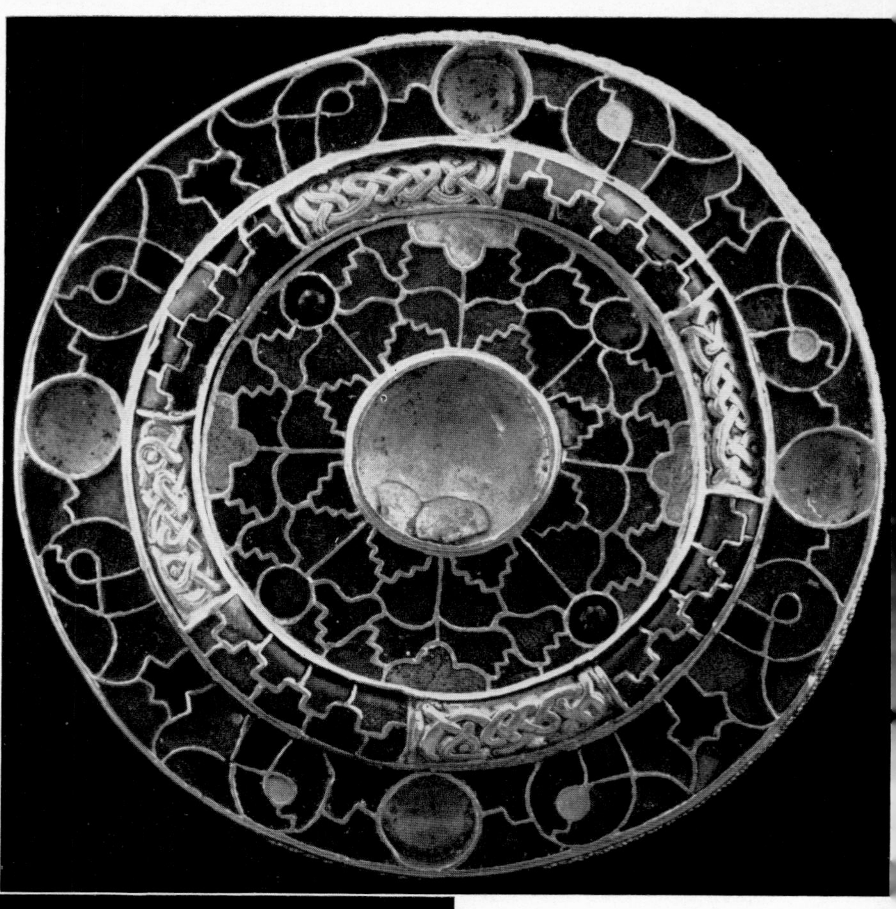

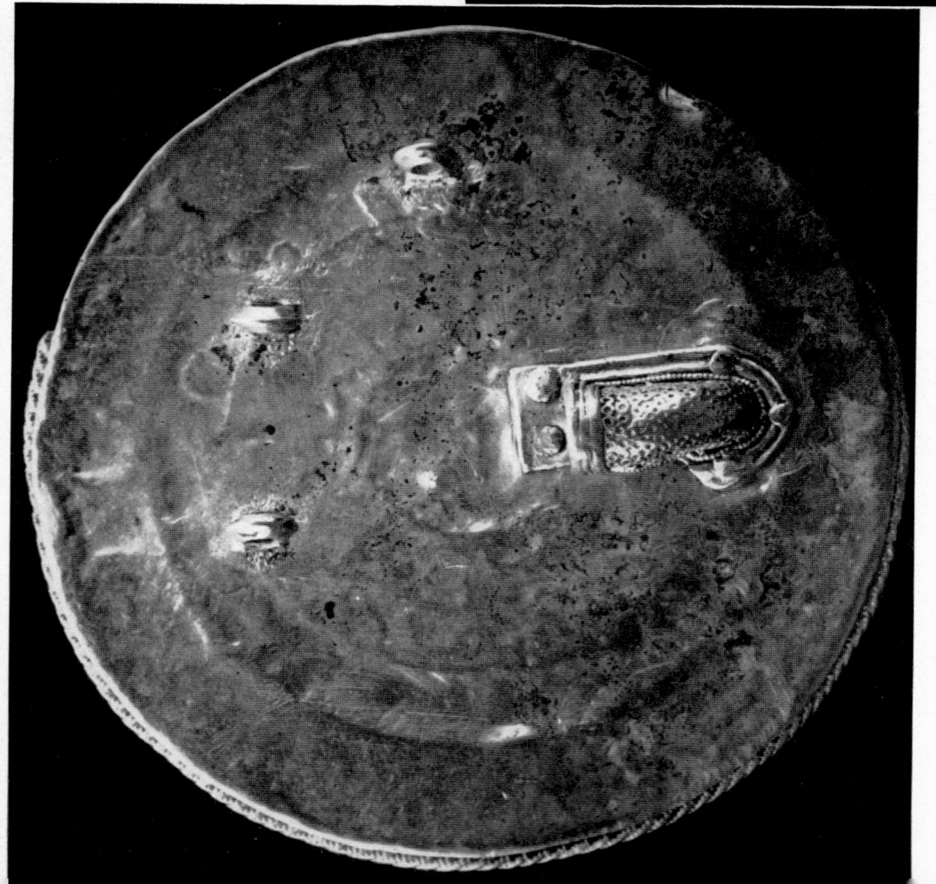

Plate 92 a,b,
The Parma Brooch
Front and back
(Scales, a little over 3 : 2)

pair found in the Sutton Hoo ship-burial. It was exhibited to the Society of Antiquaries of London on Thursday the 28th November, 1776. The text on p. 40 of Volume XV of the Society's Minute Books which accompanies the drawing reads as follows:

> Mr. Barrington exhibited, as a Matter of Curiosity, a Jewel of a Singular Form; being the Frustum, or base of a Pyramid, composed of Gold, and inlaid with Garnets on each side, and one in the Centre at the Top. It is about an Inch Square at the Bottom, and three-tenths of an inch at the Top, and its Height somewhat above seven-tenths of an Inch. In the Base are two Apertures for receiving a Catch or Spring, in order to ye adapting it to or detaching it from, the other ornamental Parts to which it may have belonged, whether a Necklace or Bracelet; for to some such Use it seems most probably to have appertained. It was found by digging under a Hedge at Dorchester in Oxfordshire.

The 'two apertures' in the base show that the mechanics of the object were the characteristic ones for such pyramids. One of the Sutton Hoo pyramids, with top and bottom views, is illustrated for comparison (Fig 45). The drawing in the text, to judge by the dimensions given, is not correctly proportioned. The shape as reconstructed from the dimensions cited is given in Fig 46, a shape closer to that of the Sutton Hoo examples and the rest of the class (Plates 86c–h). It is worth stressing this, since otherwise the tallness of the pyramid in relation to its breadth as shown in the sketch drawing (Plate 86a) could be taken as an indication

Figure 45 a, Drawing of the Dorchester pyramid in outline, according to the dimensions given in the Society of Antiquaries minute-book (Scale 1 : 1)

Figure 45 b, Drawings of the side, top and base of one of the gold cloisonné pyramids, Sutton Hoo (Scale approx. 2 : 1)

19

of the lateness of date. The tall Dalmeny pyramid, from the lowlands of Scotland, evidently a late piece, may be taken to show a late phase in the evolution of the type of object (Plate 87b). One is tempted to regard the Dorchester pyramid as a piece made in the Sutton Hoo master-goldsmith's workshop, although the description indicates that it lacked the distinctive millefiori inset at the top of the Sutton Hoo pair.

Not only are the angles and the four corners at the top apparently set with faceted stones but the pair of thick gold walls at top centre is exactly paralleled on the Sutton Hoo pyramids. The deep decorative zone at the base of the pyramid does not occur in the Sutton Hoo examples but its running design of steps linked by curves is exactly matched on mounts in the Sutton Hoo jewellery (Plates 86b, 90d). The mushroom cell is in evidence, forming the dominant central element in the cloisonné design, as well as occurring in half-mushroom cell and less clear forms. Dorchester-on-Thames was at this time a place of some substance, being given in A.D. 635 by King Cynegils of Wessex and the Northumbrian *bretwalda* Oswald to Birinus, the apostle of the West Saxons, as his see. It was described as a city ('*Civitatem quae vocatur Dorcic*', Bede III, 7) and in it Birinus built and dedicated several churches no doubt built from the ruins of Roman buildings. The Roman and early Saxon history of the place has recently been investigated by Professor Frere.[15] Birinus' establishment there would agree well in date with the time when the pyramid was made and to this extent it is a suitable find-spot for a piece evidently almost as regal as those which belong to the Sutton Hoo regalia.[16]

The second example of cloisonné work here cited is admittedly more uncertain but attention should be drawn to it. It is a bracelet of a form unparalleled so far in Anglo-Saxon archaeology and is also now lost, being known only from the drawing reproduced in Plate 86i. It was exhibited to the Society of Antiquaries on Thursday, 29th January, 1761, and the account of it given in the Society's Minute Book (Vol. VIII, p. 286) is as follows:

> Mr. Walpole exhibited a golden Bracelet, found in January 1761, in a meadow belonging to the Earl of Thomond at Shortgrove in Essex. It is composed of Chainwork like what was made for watch chains about 25 or 30 years ago. The Locket part is of red enamel or glass, ornamented with gold, and is rivetted by a small golden Pin, so as not to be opened. On different sides, but not opposite to each other, are two small rings, scarce large enough to admit a Ribband or Chain. It was found quite perfect, bright and well preserved. As Shortgrove is but two miles from Audley Inn, and the meadow where it was found, is said to have been meadow-land for near two hundred years, Mr. Walpole is of Opinion that this curious Ornament might belong to some of the noble House of Suffolk, who raised the Fabric about 150 Years ago; or to

some of the Royal Family who have lodged there. Bracelets of the same kind are worn it seems in Turkey at this time.

It seems likely to be early Anglo-Saxon for the following reasons: it was found in 1761 in an Essex meadow, said at that time, no doubt on the statements of the land-owner, the Earl of Thomond, to have been meadow land for nearly two hundred years. The emphasis laid on the fact that the ground had not been in cultivation or other use for a long time suggests that the bracelet was not a surface find but came out of the soil, otherwise there would be no point in discussing the earlier history of the land. If so, it may have lain there undisturbed from the sixteenth century and so be less likely to be an exotic piece brought back by travellers, as frequently happened in the days of the Grand Tour and in the nineteenth century era of British imperialism. The description is none too clear and does not show comprehension of techniques but the central portion seems to have been gold set with red inlays, probably garnets, since the mention of 'glass' suggests translucency. The treatment of the borders of the central solid element may suggest beaded or twisted filigree. The small projecting loops are familiar from early Saxon gold jewellery, where little loops for the attachment of security chains or pins are known from the Kingston brooch, the Sutton Hoo shoulder-clasps and a number of other instances.

The cloisonné pattern consists of four T-shaped cells with the stems of the T's meeting at the centre, a standard pattern of the time seen not only in cloisonné jewellery but in glass and enamelling[17] as a seventh-century extension of a theme rooted in the earlier Germanic technique. It is not clear what was meant by the reference to the central part of the bracelet as a 'locket' which is riveted with a small gold pin so that it could not be opened. Small gold pins were used by goldsmiths at the time, the filigree clips on the hilt of the Sutton Hoo sword being each fastened into the substance of the grip by three such gold pins (Plates 25d,e). It seems likely, if we are right in considering this as an example of early Anglo-Saxon gold cloisonné work, that the bracelet as such is a composite affair put together at a later date. Re-use of pieces of older objects in different contexts is a commonplace, well illustrated here by the Tongres Mount (Plates 90a–c and 91). The projecting gold loops on opposite sides of our mount presumably held pendants or attachment chains, neither of which would have any place on a bracelet. Anglo-Saxon goldsmiths at a somewhat later date were quite capable of fine gold chainwork such as is suggested by the flexible parts of the bracelet. The scourge from the ninth-century Trewiddle silver treasure illustrates this.[18] It is quite possible that seventh-century goldsmiths of the calibre of the Sutton Hoo master were capable of such work, although no example survives.

The general character of the piece, with the shelves at either end and the thickness suggested by its characterization as a 'locket' all suggest that it may have originally been a rectangular baldric-mount of the type illustrated by four examples in the Sutton Hoo jewellery (Plate 10b).

At either end of the panel with T-shaped cells and the two projecting loops are compartments which seem to show typical collared rivets at the outer edges. The straight elements dividing these spaces up into thin triangles may represent filigree cords or ropes, perhaps of the kind which frame the Wynaldum buckle (Plate 88a) and seal the junction of grip and quillon of the Sutton Hoo sword. Unless these end parts hinge, the rigid components of the bracelet might seem too large for the wrist. As in the case of the pyramid and other small-object drawings in the Society's Minute Books of the period, the drawing is probably approximately lifesize and is reproduced here at the same scale.

It should be said that the drawing has been submitted to the Ethnographical Department of the British Museum. They are not able to identify it so that it is unlikely to be Turkish of the sixteenth or seventeenth century as suggested, or other peasant jewellery. I am greatly indebted to the Librarian of the Society of Antiquaries, Mr John Hopkins, for drawing my attention to the pyramid and introducing me in this way to the Minute Books and their illustrations, the inspection of which subsequently led to my encountering the drawing of the bracelet.

III. A GOLD AND SILVER CLOISONNE BUCKLE FROM WYNALDUM, FRIESLAND

The buckle illustrated in Plate 88a,b was turned up by the plough on a terp-site at Wynaldum, in Friesland, in 1954.[19]

The front plate and sides of the buckle are of gold. It is a piece of very fine quality and of the first importance in the study of cloisonné jewellery of the seventh century A.D.[20]

The buckle-plate has, unusually, at the back a thick plate of silver, leaden in appearance. The front cloisonné surface, apart from injury by the plough, is remarkably well preserved. All the garnets are backed with gold foil in a plain pointillé pattern. The profile of the buckle is outlined with a thick gold filigree 'rope'. The general florid cloisonné style, in which the entire surface is covered with a continuous carpet-like spread of garnets, is one more or less universal in early Germanic Europe. It can be seen for example in Childeric's treasure, the so-called 'pectoral' of Odovacer, which was at Ravenna, the Swedish sword-pommels, the Reinstrup brooch, the Cesena treasure, at Sutton Hoo, in the two Aphaida and in the Pietroassa treasures and in a host of minor ornaments. Until

1939 nobody, at any rate in England, would have thought of calling this new buckle English but the wealth of cloisonné work in the same general all-over style found at Sutton Hoo shows that such work was also being carried out and with supreme skill and distinction, in England in the first quarter of the seventh century. We can infer that production continued in this style, though the general acceptance of Christianity results in its disappearance in the second half of the seventh century from the grave record. Extreme caution is necessary before a piece like this can be localized. Cloisonné style at this period is largely international. Skilled apprentices trained in Kent or Suffolk might go to the Continent, as we know from documentary sources, to practise their craft and take advantage of patronage and vice versa. Goldsmiths could settle[21] but were often migrant, especially in less settled societies. My impression of this buckle is that it is strongly influenced from south-east English work but more probably made in Friesland.

The buckle-plate presents a strange duality of style. The narrower lower portion bears geometric patterns in an orthodox manner easily matched in Kint and, on lesser pieces like the harness-mounts, at Sutton Hoo (Plates 10b, 89d). The step-pattern, simple zigzag and mushroom cell, the straight ligatures and parallel curves, the outer cloisonné border and the inner cloisonné field, all these features of the lower part of the Wynaldum buckle are highly characteristic of Insular work. So too are the convex cloisonné studs which sit in the middle of the white roundels (Plate 88a, Fig 46a, b). These can be exactly matched in Insular work, for example in Kentish circular brooches. The design across the broad upper part of the buckle is entirely different. It is an attempt to render Style II animal ornament in cloisonné work and consists of a complicated interlace of a most unusual kind. At first sight it gives an impression of complete, but absolutely symmetrical, confusion. On analysis it is revealed as a pair of rather tortured Durrow-type quadrupeds, looking back over their shoulders, with their hind or lower pairs of legs intertwined. One animal is shown in Fig 46*c*.

The Sutton Hoo master did this kind of interlace animal ornament too, for

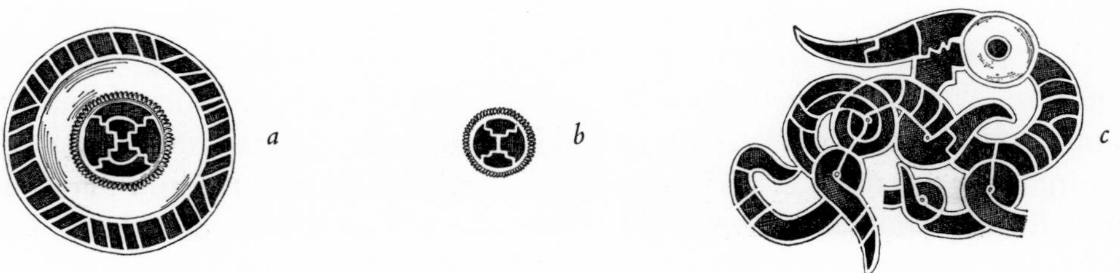

Figure 46, a–c, Line drawings of details of ornament, the Wynaldum buckle (Scale 1 : 1)

example the central dual plaque in the upper register of the purse and the border of the shoulder-clasps (Plate 89e), but with a very significant difference, an important departure from tradition which opened up new possibilities of artistic expression in the medium. He achieved clarity and emphasis of statement and brought out the animal design, by blocking out 'the background' cells, which did not form part of the subject, with plain gold lids. Similarly, when using the tiny beaded cell for purposes of effecting a twist in cloisonné work, he sealed the small beaded cell with gold, providing a more effective hub or pivot for the twist.

The absence of these technical devices, that is the lidded cells and gold-sealed beads at the heart of twisted or rotating passages, indicates that the work is not that of the Sutton Hoo master himself, for there could be no going back once this advance in cloisonné representation and techniques had been achieved. Furthermore, the small scale partitioning of the animal bodies in the Wynaldum buckle, with no adaptation of individual cell sizes and shapes to the anatomy of the animal body, shows a radically different approach to zoomorphic figural representation in cloisonné work from that seen in the Sutton Hoo boars and other figural or zoomorphic cloisonné work, where new and unique cell-shapes are devised to match the body's anatomy (Plate 89a, b). The absence of millefiori, at this time a positive hall-mark of production in England, is not a decisive feature, because it only occurs amongst the Sutton Hoo jewellery on the star pieces of the regalia-purse, shoulder-clasps and pyramids, not on the more routine items. The quadruped looking back over its shoulder, seen on the buckle, is very much an Insular theme but not exclusively so.[22] The plain cells separated by straight walls surrounding the three larger circular bosses occur in Anglo-Saxon work (for example the crests of the Sutton Hoo boars).[23]

The undulating shape of the buckle-plate is not English, but closest to the buckle is another Frisian find, that from Wieuwerd (Plate 88c).[24]

My impression after a cursory examination is that the buckle was probably not made in England, though very closely related to Insular sources, perhaps the work of a craftsman trained in Kent or Suffolk but working for a Continental patron. Its date could be anywhere between *c.* A.D. 600 and *c.* A.D. 650. The design of the upper part of the plate is not without interesting analogies with the great gold buckle, devoid of cloisonné work, in the Sutton Hoo treasure (Plate 89c), a piece which shows influences from Swedish Vendel art in its animal patterns. This analogy rests in the symmetrically outward-turned bird-heads (animal in Wynaldum) at the shoulders and the general turbulence of the zoomorphic interlace. A very remarkable feature of the Wynaldum buckle is the great fluency and flamboyance of the animal interlace, achieved with still limited technique in so static a medium.

The dating of the Wynaldum buckle is affected by the early dating now established for the Sutton Hoo burial. The buckle may be said to belong to the same general horizon and milieu as the Sutton Hoo jewellery. If it had shown the distinctive technical traits of the Sutton Hoo jeweller's achievement as seen in the purse and shoulder-clasps (lidded cells, millefiori, anatomically determined cell-shapes, sealed beads as hubs in twist patterns, etc.) one would certainly date it post *c.* 620, since these remarkable technical developments seem to have been the invention of the master-goldsmith in East Anglia in response to a great patron's demands and to the challenge of creating regalia expressly incorporating themes from Vendel art. The Wynaldum buckle shows none of these technical features, though it does reflect a generally similar competence and cell-repertoire. It also shows interest, accomplishment and practice in the representing of animal subjects in cloisonné work and the use of the beaded cell (unsealed), for rendering twists or rotation, and it shows the rich all-over style familiar from the Sutton Hoo jewellery. Might it be possible to regard the Wynaldum buckle as the work of the Sutton Hoo master before he came to East Anglia and blossomed under the royal patronage of the Wuffingas? A further factor not sufficiently considered in the archaeology of the Franco-Saxon areas at this time and later, in the period of the *sceatta* currency and of the development of wheel-made pottery (Ipswich ware), is the development of very close trading and cultural links between south-east England and the Frisian coast. The Wieuwerd hoard is a leading document for this link, recognized recently in the numismatic field by Stuart Rigold.[25]

IV. SOME OBSERVATIONS ON TWO ITEMS OF CLOISONNE JEWELLERY

1. *The Composite mount in the Cathedral Treasury, Tongres*

The unique gold cloisonné mount illustrated in Plates 90a–c and 91 was first brought to my notice by the late Professor of Archaeology in the University of Lund, Holger Arbman. It is his photographs that I reproduce here, with his kind permission. The mount, in the Cathedral Treasury at Tongres in Belgium, was referred to by Arbman in 1950.[26] As we have it, it is manifestly a composite creation, put together quite likely as late as the Carolingian period. The large cabochon stones in individual settings and the coarse outer binding of beaded filigree, seen also on the back of the mount, exhibiting the *äquatorschnitt*, a cut across the maximum circumference of each bead, are characteristic of the period. The function of the mount as made up (Plate 90a–c) is not known but it might well, in its ecclesiastical context, be an episcopal stole-weight. Our concern is with the component parts. These can, in my view, be attributed to the Sutton

Hoo workshop, without any doubt. This view was also expressed by Arbman, on p. 160 of the paper cited.

The two panels which separate the cabochons at the top of the Tongres mount are incomplete. They each depict the front half of two quadrupeds with heads turned back, biting their bodies. They have been cut down from complete panels to the depth of the required zone. The rear half of each animal is missing. In these mutilated plaques we have features otherwise uniquely seen in the Sutton Hoo regalia – cells shaped to correspond with anatomical forms such as foot, hip and leg, or jaw (Plate 91) and the background cells, which are not part of the subjects depicted, blocked out with gold lids, thus detaching the subject clearly from its background. As regards the rest of the object – the two curved L-shaped edge-pieces (Plate 90c) – these show precisely the Sutton Hoo cell-repertoire. The edges are defined in bevelled or faceted garnets separated by narrow insets, also bevelled, of opaque blue glass inserted between pairs of close-set thick gold walls, exactly as is to be seen on the Sutton Hoo gold pyramids, or in the panelled style of the small buckle and two matching strap-ends.[27] The alternation round the edges of long and short or wide and narrow simple rectangular cells can be seen in the frame of the Sutton Hoo purse-lid. The main theme of the short broad arm of the L is, in each case, a mushroom-cell design in its purest form, consisting of opposed perfectly-formed mushroom-cells joined by a straight ligature, flanked by half-mushrooms and shapes that are merely supporting or residual (Fig 47a). The patterns of the long elements of the L-shaped elements – neatly executed, step-pattern themes within semi-circles (Fig 47a) – if commonly found in Kentish cloisonné work, occur also in the Sutton Hoo jewellery (Fig 6a–d). The capacity and fashion for curved forms is seen in the Sutton Hoo jewellery in the shoulder-clasps and the curved dummy buckle (Plate 90f,g), while the florid style of setting even the edges and working parts of objects with cloisonné garnets, characteristic of the Sutton Hoo school (Plate 4d and 89d, e), is seen again on the edges of the Tongres mount (Plate 90c), while the pattern there employed, a running sequence of step motifs and curves, is paralleled on one of the Sutton Hoo mounts (Plate 90d,e). The same combination is to be found on the newly published cloisonné pyramid from Dorchester (Plate 86a). The Tongres mount then, a piece of much formal interest, both in its secondary and primary forms, should be added to the circle of products from the workshop of the Sutton Hoo master-goldsmith. An analysis of cell forms and combinations, with Sutton Hoo equivalents, is given in Figs 6a–d and 47a.

Some additional points about the Tongres mount may be made. It is quite small with an overall length of 2·2 ins (5·6 cms) and an overall strap-width of less than 1½ ins (3·7 cms). The depth of the L-shaped pieces is 4 mm, the same as that of the curved clasp in the form of a dummy buckle at Sutton Hoo. It was

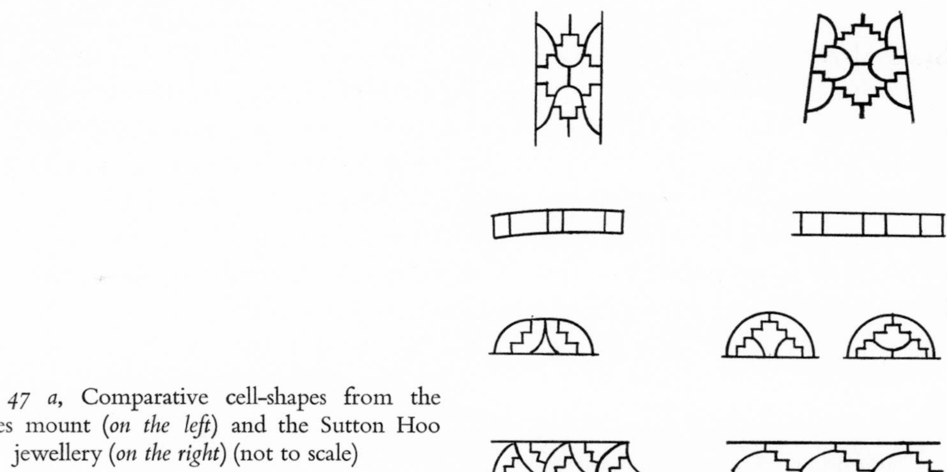

Figure 47 a, Comparative cell-shapes from the Tongres mount (*on the left*) and the Sutton Hoo jewellery (*on the right*) (not to scale)

evidently mounted on something, perhaps a belt or strip of material (not leather), which would have shown between the cloisonné edges and was presumably worth showing, that is, rich or decorated material. Two sets of rivet-holes show at the back of the L-shaped pieces (Plate 92b). Those at the bottom are slightly larger than the others and carried, incongruously enough, iron rivets. Another feature which finds a parallel, in the T-shaped strap-distributor and the shoulder-clasps from Sutton Hoo (Plate 89d), is that the L-shaped pieces are moving parts. They are attached to a hinge-pin which is terminated by the two knobs seen to either side of the head of the mount, below the large oval cabochon garnets. The L-shaped pieces, moreover, move independently of each other. The edges of the foil sheet, from which the back plates are made, seem to have been cut with shears. In the cloisonné work no inlays occur other than garnet and opaque blue glass, which is used for the eyes of the two animals, exactly as on the Sutton Hoo shoulder-clasps.

The function of this unique little piece must remain obscure. Its curvature and the independent movement of the two L-shaped elements seem inappropriate for a stole and indeed the object is too small. It is not clear whether the rivet holes refer to the primary or secondary use of the L-shaped mounts, which have clearly been re-used in making up this object. The original method of attachment is not clear, since there is no apparent gap between the back plate and the rest of the mount. If any cloth was admitted here, it can only have been the finest silk.

2. *The Parma Brooch*

In November 1950, workmen digging in the centre of Parma, Emilia, North

Italy, uncovered a richly furnished Lombardic grave of the seventh century.[28] Skeletal remains, as well as the jewellery found, indicated that it was the grave of a young woman. The disturbance caused by the workmen made it impossible to obtain a plan of the grave but excavations were undertaken by Dr Giorgio Monaco, curator of the Parma Museum of Antiquities and Superintendent of the Antiquities of Emilia, and many interesting finds were uncovered.

The grave had been laid out in a gabled cist constructed of large tiles, following the local Roman method of grave-building. The contents were typical of rich Lombardic graves of the period and consisted of the following items:

(i) A Coptic bronze bowl with solid foot-ring and no special features.
(ii) A plain gold-foil cross.
(iii) Two groups of polychrome beads.
(iv) Part of a gilt-bronze buckle-plate.
(v) Gold thread or wire, now in a ball, but showing pressure points where it had been once woven into cloth, as in the case of the gold braids from Taplow, Bucks.[29]
(vi) Two gold finger-rings, one with a bezel without its stone; the other with a broad plain hoop, decorated with punch-marks.
(vii) Five remarkable small rectangular plates of gold foil, four of which were stamped with a design of two birds back to back, the birds like miniature versions of the appliqué bird on the Sutton Hoo shield; the fifth stamped with a design in the form of a swastika of Style II birds' heads. These were probably sewn onto cloth.
(viii) A gold cloisonné disc-brooch, the subject of this note.

The most outstanding find from the grave was the disc-brooch (Plates 92, 93) measuring $2\frac{2}{3}$ ins (7 cms) across its diameter and 6 mm in thickness and encrusted with garnets and other inlays. The Parma brooch is the finest circular brooch yet found in Italy. Smaller and less rich gold disc-brooches with all-over cloisonné decoration are not uncommon in rich Lombardic graves.[30] This brooch, though, has quite unusual features which link it with Insular cloisonné work; for instance, in its use of small cabochon garnets and the introduction of plates of filigree (though the filigree is not as dominant here as on the Insular disc-brooches). The Parma brooch corresponds in size with the finest Kentish brooches. It has solid, thick cell walls and certain parts of the design are very much like English or Sutton Hoo work and would certainly cause no particular surprise had it been found in Kent, or East Anglia. Its similarity in some respects to the Faversham brooch, referred to in Chapter One (Plate 10a), should be noted.

Zoomorphic details in cloisonné (confronted animal heads) appear in the outer ring of the brooch. The eyes are formed from a cell wall bent round in a circle

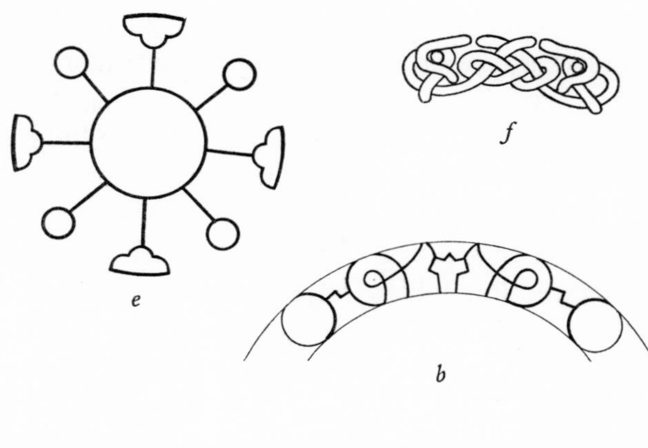

Figure 47 b–f, Parma brooch, details of cell shapes and filigree animal design (Scales 1 : 1)

and the small circular cells so formed were sealed with gold lids. The animal heads have a 'piggy' appearance. In four of them the central cell is empty (Plate 93). Presumably they originally contained garnets. The pairing of the animal representations in the interspaces of the outer zone, between the large circular cells, has English parallels, especially the Faversham empty brooch (Plate 93c, Fig 6g) but also fairly widespread parallels elsewhere. The eyes of the animals are gold-lidded cells, as already stated, but the edges of the vanes or cell-walls remain quite visible. The lids seem rather loose and sunken, like gold inlays rather than lids. Between the jaws of two of the animal heads in the outer zone are deep green glass inlays (central device, Fig 47b).

Apart from these zoomorphic details, the repertoire consists of interlocking cells (Fig 47c). As in the case of the Taplow gold buckle, the inlays have turned grey but one shows the 'lapis', blue but dark-coloured, apparently under a coating of dirt. Other cell shapes are shown in Fig 47. There are also four half quatrefoil cells on stems (Fig 47d) which are set with blue pastes. The brooch had the typical Insular arrangement of one large central and four peripheral bosses, all now missing. The quality of the work is very fine, strong and crisp.

At the centre of the brooch is a flamboyant cruciform element of floral appearance (Fig 47e), quite unlike any Anglo-Saxon work except perhaps for the petal-like effect of the Sutton Hoo scabbard-bosses. Nothing is left of the five bosses. The inset or insets have come out cleanly, leaving no trace (Plate 92a).

The filigree plates still contain mud and bear animal interlace in fully developed Style II. The use of filigree panels to break up the garnet-work is Insular in feeling. The animal bodies appear to have been built up from a thick central beaded wire with two thinner side wires, also beaded but these raised and curved filigree elements are very heavily worn. The central wire shows no trace of beading now and could have been plain. The work is a fluent and competent treatment of the Style II animal theme.

The eyes of the filigree animals are individual gold pellets, surrounded by a collar of fine beaded wire. The element coming down from the eye is odd. It does not represent a body or a leg but might be read as a kind of beard. It crosses the animal's body, going over it and under the jaw, prolonging in an irrational way the curved line which defines the eye (Fig 47f). In the central part of the filigree pattern, the interlacing jaws form a detached complete knot. The raised convex ring fitted between low upstanding walls has four matching panels with rounded or convex upper surfaces, showing identical designs of interlocked T-shaped cells. There are four convex garnets at the extremities of radii of the interior field and the central setting has an upstanding projecting flange (Plate 93). The raised zone or ring, in which the spaced filigree panels are housed, occurs on no Insular brooch but can be matched on gold disc-brooches from the Lombardic cemetery at Castel Trosino.[31]

The back of the brooch has a dull little catch-plate tightly covered with worn annular filigree. It appears to be damaged. The two loops holding the bar of the spring of the pin are set asymmetrically in relation to the catch-plate. There is a loop for a safety-chain, as in the Kingston brooch. The three loops are diamond-shaped and of faceted cross-section. The gold wire round the edge of the brooch seems to be a simple twisted beaded wire.

The unusual features of this Italian brooch, when seen in the context of its fellows of the same type from Italy, do not necessarily mean that it is of non-Italian origin but go to emphasize the international character of the goldsmith's craft at this period and illustrate, as do so many other things, the links which seem to exist between Insular archaeology and that of Italy and Scandinavia in the late sixth and early seventh centuries.

NOTES TO CHAPTER THIRTEEN

1 E. T. Leeds, *Early Anglo-Saxon Art and Archaeology*, Oxford, 1936, 118 and Pl. XXXIII, 1–3.

2 Reginald Smith called it 'a link with Kent', *Victoria County History, Suffolk*, 1, London, 1911, 330.

3 Charles Green, *Sutton Hoo*, London, 1963, 88.

4 T. D. Kendrick in *British Museum Quarterly*, XIII, 1939, 134.

5 In English and continental gold cloisonné work, that is to say. The mushroom cell becomes highly characteristic of damascened or silver plated iron brooches and buckles of the Alemanni and of the Rhineland Franks at a somewhat later period. These are essentially derivative from the cloisonné designs in the more expensive gold and garnet medium. The quotation from Kendrick is from T. D. Kendrick, *Antiquity*, XIV, 1940, 36.

6 T. D. Kendrick, *Antiquity*, XIV, 1940, 35–7.

7 Birgit Arrhenius, *Acta Universitatis Stockholmensis, Studies in North European Archaeology, Series B.* Thesis and papers published in offset, *Granatschmuck und Gemmen aus Nordischen Funden des Frühen Mittelalters*, Stockholm, 1971, Fig. 139.

8 Excavated by Faussett and in the Mayer Collection, Liverpool.

9 See Chapter II, p. 80, above, and footnote 35, p. 110.

10 E. T. Leeds, *Early Anglo-Saxon Art and Archaeology*, Oxford, 1936, Pl. XXXIII, 3.

11 For this brooch, apart from Pl. 10a and Fig. 6g, above, see George Speake, 'A seventh-century coin-pendant from Bacton, Norfolk, and its ornament', *Mediaeval Archaeology*, XIV, 1970 5–6.

12 *Victoria County History, Suffolk*, I, London, 1911, 330, and Fig. 5.

13 Rupert Bruce-Mitford, *The Sutton Hoo Ship-Burial, a Handbook*, 2nd edition, London, 1972, Fig. 1. *The Sutton Hoo Ship-Burial*, Vol. 1, Cambridge, 1974, pp. 11, 14.

14 Charles Green, '*Sutton Hoo*', London, 1963, Fig. 27.

15 *Archaeological Journal* CXIX, 114–49.

16 The drawing in the minute book of 1761 is tinted in two shades, with reddish colour now faded. Red is the only colour shown and this, combined with the lack of any reference to other colours, in the text, must indicate that the jewel contained no inlays of blue glass.

17 Cf. the glass setting associated with the Roundway Down linked pins, E. T. Leeds, *Early Anglo-Saxon Art and Archaeology*, Oxford, 1936, Fig. 23 and necklace and millefiori glass inlays in the frame of the Sutton Hoo purse-lid.

18 D. M. Wilson, *Late Saxon Ornamental Metalwork 700–1100*, British Museum, 1964, Pl. XXXV.

19 Fries Genootschap van Gescheid-, Oudheid- en Taalkunde te Leeuwarden, 126 ste Verslag (Tevens verslag van het Fries Museum) over het Jaar 1954, Dokkum, 1955, 15–17.

20 Identified as silver in the British Museum Research Laboratory, *pace* Birgit Arrhenius thesis and papers, 1971, 154, see footnote 7.

21 Cf. the goldsmith in the Anglo-Saxon poem, *Fates of Men*: 'very often he . . . adorns finely the sons of the King of Britain; and the latter in rewards grants him large estates', Eligius (*St Eloi*). Dagobert's mint master, remained at Paris until he became Bishop of Noyon.

22 The fourteen gold tremisses from the same dies from an unidentified Frisian mint in the Escharen hoard have such an animal as a reverse design. (J. Lafaurie, 'Le Trésor d'Escharen', *Révue Numismatique* VIe Série, tome II, Paris, 1960, 153–209; Pl. XII, nos. 46–59 and 59).

23 Cf. N. Åberg, *Anglo-Saxons in England*, Uppsala, 1926, 119–22.

24 The Wieuwerd buckle is illustrated in N. Åberg, *op. cit.*, Fig. 291: and also referred to in the Dutch publication, in the following footnote.

25 *The Sutton Hoo Ship-Burial*, Cambridge, 1974, Vol. I, Ch. IX. Section 3. For the Wieuwerd hoard, see J. Lafaurie and others, 'Le Trésor de Wieuwerd', *Oudheidkundige Mededelingen vit het Rijksmuseum van Oudheden te Leiden*, 1961, XLII, 78–107.

26 H. Arbman, 'Verroterie cloisonné et filigrane', *Lunds Universitets Historiska Museums Meddelanden*, 1950, 167 and Fig. 17.

27 Rupert Bruce-Mitford, *The Sutton Hoo Ship-Burial, A Handbook*, London, 1972, Pl. 33.

28 Giorgio Monaco, '*Oreficerie Longobarde a Parma*', Parma, 1955.

29 See Chapter Twelve, footnote 17.

30 S. Fuchs and J. Werner, '*Die Langobardischen Fibeln aus Italien*', Berlin, 1950.

31 Fuchs and Werner, *op. cit.* For the Parma brooch see also Birgit Arrhenius, *op. cit.* (footnote 7), 150–3 and Fig. 127.

CHAPTER FOURTEEN

The Pectoral Cross of St Cuthbert

This account of St Cuthbert's pectoral cross freely incorporates Sir Thomas Kendrick's history and classic description published in 1937.[1] Kendrick's account was the result of a minute examination of the cross on the occasion of its repair and reconditioning in the British Museum Research Laboratory in 1936. There is little to add to what Kendrick then said. His account has been modified in minor ways. Further attention has been paid to the filigree work on the (secondary) suspension-loop. The once-white substance (shell), upon which the central jewel-setting rested, has been re-examined in the light of work on such substances in pagan-period Anglo-Saxon jewellery.[2] The thickness of the garnets has been measured and in one cell at least the red inlay has been shown to be glass, presumably a replacement for a lost or damaged garnet. The depth of the cloisonné cells has also been measured. There are some observations on the type of gold used in the suspension-loop as compared with that of the cross itself. When it comes to dating the cross and assigning it a place amongst the relics of early Germanic (or British) craftsmanship, I abandon the position taken up by Kendrick. His suggestion was that the cross 'is the solitary example remaining to us of the goldsmith's work of the Britons in fifth-century Strathclyde'.[3] I do not believe this view can now be entertained for a moment. Reconsidering the old evidence and taking into account new, in particular some of the implications of the cloisonné jewellery found in such quantities in the burial at Sutton Hoo (*c.* A.D. 625) in 1939,[4] I find myself returning to the orthodox view, held by Baldwin Brown, Leeds, Åberg and others, that the cross is, like the Thurnham, Wilton and Ixworth cloisonné crosses (Plates 5, 96d, e), an expression of seventh-century Anglo-Saxon Christianity.

HISTORY AND DESCRIPTION

When St Cuthbert's tomb was opened in 1827 the jewelled pectoral cross (Plates 94a, 95a–e, 96b,c) was found 'deeply buried among the remains of the robes which were nearest to the breast of the saint'.[5] It had thus escaped disturbance in 1539 at the time of the savage ransacking of the tomb during the Dissolution[6] and it can be inferred from the circumstances in which the saint's stole and maniple were found that the Commissioners had ceased their plundering before the body had been fully stripped of its wrappings.[7]

The cross had been hung round the neck of the saint, traces of a 'silken cord, twisted with gold' whereby it was suspended being still recognizable in 1827, and it is overwhelmingly probable that it had been placed there at the time of St Cuthbert's burial in 687. As we shall see, there is not a shadow of doubt that the jewel is of sufficient antiquity to have been worn by St Cuthbert and it is also an important point that the decay of the internal silver repairing plate (Plate 95c, Fig 50a–c) can only be accounted for on the grounds that the cross had been in contact with a body at the time of its putrefaction. Furthermore, as the cross had been twice broken and repaired before it was put into the coffin, it must have been an exceedingly precious jewel, so that it could scarcely have been placed in such an intimate and honourable position on any other occasion than the first adornment of the corpse without a record of the gift being made. King Æthelstan, for instance, in 934, presented among other notable offerings the stole and maniple that were placed upon the body but Æthelstan's gifts are described in detail and we may be sure that an antique jewelled cross so important as this would have been included in the list if the king had brought it to Durham.[8]

The cross has a span of 6 cms and the thickness of the arms is 0·8 cm. It is made of thin gold and is hollow-built with soldered joints. The foundation is a single-piece base-plate cut to the shape of the cross and to the front of this at the centre is fastened a cylindrical collar which is roofed by a gold setting containing a circular garnet with a flat top (Fig 48a–b). This setting rested on a shell base (Plate 95, Fig 48a–b) to which it was secured by pins and the edge of the shell

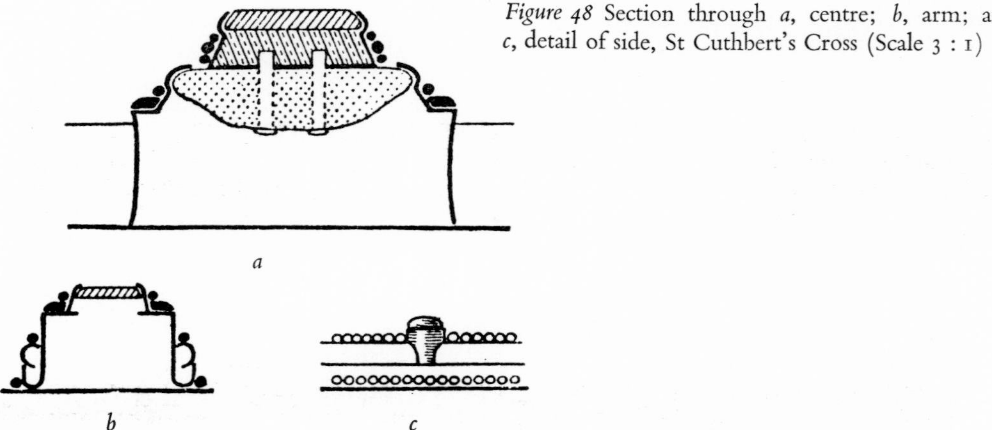

Figure 48 Section through *a*, centre; *b*, arm; and *c*, detail of side, St Cuthbert's Cross (Scale 3 : 1)

Plate 93 The Parma Brooch, enlarged detail

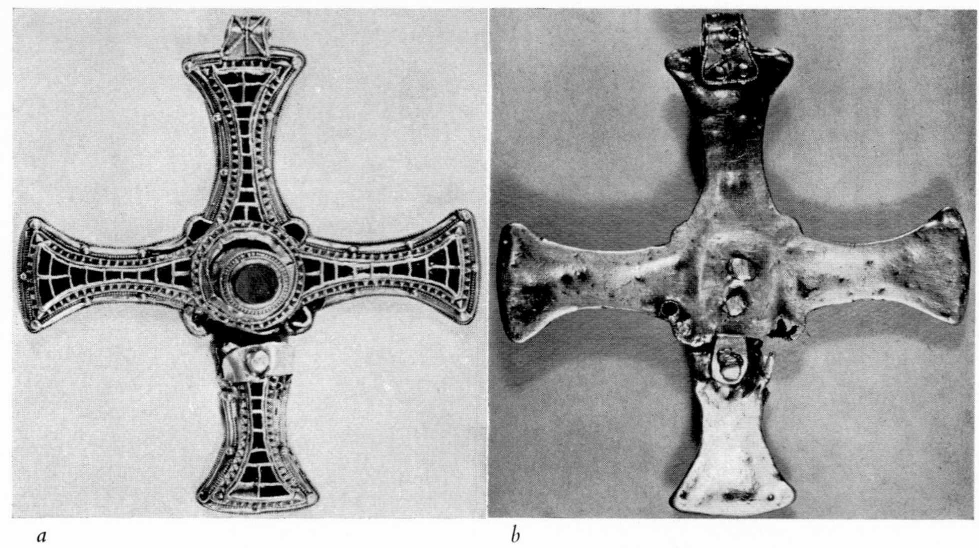

a b

c d

Plate 94 *a,b,* St Cuthbert's Cross front and back; after cleaning but before removal of nineteenth-century repair (Scales 1 : 1); *c,d,* St Cuthbert's Cross front and back, after repair in 1937 (Scale 1 : 1)

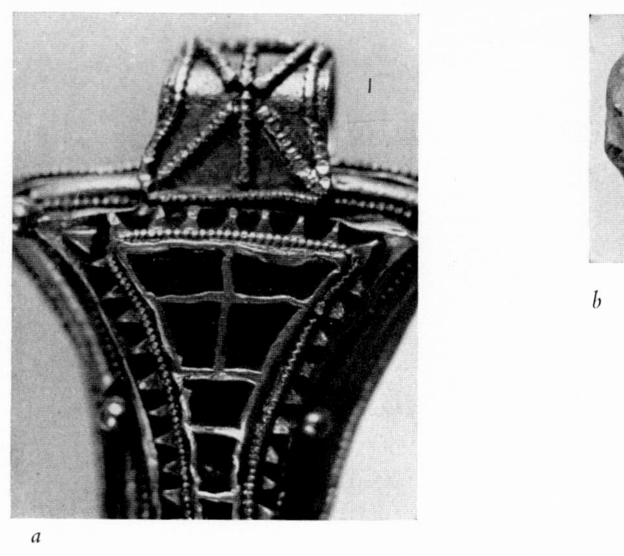

a

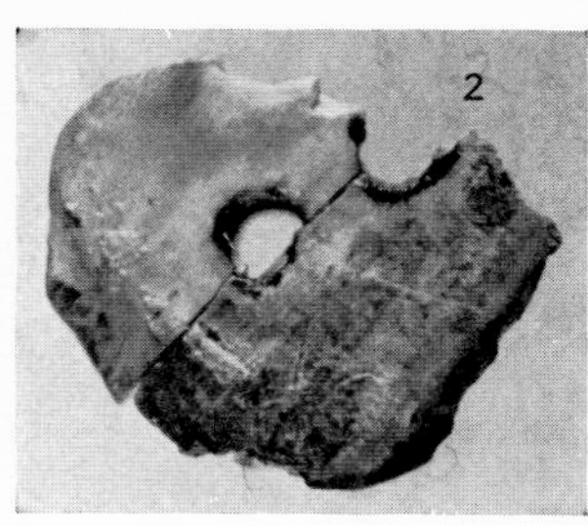

b

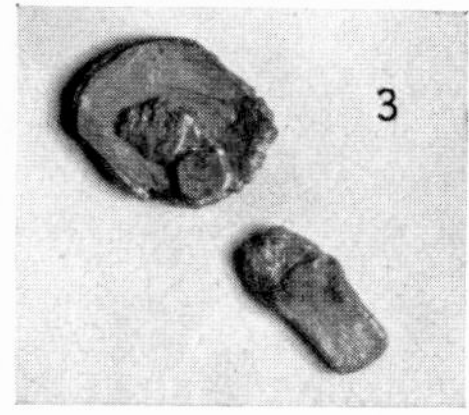

c

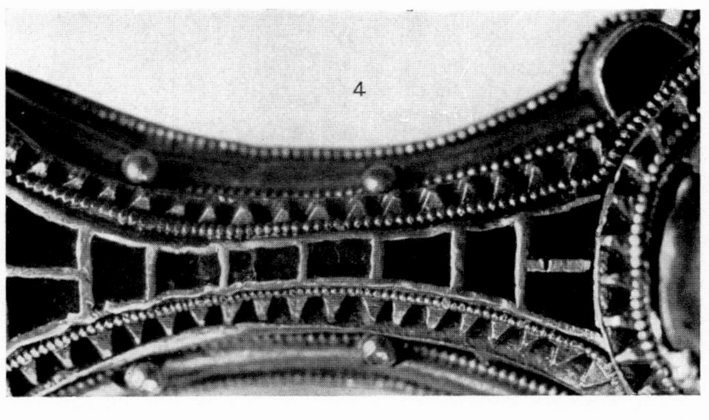

d

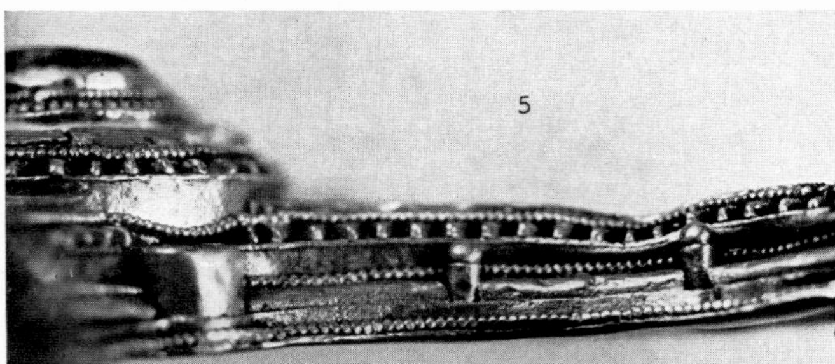

e

Plate 95 a, St Cuthbert's Cross (enlarged detail); *b*, Shell bedding-plate for central jewel (enlarged); *c*, Interior silver repair plate (Scale 1 : 1); *d,e*, Enlarged details

a

b

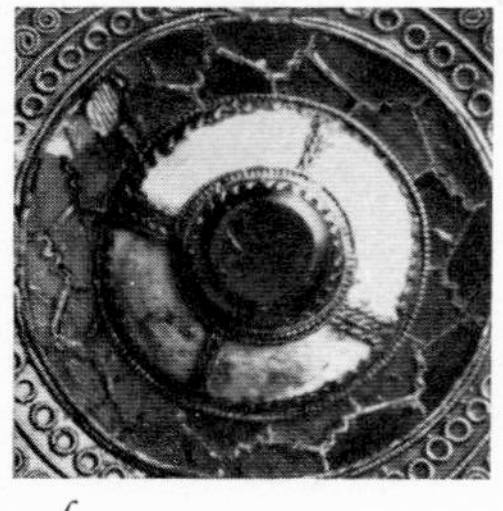

c

e

d

Plate 96 a, Buckle, Tostock, Suffolk (Scale 1 : 1); *b*, Detail of St Cuthbert's Cross (enlarged); *c*, Centre of the Sarre brooch (Scale 1 : 1); *d*, *e*, front and back views af the Wilton, Norfolk, pendant (Scale *e*, 1 : 1, *d* slightly enlarged)

fitted into the rabbeted lip of the collar, thus leaving a narrow white ring visible at the base of the central jewel. The shell base was an inverted conical lump 0·3 cm thick and there was a small cavity beneath it, not more than 0·5 cm in depth, that might have served as the receptacle for a tiny relic (Fig 48a). As this relic would have been invisible and inaccessible, there does not seem to be any justification for describing the cross as a reliquary.

Only a tiny portion of the original shell that supported the central stone-setting is now visible – a small patch opposite the gap in the gold retaining-collar at the top.[9] This original substance is now of a varying dark colour, green or yellowish[10], and it shows under magnification a uniform fine grain superficially resembling the structure of horn. The surviving fragment, removed from the cross and as seen in Plate 95b and Fig 48a, was examined by the then Keeper of Mineralogy at the British Museum (Natural History), Dr G. F. Claringbull, in February 1955. His report[10a] (see p. 295) showed that it is shell but from a species not apparently found in the waters round the British Isles or even in the Mediterranean. This identification adds another item to the group of objects (garnets, lapis-lazuli and cowrie shells – traded from the Far East) not infrequently encountered in the Anglo-Saxon graves of the pagan and transition periods. No doubt these substances came along the routes from the East that brought the well-known Coptic bronze bowls, the Byzantine buckles,[11] the soft 'cruciferous' red pottery found along the west coast of the British Isles from Cornwall to Scotland[12] and perishables such as ivory and textiles. Its interest to us is that it helps to bring St Cuthbert's cross into line with a number of important jewels, including the Kingston brooch, on which the identical substance is employed. This particular and exotic type of shell is the substance regularly used on those 'Style A' (cloisonné and filigree) jewels[13] which employ these white surrounds, whilst the less costly silver-gilt or bronze brooches in 'Style B' employ local substitutes. In other words, this identification tends to show that St Cuthbert's cross relates to 'Style A' jewellery as a whole and also to separate it from the earlier jewellery of the Continent and Britain, on which this substance (or its imitations) are not so used. The identification also places St Cuthbert's cross in the general chronological horizon of the 'orientalizing' luxury trade in North Italy, the Rhineland and south-east England, represented by the Coptic bowls, silver plate such as that at Sutton Hoo and their associated *exotica* already mentioned. It is now clear that the horizon of these in Anglo-Saxon archaeology is the late sixth and the seventh centuries, not the fifth or earlier sixth.[14] The nature of this once-white substance on the cross bears directly on the question of its date and milieu.

The gold setting that holds the flat central garnet, together with the surviving piece of shell beneath it, is now supported internally by a column of transparent plastic (perspex), inserted in the British Museum Research Laboratory during the investigation of the cross in 1954–5. This perspex column reinforces the chest of the cross without obscuring the ½ cm deep cavity beneath the central setting, the possible receptacle for an encased relic.

Another link with south English goldsmith's work is provided by the piece-work filigree on the added suspension-loop (Fig 49). Kendrick and others have described this loop as obviously of a gold different from that of the cross itself.

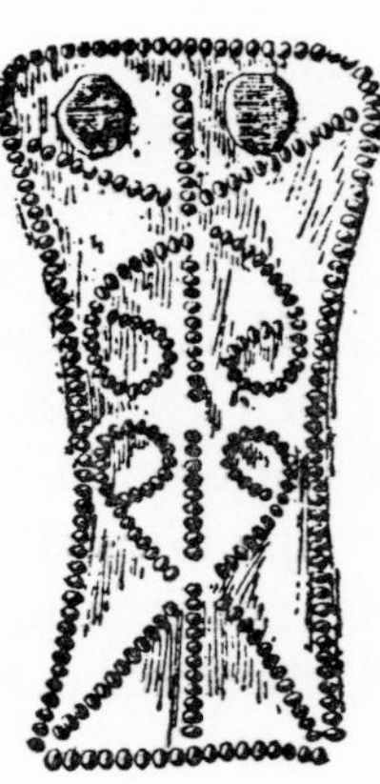

Figure 49 Filigree design on the secondary suspension-loop (Scale 3 : 1)

Deductions from the surface appearance of gold can be misleading and it is possible that the metal of loop and cross are really the same, in spite of superficial appearances. The secondary character of this loop is certain because of the damage to the top part of the cross concealed beneath it. The heart-shaped filigree motifs on the secondary loop (replacing the original suspension device) are characteristic of pagan-period gold jewellery in Kent. Convenient examples are the disc-brooches from Faversham (Plate 98b) and Teynham,[15] while an example from the north of England, though in all probability of Kentish origin, is the pendant from grave 31 at Uncleby, Yorks.[16] While not fixing the date of the cross itself, this characteristic detail on the added loop makes it virtually certain that it cannot be a late work of the eighth or ninth century. The heart-shaped motif in piece-work filigree does not occur on the known metalwork of these later periods in which wire filigree, when employed as pattern and not merely as bordering, is used often with the aid of granulation, to represent scroll-work or foliate themes.[17]

The four arms of the cross rest against the central cylindrical collar. They consist of a built-up arched structure of thin gold strips, beaded wire, solid toothing and hollow pipe-like mouldings. The tops of the arms bear straight-lined cloisonné work in 'trays', each tray carrying twelve garnets. Four more were contained in the individual external semicircular cells in the angles between the arms. Six garnets in all are now missing (two from the two lower external angle-cells, three from the lower arm where the break is and one at the end of the broken arm). Kendrick described the garnets in St Cuthbert's cross as thick and the cells containing them as deep.[18] He claims that the cross in these respects, as in others, is an established fifth-century style which 'differs markedly from the shallow cloisonné of the sixth century and later'. The cells in the arms of the cross are not deep and indeed in this respect 'differ markedly' from those few unusual cloisonné jewels from Kent which do not fit into the main series and are normally attributed to the fifth century. For example, the peculiar jewel from Milton-next-Sittingbourne in the British Museum (Plates 97b,c,d). The one undamaged empty cell in the arms of the cross is approximately 1·25 mm deep, or at most 1·5mm. This cell-depth corresponds with that of normal seventh-century Anglo-Saxon cloisonné work, for example the Ixworth cross in the Ashmolean Museum (Plate 5a),[19] the Wilton cross in the British Museum (Plate 96d,e) (a product of the workshops that produced the Sutton Hoo jewels),[20] the cloisonné tray, with T-shaped cells, from the tongue-plate of a buckle found in the barrow at Broomfield, Essex,[21] and some of the Sutton Hoo pieces, such as the rectangular strap-mounts and the purse-lid. The overall thickness of the Wilton cross is 2 mm (less than $\frac{1}{10}$ inch), and the depth of the cells approximately 1·75 mm. The pendant from Forsbrook, Staffordshire,[22] is 2·5 mm thick, giving an internal cell-depth (allowing for the thickness of the base-plate) of 1·75 mm. The garnets themselves on the arms of St Cuthbert's cross are thin. Eight were accurately measured by Dr Claringbull and the thickness varied from under 0·5 mm to nearly 0·75 mm. A loose garnet in the Forsbrook pendant, measured by eye, is 1 mm thick. In these respects, as in the nature of its central setting, St Cuthbert's cross agrees with leading examples of seventh-century 'Style A' jewellery.

There is no gold foil beneath the garnets which, according to the laboratory examination appear to rest on some light-coloured paste. It is probably for this reason (the absence of the reflecting foil-backing), and also because the individual cells are so small (the biggest are not more than 4 mm × 1·25 mm and 2·5 × 2·5 mm) that the sides of the cross and the partitioning vanes keep out the light, that the garnets on St Cuthbert's cross appear so dark a red, having an almost blackish look in certain lights. Of the eighteen garnets positively identifiable two are of the almandine type and fifteen or sixteen of pyrope type. This distinction does not appear to have any archaeological significance. One, and perhaps two, of the inserts are not garnets but red glass, presumably replacements for the lost or damaged stones. The large flat almandine garnet at the centre of the cross is thicker than the other stones and differs from them in containing very many inclusions.

The general richness of the structure is remarkable. Thus the arms in section

(Plate 95d,e and Fig 48b) show at the top the cloisonné band (the drawing shows the placing of the garnet, which is cross-hatched but not its actual thickness and the metal base of the cell is not indicated). Below this is a shoulder ornamented with beaded wire and a close toothing of a solid architectural kind, then after a short vertical drop a beaded wire resting on a curved moulding that is interrupted by ornamental points in the form of dummy cylindrical rivet-sheaths with dummy rivet-heads. Finally, a step, made of the upturned end of the vertical side-piece, at the bottom of which runs a marginal beaded wire that rests on the edge of the base-plate (Fig 48b–c).

The cross had been badly damaged before it was found in 1827. In the first place, the original means of suspension had been broken off with some violence, for beneath the present loop the end of the cross is bruised and torn and one can see the gap left by the central dummy rivet, which came away when the first ring was pulled off. There are also obvious traces of the solder whereby this original ring had been fastened to the cross.

With regard to the gold used for the secondary suspension-loop and for the cross itself it may be noted that the unworn parts of the cross, for example the bottom of the undamaged empty cell and some of the less-exposed side surfaces show a reddish tone similar to that seen on the loop. Under magnification it appears (for example at the two front bottom corners of the loop) that where the loop and the adjacent cross are identically worn and burnished, the metal is of identical colour. The beaded filigree also, where it can be seen unworn (that is in the depression at the back of the loop), appears identical with that on the body of the cross. There is little if any discrepancy between the secondary loop and the cross, either in metal or in quality of filigree.[23] There need be no great difference in date between the two and there is no reason why the cross and its secondary suspension-loop cannot be products of the same workshop. The secondary loop has been attached to the cross at the front by cutting a horizontal slot at the end of the arm under the cloisonné tray and inserting into this a tongue-projection of the loop, the loop being then folded over and riveted down at the back of the cross.[24] In addition to this somewhat crude replacement of the original suspension-loop, the cross had been broken on two occasions, both before the burial of St Cuthbert. At the time of the first break the lower vertical arm was wrenched off, a misfortune that also caused damage to the lower shoulder-cloisons, one of which was torn away and lost. This break was repaired in antiquity. First of all the missing shoulder-cloison was replaced by a new cloison,[25] and then a small metal plate attaching the loose arm to the main body of the cross was fastened by four rivets (represented by the holes *a*, *c*, *d*, *f*, on Fig 50) to the back of the cross, externally. It is not known what kind of metal was used for this repair but it is obvious that in appearance (Fig 50b) it would look exactly like the repair

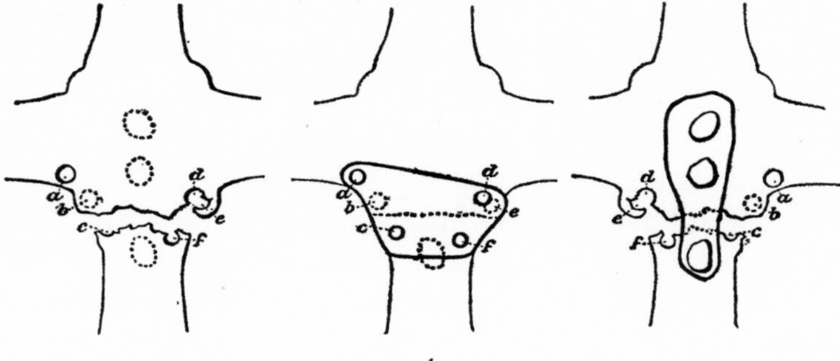

Figure 50 a, Back of St Cuthbert's Cross (seen from below), and *b* and *c*, the two repairs (*c*, seen from above) (Scale 1 : 1)

still to be seen on the back of the Ixworth cross.[26] St Cuthbert's cross was broken once again, and again roughly, because the external repairing plate was wrenched off in such a way that fragments of the base-plate were carried away with it and three of the rivet-holes were torn across. Then followed a second repair, which was effected this time by means of an internal silver plate (Plate 95c and Fig 50c) that was secured by two rivets to the upper (interior) surface of the base-plate (Fig 50c) and in order to do this the central jewel must have been removed and replaced. This internal silver plate, which was thus fastened to the main body of the cross, had a long tongue-like projection and the broken arm was then rammed home on to this tongue, so that it fitted tightly. Repaired for the second time and provided with its new loop, the cross passed into the grave of St Cuthbert.

When the cross was found in 1827, it was broken for the third time, because the interior silver repairing strip had corroded and fallen into two pieces (Plate 95c), doubtless a result of the close contact between the cross and the body during putrefaction.

Further repairs were carried out after the discovery. A narrow binding strip of gold was pinned round the broken end of the arm and plugged with a small piece of modern brass (Plate 94a,b) and the strengthened arm was placed in position against the main body of the cross and fixed to it with wax and glue.[27] The central setting and its shell bed were also repaired with modern adhesives. When the cross came to the British Museum in 1936, the binding-strip and all traces of the modern repair were removed and the jewel was restored to its condition after the second ancient repair. This was done by mending the internal repairing plate. The exact original length of this was easily determined and the missing portion made up with a piece of modern silver 0·4 cm long. The present repairing plate thus preserves the form of the old repair but now consists partly of ancient and partly of modern silver.

THE DATE AND ORIGIN OF THE CROSS

As Kendrick has said,[28] it is not easy to date St Cuthbert's cross. The reason for this (i.e. for its differences from other early Saxon jewels) is a simple one, as I suggest later. At least there can be little doubt that the cross belonged to St Cuthbert, was buried with his body in A.D. 687 and was made some time before that date. There is a possibility that the cross might have been put round the saint's neck eleven years after the burial, on the occasion of the first Translation in 698. The eye-witness account of this event in Bede's *Prose Life* (chapter xlii) is wholly credible and may be thought to dispose effectively of this possibility. The monks, who found the body incorrupt, were 'struck with fear and trembling so that they hardly dared to say anything'. They 'took away the outer garments, but did not dare to touch what was next to the skin'. As we have seen, the cross was eventually found 'deeply buried among the remains of the robes which were nearest to the breast of the Saint' and was so effectively concealed as to escape notice in all the vicissitudes that befell the body until 1827. Since the account of the 698 Translation makes no reference to the cross and specifically states that the innermost vestments were not touched, we may assume that the cross was already at that time in its position on St Cuthbert's breast. The questions we have to consider then are: how long before 687 was it made and where?

As Kendrick showed, the cross had been broken twice (in the same place) and twice repaired, before burial. The original suspension-loop and one if not two of the garnets had been replaced. These facts certainly show that the cross was not new in 687 but they do not give a clear indication of its age at that time. A violent accident, such as the breaking of an arm, might have befallen the cross at any moment after its manufacture. Nor need it have been long before the cross was broken a second time at the mend. There seems no justification, on the strength of the repairs alone, for insisting on a date for the manufacture of the cross before *c.* A.D. 650, which would give it some thirty-seven years of life when buried. It may have been made earlier but, again, it might have been made later.

St Cuthbert's cross is of the same general size and character as the well-known Wilton and Ixworth gold cloisonné pectoral crosses (Plates 5a, 96d)[29] already mentioned. Both these crosses, contrary to Kendrick's view as expressed in 1937 and 1938, can now be accepted as of seventh-century date and English manufacture.[30] The plain gold pendant cross, with central cabochon garnet from the Desborough necklace (Plate 6) and other pieces,[31] show a general fashion for pendant crosses in the early days of the Anglo-Saxon church (Plate 5b also). Baldwin Brown,[32] Åberg[33] and E. T. Leeds[34] have taken the view that St Cuthbert's cross was to be grouped with these others as an expression of seventh-century Anglo-Saxon

Christianity. Kendrick, as we have noted, came to a quite different conclusion, namely that the cross when buried in 687 was already an antique dating from the fifth century and not Anglo-Saxon at all: 'That which is certain', he writes, 'is that it is not, as has hitherto been supposed, a seventh-century piece' and he suggests that 'it is the solitary example remaining to us of the goldsmith's work of the Britons in fifth-century Strathclyde' and 'a work of the early British Church'.

Kendrick was able to take this unorthodox view of St Cuthbert's cross because, as he pointed out, it is in many respects 'not in the least like' any of the surviving English metalwork of the six and seventh centuries. It is in many respects a piece apart.

Something of its different character may be realized by comparing it with the Ixworth and Wilton crosses (Plates 5, 96). These are both flat, broad and thin. Both have enlarged central areas and short, widely expanding arms. The eye is caught by the expanses of glittering red and the complex patterns of the cloisonné work. St Cuthbert's cross, on the other hand, is thick (Plate 95e), with narrow arms. The central area is emphasized in depth, being elevated above the general plane of the arms but not enlarged and it does not interrupt the four almost continuous curves described by the arms. The thin lines of small rectangular stones, often described as 'arid', almost punched in two by the concavity of the arms, do little more than pick out the shape of the cross. The eye is held by the *structure*, which is built up in a series of superimposed steps, receding inwards, the central boss rising from the level of the cloisonné to a height greater again than the thickness of the arms (Plate 95e). Each receding step carries its embellishment. First, from the base-plate upwards, a beaded wire runs round the outline of the whole cross. Then there is a plain shelf, interrupted at regular intervals by the small pellets that form the heads of the dummy rivets, another beaded wire, then the continuous row of small dog-tooth mouldings. There is a final beaded wire, then the cloisonné level and above this again, receding inwards in concentric circles, a cog-wheel-like ring of dog-teeth and successive inner rings culminating in the flat central stone. When the cross is seen from the front each registers. It is in the variety, accumulation and shimmering effect of all these architectural embellishments that the vitality and interest of the jewel lies. Cloisonné plays a subsidiary role. The ornamental conception of St Cuthbert's cross runs in a unique way, right against the trend of the jewellery of the mid-seventh century, which is towards broad surface spreads of cloisonné. This is a tendency which the two other pendant crosses exemplify, of which the Sutton Hoo jewellery provides the classic examples and which as a fragment from Yorkshire shows[35] and the 'cloisonné' folio of the *Book of Durrow* implies,[36] also penetrated the north. In St Cuthbert's cross the media, gold and garnets, are the same as in contemporary south English jewels. The style is entirely different.

Certain of its technical features are not found on other jewels of the period. These are the solid dog-tooth mouldings, the tiny dummy rivets which are empty, fully tubular shafts external to the body of the cross surmounted by fully spherical pellets and the absence of gold foil under the garnets.

The absence of gold foil is remarkable. There are hardly any pieces of insular cloisonné work of any kind without it. One such extremely rare piece is the silver-gilt strap-end of peculiar form from Faversham illustrated in Plate 98a. In this too the garnets are about 1 mm thick, rest on a yellowish paste and are in plain rectangular cells in a narrow alignment. The Ixworth cross, though it is difficult to see through the stones, has foil backings with a distinct pointillé pattern (Plate 5a).[37] Small though the cells on the arms of St Cuthbert's cross are, they are quite big enough for gold foil. Much smaller cells on the Sutton Hoo jewellery employ it. This absence of foil is not a characteristic of fifth-century date, at any rate for gold cloisonné work, for foil was regularly used in Childeric's treasure, which was buried in A.D. 481. It is also present, for example, in a bronze buckle, with kidney-shaped plate and quatrefoil cells and dot-and-circle ornament, also from Faversham (Plate 98a) which I regard as a fifth-century piece probably of continental origin. Nor is there anything to be said in favour of connecting St Cuthbert's cross with the early British Church. There is not a shred of evidence that the Britons ever made a single piece of cloisonné jewellery, let alone practised the craft with the art and mastery which the cross displays. It is much too sophisticated a piece for the rustic milieu of fifth-century Strathclyde. We know in fact how native British art developed in early post-Roman times, first in a fine if brief Gallo-Roman tradition[38] and later in the champlevé enamelling and curvilinear styles of the hanging bowls, into St Cuthbert's own day and beyond.

In spite of the aberrant features of St Cuthbert's cross referred to above, its generally close relationship with the Anglo-Saxon goldsmith's work of the later sixth and seventh centuries cannot be denied. We have seen that the cells are in fact shallow and the garnets thin and raised on a bedding of some kind of paste and that these features are normal for Anglo-Saxon seventh-century jewellery, though not confined to that period. In the same way, the lines of simple rectangular cells, while occurring in the fifth century as Childeric's treasure shows, are even more characteristic of the seventh. The Wilton and Ixworth crosses themselves illustrate this and such lines of plain rectangular cells are to be seen in the Sutton Hoo jewellery, for instance in the crests of the boars at either end of the hinged shoulder-clasps and on the purse. The trend to sequences of plain rectangular cells is in fact highly characteristic of the decline of cloisonné work, as is illustrated in the book-covers and reliquary shrines of the eighth century.

The hollow structure, thick section, beaded peripheral wire and dome-like central setting (Plates 95 and Fig 48) of St Cuthbert's cross are features strongly reminiscent of the Kentish composite cloisonné brooches. The central boss alone, with its base of shell and collared flat stone in a beaded border, immediately gives the cross an insular character and connects it with the Kentish disc and composite brooches. The central setting itself is closely similar to those of the brooches from Faversham and Sarre (Plates 96c and 98b) and from Milton-near-Abingdon illustrated by Jessup.[39] One may possibly go further. A peculiar feature of St Cuthbert's cross which does not make sense is that the shell plays a negligible part in the decorative scheme. As we have seen, it is a rare substance, probably imported from the Indian Ocean and identical with that used in Class A Kentish circular brooches. In these it is used in broad rings or expanses as a dominant element in the decoration, strongly contrasting with the red of the jewels. Yet if St Cuthbert's cross is studied in Plate 94a–b, which shows the rabbeted retaining lip or collar complete, before the removal of the nineteenth-century repairs, it is apparent that when the cross was intact the shell was virtually invisible. It played no part in the decorative scheme. Why employ this rare shell, if it is not made to show? Underneath the gold cell that holds the central garnet the edges of the piece of shell are seen to be cut away (Fig 48a) and roughly trimmed. It seems quite possible that this central portion of St Cuthbert's cross, its thick garnet differing notably from those in the arms and looking as if it does not belong, is nothing but the centre of a Kentish disc-brooch like the Faversham one just cited, with a flat stone in a setting mounted on a thick broad flat disc of shell, cut down to fit a new setting on the cross.[40] If so, either St Cuthbert's cross must date after the development of this type of Kentish brooch, which is in turn intimately connected, by virtue of its cloisonné patterns with the Kingston brooch, or else this central setting replaces an earlier one, perhaps damaged at the time of the breaking of the lower arm of the cross, the repair of which, as we have seen, did involve removal of the central setting. There is no direct evidence for such replacement but the case for a connection between the cross and the Faversham discs is reinforced by the secondary suspension-loop, since this employs a distinctive heart-shaped filigree identical with that used on the self-same brooches (Fig 49 and Plate 98b) on which the central setting of the cross is exactly matched.[41]

The solid dog-tooth mouldings so conspicuous on the cross are unparalleled. It is worth noting that the dog-tooth device too, as a decorative theme, has parallels in south English jewellery. An illustration is provided by the Sarre brooch (Plate 96c). Here the dog-tooth surrounds the central setting in a manner rather similar to that seen in the cross, though the teeth, of gold foil, point inwards in a more functional manner, gripping the central stone. Other examples of the dog-tooth theme also in foil, sometimes thick foil rather than solid mouldings, are the buckle from Tostock in Suffolk[42] (Plate 96a), a small pendant from Barrow A, Chartham Downs, Kent,[43] and a gold pendant disc from Aclam in the East Riding of Yorkshire, in the British Museum (71, 12–7, i). A similar cog-wheel theme, used decoratively about a central setting and also in a border, appears in stamped ornament on a gold disc pendant from Faversham.[44] Collectively these examples may be said to provide a seventh-century background in south English jewellery for a theme expressed on the cross in a more solid form.

There remain the 'dummy rivets'. External collared rivets of a functional kind are not uncommon. They occur, for example, on the Swedish gold cloisonné sword pommels, on the Sutton Hoo sword pommel and on Kentish pommels, like that in the British Museum from Crundale Down. In the Milton-next-Sittingbourne jewel (Plate 97b,c,d) to which Kendrick refers, the projecting rivets like those contained within the profile are in fact functional, as our illustration shows, and not merely ornamental. The neat little dummy rivets used all round the edge on St Cuthbert's cross are a different matter. I can find no parallel except that which Kendrick himself adduced, a Roman ring in the British Museum, found at the Roman Wall base at Corbridge in a hoard of fourth-century coins (Plate 97a). The dummy rivets on the Corbridge ring do not exactly match those on St Cuthbert's cross, for they are not detached tubes but re-entrants or bulges in the wall of the circular bezel. Nevertheless the parallel is striking, the 'heads' of the 'rivets' on the Corbridge ring being, as on the cross, fully spherical pellets and this 'preservation of the Roman vestigial rivet' was one of Kendrick's stronger arguments for the fifth-century date of St Cuthbert's cross. Underlying this is a fallacy which, I believe, underlies the case for British origins and early date of our cloisonné jewellery as a whole, namely that Roman ideas occurring in post-Roman art must imply early date. It is becoming increasingly clear that borrowings from Roman art occur late. The designs of some of the silver coins (*sceattas*) of the late seventh and early eighth century are based on early Roman coin-types. Millefiori glass characteristic of the earlier Roman period suddenly appears at Sutton Hoo in seventh-century Saxon jewellery. Saxon kings, like Raedwald of East Anglia and Edwin of Northumbria, adopted standards in the Roman manner,[45] or inserted Caesar into their barbarian genealogies after Woden,[46] not in the confused hand-to-mouth era of invasion and settlement but in the full seventh century, when kingdoms had emerged, trade was revived and the authority and prosperity of a Bretwalda required outward expression. Roman monuments still stood or lay all over Britain and the discovery of Roman hoards must have been a common occurrence. The ideas they contained were taken up when patronage and wealth produced and encouraged enterprising and imaginative craftsmen. The importance of the dummy rivets on the Corbridge ring (Plate 97a) seem not so much chronological but, as suggested below, geographical, as giving perhaps a local slant to the workshop that produced the cross.

There is a simple and straightforward explanation of the unusual features of St Cuthbert's cross. Why should it follow at all closely jewels made in the extreme south? Worn and buried at Lindisfarne, it is the most northerly piece of jewellery of its kind known. No one suggests that it was made in Kent or Suffolk and brought north, nor can it be matched abroad. Can we not then take the natural view that it is the product of a northern Saxon workshop, perhaps working for Northumbrian court circles? The great difficulty is that, if so, the cross is its solitary surviving product. Grave goods of the pagan Saxon era are notoriously scarce in the far north and it would also be reasonable to think that the goldsmith's craft only developed in this area with the growth of Northumbrian political power and in courtly circles. This is within the phase and the sphere of Christian culture, so that it would hardly be expected to show amongst the few finds from pagan period graves in that part of Northumbria. Certainly besides the stream of Mediterranean objects – illuminated books, silver ware, ivory and textiles – flowing into Northumbria from the new horizons of the Christian church, notable antiquities from the South of England characteristic of the pagan cemeteries, like the Castle Eden claw-beaker (now in the British Museum), found their way as far north as the modern County Durham and beyond. If the centre of St Cuthbert's cross was indeed, as we have considered possible, once part of a Kentish disc-brooch (Plate 96b,c) this would be another instance. There is also indirect evidence already alluded to, inferred from political circumstances and the remarkable connection between the 'cloisonné page' (folio i *b*) of the *Book of Durrow* and the Sutton Hoo clasps, of the existence of an important late school of cloisonné goldsmith's work in Northumbria at this time.[47] We can hardly imagine that the beginnings of the Northumbrian renaissance were without fine examples of gold cloisonné craftsmanship. I suggest that St Cuthbert's cross is an expression, not merely of the seventh-century Anglo-Saxon but of the seventh-century Northumbrian church.

The most important thing about St Cuthbert's cross seems to me to be its shape. The long bar-like outstretched arms with gently expanded ends and the unweighted centre, give it a reaching crucifix-like character, a taut quality, absent from the equal-armed crosses of the south-east, even those of rather similar 'Celtic' type. It was Kendrick who pointed out that this form of cross, with narrow straight arms and slightly expanded ends, had roots in the traditions of the Celtic church in the north-west and it was this that led him to refer St Cuthbert's cross to Strathclyde. Similar crosses, with straight rather than curved arms, occur at an earlier period on the Kirkmadrine stone[48] (in Chi-Rho monogram form) and on some of the earlier Irish monuments at Clonmacnoise,[49] forms easily incised on stone or metal but less suited to an independent existence or to the embellishments of the goldsmith's craft. There is no such tradition in the south-east. The form of St Cuthbert's cross in which, as Baldwin Brown says,[50] 'the arc of the circle is used to give a common outline to two adjacent arms, instead of two opposite ones', is developed beyond the simple shapes of the Galloway stones and in its general type is more widespread in Saxon and Celtic areas alike.[51] St Cuthbert's cross retains a special thin, straight-armed look. The slight angularity between the arms, the pinched-in straight lines of cells and even the small lateral vane which separates the four cells at the expanding ends of the arms, accentuate their straightness and narrowness. This straight and narrow form seems to stem from the Celtic Christian tradition of the Galloway and Clonmacnoise stones. Its popularity in Northumbria in St Cuthbert's day (alongside the form with thin straight arms, expanded terminals and lightly developed centre, evolved from the same essentials and seen on the pillow-stones and on the silver case of St Cuthbert's portable altar) is shown by its frequent occurrence amongst the finds from the monastery at Whitby, founded by St Hild in A.D. 657.[52] In shape St Cuthbert's cross seems to belong to the Northumbrian milieu and also to fit a seventh-century date.

If we can suppose that this special shape was stipulated by a Northumbrian patron (because traditionally favoured in the early Church of the Ninianic and Scottic West), a very natural supposition, then the unusual features of St Cuthbert's cross are largely explained. The thinness of the required shape dictates solid construction and the cross is designed in depth. The narrowness of the field for decoration on the arms leads to a concentration of ornamental attention on the mouldings, accenting the architectural qualities. Flat foil triangles became solid teeth. The cloisonné is arid of necessity, though brilliantly effective in its function of picking out the wanted shape. The narrow field for the cells, the reduced role of the cloisonné and perhaps the independence of a northern workshop, may explain the absence of the habitual foil backings. The form of the cross, then, seems to go far towards accounting for its other special characteristics. Since the only parallel to the dummy rivets is found in a Romano-British gold ring from the same area, we may reasonably suggest that the Northumbrian goldsmith was not slow to turn to his purpose an idea seen in some example that had fallen into his hands of the work of one of his Romano-British predecessors who worked in the same locality.

We have put forward, for the first time, the not very startling view that St Cuthbert's cross, different in shape, style of ornament and some technical details from its counterparts in the south and worn by a Northumbrian bishop in a Celtic monastery, was a local product, made in a Northumbrian workshop. It was of some age when buried but the damage it sustained can have occurred within a generation. If we accept the 'overwhelming probability' that the cross was buried with the saint in 687, which purely archaeological considerations entirely support, and if we consider on the one hand the probable dating advocated here of its southern counterparts (Wilton and Ixworth) in the second quarter of the seventh century and on the other that of the founding of Lindisfarne (635), the milieu of Celtic Christian patronage in which the cross appears, a date for the manufacture between A.D. 640 and 670 seems secure. St Cuthbert's cross, Celtic in fundamental form, southern in fashion and in the goldsmith's craft-traditions it exemplifies, yet with a strong local complexion, seems to be like St Cuthbert himself and the famous monastery he adorned, essentially Hiberno-Saxon.

APPENDIX

The pectoral cross received treatment in the British Museum Research Laboratory in 1936, when some of the stones were fixed with lacquer. Special attention was paid on this occasion to the central stone which, although complete, was badly cracked.

Fragments only had survived of the original white material that once surrounded the central stone and in order that these fragments should not be lost they were set in a pillar of dental plaster fixed in the hollow centre of the cross between the back plate and the central stone.

When the opportunity was presented of making a detailed study of the materials it was decided at the same time to replace the plaster support by one of perspex in order to expose to view the inner cavity which was of significance in suggesting that the cross might at one time have been a reliquary.

The white material was made the subject of special study by Dr G. F. Claringbull (Keeper of Mineralogy) who reports as follows:

> The originally white material, now stained, is exactly comparable with the white decoration of type 'A' Kentish brooches, and particularly well seen on the Kingston Brooch. I am now convinced that this white substance showing structure is shell. I think it most unlikely that pieces as large as those in the Kingston Brooch can be derived from any species normally found in temperate or Mediterranean waters.

The stones were examined individually by Mr R. M. Organ of the British Museum Research Laboratory who presents the following report:

EXAMINATION OF THE GEM-STONES IN THE CUTHBERT CROSS
(by R. M. Organ)

There is evidence to show that this cross originally contained fifty-three stones, all but the centre one being recessed in gold cells. All the stones remaining were examined by means of a Vickers projection microscope in both ordinary and plane-polarized light by vertically incident illumination with the object of determining whether they were gem-stones or glass. In addition it was determined whether the refractive index of the stone was above or below 1·66, this figure being the generally accepted upper limit for ancient glasses and well below the 1·74 to 1·89 found in the various minerals known as garnet. This determination was made by observing the Becke effect[53] at the edge of a droplet of liquid of R.I. 1.66 placed on the surface of the stone. Observation of the effect was often rendered uncertain because the surface of the gem-stone was weathered and because traces of lacquer were present even after cleaning. The thickness of eight of the stones was measured by focusing with an 8-mm. objective alternately on their upper and lower faces, measuring this apparent depth and calculating their real depth from the estimated R.I. of the stone. During this measurement the absorption spectrum of the stone was observed using a direct vision spectroscope with the object between crossed polars. Three types of spectra were observed: that of Almandine[54] showing one orange band and two bands in the green-blue; that of Pyrope —a broad band in the yellow and yellow-green; and a general absorption in the yellow, green, and blue characteristics of a red glass.

The result of the observations are tabulated below, the number of the stone indicating its position on the cross (Fig 51). The unnoted stones show no remarkable features.

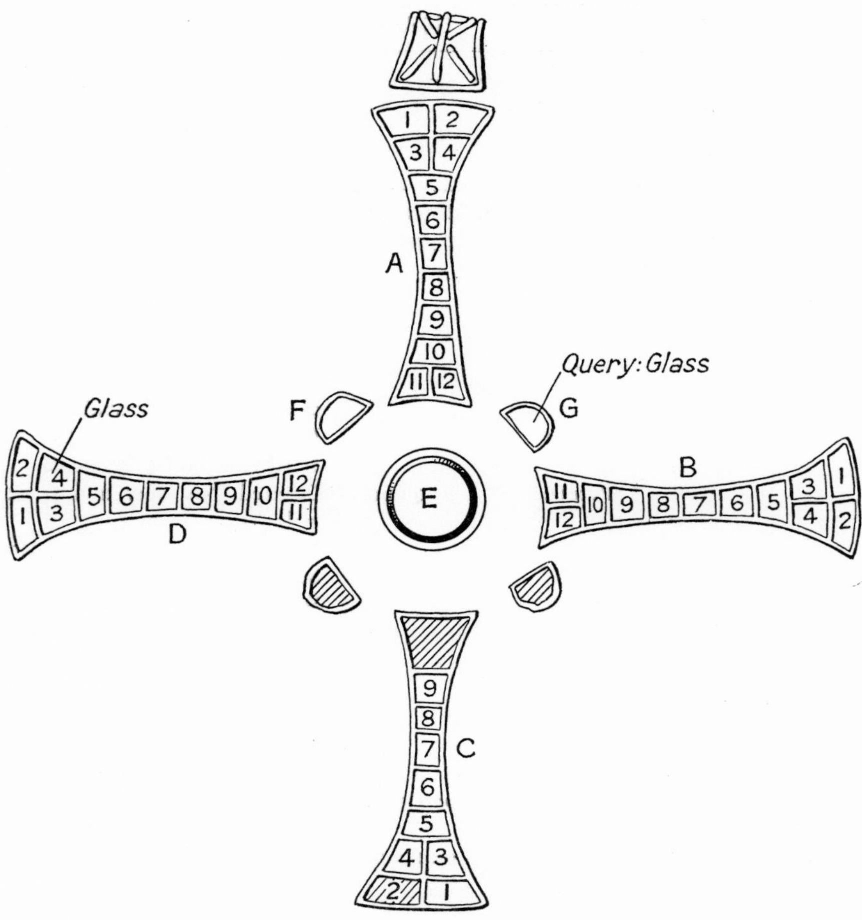

Figure 51 Arrangement and identification of gemstones in the pectoral cross (Scale nearly 2 : 1)

No.	R.I.	Spectrum	Thickness	Notes
		FOR REFERENCE		
Known Almandine	1·74	Almandine		A fractured face exhibits ladder-like breaks across a conchoidal fracture. See Pl. 98c.
		STONES FROM THE PECTORAL CROSS		
E	1·75	Almandine	1·7 mm.	Cracked completely across. Contains very many inclusions in the form of needles having three axes with an included angle of 60° and also in the form of faceted bubbles. See Pl. 98d. The inclusions are probably of rutile and in this form are characteristic of almandine.
A.1	1·66	Pyrope	0·65 mm.	Brownish-red ladder-like fracture. Cracks and surface scratches.
A.2	1·66	Pyrope	0·60 mm.	Cracked. Not very transparent. Surface inclusions.
A.3				Very rough surface. No scratches or bubbles.
A.4	1·66	Pyrope		Worn and scratched surface. One needle-like inclusion. Surface pits with 60° facets.
A.5	1·66			No scratches. A hole of 'water-worn' appearance.
A.6		Pyrope		Orange-brown colour. Ladder fracture.
A.7				Not examined; surface too rough.
A.8	1·66	Almandine	0·72 mm.	Not very translucent. Rough and uneven surface.
A.9	1·66	Pyrope	0·61 mm.	Deep red colour slightly different from other stones.
A.10	1·66			Very deep red.
A.11	1·66	Pyrope		Surface scratches and tool mark near mount.
A.12	1·66	Pyrope	0·64 mm.	Deep colour. Patches of anomalous double refraction.
B.1	1·66	Pyrope		Surface of weathered appearance.
B.2	1·66	Pyrope		Dull colour. Hair-like groove at corner.
B.3	1·66	Pyrope		A group of five parallel scratches curved in a short arc.
B.4	1·66	Pyrope		Scratches and ladder-like broken surface.
B.5	1·66			Grey colour but bright red anomalous double refraction near the mount. Surface of weathered appearance.
B.6	1·66			Greyish but translucent. Surface pits and irregular crevices.
B.7	1·66			Orange colour.
B.8	1·66			Laddered conchoidal fracture at one corner. Groove filled with organic and green debris.

B.9	1·66			Surface 'weathered', showing a few parallel lines.
B.10	1·66			'Weathered' surface with green debris in the pits.
B.11	1·66	Pyrope		An optically active needle-shaped red inclusion is present.
B.12	1·66			Very 'weathered' with surface crevices.
C.1		Pyrope	0·48 mm.	Badly cracked.
C.3		Pyrope	0·47 mm.	
C.8				Colour rather dark.
D.1				Shows strong anomalous double refraction.
D.4	1·66	Glass		Dark colour and not very transparent to polarized light. Contains obvious bubbles.
D.5				Rather dark in colour with a group of small white circles upon its surface. See D.6.
D.6				Has a group of white circular markings upon its surface, all of about the same size. Three were measured and had diameters of 2·2, 2·4, and 3·μ. They are possibly the remains of bubbles in lacquer.
D.8				Colour rather grey.
F		Pyrope		Is too near the central projecting boss for proper observation with the objectives available.
G		Like Pyrope		Observation very difficult but is of dull colour and has many dark patches. V-shaped piece out of flat side.

Conclusions: Of the forty-seven stones remaining in the cross, one (D.4) is undoubtedly of glass and one other (G) may also be of glass. There is no evidence as to whether the glass is original or is a reset. The other stones, except A.7, are garnets of the Pyrope or (E. and A.8) of the Almandine variety. The central stone, E, differs from the others in being thicker and of Almandine containing many inclusions. The stones do not rest on foil but on some light-coloured composition.

Acknowledgments for assistance in identification of the stones are made to members of the staff of the Mineralogy Department, British Museum (Natural History).

NOTES TO CHAPTER FOURTEEN

1 *Antiquaries Journal*, XVII, 1947, 283–93.

2 *Antiquaries Journal*, XXI, 1951, 197–200, and further work which in part supersedes this.

3 *Op. cit.*, 228.

4 See Rupert Bruce-Mitford, *Sutton Hoo – A Handbook*, London, 1972, and *The Sutton Hoo Ship-Burial*, Volume 2, Cambridge, 1974, in preparation. R. H. Hodgkin, *A History of the Anglo-Saxons*, 3rd edition, 1952, Appendix, The Sutton Hoo Ship-Burial.

5 Canon James Raine, *St. Cuthbert*, Durham, 1828, 211.

6 *Ibid.*, 217.

7 Even in the translation of 1104, only the ends of the stole had been exposed: cf. the evidence of Reginald of Durham (J. Raine, *op. cit.*, 88).

8 We cannot regard it as probable that the eleventh-century sacrist, Ælfred Westou, put the cross into the coffin. For this man see J. Raine, *op. cit.*, 88.

9 For the work carried out on the cross in the British Museum Research Laboratory in 1955, see Appendix, p. 295, the first part of which is by Dr H. J. Plenderleith.

10 Originally, Dr Claringbull informs me, it must have been a brilliant clean white and presumably because of its scarcity and high cost it must have been a more effective substance than the various types of white paste made up locally and used in the cheaper jewellery.

10a Dr Claringbull's report is included with Dr Plenderleith's account of the technical work on the cross (see footnote 9).

11 N. Åberg, *The Anglo-Saxons in England*, Uppsala, 1926, 102–6 and 207–8.

12 C. A. Ralegh Radford, in *Dark Age Britain: Essays presented to E. T. Leeds*, Methuen, 1955, ed. D. B. Harden.

13 For this classification see T. D. Kendrick, 'Polychrome Jewellery in Kent', *Antiquity*, VII, 1953, 429–52.

14 Cf. R. L. S. Bruce-Mitford in *Antiquaries Journal*, XXX, 1950, 78–99 (review of W. B. Emery, *Nubian Treasure*). The late horizon of luxury goods in Saxon graves is confirmed by their regular association with rich gold jewellery of 'Class A' type. The renewed flow of gold from the continent into Britain has been shown by Dr C. H. V. Sutherland to be a phenomenon of the later sixth and seventh centuries. (*Anglo-Saxon Gold Coinage in the Light of the Crondall Hoard*, Ashmolean Museum, 1948, *passim.*)

15 R. F. Jessup, *Anglo-Saxon Jewellery*, London, 1950, Pls. xxii and xxiii.

16 E. T. Leeds, *Early Anglo-Saxon Art and Archaeology*, Oxford, 1936, Pl. xxvii.

17 e.g. the Kirkoswald trefoil brooch, British Museum *Guide to Anglo-Saxon Antiquities*, 1923, 102, Fig. 122.

18 *Op. cit.*, 284 and 287–8. The reference he makes to the Spanish (Visigothic) buckle in the British Museum (our Pls. 97c,d) (also illustrated by H. Zeiss, *Grabfunde aus dem Spanischen Westgotenreich*, 1934, Pl. 7.3) is somewhat misleading. Its cells-large, thick-walled pits are 4 or 5 mm deep, as against just over 1 mm on St Cuthbert's cross. In construction and effect they are wholly unlike the shallow tray of flat cell-work in the tops of the arms of St Cuthbert's cross. The peripheral rivets with globular heads round the buckle-plate are not dummy rivets, as Kendrick says, but functional, attaching the base plate to the walls of the buckle.

19 I am indebted to Miss Joan Kirk, F.S.A., for particulars of this cross.

20 See Chapter I, pp. 28–32.

21 In the British Museum, *Victoria County History*, *Essex*, London, 1903, Vol. I.

22 In the British Museum, E. T. Leeds, *op. cit.*, Pl. xxx(a).

23 This is contrary to the opinions expressed by T. D. Kendrick, *op. cit.*, 285, 287, and R. F. Jessup, *op. cit.*, 123.

24 It was presumably necessary to remove one or two of the garnets in order to fix these rivets.

25 It seems to have been provided with a shank that passed through a hole punched for the purpose (*b* on Fig. 50) and was then hammered down. There was probably a corresponding hole (*e* on Fig. 49) that was made for the repairs to the damaged cloison on the other side.

26 T. D. Kendrick, *op. cit.*, Pl. LXXVII, D.

27 Dr Raine says that the arm was 'found broken off' and that 'upon examination it appeared to have been broken once before, as there were

evident proofs that it had been repaired by means of small rivets, some of which were remaining'. I take it to be quite clear from this that the binding-strip was not in position when the cross was found, as otherwise it would have been mentioned as the most obvious sign of the repair to which he alludes. Raine's engraving shows the cross unbroken. In the Conway Library there is another very old engraving that shows the strip in position. I have not been able to trace the work in which this appears but it is certainly not much later than Raine's engraving and suggests that the modern repair took place very soon after the discovery in 1827.

28 *Op. cit.*, 287; T. D. Kendrick, *Anglo-Saxon Art to A.D. 900*, London, 1938, 72–3.

29 See Chapter 1, pp. 28–32. For these crosses see also N. Åberg, *The Anglo-Saxons in England*, Uppsala, 1926, p. 136; T. D. Kendrick, 'St. Cuthbert's Pectoral Cross and the Wilton and Ixworth Crosses', *Antiquaries Journal*, XVII, 1947, 283–93.

30 Chapter One, p. 31; T. D. Kendrick, *op. cit.*, and *Anglo-Saxon Art*, 72–3, regarded the Wilton pendant as Merovingian work of the sixth century and the repaired Ixworth cross as an heirloom of comparable date.

31 Chapter 1, p. 31. N. Åberg, *op. cit.*, Figs. 261, 262.

32 G. Baldwin Brown, *The Arts in Early England*, London, V, 1921, p. 96.

33 *Loc. cit.*

34 E. T. Leeds, *Early Anglo-Saxon Art and Archaeology*, Oxford, 1936, 121.

35 From Uncleby in the East Riding; Leeds, *op. cit.*, Pl. XXVII, Grave 65.

36 Cf. R. H. Hodgkin, *A History of the Anglo-Saxons*, 3rd edition, London, 1952, 731–2.

37 Not as in *Antiquaries Journal*, XVII, 1947, 291.

38 E. T. Leeds, *op. cit.*, Chapter I and Pls. II and III.

39 *Op. cit.*, Pl. XXV. I.

40 If so, the presence of the shell would be more or less fortuitous but convenient, since it would have formed a ready-made base to which the garnet setting was already riveted and would also have served to fill out the small gap between the old retaining collar and smaller new setting. It must be admitted that such central cells on Kentish disc-brooches of Kendrick's Class A are so far as I know not riveted to the underlying shell but are usually supported on cylinders, fitted through a central hole in the shell disc and held at the back by a flange or by flat radiating metal strips. There is no reason why a particular craftsman might not have decided on some occasion to use a couple of rivets instead of what is often a cumbrous device.

41 Cf. also R. F. Jessup, *op. cit.*, Pls. XXII and XXIII.

42 Also E. T. Leeds, *op. cit.*, Pl. XXX, g.

43 *Ibid.*, Pl. XXIX, *a*.

44 *Ibid.*, Pl. XXX, *b*.

45 Chapter 1, 11.

46 Chapter 1, 58.

47 We know that silversmiths of originality were working at Lindisfarne at a slightly later date, since it has now become apparent that the silver shrine that contains St Cuthbert's portable altar may be as early as 698.

48 G. Baldwin Brown, *The Arts in Early England*, Vol. V, London, 1921, Pl. II; Romilly Allen, *Early Christian Monuments of Scotland*, Edinburgh, 1903, Vol. III (Plates), Fig. 532.

49 G. Baldwin Brown, *op. cit.*, Pl. IX, 1–3.

50 *Ibid.*, 95.

51 In the seventh to ninth centuries it occurs, for example, on the base of the Ormside bowl, G. Baldwin Brown, *op. cit.*, Vol. V, Pl. XXX, top; on Saxon silver *sceattas*, British Museum *Catalogue of English Coins*, Anglo-Saxon Series, Vol. I, Pl. IV, No. 2; Pl. III, Nos. 25, 9, 10 and 13; on standing stones in the Celtic west, V. E. Nash-Williams, *Early Christian Monuments of Wales*, Pl. XX, 302, 388, and on the wheel crosses, Pls. XLI and XLVIII, 233; and, in rather fatter form, on the Sutton Hoo scabbard-bosses. A good example is the disc-pendant of pale gold with filigree decoration from Wye Down, Kent, in the British Museum.

52 Sir C. Peers and C. A. Ralegh Radford, 'The Saxon Monastery at Whitby', *Archaeologia*, Vol. 89, 1943, Fig. 6 (Pl XX), p. 51, No. 16 (Pl. XXVII, No. 19) and (in a slightly stylized version) No. 14: and Pl. XXVI, *a* and *b* (each showing two crosses of this type superimposed), and *c*, No. 1 (the Kirkmadrine type on a hanging-bowl escutcheon).

53 Examination of the refractive index by use of the Becke effect does not enable an exact result to be obtained, and it is only possible to quote a range, depending on what standard

liquids are available. Hence in the table on pp. 298–9, in no case can the R.I. of the pyropes have been as low as 1·66, but presumably the results should read >1·66 (i.e. greater than 1·66)' (W. A. Oddy, British Museum Research Laboratory, in a letter to the writer, 19/2/71).

54 Three red forms of garnet are known, and of these almandine [$Fe_3Al_2(SiO_4)_3$] and pyrope [$Mg_3Al_2(SiO_4)_3$] are commonly found in jewellery. These formulae represent the 'pure' or ideal composition of the minerals, but in nature the minerals are often slightly mixed in composition, with one form predominating.

Both almandine and pyrope are widely distributed throughout the world and it is not normally possible to identify the source of the mineral from an identification of the type.

The two stones can be distinguished by examination of the absorption spectrum or by measurement of the refractive index. The R.I. of pyrope is the range 1·730 to 1·750 and that of almandine 1·750 to 1·811. The range 1·750 to 1·760 represents mixtures of the two forms. However, the measurement of refractive index is rather difficult for mounted stones. An identification can be made by observing the absorption spectrum or reflected plane polarized light with a direct vision spectroscope mounted on a Vickers projection microscope.

(W. A. Oddy, British Museum Research Laboratory, in a letter to the writer, 19/2/71.)

CHAPTER FIFTEEN

Late Saxon Disc-Brooches

INTRODUCTION

Since the discovery in 1925 of the Beeston Tor treasure,[1] late Saxon disc-brooches, usually of silver but also known in bronze, have grown as a class in number and importance. They are direct descendants, in an age of silver, of the gilt and gold circular brooches of the later pagan period and of the conversion. The Kentish circular brooches of the seventh century are themselves progenitors of a long series of less costly but no less pretentious circular ornaments which continued to be made (as the Sutton, Isle of Ely disc, Plates 107, 108a, shows) at least into the eleventh century.

After *c.* 675 gold was scarce, and is known in late Saxon metalwork only in a long but outstanding series of royal, episcopal or aristocratic finger-rings; in a few jewels, such as the Alfred and Minster Lovel jewels in the Ashmolean Museum[2] or the Hamilton and Dowgate Hill brooches in the British Museum,s and one or two twisted or wire armlets.[4] There was, however, throughout the period, a plentiful silver currency and a comparative profusion of silver treasures. The inclusion of gold, in the form of thick slabs of the pure metal, in a silver disc-brooch (Plate 105a,b), the Strickland brooch, as I propose to call it, and in the sword-pommel from Ingleton (Plate 109d) is a rare touch which confers on these pieces an extra richness and distinction.

Ornamental discs that are not brooches are common enough in the pagan period and examples from the fronts of wooden chests (the discs from Caenby, Lincs.,[5] and the small Sutton Hoo 1938 boat-grave[6]) or of unknown use (the Allington Hill and Hardingstone discs[7]) or in the form of supposed horse-trappings (the Faversham mounts,[8] Fig 52f) may be quoted. The Allington Hill, Hardingstone and Faversham discs are all seventh-century pieces and all show affinities with the late Saxon discs and illustrate stages in their formal development. Ultimately it is from a common type of Kentish circular brooch that most late Saxon discs (cf. Figs 53a,b, 56) are descended – that is, the type with a central and four peripheral

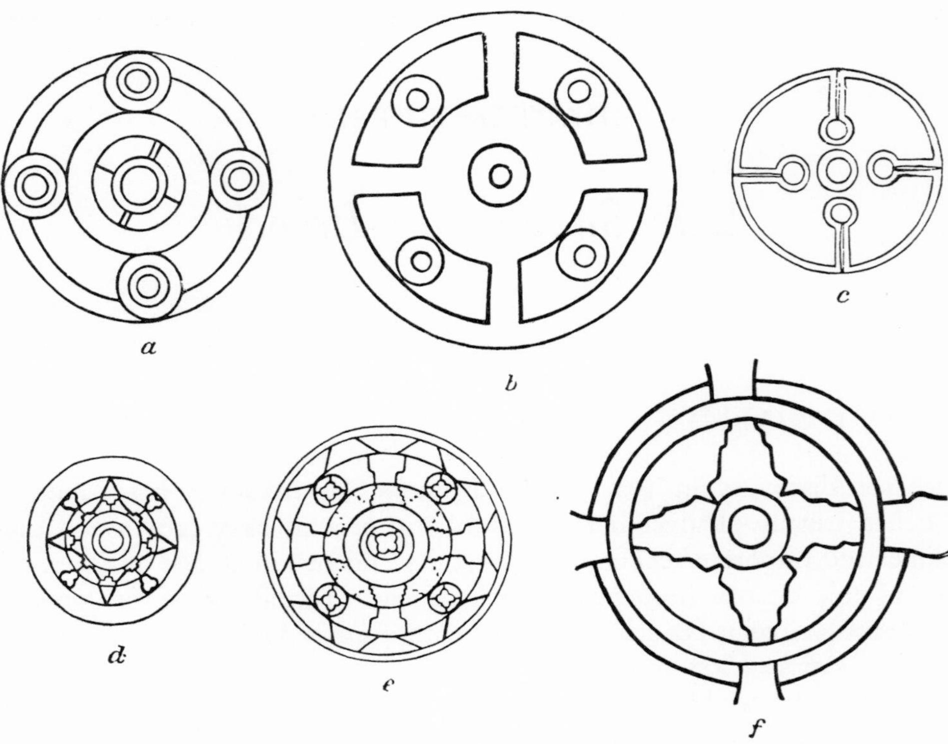

Figure 52 Basic designs of brooches and disc-ornaments of the pagan and early post-pagan periods: *a*, Sarre I, Kent; *b*, Milton near Abingdon, Berkshire; *c*, Fiskerton, near Lincoln; *d*, Faversham, Kent; *e*, Sarre II, Kent; *f*, Mount, Faversham, Kent. (Scales 1 : 2)

bosses in which is established a fundamentally quadripartite design. A late example of the basic type is the brooch known as Sarre I (Fig 52a).[9] The Kingston Brooch,[10] and another important piece which, so far as basic design is concerned, stands in close relationship with it, the upper plate of a 'composite' brooch with empty settings from Faversham, Kent,[11] and also the Milton, near Abingdon, honeycomb cell brooch (Fig 52b),[12] the Faversham honeycomb cell brooch[13] and others show a development of this simple quadripartite design with bosses. Straight elements run from the centre out between the peripheral bosses to the circumference, dividing the brooch into four segments. These straight elements, with four outlying bosses, though in a different grouping, can be seen in the late Saxon material in the late eighth- or early ninth-century bronze disc turned into pin-heads found at Fiskerton on the River Witham near Lincoln, now in the British Museum[14] (Fig 52c). The pagan-period circular brooch known as Sarre II[15] (Fig 52e), in which bosses are replaced in the design by circles each containing a quatrefoil, has this same basic design, of elements running out from the centre between the peripheral bosses (in this case, the circles with quatrefoils) to the circumference but, in addition, the central ornamental nucleus with its projections has been elaborated into a device not unlike that to be seen on the late Saxon Strickland and Fuller discs. The omission of four small elements in the pattern (dotted in Fig 52e) produces a design essentially the same as that of the Strickland brooch (Fig 56a,b). Indeed, the germ of the basic design of the Fuller and Strickland brooches can be seen in familiar disc-brooches like those from Faversham and Teynham (close to Faversham).[16] The Faversham 'horse-trappings' already referred to have no peripheral bosses but they have a developed central four-armed motive (Fig 52f) of the same sort as on the discs, a quadrangular field with hollow sides, leaving four residual segments. In Sarre I (Fig 52a) and the Faversham brooch with empty settings, the peripheral bosses, or rather the decorative roundels in which these are set, encroach upon the cloisonné borders; while in the Sarre II brooch (Fig 52e) something more specific may be seen of a tendency to break up the border into pendant triangles which incorporate the peripheral bosses, which we later encounter fully developed in the late Saxon Strickland Brooch (Fig 56a).

In the circular brooches and ornaments of the end of the pagan period can thus be seen not only a general source for the late Saxon discs but also specific trends in design which the discs exemplify in developed form.

No similar group of circular discs or disc-brooches exists on the continent. The circular brooches of the Merovingian period develop in Carolingian times on other lines,[17] and do not show the five bosses or nuclei, the quadripartite design or the distinctive development of the central nucleus as seen in the Fuller and Strickland brooches. Certainly these elements can be found on the Scandinavian box brooches[18] but these are a different category of object. The plain silver disc does not appear as a continental type. This type of disc-brooch is thus an Insular development, derived from exclusively Anglo-Saxon roots and discs of this type found on the continent can be regarded as exports from England, or copies of English models. For this reason, as well as for the details of its ornaments which he cited, Thorleif Sjøvold was certainly correct in regarding the bronze disc from Hillesøy, Lenvik, Norway (Plate 110b), as of English origin.[19]

This chapter describes important new members of the class, including the Fuller, Strickland, Sutton, Isle of Ely, and Canterbury brooches, and is intended to draw attention afresh to this group of documents in late Saxon metalwork, which now bulks larger and is more intelligible than when Reginald Smith first recognized it in 1925.[20] Because of its complex iconography and controversial nature, the Fuller brooch, the first to be described, is discussed at greater length than the others. Some of the comparative material, both English and continental, is also discussed.

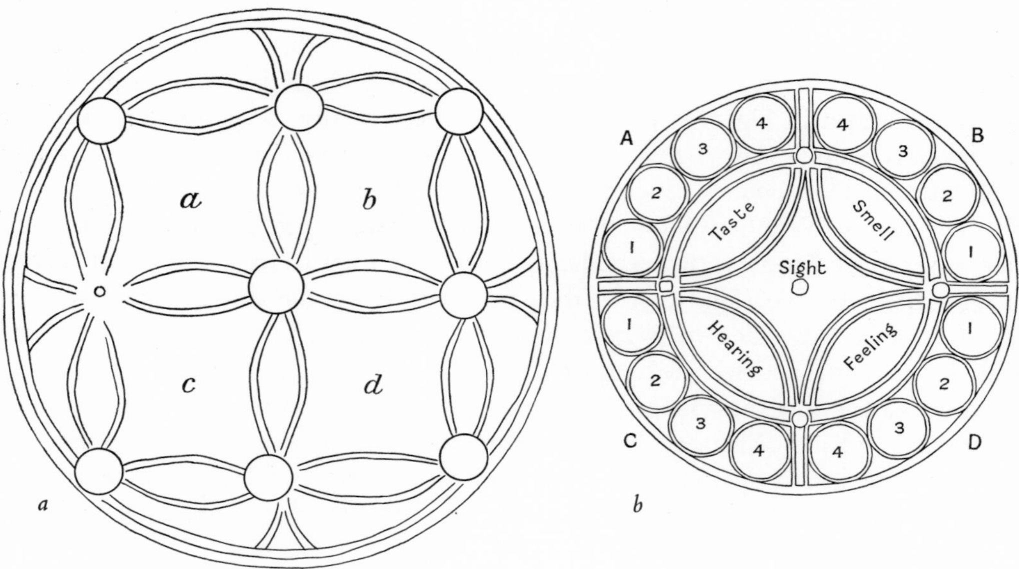

Figure 53 Basic design of *a*, the Sutton, Isle of Ely, and *b*, the Fuller brooches. (Scale, 1 : 2)

I: THE FULLER BROOCH

History

The Fuller brooch (Plate 99 and Figs 53b, 54, 55), a large silver disc inlaid with niello, first came to notice in 1910, when a photograph and short description of it were published by Sir Charles Robinson.[21] Sir Charles said that it came into his possession from a previous owner, who had purchased it from a London bric-à-brac dealer who apparently knew nothing about it and could not, or would not, give any account of its provenance. Nothing more can now be said of its origins. Some years later E. Hockligge, Sir Charles's son-in-law, visited the Ashmolean Museum and offered to deposit the brooch there on loan. E. T. Leeds sensed the genuineness of the piece and persuaded the then Keeper, D. G. Hogarth, to accept the loan. Later Reginald Smith, seeing the brooch exhibited in the Ashmolean, said that Sir Hercules Read (at that time Keeper of British and Mediaeval Antiquities at the British Museum and also President of the Society of Antiquaries) had pronounced it to be a fake and that it ought to be withdrawn. This was done after W. H. Young, the Ashmolean's technical specialist, had agreed with Reginald Smith. The brooch was wholly discredited and eventually purchased by Captain A. W. F. Fuller 'for the price of the metal'. It had received an occasional mention since then[22] but had never been taken seriously. When,

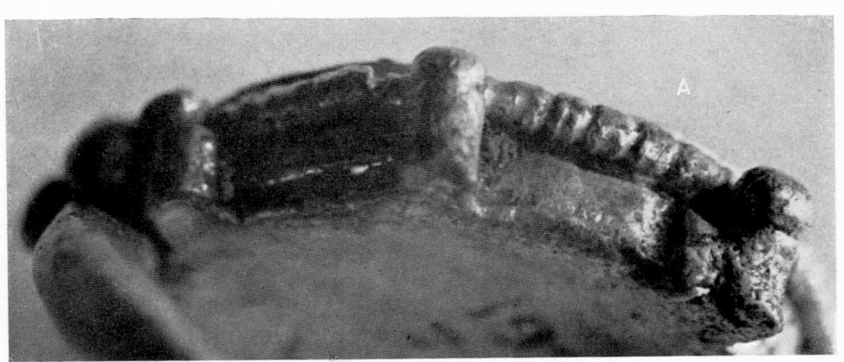

a

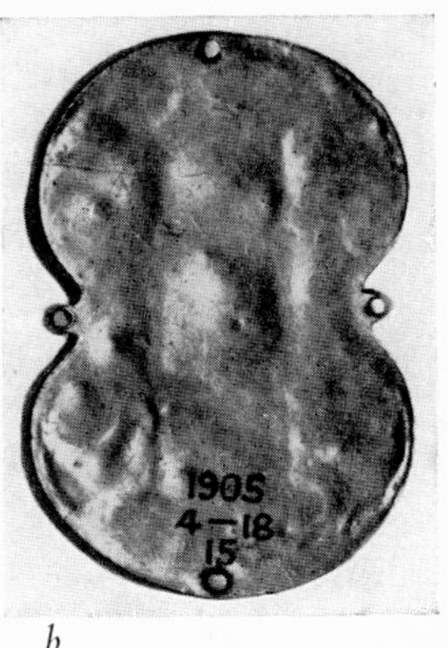

b

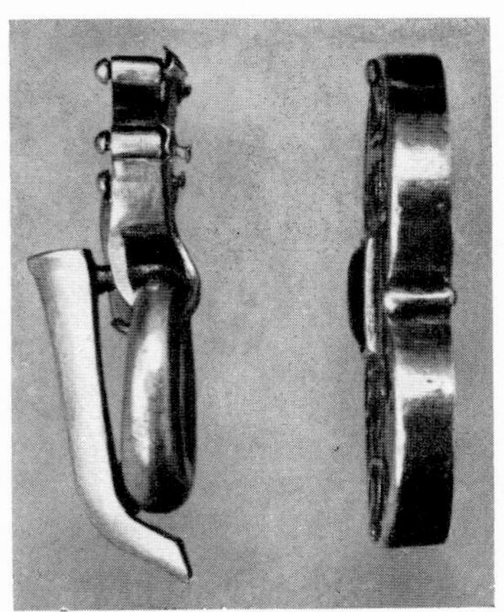

c

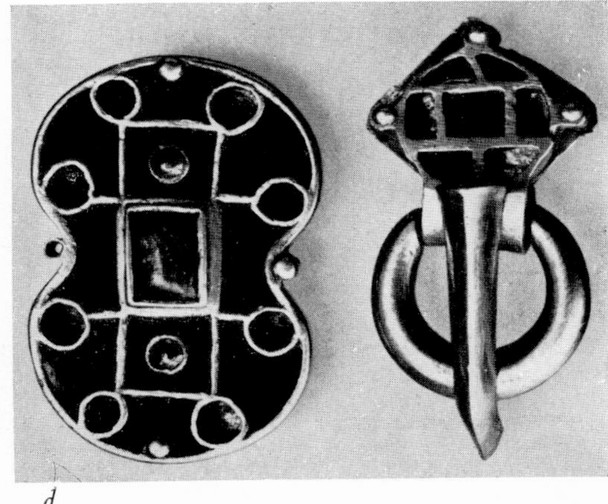

d

Plate 97 a, Detail of gold finger ring, Corbridge, Northumberland (enlarged); *b*, Ornament, Milton-next-Sittingbourne, Kent (back view) (Scale 1 : 1); *c*, Side views of Visigothic buckle, Spain, and ornament, Milton-next-Sittingbourne, Kent (Scale 1 : 1); *d*, Ornament, Milton-next-Sittingbourne, Kent and Visigothic buckle, Spain (front views) (Scale 1 : 1)

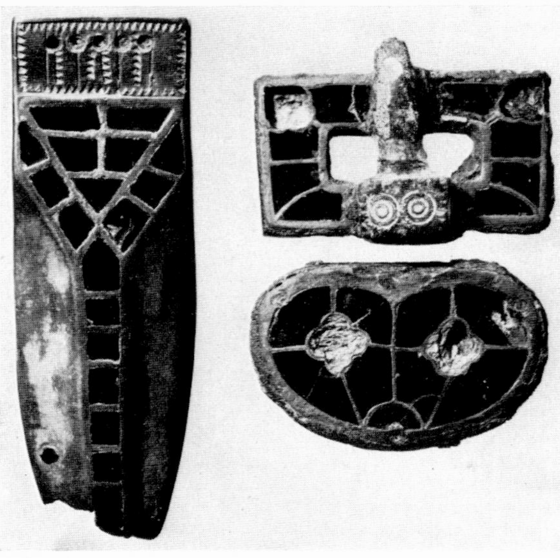

a

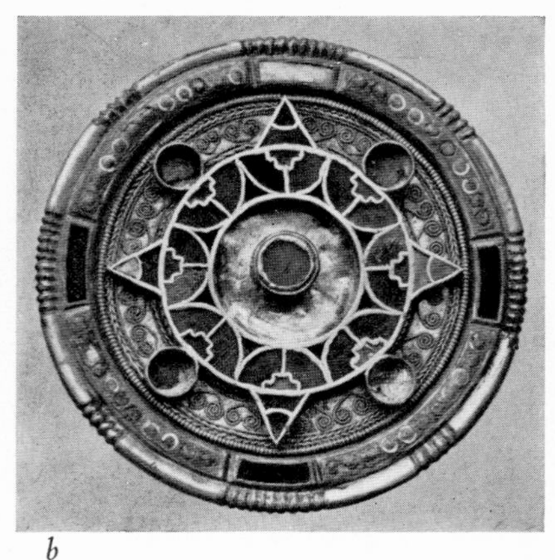

b

c

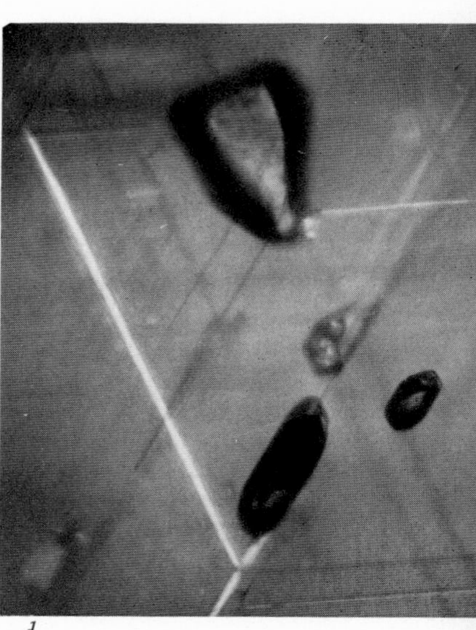

d

Plate 98 *a*, Strap-end and buckle, Faversham, Kent (Scale 1 : 1); *b*, Disc-brooch, Faversham, Kent (Scale 1 : 1); *c*, Surface fracture on Indian Almandine for comparison with the stones on St Cuthbert's cross. x200; *d*, Stone E, Fig. 51, needle-like and bubble-like inclusions (rutile) at four levels in the stone. Viewed between crossed polars by scattered vertical illumination (Scale × 188)

Plate 99 The Fuller Brooch (Scale approx. 8 : 7)

Plate 100 Saxon Sword hilts: *a,b*, Abingdon, Berkshire (Ashmolean Museum; *c*, Hoven, Norway (Oslo Museum (Scale 1 : 1)

a

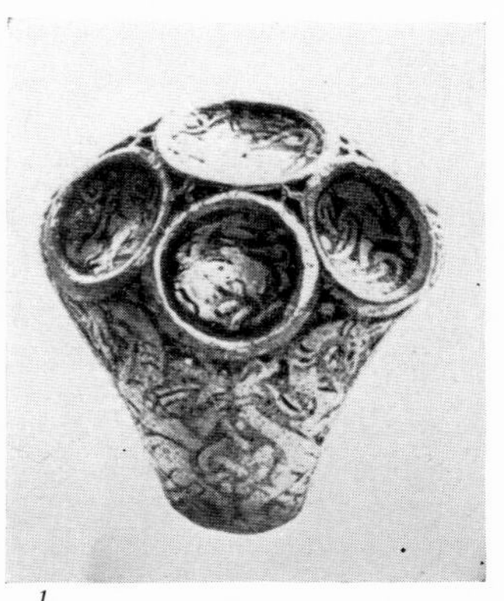

b

c

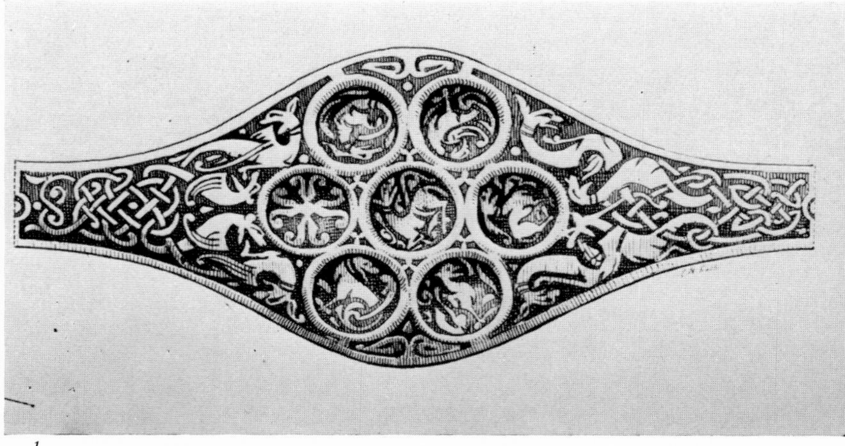

d

Plate 101 Gold nielloed finger-rings: *a*, Malton, Yorks; *b–d*, R. Reno, Bologna (Scales *a*, enlarged, *b* 1 : 1)

a

c

102

Plate 102 Anglo-Saxon sword pommels with nielloed silver mounts: *a*,*b*, Dolven, Norway *c*,*d*, Gronneberg, Norway; (Slightly enlarged)

b

d

Plate 103 St Matthew Portrait and Symbol from the Book of Cerne, *c.* 820 A.D.

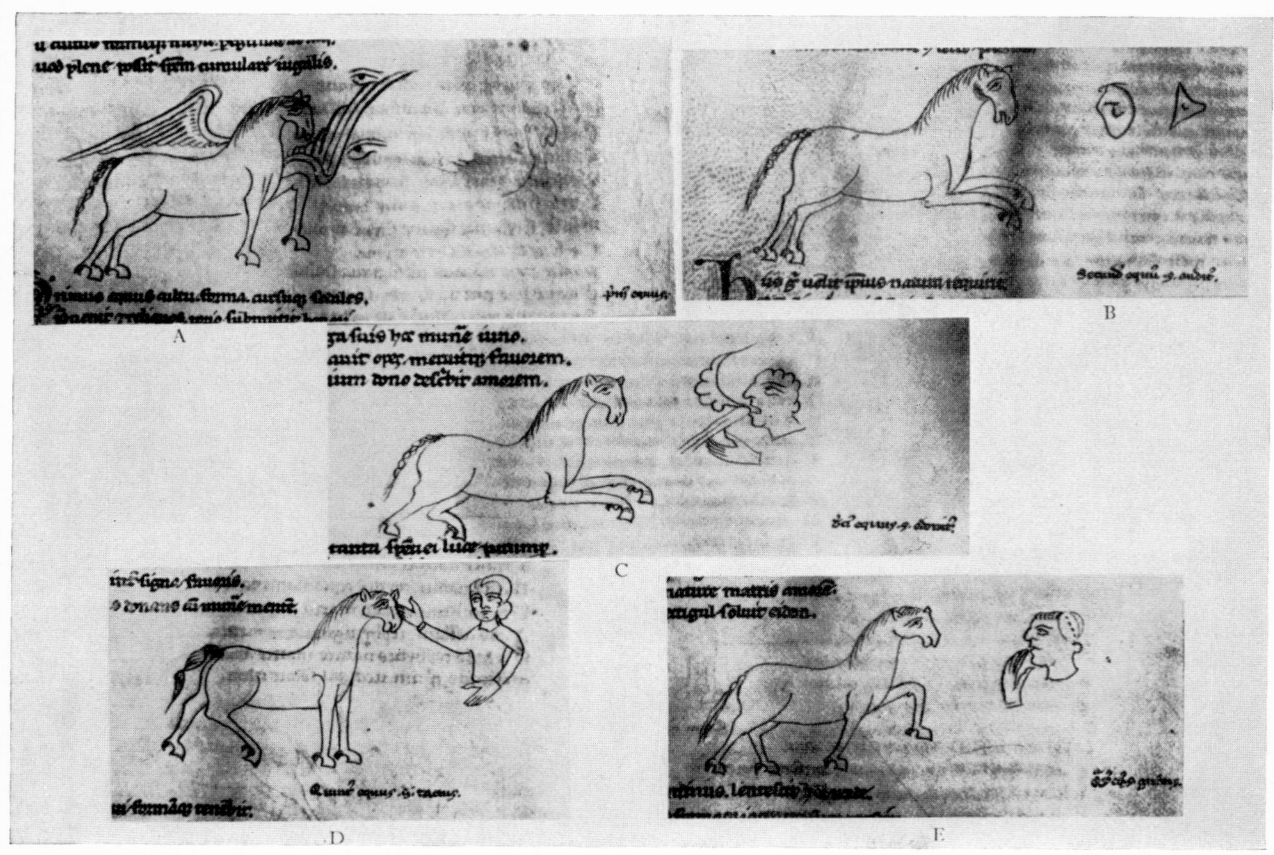

Plate 104 The Five Senses as illustrated in the Verona MS of the *anticlaudianus* of Alanus ab Insulis: *a*, Sight; *b*, Hearing; *c*, Smell; *d*, Touch; *e*, Taste

in 1949, the Strickland brooch (Plate 105a,b), a piece of the same class and practically the same size, came to light, Sir Charles Robinson's piece was remembered by Sir Thomas Kendrick and traced by me. It was still in the possession of Captain Fuller, who brought it for re-examination to the Museum, where its genuineness was quickly established. The Museum subsequently acquired it from Captain Fuller as part-gift, part-purchase (1952, 4–4, 1) with the stipulation that it should be known as the Fuller brooch, to signalize Captain Fuller's faith in it at a time when it was otherwise discredited by everyone except, as we shall see later (p. 318 below), E. T. Leeds.[23]

Description

The brooch, of which the pin, pin-hinge and catch-plate are missing, is a large silver disc, 4·5 in (11·4 cm) in diameter, not flat, but slightly dished. It has a broad openwork border containing roundels. Both in the roundels and in the interior of the brooch are figural and foliate designs reserved in silver against a background of niello. This extensive niello work is of quite exceptional quality and competence. The disc now weighs 68·5 grm (2⅜ oz approximately).

The basic design (Fig 53b) is that of two concentric rings about a central field, the whole being divided into four segments by four equal curves disposed back-to-back, leaving a pointed space with four hollow sides in the centre. The four back-to-back curves, with their straight extensions across the outer openwork border and also the inner ring, take the form of slightly raised mouldings within plain borders (Plate 99). They are scored with closely-set parallel lines giving a finely 'milled' effect quite unlike the grosser and normal beaded borders of contemporary metal work (see Plates *passim*). There is a very small vestige of a central boss and four similar peripheral ones at the points where the back-to-back curves intersect the inner ring. In the central pointed field is the figure of a man with wide-open eyes and inverted eyebrows (Fig 54a) carrying in each hand a branch, the stems of which terminate symmetrically at the edges of his coat. He appears to be clad in a round-necked shirt and over it a buttonless open jacket with long sleeves. This costume is not essentially different from that of the four subsidiary full-length human figures whose clothes are best displayed in the two to the left in Plate 99 and Fig 54b,d, except that the coat of the central figure seems longer and more ample. Its sleeves, too, are more baggy and a fold is indicated at each wrist. The exposed portion of the under-garment shows (between the hands) two horizontal lines (too high up to be intended for a belt) and below these a small cross and what appear to be sketchy suggestions of folds or puckers, lightly incised. At first sight this central element might suggest a *pallium* but none

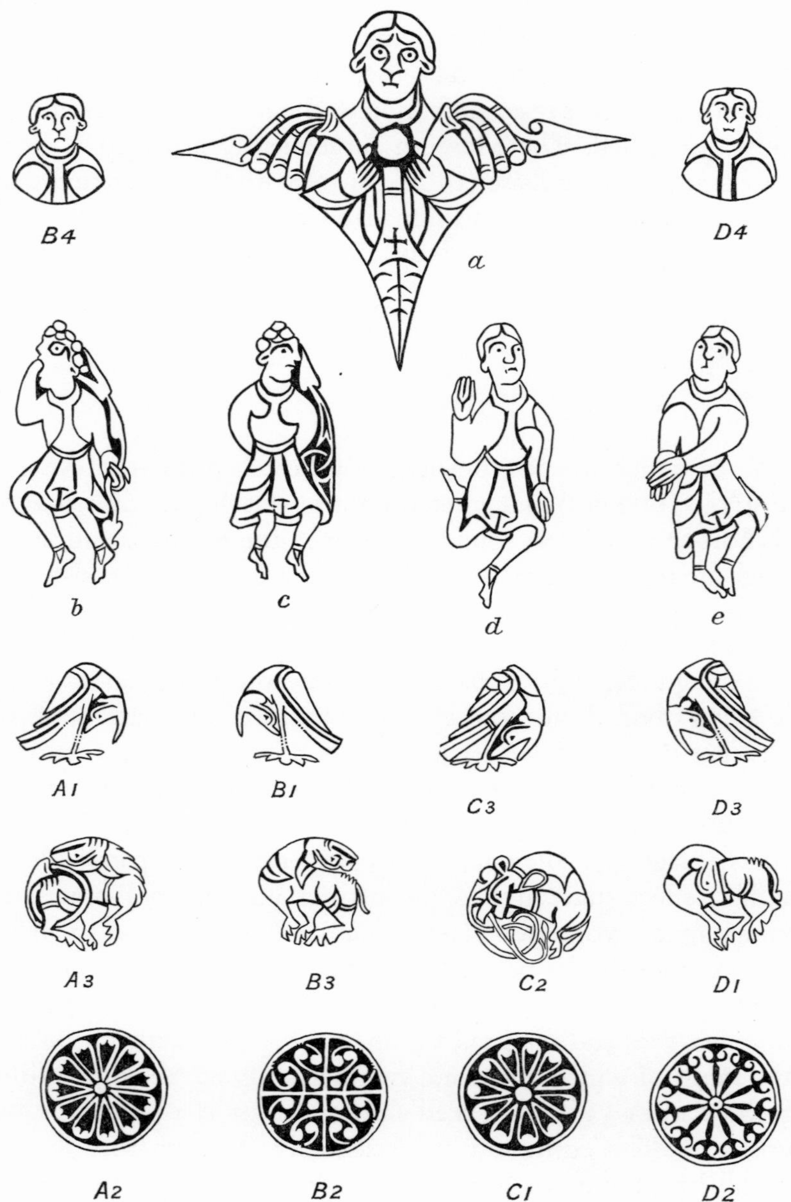

Figure 54 Human figures and subjects from the border-roundels on the Fuller brooch. (Scales 1 : 1)

is indicated at the neck, where the garments can be seen to be the same as on the other figures. This central figure certainly shows no trace of the belt and skirt worn by the four full-length figures. Perhaps these differences are due to the way in which the field that contains the central figure contracts to cut out the lower part of the body and to the need (failing belt and skirt folds) for some other relief or interest in so conspicuous a part of the design. The fuller cut of the garments and perhaps these other differences also, may be meant to emphasize, or at least to be in keeping with, the special prominence given to the cenratl figure.

The branches which the figure holds develop symmetrically on either side into bell-shaped mouths from which emerge three drooping bud-like lobes and above them a long pointed leaf with basal scrolls. The eyes of the figure are circles with a dot in the middle and the staring expression thus achieved is accentuated by the inverted eyebrows. This treatment of the eyes is in marked contrast to that of the six other full-face or nearly full-face figures on the brooch (Plate 99 and Fig 54, B4, D4, d and e), although one of the two profile heads has a circle for an eye but with a normal or drooping eyebrow. The hair of the central figure is parted in the middle and rendered as two simple shapes. The ears protrude from under the hair as downward-pointing lobes. This is a distinctive convention followed on all the nine human figures on the brooch. The ear-lobes of the two figures below the central figure are plain, that is, without any central mark or nick. This is possibly an oversight but perhaps intentional. Above the head is a fill-up device of foliate character. A similar sequence of broad-based leaves, each resting on the tip of the preceding one but narrower and more attenuated because of the confined space, may be seen above the human figures in the two oval fields below the central area. One of these motives is illustrated in Fig 55 *Hearing*.

The four pointed ovals around the central figure, which complete the central part of the brooch, each contains a male human figure (Fig 54b–e). The heads of the two above are seen in profile and their hair is represented in a pellet-like convention. The heads of the two below are seen slightly from one side and their hair is shown, as in the central figure, in two simple lobes centrally parted. The two figures above face outwards. The two below face inwards. The four figures all glance upwards, as if to stress the vertical axis of the ornament. The heads of the two above point inwards, of those below, outwards. The four figures are similarly dressed. Each wears a round-necked shirt or vest, tucked-in or belted at the waist to a heavy skirt which hangs in folds. Each wears a short open jacket with long sleeves and a pair of shoes with V-shaped openings and ankle-straps. All are simply clad, bare-headed, without weapons or attributes. The two on the right (Fig 54c,e) have three curving lines on the left-hand side of their skirts indicating drapery folds and the figure below right (Fig 54e) has certain other small differences – one line showing at the belt or waist instead of two and a closed neck-line with no vertical junction indicated at the neck of the jacket. Whether this represents a difference in the upper garment, or merely results from the attitude of the figure, which alone of the four has his arms brought together in front of the body, is not clear. But the difference is there. The four busts in the border-roundels (Fig 54, B4, D4) all have the central neck-opening of the outer garment. This is the only one of the human figures to be treated in this way.[24] The four figures, in other respects similar, are all shown in different and studied attitudes (Fig 54b–e). One holds a branch in his left hand, while his right hand is inserted in his open mouth. One has his hands behind his back, while his head is turned to one side towards a plant which passes just in front of his nose. One is shown running, with a hand raised to his ear and the fourth rubs his hands together. The backgrounds to all the figures are completely filled with pellets, branches, odd leaves and knots pointed and thickened at the extremities in the Celtic manner and in several cases developing into leaves or flowers, a tendency observed on the larger of the two Beeston Tor disc-brooches by Reginald Smith.[25] The right-hand bottom figure (Plate 99) has five parallel billets filling up the space between his legs.

The openwork border of the brooch contains sixteen roundels in groups of four. Slender triangles of plain metal run in between the roundels run from the outer edge of the brooch and opposite these, similar but smaller triangles from the inner ring outwards. The groups of four are separated by the straight 'milled' mouldings that extend the back-to-back curves.

The design of the brooch thus falls into five parts, a central and dominant figure and in each of the four surrounding segments a subsidiary figure associated with four border-roundels. In each segment the four roundels contain severally a man, an animal, a floral device (rosette) and a bird. In the upper half of the brooch the roundels occur in the two groups in the same order – from top downwards, man, animal, flower, bird. In the lower half of the brooch, reading from the bottom upwards, the bird and animal roundels are transposed in the right-hand group, while in the left there is a further change of order – man, bird, animal, flower. The bird and animal roundels, separated in the other segments by a rosette, here come together. Whether these changes were introduced merely for the sake of variety, or to show that the order of the roundels is immaterial, or for any other purpose, is not apparent.

The Fuller brooch thus presents an elaborate but clear-cut and carefully worked out iconography. This alone gives it a unique place in late Saxon metalwork, for it is the only piece of that period in this country with representations of the human figure, apart from the single small and highly stylized man on the pommel guard of the Wallingford sword[26] which must now be called the Abingdon sword[27] and the rudimentary cloisonné enamel portraits of the Alfred jewel and the Dowgate Hill (London) brooch.[28] The only objects that compare with the Fuller brooch abroad in respect of its human figures are the Tassilo chalice (A.D. 777 or shortly after)[29] which, whether made in southern England or Bavaria, was made under strong English influences,[30] and the Lindau book-cover in the Pierpont Morgan collection in New York (usually dated to the early ninth century), an English or south German piece.[31] The Tassilo chalice has a Christian iconography (a Christ-figure, with four evangelists and four saints) appropriate to a chalice and the cross-limbed figures on the Lindau book-cover are also religious. The lay iconography of the Fuller brooch is something altogether different and unparalleled.

Finally we may note the insignificance of the five bosses on the brooch (Plate 99). They are as originally designed, for the decoration is carried up to their edge. These studs are, as it were, obligatory, partly out of convention (five bosses are, as we have seen, an integral part of the traditional design of this class of brooch and they persist as a prominent feature to the end of the series) and partly to emphasize the quadripartite nature of the design. Two of them, those to the left and right, are also functional. Here the rectangular shafts of silver blocks for the spring and catch-plate on the back of the brooch were inserted through the disc and unobtrusively clenched on its front. But clearly bosses have been deliberately played down on this brooch. This was no doubt because all available space was needed for the deployment of the elaborate iconographic scheme and features which had been exploited on brooches that were merely ornamental had to suffer.

The straight 'milled' moulding that divides the border at the top of the brooch has two small holes in it. They belong to the later history of the brooch. The pin-hinge, catch-plate and pin were at some stage removed (shorn off low down from their blocks) and the remaining silver stumps filed and rubbed down to innocuous projections. The brooch then ceased to be a brooch and was perforated for suspension. It appears to have been of considerable age when this took place. The front now shows considerable wear and is highly burnished but apart from a deficiency of niello here and there and one silver triangle broken away in the border (top centre, next to the moulding with the two small holes), it is in perfect condition. It would appear to have come down from hand to hand and never to have been buried in the ground.

Authenticity

The notion that this brooch is a fake is extraordinarily persistent. The chief reason is the over-smooth and highly burnished appearance of the front. The brooch *looks* new. The unusual and close-set 'millings' of its mouldings have a machined appearance at first sight and, as virtually all the niello is present, black, rubbery, slick-looking surfaces surround the ornament. The fact is that the front of the brooch, where the low studs offer no impediment, has been kept polished by its owners and this, with the smoothness and facile assurance of all the ornament and the ingenuous look of the figures, gives at first sight a specious impression. The plain back of the brooch, which is untouched, has a different and genuinely antique look. There are numerous patches of green substance (malachite) that have worked out from the alloy and the surface of the metal is cracked and stained. The tendency to regard the brooch as a fake is also due to the strangeness of the iconography and the unfamiliar figure style. These are really points in its favour. Forgers do not favour original conceptions that do not appear plausible. They may go in for esoteric touches here and there but in general they play for probability, carefully building up their work from known ingredients. As for the certitude of the ornament, there is nothing modern about that. As T. C. Lethbridge aptly put it to the writer, 'it must take years of practice to fit Anglo-Saxon animals so neatly into spaces'.

The brooch was examined with especial care in the British Museum Research Laboratory in view of its history and the then Keeper, Dr H. J. Plenderleith, reported as follows:

> The brooch has been so cleaned and burnished on the obverse as at first glance to appear to be modern, but the reverse suggests that it has a history. Here the metal is seen as a base silver, which has been in contact with leather (?pigskin), and this has left a black imprint of the pore structure. There are traces of copper carbonate in a mineralized condition (malachite) arising from the segregation of the copper constituent of the silver. One can deduce that the metal is in the brittle crystalline condition which is characteristic of silver of some considerable age by the fractures to be seen where a small triangular piece is missing near the top. It may well be that the two small holes in this part of the brooch were bored at a late date in its history when the silver was already brittle and that this was done so that the object could be suspended vertically as an ornament. The tooling is all craftwork carried out with primitive implements in a free-hand manner: and under slight magnification it can be seen that there is no mechanical regularity anywhere. Such technical evidence as this object affords is, therefore, in my view entirely in favour of its antiquity.

Plenderleith further described the cracks on the back of the brooch to the writer as 'a typical surface regrouping of ancient silver'. Subsequently an analysis of the niello on the brooch was made in the Laboratory by Dr A. A. Moss in the course of his general investigation into the composition of niellos, which has been published in full[32] and in a short note[33] elsewhere. Moss had been able to show that a radical change took place in the composition of niello and in the technique of its application, in the tenth century. The niello on the Fuller brooch is of the primitive pre-eleventh-century type and identical in composition with that on King Æthelwulf's ring.[34] In one place (Fig 54, C2), where the niello has fallen out, the deeply scored ground associated with the early niellos, that consist of silver sulphide only, can be seen. The niello test alone proves the Fuller brooch genuine, for it is inconceivable that a forger before 1910 (assuming that one could ever have evolved such an object to forge) should have gone to the trouble of making a quantitative chemical analysis of pre-eleventh-century niellos, or had the knowledge, opportunity or technique to do so. Common sense amply reinforces the technical evidence. In 1910, when the disc first came to light, no such object existed, except an obscure piece in Stockholm (Plate 110a) of different style and appearance, small, flat (not dished, as is the Fuller brooch) and with foliate ornament only. Late Saxon disc-brooches as a class did not exist until Reginald Smith assembled the known examples and drew attention to them in 1925 in the paper on the Beeston Tor treasure already referred to. None of the early works discussing late Saxon ornament, Baldwin Brown's relevant volumes, the British Museum's *Anglo-Saxon Guide* (1923), or Brøndsted's *Early English Ornament* (1924), had been written. Some ninth-century metal work of course existed, notably the Trewhiddle hoard, the Abingdon sword, the Alfred jewel and some rings, but nothing that could possibly serve as a model for the Fuller disc and especially for its figure. No special market existed for minor arts of the late Saxon period. Looking back in the light of new knowledge and finds since 1910, we can see that while no single detail on the Fuller brooch has been directly copied from anything else, many of its features are on the other hand remarkably paralleled in authentic pieces that have only come to light since it was discovered. Finally, the last thing a forger might be expected to do would be to devise a unique and puzzling iconography out of his head. How odd, for example, are the four human half-figures in the border roundels above and below the central figure (Plate 99 and Fig 54, B4, D4). They do nothing and bear no marks of identification. A forger, who aims at selling his work, would surely have made something more attractive and plausible using evangelists, saints, or figures of seasons. When the brooch arrived at the Museum it was in a wooden skin-covered case of the seventeenth or eighteenth century apparently made to fit.

Ornament, Style and Date

We need have no hesitation, then, in accepting the Fuller brooch as a genuine piece of Anglo-Saxon silversmith's work. Not only is the form of disc-brooch, with its one central and four peripheral bosses and other features, characteristic of and, so far as we know, confined to the Saxon period but every detail of the ornament and style of the brooch fits into the art-milieu of ninth-century Anglo-Saxon England. A series of coin-dated hoards (in particular the Trewhiddle hoard from Cornwall, buried *c.* 875, and the Beeston Tor hoard from Staffordshire, buried *c.* 871–874) and of finger-rings or jewels unambiguously identified by their inscriptions with historical personages (in particular the finger-rings of Ælfred the Great's father, King Æthelwulf of Wessex (made for him as king between 839 and 858) and of Ælfred's sister Æthelswith (d. 888) and the Alfred jewel itself, between 871 and 899) together with a considerable assemblage of closely related if not dated pieces, make the ninth century and more especially its second half, the period in which the applied art of late Saxon metalwork is best known. The ornament of the Fuller brooch fits into this context. The manuscripts of the 'Canterbury School', which can mostly be assigned to the first half of the ninth century (in particular the British Museum Gospels Royal I E VI and the Codex Aureus at Stockholm and also such manuscripts as the British Museum Psalter Cotton Vespasian A I and the Book of Cerne at Cambridge), provide sources or analogies for the Trewhiddle-style ornament of the metalwork, as well as, where the Fuller Brooch is concerned, comparative material for the study of the human figure and draperies. There is ample and fairly well dated material of all kinds with which the brooch may be compared. Nearly all this material is illustrated in the works of Brøndsted and Kendrick.[35] By the ninth century craftsmen of the mixed Anglo-Saxon and British races with something inherited of the early Celtic genius and practice in curvilinear ornament, with long experience of the neat filling of spaces with zoomorphic designs and interlace, and with plenty of practice with the inhabited vine-scroll, had become extraordinarily expert in fitting animals and birds into frames of all shapes. Their designs are balanced, animated, ingenious and neat. To appreciate this insular facility and style, one has only to compare the assured and expertly drawn fauna of the manuscript Royal I E VI of the Fuller brooch, with their gauche if charming counterparts in such Frankish-Merovingian manuscripts as the *Sacramentarium Gelasianum* in the Vatican,[36] or the Augustine MS. 12168 in the Bibliothèque Nationale.[37] Good examples of Saxon animals in roundels which may be compared with those of the Fuller brooch are to be seen on the silver ring from the Thames at Chelsea in the Victoria and Albert Museum,[38] on the pommel of the Saxon sword found at Hoven in Norway[39] (Plate 100c), now in the Universitetets Oldsaksamling in Oslo; in the Gospel book Royal I E VI, e.g. fol. 4a[40] (a close parallel to Queen Æthelswith's ring) and in more stolid style associated (as on the brooch) with rosette-like foliage, on the Ramsbury cross-shaft,[41] dated by Kendrick to *c.* 850. Another example is the gold ring found at Malton in Yorkshire in 1774, known only from a drawing (Plate 101a).[42] The Hoven sword, with its contorted birds and animals in individual curved frames, the birds with feathers treated (to judge by Brøndsted's

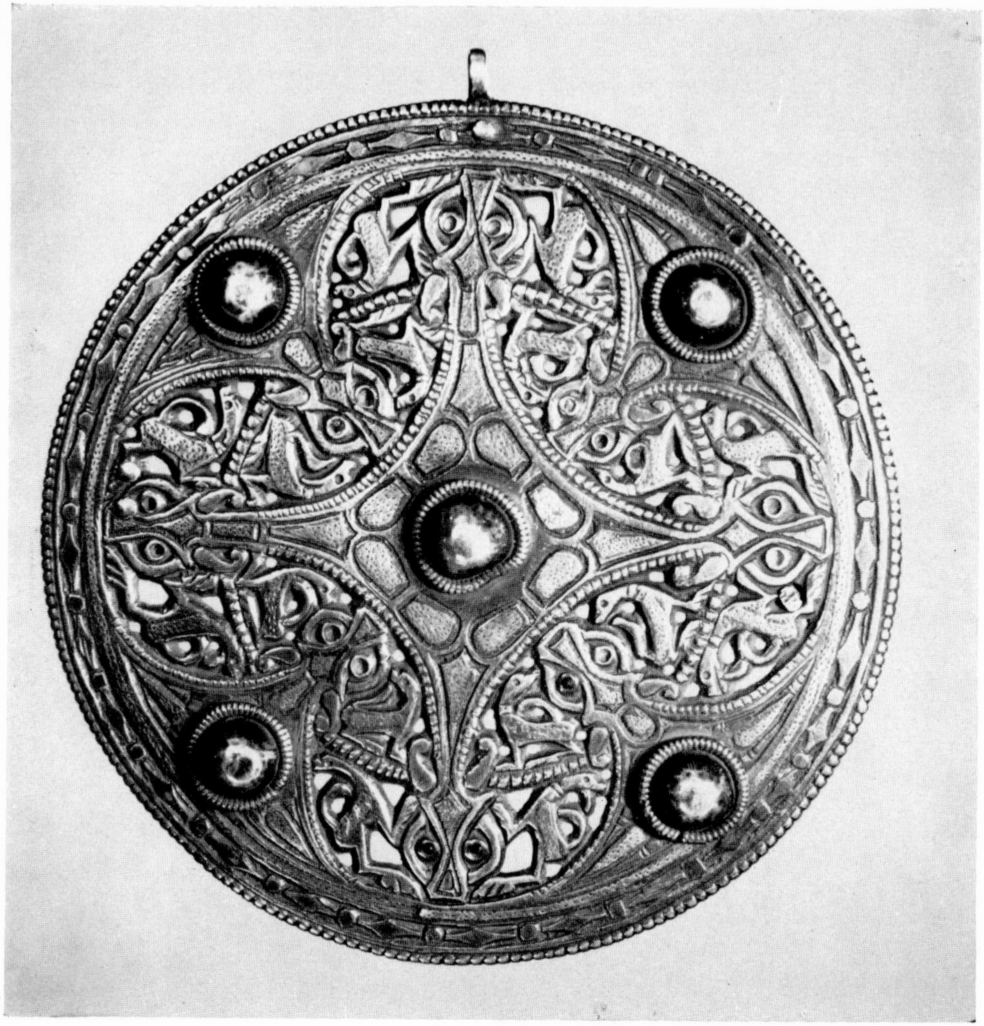

a

b

Plate 105 The Strickland Brooch: *a*, Front view (Scale 1 : 1); *b*, Enlarged detail

a

b

d

c

Plate 106 a,b, Silver nielloed disc-brooches, Beeston Tor, Staffs (Scale 1 : 1); *c*, Detail from the Genoels Elderen diptych, bust of Christ, probably made in Northumbria; *d*, Gold filigree pendant, Hon find, Norway (Scale enlarged)

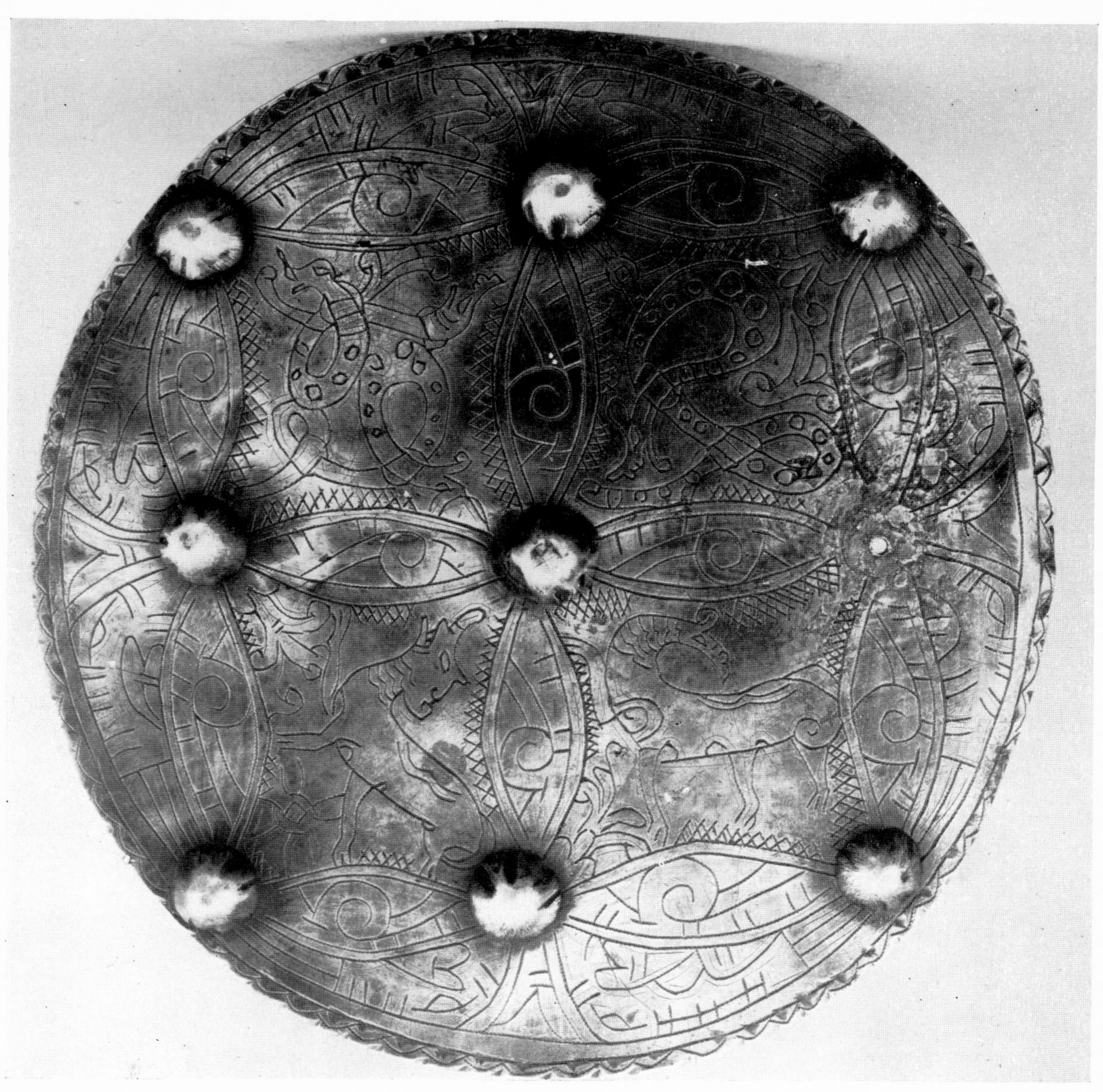

Plate 107 Engraved silver disc-brooch, Sutton, Isle of Ely (Scale 1 : 1)

a

b

Plate 108 a, Detail of back of Sutton, Isle of Ely Brooch, showing inscriptions (slightly enlarged); *b*, Back view of smaller Beeston Tor Brooch (Scale 1 : 1)

drawing) in the same scale-like convention as in C3 and D3 on the Fuller brooch (Plate 99 and Fig 54); with a creature in a roundel like our C2 (Fig 54), with one leg showing and tailing off into an interlace, and with small foliate fill-ups between the frames, is a good general parallel for the Fuller brooch. The general character of the panelling, the beaded borders especially, and of the animal ornament on the Hoven sword, relate it closely to the Trewhiddle find (buried *c.* 875), as Brøndsted pointed out, and this suggests a mid-ninth-century, or somewhat earlier date for its manufacture. The closest parallel of all to the Fuller brooch is the nielloed gold finger-ring found in the River Reno near Bologna in 1923.[43] I am grateful to my friend Professor Günther Haseloff of Würzburg for generously allowing me to use his photographs of this piece and for calling my attention to it in this connection. This remarkable ring (Plate 101b–d) has seven roundels in which individual animals and birds, with small accompanying foliate and pellet fill-ups are reserved, as on the Fuller brooch, against a niello ground. One roundel contains a rosette theme completely filling its roundel like those on the Fuller brooch. The two birds on the ring have the same feet as the birds on the brooch, the muscles of the animals on the two pieces are treated in the same distinctive way and the convention of a pair of parallel lines across the neck or body seen on the Fuller brooch in Fig 54, C2, A3 (and across the tail in C3 and the rear hip or hindquarters in A3, B3 and D1) can be seen also on the ring. One of the winged animals on the shoulders of the ring, outside the cluster of roundels, has the scale-like treatment of wing-feathers already referred to, a detail which may also be seen on the Saxon gold finger-ring from the heterogeneous hoard found at Hon in Norway, the deposit of which can be dated by its coins to about the end of the ninth century.[44]

The heavy leaves with bud-like ends that hang from the stems held by the central figure on the Fuller brooch are closely similar to the leaves on the quillon of the Abingdon sword (Plate 100b). Apart from general similarities, the pair of incised lines that define the curl of the tip, with a further pair lower down the leaf, occur on both pieces. The small foliate fill-ups that appear with the busts in the roundels in the Fuller brooch (Fig 55, D4) are exactly paralleled on the larger of the Beeston Tor brooches (Plate 106a) and occur on the Saxon sword pommel found at Dolven in Vestfold, Norway[45] (Plate 102a,b).

The rosette theme is common enough in English pagan Saxon material and later appears, to quote only a few instances, on the Franks casket (the star in the Adoration scene), the Lindisfarne gospels (the central device in the cruciform page facing the opening of St Matthew)[46], St Chad's gospels (the centre of the head of the portable cross held by St Luke, folio 218)[47], and commonly in the Book of Kells (e.g. ff. 129v, 130r).[48] In the Merovingian manuscripts such devices may be seen liberally used in the Würzburg St Paul MS. fol. 7r (Zimmerman,

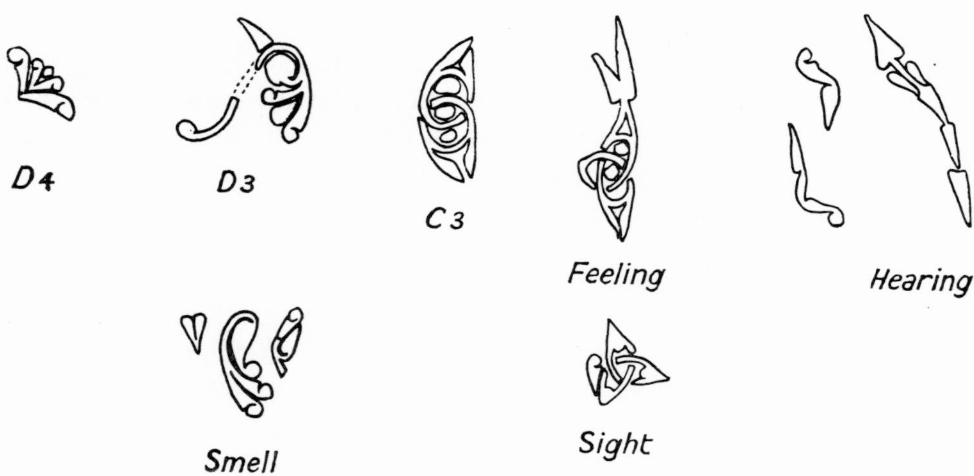

Figure 55 Foliate details, Fuller brooch. (Scales 3 : 2)

Vorkarolingische Miniaturen, pl. cxx) and elsewhere. Good parallels for the Fuller brooch rosettes, closer to it in date and in which the rosettes can be recognized as representing floral themes, occur in the *Sacramentarium Gelasianum* (e.g. fol. 172(b), in the capitals of the arch),[49] the Augustine MS. Paris Bibliothèque Nationale lat. 12168 (e.g. the central device on fol. C(b))[50], and (seen also on the Fuller brooch) in the arch above the well-known composition showing David the Musician on fol. 30(b) of British Museum psalter Cotton Vespasian A 1.[51] Rosettes representing floral details are also used on the tree-of-life motive separating the two birds on King Æthelwulf's ring.

The above observations should suffice to show that the Fuller brooch is quite at home in this ninth-century milieu and that from the point of view of its ornament – foliate, animal and geometric – there is no need to date its manufacture any later than *c.* 850. All its elements can be paralleled in pieces whose manufacture (as distinct from their burial in the ground, or their latest possible date) can safely or reasonably be placed at that date or before.

The human figures and their draperies dominate the brooch but it is easier and safer to assess its date, as we have, on its smaller ornamental details taken together. Well-dated metalwork parallels exist for these details, which, however persistent an individual theme may be, are in general more sensitive to changes of taste and to stylistic evolution and are less faithfully copied than the human figures. We can say that the human figures and their draperies are also wholly in keeping with the date for the brooch suggested by its ornament. The figures and their faces are in the simple northern barbaric tradition descended from St Cuthbert's coffin. The faces are not far removed from those of the cross-nimbed figures of the Lindau book-cover,[52] or of the David folio (30b) already referred to in the

British Museum psalter Cotton Vespasian A I. The closest parallels to the Fuller brooch figures are to be found in the Book of Cerne. In this Mercian MS. of *c.* 820 (Cambridge University Library L.C.I. 10) the half-length evangelist 'portraits' in roundels and in the case of St Matthew, the full-length man-symbol (Plate 103), provide near enough exact manuscript equivalents in style to the metalwork figures.[53] Both show the same serious, rather blank, often long faces with round chins, centrally parted hair, straight-line or curved-line mouths and rudimentary hands. In particular, the distinctive and unusual downward-pointing ears projecting from beneath the hair, with a central black mark or opening – a pen stroke in the manuscript, a niello-filled nick on the brooch. This is a very peculiar trick of style. Something similar but less stylized than on the brooch occurs occasionally in later Winchester manuscripts like the New Minster Psalter of *c.* 1160 (e.g. the Crucifixion folio),[54] the late twelfth-century Winchester Bible (e.g. vol. I, fol. 21v; vol. II, fol. 135v)[55] and the Bury St Edmunds Bible (e.g. fols. 94 and 254v, 281v, the figures of Christ and Moses).[56] In the Book of Cerne it occurs in a manuscript contemporary with the brooch, in precisely similar form and together with further parallels in features and drapery. The linear treatment of the draperies on the brooch and in the manuscript is very similar (though the lay costume of the Fuller brooch differs from that of the sacred figures of the manuscript). One may in particular compare the lines on the right shoulder and on the drapery held in the left hand of the Matthew-symbol (fol. 26) of the manuscript with those on the sleeve of the central figure and on the skirts of the two figures to the right (Plate 99 and Fig 54a,c,e) on the Fuller brooch. The T-shaped marks that pick out the bottoms of the central fold of the skirts of the Fuller brooch figures are simplified metalwork versions of the same theme as seen for example on the St Matthew symbol, while the sketchy lines indicating puckers on the lowest portion of the dress of the figure of St Matthew and on the legs and skirt of his symbol are the equivalent of the similar marks below the little cross on the dress of the central figure of the Fuller brooch. In its ornament, therefore, in both the figures and the animal and foliate details, the Fuller brooch suggests a date for its manufacture in the second quarter of the ninth century, or perhaps *c.* 850.

Iconography

General. Early attempts to explain the iconography of the Fuller brooch were rather ingenuous. Sir Charles Robinson, in his note in the *Antiquary* already referred to, recorded suggestions that the four roundels with busts represented the four evangelists, that the central figure 'held two scourges of leather thongs tipped with leaden balls' and that two of the four subsidiary figures (those to the right of Plate 99) were bound hand and foot, while those to the left in the acts of running and eating were free, so that these four figures 'typify the pretensions of the Church to bind and loose its votaries', while the 'contorted and involved monsters in the marginal roundels may probably represent evil spirits of paganism'. Sir Alfred Clapham did not venture any suggestions on the iconography. It was E. T. Leeds who, with characteristic acumen, perceived long ago the correct explanation of the five central figures. In a letter to the writer, dated 18th April, 1949, Leeds gave his views on the brooch, supplied the details of its earlier history and went on to say that he had always believed it genuine (even when it was withdrawn from exhibition at the Ashmolean) and why. After drawing attention to the affinities of the ornament of the roundels with the Trewhiddle treasure (which he felt might be cited as a source from which a hypothetical forger might have drawn some of the ideas) he continued with characteristic forthrightness:

> But the five figures in the middle are another story, and no one, I hold, could possibly have invented them in modern times. To put it frankly, these figures are as genuinely Saxon as anything I know. There is, as I have always maintained, an element in Anglo-Saxon art, early or late, that is inimitable, and my instinct tells me that the Robinson piece has got it. . . . One point that bothered me was the geometrical roundels in the borders (i.e. the 'rosettes' or 'floral themes', R.B-M.). They did not quite seem to harmonize with the rest, and I could not quite place them. . . . To return to the figures – there I felt I was safe, an opinion all the more decided when I studied them nearer. I had already on the Wallingford (now Abingdon, R.B-M.) sword detected the four symbols of the evangelists, and wondered if the disc could yield some similar interpretation. But the figures round the centre had an almost too jaunty look to be biblical. They seemed to belong to civil life. And yet they are symbolic enough; for I have no doubt whatever that they can, with the central figure, be interpreted as the five senses, read as follows
>
> Taste   Smell
>
> Sight
>
> Hearing   Touch
>
> And if you will argue that any modern forger could have evolved that idea in Saxon spirit out of his inner consciousness, then it is as well I should have retired to sit in the sun, as now, in my garden, and contemplate on the amount of learning that drives away common sense.

There is no doubt that Leeds's explanation of the five central figures is correct and that this is the key to the whole iconographic scheme. This being so, this ninth-century brooch is by far the earliest illustration of the five senses in any guise, the next representations of them dating from the thirteenth and fourteenth centuries. It is further unique both in its representation of the senses as human beings and in its association with them of the four vital factors of human, animal, bird and plant life, for this, it seems, is what the border roundels must represent.

In dealing with the iconography I am greatly indebted to Mr Chu-tsing Li, of the State University of Iowa, for much valuable advice and many useful bibliographical references to the senses in allegory and art, a subject of which he is making a special study. I also acknowledge my debt to Miss Dorothy Whitelock for advice and to Miss Enid M. Raynes for references to the five senses in Ælfric. Mr Peter Clemoes of King's College, Cambridge, supplied further references in Ælfric and referred me to Isidore's *Etymologies* and to Byrhtferth's *Manual*.

Even with this assistance and after consulting the Index of Christian Art at Princeton and the Warburg Institute, I have not been able to clinch this identification by finding any earlier illustration dealing with the five senses in the manner of the brooch, or any text linking them with the four factors of human, animal, bird and plant life. The senses enter frequently into mediaeval allegory but usually in other guises, roles or contexts – as guardians of the soul and ruled over by reason, or associated with the four elements, earth, air, fire and water; with the four humours; with the idea of *microcosmus*; or with the Seven Deadly Sins and other things. Perhaps no iconographic model or text specifically linking the senses with the four aspects of life exists, or is necessary. The roundels might have been invented by the artist himself or his patron as a fairly obvious way of symbolizing the external world of living things, which we know only through the senses and the iconography may have been largely determined, as suggested below, by the form of the brooch on which the subject had to be depicted. There are, nevertheless, other difficulties beyond the lack of a prototype or model in the way of accepting the five senses as a complete explanation of the iconography. Is a quadripartite design, with a dominant central figure, an appropriate way of illustrating the five senses, which one might suppose to be equals? Why is the inanimate world which is equally perceived with the senses, excluded from the iconography? If the figures are the five senses, is there any method in their arrangement or sequence? It is necessary to look into the matter more closely before the identification can be taken as established, particularly when we remember that our brooch is four hundred years earlier than the first known appearance of this subject in the graphic arts in any form.

The figures. The principal figures on the Fuller brooch may, at first sight, seem comical to modern eyes but their ingenuousness will not surprise anyone familiar with early mediaeval allegorical illustration as seen, for example, in the many *Psychomachia* manuscripts. The senses after all have no fixed iconography, no special symbols or attributes by which they can be readily identified without having to be depicted performing some sort of rudimentary and pointed actions (cf. Plate 104c,e). They are not easily conveyed and we can greatly admire the success and ingenuity with which the artist of the Fuller brooch has solved his problem. I say the artist of the Fuller brooch, rather than of his model or prototype, for iconography of the Fuller brooch has the stamp of complete originality. There is, in the first place, nothing of the late antique about it. The animals, birds, rosettes and foliate details, fill-ups and scraps of interlace and even the figures are pure Saxon and quite masterly in their clear, perfectly balanced, vital and cleanly finished rendering. They are not the work of a copyist. Secondly, the whole *schema* clearly is thought out with reference to, or adapted to suit, an established Saxon brooch-type. The quadripartite design is inherent, as has been explained, in this brooch-series, in which it persists from start to finish, making the differentiation between the central field and the four equal segments and the distribution of the five figures inevitable in this case and unlikely to have originated in this form in any other way. Moreover, each figure is exactly designed to fit the space provided for it and not only designed to fit the space but also with reference to the position on the brooch which the space is to occupy. Thus the two uppermost of the four subsidiary figures (Taste and Smell) form a pair. Both are in profile, with pellet-hair and ear-lobes with central nick and both, as positioned, face outwards. The two lower figures (Hearing and Feeling) are also a pair, heads seen half from the front, hair in plain lobes, ear-lobes plain (no nicks). Both, as positioned, are facing inwards. All four, as placed, face upwards, stressing the vertical axis of the brooch, the consistency of which is maintained in the bird and animal roundels but depends primarily on the ingenious placing of the four static, rigid busts in the border at top and bottom, set off by foliate sprays and with vertical lines stressed in the openings of their tunics and their general upright positioning; and on the central figure and the tapering fill-up over its head. These details anchor the circular disc in one position. With design of such purposefulness in evidence, we must suppose that the details and emphasis of the figures are deliberate and meaningful and with this in mind we may consider the appositeness of the drawing of each to the interpretation put forward. The strength of Leeds's interpretation is simply that the figures do, by their attitudes and actions, illustrate the senses. Other suggested interpretations – that they might represent, for example (with *Annus*, *Helios* or *Terra Mater* for the central figure), the four seasons or the four parts of the earth, or the four elements – have nothing concrete whatever to support them, except for a possible reading of the bottom right-hand figure (Feeling), considered alone, as Winter warming his hands. This is an interpretation with which neither his bare head, nor his clothes (apparently essentially the same as those of the other figures, although what has been said on pp. 309–10 above on this point may be noted) nor the accompanying foliage very well agree. The fact is that the only essential differentiation between the figures lies in their gestures or actions. The whole emphasis of the central figure, which is otherwise symmetrically composed and at rest, is in the eyes. These contrast with those of the other figures and the staring expression, marked by inverted eyebrows, is obviously deliberate. Of the other figures, Feeling is well indicated by the gesture of the hands and Taste by the hand in the mouth (the gesture perhaps emphasized by the absence of any lateral line marking the end of the sleeve). The branch which Taste holds in his hand is no doubt intended to represent the source of what is being tasted. Smell and Hearing are less obvious but just as unequivocal. They are inherently more difficult to convey than Touch and Taste. The hands of Smell are carefully and necessarily concealed behind his back, in order to avoid confusing the issue and to concentrate attention on the head. Here the mouth and eye remain negative, the only gesture being the turning of the head, which brings the nose towards one of the two plants that flank the figure. If this figure does not represent Smell, it represents nothing. Hearing is somewhat cramped for space but one hand is raised towards the ear, while the figure is shown running. He can be regarded as having heard a cry and shown as moving in answer to it. Of the figures in the border roundels the human figures, by the same negative device as is employed in Smell, are carefully and uniformly shown doing nothing at all. They are merely a symbol of humanity, repeated four times. The other roundels contain in each quadrant a bird, an animal and a rosette or floral theme so that each of the four subsidiary senses is shown in connection with the four manifestations of life on earth. The iconography thus recognizes animate, or living, but not inanimate creation, as associated with the senses.

The finding of a precise source of this idea, if one exists, as uniquely expressed in the Fuller brooch, must be left to specialists in early mediaeval texts and ideology and to art historians expert in iconography and the illustrations of early encyclopaedias, patristic writings and allegorical treatises. Some preliminary observations which seem sufficient to settle the identification may be offered here.

The figures on the Fuller brooch are lay figures, nor has any of the disc-brooches any specifically religious context or content. Nevertheless the Fuller brooch seems to have a Christian background. In the works of Abbot Ælfric, the tenth-century Saxon homilist, whose first work was issued about 990,[57] when he was a monk at Cerne Abbas, Dorset, and most of whose writings are believed to precede his becoming abbot of Eynsham in 1005, the five senses are referred to on many occasions. Ælfric writes at least a century after the Fuller brooch was devised but his *Homilies* serve to show that the five senses had a place in the religious teaching of Saxon England at this time and his reference to Gregory the Great's elucidation of a biblical allegory in terms of the five senses[58] quoted below, further implies a continuity of religious teaching on the subject from earlier times and so an earlier background to explain the theme on the brooch.

In the homily for the third Sunday after Pentecost,[59] on the text 'A certain man prepared a great feast and thereto invited many', Ælfric gives Gregory the Great's interpretation of this parable. One of those invited made the excuse 'I have bought five teams of oxen and I wish to go to try them'. Gregory's interpretation is given by Ælfric as follows (the italics are mine):

> The five teams of oxen betoken the five senses of our body, which are Sight, Hearing, Taste, Smell, Touch. These five senses he who has is whole. *Through our eyes we see and distinguish all things*; *through the ears we hear*; *in the mouth* (on ðam muðe) we have taste and distinguish whether it be sweet or bitter, what we eat; *through the nose* we smell what is clean, what foul; *in the hands* and in all the body we have touch, that we may feel what is hard, what smooth, what unsmooth, and so everything. These senses are rightly compared with the five teams of oxen, because they are doubled in the two persons, that is, in man and in woman. He goes and tries these five senses who through curiosity or unstillness wastes them uselessly. Immoderate curiosity is a grave sin; for we should turn our look from evil sight, our hearing from evil speech, our taste from unhallowed aliments, our nose from hurtful smells, our hands and whole body from foul and sinful contacts, if we are desirous of coming to the delicacies of the eternal refection. . . .

Ælfric's homily for December 25, the Nativity,[60] contains the following:

> The soul is mistress of the body and governeth the five senses of the body. The senses are thus named: Visus, that is, Sight; Auditus, Hearing; Gustus, Taste, *with the mouth*; Odoratus, Smelling, *with the nose*; Tactus, Touching or Feeling, with all the limbs *but most usually with the hands*. The Soul directeth these five senses according to its will and it behoveth it that, as a mistress, it should carefully consider what it will commend each limb to do, or what it permitteth to each limb as regards its natural desire, that nothing unseemly should befall by means of any limb's service.

The homily on the Nativity of a Confessor[61] refers to the parable of the rich man who would go into a strange country and, calling his servants, committed to one five pounds, to one two, to another one . . . 'the five pounds are the five senses of our body, that is, sight and hearing, taste, smell and touch.'

In the homily on the Nativity of Holy Virgins,[62] in which the Church is compared to the five wise and five foolish virgins, Ælfric says:

> With five senses, as we have often said to you, every man lives that has his health; that is, sight and hearing, taste, smell and touch. Everyone who abstains from unallowed sight, from unallowed hearing, from unallowed

> taste, from unallowed smell, from unallowed touch, has the name of maiden for that purity.

In the Homily for February 2 on the Purification of St Mary[63] the following occurs:

> God, in the Old Law, commanded his people that they should offer to him the first born male child, or redeem it with five shillings. . . . Our evil thoughts or actions we should redeem with five shillings; that is we should repent of our wickedness with our five senses,[64] which are sight, and hearing, and taste, and smell, and touch.

In addition to these extracts there are plentiful references in Ælfric to the senses in general, or to one or other of them, particularly to the New Testament miracles in which sight was restored to the blind, hearing to the deaf, etc.

Three points in these five extracts from Saxon texts are directly relevant to the iconography of the Saxon brooch. In each, Sight is mentioned first and seems to have primacy – *Through our eyes we see and distinguish all things.*

In each reference the senses are placed in the order in which they appear on the brooch: Sight first, following by Hearing, Taste, Smell and Touch. Thirdly, the *organs* of sense are stressed, Sight *through the eyes*; Taste, *in the mouth*; Feeling, *especially in the hands* and *the nose* and *ears* for Smell and Hearing. This association of the senses with the human body and its sensory organs is important, for we shall see that in the only other representations of the senses in the mediaeval era, this is not so. In the text of Alanus ab Insulis's *Anticlaudianus*[65] and its illustrations published by[66] Florentine Mütherich (Plate 104) they appear as horses pulling a chariot driven by Reason (*ratio*). In the *De Natura Rerum* of the mid-thirteenth-century encyclopaedist Thomas de Cantimpré and the early fourteenth-century Longthorpe Tower illustration of his text[67] they are represented by animals (the 'sensory champions' – cock or lynx, sight; pig or boar, hearing; monkey, taste; vulture, smell; spider, feeling) sitting on a wheel, which is turned by Reason. The correspondence of the *Homilies* of Ælfric with the brooch is thus notable. In the only other mediaeval illustration of the senses known, in the Pierpont Morgan Library's manuscript of Richard de Fournival's *Bestiaire d'Amour*, they are again represented as animals but in a simpler version appropriate to the bestiary, without the introduction of Reason or other philosophic trappings.[68] The *Homilies* not only show an emphasis on the five senses in Saxon religious teaching at a date not far removed from the brooch but a conception of the senses as on the brooch, in terms of the human body and its functioning; precedence given to Sight; a consistently maintained sequence or precedence of the senses identical with that on the brooch and emphasis on those sensory organs that are emphasized on the brooch. The same sequence of the senses is found at the same date (1011) in

Byrhtferth of Ramsey's scientific *Manual*.[69] In the section 'Of the Symbolism of Numbers' under the number 5, we have 'Five doubled up makes ten; There are five books of Moses; There are five Senses of Man, viz. Sight, Hearing, Taste, Smell, Touch'. Both Byrhtferth and Ælfric used Alcuin's pupil Rabanus Maurus (d. 856) as a source. It is very probable that Rabanus discusses the senses also but I have not as yet found the passage.

In the quadripartite arrangement of the brooch, Sight is not directly associated with the four forms of life, as are the other senses, but it may in its central position facing directly to the front and at the centre of the scheme be fairly taken as cognizant of the emblems that surround it. Since we have seen how carefully every detail of the iconography is worked out, we must suppose that the branches held by Sight are more than mere foliage. He is probably intended to be shown possessing the fruits of the earth – in other words, these are *cornucopia*.

As we have said, a striking feature of the Fuller brooch is the dominance of the central figure. Why should Sight be accorded such primacy over the other senses? It is natural enough, for sight is the Sense *par excellence* by which we comprehend the outside world. Apart from this, Sight's primacy was consistently assumed, as we have seen in Anglo-Saxon sources more or less coeval with the brooch. Sight seems invariably to be mentioned first in mediaeval or antique sources that refer to the five senses. It does not necessarily follow that Sight is the most important. In the *Anticlaudianus* of Alanus, although the senses are mentioned in the sequence Sight, Hearing, Smell, Taste, Touch (Smell and Taste, incidentally, transposed from the normal sequence as seen on the brooch), it is in the final event Hearing which alone is able to carry Prudence into the heavenly kingdom and to the throne of the Almighty.[70] There is a tradition in which Sight is supreme over the other senses. It is embodied in the mid-twelfth-century *De Mundi Universitate* of Bernardus Silvestris of Chartres.[71] In his second book, the *Microcosmus*, the creation of man is described, the final stage being the making of the five senses and man's endowment with them. The work is discussed and in part translated by C. S. Lewis in his *Allegory of Love*[72] and Sight's primacy is described in the following words:

As the world's eye, the Sun, exceeds by far,
And claims the heaven from every vulgar star,
So doth the eye all other senses quite
Out-go, and the whole man is the Sight.[73]

The next in the hierarchy, Hearing, is on a lower plane altogether:

Auditus sede inferior, virtuitibus inpar,
Tardior in sensu, commoditate minor.

Taste and Smell follow, in that order; 'Touch comes last, even as, among the organs, those of generation come last'.[74] Later by some centuries though it is, this passage fully justifies the treatment of Sight on the Fuller Brooch, its dominance in the iconographic scheme. For the tradition of primacy of Sight goes back at least to the end of the sixth century A.D. In the *Etymologies* of Isidore of Seville (570–636), book XI, *De Homine et partibus eius*, after the naming of the five senses, the following occurs:

> Visus dictus, quod vivacior sit ceteris sensibus, ac praestantior sive velocior, ampliusque vigeat, quantum memoria inter cetera mentis officia. Vicinior est enim cerebro, unde omnia manant . . .

Summary. The conception of the senses expressed in the Fuller brooch seems to have no relation to the classical treatment of the subject, as in Pliny, in which two senses (Taste and Touch) are most acute in man, but the others in various beasts: nor to the Christian version of it, as in the *Bestiaire d'Amour* and in Thomas de Cantimpré, in which these vehicles of temptation are all found at their acutest, not in man but in creatures. Nor is there any connection in the iconography of the brooch with the philosophic schemes that relate the senses to *microcosmus*, to the elements, the humours, the seasons and other concepts, except that *microcosmus* is concerned with the senses in man and (in Bernardus Sylvestris at any rate) stresses emphatically the primacy of Sight. On the contrary, these are the traditions which lie behind the mediaeval representations of the senses in animal form and their inclusion (by name only) in cosmological diagrams.[75] The Fuller brooch, which depicts the senses in man and associated with organs of the human body and which is some seven hundred years earlier than the next known representation of the senses in human form,[76] except for the explanatory or identifying sketches that accompany the horses in the Italian (Verona) *Anticlaudianus* MS. (Plate 104),[77] stands apart and seems rather to reflect the moral teaching of the early Church, perhaps especially of the Saxon church. It must be admitted that the brooch, apart from the small casual-looking cross on the garments of Sight, seems to dwell on the senses for their own sakes in an almost secular way with no indication of the essential theme of the homilist, namely that they are sources of temptation which must be kept under control. Nor do the homilies (so far as I have been able to discover) anywhere associate the senses with the four forms of life, which are reiterated round the brooch. Even so, while the texts adduced do not explain the iconography in every particular, there can now be no doubt that it is the five senses that are depicted on the Fuller brooch and furthermore that this subject is in no way out of place in the ninth century.

II: THE STRICKLAND BROOCH

The Strickland brooch (Plate 105a,b and Fig 56), a large silver disc of the same size as the Fuller brooch with inlays of gold, blue glass and niello, was acquired by the British Museum in 1949 (1949, 7–2, I) after a sale at Sotheby's.[78] It had been purchased on behalf of an American collector who ceded it to the British Museum (the underbidder) at the international sale price, after an export licence had been refused. It was formerly the property of Mrs Strickland of Boynton Hall, Bridlington, Yorkshire. Nothing is known of its origin but it was considered by this owner to have been part of the collections of Sir William Strickland, the 6th Baronet (1753–1834). Sir William, who collected Yorkshire antiquities and historical and literary manuscripts, minor Italian arts and other things, was the owner of Boynton Hall. After his death in 1834, his collections remained in the house, finally passing with it to the vendor in 1945. The brooch was acquired by the vendor in this way. It was a natural assumption that it had formed part of Sir William's collection, since he was the only occupier of the house known to have collected antiquities and the antiquarian pieces and *objets d'art* that were in the house had almost all been collected either by him or by his forebears. The probability is that Sir William acquired the brooch, quite likely as a Yorkshire find and that it had been at Boynton Hall at least since 1834.

Authenticity

The history of the brooch will probably be thought a sufficient guarantee of its genuineness. It was examined before the sale in the British Museum Research Laboratory and the then Keeper, H. J. Plenderleith, reported as follows:

> I have examined the silver brooch with care and it seems to me to be original. The metal (gold and silver), the niello, the blue glass eye inlays, and the method of construction (punch and chisel work) all seem to me to be in keeping. I consider the marks of wear to be old. The hanging ring is obviously later, and the brooch has been cleaned with rouge, not recently. I feel there are grounds for assigning it considerable antiquity, apart from the ornament, and this being so it is probably authentic.

Subsequently A. A. Moss analysed the niello inlay on the brooch in the course of the investigation referred to above (p. 312) and showed that it was of the tenth-century or earlier type and of the same character as that on the Fuller brooch

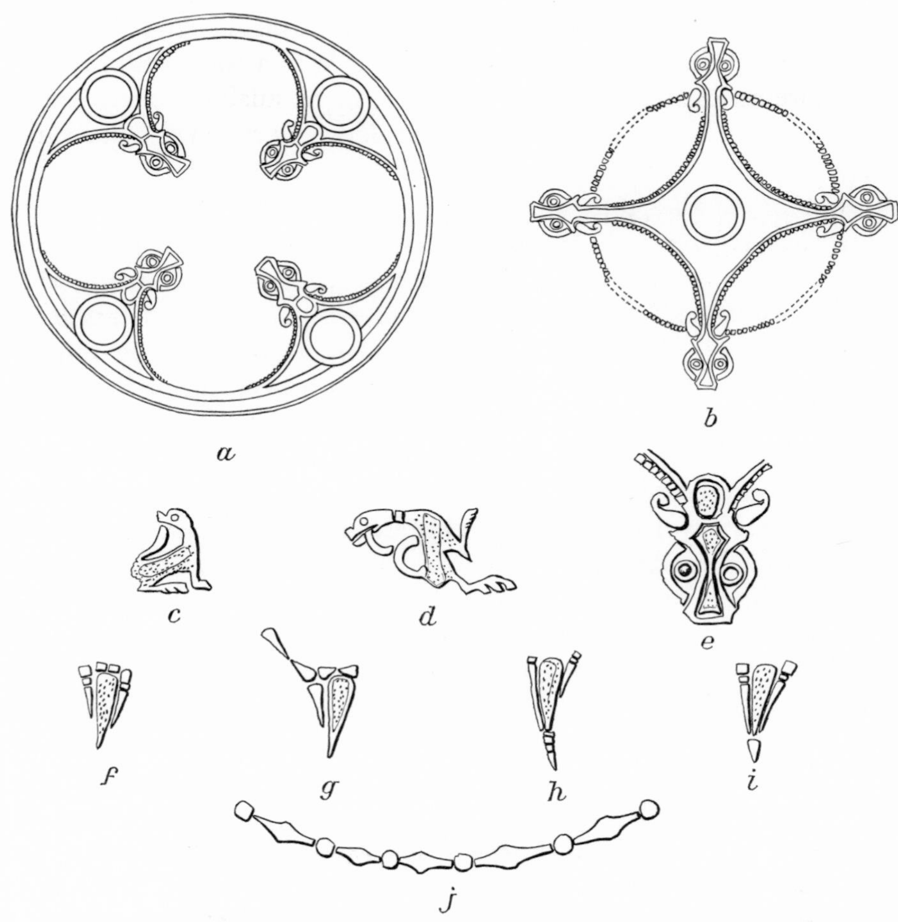

Figure 56 Basic design and ornamental details, Strickland brooch. (Scales: *a*, *b*, 1:2; *c–j*, 1 : 1)

and the Æthelwulf ring. There can therefore be no doubt as to the genuineness of the brooch, which is in any case apparent in every detail of its form, technique and decoration.

Description

The Strickland brooch is a large circular silver disc, 4·35 in (11·0 cm) in diameter, slightly curved and ornamented on the convex surface, the plain concave back carrying a swivelling attachment for a hinged fastening-pin. The loop at the top may indicate secondary use as a pendant but could also be the attachment for a safety-chain such as was sometimes worn with the more precious personal ornaments (such as the Kingston brooch). A geometric outer border carries, in pendant triangular fields that terminate in inward-facing animal masks, four prominent bosses with beaded collars (Fig 56a). Within the border is a rosette-shaped openwork area in which are arranged, in two zones, sixteen small dogs with collars, all looking back over their shoulders. Those in the inner zone are sitting, those in the outer rampant or leaping. In some cases the dogs in the outer zone have long hanging tongues. The dogs' feet (Plate 105b and Fig 56d) are represented in a conventional manner that goes back to the pagan period[79] and is to be seen in the animals of the Fuller brooch (Fig 54, A3, B3, C2, D1). The dogs' eyes are small circular punched depressions which do not appear to have contained any inlay, although on the Witham-pin animals even smaller eye-sockets carry glass inlays. The centre of the brooch is occupied by a cruciform motive, a rectangular field with hollow sides (Fig 56b), like that on the Fuller brooch. The arms of this cruciform motive terminate in outward-facing animal masks of the same character as the inward-facing masks of the border (Fig 56a). There is a central boss similar to the other bosses. The ornament is chased and carved and the background filled with niello. The eye-sockets of the animal masks originally contained convex studs of blue glass which remain in five of them (Plate 105b). A remarkable feature of the brooch not paralleled in other pieces of its class is the extensive use of gold. The many speckled areas (Plate 105b) – the bodies of the dogs, the 'petals' round the central boss, on the animal masks, a continuous ring in the border and the large leaves of its pendant triangles – are plates of solid gold hammered into cut-away fields and then ornamentally spotted with small stabs which often overrun the limits of the gold inlay and appear on the adjacent silver (Plate 105b and Fig 56c,d). The execution of the ornament is often crude but the general effect is rich and alive. Foliate and animal details are shown in Fig 56. The niello only survives in a few places. Originally it completely filled the cut-away backgrounds of the border and of the central device (Plate 105) except for the cheeks or eye-surrounds of the animal masks but was wholly absent from the openwork areas. The ragged chasing of the channels, designed to grip the niello, can be seen in Plate 105b. The bosses are prominent and project 7 mm (rather over $\frac{1}{4}$ in) from the face of the brooch. The present weight of the brooch is 124.3 grm (approximately $4\frac{3}{8}$ oz), or nearly twice that of the Fuller brooch, which has the same diameter.

The Strickland brooch is, and must always have been, a striking and effective piece. Its solidity, deep carving, heavy bosses and punched openwork give a rich plastic feeling and the interest is enhanced by the polychrome effect of dispersed gold, black, silver and blue, while the slight curvature of the brooch adds to the glitter of light and shade. It stands in sharp contrast to the flat smoothness and linear ideas of the Fuller and Ely brooches.

Date

The roughly-beaded borders of the brooch are very similar to those of the Trewhiddle pieces, the two Beeston Tor brooches (Plate 106a,b), the Dolven and Grønneberg pommels (Plate 102a–d), the Talnotrie strap-end (deposited *c.* 900),[80] the Æthelwulf and Æthelswith rings and other dated pieces of the ninth century. Speckling of animal bodies occurs on the Ixworth disc (Plate 109a) and the Ingleton pommel (Plate 109d),[81] the Witham pins, the Victoria and Albert ring,[82] the Trewhiddle 'drinking-horn mounts'[83] and of birds, borders and foliate details on the Æthelwulf ring,[84] where also the 'collars' of the neck can be matched. The central element of the design (Fig 56b) matches that of the Fuller brooch. A more striking parallel, in which the animal masks at the points of the central hollow-sided rectangular motive occur, is an Anglo-Saxon gold pendant in the Hon Treasure (Plate 106d). This piece is made of gold with filigree decoration, including collared granules (eyes), vine-scroll ornament (retained by little clips in the manner of the Kirkoswald trefoil brooch) and a central cabochon garnet, and it should, in spite of the late date of deposition be of eighth-century date and ancestral to the Strickland brooch. The terminals of the Trewhiddle 'drinking-horn mounts' provide particularly close parallels for the animal masks on the Strickland brooch, allowing for the fact that they are modelled and not flat and inlaid. The prominent eyes, the incurved and clubbed ears and the geometric fields on nose and forehead, all occur.[85] The rough leaf fill-ups are in the general manner already noted on the Fuller brooch and the larger of the two from Beeston Tor (Plate 106a).

Blue-glass studs which can be seen as a decorative theme as early as the mid-seventh-century Crundale Down sword-pommel, occur on the Tassilo chalice[86] in form and setting as in the Strickland brooch. Finally, attention may be drawn to the lozenge and pellet border (Fig 56j). Geometric borders with lozenges separated by vertical billets (usually in pairs) occur in late Roman art, for example, on bracelets in the Gallo-Roman cemetery at Vermand[87] and amongst the Nydam bog-finds.[88] They occur also on Byzantine and early Christian ivories,[89] and in Coptic art.[90] From one or more of these sources the theme passed into Germanic and late Celtic art where it can be found in precisely the classical form and also in stylized and variant versions, over a wide range of time and space.[91] At the period of the Strickland brooch, the theme can be seen on the upper edge of the topmost of three similar knobs of ninth-century date on the Kells crozier in the British Museum and in a variant form (pellets separated by vertical bars) forming the wheel-head of the cross on the contemporary binding-strip above it. A similar theme occurs on the two Saxon sword-pommels from Norway (Plate 102a–d), on strap-ends from horses' headstalls in the Borre and Gokstad finds and elsewhere. The exact form seen on the border of the Strickland brooch, a continuous line of alternating lozenges and pellets, seems chiefly to be found in ivories (Plate 106, a work which I attribute firmly to Northumbria)[92] and in manuscripts[93] of the Ada group of the early ninth century but also occurs in Anglo-Saxon metalwork in the dated gold and niello ring of Alhstan, bishop of Sherborne (823–867) – the earliest English episcopal ring – which itself takes this form,[94] and one of the Oseberg sledge panels[95] of 800–850. All the ornamental themes of the Strickland brooch thus fit a date in the ninth century and probably in its first half.

III: THE SUTTON, ISLE OF ELY, BROOCH

History

In 1694, the remains of a lead casket were turned up by the plough at Sutton in the Isle of Ely. From it were recovered a hundred silver coins of William the Conqueror, five heavy gold rings, a plain silver dish or disc and another decorated silver disc, six inches across, with Anglo-Saxon and runic inscriptions on the back. Ten years later, this latter piece was sent to George Hickes by the learned vicar of Harlow in Essex, John Taylor, also canon of Peterborough, at a time when Andrew Fountaine's *Dissertatio de Numismatibus Saxonicis and Dano-Saxonicis* (Oxford, 1705) was in the press. Hickes wrote a supplementary letter in Latin dated 30 September 1704, which he appended to Fountaine's numismatic treatise and which became pp. 186–8 of his *Dissertatio De Linguarum Veterum Septentrionalium Usu* (Oxford, 1705), in which Fountaine's treatise is incorporated. In this letter he described the discovery of the silver disc and illustrated its front and back (Fig 57), also transcribing the Saxon inscription. Hickes's account was used as the basis of a paragraph in Gibson's edition of Camden's *Britannia* (2 ed., I, 493), where the back of the brooch was reproduced. Sir Cyril Fox lists the find in his *Archaeology of the Cambridge Region* (I ed., 1923), p. 300, and Reginald Smith reproduced Hickes's drawings and discussed the Sutton disc in his paper on the Beeston Tor treasure (1925). The brooch itself and the things found with it had disappeared.

In November 1950, a rubbing of an inscription 'on a silver plate' was brought into the Department of British and Mediaeval Antiquities of the British Museum, by Mr John Hunt of Co. Limerick. It was the inscription of the Sutton disc.[96] The presence of the original in the Paris collection of Mr O'Connor of Dublin was subsequently established. Mr O'Connor kindly arranged for the disc to be

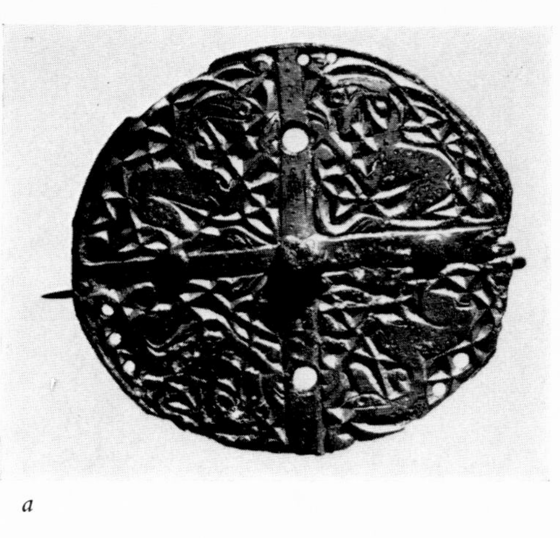

a

b

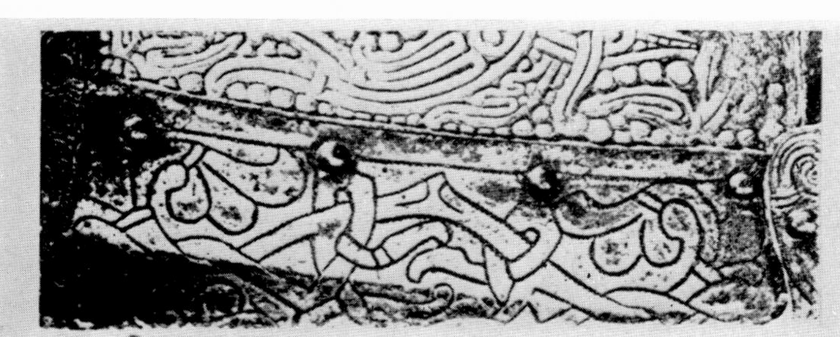

c

d

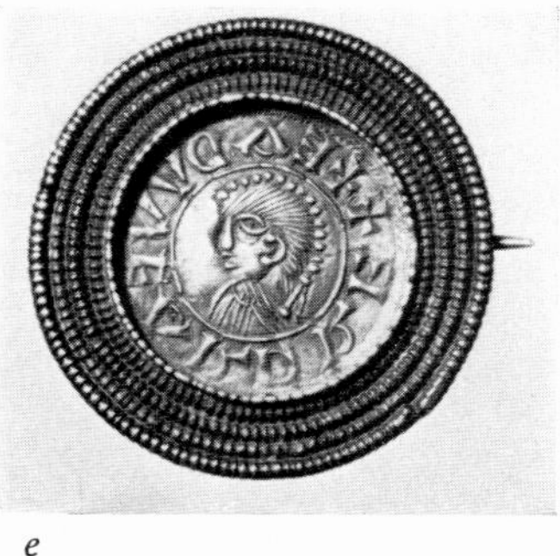

e

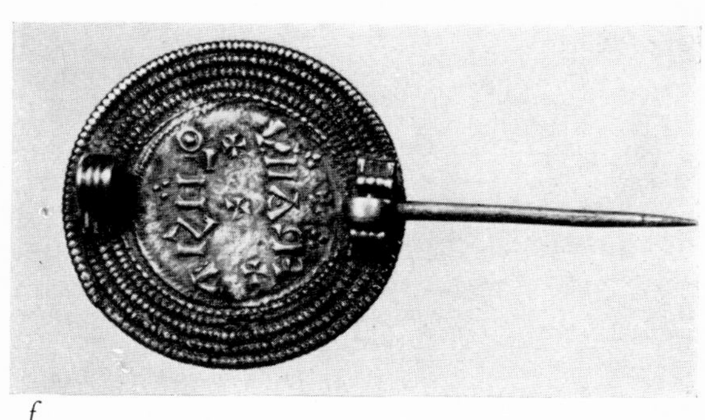

f

Plate 109 a, Gilt-bronze brooch, Ixworth, Suffolk (Scale 1 : 1); *b,c*, Details of metal mounts, Cammin casket (enlarged); *d*, Sword pommel, Ingleton, Yorks (Scale 1 : 1); *e,f*, Silver coin-brooch, Rome (Scale 1 : 1)

a

b

Plate 110 a, Silver disc-brooch, Stockholm (Scale 1 : 1); *b*, Gilt-bronze disc-brooch, Hillesøy, Lenvik, Norway (Scale 1 : 1)

Plate 111 Disc-brooch, silver with gold and niello inlays, King's School, Canterbury (Scale 1 : 1)

Plate 112 Squat jar in dark blue glass, Deal, Kent (slightly reduced)

brought to the British Museum for identification and it was subsequently purchased (Plate 107).

It is always highly interesting and satisfactory to recover an important lost antiquity and the Sutton brooch, a remarkable piece with known find-spot and impeccable history, dated by associated coins to before 1088 and with the two inscriptions, came to light again at an opportune moment, following immediately upon the discovery of the Strickland and Fuller brooches. It is the largest of all these disc-brooches, the latest in date and the only one ornamented in Viking style. Study of the original shows that Hickes's engravings (Fig 57) were exactly full-scale and of an extremely high degree of accuracy.

Description and Stylistic Affinities

The Sutton, Isle of Ely, brooch is a thin silver disc, not flat but as in the case of the Fuller and Strickland brooches, dished in a shallow curve. It is not quite circular, the diameter varying between 5·8 and 6·1 in (14·9–16·4 cm). One of the conical silver bosses is missing from the front and the pin, spring-coil and catch-plate are missing from the back. Part only of a flat silver strip that ran across the brooch from which the spring, pin and catch developed, survives (Plate 108a). It was this strip which bore the runic inscription. The missing boss is in line with this strip and concealed one of the three rivets by which the strip was affixed to the disc. The fastening mechanism of the brooch must have been similar to that which survives intact on the back of the smaller of the two Beeston Tor brooches (Plate 108b). Boss, strip and pin were already missing (except for the part of the strip that survives with the runes) when the brooch was engraved in 1704, it being then in exactly the condition it is today. The lead casket had no doubt been buried in a time of danger and the nature of the damage to the brooch suggests that it had been hastily and forcibly torn from the clothing, perhaps from a body, by someone who had no time to get the pin undone. If the corpse we have postulated was that of the lady who owned the brooch, the curse on the back may have come into operation in more dramatic circumstances than were probably imagined when it was written. The weight of the brooch in its present condition is 4¾ oz (134 grm).

The general design of the front (Fig 53a) bears, as Reginald Smith pointed out,[97] a remarkable resemblance to that of the larger of the two Beeston Tor brooches (Plate 106a). In both, the basic design is that of four intersecting circles and in both, nine small bosses are evenly spaced over the surface (at the intersections of the circles) and linked by twelve pointed oval fields, resulting from the intersection of the circles, made up with eight extra arcs, thus leaving four four-sided

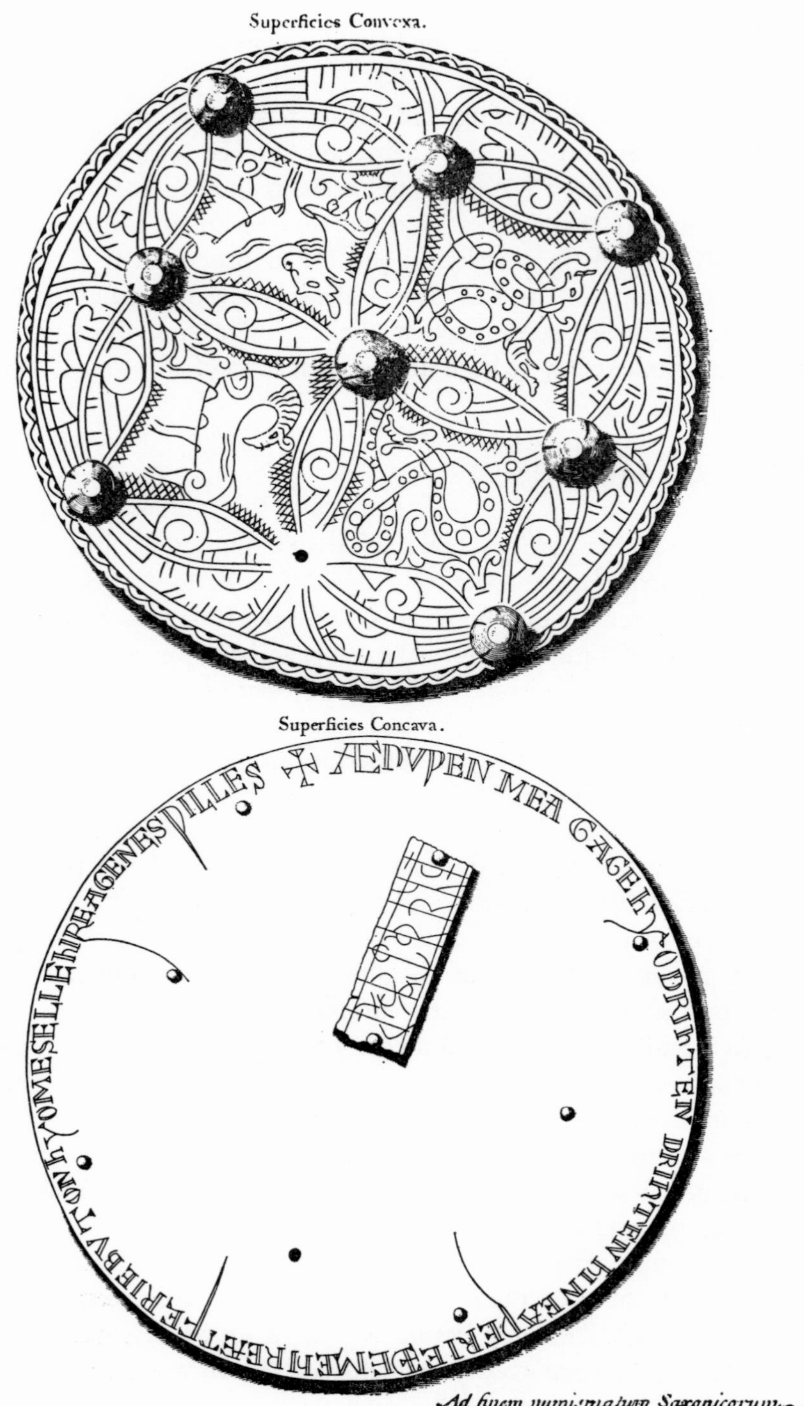

Figure 57 The Sutton, Isle of Ely, brooch, as illustrated in Hickes' *Thesaurus* (Scale: reduced)

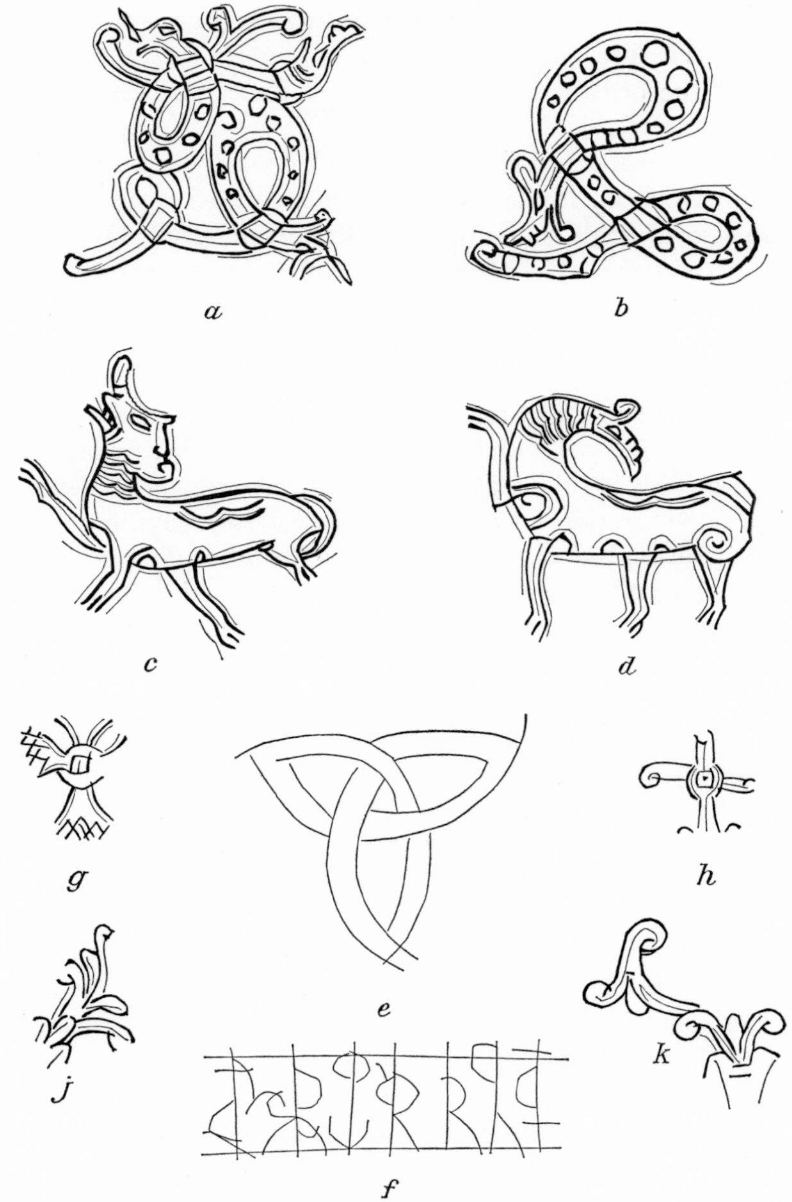

Figure 58 Details of ornament and runic inscription, Sutton, Isle of Ely, brooch. (Scales 1 : 1)

internal spaces to be filled. In the Beeston Tor brooch, these spaces are filled with leaves and other small foliate and geometric details. In the Sutton brooch, while scrolls and foliate details in late Viking Ringerike style and (apparently) vestigial animal elements fill other spaces, two of the four central fields carry a grotesque quadruped, the other two a dragon and two dragons (one with a head at both ends) interlacing (Fig 58).

The whole of the ornament is engraved and there has been no attempt at niello inlay.

The foliate and animal ornament is all in late Viking style, animated but crude and sketchy in execution. It can hardly be placed more precisely. The twelve narrow, pointed oval fields contain similar degenerate scrolls in what Reginald Smith called a Ringerike style. Outside them in the outer parts of the brooch are doubtful but symmetrically balanced patterns without any obvious foliate character, to which eight rather deliberately drawn eyes give a zoomorphic touch suggesting pairs of affronted beasts. Double contouring is present throughout the ornamentation of the brooch, in the form of a very faintly-cut line following the main engraved lines (Fig 58), except in the pointed oval fields where it does not occur. The foliate and knot details in the four main rectangular spaces have a more definite style-character. It remains difficult to claim anything more specific for the art of the Sutton brooch than that it is an English equivalent of late Viking style. The technique and style of the engraving is matched on the metal mounts of the Cammin casket,[98] (Plate 109b), a house-shaped casket formerly in the cathedral of Cammin in Poland, destroyed during the Second World War. The animals carved on the elk-horn panels (not illustrated here) were in typical Danish Mammen style (*c.* A.D. 970–1010). The engraved animals on the metal frames are more akin to Jellinge style and a date of A.D. 1000 may be suggested. The quadrupeds and foliate details in the main rectangular fields are akin to these themes on the Jellinge stone.[99] The affinities which Reginald Smith perceived with the Norwegian Urnes style of *c.* 1050–1100 are not pronounced but the interlacing snakes or dragons in the upper rectangular fields have a distinct kinship with the Swedish runestone style.[100] Whatever its precise affinities, the Sutton brooch is a piece made in the English Danelaw. Its place of discovery, its insular and traditional character (one of the Saxon disc-brooch series and closely related in design and construction to the Beeston Tor brooches) and its Anglo-Saxon inscription, all demonstrate this. As such and as a piece buried in *c.* 1088 and datable with probability to the period *c.* 1025–1050, it stands in its own right as an important minor document in the history of Viking style in Britain.

The Inscriptions

Anglo-Saxon. The Anglo-Saxon inscription, certain of whose spellings are said to indicate an eleventh-century date, in agreement with the other evidence, was read as follows by Bruce Dickens.[101]

+AEDVWEN ME AG. AGE HYO. DRIHTEN, DRIHTEN HINE AWERIE DE ME HIRE AETFERIE BUTON HYO ME SELLE HIRE AGENES WILLES. (+Ædwen owns me. May she own me. Lord, Lord mayest Thou curse him who takes me from her, unless she give me of her own accord.)

This interpretation rests to some extent upon punctuation and G. M. Young has offered a different reading which seems preferable both in sense and when the epigraphy is studied in the original. His reading punctuates the opening of the inscription

+AEDVWEN ME AG. AGE HYO DRIHTEN. DRIHTEN HINE AWERIE etc. (+Ædwen owns me. May the Lord own her. Lord, mayest Thou curse him, etc.)

From a study of the original it appears that two factors affected the spacing and *ductus* of the inscription – its sense and obstacles represented by the presence of casting flaws in the metal and the ends of the rivets associated with the outer bosses on the front. Here Hickes's engraving is not absolutely faithful to the original and the recovery of this helps. In the original there is a gap between the words HIRE and AGENES (not shown in the 1704 engraving, Fig 57). This is to avoid a flaw in the metal. The LE of WILLES at the end of the inscription is spaced to either side of a rivet (not shown in the 1704 engraving). The arms of the Y of HYO in the phrase AGE HYO DRIHTEN are unduly spread in order to use up the awkward space outside a rivet. In the material part of the inscription, the space between the A and the G of AG in the phrase AEDVWEN ME AG, where it is not required, is due to a flaw in the metal. The phrase AGE HYO DRIHTEN starts in rather smaller lettering than the end of the preceding phrase and is written without a break. A clear break and one not conditioned by an obstacle follows the DRIHTEN. It is true that there is a small flaw at this point but it is not sufficiently large to account for the extent of the space, or for a space at all. It is, in fact, small enough to have been ignored. Another smaller space, not conditioned by any flaw, occurs after the second DRIHTEN. A similar space occurs after the name of the owner, AEDVWEN. A small space after the second DRIHTEN could also be desirable from the point of view of the sense, for the word is an invocation (Lord, mayest thou curse him, etc.) which prefaces the phrase, which itself is written continuously without any break other than those conditioned by obstacles of the kind described. Bruce Dickens, to whom Young's suggestion was submitted, said that it was certainly possible 'unless there is punctuation standing in the way'. There is no such punctuation. The suggestion is, on the contrary, directly supported by the spacing of the phrases and makes better sense. It may accordingly be taken as the correct interpretation.

Runic. The strip on which the runes occur (Plate 108a) is broken at both ends. Originally it must have extended, as on the smaller Beeston Tor brooch (Plate 108a), right across the disc. The portion of the inscription preserved is its latter part, the runes, as shown in Fig 58f, reading from left to right. They run right up to the outer rivet and the commencement of the inscription may be assumed to have begun close to the corresponding (missing) rivet at the other end. At least half the inscription, its beginning, is therefore lacking. The silver strip on the Beeston Tor brooch can be seen to extend some way beyond its outer retaining rivets, before it narrows in and develops into coil and catch-plate. It extends to the edges of the disc before it narrows. If this were so on the Sutton brooch, another 1·8 in in all (nearly 1 in at either end) would have been available for additional runes. It certainly seems from the continuing marginal lines above and below the runes, that the inscription may have carried on beyond the outer rivet. The whole inscription was then probably at least 3½ in long and might have extended for a maximum length of approximately 5½ in. The runes are unfortunately unintelligible. R. W. Chambers expressed the view that they were an attempt to write Scandinavian runes by someone who did not understand them. A careful new transcription from the original is given in Fig 58f and this adjusts that published by Hickes (Fig 57) in some particulars. In spite of this the runes remain unintelligible. The new transcription with photographs was submitted to the Swedish runologist, Sven B. Janson, whose comments are:

> These are not eleventh-century Scandinavian runes, nor an ignorant attempt to imitate them. It is more a case of degenerate Anglo-Saxon runes. In many cases the writer has tried to make bind-runes. It seems to me that certain lines are thinner than others, but this may be due to the photograph. Two r-runes of a late type, one *þ* and possibly one *oe* might be read, but I cannot get any intelligible meaning from the damaged inscription.

IV: THE HILLESØY AND STOCKHOLM DISCS

The discs found at Hillesøy in the parish of Lenvik (in Rogaland, West Norway) and in Stockholm are illustrated in Plate 110a,b. Both are Anglo-Saxon pieces. The Hillesøy disc has been admirably and accessibly described by Sjovøld,[102] and it need only be said here that although found in a burial dated by its pair of tortoise brooches to the ninth century, the disc itself is more likely to be in the eighth. It stands in close relationship with the Brunswick casket, the Witham pins and the Ixworth disc (Plate 109a).[103] This group of material is not itself dated but its differences in themes and style from all the dated ninth-century metalwork (already discussed in connection with the Fuller and Strickland brooches), are so marked that it seems legitimate to regard these styles as characteristic of the latter part of the eighth rather than of the ninth century. The relationship of the Hillesøy disc with the mutilated Ixworth disc lies chiefly in the fact that both are in gilt-bronze (all the other discs discussed being of silver or silver and gold) and slightly curved and that the surviving knob at the centre of the Ixworth piece is knurled in the distinctive manner of those of the Hillesøy disc. The Ixworth piece, whatever it sultimate fate, was designed as a brooch since the impression (pointed at one end), across a diameter, of a metal strip which carried the attachment mechanism (Plate 109a) survives.[104] From this it seems likely that the Hillesøy disc also was originally a brooch, although Sjovøld's account implies that it was a mounting (e.g. for a shrine or casket) adapted as a brooch by Vikings who had looted it.

The Stockholm disc (Plate 110a)[105] was also a brooch. It is flat but so are the two Beeston Tor brooches (Plate 106a,b). There are no indications on the disc of any other use. The three extra holes piercing the ornament (Plate 110a) are clearly secondary but they are not disposed in a manner appropriate to the attachment of the disc as an appliqué mounting. They form an alignment on a diameter of the brooch from which three of the original bosses or studs are missing. They must represent rivets driven through the silver to reinforce, or to fix a replacement for, a metal strip across the back like those of the Ely, Beeston Tor and Ixworth discs which carried the fastening mechanism. The back of the brooch, to judge from a photograph, shows above and below these holes two faint parallel lines, which come together to a point at either end. These seem to delineate a short metal strip associated with the two secondary holes on this alignment. The function of the third hole, slightly off the alignment, is not clear. It is on the line of a severe crack across the disc and may perhaps, with the other two, represent an attempt to repair it after damage.

The burial of the Stockholm brooch (as I propose to call it) can be dated by the associated coins (thirty-nine Arab and Sassanian, twenty-seven Anglo-Saxon of Æthelred II and Canute) to shortly after 1016. It had travelled from England and was not in mint condition, as the repair shows. The general resemblance to the larger of the Beeston Tor brooches, which also has foliate ornament only, with some interlacing, similar smooth low studs or bosses (Plate 106a) and roughly 'beaded' borders, is notable. The foliage has many details – curls, nicks and frets on the leaves, pointed 'Celtic' knots with pellet fill-ups and so on, which relate it to the foliage of such pieces as the Ormside bowl and the Fuller brooch and other related metal work of the ninth century like the Abingdon sword. This lush, close-knit, angular foliage of the Stockholm brooch, spreading to fill up its frames, is in a distinct and developed style. It must be appreciably later than any of the ninth-century metal work cited but it is clearly closely dependent on it and bears no trace of Viking style. I should be disinclined to date this brooch later than early in the tenth century and the style of its foliage may prove to be characteristic for that period.

V: A COIN-BROOCH FOUND IN ROME

This chapter does not set out to discuss the numerous small disc-brooches of the late Saxon period in bronze, lead and pewter with simple pellet and geometric ornament and in one series enamelled, nor will the small but important late eleventh-century openwork circular ornament from Pitney in Somerset in Anglo-Irish Urnes style,[106] which is in a somewhat different category, be discussed. This is, though, an opportunity for introducing to the archaeological literature a small coin-brooch, (diameter 1·4 in) found about twenty-five years ago in Rome, with a large hoard of Anglo-Saxon silver pennies[107] and acquired by the British Museum (1951, 2–6, 1; Plate 109e,f). The coin appears (from its irregular workmanship, lettering and legend) to be a Danish imitation struck in this country of a coin of Edward the Elder (899–925). Both legends have been copies from a normal coin straight on to the die, with the result that they come out retrograde on the new coin. The brooch must date from the earlier part of the tenth century and provides a useful fixed point for the style of the plain contemporary setting of beaded silver wire and for the details of the fastening mechanism on the back. It also serves as a reminder of another similar but considerably larger silver medallion-brooch of the same century on which the medallion is in the style of the coins of Edgar the Peaceful, 959–975. This is the well-known piece believed to have been found in Canterbury, which bears the legend WVDEMAN FECID on the obverse and has a remarkable back reinforced with silver strips.[108] It has been acquired by the Ashmolean Museum. In considering the larger and more sumptuous disc-brooches, these smaller disc-brooches of quality must not be forgotten, for they help to show in the somewhat scanty archaeological record how typical and regular a feature of the late Saxon scene the disc-brooch, large and small, must have been.

VI: THE IGELÖSA DISC

A fragmentary disc found at Igelösa in Skane, with a hoard of Saxon coins whose deposition is dated 1006 by R. M. Dolley, has very kindly been brought to my notice by David Wilson. It is much broken and folded and appears in the hoard

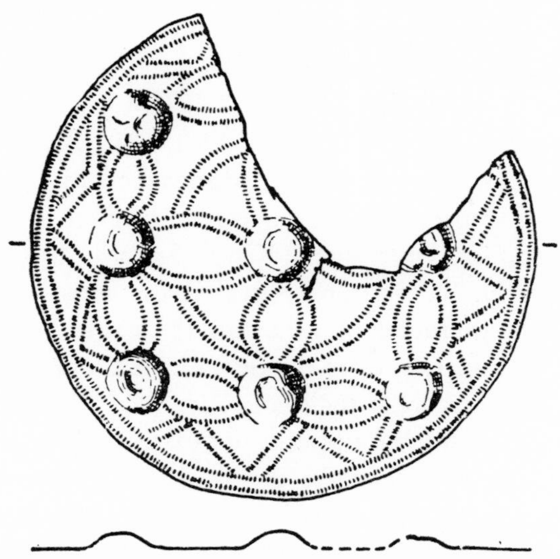

Figure 59 Silver disc, Igelösa, Skåne, Sweden (Scale 1 : 1)

as scrap. It no doubt dates from the tenth century. This disc is now in Lund, on loan from the Statens Historiska Museum, Stockholm and I am grateful to the Authorities of the Universitets Historiska Museum, Lund for permission to publish it and to Mrs D. M. Wilson for providing the drawing (Fig 59).

The disc, diameter 7 cm, is flat and only 0·6 mm thick. It weighs, as extant, 9·02 grammes. When complete it had nine bosses like the larger Beeston Tor disc (Plate 106a). The workmanship is rough and the edge uneven. A basic geometric pattern, very like that of the Stockholm (Plate 110a) and the larger Beeston Tor discs is picked out with punch-marks but the spaces between are not filled with ornament. The repoussé character of the bosses, well seen in profile (Fig 59), is not paralleled on any of the other discs here described. As Wilson has suggested to me they would seem to be skeuomorphs of the traditional bosses of the Insular series. On the back, there is no trace of an attachment for fastening and this and the rough edge and exceptional thinness suggest that the disc may have been cut down from a mounting of some other kind.

In the absence of distinctive decoration which might help to place or date it, we may note that the disc seems to have close affinities in size and design with the Stockholm and larger Beeston Tor examples. Like Stockholm, it has an inner ring. Its diameter and number of bosses are the same as Beeston Tor and both brooches are also alike in having four pointed oval fields radiating from the centre, with others joining the bosses and in having triangular motives in the outer border. The geometric design with nine bosses is also akin to that of the Isle of Ely brooch.

VII: THE CANTERBURY BROOCH

For the sake of completeness I add here an illustration (Plate 111) and brief note of the King's School, Canterbury, brooch, discovered in 1957 in Palace Court, within the precincts of Canterbury Cathedral, and given to the British Museum by the Headmaster and Governors of the King's School. It was subsequently fully published by Professor D. M. Wilson[108a] and is the most baroque and evolved example of the type. Its diameter of 14·2 cms ($5\frac{1}{2}$ inches) places it amongst the largest examples. It combines, as does the Strickland brooch, the two metals gold and silver, but in a very different technique. Its gold filigree ornamental panels appear through openings cut in an upper silver plate, and were held in position by a silver back plate of the same size as the front plate. The spaces between the filigree panels are incised with interlace and animal interlace in a tortured tenth-century Jellinge style (Fig 60). There is a massive attachment pin at the back.

Figure 60 The ornament in Ringerike style of the nielloed fields, Canterbury brooch (Scale 1 : 1)

CONCLUSIONS

From this survey it appears that the flat or slightly curved disc-brooch, not 'composite' but made from a thin sheet of metal, is the characteristic brooch-form throughout the late Saxon period. If the chronological arguments here set forward are accepted, the leading brooches give the following picture:

Eighth century	*Ninth century*	*Tenth century*	*Eleventh century*
Hillesøy brooch	Strickland brooch	Stockholm brooch	Sutton, Ise of Ely, brooch
Ixworth brooch	Fuller brooch	Rome coin-brooch	Pitney brooch
Witham pins	Beeston Tor brooches (2)	Canterbury medallion-brooch	King's School, Canterbury brooch
		Igelösa disc	

The three large brooches, the main subject of this chapter, add greatly to our knowledge and by their inter-relationships with the already known material, give a new cohesion to the whole subject of late Saxon ornament in metalwork. All, except the Witham pins, seem originally to have been brooches. They illustrate all the styles of late Saxon ornament. The Fuller brooch in particular, with its magnificent niello-work, the precision and finish of its ornament and its elaborate and original design, reveals new levels of technical ability and imagination, amidst the small-scale ornament characteristic of the metalwork of its century.[109]

NOTES TO CHAPTER FIFTEEN

1 Reginald A. Smith, 'The Beeston Tor Hoard', in *Antiquaries Journal*, V, 1925, 135–40.

2 J. R. Kirk, *The Alfred and Minster Lovel Jewels*, Ashmolean Museum, Oxford, 1948; R. F. Jessup, *Anglo-Saxon Jewellery*, London, 1950, 38, Pl. B (in colour).

3 For the Hamilton (or Townley) brooch, see Reginald A. Smith, *British Museum Guide to Anglo-Saxon Antiquities*, London, 1923, Pl. X a; for the Dowgate Hill brooch, see R. F. Jessup, *op. cit.*, Pl. XXXII, I; for both see O. M. Dalton in *Proceedings of the Society of Antiquaries*, Second Series, XX, 1903–5, 64–76.

4 One such armlet was deposited with the Douglas, Isle of Man, hoard, *c.* 975 (British Museum 95, 8–9, I). Others also in the British Museum were found at Wendover, Bucks. (49, 2–10, I), *Archaeologia*, XXXIII, 347; *Archaeological Journal*, VI, 48, and Virginia, Co. Cavan, Eire (49, 3–1, 2).

5 R. A. Smith, *op. cit.*, 1923, Fig. 104.

6 *The Sutton Hoo Ship-Burial*, Vol. I, Cambridge, 1974, Chapter 2.

7 Sir Thomas Kendrick, *Anglo-Saxon Art to A.D. 900*, London, 1938, Pl. XXXVI.

8 T. D. Kendrick, *op. cit.*

9 R. F. Jessup, *op. cit.*, Pl. XXVII; T. D. Kendrick, *op. cit.*, 1938, Pl. XXXI, 5; R. A. Smith, *op. cit.*, 1923, Fig. 60.

10 T. D. Kendrick, *op. cit.*, 1938, Pl. XXXI, 3; R. F. Jessup, *op. cit.*, 1950, frontispiece (in colour) and Pl. XXIV.

11 *Antiquity*, VII, 1933, 448, Pl. V; T. D. Kendrick, *op. cit.*, 1938, Pl. XXXI, 2; Chapter One, pp. 40–1 in this volume.

12 R. F. Jessup, *op. cit.*, 1950, Pl. XXV, 1.

13 R. F. Jessup, *op. cit.*, 1950, Pl. XXV, 2.

14 T. D. Kendrick, *op. cit.*, 1938, Pl. LXXI; R. A. Smith, *op. cit.*, 1923, Pl. IX.

15 R. F. Jessup, *op. cit.*, 1950, Pl. XXVI a; E. T. Leeds, *Early Anglo-Saxon Art and Archaeology*, Oxford, 1936, Pl. XXXIII, 5.

16 Cf. R. F. Jessup, *op. cit.*, 1950, Pls. XXII, XXIII, 2; particularly the lower (Faversham) brooch on Pl. XXII (our Fig 52d).

17 Cf. the Carolingian circular ornaments from Molsheim (H. Arbman, *Schweden und das Karolingische Reich*, Stockholm, 1937, Pl. LIX, 2; from Schonen, Sweden (*ibid.*, Pl. LI), and the Hon find, Norway (*ibid.*, Pl. LIX, 3).

18 R. A. Smith, *op. cit.*, 1923, Pl. XVI, 1.

19 Thorleif Sjovøld, 'A Bronze Ornament of Western European Origin found in Northern Norway', *Antiquity*, XXV, 1951, 127–30: originally published in *Stavanger Museums Årbok*, 1946, 87–91.

20 R. A. Smith, *op. cit.*, 1925.

21 *Antiquary*, XLIX, No. 10 (n.s. VI, 1910), 268–9.

22 A. W. Clapham, *English Romanesque Architecture before the Conquest*, Oxford, 1930, 130; D. Talbot Rice, *English Art 871–1100*, Oxford, 1952, 229.

23 A preliminary note on the Fuller brooch appears in *British Museum Quarterly*, XVI, 1952, 75–6.

24 The difference might possibly have some significance if, for example, the figure could be thought to represent Winter warming his hands.

25 R. A. Smith, *op. cit.*, 1925, 136.

26 J. Brøndsted, *Early English Ornament*, London, 1924, Fig. 105.

27 Cf. *Oxoniensia*, XVII/XVIII, 1952–3, 261 ff., where it is shown that this well-known sword has no connection with Wallingford and no title to that name. In *Proceedings of the Oxford Architectural and Historical Society*, N.S. III, 1874, 171, A. J. (later Sir Arthur) Evans reported to the Society the discovery of a sword, which can only be this one, at Bogs Mill on the River Ock, about one mile above Abingdon. Bogs or Buggs Mill is now known as New Cut Mill.

28 These two last may be conveniently seen, together with King Æthelwulf's ring, referred to below, in R. H. Hodgkin, *A History of the Anglo-Saxons*, London, 1952, II, Pl. IV (in colour in 1 and 2 ed).

29 J. Brøndsted, *op. cit.*, 1924, Fig. 126.

30 For the latest and most profound description and art-historical analysis of this chalice see G. Haseloff, *Der Tassilokelch*, Munich, 1951.

31 J. Brøndsted, *op. cit.*, 1924, Fig. 129; G. Haseloff, *op. cit.*, in note 28, 44, 67.

32 *Journal of the International Institute for the Conservation of Museum Objects*, II, London, 1953, 49–62.

33 *Antiquaries Journal*, XXXIII, 1953, 75–7.

34 R. A. Smith, *op. cit.*, 1923, Fig. 143; R. F. Jessup, *op. cit.*, 1950, Pl. XXXVI, I; R. H. Hodgkin, *op. cit.*, in note 26, II, Pl. IV (in colour n. 1 and 2 ed).

35 J. Brøndsted, *op. cit.*, 1924; T. D. Kendrick, *op. cit.*, 1938. Except for the Alfred Jewel (Ashmolean Museum) all the metalwork referred to above is in the British Museum.

36 J. Brøndsted, *op. cit.*, 1924, Figs. 83, 90, 91.

37 *Ibid.*, Fig. 87.

38 *Ibid.*, Fig. 130; R. F. Jessup, *op. cit.*, 1950, Pl. XXXVI, no. 6.

39 J. Brøndsted, *op. cit.*, 1924, Fig. 124.

40 *Ibid.*, Fig. 29.

41 *Ibid.*, Fig. 103.

42 Published by D. M. Waterman, *Antiquaries Journal*, XXXI, 1951, 192, Pl. XXXI. The early engravings of this ring discussed by Waterman apparently all show between the four roundels small tightly-knotted snakes, whose eyes and mouths are in most cases clearly indicated. These knotted snakes are not known elsewhere and the foliate knots on the Saxon sword-pommel from Gronneberg (Pl. 102a,b) are so similar in general appearance as to suggest that the snakes on the Malton ring may in reality be foliate details misunderstood by the engraver. The sword-pommel from Ingleton (Pl. 109d), a Yorkshire find like the ring, shows a fauna close to that of the ring and its zoomorphic details have minute dots for eyes like those of the snakes on the ring and similar mouths. The Ingleton pommel see *British Museum Quarterly*, XV, 1941–50, 74, Pl. XXXIII d.

43 T. D. Kendrick and C. F. C. Hawkes, *Archaeology in England and Wales*, London, 1930, Figs. 117, 333; *Bollettino d'Arte*, 2 ser. III, 1923, 241.

44 J. Brøndsted, *op. cit.*, 1924, Fig. 125; Chr. A. Holmbøe, *En maerkvaerdig Samling, af Smykker etc.*, Christiania, 1835; S. Grieg, 'Vikingetidens Skattefund', *Universitetets Oldsaksamlingens Skrifter*, Bd. II, Oslo, 1929, 182–98, Fig. 7.

45 The three Saxon swords found in Norway referred to in this chapter from Hoven, Dolven and Gronneberg (Pls. 102a–d, 100a) were all from burial-mounds but none had datable associations (cf. J. Brøndsted, *op. cit.*, 1924, 149, note 1). All three are illustrated and discussed by A. W. Brøgger, 'Rolvsøyaetten', *Bergens Museum Årbok* (Historisk-Antikvarisk Raekke), 1920–1, 15–17. The Dolven sword is illustrated in O. Rygh, *Norsk Oldsager*, Fig. 505, and both it and Gronneberg by Jan Peterson in Haakon Shetelig, *Viking Antiquities in Western Europe*, v. (*British Antiquities found in Norway*).

46 T. D. Kendrick, *op. cit.*, 1938, Pl. XLI; E. G. Millar, *The Lindisfarne Gospels*, Pl. XXI.
47 T. D. Kendrick, *op. cit.*, 1938, Pl. LIII.
48 e.g. Sir Edward Sullivan, *The Book of Kells*, 1914, Pls. XII, XIII. For rosette themes in the Book of Kells see also F. Henry, *Irish Art*, London, 1940, Pls. LX, LXIb, LXII.
49 J. Brøndsted, *op. cit.*, 1924, Fig. 90.
50 *Ibid.*, Fig. 87.
51 *Ibid.*, Fig. 84; T. D. Kendrick, *op. cit.*, 1938, Pl. LXV, 2.
52 J. Brøndsted, *op. cit.*, 1924, Fig. 129.
53 T. D. Kendrick, *op. cit.*, 1938, Pl. LXVIII, 4.
54 E. G. Millar, *English Illuminated Manuscripts, Vol. I, from the Xth to the XIIIth centuries*, Pl. XXXI.
55 *Ibid.*, Pls. XLVI, XLVII.
56 *Ibid.*, Pls. XXXVIII, XXXIX.
57 Dorothy Whitelock, *The Beginnings of English Society*, 1952, 220.
58 Gregory, *XL Homiliarum in Evangelia Libri Duo*, Liber Secundus, Hom. XXXVI (Migne, *Patr. Lat.*, LXXVI, 1268, col. 2).
59 Benjamin Thorpe, *Homilies of the Anglo-Saxon Church*, I-II, 1846, pp. 372–5.
60 Rev. W. W. Skeat, *Ælfric's Lives of the Saints, being a set of sermons on saints' days formerly observed by the English Church*, 1881, I, 22.
61 B. Thorpe, *op. cit.*, 1846, 549–53.
62 B. Thorpe, *op. cit.*, 1846, 562–4.
63 B. Thorpe, *op. cit.*, 1846, I.
64 'We sceolon ure yfelnysse behreowsian mid urum fig andgitum, ðaet synd gesihþ, and hylst, and swaec, and stenc, and hrepung.'
65 Alanus ab Insulis, IV, cap. iii (Migne, *Patr. Lat.* CCX).
66 *J. Warburg and Courtauld Inst.*, XVIII, 1955. Also noted by Audrey Baker, see H. W. Janson, *Apes and Ape-lore in the Middle Ages and the Renaissance*, Warburg Institute, London, 1952, 255, note 12.
67 E. Clive Rouse and Audrey Baker, 'The Wall-paintings at Longthorpe Tower, nr. Peterborough', *Archaeologia*, XCVI. H. W. Janson, *op. cit.*, 240–1, Pl. XLIV, a.
68 H. W. Janson, *op. cit.*, 241, Pl. XLIV, a.
69 Byrhtferth's *Manual* (A.D. 1011), ed. S. J. Crawford, I (Early English Text Society, London, 1929), 207.
70 C. S. Lewis, *The Allegory of Love*, Oxford, 1936, 101.
71 Bernardus Silvestris, *De Mundi Universitate, Libri Duo, Sive Megacosmus et Microcosmus*, herausgegeben von Dr Carl Sigmund Barach und Dr Johann Wrobel, Innsbruck, 1876, 65–9.
72 *Op. cit.*
73 Sed oculus mundi quantum comminibus astris
Praeminet et Caelum vindicat usque suum,
Non aliter sensus alios obscurat honore
Visus et in solo lumine totus homo est.

Cf. also the *Reductorium Morale* of Petrus Berchorius, written 1340–2, which contains a lengthy discourse on the senses. 'Visus est sensus subtilior et nobilior inter sensus et ideo remotiora potest percipere, et de objectis coloribus a longe judicare' (*R.P. Petri Berchorii Opera Omnia*, ed. no. v, I, Cologne, 1730, cap. vii).
74 C. S. Lewis, *op. cit.*
75 *Isidori Hispalensis Episcopi Etymologiarum Sive Originum, Libri XX*, ed. W. M. Lindsay, II, Oxf. Class-Texts, 1911, Liber XI, De Homine et Portentis, De Homine et partibus eius, sections 18, 21. Cf. F. Saxl, *Verzeichnis astrologischer und mythologischer illustrierter Handschriften des lateinischen Mittelalters, II, Die Handschriften der National Bibliotek in Wien* (*Sitzungsberichte der Heidelberger Akademie der Wissenschaften*), Phil. Hist. Klasse, Heidelberg, 1927, Abb. 24, 43.
76 Mr Chu-tsing Li refers me to a seventeenth-century painting in the Prado by J. A. Escalante, 'The Triumph of Faith over the Senses', as the only comparable representation of the senses (personified, not symbolized) known to him.
77 I am indebted to Dr Mütherich for very kindly allowing me to reproduce her photographs of this MS., to which she drew my attention.
78 Sotheby Sale, 9 May 1949, lot 128, Pls. III–IV; and, for a preliminary note, cf. *British Museum Quarterly*, XV, 1941–50, 74, Pl. XXXIII a.
79 Cf. e.g., Rupert Bruce-Mitford, *The Sutton Hoo Ship-Burial*, A Provisional Guide, British Museum, 1947, Fig. 15.
80 J. Brøndsted, *op. cit.*, 1924, Fig. 108.
81 J. Brøndsted, *op. cit.*, 1924, Fig. 114, and *British Museum Quartley*, XV, 1941–50, 7, Pl. XXXIII.
82 J. Brøndsted, *op. cit.*, 1924, Fig. 130.
83 T. D. Kendrick, *op. cit.*, 1938, Pl. LXXVIII, top.
84 *Ibid.*, Fig. 25.
85 J. Brøndsted, *op. cit.*, 1924, Fig. 104; R. A. Smith, *op. cit.*, 1923, Fig. 120.

86 Cf. for illustration in colour, G. Baldwin Brown, *The Arts in Anglo-Saxon England*, Vol. VI, London, 1921, frontispiece; P. Stollemayer, 'Der Tassilokelch', *Professorenfestschrift zum 400-jährigen Bestande des öffentlichen Obergymnasiums der Benediktiner zu Kremsmunster*, 1949. Also G. Haseloff, *Der Tassilokelch*, Taf. 8 B.

87 T. Eck, *La Cimitière gallo-romain de Vermand, Aisne: Suite et Fin, Mémoires de la Société* Académique de St Quentin, ser. 4, IX, 1891, p. 240, Pl. XVIII, nos. 10, 16: Pl. XIX, no. 10. A thin bronze bracelet embodying the theme from disturbed levels in the Jewry Wall Roman site, Leicester, may be of this period; K. M. Kenyon, *Excavations at the Jewry Wall Site, Leicester, Society of Antiquaries Research Report*, XV, 1948, Fig. 86, 6.

88 A. Riegl, *Die Spätrömische Kunstindustrie*, Vienna, 1901, Pl. I, no. 9.

89 A. Goldschmidt, *Die Elfenbeinskulpturen*, Berlin, 1914 ff., I, no. 94c (Diptych leaf, fourth–fifth cent.), IV, no. 112 (Alexandrian *c.* A.D. 600). Also the well-known late fourth-century ivory panel in the British Museum with the apotheosis of an emperor, O. M. Dalton, *Catalogue of the Ivory Carvings of the Christian Era in the British Museum*, London, 1909, Pl. I; E. Kitzinger, *Early Medieval Art*, British Museum, 1940, Pl. VI.

90 J. Strzygowski, *Koptische Kunst*, no. 7063 (Brautkasten) and 8842 (Löffel).

91 Cf. (1) a Burgundian iron and silver buckle of the late seventh century (P. Bouffard, *Nécropoles burgondes de la Suisse*, Geneva, 1945, Pl. VII, I); (2) In the Vendel material, on the famous enamelled harness from grave III (H. Stolpe and T. J. Arne, *La Nécropole de Vendel*, Stockholm, 1927, Pl. XIII, 3) and a rather similar theme on the harness mounts from Vendel VII (*ibid.*, Pls. XIX, XX, Fig. I); (3) on the upper guard of the sword from Valsgärde 6 (E. Behmer, *Das Zweischneidige Schwert der Germanischen Völkerwanderungzeit*, Stockholm, 1939, Taf. XLVIII; H. Shetelig and H. Falk, *Scandinavian Archaeology*, Oxford, 1937, frontispiece b); (4) the Söndersö Viking sword-grip and pommel in the National Museum, Copenhagen.

In ninth to twelfth century ivories the motive occurs in A. Goldschmidt, *op. cit.*, I, nos. 5, 32, 33, 34 (Ada Group, ninth century); II, nos. 87, 88; III, no. 17a–d (Cologne) and nos. 42–6; IV, nos. 44, 126, 168a. Also on the cover of Queen Melissenda's psalter (twelfth century).

92 A. Goldschmidt, *op. cit.*, I, Pl. I.

93 A. Boinet, *La Miniature carolingienne*, 1913, Pl. XII (Canon Table of the Ada MS. known as the Harley Gospels, the rectangular border at the top).

94 J. Brøndsted, *op. cit.*, 1924, 134, Fig. iii.

95 Cf. H. Shetelig and H. Falk, *op. cit.*, XLVIII, b.

96 The rubbing was also seen and independently identified by R. F. Jessup.

97 R. A. Smith, *op. cit.*, 1925, 137.

98 A. Goldschmidt, *op. cit.*, ii, II, Pls. LXV–LXIX.

99 Sir Thomas Kendrick, *Late Saxon and Viking Art*, London, 1923, Pl. LVIII, and Fig. 9, p. 89; J. Brøndsted, *op. cit.*, 1924, Fig. 198.

100 As Miss Elizabeth Munksgaard has reminded me: cf. the Tullstorp, Skåne, Stone: J. Brøndsted, *op. cit.*, 1924, Fig. 200; T. D. Kendrick, *op. cit.*, 1949, in note 99, Pls. LXXV, LXXVI.

101 *Antiquaries Journal*, v, 1925, 138. Since Bruce Dickens wrote, the two inscriptions have been dealt with by Dr Elisabeth Okasha in her book *Handlist of Anglo-Saxon Non-Runic Inscriptions*, Cambridge University Press, 1971, as follows:

(i) + ÆDVÞEN MEAG AGEHYODRIHTEN
DRIHTEN HINEAÞERIE DEMEHIRE
ÆTFERIEBVTONHYOMESELLEHIRE-
AGENES ÞILLES/I

Text (i) is in verse and reads:

+ ÆDVÞEN ME AG
AGE HYO DRIHTEN
DRIHTEN HINE AÞERIE
DE ME HIRE ÆTFERIE
BVTON HYO ME SELLE
HIRE AGENES ÞILLES

It is probably to be translated, '+ Aedven owns me, may the Lord own her. May the Lord curse him who takes me from her, unless she gives me voluntarily'. ÆDVÞEN is a feminine name, a form of either the recorded ĒADWYNN or the unrecorded *AEDWYNN. The owner formula is followed by a Christian curse, as occurs in wills and charters. The first line appears to be alliterative, the second two rhyming. (ii) Text (ii) is uninterpreted; it consists of seven characters in cryptic script, possibly based on the runic *fuþarc*.'

102 *Op. cit.*

103 For the Ixworth brooch see J. Brøndsted,

op. cit., 1924, Fig. 114. The disc is now in the British Museum, 1927, 12–12, 23. On the uppermost disc of the Witham pins (T. D. Kendrick, *op. cit.*, 1949, Pl. LXXI) a vine-tree motive with interwoven animals can be seen. On the middle disc, the spirited animals are akin to those of the Hillesøy disc. The parallel on the Brunswick casket (T. D. Kendrick, *op. cit.*, 1949, Pl. LXX), apart from the more composed winged creatures in the bottom left- and right-hand panels, is on the slope of the lid not illustrated by Kendrick (A. Goldschmidt, *op. cit.*, II, Pl. LIX, b, e) where winged animals of a more active kind, possessing only front legs appear to either side of a vine plant in which other animals are interlaced. As on the Hillesøy disc, these floral and animal themes are on the Brunswick casket surrounded by borders of ribbon interlace. Similar interlace borders are a feature of the Tassilo chalice.

104 The fastening mechanism of the Ixworth brooch, now missing, can be seen projecting at either edge of the disc on the old photograph used in Pl. 102a.

105 *Månadsbladet* (Stockholm, K. Vitterhets Historie och Antikvitets Akademie), Oct.–Dec. 1892, pp. 173–4; Reginald Smith, *op. cit.*, 1925, 139–40, Fig. 3.

106 T. D. Kendrick, *op. cit.*, 1949, Pl. LXXXII, 2. 116–17. *Victoria County History, Somerset*, London, 19—, I, colour-plate facing p. 278, no. 5. The Pitney brooch is deposited on loan at the British Museum, by its owners, Capt. T. J. Hardinge, R.N., and Mrs Hardinge.

107 *British Numismatic Journal*, 1950, Pl. B (opposite 234).

108 *Proceedings of the Society of Antiquaries*, 2 ser. XIX, 1903, 210; Burlington Fine Arts Club Catalogues, *Exhibition of Art of the Dark Ages*, 1930, Pl. II (A44); *Victoria County History, Kent*, London, 1908, 382, Fig. 27; R. F. Jessup, *op. cit.*, 1950, 112, and Pl. XX, 2; *Ashmolean Museum Report*, 1951, Pl. V; Okasha, *op. cit.* in footnote, 101, No. 19 (text and plate).

108a D. M. Wilson, *Catalogue of Anglo-Saxon Ornamental Metalwork 700–1100 in the British Museum*, 1964, No. 10.

109 The drawings from which Figs. 52, a–f, 53, 54, 55 and 56 are taken are by Mr C. O. Waterhouse, M.B.E., and the author is deeply indebted to him for the great care and attention with which he executed them.

CHAPTER SIXTEEN

Note on a Squat Jar in Blue Glass from Deal, Kent

The glass jar illustrated in Plate 112 and Fig 61 belongs to a small but distinctive group, type A iv in Dr Harden's classification under his class viii (squat jars).[1] It is the ninth or tenth example of this type of jar known[2] depending upon whether the fragment of thick dark blue glass recorded from the Snape boat-grave (Chapter Three, pp. 126, 129) is taken, as seems likely, to represent a vessel of this type. The jar here described was found by Mr F. Oliver in 1970 in the front garden of his house, The Beeches, St Richard's Road, Deal, when digging a large hole to plant a tree. Mr Oliver was digging down to find the level of the natural chalk rock, so that his tree could be planted well clear of it and had evidently struck a grave pit excavated in the chalk. The vessel was found close to bedrock at a depth of about 7 ft (2·13 metres). The grave pit filling showed in the section of his hole like a tunnel, aligned in a north-western direction across the lawn. Mr Oliver records the discovery of 'unusual coins' and of bones in various parts of his two and a half acres of land. It is evident that this is the site of a hitherto unrecorded Anglo-Saxon cemetery.

The jar has a diameter of $4\frac{11}{12}$ inches (12·4 cms) and a height of $3\frac{1}{4}$ inches (8·5 cms). The vessel is slightly unevenly blown so that one side of the neck is lower than the other. The external width of the neck is $2\frac{1}{2}$ inches (6·3 cms). The form is identical with that of other examples. The neck is vertical and plain, without any sort of rim-development. The kick under the base is pronounced and of a regular conical form when seen from the inside. Externally the kick is masked by an applied rosette of seven lobes, executed in a blue glass overtrail. The reticulated overtrails on the shoulder and below it form a somewhat uneven pattern of lozenge or ovoid shapes (Plate 112, Fig 61).

These overtrails form in effect a zone of two lines of interlocking ovoid shapes, the lower ones (there are twelve at each level) being pinched and drawn downwards into points. The design is very similar to that of the fragmentary vessel of the same type found in the boat-grave in Mound No. 2 at Sutton Hoo in 1938 and close also the the more fragmentary of the two from the rich burial at

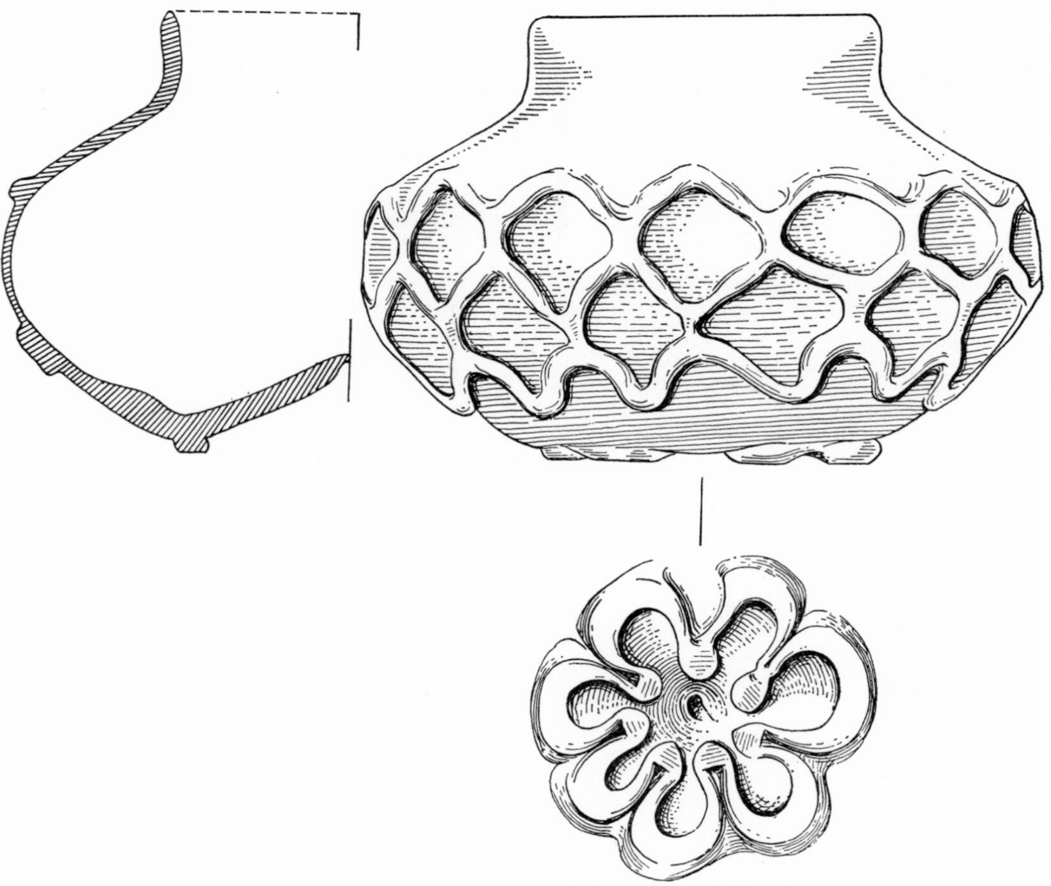

Figure 61 Squat blue glass jar, Deal, Kent (Scale approx. 3:4)

Broomfield, near Colchester. The metal of the Deal jar differs somewhat from that of both the Broomfield jars, the more complete of which also has a simpler design of overtrails.

The neck of the Deal jar is broken off at one side. The thickness of the metal at the base of the vertical neck is 3–4 mm. The metal is fairly full of bubbles, some few of which are of large size – one 5 mm in length, another 3 mm. Spiral threads or trails in the metal are conspicuous round the base and on the upper part of the shoulder and the neck.

This vessel is the eighth of its kind to be found in England, the other two examples of the ten cited being from Norway. All are from the south-east (Kent,

Essex, Suffolk and Oxfordshire). As the type is wholly unrepresented on the Continent and in the Scandinavian trading area, with the exception of Norway, it is highly probable that the group is of English manufacture. Faversham in Kent is thought to be a likely place for the glass works.

NOTES TO CHAPTER SIXTEEN

1 D. B. Harden, 'Glass Vessels in Great Britain and Ireland A.D. 400–1000', *Dark Age Britain*, London, 1956, 138 and Fig. 25.

2 For details of all known examples see the British Museum definitive publication, *The Sutton Hoo Ship-Burial*, Cambridge, 1974, Vol. I, Ch. 2, Appendix A (pp. 132–4).

Index

(The numerals in italics refer to the figures in the text and those in bold type refer to the plates)